This book is a survey of literature by North American writers of Asian descent, in terms of both national origins (Chinese, Filipino, Japanese, Korean, South Asian, Vietnamese) and shared concerns. It introduces readers to the distinctive literary history of each group of writers and discusses issues that connect or divide these different groups. Part One provides a literary history of each constituent national group and underlines salient historical events that have affected its writing. Part Two, addressing common racial issues such as nationalism, representation, and crises of identity, explores the forces that bind, divide, and foster exchange among writers and critics of diverse origins. The volume is an original and valuable guide and reference work for students, teachers, and scholars in Asian American studies, ethnic studies, and American studies.

An Interethnic Companion to
Asian American Literature

AN INTERETHNIC COMPANION TO ASIAN AMERICAN LITERATURE

Editor

King-Kok Cheung
University of California, Los Angeles

CAMBRIDGE
UNIVERSITY PRESS

Published by the Press Syndicate of the University of Cambridge
The Pitt Building, Trumpington Street, Cambridge CB2 1RP
40 West 20th Street, New York, NY 10011-4211, USA
10 Stamford Road, Oakleigh, Melbourne 3166, Australia

© Cambridge University Press 1997

First published 1997

Printed in the United States of America

Typeset in Meridien and Optima

Library of Congress Cataloging-in-Publication Data
An interethnic companion to Asian American literature / edited by
King-Kok Cheung.
p. cm.
Includes bibliographical references (p.) and index.
ISBN 0-521-44312-1 (hard). – ISBN 0-521-44790-9 (pbk.)
1. American literature – Asian American authors – History and
criticism.   2. Asian Americans – Intellectual life.   3. Asian
Americans in literature.   I. Cheung, King-Kok, 1954– .
PS153.A84I58   1996
810.9′895 – dc20   95-43092
                                                                     CIP

A catalog record for this book is available from the British Library.

ISBN 0-521-44312-1 Hardback
ISBN 0-521-44790-9 Paperback

CONTENTS

ACKNOWLEDGMENTS

An Interethnic Companion to Asian American Literature was partially prepared while I was a fellow at the Center for Advanced Study in the Behavioral Sciences at Stanford; I am grateful for the financial support provided by the Andrew W. Mellon Foundation. The project was also funded in part by grants from the UCLA Academic Senate and Asian American Studies Center. My special thanks to Don Nakanishi, director of the center, for his abiding support.

Julie Greenblatt, the former literature editor of Cambridge University Press, started me off on this volume. T. Susan Chang, her successor, read the manuscript with great care, insight, and understanding. It has been a rare blessing to work with an editor who is both informed and interested in the subject matter as well as always inspiring and encouraging. Barbara Folsom's expert copyediting has improved the manuscript in numerous ways. Eric Newman, the production editor, guided me through the final stages of putting the book together.

Sau-ling Wong perused a draft of "Re-viewing Asian American Literary Studies" and provided detailed and incisive criticism as well as wise counsel. Eric Sundquist's comments further helped to clarify some hazy ideas. Rosalind Melis gave superb advice.

The cumulative bibliography at the end of the book is built on the contributors' suggestions. I am also indebted to Wen-ching Ho for supplying me with a list of research articles published in Taiwan on Chinese American literature; to Tomo Hattori, Dharini Rasiah, and Rapee Thongthiraj for furnishing me with bibliographical data on Asian Canadian, South Asian American, and Thai American literature, respectively; and to Grace Kyung Won Hong, Brenda Lee Kwon, and James Kyung-Jin Lee for devoting countless hours to intelligent and meticulous research assistance.

Gerard Maré uplifted me with his good humor when the task seemed interminable. Stimulating discussions with my students made the research come alive for me.

My deepest gratitude goes to all the contributors for making the *Interethnic Companion* possible and for our companionship.

CONTRIBUTORS

Oscar V. Campomanes is an assistant professor of English at the University of California, Berkeley. His essays have appeared in *Critical Mass, MELUS, Positions*, and critical anthologies of Asian American literary criticism and Filipino cultural studies.

King-Kok Cheung is an associate professor of English and Asian American Studies at the University of California, Los Angeles. She is author of *Articulate Silences: Hisaye Yamamoto, Maxine Hong Kingston, Joy Kogawa* (1993); editor of *"Seventeen Syllables"* (1994); and coeditor of *Asian American Literature: An Annotated Bibliography* (1988). Her articles and essays have appeared in such journals as *American Literary History, MELUS*, and *PMLA*, as well as in anthologies of feminist theory and Asian American literary criticism.

Donald C. Goellnicht is a professor in and chair of the English Department at McMaster University. He is author of *The Poet Physician: Keats and Medical Science* (1984) and coeditor of *New Romanticisms: Theory and Critical Practice* (1994). He has published in such journals as *Tulsa Studies in Women's Literature, Mosaic*, and the *African American Review* and has contributed essays to several critical collections.

N. V. M. Gonzalez is Professor Emeritus of English at the California State University in Hayward and International Writer-in-Residence at the University of the Philippines System Writers' Workshop. He is the author of three novels, five short-story collections, and numerous essays on Philippine literature and culture. Recent publications include *The Bread of Salt and Other Stories* (1993) and *Work on the Mountain* (1995).

Ketu H. Katrak is a professor and director of Asian American Studies at the University of California, Irvine. She is author of *Wole Soyinka and Modern Tragedy* (1986); *Exiling the Body: African, Indian, and Caribbean Women Writers in English* (forthcoming); and coeditor of *"Desh-Videsh:*

South Asian Expatriate Writing and Art," a special issue of the *Massachusetts Review* (1988–9). Her articles and essays have appeared in such journals as *Modern Fiction Studies* and *College Literature*, and in critical collections.

Elaine H. Kim is a professor of Asian American Studies and chair of Comparative Ethnic Studies at the University of California, Berkeley. She is author of *Asian American Literature: An Introduction to the Writings and Their Social Context* (1982); coeditor of *Making Waves: Writings by and about Asian American Women* (1989); coeditor of *Writing Self Writing Nation* (1994); and coauthor of *East to America: Korean American Life Stories* (1996).

Rachel C. Lee is an assistant professor of English and Women's Studies at the University of California, Los Angeles. Her essays have appeared in the *African American Review* and in critical collections. She is currently working on a book that examines discourses of nationalism, gender, and sexuality in Asian American fiction.

Shirley Geok-lin Lim is a professor of English and Women's Studies at the University of California, Santa Barbara. She is a poet and short-story writer whose most recent work is *Among the White Moon Faces: An Asian-American Memoir of Homelands* (1996). She is the editor of *Approaches to Teaching Kingston's "The Woman Warrior"* (1991); coeditor of *The Forbidden Stitch: An Asian American Women's Anthology* (1988); and coeditor of *Reading the Literatures of Asian America* (1992). Her articles have appeared in such journals as *Feminist Studies, New Literary History,* and *World Englishes.*

Jinqi Ling is an assistant professor of English and Asian American Studies at the University of California, Los Angeles. He is author of *Negotiating Transformations: Ideology and Form in Post–World War II Asian American Literary Discourse* (forthcoming). His articles have appeared in *American Literature* and *MELUS.*

Stephen H. Sumida is an associate professor in the Program in American Culture and the Department of English Language and Literature at the University of Michigan, Ann Arbor. He is author of *And the View from the Shore: Literary Traditions of Hawai'i* (1991) and coauthor of *Asian American Literature of Hawaii: An Annotated Bibliography* (1979).

Monique T. D. Trương is an attorney and writer in New York City. Her short stories and critical essays have appeared in *Amerasia Journal, Viet Nam Forum,* and *New York Asian News,* as well as in literary and critical anthologies.

Sau-ling C. Wong is an associate professor in the Department of Comparative Ethnic Studies, University of California, Berkeley. She is author of *Reading Asian American Literature: From Necessity to Extravagance* (1993). Her essays have appeared in journals such as *Amerasia* and *MELUS* and in various critical collections of cultural and Asian American literary studies.

Stan Yogi is an independent scholar. He is coauthor of *Asian American Literature: An Annotated Bibliography* (1988). His articles have appeared in journals such as the *French Review of American Studies, MELUS,* and *Studies in American Fiction,* as well as in several critical collections.

An Interethnic Companion to
Asian American Literature

RE-VIEWING
ASIAN AMERICAN
LITERARY STUDIES

KING-KOK CHEUNG

Asian American literature – defined here as works by people of Asian descent who were either born in or who have migrated to North America – has undergone dramatic changes since it emerged as a distinctive field in the wake of the civil rights movement in the late 1960s. The most visible difference arises from its rapid and extensive growth over the past three decades. There was a time when teachers and scholars moaned at having to teach or write about the same works, mostly by Chinese American and Japanese American writers, over and over again. Today the difficulty lies in representing and selecting among writers of diverse national origins. As this literature – along with the theory and criticism accompanying it – expands, original parameters are modified and contested; paralleling the explosion in volume is a proliferation of perspectives.

A significant switch in emphasis has also occurred in Asian American literary studies. Whereas identity politics – with its stress on cultural nationalism and American nativity – governed earlier theoretical and critical formulations, the stress is now on heterogeneity and diaspora. The shift has been from seeking to "claim America" to forging a connection between Asia and Asian America; from centering on race and on masculinity to revolving around the multiple axes of ethnicity, gender, class, and sexuality; from being concerned primarily with social history and communal responsibility to being caught in the quandaries and possibilities of postmodernism and multiculturalism. The term "shift" can be misleading, however, for the recent critical moves have by no means replaced earlier exigencies. The two phases of Asian American cultural criticism may more accurately be characterized as a dialectic that continues to spark debate. I shall attempt to map some major courses this discursive development has taken. As scholars in the field, we know literary and critical anthologies are often inflected by the editors' particular beliefs and interests – biases that surface most clearly in the books' introductions. What follows is therefore less an objective review than a subjective re-viewing of Asian American literary studies. Rather than "defining" the field, I will grapple with its crosscurrents.[1]

IDENTITY, CULTURAL NATIONALISM, HETEROGENEITY

The umbrella term "Asian American" was coined in the late 1960s to promote political solidarity and cultural nationalism. This movement was a broad-based one, appealing to immigrants and American-born Asians alike. By contrast, early Asian American cultural criticism – which emerged during this period as part of the larger movement – placed a much greater emphasis on American nativity. In the influential introduction to *Aiiieeeee! An Anthology of Asian-American Writers* (1974), edited by Frank Chin, Jeffery Paul Chan, Lawson Fusao Inada, and Shawn Wong, the editors regarded American nativity as crucial to what they considered to be Asian American "sensibility" – one "that was neither Asian nor white American" (1974/1983, xxi). They also decried the notion of a "dual personality, of going from one culture to another" (vii, xi). Only writers of Chinese, Filipino, and Japanese descent were included in their anthology.

More recently, however, critics such as Lisa Lowe (1991), Oscar Campomanes (1992), Shirley Lim (1993), and R. Radhakrishnan (1994) have challenged the idea of a unifying Asian American sensibility and underlined the need to take into account "heterogeneity," "exile," and "diaspora" when reading Asian American literature. These alternative modes of reading suggest that the editors of *Aiiieeeee!*, in rejecting the concept of the dual personality, also discounted the work of most foreign-born Asians and discredited the bicultural tension that often does surface in literature by both immigrant and American-born writers. Amy Ling, for example, notes that Chinese American women are frequently caught "between worlds": "Their facial features proclaim one fact – their Asian ethnicity – but by education, choice, or birth they are American" (1990, 20). Ling acknowledges the reality of a double consciousness in the writers she analyzes. The writers examined in *Articulate Silences* likewise draw freely from Asian and Anglo-American traditions, as I demonstrate, "but refuse to be defined or confined by either" (1993, 170).

Elaine H. Kim, author of the ground-breaking work of criticism in the field, *Asian American Literature: An Introduction to the Writings and Their Social Context* (1982), explains in her foreword to *Reading the Literatures of Asian Ameria* (Lim and Ling 1992) why cultural nationalism was important to her earlier conception of Asian American literature and why that conception should now be revised:

> In the late 1970s . . . I sought delimitations, boundaries, and parameters because I felt they were needed to establish the fact that there was such a thing as Asian American literature. . . . That is why cultural nationalism has been so crucial. . . . Insisting on a unitary identity seemed the only effective means of opposing and defending oneself against marginalization. . . . *Yet Asian American identities have never been exclusively racial.* (1992, xi–xii; emphasis added)

Adverting to race alone also obscures the variety of generational and ethnic constituencies within Asian American communities. The fluctuating parameters of this literature reflect this complexity. Largely as a result of the 1965 Immigration and Nationality Act, which abolished quotas favoring northwestern European nations, the number of Asian immigrants has risen so sharply that it is no longer practical to stress American nativity as the sine qua non for Asian American sensibility. As the label "Asian American" stretches to accommodate new subgroups, so does Asian American literature, which has now broadened to include writings by Americans of Bangladeshi, Burmese, Cambodian, Chinese, Filipino, Japanese, Korean, Indian, Indonesian, Laotian, Nepali, Pakistani, Sri Lankan, Thai, and Vietnamese descent.[2]

Cultural nationalism, far from being dissipated by growing heterogeneity, has taken plural forms. Ethnic and regional groups formerly eclipsed by the critical focus on Chinese and Japanese American writers on the West Coast are beginning to call for specific forms of cultural alliances. Oscar Campomanes advocates a historical and literary paradigm specific to Philippine writings in English, one that takes into account the experience of direct colonization by the United States (1992). Naheed Islam protests against the homogenization of diverse groups and the domination of Indian Americans within the "South Asian" category: "But why would I be South Asian when I could be Bangladeshi? And the Tripuras, Shantals and Chakmas living within the borders of Bangladesh, brutally suppressed by the military, may choose to distinguish their identity from that nation-state" (242). Elaine Kim stresses the importance of Korean political and cultural solidarity during the 1991 Los Angeles uprising: "Korean national consciousness, the resolve to resist and fight back when threatened with extermination, was all that could be called upon when the Korean Americans in Los Angeles found themselves abandoned" (1993, 229). Stephen Sumida points out the need for a separate critical lens to bring out the inextricability of history and place in the local literature of Hawai'i: "History and place are not simply two separate elements. . . . [I]n Hawaii's island culture *place* is conceived *as history* – that is, as the story enacted on any given site" (1992, 216). Still others are contesting for the recognition of writers "East of California" (title of a conference at Cornell in 1991), such as those from the Midwest and the East Coast. However, even scholars who insist on the distinctness of each Asian subgroup recognize the importance of interethnic cohesion. Thus, although E. San Juan, Jr., urges Filipino Americans to assert "autonomy from the sweeping rubric of 'Asian American,'" he also concedes the importance of uniting with other Asians for "common political demands" (1994, 206). Similarly, despite Islam's annoyance with the "South Asian" tag, she "continue[s] to work with others of South Asian descent on certain issues" (244). Without such broader consortium the voice of each sector would remain inaudible in America.

Sau-ling Cynthia Wong uses an incident prior to the 1990 census to epitomize Asian Americans' need to remain both culturally distinct and politically unified. When the Bureau of the Census proposed to dispense with the listing of different ethnicities by lumping them together under the category of "Asian or Pacific Islander," diverse Asian Americans vehemently opposed the idea: "they *united* with each other in order to protect their *separate* interests" (1993, 7). But Wong herself goes beyond championing solidarity on just the political front. In *Reading Asian American Literature: From Necessity to Extravagance*, she attempts to forge a "textual coalition" across different national literatures, arguing that although Asian American writers, like their "mainstream" counterparts, evoke common literary motifs such as food, the doppelgänger, mobility, and art, "Asian American deployments of [these motifs], when contextualized and read intertextually, form distinctive patterns" within themselves (1993, 12). These patterns, according to Wong, are rooted in the race-specific American historical experience of people of Asian descent. Wong's book represents a valiant and ambitious critical effort to build an Asian American literary network, though some will quarrel with her focus on what Campomanes calls "U.S.-centric narrations" (see Chapter 2).

"Asian American panethnicity" (to borrow Yen Le Espiritu's term) is undoubtedly crucial to our political visibility. Conscious as most Asian Americans are about their ethnic differences from one another, they still look very much alike to the larger American populace, and they still confront hate-crimes perpetrated indiscriminately against them by those unable or unwilling to make distinctions. (In the now notorious case of Vincent Chin, a Chinese American was mistaken for a Japanese autoworker and was clubbed to death with a baseball bat in Detroit.) As Victor Bascara puts it, "It is this ignorance and prejudice that makes for some semblance of an Asian American collectivity forged by racism" (8). But a literary collectivity is a different matter. Trying to link the literatures of historically, culturally, and linguistically diverse ethnic groups will become increasingly straining as these communities multiply.

Nevertheless, one must not overlook the interdependence of politics and literature. Without the initial naming, subsequent institutionalizing, and continuous contestation over this literature, the many voices that are now being heard might have remained mute. Perhaps the most important reason to maintain the designation of "Asian American" literature is not the presence of any cultural, thematic, or poetic unity but the continuing need to amplify marginalized voices, however dissimilar.

AMERICAN, ASIAN, ASIAN AMERICAN

Historically, the appellation "Oriental" was used in North America both for peoples across the Pacific and for Asian inhabitants of the "New World." "Asian American," on the other hand, accentuates the American status of immigrants from Asia and their descendants. The term grows out of the frustration felt by many American-born citizens of Asian extraction at being treated as perpetual foreigners in the United States despite the fact that their roots in this country go back as many as seven generations. Such racist treatment, along with Orientalist tendencies that fetishize Asian objects, customs, and persons, has also engendered in many Asian Americans an internal ambivalence about their Asian heritage. Because of the dominant perception that what constitutes "American" is white, mainstream, and Western, the desire to reclaim a distinctive ethnic tradition seems forever at odds with the desire to be recognized as fully "American."

The most glaring example of the danger of lumping Asians and Americans of Asian ancestry together was the internment of people of Japanese descent in both the United States and Canada during World War II, after the bombing of Pearl Harbor. The American and Canadian governments not only refused to distinguish between Japanese people and those of Japanese descent born or residing permanently in North America, but also conflated national and cultural allegiances. In the United States, after war was declared with Japan, Japanese Americans on the West Coast who observed Japanese customs or religions, who organized social functions for the ethnic community, or who engaged in Japanese art or literature became the FBI's prime suspects. Many families, in order to avoid being incriminated, destroyed nearly everything associated with their culture of origin, from heirlooms and artwork to books, manuscripts, and diaries written in Japanese. The self-hatred induced by the psychic strain of being denied American civil rights and of having to choose between being Japanese and being American are graphically depicted in John Okada's *No-No Boy*, which, in Gayle K. Fujita Sato's words, "attempts to affirm 'Japanese American' through a character who rejects everything Japanese" (1992, 239).[3] Japanese Canadians fared no better. Joy Kogawa, author of *Obasan* and *Itsuka* (both of which deal with the Japanese Canadian internment and its aftermath), discloses in an interview that after the war Japanese Canadians similarly tried to distance themselves from their ethnicity: "We learned to shun one another and to view any Japanese-Canadian gathering as a gaggle of ghettoized geese" (1985, 60).[4]

It is therefore not surprising that writing by Asian Americans has coalesced around the theme of "claiming an American, as opposed to Asian, identity" (E. Kim 1987, 88). This imperative accounts for the deliberate omission of the hyphen among most Asian American intellectuals. In Maxine Hong Kingston's words, "We ought to leave out the hyphen in 'Chinese-American,' because the hyphen gives the word on either side equal weight. . . . Without the hyphen, 'Chinese' is an adjective and 'American' a noun; a Chinese American is a type of American" (1982, 60). This desire to be recognized as American has sometimes been achieved at the expense of Asian affiliation. The obsessive desire to claim America has induced a certain cultural amnesia regarding the country of ancestral origin. In Kingston's *China Men* – a book admittedly designed to "claim America" – the narrator puzzles over her father's reluctance to divulge his past: "Do you mean to give us a chance at being real Americans by forgetting the Chinese past?" (14). Her question, which implies that jettisoning Asian cultural baggage augments a Chinaman's chance of being acknowledged as a "real" American, explodes the myth of a pluralist country.

Children of immigrants are perhaps made even more acutely aware of their ethnic differences. The pain of maintaining traditional Asian customs is evoked in Chitra Divakaruni's poem "Yuba City School" (in northern California). The speaker's son – who has long hair in keeping with Sikh customs – is mercilessly harassed by his classmates: "In the playground . . . invisible hands snatch at his uncut hair, / unseen feet trip him from behind, / and when he turns, ghost laughter / all around his bleeding knees" (80). He is also repeatedly called "idiot" on account of his broken English, his second language (79). Even American-born Asians are not immune to linguistic self-doubts, however, as intimated in Chang-rae Lee's *Native Speaker*, in which the fully acculturated Korean American protagonist observes wryly that people like him are "always thinking about still having an accent" (11). Many people of Asian descent feel, to this day, the need to prove their Americanness by shedding their originary culture and by setting themselves apart from new Asian immigrants. Though different sensibilities admittedly characterize the American-born and the foreign-born, insistence on American nativity can result in the double exclusion of current Asian immigrants – by non-Asians and by American-born Asians alike.

Both the altered demography in recent years and the prominence of some immigrant writers are beginning to unfix the border of Asian American literature. In Elaine Kim's words, "The lines between Asian and Asian American, so important to identity formation in earlier times, are increasingly being blurred" (1992, xiii).[5] The 1965 change in the immigration quota has resulted in the number of foreign-born Asians now exceeding that of the American-born. Asian American literature has been enriched by the voices of writers of diverse ethnic origins. Especially notable is the emergence of South Asian and Southeast Asian American authors, including Wendy Law-Yone (Burmese); Agha Shahid Ali, Meena Alexander, and Bharati Mukherjee (Indian); Bapsi Sidhwa and Sara Suleri (Pakistani); Rienzi Crusz and Michael Ondaatje (Sri Lankan); Cecilia Brainard, Jessica Hagedorn, and Ninotchka Rosca (Filipino); Le Ly Hayslip, Jade Ngọc Quang Huỳnh, and Nguyễn Qúi Đứ'c (Vietnamese); and S. P. Somtow and Wanwadee Larsen (Thai). The competing impulses of claiming America and maintaining ties with Asia are especially pronounced among some of these immigrants. Mukherjee believes that such authors should draw on their American experience instead of writing as expatriates and indulging in nostalgia: "Immigration is the opposite of expatriation. . . . I've come to see expatriation as the great temptation, even the enemy, of the ex-colonial, once-third-world author. . . . Turn your attention to this [American] scene, which has never been in greater need for new perspectives" (Mukherjee 1988, 28–9). Hagedorn takes the opposite view: "I'm not interested in just writing 'an American novel.' . . . Though I've been living in America for 30 years now, my roots remain elsewhere . . . back there" (Hagedorn 1994, 181). Nguyễn, who has spent two decades in America, likewise identifies himself as a Vietnamese man, because "A psychological sense of home is the most important sense of home" (Vinh 1994, 1). Alexander describes herself in *Fault Lines* as "a woman cracked by multiple migrations," who is impelled to revisit figuratively "all the cities and small towns and villages" in which she has lived to come to terms with her fragmented life history (2–3).

Even some American-born Asians who grew up trying to distance themselves from their originary cultures have begun to take renewed interest in their Asian legacy. The protagonist in Peter Bacho's *Cebu* shuttles between the Philippines and the United States; both his visit to his "motherland" and his return to Seattle are fraught with unpleasant surprises. In *Turning Japanese* David Mura chronicles his literal and psychological odyssey of coming to terms with his ethnicity. In his own words: "Up until my late twenties, I mainly attempted to avoid dealing with my *sansei* identity, and tended to think of myself as a middle class white person. The result . . . was self-hatred and self-abuse. . . . If I had not become self-conscious about my identity, I might have destroyed myself" (1994, 187).

Clearly the Asian American movement, together with the recent emphasis on multiculturalism, has been inspiring Americans of Asian descent to explore their composite heritage. Cultural criticism is undergoing corresponding changes, and the terms of what constitutes "America" are being re-visioned in the light of its multicolored citizenry. Some scholars, mindful that many Asians have settled in North America not necessarily by choice but because of political instability (not infrequently caused by U.S. interventions) in their Asian homelands, have gone as far as to deny the United States as the psychic center for Asian Americans and to embrace instead a "diasporic" or "exilic" identity. In addition, writers and critics who view Asia and Asian America conjunctively are exploring the relationship between Asian American and postcolonial studies, especially with regard to such countries as India, Korea, Vietnam, and the Philippines.[6]

The new diasporic emphasis coincides with growing interest in Asian American literature among overseas scholars as well as with deepening interest in East Asia among scholars in the United States. An organization called the Asian American Literature Association was founded in Japan in 1989; the inaugural issue of its publication, the *AALA Journal*, appeared in 1994. A conference on Chinese American literature has been sponsored biennially since 1993 by the Institute of European and American Studies, Academia Sinica, in Taiwan; selected papers are published in an anthology (in Chinese) after each conference. Journals such as *Muae: A Journal of Transcultural Production* and *Positions: Each Asia Cultures Critique*, which are based in the United States, cover cultural and political events in the "Asian diaspora" and feature work by writers and artists on both sides of the Pacific. These trends point to strengthening ties between Asia and Asian America as well as the internationalization of Asian American literary studies.[7]

Although excited by these new critical currents in Asian American literary studies, I hold with Sau-ling Wong that the shift from claiming America to writing diaspora should not be seen as a "teleological" progression (Wong 1995b, 17). When I first entered the field almost a decade ago as a foreign-born Asian, I felt at times like an interloper because American nativity was so central to the definition of Asian American literature. As the voices of immigrant writers become more prominent and as critical paradigms change to accommodate these new voices, my bicultural training is increasingly germane to my teaching and research. Although I take issue with the editors of *The Big Aiiieeeee!* for valorizing the Asian heroic tradition (see next section), I appreciate their effort to look beyond European American traditions for influences that have

shaped Asian American writing. I also enjoy the opportunity to revisit
Chinese classics – which were never a part of my American university
education – in my work on Chinese American literature.

Nevertheless, I am aware that the current emphasis on diaspora has
uneven material consequences for people who have lived and studied on
different continents and for people who were born and raised in North
America. I am less certain how American-born Asians – the very people
who spearheaded Asian American studies in defiance of their political
and cultural invisibility – can avail themselves of a diasporic identity. For
instance, though bilingualism is undeniably a valuable asset in tackling
Asian American literature, it is disturbing to see some highly qualified
American-born candidates being denied teaching jobs on the ground that
they are not fluent in any Asian languages. Many of these candidates,
growing up in the United States or Canada, were never encouraged or
given adequate opportunity to learn their ancestral tongue(s). Furthermore, if American-born Asians discriminate against so-called FOBs
(Fresh-off-the-Boats), some new immigrants from professional classes
also tend to look down on the less privileged old-timers and their monolingual children and to distance themselves from community involvement generally.[8] Thus while I welcome the growing recognition of the
crossover between Asia and Asian America – a crossover that permits a
more fluid sense of identity – I believe Asian American literary studies
must also keep alive the impetus to claim America. Otherwise the field
may swing from excluding the voices of immigrants to marginalizing
those of American-born Asians.[9]

Unlike Sau-ling Wong, who suggests that a "location" or "nation" must
be the focal point for any political struggle (1995b, 19), or Shirley Lim,
who argues from the opposite viewpoint that the effort to "claim
America" only spurs assimilation into the majority culture and feeds
American national pride and prejudice (see Chapter 9), I believe that we
can both "claim America" – assert and manifest the historical and cultural
presence of Asians in North America – and use our transnational consciousness to critique the polity, whether of an Asian country, Canada,
the United States, or Asian America. Individuals may feel empowered by
an ethnic American identity, by a diasporic identity, or by both, but the
field of Asian American literary studies can certainly afford to incorporate
these divergent perspectives. An Asian American consciousness fueled by
the urge to claim America has allowed some writers to rupture a racist
and patriarchal definition of an American national identity (see Lowe
1995). Similarly, an exilic or diasporic identity can enable others to
contest the exclusiveness of state or cultural nationalism. To reckon
with these sometimes contradictory stances is not to take refuge in a
postmodern protean identity that flits from one location to the next, but

to make room for reciprocal critique and multiple commitments. Straddling these positions may involve painful alienation that renders oneself ill at ease within one's own communities. But assuming such vantage points also makes it possible to rally around our concerns as an ethnic minority in North America while avoiding the pitfalls of chauvinism and separatism that can at times accompany unconditional national allegiances. To my mind, the works of Meena Alexander, Peter Bacho, Marilyn Chin, Jade Ngọc Quang Huỳnh, Younghill Kang, Fae Ng, and Wendy Law-Yone, for example, often exemplify the simultaneous claiming and disclaiming of both Asia and America.

RACE, GENDER, SEXUALITY, CLASS

From the beginning, race and gender have been intertwined in Asian American history and literature. The editors of *Aiiieeeee!* considered "emasculation" to be one of the most damaging stereotypes about Asian Americans: "Good or bad, the stereotypical Asian is nothing as a man. At worst, the Asian-American is contemptible because he is womanly, effeminate, devoid of all the traditionally masculine qualities of originality, daring, physical courage, and creativity" (Chin et al. 1974/1983, xxx). The editors saw this affront as bound up with language and culture: "The deprivation of language in a verbal society like this country's has contributed to the lack of a recognized Asian American cultural integrity . . . and the lack of a recognized style of Asian-American manhood" (xxxviii). Outraged by Hollywood's representation of Asian Americans as either sinister or subservient, they resolved to invent a form of ethnopoetics that is specifically masculine.

This androcentric solution to racist representation was bound to be challenged sooner or later. The catalyst came in the form of Maxine Hong Kingston's *The Woman Warrior* (1976), the first Asian American work to receive astounding national acclaim. "The literary decade which had begun on a note of brash machismo with the liberating outcry from the editors of *Aiiieeeee!* . . . ended on a deeply plangent note of powerful feminist independence and literary vision," Garrett Hongo observed (1993, xxix–xxx). Yet *The Woman Warrior* was severely attacked by Frank Chin, who accused Kingston of falsifying Chinese myths and catering to a racist white audience in the name of feminism. The ensuing pen war that raged between the defenders of Kingston on the one side and Chin and his supporters on the other became one of the most protracted and notorious in the field.

Feminist critics such as Elaine Kim, Shirley Lim, Sau-ling Wong, and myself have taken the *Aiiieeeee!* editors to task for their preoccupation with reasserting Asian American manhood, their classification of desirable attributes as masculine, and Chin's blistering attack on Kingston (Cheung 1990, Kim 1990, S. G. Lim 1990, S. C. Wong 1992). We have further pointed out the reality of sexism in both Asian and American cultures and the imperative for Asian American women to engage in gender politics. The hyperfeminization of Asian women in popular American culture, for instance, is no less demeaning than the emasculation of Asian American men and is in as much need of refutation. In Kim's words, "Asian men have been coded as having no sexuality, while Asian women have nothing else. . . . Both exist to define the white man's virility and the white race's superiority" (1990, 69). The stereotype has been responsible in part for the continuing boom of the mail-order Asian bride business. Rapee Thongthiraj, in her study of Wanwadee Larsen's *Confessions of a Mail Order Bride*, demonstrates how the narrator – a Thai woman – must overcome the constraints exerted on her by both a feudal Thai society and an American culture that exoticizes her.

The feminist intervention has had little impact on the direction of the *Aiiieeeee!* editors. Seventeen years after the publication of *Aiiieeeee!* (1974) the editors made good their commitment to discovering a style for Asian American manhood in *The Big Aiiieeeee!* (1991). This sequel presents selected Chinese and Japanese heroic epics as the sources of the "Asian heroic tradition" and maintains that "authentic" Asian American writing must hark back to these heroic tales and to early immigrant annals. Such tenets infuse Chin's *Donald Duk*, in which a Chinese American boy regains his cultural pride by learning about the heroic exploits of classical heroes and of the Chinese railroad builders in America. Alongside the editors' endorsement of the Asian heroic tradition is their vehement denouncement of highly publicized Chinese American writers such as Jade Snow Wong, Maxine Hong Kingston, David Henry Hwang, and Amy Tan for being complicit with the white publishing industry in distorting Asian legends and creating unflattering portraits of Asian and Asian American men. These editors, so instrumental in launching the literature, have subsequently vilified much of it by arbitrating what is "real" and what is "fake" Asian American writing; to them, seemingly every work that has become a national bestseller falls into the "fake" category. To question their arbitrary distinction of the "real" and the "fake" is not, however, to dismiss many of their astute observations about the dubious ways in which the publishing establishment promotes certain Asian American texts and scants others, a topic I shall discuss in a later section.

The skirmishes between feminist critics and the editors of *Aiiieeeee!* and *The Big Aiiieeeee!* bespeak a more general conflict between feminism and state or cultural nationalism.[10] Both Theresa Cha's *Dictée* and Sara Suleri's *Meatless Days* have in their different ways shown how state nationalism – in Japan/Korea, the Indian subcontinent, and the United States – is at times fought over the bodies of women (see Lowe 1994, Sadana 1993). More complex is the relationship between feminism and cultural nationalism. Many Asian American feminist critics champion cultural nationalism in their own way by contending not only against Asian and white patriarchy but also against Eurocentric feminism. Some of these critics have taken women writers to task for espousing white liberal feminism at the expense of "third world" cultures. Bharati Mukherjee's *Jasmine*, for instance, has been interrogated by Inderpal Grewal and Susan Koshy, among others, for its hierarchical comparison of women in India and the United States, with India coded as an oppressive place for women and the United States emerging as a land of hope and freedom. "The problem of such a formulation," Grewal observes, "is that it enables the erasure . . . of women's exploitation and oppression in the U.S., and the denial of women's agency in India" (226). Koshy further notes how Mukherjee's unqualified celebration of a self-determining subject in *Jasmine* is complicit with Western liberal feminism in masking class differences in both India and the United States: "In a strange alliance of liberal feminism, capitalism, and neocolonialism, Mukherjee's critique of the patriarchal practices of indigenous and diasporic Indian culture gets narrativized . . . as the emancipatory journey from Third to First World, a journey into the possibilities of a 'developed' subjectivity characterized by individualism, autonomy, and upward mobility" (71). Another widespread Anglo-American assumption – the notion that silence is synonymous with submissiveness and passivity and that voice is tantamount to power and truth – has been variously challenged by critics such as Gayle Fujita, Donald Goellnicht, and myself (1993).

Feminism and cultural nationalism have thus infiltrated and refined one another. Feminism has gone through much internal revamping to take into consideration differences in race, class, and culture; both patriarchal and Eurocentric constructions of femininity and masculinity are currently being questioned in cultural studies and gender studies. Similarly, nationalism (increasingly exposed as being complicit with patriarchy and compulsory heterosexuality) is being revaluated in ethnic studies, and gay and lesbian studies (see, for example, Eng 1994; J. Lee 1995; R. Lee 1995; Lowe 1995). These ongoing investigations may enable scholars and critics of Asian American literature to go beyond the binarism of feminist and masculinist agendas, to extend feminist concern to men of color who have been subordinated by the dominant culture, and to dispel stereotypes by inventing alternative models that do not simply conform to patriarchal templates.

Whereas debates about gender have been seething for more than two decades, discussions around themes of sexual orientation have remained relatively hushed until recently. Notable literary exceptions include Merle

Woo's "Letter to Ma" (1981), Kitty Tsui's *The Words of a Woman Who Breathes Fire* (1983), Barbara Noda's *Strawberries* (1986), Paul Stephen Lim's plays (1977, 1985a, 1985b, 1989), and *Between the Lines: An Anthology by Pacific/Asian Lesbians*, edited by C. Chung et al. (1987); these were published by small presses with limited circulations. Self-censorship and the repressive attitudes of both Asian American communities and American society at large no doubt kept Asian American lesbian and gay writers and critics from reaching wider audiences earlier. The situation has changed dramatically in the last few years. Acclaimed works with gay or lesbian themes have flooded the cultural scene. These works include Jessica Hagedorn's *Dogeaters* (1990), Ginu Kamani's *Junglee Girl* (1995), Timothy Liu's *Vox Angelica* (1992), David Wong Louie's title story in *Pangs of Love* (1991), Russell Leong's *The Country of Dreams and Dust* (1993a) and "Geography One" (1993b), Anchee Min's *Red Azalea* (1994), and Norman Wong's *Cultural Revolution* (1994), along with anthologies such as *A Lotus of Another Color: The Unfolding of the South Asian Gay and Lesbian Experience*, edited by Rakesh Ratti (1993); *Piece of My Heart: A Lesbian of Colour Anthology*, edited by Makeda Silvera (1993); and *The Very Inside: An Anthology of Writing by Asian and Pacific Islander Lesbian and Bisexual Women*, edited by Sharon Lim-Hing (1994). In 1994 *Amerasia Journal* launched a special issue entitled "Dimensions of Desire: Other Asian & Pacific American Sexualities." With respect to literary theory and criticism, David Henry Hwang's *M. Butterfly* – a play at once popular and highly controversial – has generated some sophisticated analysis of the intersection of race, gender, nationalism, and sexuality (see, for example, Eng, Garber, Kondo, Lye, Moy, Pao, and Shimakawa).

Of the vectors in Asian American literary studies discussed in this section, class issues have perhaps been the most neglected to date. Aside from E. San Juan, Jr.'s *Carlos Bulosan and the Imagination of the Class Struggle* (1972/1975), there is hardly any sustained materialist analysis of Asian American literature. The diverse nationalities and disparate incomes of Asian Americans make any generalization in this area difficult. In addition, the prevailing perception of Asian Americans as the model minority clouds the tremendous economic variation among and within Asian American ethnic communities. Nevertheless, the literature itself offers many examples of capitalist exploitation, class privilege, and penury, as well as of the interplay between class and ethnicity. H. T. Tsiang's *And China Has Hands* (1937) describes the ordeal of a Chinese laundryman hounded by city officials and beleaguered by racist ordinances in New York's Chinatown, and who becomes increasingly involved in the labor movement of his day. Bulosan's *America Is in the Heart* (1943) confronts head-on the appalling working conditions of Filipino farmworkers in California, the fierce collisions between labor and capital, and the uneasy alliances between Filipino and white workers. Milton Murayama's *All I Asking For Is My Body* (1959) exposes the pyramidal structure of the Hawaiian plantation system, with white foremen at the top and Filipino laborers at the bottom. Surjeet Kalsey's "Siddhartha Does Penance Once Again" (1977) evokes the hardship of early Punjabi immigrant workers; this poem also shows the parallels between the experiences of workers in India and immigrant workers in North America (Grewal). Kim Ronyoung's *Clay Walls* (1987) recounts the vicissitudes of a déclassé Korean immigrant family; the mother, member of a Yangbang (aristocratic class) in Korea, survives by being first a domestic and then a sweatshop worker in California. Wendy Law-Yone's *The Coffin Tree* (1987) provides vivid glimpses into the schizophrenia suffered by two siblings uprooted from their relatively comfortable circumstances in Burma to live in harrowing poverty in the United States. Gary Pak's "The Trial of Goro Fukushima" (1992) shows how the combined prejudice of classism and racism leads to the unjust lynching of a Japanese gardener. As suggested earlier, the new waves of immigrant professionals may also feel estranged from their working-class compatriots, especially the old-timers who came before them; such cleavages are poignantly delineated in Bienvenido Santos's "The Day the Dancers Came" (1979) and *What the Hell For You Left Your Heart in San Francisco* (1987). All the works above manifest the various ways in which social and economic inequality engenders interracial, interethnic, and intra-ethnic friction.

As Asian American literary criticism evolves, class analysis will take on increasing importance.[11] Such analysis is likely not only to reveal the unequal material conditions of Asian Americans but also to prompt a refinement of current critical concepts such as hybridity and diaspora. Bilingual and biliterate writers and academics may thrive on hybridity, whereas those who are less fluent and less privileged may find their biculturalism to be a handicap that marginalizes them in both dominant and ethnic cultures. Similarly, diasporic experience may be enabling for metropolitan intellectuals who can afford to travel back and forth across the Pacific but debilitating for migrant workers and those who suffer drastic occupational "demotion" in the transition from Asia to America. At the same time, a transnational class analysis can unveil analogous or interrelated structures of class and gender oppression in Asia and America, as exemplified in the works of Bulosan and Kalsey, as well as those of Meena Alexander and Le Ly Hayslip (see also Grewal 1993; Mohanty 1993; San Juan 1995). With the rise of global corporatism in which Asia plays a significant role (see Miyoshi 1993), Asians and Asian Americans are seen as occupying not just exploited but exploiting positions.

COMMUNAL RESPONSIBILITY, ARTISTIC FREEDOM

"Must the multicultural writer/artist be totally and exclusively answerable to his or her ethnic community . . . [or] can she or he claim the right to express an individual vision and personal concerns?" asked Amy Ling (1991, 195). This question has haunted writers of every emerging canon. Given the ideological genesis of the term "Asian American" – a self-designation that implies a certain political awareness – and its subsequent use as a neutral descriptive label, the perspectives of those who expect Asian American literature to be primarily socially dedicated and those who believe literature to be essentially personal and experimental inevitably clash.

Elaine Kim's subtitle for her classic – *Asian American Literature: An Introduction to the Writings and Their Social Context* – makes plain the nexus between this literature and society. The editors of *Aiiieeeee!* likewise argue that "the distinction between social history and literature is a tricky one, especially when dealing with the literature of an emerging sensibility. The subject matter of minority literature is social history, not necessarily by design but by definition" (xxxv). Texts that contain implicit or explicit social commentary (for example, Bulosan's *America Is in the Heart*, Louis Chu's *Eat a Bowl of Tea*, and John Okada's *No-No Boy*) have long been staples in courses on Asian American literature. Many scholars and students have almost come to assume that Asian American writers furnish material that reflects ethnic experiences. In the wake of poststructuralism and postmodernism, however, not only is identity perceived as unstable and multiple, but history itself becomes suspect – a human construct not to be equated with "truth." Thus the earlier view of Asian American literature as mirroring society has been unsettled.

George Uba, in tracing the evolution of Asian American poetry, has remarked that, unlike the "activist" poets of the late sixties and early seventies (for instance, Janice Mirikitani and Merle Woo, both of whom evoke a "tribal" identity and shun the "conventional finesse of Euro-American poetry" in their attempt to "deliver poetry to the People"), "postactivist" poets such as Marilyn Chin, David Mura, and John Yau have lost their "faith in the efficacy of language as an agent of social reform and as a reliable tool of representation," though they continue to wrestle with issues of identity (33–5).

The impetus to dispel the notion of a unitary identity and to extend the boundaries is evident in the two recent anthologies of Asian American literature: *Charlie Chan Is Dead: An Anthology of Contemporary Asian American Fiction*, edited by Jessica Hagedorn (1993), and *The Open Boat: Poems from Asian America*, edited by Garrett Hongo (1993). Both Hagedorn and

Hongo aim at contradicting existing stereotypes. In her introduction Hagedorn trots out the offensive images of Asians and Asian Americans propagated by the mainstream cinema then and now: "The slit-eyed, bucktooth Jap. . . . The inscrutable, wily Chinese detective. . . . The child-like, indolent Filipino houseboy . . . the greedy, clever *Japanese Business-man* . . . the *Ultimate Nerd*, the model minority Asian American student . . . *Miss Saigon*" (xxii).

Whereas Hagedorn lambasts the popular media for stereotyping Asian Americans, Hongo criticizes Asian American critics for regulating and policing Asian American expression. He challenges what he calls a "secondary system of literary authority *within* Asian America that has arisen since the early seventies" (xxx–xxxi). Although he does not name names, Hongo's criticism seems directed, inter alia, at the editors of *Aiiieeeee!* and *The Big Aiiieeeee!* for having "created a profile of what the Asian American writer was supposed to be": "The Asian American writer was an urban, homophobic male . . . who identified with Black power and ethnic movements in general . . . he was macho; he was crusading; he professed community roots and allegiances . . . his work was widely unrecognized by 'the mainstream'" (xxxi). Hongo allegedly detects an unspoken mandate for the Asian American writer to write for "an idealized fiction called 'the community'" and to adopt "a predominantly political or sociological construction of Asian American identity" (xxxiv).

In their attempts to break out of the rigid molds cast by the mainstream media and the ethnic community, respectively, both Hagedorn and Hongo stress the dazzling array of their selections. "The writers . . . are exhilarating in their differences," Hagedorn remarks. "The resulting range is enormous" (xxviii). Her writers hail from so many places that she muses: "Asian American literature? Too confining a term, maybe. World literature? Absolutely" (xxx). Hongo similarly notes: "For the thirty-one poets included here, our own individual literary odysseys differ and diverge. . . . Each poet defines for us a world, and those worlds are as varied as the dreams of ten thousand saints imagining ten thousand worlds. . . . It is a plain fact that recognition has come to us and to our work as part of the American voice that is great within us," (xxxvii–xxxviii, xlii).

I agree with Hagedorn that, as Asian Americans, our choice is "more than whether to hyphenate . . . more than gender, race or class. . . . who is authentic or fake. . . . Mainstream or marginal" (xxx). I also agree with Hongo that the category of Asian American literature has previously been "too narrowly defined" and that "it is arguable whether or not we can agree on an identifiable model for the *culture* of Asians in America from which we must derive our work" (xxxiv). Yet those socially committed forerunners with whom Hagedorn and Hongo differ have nevertheless been instrumental in securing the freedom and diversity of expression enjoyed by Asian American writers at present. Without those pioneers who first gave Asian American literature a name, without the ethnic studies programs and community centers that gave it a habitation – not to mention the community activism that engendered both – today's flowering of Asian American literature and the concomitant multiplication of venues for writers and critics could hardly have occurred. The profusion attests to the power of naming and to the efficacy of communal effort.

THE PUBLISHING MARKETPLACE

Even as we marvel at this burgeoning, we must not assume that the constraints on Asian American writers have lifted completely. Just because some writers have been recognized by the literary establishment does not mean that the mainstream publishing industry is now open to the full range of Asian American sensibilities and tonalities. If, as Hongo charges, ethnic presses and ethnic studies programs in the past tended to valorize texts that are bitter, brashly political, and accountable to an ethnic community (xxxi, xxxv), the commercial presses seem to have favored works at the other end of the spectrum: those that are optimistic, apolitical, autobiographical.

To be sure, a work can be at once autobiographical and political, as exemplified by Bulosan's *America Is in the Heart*. But both commercial presses and the mainstream American reading public seem lukewarm toward that kind of writing by Asian Americans. The highly uneven receptions of Maxine Hong Kingston's three major works further illustrate my point. *The Woman Warrior*, originally classified as "autobiography," was an overnight, resounding success. *China Men* (also autobiographical) and *Tripmaster Monkey*, both of which are much more concerned with collective identity and racial politics, were accorded scant attention. As all three works are by the same writer, the difference in reception may have more to do with content than with artistic merit.[12]

Although we must not detract from the achievement of writers who have received national acclaim, we need to question whether there is some unspoken formula for Asian American literary success that prevents those who deviate from it from being heard. Why, for instance, is there such a preponderance of autobiographical works by Asian Americans? Why is it that, unlike works by other peoples of color, Asian American works that are commercial triumphs seem to be those the least overtly concerned with racial politics? Why are the few Asian American writers who do rage about racism (Frank Chin, Lawson Inada, Janice Mirikitani) so neglected by a general readership? To what extent are Asian American writers complicit with Orientalism in order to meet mainstream expectations? I ask these questions not in any attempt to prescribe literary creativity, but to suggest that there are still invisible limits placed on Asian American writers.[13]

Unlike Frank Chin, who categorically denounces the genre of autobiography as being a form of Christian confession, I have no qualms about autobiography and autobiographical fiction. What troubles me is the trade publishers' predilection for Asian American personal narratives that lend themselves to what Brian Niiya, in his survey of Asian American autobiography, calls "open-minded conservative" political orientation, works that stress the ability of Asian Americans to assimilate and to accommodate to the basic rules of American society. Niiya believes these books collectively contribute to the current image of Asian Americans as the "model minority": "If one were trying to prove that the American system works for everyone and that, consequently, it's their own fault if certain groups fail to achieve 'success,' then one could hardly come up with a better vehicle than the Asian American autobiography." Because young Asian American writers often look to their predecessors for inspiration, this "success" story, in all senses of the word, tends to reproduce itself (Niiya 1990, 127–8, 132).

Although the recent works touted by the mainstream are much more multifarious in content and genre, many of them still fall under what David Palumbo-Liu calls "model minority discourse": "The most popular texts tend to be perceived as resolutions to a generalized 'problem' of race, ethnicity, and gender." He observes that there is a "doubleness" in texts such as *The Woman Warrior*, Gus Lee's *China Boy*, and Gish Jen's *Typical American*, which "at once serve as representatives of 'ethnic' literature and as models of assimilation into the dominant." Niiya's remarks regarding Asian American autobiography are echoed in Palumbo-Liu's observations concerning these contemporary texts, in which "the sociopolitical apparatuses that perpetuate material differentiations remain unchallenged and sometimes even fortified" (forthcoming).[14] In a parallel vein, Sau-ling Wong observes that both *The Joy Luck Club* and *The Kitchen God's Wife* by Amy Tan "tacitly subscribe to a worldview in which the inverse relationship between political power and cultural visibility is deemed natural." She further argues that Tan's novels plug into certain "discursive traditions" that contribute to their sensational success; these include "'mainstream' feminist writing; Asian American matrilineal literature; quasi ethnography about the Orient; Chinese American 'tour-guiding' works" (S. C. Wong 1995a, 201, 202).

Perhaps the time has come to reflect on how the label "Asian American literature," so instrumental in instituting the literature, can also regulate

creativity. Both ethnic studies programs and mainstream literary estab-
lishments may, in different ways, have essentialized and commodified the
Asian American writer. For entirely different reasons, both institutions
have come to expect a strong "ethnic" quotient in Asian American literature. The earlier emphasis on social history and communal responsibility
in ethnic studies has led to the privileging of writers (such as Bulosan and
Okada) who can speak out of a collective identity; it has also occasioned
a distrust or neglect of the formal dimensions of writing.

If community activists at times distrust "high-brow" art, the literary
establishment seems to think that Asian American writers are incapable
of it. The die-hard tendency to value Asian American works primarily as
autobiography or ethnography has perhaps prevented these works from
being taken seriously as literature. In tandem with the reading public's
preference for autobiographical works is readers' tendency to take
selected Asian American texts as representative of an entire ethnic
group, a tendency that is reinforced by the current implementation of
multiculturalism in the American classroom.[15] Ironically, while Asian
American writing that emerged after the civil-rights movement was bent
on claiming America, educators and publishers who are currently seeking
to integrate works by Asian Americans into their offerings tend to fasten
on texts with a strong "Asian" (exotic) flavor. In the popular consumption
of East Asian and South Asian American literature, the focus has been on
putative Asian lore, picturesque details, and outlandish practices. Such a
predilection has the effect of distracting from what Asian American writers have to say about America at large.[16]

Works that do not dwell on being Asian or Asian American, including
José García Villa's *Have Come Am Here*, Holly Uyemoto's *Rebel without a
Clue*, Vikram Seth's *Golden Gate*, Arthur Sze's *Dazzled*, Karen Yamashita's
Through the Arc of the Rain Forest, have also been elided in both ethnic
studies and multicultural studies. Because American minority writers are
often judged primarily by the ethnic content in their work, those interested in taking up other subjects are seldom given critical attention. Asian
American writers thus may find little incentive to explore different chan-
nels of creativity.

These reflections are not meant to downplay the tremendous strides
made in Asian American literary studies in the last three decades, but to
provoke Asian and non-Asian scholars alike to rethink the many in-
grained assumptions about Asian American literature. Cultural critics,
being partly responsible for the reception and dissemination of this literature, must avoid ghettoizing it while remaining vigilant about the terms
of its production and circulation. We may find ourselves juggling different
tasks: uncovering the distinctive Asian ethnic traditions that inform this
literature as well as attending to what it says about the larger American

society; exploring its historical and political specificity as well as analyzing the writing in interethnic, interracial, trans-Pacific, and international contexts; refraining from setting up arbitrary standards that circumscribe creativity as well as exposing and resisting dominant forces that contain Asian American literature and sanction "model minority discourse" at the expense of dissident voices. "We've come a long way" (Hagedorn 1993, xxviii). But is it far enough?

INTERETHNIC LITERACY

Despite the mounting interest in Asian American literature, not only among "insiders" but also among scholars seeking to broaden the American canon, many have found this literature especially difficult to teach because of the lack of background knowledge, the scarcity of secondary sources, and the variety of cultures involved. Most instructors, familiar with only a few luminaries, are unable to place these writers within cultural and historical contexts, let alone within a literary tradition. Even specialists in the field are not fully conversant with its numerous components.

This collection seeks to fulfill the dual purpose of introducing the distinctive literary history of constituent Asian American groups and of bringing out issues that connect them. Each contributor in Part One provides a literary survey of a subgroup of writers and describes salient historical events (for instance, the Chinese exclusion laws, the Japanese internment, the Vietnam War) that have affected the writers. The contributors in Part Two delineate some of the shared theoretical and critical concerns and reciprocal influences in literary texts by writers of different ethnic extractions, as well as issues that set them apart. By presenting Asian American writers according to ethnic descent and in comparative terms, this volume calls attention both to the many strains of Asian American literature and to their points of intersection. The book is intended both for nonspecialists seeking a broad introduction to the field and for veteran scholars wishing to learn more about the literature of a particular group or about new ways of reading, theorizing, and comparing Asian American literary texts.

There are two limits to this volume. First is the concentration on texts written in English, the only common language among people of diverse Asian lineage in North America. Though it is possible and highly desirable to have a bilingual literary or critical anthology devoted to one subgroup, it is not feasible to encompass in a single volume works written in many dissimilar tongues. This practical consideration must not obscure the fact that in every group there is a sizable body of literary production in the corresponding Asian language(s). The second limit concerns the selective coverage of ethnic groups in Part One. I have been unable to find scholars who feel equipped to discuss writings by Americans of Burmese, Cambodian, Indonesian, Laotian, or Thai descent, as well as by those of mixed descent. My hope is that future scholars will be goaded into launching a study of these missing traditions.

CHAPTERS BY CONTRIBUTORS

In the spirit of decentering authority and promoting multiple points of view, I have in large part refrained from editorial interference. The contributors – many of whom are more knowledgeable about the particular topics they address than I am – were urged to present their ideas in whatever way they saw fit. They were also encouraged to come up with their own analytical frames and critical angles instead of merely providing a survey of a specific literature or a chosen topic.

Sau-ling Wong starts with a brief examination of the history of Chinese in the United States and traces the coinage of the term "Chinese American." Her survey of Chinese American works pays close attention to the historical periods from which individual works emerge, though she does not treat them as mere reflections of social reality. Instead she brings out "the complex and reciprocal interactions of material and discursive forces," taking into account the social conditions that impinge on the texts and noting the ways in which some of the writers challenge the dominant reception and containment. In reviewing writers with varying degrees of political consciousness and concern, Wong reveals the dialectical relationship between particular works and the social climates in which they are written. She also highlights certain texts that generated cultural debates and transformed previous literary criteria. A notable case in point has been the polemical writing of the *Aiiieeeee!* editors, who called for a revolutionary cultural nationalism. Wong considers their writing to be the "first clear articulation of the possibilities of Chinese American literary identity." She believes that new perspectives such as those of gay and lesbian writers, Chinese Canadian writers, and writers from other Asian ethnic communities will provide further opportunities for opening up and challenging the existing canon of Chinese American literature.

Stan Yogi divides the chapter on Japanese American literature into three main sections according to the writers' generations – issei (first), nisei (second), and sansei (third) – and traces the cultural and political events that have affected each group. The issei section introduces three authors who wrote in English: Sadakichi Hartman, Etsu Sugimoto, and Bunichi Kagawa (whom Yogi regards as the first to have taken on the concept of a Japanese American identity). The nisei section is subdivided chronologically: prewar, internment, and postwar. Yogi notes that, before the war, published works by issei and nisei were confined mostly to Japanese American periodicals, which provided a forum for writers such as Taro Katayama, Chiye Mori, Toshio Mori, and Mary Oyama. The segment on literature about the internment underscores the tension between the "optimistic" and the "critical" in the works printed in camp journals, notably *Tulean Dispatch*, *The Pen*, and *Trek*. The sansei section is subdivided by theme: activism, place, and postmodernism. These headings refer to activist poets, writers who evoke a specific locale, and writers who evince postmodernist aesthetics, respectively. Throughout the chapter Yogi illuminates the role played by literature in creating and maintaining Japanese American identity.

Elaine Kim presents writings by Koreans in the United States as an ever-dynamic corpus, resistant to racism in American society, sexism in the Korean American community, and classism within a seemingly monolithic group. The works are divided into four sections. In the first section, the authors described write in different periods and about vastly different subjects, but they all, according to Kim, look back to Korea as their "homeland" and offer an incisive critique of racism in the United States. The second section concentrates on immigrants' daughters who write about their struggle to maintain the cultural integrity of Koreans even as they are beset by poverty and discrimination. These writers offer a narrative of what Kim calls "(female) difference" from the centralized narrative of whiteness and maleness in the United States. In the third section Kim discusses the emerging possibilities of identity formation for Korean Americans, particularly writers from Hawai'i who are "distinct from their mainland counterparts" in that they can "claim to be both Asian and American." These writers partake of the cultural hybridization that occurs in Hawai'i and refuse to allow a single frame of reference to determine their identity as writers. The last section points to the future of Korean American writing by invoking Theresa Hak Kyung Cha's *Dictée*, noting that by subverting the very notion of narrative, Cha poses a challenge to all future writers to remain critically engaged as Korean Americans while being open to the multiple dimensions of identity.

The collaborative essay by N. V. M. Gonzalez and Oscar V. Campomanes sketches the permeable yet irreducible boundaries between Filipino English and American literatures, as well as between postcolonial and ethnic studies. Both contributors agree that "engagement with the legacy of colonialism . . . charges the Filipino (American) literary tradition with its singular tensions." Gonzalez, a second-generation Filipino English writer, uses the term "Filipino Writing in English" to describe the work of writers who have either settled in the United States or maintained dual residence in the Philippines and North America. This writing is informed by various Philippine folkloric and vernacular traditions as well as by the colonial languages of Spanish and English. The American legacy of English functions paradoxically as both "the deterrent and medium of 'Filipino imagination' seeking to break out of colonial fetters." Unlike immigrant writers who see America as the "promised land," Filipino writers often construct a fictive "homeland" for "moorings in their exilic writings and peripatetic journeys." Campomanes, an immigrant scholar of Filipino descent, refers to the writing by Filipinos in the United States as "Filipino American" only to expose the slipperiness of that terminology. He argues that this writing "falls within, while exceeding the discursive borders" of both Asian American and postcolonial discourse. Writers such as Carlos Bulosan, Gonzalez, Bienvenido Santos, and José García Villa have been studied as being both Filipino English and Filipino American authors.

Ketu Katrak announces at the outset that South Asian American literature is not "a monolithic whole but a collection of differences." The authors she covers exhibit differences in class, religion, education, and gender, dispelling the notion of a unitary identity. Katrak provides a broad historical survey of writers of the 1950s and 1960s and a much more detailed analysis of authors writing during and after the 1970s, particularly Agha Shahid Ali, Meena Alexander, and Bharati Mukherjee. Borrowing Edward Soja's argument in *Postmodern Geographies*, Katrak observes that identities are negotiated along the axes not only of race, class, gender, and language but also of region. This attentiveness to geographical surroundings informs Katrak's discussion of authors in whose works she discerns the violence of dislocation accompanied by a poetics of loss, as well as a sensibility enriched by the "simultaneity of geography": "the possibilities of living here, in body, and elsewhere in mind and imagination."

Monique T. D. Trường frames the emergence of Vietnamese American literature in the context of the Vietnamese conflict and its aftermath. Throughout her chapter, which is divided into five sections, she exposes the "U.S.-centric" approach to the Vietnam War and to Vietnamese Americans. The first two sections critique European American editors' appropriation and manipulation of Vietnamese American voices in several collections of oral history. The third section analyzes *Shallow Graves* by Wendy Wilson Larsen and Tran Thi Nga; Trường detects an imbalance of power in the relation between Larsen and Tran, an imbalance which replicates that of the interviewer-respondent relationship in the edited collections. The fourth section demonstrates how an analogous subordination of Vietnamese American subjectivity takes place in Oliver Stone's film *Heaven and Earth*, in which Le Ly Hayslip's narratives are reduced into "fragments of American popular culture" and codified as a "definitive

Vietnamese American perspective." The chapter's coda celebrates the advent of autonomous literary voices in Jade Ngọc Quang Huỳnh's *South Wind Changing* and Nguyễn Qúi Đức's *Where the Ashes Are.*

The essays in Part Two of the *Interethnic Companion* address common issues that affect writers from different subgroups and suggest various ways of reading and theorizing Asian American literature. Rachel Lee examines how four writers respond to the portrayals of Asians and Asian Americans in the popular press from 1910 to 1920. She observes that American journals of the time, including *Collier's,* the *Masses,* and *Good Housekeeping* typically characterized Asians as less evolved, unclean, unknowable, and unassimilable. She notes that the threatening descriptions of Asians found in the texts of these journals were juxtaposed with pictorial advertisements in which Asian emblems were used to sell domestic goods. The writers Lee discusses (Sax Rohmer, Onoto Watanna, Paz Marquez, and Sui Sin Far) each responded directly but very differently to the negative images of Asians produced in the press. Whereas Rohmer fuels those images, the other three challenge the popular constructions to varying degrees. By comparing journalistic and literary representations, Lee presents a spectrum of contending perspectives on Asian American identity in the early twentieth century.

Stephen Sumida argues that the notion of postcoloniality only imperfectly describes the relations between colony and nation in Asian Pacific American literatures. He asserts that Native Hawaiian literature today, for instance, is created and studied under conditions not of postcolonialism but of a colonialism that commenced with the overthrow of the Hawaiian nation in 1893. Asian American literature as a whole, according to Sumida, is still a literature of internal colonization, because a point of "liberation" from a colonizing nation's racial and cultural oppressiveness has not yet been reached. He observes that with the notable exception of Native Hawaiian literature – which assumes a "nation" apart from the United States and which expresses resistance and opposition to colonization in both content and form – the "nation" generally assumed in Asian American literary studies has been the United States, albeit in its idealized form as a country built on equality and democracy. This sanguine vision of the United States, he adds, distinguishes Asian American literature from Native American, African American, and Latina/Latino literatures.

Shirley Lim deplores the tendency of critics and publishers to disregard works by ethnic writers who do not center on stock American topics and proposes a diasporic model of reading that seeks to illuminate how works by Asian Americans shuffle notions of "identity, home, and nation." Borrowing Edward Said's notion of "filiation and affiliation," she shows how the tension between natal ties (filiation) and social relations (affiliation) surfaces rather differently in works by immigrants and in works by second-generation authors.[17] Lim discerns in immigrant texts (for instance, the poems on the walls of Angel Island) a "cultural di/stance toward U.S. society." She notes by contrast that the narratives produced by American-born writers (for example, Jade Snow Wong, Pardee Lowe, Maxine Hong Kingston, Amy Tan, and Gish Jen) advance an assimilationist narrative position.

Jinqi Ling explores ways of undermining gender binarism by discussing three interrelated issues: the "emasculation" of Asian American men, the simultaneous articulations of multiple oppressions, and the transgression of gender norms to disrupt heterosexism. He argues that when the term "emasculation" is used to epitomize the identity crisis of Asian American men, it entraps the user in "an endless repetition of the oppressor's logic." To remain constructive, the metaphor must be detached from its familiar contexts. Ling illustrates how this concept is put to different uses in the works of David Henry Hwang, Carlos Bulosan, and Frank Chin. He then analyzes how the writing of Maxine Hong Kingston concurrently resists racism and sexism. Finally, he demonstrates how Wendy Law-Yone and Jessica Hagedorn refigure gender in their work.

Donald Goellnicht, after pondering on his own position as a white male engaged in Asian American literary discourse, proposes a method of reading that blurs the generic line between literature and theory and permits Asian American works to stand as significant narratives of resistance. He argues that writers such as Maxine Hong Kingston, Joy Kogawa, Theresa Cha, and Trinh Minh-ha challenge "traditional, patriarchal hierarchies of genre"; these writers, though seeking to recover repressed ethnic histories, are "acutely cognizant of the difficulty of knowing the past through language." Their works discourage a universalist and singular mode of reading, writing, or theorizing history.

Interethnic Companion likewise discourages a homogeneous approach to Asian American literature. It does not strive toward arriving at a consensus of what "Asian American literature" is. As indicated earlier, both the literature and the criticism are undergoing unprecedented growth and flux. Many of the essays here reflect some of the aforementioned "shifts" in paradigms, especially the changing emphasis from a unifying cultural nationalism grounded in North America to an insistence on heterogeneity and diaspora. Heterogeneity is also manifest in the variety of organizing themes that emerge in Part One, revealing the historical concerns particular to each subgroup. But whether the focus is on generational peculiarity (Yogi), geographical instability (Katrak), or the difficult emergence of an autonomous voice (Trường), there is a concerted accent on differences *within* the subgroup covered.

The essays in Part Two more directly challenge or complicate earlier critical paradigms. Lee's analysis of the narratives set in Japan and the Philippines demonstrates how asymmetrical race relations in the United States are replicated outside American borders; her essay furnishes another vantage point for viewing parallel phenomena in Asia and Asian America. Sumida holds that cultural nationalism takes very different forms in Hawai'i and on the continent. Lim reverses the trend of earlier critics (who stressed American nativity as crucial to an Asian American sensibility) by placing a premium on the diasporic consciousness of immigrant writers. Ling recasts the concept of "emasculation" to take into account the perspectives of women and gay men. Goellnicht moves away from the critical tendency that conflates ethnic literature and social history by showing how women writers question traditional historiography.

Certain concerns run through both parts, providing material for further dialogue or debate. Lee and Trường unmask the skewed representation of Asia in U.S. print and cinematic media; Lim and Wong analyze the assimilationist and resistant dimensions in Asian American texts; Goellnicht, Kim, and Ling map out the intersection of gender and race in positioning writers and critics; Campomanes, Gonzalez, and Sumida investigate the conjunction and disjunction of Asian American and postcolonial studies; Katrak and Yogi show the centrality of geographical sites in shaping or unsettling ethnic identity. Considered together, these approaches will enable students and scholars to explore many of the tributaries and confluences in Asian American literary studies.

The boundaries of Asian American literature are likely to continue to stretch and be contested as its constituency expands and new voices emerge. The question remains whether the label "Asian American" can continue to hold together the multitude of ethnic groups and "consent" (to give an ethnic twist to Werner Sollors's term) is possible amid such diversity.[18] This question is not unlike the one raised by those critics of multiculturalism who worry about the "balkanization" of America. Other issues broached earlier – the competing claims of wanting to embrace an ethnic heritage and wishing to be recognized fully as an "American"; the politics of race, gender, class, and sexuality; and the concerns about representation, communal responsibility, artistic freedom, and the literary marketplace – also have much in common with the study of Native American, African American, and Mexican American literatures. Hence I would like to conclude by reflecting on Asian American literary studies in conjunction with a multicultural curriculum.

When teaching courses on Asian American literature at UCLA, I encounter students of all colors as well as students from practically every extant Asian American group. I have come to see that for most Asian American students, and for myself, identification with Asians who belong to different subgroups is not so much "natural" as learned or acquired. As Espiritu points out, "pan-Asian ethnicity was the product of material, political, and social processes rather than cultural bonds. But . . . once established, the panethnic group – through its institutions, leaders, and networks – produces and transforms panethnic culture and consciousness. In the process, the panethnic idea becomes autonomous, capable of replenishing itself" (164). Although Asian American students may readily feel a certain affinity with one another because they have faced similar forms of discrimination, a deeper sense of mutual understanding emerges only after exposure to the different material histories, cultures, and literatures of the various groups. Perhaps that is why a much greater degree of solidarity can be discerned among Asian Americans in academic communities than among those outside these settings. Similar dynamics are also at work in courses covering writers from diverse racial groups. Paradoxical as it may seem, learning about differences is an effective way to foster empathy.

Knowledge, to be sure, can also divide. For instance, in connecting Asia and Asian America, Asian Americans must confront the conflicted histories that have split nations such as Japan and Korea, Pakistan and India, and Vietnam and Cambodia. Similarly, a multicultural education that does not simply scratch the surface of cultural diversity must grapple with historical injuries – for instance, the dislocation and the dispossession of Native Americans and Mexican Americans, the enslavement of African Americans, the internment of Japanese Americans – not to mention the economic asymmetry and unequal power relations that continue to pit one group of people against another. These painful legacies will fissure and embitter. But acquiring such knowledge in the hope of eventual reconciliation and cooperation is surely preferable to accepting any false harmony imposed by the repression of history.

This volume, published at a time when the Asian American population in North America has been escalating and when the call for multiculturalism can no longer be ignored, works toward a historically and culturally informed reading of Asian American literature. It aims at facilitating interethnic approaches to American literature, not only in relation to the nationalities covered but, conceivably, also to other marginalized groups. I hope the *Interethnic Companion* will encourage those not of Asian American backgrounds to know us and help us to know ourselves.

NOTES

1. Sau-ling Cynthia Wong and I discovered upon exchanging our works-in-progress that independently we had been wrestling with similar "shifts" in Asian American studies (see Wong, 1995b). Wong's valuable suggestions inform this essay; I am especially grateful to her for alerting me to the slippage between how the term "Asian American" was used in cultural criticism and how it was used in the general Asian American movement (see next section).
2. This list is not meant to be exhaustive. Asian American groups are continuing to proliferate and to redefine themselves. For instance, Pacific Islanders, who are currently bidding to be placed in the same category as "Native Americans" in the U.S. census, are not listed here (though some of their works are included in the cumulative bibliography). Senator Daniel K. Akaka, a Native Hawaiian, observes: "There is the misperception that Native Hawaiians, who number well over two hundred thousand, somehow "migrated" to the United States like other Asian or Pacific Island groups. . . . This leads to the erroneous impression that Native Hawaiians, the original inhabitants of the Hawaiian Islands, no longer exist" (quoted in Wright 1994). There is also disagreement over whether the many national groups who hailed from the Indian subcontinent should be classified as Asian Americans or even as South Asians (see Islam, Sharpe, Wright).
3. "No-no boys" were nisei who refused to fight for the United States. Internees were asked to fill out a so-called Loyalty Questionnaire administered in conjunction with an army recruitment drive. "No-No" refers to the responses given to two of the questions: 'Are you willing to serve in the armed forces of the United States in combat duty wherever ordered?" and "Will you swear unqualified allegiance to the United States of America and faithfully defend the United States from any or all attacks of foreign or domestic forces, and forswear any form of allegiance or obedience to the Japanese emperor, to any other foreign government, power, or organization?" See also Monica Sone's *Nisei Daughter* (155) for a moving description of the burning of Japanese textbooks and other items during the war.
4. Partly because of the parallel experience of Japanese Americans and Japanese Canadians during World War II, Kogawa's works have often been considered as a part of the Asian American canon.
5. As E. Kim (1992) and S. Wong (1995b) have pointed out, the growing fluidity between "Asian" and "Asian American" is also facilitated by material factors such as increasingly affordable air travel and phone services across the Pacific, fax machines, e-mail, and the easy rental of Asian films and videos.
6. Outside the literary realm, the connection between Asia and Asian America was there from the start. As historian Sucheta Mazumdar points out, the activists who spearheaded Asian American studies in the late 1960s were influenced no less by the Cultural Revolution in China than by the civil-rights movement and the Black-Power movement. Similarly, the anti–Vietnam War movement and the internal colonialism model have maintained a transnational perspective (1991). The term "Asian American literature" has itself

become a site of debate, either because many early Asian inhabitants in North America do not perceive themselves as "Americans," or because the term homogenizes different groups, or because it presupposes the desirability of be(com)ing Americans. For these various points of view, see E. San Juan 1995, S. Wong, 1995b, as well as the essays by Campomanes, Gonzalez, Lim, and Sumida in this volume. I discuss the ambivalence among Asian Americans toward their ancestral homeland at much greater length in Cheung 1992.

7. Interest in Asian American literary studies in Europe is also mounting. The first book-length work of criticism on Chinese American literature, Karin Meissenburg's *The Writing on the Wall* (1987), was published in Germany. More recently, students from Italy, Poland, France, and Spain have come to the United States specifically to study Asian American literature. The spread of Asian American literary studies abroad reflects the internationalization of American Studies in general. Paul Lauter asks, "What are the borders within which the study of 'America' has been conducted? Does it make sense, especially when we talk of multiculturalism and cultural study, to define these borders by nationalist geography or by language? Or does 'America' have to be seen within a world system, in which the exchange of commodities, the flow of capital, and the interactions of culture know no borders?" These questions are obviously relevant to Asian American Studies as well (see also Kroes).

8. David Henry Hwang's *FOB* dramatizes the tension between American-born and foreign-born Chinese; see also Hom on their mutual discrimination. Grewal discusses the disinclination of upper-class Indian immigrants to associate with Asian Americans and other peoples of color.

9. Either of these extremes is complicit with the exclusive forces of the dominant culture. The hiring pattern described above (preference for foreign-born Asians who are bilingual over American-born Asians who are not fluent in any Asian languages) gives the impression that Asian Americans have done well in institutions of higher learning, even in the unlikely fields of the humanities, thereby reinforcing the myth of the model minority while perpetuating the invisibility of Asians born and raised in North America.

10. In both anthologies there are twice as many male as female writers represented. As though to make up for this imbalance, successive anthologies of Asian American women writers have appeared, including *Making Waves: An Anthology of Writing by and about Asian American Women*, ed. Asian Women United of California (1989), *The Forbidden Stitch: An Asian American Women's Anthology*, ed. Shirley Geok-Lin Lim and Mayumi Tsutakawa (1989), and *Home to Stay: Asian American Women's Fiction*, ed. Sylvia Watanabe and Carol Bruchac (1990).

11. As Lisa Lowe has pointed out, a number of young scholars – Jeff Chang, Colleen Lye, Michael Murashige, Viet Nguyen, Shelly Wong – have been working on the intersection of class and race, though much of their work still remains unpublished (1995b).

12. *Tripmaster Monkey* may have deterred some readers because of its many layers of allusion. Unfolding these layers requires knowledge of Chinese and English

classics, the culture of the late 1960s, as well as various "inside stories" about Asian Americans (including a re-creation of Frank Chin as the protagonist). Yet similar complexity in work by Euro-American writers such as T. S. Eliot and James Joyce has always inspired scrupulous scholarship.

13. In asking these questions I am indebted to critics such as Tomo Hattori, Brian Niiya, David Palumbo-Liu, E. San Juan, Jr., Monique Trưởng, and S.C. Wong.

14. That Asian American literature exudes a sanguine tone is apparently a widespread assumption. Responding to a call in the T-AMLIT e-mail bulletin board for suggestions of texts that are "humorous and affirming," which will make readers "feel good" afterwards, A. Keith Lawrence writes: "Many contemporary Asian American writers fit the bill" (quoted with Lawrence's permission). He goes on to list the works of Jade Ngọc Quang Huỳnh, David Henry Hwang, Gish Jen, Maxine Hong Kingston, Gus Lee, Sky Lee, David Wong Louie, Lydia Minatoya, Michael Ondaatje, Ruth Sasaki, and Amy Tan.

15. One must not dismiss the sincere effort of many educators to transform the curriculum by including the voices of hitherto marginalized minorities. However, as scholars such as Hazel Carby, Henry Giroux, Chandra Mohanty (1989–90), and Cornell West have pointed out, the liberal notion of multiculturalism, which stresses merely *cultural* differences, clouds the highly uneven economic conditions and asymmetrical power relations among races. In contrast to this form of multiculturalism, David Palumbo-Liu advocates a "critical multiculturalism [that] explores the fissures, tensions, and sometimes contradictory demands of multiple cultures, rather than (only) celebrating the plurality of cultures by passing through them appreciatively" (1995, 5).

16. Cutting a piece of one's own flesh and serving it in a broth to one's mother – a scene that occurs in both the text and film version of *Joy Luck Club* and passes for a time-honored Chinese expression of filial piety – is one that I find particularly vexing. As far as I know, there is no such Chinese custom.

17. For another application of Said's concept to Asian American literature, see Li.

18. Sollors describes the ethnic characteristics inherited by American immigrant writers from their ancestors as "descent" and the common American characteristics adopted by them in the New World as "consent."

■■■■ WORKS CITED

Alexander, Meena. 1993. *Fault Lines: A Memoir*. New York: Feminist Press.

Asian Women United of California, eds. 1989. *Making Waves: An Anthology of Writing by and about Asian American Women*. Boston: Beacon Press.

Bacho, Peter. 1991. *Cebu*. Seattle: Univ. of Washington Press.

Bascara, Victor. 1993. "Hitting Critical Mass." *Critical Mass: A Journal of Asian American Cultural Criticism* 1.1:3–38.

Bulosan, Carlos. 1943/1977. *America Is in the Heart: A Personal History*. Seattle: Univ. of Washington Press.

Campomanes, Oscar V. 1992. "Filipinos in the United States and Their Literature of Exile." In Lim and Ling, 49–78.

Carby, Hazel. 1980. "Multi-Culture." *Screen Education* 34:62–70.

Cha, Theresa Hak Kyung. 1982/1994. *Dictée*. Berkeley: Third Woman Press.

Chan, Jeffery Paul, Frank Chin, Lawson Fusao Inada, and Shawn Wong, eds. 1991. *The Big Aiiieeeee! An Anthology of Asian American Writers*. New York: New American Library-Meridian.

Cheung, King-Kok. 1990. "The Woman Warrior versus the Chinaman Pacific: Must a Chinese American Critic Choose between Feminism and Heroism?" In *Conflicts in Feminism*, ed. Marianne Hirsch and Evelyn Fox Keller, 234–51. New York: Routledge.

———. 1992/1993. "Asian and Asian American: To Connect or Disconnect?" Conference paper delivered at the American Studies Association Annual Convention; a version of this paper was also presented at National Taiwan University, Taipei.

———. 1993. *Articulate Silences: Hisaye Yamamoto, Maxine Hong Kingston, Joy Kogawa*. Ithaca, NY: Cornell Univ. Press.

Chin, Frank. 1991. *Donald Duk*. Minneapolis: Coffee House Press.

———. 1991. "Come All Ye Asian American Writers of the Real and the Fake." In Chan et al., 1–92.

Chin, Frank, Jeffery Paul Chan, Lawson Fusao Inado, and Shawn Wong, eds. 1974/1983. *Aiiieeeee! An Anthology of Asian-American Writers*. Washington, D.C.: Howard Univ. Press.

Chu, Louis. 1961/1979. *Eat a Bowl of Tea*. Seattle: Univ. of Washington Press.

Chung, C., Alison Kim, and A. K. Lemshewsky, eds. 1987. *Between the Lines: An Anthology by Pacific/Asian Lesbians*. Santa Cruz, CA: Dancing Bird Press.

Divakaruni, Chitra Banerjee. 1993. "Yuba City School." In Hongo, 79–80.

Eng, David. 1994. "In the Shadows of a Diva: The Commitment of Homosexuality in David Henry Hwang's *M. Butterfly*." *Amerasia Journal* 20.1:93–116.

Espiritu, Yen Le. 1992. *Asian American Panethnicity: Bridging Institutions and Identities*. Philadelphia: Temple Univ. Press.

Fujita, Gayle Kimi. 1985. " 'To attend the sound of stone': The Sensibility of Silence in *Obasan*." *MELUS* 12.3:33–42.

Garber, Marjorie. 1992. "The Occidental Tourist: *M. Butterfly* and the Scandal of Transvestitism." In *Nationalism and Sexualities*, ed. Andrew Parker et al., 121–46. New York: Routledge.

Giroux, Henry. 1992. *Border Crossings*. New York: Routledge.

Goellnicht, Donald C. 1989. "Minority History as Metafiction: Joy Kogawa's *Obasan*." *Tulsa Studies in Women's Literature* 8.2:287–306.

Grewal, Inderpal. 1993. "Reading and Writing the South Asian Diaspora." In Women of the South Asian Descent Collective, 226–36.

Hagedorn, Jessica. 1990. *Dogeaters*. New York: Penguin.

———. 1994. "The Exile Within/The Question of Identity." *The State of Asian America: Activism and Resistance in the 1990s*, ed. Karin Aguilar-San Juan, 173–82. Boston: South End Press.

———, ed. 1993. *Charlie Chan Is Dead: An Anthology of Contemporary Asian American Fiction*. New York: Penguin.

Hattori, Tomo. 1994. "Orientalist Typologies: The Cultural Politics of the Female

Subject in Maxine Hong Kingston's *The Woman Warrior* and Joy Kogawa's *Obasan*." Ph.D. diss., McMaster Univ.

Hom, Marlon K. 1984. "A Case of Mutual Exclusion: Portrayals by Immigrants and American-born Chinese of Each Other in Literature." *Amerasia Journal* 11:29–45.

Hongo, Garrett, ed. 1993. *The Open Boat: Poems from Asian America*. New York: Anchor-Doubleday.

Huỳnh, Jade Ngọc Quang. 1994. *South Wind Changing*. St. Paul, MN: Graywolf Press.

Hwang, David Henry. 1983. *FOB*. In *Broken Promises: Four Plays*, 5–56. New York: Bard/Avon.

———. 1989. *M. Butterfly*. New York: Plume/Penguin.

Islam, Naheed. 1993. "In the Belly of the Multicultural Beast I Am South Asian." In Women of the South Asian Descent Collective, 242–5.

Jen, Gish. 1991. *Typical American*. Boston: Houghton Mifflin.

Kalsey, Surjeet. 1977. "Siddhartha Does Penance Once Again." *Contemporary Literature in Translation* 26:32–4.

Kamani, Ginu. 1995. *Junglee Girl*. San Francisco: Aunt Lute Books.

Kim, Elaine H. 1982. *Asian American Literature: An Introduction to the Writings and Their Social Context*. Philadelphia: Temple Univ. Press.

———. 1987. "Defining Asian American Realities through Literature." *Cultural Critique* 6:87–111.

———. 1990. "'Such Opposite Creatures': Men and Women in Asian American Literature." *Michigan Quarterly Review* (Winter):68–93.

———. 1992. "Foreword. " In Lim and Ling, xi–xvii.

———. 1993. "Home Is Where the *Han* Is: A Korean American Perspective on the Los Angeles Upheavals." In *Reading Rodney King/Reading Urban Uprising*, ed. Robert G. Williams, 215–35. New York: Routledge.

Kim, Elaine H., and Norma Alarcón, eds. 1994. *Writing Self, Writing Nation: A Collection of Essays on DICTEE by Theresa Hak Kyung Cha*. Berkeley: Third Woman Press.

Kim, Ronyoung. 1987. *Clay Walls*. Sag Harbor, NY: Permanent Press.

Kingston, Maxine Hong. 1976/1977. *The Woman Warrior: Memoirs of a Girlhood Among Ghosts*. New York: Vintage Books.

———. *China Men*. 1981. New York: Vintage-Random House, 1989.

———. 1982. "Cultural Mis-readings by American Reviewers." *Asian and Western Writers in Dialogue: New Cultural Identities*, ed. Guy Amirthanayagam, 55–65. London: Macmillan.

———. 1989. *Tripmaster Monkey: His Fake Book*. New York: Knopf.

Kogawa, Joy. 1981. *Obasan*. Toronto: Lester & Orpen Dennys.

———. 1985. "The Japanese-Canadian Dilemma." *Toronto Life*, December, 29–33, 58, 60.

———. 1992. *Itsuka*. Toronto: Viking.

Kondo, Dorinne K. 1990. "*M. Butterfly*: Orientalism, Gender, and a Critique of Essentialist Identity." *Cultural Critique* 16:5–29.

Koshy, Susan. 1994. "The Geography of Female Subjectivity: Ethnicity, Gender, and Diaspora." *Diaspora* 3.1:69–84.

Kroes, Rob. 1995. "Internationalizing the Study of the United States." *American Studies Association Newsletter* 18.2:1, 3–4.

Larsen, Wanwadee. 1989. *Confessions of a Mail Order Bride: American Life Through Thai Eyes*. Far Hill, NJ: New Horizon.

Larsen, Wendy Wilder, and Tran Thi Nga. 1986. *Shallow Graves: Two Women and Vietnam*. New York: Perennial Library.

Lauter, Paul. 1995. "A Call for (At Least a Little) American Studies Chauvinism." *American Studies Association Newsletter* 18.2:1–3.

Law-Yone, Wendy. 1987. *The Coffin Tree*. Boston: Beacon Press.

Lee, Chang-rae. 1995. *Native Speaker*. New York: Riverhead Books.

Lee, Gus, 1991/1994. *China Boy*. New York: Penguin/Plume.

Lee, James Kyung-Jin. 1995. "The Poetry of Myung Mi Kim." M.A. thesis, Univ. of California, Los Angeles.

Lee Marie G. 1992. *Finding My Voice*. Boston: Houghton Mifflin.

Lee, Rachel. 1995. "The Americas of Asian American Literature: Nationalism, Gender, and Sexuality in Bulosan's *America Is in the Heart*, Jen's *Typical American*, and Hagedorn's *Dogeaters*." Ph.d. diss., Univ. of California, Los Angeles.

Leong, Russell. 1993a. *The Country of Dreams and Dust*. Albuquerque, NM: West End Press.

———. 1993b. "Geography One." In Hagedorn, 215–29.

———, ed. 1994. "Dimensions of Desire: Other Asian and Pacific Sexualities: Gay, Lesbian and Bisexual Identities and Orientations." *Amerasia Journal* (special issue) 20.1.

Li, David Leiwei. 1992. "Filiative and Affiliative Textualization in Chinese American Literature." In *Understanding Others: Cultural and Cross-Cultural Studies and the Teaching of Literature*, ed. Joseph Trimmer, 177–200. Urbana, IL: National Council of Teachers of English.

Lim, Paul Stephen. 1977. *Conpersonas: A Recreation in Two Acts*. New York: Samuel French.

———. 1985a. *Homerica: A Trilogy on Sexual Liberation*. Louisville, KY: Aran Press.

———. 1985b. *Woe Man: A Recreation in Two Acts*. Louisville, KY: Aran Press.

———. 1989. *Figures in Clay: A Threnody in Six Scenes and a Coda*. Louisville, KY: Aran Press.

Lim, Shirley Geok-lin. 1990. "Japanese American Women's Life Stories: Maternality in Monica Sone's *Nisei Daughter* and Joy Kogawa's *Obasan*." *Feminist Studies* 16.2:289–312.

———. 1993. "Feminist and Ethnic Literary Theories in Asian American Literature." *Feminist Studies* 19.3:571–96.

Lim, Shirley Geok-Lin, and Mayumi Tsutakawa, eds. 1989. *The Forbidden Stitch: An Asian American Women's Anthology*. Corvallis, OR: Calyx Books.

Lim, Shirley Geok-Lin, and Amy Ling, eds. 1992. *Reading the Literatures of Asian America*. Philadelphia: Temple Univ. Press.

Lim-Hing, Sharon, ed. 1994. *The Very Inside: An Anthology of Writing by Asian and Pacific Islander Lesbian and Bisexual Women*. Toronto: Sister Vision Press.

Ling, Amy. 1990. *Between Worlds: Women Writers of Chinese Ancestry*. New York: Pergamon Press.

Ling, Amy. 1991. "'Emerging Canons' of Asian American Literature and Art." In *Asian Americans: Comparative and Global Perspectives*, ed. Shirley Hune et al., 191–7. Pullman: Washington State Univ. Press.

Liu, Timothy. 1992. *Vox Angelica*. Cambridge, MA: Alicejamesbooks.

Louie, David Wong. 1991. *Pangs of Love*. New York: Knopf.

Lowe, Lisa. 1991. "Heterogeneity, Hybridity, Multiplicity: Marking Asian American Differences." *Diaspora* 1.1:24–43.

———. 1994. "Unfaithful to the Original: The Subject of *Dictée*." In Kim and Alarcón, 35–69.

———. 1995a. "Canon, Institutionalization, Identity: Contradictions for Asian American Studies." In Palumbo-Liu, 48–68.

———. 1995b. "On Contemporary Asian American Projects." *Amerasia Journal* 21.1, 2:41–52.

Lye, Colleen. 1995. "*M. Butterfly* and the Rhetoric of Antiessentialism: Minority Discourse in an International Frame." In Palumbo-Liu, 260–89.

Mazumdar, Sucheta. 1991. "Asian American Studies and Asian Studies: Rethinking Roots." In *Asian Americans: Comparative and Global Perspectives*, ed. Shirley Hune et al., 29–44. Pullman: Washington State Univ. Press.

Meissenburg, Karin. 1987. *The Writing on the Wall*. Frankfurt: Verlag für Interkulturelle Kommunikation.

Min, Anchee. 1994. *Red Azalea*. New York: Pantheon.

Miyoshi, Masao. 1993. "A Borderless World? From Colonialism to Transnationalism and the Decline of the Nation-State." *Critical Inquiry* 19:726–51.

Mohanty, Chandra Talpade. 1989–90. "On Race and Voice: Challenges for Liberal Education in the 1990s." *Cultural Critique* 14:179–200.

———. 1993. "Defining Genealogies: Feminist Reflections on Being South Asian in North America." In Women of the South Asian Descent Collective, 351–8.

Moy, James S. 1993. *Marginal Sights: Staging the Chinese in America*. Iowa City: Univ. of Iowa Press.

Mukherjee, Bharati. 1988. "Give Us Your Maximalist." *Los Angeles Times*, 28 August, 1, 28–9.

———. 1989. *Jasmine*. New York: Grove Press.

Mura, David. 1991. *Turning Japanese*. New York: Atlantic Monthly Press.

———. 1994. "A Shift in Power, A Sea Change in the Arts." In *The State of Asian America: Activism and Resistance in the 1990s*, ed. Karin Aguilar-San Juan, 183–204. Boston: South End Press.

Murayama, Milton. 1959/1975. *All I Asking For Is My Body*. San Francisco: Supa Press.

Ng, Fae Myenne. 1993. *Bone*. New York: Hyperion.

Nguyễn Qúi Đứ'c. 1994. *Where the Ashes Are: The Odyssey of a Vietnamese Family*. Reading, MA: Addison-Wesley Publishing Company.

Niiya, Brian T. 1990. "Open-Minded Conservatives: A Survey of Autobiographies by Asian Americans." M.A. thesis, Univ. of California, Los Angeles.

Noda, Barbara. 1979. *Strawberries*. Berkeley: Shameless Hussy.

Okada, John. 1957/1979. *No-No Boy*. Rutland, VT: Charles E. Tuttle; Seattle: Univ. of Washington Press.

Pak, Gary. 1992. "The Trial of Goro Fukushima." In *The Watcher of Waipuna and Other Stories*, 95–112. Honolulu: Bamboo Ridge Press.

Palumbo-Liu, David. Forthcoming. "Model Minority Discourse and the Course of Healing." In *Minority Discourse: Ideological Containment and Utopian/ Heterotopian Potentials*, ed. Abdul JanMohamed. New York: Oxford Univ. Press.

———, ed. 1995. *The Ethnic Canon: Histories, Institutions, and Interventions*. Minneapolis: Univ. of Minnesota Press.

Pao, Angela. 1992. "The Critic and the Butterfly: Sociocultural Contexts and the Reception of David Henry Hwang's *M. Butterfly*." *Amerasia Journal* 18.3:1–16.

Redhakrishnan, R. 1994. "Is the Ethnic 'Authentic' in the Diaspora?" In *The State of Asian America: Activism and Resistance in the 1990s*, ed. Karin Aguilar-San Juan, 219–33. Boston: South End Press.

Ratti, Rakesh, ed. 1993. *A Lotus of Another Color: The Unfolding of the South Asian Gay and Lesbian Experience*. Boston: Alyson Press.

Sadana, Rashmi. 1993. "Making a Space for Women in the Third World: Displacement and Identity in Sara Suleri's *Meatless Days*." In Women of the South Asian Descent Collective, 320–4.

San Juan, E., Jr. 1975. *Carlos Bulosan and the Imagination of the Class Struggle*. Quezon City: Univ. of the Philippines Press.

———. 1991. "Beyond Identity Politics: The Predicament of the Asian American Writer in Late Capitalism." *American Literary History* 3.3:542–65.

———. 1994. "The Predicament of Filipinos in the United States." In *The State of Asian America: Activism and Resistance in the 1990s*, ed. Karin Aguilar-San Juan, 205–18. Boston: South End Press.

———. 1995. "In Search of Filipino Writing: Reclaiming Whose 'America?'" In Palumbo-Liu, 213–40.

Santos, Bienvenido N. 1979. "The Day the Dancers Came." In *Scent of Apples: A Collection of Stories*, 113–28. Seattle: Univ. of Washington Press.

———. 1987. *What the Hell For You Left Your Heart in San Francisco*. Quezon City, Philippines: New Day Publishers.

Sato, Gayle K. Fujita. 1992. "Momotaro's Exile: John Okada's *No-No Boy*." In Lim and Ling, 239–58.

Seth Vikram. 1986. *Golden Gate*. New York: Random House.

Sharpe, Jenny. 1995. "Is the United States Pcostcolonial? Transnationalism, Immigration, and Race." *Diaspora* 4.2:181–99.

Shimakawa, Karen. 1993. "'Who's to Say?' Or, Making Space for Gender and Ethnicity in *M. Butterfly*." *Theatre Journal* 45.3:349–62.

Silvera, Makeda, ed. 1993. *Piece of My Heart: A Lesbian of Colour Anthology*. Toronto: Sister Vision Press.

Skloot, Robert. 1990. "Breaking the Butterfly: The Politics of David Henry Hwang." *Modern Drama* 33.1:59–66.

Soja, Edward. 1989. *Postmodern Geographies: The Reassertion of Space in Critical Social Theory*. New York: Verso.

Sollors, Werner. 1986. *Beyond Ethnicity: Consent and Descent in American Culture*. New York: Oxford Univ. Press.

Sone, Monica. 1953/1979. *Nisei Daughter*. Seattle: Univ. of Washington Press.

Suleri, Sara. 1989. *Meatless Days*. Chicago: Univ. of Chicago Press.

Sumida, Stephen H. 1991. *And the View from the Shore: Literary Traditions of Hawai'i*. Seattle: Univ. of Washington Press.

———. 1992. "Sense of Place, History, and the Concept of the 'Local' in Hawaii's Asian/Pacific American Literatures." In Lim and Ling, 215–37.

Tan, Amy. 1989. *The Joy Luck Club*. New York: Putnam.

———. 1991. *The Kitchen God's Wife*. New York: Ballantine.

Thongthiraj, Rapee. 1955. "Breaking Silence and Remaking the Self in Wanwadee Larsen's *Confessions of a Mail Order Bride*." M.A. thesis, Univ. of California, Los Angeles.

Tsiang, H. T. 1937. *And China Has Hands*. New York: Robert Speller.

Tsui, Kitty. 1983. *The Words of a Woman Who Breathes Fire*. San Francisco: Spinsters Ink.

Uba, George. 1992. "Versions of Identity in Post-Activist Asian American Poetry." In Lim and Ling, 33–48.

Uyemoto, Holly. 1989. *Rebel Without a Clue*. New York: Crown.

Villa, José García. 1942. *Have Come, Am Here*. New York: Viking.

Vinh Do. 1994. "The Search for Home: An Interview with Bay Area Writer Nguyễn Qúi Đức." *Pacific Reader: International Examiner Literary Supplement* (Spring), 1.

Watanabe, Sylvia, and Carol Bruchac, eds. 1990. *Home to Stay: Asian American Women's Fiction*. Greenfield Center, NY: Greenfield Review Press.

West, Cornell. 1993. *Beyond Eurocentrism and Multiculturalism*. Monroe, ME: Common Courage Press.

Women of the South Asian Descent Collective (Sheela Bhatt, Preety Kalra, Aarti Kohli, Latika Malkani, Dharini Rasiah, eds.). 1993. *Our Feet Walk the Sky: Women of the South Asian Diaspora*. San Francisco: Aunt Lute.

Wong, Norman. 1994. *Cultural Revolution*. New York: Persea.

Wong, Sau-ling Cynthia. 1992. "Autobiography as Guided Chinatown Tour? Maxine Hong Kingston's *The Woman Warrior* and the Chinese American Autobiographical Controversy." *Multicultural Autobiography: American Lives*, ed. James Robert Payne, 248–79. Knoxville: Univ. of Tennessee Press.

———. 1993. *Reading Asian American Literature: From Necessity to Extravagance*. Princeton, NJ: Princeton Univ. Press.

———. 1995a. " 'Sugar Sisterhood': Situating the Amy Tan Phenomenon." In Palumbo-Liu, 174–210.

———. 1995b. "Denationalization Reconsidered: Asian American Cultural Criticism at a Theoretical Crossroads." *Amerasia Journal* 21.1, 2:1–21.

Woo, Merle. 1981/1983. "Letter to Ma." In *This Bridge Called My Back: Writings by Radical Women of Color*, ed. Cherríe Moraga and Gloria Anzaldúa, 140–7. Latham, NY: Kitchen Table/Women of Color Press.

Wright, Lawrence. "One Drop of Blood," *New Yorker*, 25 July 1994, 46–55.

Yamamoto, Hisaye. 1988. *"Seventeen Syllables" and Other Stories*. Latham, NY: Kitchen Table/Women of Color Press.

Yamashita, Karen Tei. 1990. *Through the Arc of the Rainforest*. Minneapolis: Coffee House Press.

PART ONE

1

CHINESE AMERICAN LITERATURE

SAU-LING CYNTHIA WONG

A survey of a literature typically begins with an attempt to pin-point its origins, then proceeds to trace its "growth" (implying a matura-tional model of literary production). In the case of Chinese American literature, however, it would be misleading to plunge into a positivistic, unproblematized chronological account without first addressing defini-tional issues, for the term "Chinese American literature" is itself a product of a specific historical moment. Just as ambiguities surround the term "Chinese Americans," so there exists no consensus on what properly falls within the purview of Chinese American literature; indeed, the bound-aries of the field, as inferred from critical practice, have fluctuated with changing historical conditions. It is only when the definitional debates are understood that statements about the significance of specific works and authors, as well as efforts at periodization (virtually inescapable in an overview this brief), become meaningful.

The usage of "Chinese Americans," currently accepted by a majority of the community and by the American political structure, to refer to per-sons of Chinese ancestry residing permanently in the United States re-gardless of nativity, is of recent coinage. The group now known as Chinese Americans can trace a long history in this country dating back to the first influx after the Gold Rush of 1848 and the massive importation of laborers to build the transcontinental railroad in the 1860s. Despite its contributions, however, the group was regarded by the dominant society as foreign – at best exotic, at worst terminally unassimilable. The policy of Exclusion (1882–1943), which banned the entry of Chinese laborers to and prevented the formation of Chinese families in the United States, was just the most visible institutional expression of such an othering attitude; its effects were not significantly reversed until the liberalization of the immigration laws in 1965. Because of American political rejection, no less than Chinese cultural imperatives, even those immigrants who had man-aged to put down roots on American soil tended to think of themselves as *huaqiao*, "overseas Chinese." It was only with the pan-Asian movement of the late 1960s and early 1970s, which highlighted the importance of recognizing Asians in America as an internally colonized ethnic minority, that the term "Chinese Americans," like its superordinate "Asian Americans," began to take on its current meaning, connoting at once a claim to full membership in American society and intragroup coalition based on similarities in historical circumstances.

When the sixties generation of Asian American activists turned their attention to literature, their interest was not abstract or academic. In this period of profound demographic, social, and political change, they saw the building of an Asian American cultural tradition, with its concomitant challenge to the Anglo-American canon, as an integral part of the group's larger struggle for a rightful place in this country. In this movement Chinese Americans played a key role. Many of the first anthologizers were Chinese: Kai-yu Hsu (1972); David Hsin-fu Wand (1974); and, in particular, Frank Chin, Jeffery Paul Chan, and Shawn Wong, who, with Japanese American poet Lawson Fusao Inada, created a manifesto for Asian American literature in their landmark volume *Aiiieeeee! An Anthology of Asian-American Writers* (1974).

It was Frank Chin and his associates who, in their prefatory essays affirming cultural dynamism, set forth most of the terms of debate on what counts as Chinese American literature. Controversial as these views are, they represent the first clear articulation of the possibilities of a Chinese American literary identity. Briefly stated, the *Aiiieeeee!* group valorizes works written in English by American-born writers on American subjects addressed primarily to fellow Asian Americans, preferably with a pronounced anti-Orientalist agenda, working-class sympathies, and an interest in rehabilitating Chinese American masculinity. Several overlapping criteria, of varying degrees of elusiveness, are at work here (although some of the group's favorite writers are exempted from their rigid application): author's nativity, language of composition, intended audience, subject matter, and sensibility. Shaped by an acute awareness of Chinese American history, the prevailing ideology of the anti–Vietnam War and civil rights movement era, as well as the *Aiiieeeee!* writers' own American-born backgrounds, these criteria have been shared implicitly or explicitly by many critics and remain influential today.

To speak of "the emergence of Chinese American literature," then, is not so much to label a cultural event as to recognize, and by recognizing sustain, a cultural creation. While the boundaries of this creation continue to be contested – the *Aiiieeeee!* tenets have been increasingly challenged from a number of directions – the existence of Chinese American literature has been naturalized to such an extent that a group-specific reference piece like this chapter is now possible. The Chinese American tradition, young to begin with, is ceaselessly being reconfigured. My decision to commence this narrative with issues of nomenclature may detract from its smooth linearity but does keep the constructed and open-ended nature of canon formation in view. In accordance with the general policy of this volume, I will emphasize writings in English; however, as translation can play, has played, and will continue to play a decisive role in the formation of the Chinese American canon, important Chinese-language works will be noted as well.

After this clarification, in the rest of the chapter I will give a loosely chronological account of Chinese American literature along more conventional lines. I follow King-Kok Cheung and Stan Yogi, authors of *Asian American Literature: An Annotated Bibliography* (1988), in favoring an inclusive view of Chinese American literature, within constraints of space. Periodization correlates broadly with changes in the political, social, and economic conditions of Chinese Americans, but this should not be taken to imply a concept of literature as a mechanistic reflection of social reality. Rather, my account tries to emphasize the complex and reciprocal interactions of material and discursive forces.

Few firsthand records are left by nineteenth-century Chinese immigrants. Except for a small number of women and some merchants, immigrants of this period were predominantly male laborers, poorly educated peasants charged with supporting their families left behind in Guangdong Province in southern China. Exclusion and other discriminatory laws created gender-imbalanced "bachelor societies" in Chinatowns; prolonged family separation was often ended only through fraudulent entry with purchased immigration papers (creating "paper sons" and, less commonly, "paper daughters"). Extreme physical and psychological hardships, coupled with limited schooling, did not favor artistic creation. However, a glimpse of the early Chinese Americans' original cultural milieu, elements of which must have been brought over, can be gained from *Chen* Yuanzhu's *Taishan geyao ji* (A collection of Taishan folk rhymes) (1929; rpt. 1969) and *Hu* Zhaozhong's *Meizhou Guangdong huaqiao liuchuan geyao huibian* (A collection of folk rhymes popular among Cantonese in America) (1970).[1] These folk rhymes exhibit characteristics of oral compositions: formulaic opening lines, simple prosodic structures, directness of language, anonymous authorship, and depictions of rural life. Many pieces speak of the harsh conditions that forced young men to emigrate, the pain of leave-taking, and wishes for success in "Gold Mountain."

Despite the efforts of scholars such as Marlon K. Hom, the oral tradition among Chinese Americans is, by and large, under-researched and ill-understood. The *Aiiieeeee!* group mentions nonprint literary sources, such as "wooden fish songs," gathered for the Combined Asian Resources

Project (CARP) (Jeffery Paul Chan et al., 1981), but gives few substantial examples of oral transmissions. Later, the popular success of Maxine Hong Kingston's *The Woman Warrior* (1976) and Amy Tan's *The Joy Luck Club* (1989), both putatively elaborated from "talk-story" passed on from mother to daughter, has occasioned discussion of the Chinese American oral tradition among critics (for example, Sledge 1990), but the empirical basis for most such generalizations is weak.

Still, even to this day, vestiges of a Chinese American oral tradition can be found. For example, the genre of the "wooden fish song" (the "wooden fish" or *muyu* [*muk-yu* in Cantonese] is a small percussion instrument) finds a contemporary exponent in *Ng* Sheung Chi, known as "Uncle Ng," a New York Chinatown inhabitant from Taishan. Admittedly a rarity and an anachronism, this folk artist recently caught the attention of a Chinese American historian, Robert Lee; some of his songs were transcribed and translated; and a videotape about him, *Singing to Remember*, was released by New York's Asian American Arts Centre (Robert Lee 1992).

The fate of "Uncle Ng's" songs illustrates the crucial role played by textual recovery, preservation, dissemination – especially translation – in the Chinese American canon formation process. Despite images of cultural tenacity, language shift in the Chinese community as a whole has been no slower than among European immigrant groups. Although Chinese language retention has been somewhat more successful in recent years with the arrival of affluent, determinedly bicultural immigrant families from Taiwan and the institutional recognition of Chinese as a foreign language in certain sectors of the American educational system, it is still unusual for third-generation Chinese to be able to read Chinese. Thus, unless translated, first-generation works in Chinese are inaccessible to Anglophone scholars. Some of the texts now considered landmarks in Chinese American literary history were, in the very recent past, in danger of being annihilated, or else relegated to dusty corners of special library collections. However, labors of love by scholars and the community led to their translation into English and publication in book form, and these once obscure works immediately became part of the Chinese American canon.

One such work is the collection *Island* (Him Mark Lai et al. 1980), consisting of poems carved by detained immigrants into the wooden walls of barracks on Angel Island (in San Francisco Bay), which was used as an immigration station between 1910 and 1940 in which to interrogate Chinese entrants and screen out "paper sons" with forged documents. Almost lost when the barracks fell into disrepair, the poems were preserved through community effort: studied (Wang 1976), transcribed and translated, then published in bilingual format. The angry and poignant voices of these early Chinese immigrants constitute a powerful counterdiscourse to the myth of America as a nation open to all immigrants.

Another noteworthy translation is *Jinshan geji*, which appeared in two volumes in 1911 and 1915 but remained unknown outside of specialist circles until 1987, when Marlon K. Hom rendered selected poems into English and published them as *Songs of Gold Mountain: Cantonese Rhymes from San Francisco Chinatown* (1987). Unlike the rhymes in Chen's and Hu's collection, these "songs" were not transcriptions of oral recitations; rather, they were composed in written form by members of "poetry societies" then active in San Francisco Chinatown. These anonymous authors were most likely members of the better-educated merchant class (one of the handful of exempt categories under the Exclusion Act). The poets' voices are unpretentious, exuberant, and candidly patriarchal; they cover topics ranging from American hardships to fantasies of triumphant return to China, from the pain of family separation to the allures of Chinatown prostitutes, from support for Dr. Sun Yat-sen's Republican Revolution (1911) to outrage at the un-Confucian ways of "emancipated women." The prefaces to the two volumes of *Jinshan geji*, as yet untranslated, are in fact key documents in the evolution of Chinese American literature. Arguing that the homeland literati's rigid aesthetic standards are no longer relevant to "Gold Mountain" poets, because of the latter's Cantonese origin, use of dialect, and American experiences, the preface writers affirm the validity of cultural transformation in a new land. The *Gold Mountain* songs' innovative mixture of Cantonese slang, translations from English, and classical poetic diction is a compelling example of heteroglossia.

If *Songs of Gold Mountain* represents the early immigrants' most sustained and distinctive literary production on American soil, *Kuxuesheng* (The industrious student), a well-crafted novella published in China under the pseudonym of Qiyouzi, contains perhaps the first fictional character with a clearly non-sojourner mentality. The novella is part of a vast body of anti-Exclusion literature arising from the 1905 Chinese protest boycott of American goods and collected in Aying's *Fanmei huagong jinyue wenxueji*, an enormous, multigenre compilation published in 1960. *Kuxuesheng* descibes a patriotic student who travels to America in order to acquire the knowledge needed to save his crumbling country from corrupt Manchu rule as well as economic and military invasion by foreign powers. Before the protagonist returns home, he receives help from an extraordinary old man, a wealthy Chinese immigrant who has managed to create his own utopian estate in an inhospitable, often overtly racist, society. Significantly, the old man is named *Huasheng*, evoking Washington, "father of the American nation"(*Huasheng* forms part of *Huashengdun*, the Chinese translation of Washington's name), but also meaning "prosperity for China," a cause to which he contributes but in which he does not personally participate. This doubleness of vision and commitment is the earliest example I can find of the sensibility later described as Chinese American by the sixties generation.

Out of Aying's vast compilation, only a short excerpt on the United States from *Kushehui*, a rambling novella on the plight of Chinese "coolies," has been translated as "The Bitter Society" (Mei, Yip, and Leong 1981). The authors of both *Kuxuesheng* and *Kushehui* appear to be "returnees" rather than settlers in the United States. Their works show somewhat greater familiarity and empathy with Chinese American life than visitors' accounts penned by members of the Chinese elite, such as *Huang* Zunxian and *Liang* Qichao. (Translated excerpts from their accounts are found in Arkush and Lee's *Land Without Ghosts* [1989], an anthology on Chinese impressions of America.) Still, the "permanent residency" criterion for Chinese American authorship becomes problematic when applied to the Exclusion period.

A similar case can be made for works written by Chinese in English in roughly the same period. *Lee* Yan Phou, author of *When I Was a Boy in China* (1887), may or may not have returned to settle in China. The author of *My Life in China and America* (1909), *Yung* Wing, like Lee among "China's first hundred" young students sent to study in the United States, and *Huie* Kin, whose *Reminiscences* (1932) chronicles his life as a Christian minister in the United States, both returned to settle in China. Yet these men's accounts cannot be ignored when tracing the lineage of Chinese American literature. Even Frank Chin's attack on Yung Wing for having initiated a feminized, Christianized, and assimilationist tradition of Chinese American autobiography (Frank Chin 1985) is in its own way an indication of the importance of *My Life in China and America*.

Current scholarly practice tends to designate *Sui* Sin Far – a Eurasian writer who had lived in Britain and Canada before immigrating to the United States – as the first Chinese American writer in English. Sui Sin Far is the pen name of Edith Eaton, daughter of an English father and a Chinese mother. Because of her Chinatown subject matter and nonstereotypical portrayals of the Chinese (to the extent allowed by the prejudices of her times and the stylistic conventions of sentimental fiction), her prose narratives – notably the autobiographical account "Leaves from the Mental Portfolio of an Eurasian" (1909) and short-story collection *Mrs. Spring Fragrance* (1912; rpt. 1995) – have been accepted as key contributions to the Chinese American literary tradition. The efforts of critics have made Sui Sin Far's works accessible to the contemporary reader. The canonization of Sui Sin Far points to a question of boundary similar to that raised by residency: the extent to which an author's ancestry or "blood" should – or should not – figure in a definition of Chinese American literature.

The significance of Sui Sin Far's work cannot be fully appreciated unless one knows something of the blatantly racist depictions of Chinese during the late nineteenth and early twentieth century. As Elaine Kim notes, early Chinese Americans typically appear in Anglo-American literature as unassimilable aliens: either docile, grunting brutes or corrupt villains "too clever for their own good." The setting is usually a phantasmic Chinatown of ornamental Orientalia and heathen rituals, of intrigues, savagery and sexual degradation. Other Asians suffered a similar literary fate (Kim 1982, 3–22). It is not surprising, therefore, that defending and explaining the Chinese to white readers became a preoccupation of "ambassadors of goodwill": highly educated, often aristocratic, Asians who used their knowledge of the English language and American culture to dispel negative images about their ethnic group (Kim 1982, 24–32). This type of writing was common from the turn of the century past the Exclusion Act's repeal in 1943, down through World War II and the postwar period; the cultural stance it represents continues to exist in various guises even today. The term "ambassadors of goodwill" captures the writers' subjective intentions as well as the tenor of their presentation; nevertheless, because of the writers' privileged backgrounds and their investment in maintaining the role of cultural mediator, their writing often trades one kind of Orientalism for another. This is the historical basis for the sixties writers' vehement reaction against exoticization and insistence on the problematic litmus test of "intended audience."

The Chinese American writers whom Kim classifies as "ambassadors of goodwill" include Lee Yan Phou; Wu Tingfang, author of *America through the Spectacles of an Oriental Diplomat* (1914); Lin Yutang, who enjoyed a long and lucrative American career as a humorist, a living embodiment of Chinese high culture, and a popularizer of traditional Oriental wisdom, and wrote a novel about an immigrant family in New York, *Chinatown Family* (1948); and Chiang Yee, whose *Silent Traveler* series contains his own illustrations.

Not all Chinese American writing produced during the first few decades of the twentieth century can be subsumed under the cultural politics outlined above. H. T. Tsiang (Jiang Xizeng), a first-generation leftist writer active in the 1930s, left behind novels, poems, and a play supportive both of the international proletarian movement and the Communist cause in China; his *And China Has Hands* (1937), a short novel about the life of a New York laundryman, is credited by Kim as the "first fictional rendition of the bachelor society in English by a Chinese immigrant" (Kim 1982, 109). In Hawai'i since the 1920s, Chinese students at the University of Hawai'i (among them James H. Chun, Phoebe Chun Chang, Wai Chee Chun Yee, and *Li* Ling-Ai) had been composing stories, poems, and plays about plantation life, generational conflict, and other "local" subjects; some experimented with the use of pidgin. These and other writings are collected in *Paké* (1989), a special issue of *Bamboo Ridge: The Hawaii Writers' Quarterly* edited by Eric Chock and Darrell Lum to commemorate the two hundredth anniversary of Chinese immigration to Hawai'i.

The Second World War marked a turning point in the fortunes of Chinese Americans, which in turn had an effect on the type of Chinese American literature favored by the reading public and the publishing establishment. China being America's ally in the war, Chinese Americans suddenly became the "good" Asians as distinguished from the "bad" Japanese; the Exclusion Act was repealed in 1943 (although large-scale Chinese immigration did not resume until 1965); and Chinese were allowed into certain occupations previously barred to them. Pro-Chinese sentiments made it possible for a small group of Chinese-born, Westernized women – Helena Kuo, Lin Yutang's daughters Adet Lin and *Lin* Taiyi (or Anor Lin), Mai-mai Sze, and *Han* Suyin – to publish as many as ten books in the 1940s (Ling 1990, 59). The 1940s also saw the coming of age of a small American-born generation: biliterate men and women who grew up in Chinatown but were socialized into the assimilationist ethos of the time. Like the foreign-born "ambassadors of goodwill," they were positioned to be cultural mediators. From the ranks of this second generation came Stanford- and Harvard-educated Pardee Lowe, whose *Father and Glorious Descendant* (1943) interprets Chinese customs to white readers, and Jade Snow Wong, whose *Fifth Chinese Daughter* (1945) became a hit, earned the author a State Department–sponsored speaking tour in Asia, has been widely taught in American schools as a young adult book, and remains in print today.

Both Lowe and Wong can be said to practice a type of writing I have elsewhere termed "autobiography as guided Chinatown tour" (S. C. Wong 1992). Both owed their success in no small measure to the greater receptivity toward things Chinese – including exotic foods and customs previously deemed repulsively alien – induced by shifting international politics; and both chart a trajectory of Chinese American life from tradition to modernity, from conformity to individual freedom, that fits neatly into mainstream myths about the inevitable "progress" of the immigrant family. Nevertheless, as shown by some of Jade Snow Wong's poignant observations about her lowly status, growing up Chinese American meant vastly different things for the male child than for the female.

In general, the female writer's relationship to American culture is much more vexed than the male's, for, given her subjected position in

Chinese patriarchy, the woman's first contacts with Western ways typically had some liberating effects, however the imperialistic or racist aspects of Westernization might play out in the long run. This is true for both Chinese- and American-born women, even for women whose class advantages might have partially compensated for sexist deprivations, such as Helena Kuo, author of the autobiographical *I've Come a Long Way* (1942). Thus, not unlike African American slave narratives beginning with the acquisition of literacy, Chinese American women's life stories such as Jade Snow Wong's and Kuo's, as well as later ones like Su-ling Wong's *Daughter of Confucius* (1952) and Katherine Wei's *Second Daughter* (1984) (cowritten with E. H. Cressy and Terry Quinn, respectively), tend to contain accounts of how the author, contrary to prevailing gender norms, came to be highly educated and to learn English. (The feminist sentiments and counter-stereotyping practices of Chinese American women writers are explored in Amy Ling, *Between Worlds* [1990].) This complex interaction of gender, racial, ethnic, and class politics is at the root of the conflict between feminism and cultural nationalism that was to erupt in the 1970s (see Cheung [1990] for a succinct analysis of this debate).

After the Second World War, the Chinese American community was transformed by the entry of "war brides," which began to correct the gender imbalance in Chinatowns and made nuclear families prevalent for the first time in many years. Soon, however, the glow faded as communism triumphed in China, the Korean War broke out, and the Cold War began to cast suspicions on Chinese Americans – now the "bad" Asians again. Some of these changes are captured in a series of short stories in a leftist journal, *Xinmiao* or *The Bud*, which lasted only from 1947 to 1948 but managed to produce a multifaceted picture of New York Chinatown in the social realist tradition; the stories depict waiters, gamblers, students, war brides, family and district association leaders, and a handful of whites and blacks with whom they come into contact. The short burst of creativity among immigrants before the Cold War is detailed in Wenquan's essay "Huaqiao wenyi shinian," which has been translated into English by Marlon Hom (1982). However, the *Bud* stories, as well as some novellas written by the members of the *Bud* group, remain untranslated. (See S. C. Wong [1988] for synopses of the stories and an analysis.)

Fortunately for the Anglophone reader, Louis Chu's *Eat a Bowl of Tea*, though first published as late as 1961, fills the gap by providing a comic tale of romantic love and community renewal during the postwar period. Set in New York Chinatown like the *Bud* stories, and exhibiting a very similar working-class, realist "Chinatown" sensibility, Chu's novel revolves around the impotence of Ben Loy, a second-generation Chinese

American veteran who brings over Mei Oi as his "war bride" but is unable to produce an heir for his watchful elders. Mei Oi is seduced by a Chinatown ne'er-do-well; her pregnancy wreaks havoc on the community, but when a son is born, the young people are forgiven, free to start a new life in San Francisco. Thus is the dying "bachelor society," a legacy of the Exclusion era, transformed into a community with a future, one not defined exclusively by "bloodline." *Eat a Bowl of Tea* is an important Chinese American text in a number of ways: it departs from the autobiographical imperative as well as the mediational cultural stance prevalent in many previous tales of Chinatown; provides a narrative of community life at a critical historical moment; and employs a "Chinatown English" without overtones of caricature. Chu's artistic accomplishments can be appreciated when *Eat a Bowl of Tea* is contrasted with Monfoon Leong's *Number One Son* (1975), a collection of short stories written in the 1950s and early 1960s, where the desire to represent Chinatown life sympathetically is not matched by linguistic skill and formal command.

The characteristics of *Eat a Bowl of Tea* are especially striking when one recalls that it was roughly contemporaneous with C. Y. Lee's *The Flower Drum Song* (1957), whose unabashed catering to white stereotypes of the Chinese earned it great popularity (including adaptation into a Rodgers and Hammerstein musical and a film). To the *Aiiieeeee!* group, Chu's novel represents the affirmation of a male literary tradition, an emblem of incorruptible Chinese American cultural integrity (for example, Jeffery Paul Chan et al. 1991, xii). However, it would be simplistic to see the development of Chinese American literature in terms of a unidirectional "improvement" away from the distortions of Orientalism into the sunshine of ethnic pride and historically accurate representations. Frank Chin himself, self-proclaimed heir to Louis Chu's Chinatown tradition, provides good illustrations of how contestation between discursive formations, not simple filiation or supersession, shapes even those works with an explicitly revisionist political agenda.

Chin's plays *Chickencoop Chinaman* and *The Year of the Dragon* (first performed in 1972 and 1974, respectively; published in 1981), as well as his short stories first published between 1970 and 1978 and later collected in *The Chinaman Pacific & Frisco R.R. Co.* (1988), bear the mark of the turbulent 1960s. In revolt against institutional racism and white cultural hegemony, and inspired by the heroics of the Black Power movement, Chin is determined to forge a uniquely "Chinaman" language fusing the cadences of Cantonese and urban black vernacular to the English language. His verbal pyrotechnics impressed even as its hybridity baffled mainstream critics and outraged some Chinese readers. In their boldness, Chin's works of this period can be said to exemplify the spirit of the

Aiiieeeee! manifesto: "An American-born Asian . . . does not reverberate to gongs struck hundreds of years ago or snuggle into the doughy clutches of an America hot to coddle something ching chong" (Frank Chin et al. 1974, xxiv). But in them programmatic ideological lucidity is also constantly overrun by dark psychic forces, as the author seeks to articulate a viable minority identity among multiple discourses, under contradiction-ridden material conditions. Chin glamorizes – highly selectively – certain aspects of Chinese tradition, for instance, by identifying the heroic fraternity of Chinese classics *The Romance of the Three Kingdoms* and *Outlaws of the Marsh* as the authentic essence of "Chinaman" culture. At the same time, his fictional Chinatown is peopled with the same cast of tradition-bound, moribund elders as are found in *The Flower Drum Song* or rebellious Americanized youngsters as are found in *Fifth Chinese Daughter*. Fiercely anti-assimilationist, he yet builds an oeuvre rich in allusions to icons of American myth and popular culture (like Paul Bunyan, John Wayne, or the Lone Ranger), which he at once invokes and subverts.

It is perhaps this kind of responsiveness to historical and discursive complexity, rather than any single event or publishing "landmark," that most clearly marks the coming-of-age of Chinese American literature. Some of Jeffery Paul Chan's short stories, such as "Auntie Tsia Lays Dying" (1971) and "Jackrabbit" (1974), and Ashley Sheun Dunn's "No Man's Land" (1978), share in Frank Chin's masculinist, angst-ridden vision. So does Shawn Wong's *Homebase* (1979), though to a lesser extent and in a different shading. A lyrical invocation of Chinese ancestry, American land, and Chinese American history, *Homebase* interweaves personal history and collective trauma to achieve cultural healing (in language if nowhere else).

As American-born writers negotiated one set of cultural terrain, a "diasporic" group of Chinese-born writers in the 1960s and 1970s explored the experience of global dispersal beyond the "ambassadors of goodwill" genre. *Chuang* Hua published the paradigmatically titled novel *Crossings* in 1968. Perhaps the only sustained example of high modernism in Chinese American literature, the fragmented narrative jumps between America, Europe, and memories of China, as the upper-class protagonist, Fourth Jane, attempts to come to terms with her deracination. Reissued in 1986, *Crossings* shows thematic and formal affinities with Hualing Nieh's *Mulberry and Peach* (1981/1988), whose publication history is even more circuitous. Originally written in Chinese and published in 1976, in its Chinese version the book is read both as a political allegory (it was banned by the Nationalist government) and as part of an exile or émigré tradition; Nieh is seen as a peer of *Pai* Hsien-yung (Bai Xianyong) and *Yu* Lihua, who have written extensively on the lives of transplanted intellectuals in the 1960s and 1970s.[2] But as American critical interest grew in feminist, non-Western works and in literatures of displacement and border-crossing, the translation of *Mulberry and Peach*, which first appeared in the United States in 1981, was reissued as a paperback in 1988. *Mulberry and Peach* chronicles the physical and psychological travails of a refugee woman who ends up as an illegal alien wandering across the United States; unable to resolve her conflicts, she splits into two personalities, Mulberry and Peach. The book's multiple discursive locations are a reminder of the complexity of Chinese American literature.

To American readers unaware of this complexity, it is often Maxine Hong Kingston's *The Woman Warrior* (1976) that serves as their first introduction to – unfortunately, for many also their only glimpse into – the tradition. By now canonized and estimated by some to be the most widely taught work by a living American author, *The Woman Warrior* is a key – if highly controversial – Chinese American text in many ways. Subtitled *Memoirs of a Girlhood among Ghosts*, first marketed under an "autobiography" label, and featuring a blend of personal reminiscences, imaginative reconstructions of family events, and outright fantasies, it problematizes generic definitions and the idea of representational responsibility in "ethnic" writing. The book's focus on the mother–daughter relationship, and on concerns such as sexism in Chinese culture and the need to break silence, marks it as a feminist text, aligning it with not only middle-class white feminism but also such women-of-color works as Alice Walker's *The Color Purple* (1982). The intricacy of its formal structure, with its attendant epistemological issues, also places it within the "postmodern metafiction" category. Finally, its popularity – greater among mainstream readers than Chinese Americans – raises questions of misreading and appropriation. In freely altering aspects of Chinese tradition to suit her purpose of depicting the cultural predicament of the American-born Chinese, Kingston has been read as both anti-Orientalist and neo-Orientalist. Frank Chin, Jeffery Paul Chan, and others, taking the latter point of view, have been vocal in attacking *The Woman Warrior* as a contemporary representative of a "fake" Chinese American tradition – misogynist, exoticized, and inauthentic. Kingston's next book, *China Men* (1980), partly in response to such criticism, attempts to delineate a new kind of Chinese American male heroism and to incorporate historical information on discrimination against Chinese Americans while continuing to engage in formal experimentation. But the controversy rages on; every issue raised by *The Woman Warrior* touches a nerve and exposes a fundamental tension in the Chinese American experience that cannot be resolved through debate. (Shirley Lim, ed. 1991, presents a variety of viewpoints on the book.)

The high visibility of *The Woman Warrior* tends to obscure for the nonspecialist reader the fact that Chinese American "feminist" writing was not invented by Kingston; instead, as alluded to in the section above on literacy in women's autobiography, it has been shaped by the uneasy positioning of Chinese American women vis-à-vis patriarchal values in Chinese tradition and American political and ideological colonization since the early days of East–West contact. Works by women writers with a focus on matrilineality, be it biological or cultural, continue to be an important component of Chinese American literature, ranging from Ruthanne Lum McCunn's fictionalized biography of a Chinese pioneer woman, *Thousand Pieces of Gold* (1981); Alice Lin's autobiographical *Grandmother Had No Name* (1988); the short stories by Chinese American women in Watanabe and Bruchac's 1990 anthology *Home to Stay*; to Fae Myenne Ng's novel on a Chinatown immigrant family of three daughters, *Bone* (1993). Within this strand, Amy Tan's *The Joy Luck Club* (1989) stands out as yet another crossover bestseller like *The Woman Warrior*. Made up of stories about four mother–daughter pairs, it is less taxing to read than *The Woman Warrior*; it also appeals to a wide spectrum of readers by drawing upon a number of popular discourses in the 1980s, including those related to the recovery movement, yuppie life, and liberal pluralism. In the shadow of Tan's blockbuster, Kingston's inventive *Tripmaster Monkey: His Fake Book*, which appeared the same year, was overshadowed. *Tripmaster Monkey* is a formally and stylistically innovative narrative centered upon Wittman Ah Sing, a 1960s Chinese American playwright modeled on Frank Chin. Through chronicling his attempt to put on a show for his friends and family, Kingston alludes to Asian American cultural history and the San Francisco Bay Area counter-cultural scene, plays with both Chinese literary classics and the Euro-American canon, and gestures toward the possibility of a community-building, mythmaking Chinese American art.

The Kingston–Chin controversy was rekindled by both *The Joy Luck Club* and David Henry Hwang's award-winning Broadway play, *M. Butterfly* (first performed 1988; published 1989). A theatrical tour de force combining spectacular visual effects, biting dialogue, and gender-bending shocks, *M. Butterfly* is based on the true story of a French diplomat in China who maintained a twenty-year relationship with a Communist Chinese spy, a transvestite opera singer, without (so the diplomat claimed) knowing that "she" was a man. Although not set in Asian America, *M. Butterfly* was immediately hailed by some as a central text in Asian American literature because, in fusing this story to the outlines of Puccini's opera *Madama Butterfly*, it works to deconstruct sexism, Orientalism, and imperialism, which are ongoing concerns in the literary tradition. Yet applause for this deconstruction is countered by bitter criticism, especially from Asian American men, against the play's restaging of Orientalist stereotypes (the wimpy man, the sneaky spy, and so on). Finally, because the relationship depicted is in fact a homosexual one, *M. Butterfly* raises questions about how sexual orientation intersects with race and gender in Asian American identity and cultural politics. Although David Henry Hwang had been an acclaimed playwright for some time before (his *FOB* and *The Dance and the Railroad*, both about specifically Chinese American subject matter, premiered in 1979 and 1981, respectively, and are collected in *Broken Promises* [1983]), and although he has continued to work in theater and film since, *M. Butterfly* remains the title with which he is the most closely identified.

Before Hwang, the last time a Chinese American playwright gained mainstream critical attention was when Frank Chin burst on the scene with *The Chickencoop Chinaman* and especially *The Year of the Dragon*. Thus the debate surrounding *M. Butterfly* became particularly acute, with an element of professional competition thrown in. Although drama is a less developed genre than prose fiction within the Chinese American tradition, there have in fact been a sizable number of playwrights active over the years, associated with East/West Players in Los Angeles, the Asian American Theater Company in San Francisco, the Asian Exclusion Act in Seattle, and other companies. Only a small proportion of their plays have been published in book form; the rest either appeared in journals or else remain unpublished. Among the published titles are Laurence Yep's *Pay the Chinaman* (1990), set in the Sacramento Delta at the end of the nineteenth century; and Genny Lim's *Paper Angels* (1991), about early Chinese immigrants in the Angel Island Detention Station, and *Bitter Cane* (1991), about the lives of Chinese contract laborers on a Hawaiian sugar-cane plantation. As can be seen from this cursory list, reconstruction of certain canonical historical experiences is a popular project among Chinese American dramatists; style tends toward realism while staging is adapted to the paucity of material resources with which ethnic theater usually has to contend. A notable exception is Ping Chong, whose multimedia theater pieces defy ready classification and are unmoored from direct references to the Chinese American experience (see Westfall 1992 for an analysis).

Like drama, Chinese American poetry has been receiving much less critical attention than prose fiction, even though there exists a rich poetic corpus that would require a separate study to do it justice. Through a dazzling range of stylistic ventures, Chinese American poets negotiate what editors L. Ling-Chi Wang and Henry Yiheng Zhao call "the necessity of embracing, but at the same time distancing themselves from, their cultural roots" (xxviii) in their *Chinese American Poetry: An Anthology* (1991), thus far the only book-length collection on the subject.[3] Among the twenty-two poets included are Mei-Mei Berssenbrugge (*Empathy*, 1989), who describes her poetics in terms of "the material sensation of placing one word next to another word"; Diana Chang (*What Matisse Is After*, 1984), also a novelist and painter, who aspires to being imagistic; Alan Chong Lau (*Songs for Jadina*, 1980), for whom memory, heritage, and history (especially of California and the Pacific Northwest) are important subjects; Genny Lim (*Winter Place*, 1989), also a playwright and performance artist, who explores feminist and cultural concerns through experiments with rhythm and image; Shirley Lim (*Modern Secrets*, 1989), who draws upon both her Chinese-Malaysian roots and the Western literary tradition; Wing Tek Lum (*Expounding the Doubtful Points*, 1987), who writes intimately of family and love, mostly in a Chinese Hawaiian context; and John Yau (*Radiant Silhouettes*, 1989), art critic by profession, who investigates the paradoxes and limitations of language through deformation and variation. Marilyn Chin (*Dwarf Bamboo*, 1987), Chinese-literate but open to a host of poetic influences, writes with a passionate sense of craft. Arthur Sze (*Dazzled*, 1982), likewise conversant with classical Chinese poetry, evinces a sensibility toward nature that also resonates with a Native American worldview. Others in the anthology edited by Wang and Zhao include Shalin Hai-Jew, Jason Hwang, Alex Kuo, Carolyn Lau, Amy Ling, Stephen Liu, Laureen Mar, Diane Mark, and S. Lee Yung. In addition, San Franciscans Kitty Tsui (*The Words of a Woman Who Breathes Fire*, 1983), Nellie Wong (*The Death of Long Steam Lady*, 1986), and Merle Woo (*Yellow Woman Speaks*, 1986) seek to give voice to Asian American women's experiences; on the East Coast, Fay Chiang (*In the City of Contradictions*, 1979) engages in a similar enterprise to fuse art and politics. Among the younger generation of Chinese American poets, Indonesian-born Li-Young Lee dazzles with his lyrical intensity in *Rose* (1986) and *The City in Which I Love You* (1990). Two sets of recent publications indicate the thematic range of Chinese American poetry. A diasporic outlook is found in *The Country of Dreams and Dust* (1993) by Russell Leong, a veteran of the Asian American movement, and in *The Naturalization of Camellia Song* (1993) by Chin Woon Ping, a Chinese Malaysian poet. At the opposite end is a poetics of place of Chinese Hawaiian poet Eric Chock, in *Last Days Here* (1990).

Some of the poets mentioned above are also significant in establishing a gay and lesbian presence in the Chinese American literary tradition, which includes works in a variety of genres.[4] Kitty Tsui, Nellie Wong, and Merle Woo have long been outspoken on lesbian politics. Timothy Liu's volume of poetry, *Vox Angelica*, appeared in 1992. Chinese-Filipino playwright Paul Stephen Lim published *Figures in Clay*, a play on Asian–white gay relationships, in 1989. A number of pieces on homosexual themes by writers such as Russell Leong and Han Ong appeared in *Charlie Chan Is Dead* (1993), a fiction anthology edited by Jessica Hagedorn. Fiction writer Norman Wong published *Cultural Revolution* in 1994, which also saw Sharon Lim-Hing's anthology, *The Very Inside*, featuring (among others) Chinese American lesbian and bisexual writers.

No survey of Chinese American literature would be complete without mentioning Chinese Canadian literature, which is becoming increasingly vibrant and visible.⁵ A series of prose works appeared in the late 1980s and 1990s: Evelyn Lau's autobiographical *Runaway: Diary of a Street Kid* (1989); Sky Lee's novel *Disappearing Moon Cafe* (1990) and short-story collection *Bellydancer* (1994); Yuen Chung Yip's novel *The Tears of Chinese Immigrants* (1990), translated from Chinese; Ivy Huffman and Julia Kwong's composite account of early immigrants, *The Dream of Gold Mountain* (1991); and *Many-Mouthed Birds*, an anthology edited by Bennett Lee and Jim Wong-Chu (1991). Among the poets are Jamaila Ismail (*sexions*, 1984); Laiwan (*CAVE caveat*, 1984–5); Evelyn Lau (*You Are Not Who You Claim*, 1990); Jim Wong-Chu (*Chinatown Ghosts*, 1986); and Fred Wah, who has published since the 1960s and whose latest volume is *Alley Alley Home Free* (1992).

In an increasingly diverse Asian American culture representing many ethnic subgroups, Chinese American literature has lost some of its earlier dominance, and new themes embodying current demographic realities are emerging. For example, among the works published in 1991 – a particularly productive year for Asian American literature, marked by a surge of attention from the mainstream media – Frank Chin's *Donald Duk* (as well as his 1994 novel, *Gunga Din Highway*) reprises issues of historical recuperation and male heroism, while Gus Lee's *China Boy* and Gish Jen's *Typical American* both focus on a type of Chinese immigrant very different from Chin's Cantonese, railroad-building ancestors: Shanghainese refugees of the elite class fleeing the Communist Revolution. David Wong Louie's short-story collection, *Pangs of Love*, which contains some "postmodern" or "metafictional" pieces, gives voice to a younger generation of hip, affluent, and assimilated Chinese Americans who are, however, still marginalized in American society. In 1995, Sigrid Nunez published *A Feather on the Breath of God*, which highlights the life of a Chinese American of mixed descent and lends contemporary inflections to a tradition started by Sui Sin Far, while Shawn Wong published *American Knees*, which features heterosexual (including erotic) relations between adult Asian Americans far removed from the coming-of-age concerns of his earlier *Homebase* and many other Asian American works in a bildungsroman tradition. The latest Asian American anthologies, such as *The Open Boat: Poems from Asian America* (1993) and *Under Western Eyes: Personal Essays from Asian America* (1995), edited by Garrett Hongo; *Charlie Chan Is Dead: An Anthology of Contemporary Asian American Fiction* (1993), edited by Jessica Hagedorn; *American Dragons: Twenty-Five Asian American Voices* (1993), edited by Laurence Yep; and *Premonitions: The Kaya*

Anthology of *New Asian North American Poetry* (1996) edited by Walter Lew, continue to reveal exciting new Chinese American talents.

■■■ NOTES

1. Some of the authors cited in this essay have kept the Chinese practice of placing the surname before the given name. In such cases, italicization is used to indicate the surname, alphabetized in the bibliography. In the case of a pseudonym such as Sui Sin Far, where the surname–given name distinction does not apply, the word used for alphabetization will be italicized.
2. These writers' works with American settings are far less commonly available in English translation than their works with Chinese settings; the latter are perceived to have a clearer location in the "mainstream" of contemporary Chinese literature and command greater recognition from Chinese studies scholars. The same is true of works by other well-known transplanted intellectuals such as *Chen* Jo-hsi (*Chen* Ruoxi), *Chang* Hsi-kuo (*Zhang* Xiguo), and *Li* Li. Some English translations for short fiction by the aforementioned writers, as well as by younger ones like Philip Chou (*Zhou* Feili) and Dschau-Sen J. Ku (*Gu* Zhaosen), are listed in the Selected Bibliography. Since diplomatic relations between the United States and the People's Republic of China resumed in 1979, leading to renewed immigration from the mainland, mainland-origin immigrant writers have been producing literary works with concerns that both overlap and contrast with those of Taiwan-origin writers. These have yet to be translated into English.
3. In the following discussion, because of space limitations, only one volume by each poet will be cited; a degree of arbitrariness of choice cannot be avoided.
4. I am indebted to David Eng for his generous help with this section of the chapter.
5. I am indebted to Shelley Wong for her generous help with this section of the chapter.

■■■ WORKS CITED AND SELECTED BIBLIOGRAPHY

Arkush, R. David, and Leo O. Lee, eds. 1989. *Land Without Ghosts: Chinese Impressions of America from the Nineteenth Century to the Present*. Foreword by John K. Fairbank. Berkeley and Los Angeles: Univ. of California Press.

Aying. 1960. *Fanmei huagong jinyue wenxue ji* [A collection of literature against the American exclusion of Chinese laborers]. Beijing: Zhonghua shuju.

Berssenbrugge, Mei-Mei. 1989. *Empathy*. Barrytown, NY: Station Hill Press.

Chan, Jeffery Paul. 1971/1972. "Aunt Tsia Lays Dying." Rpt. in *Asian-American Authors*, ed. Kai-yu Hsu and Helen Palubinskas, 77–85. Boston: Houghton Mifflin.

———. "Jackrabbit." In *Yardbird Reader* 3 (1974): 217–38. A special Asian American issue edited by Shawn Wong and Frank Chin.

Chan, Jeffery Paul, et al. 1981. "Resources for Chinese and Japanese American Literary Traditions." *Amerasia Journal* 8.1:19–31.

Chan, Jeffery Paul, Frank Chin, Lawson Fusao Inada, and Shawn Wong, eds. 1991. *The Big Aiiieeeee!: An Anthology of Chinese American and Japanese American Literature.* New York: Meridian.

Chang, Diana. 1984. *What Matisse Is After.* New York: Contact II.

Chang, Hsi-kuo. 1983. "Red Boy." Trans. Jeannette L. Faurot. In *The Unbroken Chain: An Anthology of Taiwan Fiction since 1926,* ed. S. M. Lau, 218–31. Bloomington: Indiana Univ. Press.

Chang, S. K. [Chang Hsi-kuo]. 1987. "The Banana Freighter," trans. Jeffrey Toy Eng. *The Chinese PEN* (Summer): 82–92.

Chen, Ruoxi [Chen Jo-hsi]. 1986. "Another Fortress Besieged." *The Old Man and Other Stories,* 113–41. Hong Kong: Renditions Paperbacks, The Research Centre for Translation, The Chinese Univ. of Hong Kong.

Chen, Yuanzhu ed. 1929/1969. *Taishan geyao ji* [A collection of Taishan folk rhymes]. Rpt. Taipei: Folklore Books.

Cheung, King-Kok. 1988. "'Don't Tell': Imposed Silences in *The Color Purple* and *The Woman Warrior.*" *PMLA* 103.2:162–74.

———. 1990. "The Woman Warrior versus the Chinaman Pacific: Must a Chinese American Critic Choose between Feminism and Heroism?" In *Conflicts in Feminism,* ed. Marianne Hirsch and Evelyn Fox Keller, 234–51. New York: Routledge.

———. 1993. *Articulate Silences: Hisaye Yamamoto, Maxine Hong Kingston, Joy Kogawa.* Ithaca, NY: Cornell Univ. Press.

Cheung, King-Kok, and Stan Yogi. 1988. *Asian American Literature: An Annotated Bibliography.* New York: Modern Language Association.

Chiang, Fay. 1979. *In the City of Contradictions.* New York: Sunbury Press.

Chiang, Yee. 1950. *The Silent Traveller in New York.* New York: John Day.

———. 1959. *The Silent Traveller in Boston.* New York: Norton.

———. 1964. *The Silent Traveller in San Francisco.* New York: Norton.

Chin, Frank. 1976. "Backtalk." *Counterpoint: Perspectives on Asian America,* 556–7. Los Angeles: Asian American Studies Center.

———. 1981. *The Chickencoop Chinaman* and *The Year of the Dragon.* Intro. by Dorothy Ritsuko McDonald. Seattle: Univ. of Washington Press.

———. 1985. "This Is Not an Autobiography." *Genre* 18.2:105–30.

———. 1988. *The Chinaman Pacific & Frisco R.R. Co.* Minneapolis: Coffee House Press.

———. 1991. *Donald Duk.* Minneapolis: Coffee House Press.

———. 1994. *Gunga Din Highway.* Minneapolis: Coffee House Press.

Chin, Frank, et al. 1974/1983. *Aiiieeeee! An Anthology of Asian-American Writers.* Washington, D.C.: Howard Univ. Press.

Chin, Marilyn. 1987. *Dwarf Bamboo.* Greenfield Center, NY: Greenfield Review Press.

Chin, Woon Ping. 1993. *The Naturalization of Camellia Song.* Singapore: Time Books International.

Chiu, Jeannie. 1993. "Uncanny Doubles: Nationalism and Repression in Frank Chin's 'Railroad Standard Time.'" *Critical Mass* 1.1(Fall):93–107.

Chock, Eric. 1990. *Last Days Here*. Honolulu: Bamboo Ridge Press.

Chock, Eric. and Darrell H. Y. Lum, eds. 1989. *Paké: Writings by Chinese in Hawaii*. Honolulu: Bamboo Ridge Press.

Chou, Philip [Zhou Feili]. 1986. "The Big Event of the Week," trans. Howard Goldblatt. *The Chinese Pen* (Autumn), 1–30.

Chu, Louis. 1979. *Eat a Bowl of Tea*. 1961. Intro. by Jeffery Paul Chan. Seattle: Univ. of Washington Press.

Chua, C[heng] Lok. 1981. "Two Chinese Versions of the American Dream: The Golden Mountain in Lin Yutang and Maxine Hong Kingston." *MELUS* 8.4:61–70.

Chuang Hua [pseud.]. 1968/1986. *Crossings*. Foreword by Amy Ling. Boston: Northeastern Univ. Press.

Dunn, Ashley Sheun. 1978. "No Man's Land." *Amerasia Journal* 5.2:109–33.

Eng, David L. 1996. "In the Shadows of a Diva: Committing Homosexuality in David Henry Hwang's *M. Butterfly*." In *Asian American Sexualities: Dimensions of the Gay and Lesbian Experience*, ed. Russell Leong, 131–52. New York and London: Routledge.

Gong, Ted. 1980. "Approaching Cultural Change through Literature: From Chinese to Chinese American." *Amerasia Journal* 7.1:73–86.

Hagedorn, Jessica, ed. 1993. *Charlie Chan Is Dead: An Anthology of Contemporary Asian American Fiction*. New York: Penguin.

Hom, Marlon K. 1983. "Some Cantonese Folksongs on the American Experience." *Western Folklore* 42.2:126–39.

——. 1984. "A Case of Mutual Exclusion: Portrayals by Immigrants and American-born Chinese of Each Other in Literature." *Amerasia Journal* 11:29–45.

——. 1987. *Songs of Gold Mountain: Cantonese Rhymes from San Francisco Chinatown*. Berkeley and Los Angeles: Univ. of California Press.

Hongo, Garrett, ed. 1993. *The Open Boat: Poems from Asian America*. New York: Anchor/Doubleday.

——, ed. 1995. *Under Western Eyes: Personal Essays from Asian America*. New York: Anchor Books.

Houn, Fred [Fred Ho]. 1987. "The Revolutionary Writings of H. T. Tsiang." *East Wind* 6.1:39–40.

Hsu, Kai-yu, and Helen Palubinskas, eds. 1972. *Asian-American Authors*. Boston: Houghton Mifflin.

Hu, Zhaozhong, ed. 1970. *Maizhou Guangdong huaqiao liuchuan geyao huibian* [A collection of folk rhymes popular among Cantonese in America]. Hong Kong: Zhendan tushu gongsi.

Huffman, Ivy, and Julia Kwong. 1991. *The Dream of Gold Mountain*. Winnipeg, Mani.: Hyperion Press.

Huie, Kin. 1932. *Reminiscences*. Peiping: San Yu Press.

Hwang, David Henry. 1983. *Broken Promises: Four Plays* [*FOB*; *The Dance and the Railroad*; *Family Devotions*; *The House of Sleeping Beauties*]. New York: Bard/Avon.

——. 1989. *M. Butterfly*. New York: Plume/Penguin.

Ismail, Jam (Jamaila). 1984. *sexions*. Kitsilano: n.p.

Jen, Gish. 1991. *Typical American*. Boston: Houghton Mifflin/Seymour Lawrence.

Kim, Elaine H. 1982. *Asian American Literature: An Introduction to the Writings and Their Social Context*. Philadelphia: Temple Univ. Press.

Kingston, Maxine Hong. 1976/1977. *The Woman Warrior: Memoirs of a Girlhood among Ghosts*. New York: Vintage Books.

———. 1980/1981. *China Men*. New York: Ballantine.

———. 1989. *Tripmaster Monkey: His Fake Book*. New York: Knopf.

Kondo, Dorinne K. 1990. "*M. Butterfly*: Orientalism, Gender, and a Critique of Essentialist Identity." *Cultural Critique* 16 (Fall): 5–29.

Ku, Dschau-Sen J. [Gu Zhaosen]. 1988. "Ming-te Wang," trans. Ying-tsin Hwang. *The Chinese Pen* (Autumn): 1–24.

Kuo, Helena (Kuo Ching Ch'iu). 1942. *I've Come a Long Way*. New York: Appleton.

Lai, Him Mark, Genny Lim, and Judy Yung. 1980. *Island: Poetry and History of Chinese Immigrants on Angel Island 1910–1940*. San Francisco: HOC DOI [History of Chinese Detained on Island] Project.

Laiwan. 1984–5. *CAVE caveat*. Vancouver: Laiwan.

Lau, Alan Chong. 1980. *Songs for Jadina*. Greenfield Center, NY: Greenfield Review Press.

Lau, Evelyn. 1989. *Runaway: Diary of a Street Kid*. Toronto: Harper Collins.

———. 1990. *You Are Not Who You Claim*. Victoria: Porcepic Books.

Lee, Bennett, and Jim Wong-Chu. 1991. *Many-Mouthed Birds: Contemporary Writing by Chinese Canadians*. Vancouver: Douglas & McIntyre; Seattle: Univ. of Washington Press.

Lee, C. Y. 1957. *The Flower Drum Song*. New York: Farrar Straus.

Lee, Gus. 1991. *China Boy*. New York: Dutton.

Lee, Li-Young. 1986. *Rose*. Brockport, NY: BOA Editions.

———. 1990. *The City in Which I Love You*. Brockport, NY: BOA Editions.

Lee, Robert. 1992. *Singing to Remember*. Produced and directed by Tony Heriza. New York: Asian American Arts Centre.

Lee, Robert G. 1992. "In Search of the Historical Guan Gong." *Asian America: Journal of Culture and the Arts* 1:28–47.

Lee, Sky. 1990. *Disappearing Moon Cafe*. Vancouver: Douglas & McIntyre.

———. 1994. *Bellydancer*. Vancouver: Press Gang Publishers.

Lee, Yan Phou. 1887, *When I Was a Boy in China*. Boston: D. Lothrop Co.

Leong, Monfoon. 1975. *Number One Son*. San Francisco: East/West Publishing Company.

Leong, Russell. 1993. *The Country of Dreams and Dust*. Albuquerque, NM: West End Press.

Lew, Walter, ed. 1996. *Premonitions: The Kaya Anthology of New Asian North American Poetry*. New York: Kaya Publications.

Li, David Leiwei. 1990. "*China Men*: Maxine Hong Kingston and the American Canon." *American Literary History* 2.3:482–502.

Li, Li. 1989. "Bird of Paradise," trans. Michelle Yeh. *The Chinese Pen* (Summer): 70–95.

Lim, Genny. 1989. *Winter Place*. San Francisco: Kearney Street Workshop Press.

————. 1991. *Paper Angels* and *Bitter Cane*. Honolulu: Kalamaku Press.

Lim, Paul Stephen. 1989. *Figures in Clay: A Threnody in Six Scenes and a Coda*. Louisville, KY: Aran Press.

Lim, Shirley Geok-lin. 1989. *Modern Secrets*. London: Dangaroo.

————, ed. 1991. *Approaches to Teaching Kingston's "The Woman Warrior."* New York: Modern Language Association.

Lim, Shirley Geok-lin, and Amy Ling, eds. 1992. *Reading the Literatures of Asian America*. Philadelphia: Temple Univ. Press.

Lim-Hing, Sharon, ed. 1994. *The Very Inside: An Anthology of Writing by Asian and Pacific Islander Lesbian and Bisexual Women*. Toronto: Sister Vision Press.

Lin, Alice Murong Pu. 1988. *Grandmother Had No Name*. San Francisco: China Books and Periodicals.

Lin, Yutang. 1948. *Chinatown Family*. New York: John Day.

Ling, Amy. 1982. "A Rumble in the Silence: *Crossings* by Chuang Hua." *MELUS* 9.3:29–37.

————. 1990. *Between Worlds: Women Writers of Chinese Ancestry*. New York: Pergamon Press.

Liu, Timothy. 1992. *Vox Angelica*. Cambridge, MA: Alicejames/books.

Louie, David Wong. 1991. *Pangs of Love*. New York: Knopf.

Lowe, Lisa. 1991. "Heterogeneity, Hybridity, Multiplicity: Marking Asian American Differences." *Diaspora* 1.1:24–44.

Lowe, Pardee. 1943. *Father and Glorious Descendant*. Boston: Little, Brown.

Lum, Darrell H. Y. 1990. *Pass On, No Pass Back!* Honolulu: Bamboo Ridge Press.

Lum, Wing Tek. 1987. *Expounding the Doubtful Points*. Honolulu: Bamboo Ridge Press.

Lye, Colleen. 1995. "*M. Butterfly* and the Rhetoric of Antiessentialism: Minority Discourse in an International Frame." In *The Ethnic Canon: Histories, Institutions, and Interventions*, ed. David Palumbo-Liu. 260–89. Minneapolis: Univ. of Minnesota Press.

McAlister, Melani. 1992. "(Mis)reading *The Joy Luck Club*." *Asian America: Journal of Culture and the Arts* 1:102–18.

McCunn, Ruthanne Lum. 1981. *Thousand Pieces of Gold*. San Francisco: Design Enterprises.

Mei, June, and Jean Pang Yip, with Russell Leong. 1981. "The Bitter Society: *Ku Shehui*. A Translation, Chapters 37–46." *Amerasia Journal* 8.1:33–67.

Meissenburg, Karin. 1987. *The Writing on the Wall*. Frankfurt: Verlag für Interkulturelle Kommunikation.

Moy, James S. 1993. *Marginal Sights: Staging the Chinese in America*. Iowa City: University of Iowa Press.

Ng, Fae Myenne. 1993. *Bone*. New York: Hyperion.

Nieh, Hualing. 1981/1988. *Mulberry and Peach: Two Women of China*. Trans. Jane Parish Yang with Linda Lappin. Boston: Beacon.

Nunez, Sigrid. 1995. *A Feather on the Breath of God*. New York: HarperCollins.

Pai, Hsien-yung. 1971. "Li T'ung: A Chinese Girl in New York." In *Twentieth Century Chinese Stories*, ed. C. T. Hsia with S. M. Lau, 220–39. New York: Columbia Univ. Press.

————. 1981. "A Day in Pleasantville." In *Born of the Same Roots: Stories of Modern Chinese Women*, ed. Vivian Ling Hsu, 184–92. Bloomington: Indiana Univ. Press.

Palumbo-Liu, David, 1995. "The Ethnic as 'Post-': Reading *Reading the Literatures of Asian America*." *American Literary History* 7.1:161–8.

————. Forthcoming. "Model Minority Discourse and the Course of Healing." In *Minority Discourse: Ideolgical Containment and Utopian/ Heterotopian Potentials*, ed. Abdul JanMohamed. New York: Oxford Univ. Press.

Pao, Angela. 1992. "The Critic and the Butterfly: Sociocultural Contexts and the Reception of David Henry Hwang's *M. Butterfly*." *Amerasia Journal* 18.3:1– 16.

Shih, Shu-mei. 1992. "Exile and Intertextuality in Maxine Hong Kingston's *China Men*." In *The Literature of Emigration and Exile*, ed. James Whitlark and Wendell Aycock, 65–77. Lubbock, TX: Texas Tech Univ. Press.

Sledge, Linda Ching. 1980. "Maxine Hong Kingston's *China Men*: The Family Historian as Epic Poet." MELUS 7.4:3–22.

————. 1990. "Oral Tradition in Kingston's *China Men*." In *Redefining American Literary History*, ed. A. LaVonne Brown Ruoff and Jerry W. Ward, Jr., 142– 54. New York: Modern Language Association.

Solberg, S. E. 1981. "Sui Sin Far/Edith Eaton: First Chinese-American Fictionalist." *MELUS* 8.1:27–40.

Sui Sin Far [Edith Eaton]. January 1909. "Leaves from the Mental Portfolio of an Eurasian." *Independent* 7:125–32.

————. 1912/1995. *Mrs. Spring Fragrance*. Ed. Amy Ling and Annette White-Parks. Urbana-Champaign: University of Illinois Press.

Sze, Arthur. 1982. *Dazzled*. Point Reyes Station, CA: Floating Island Publications.

Tan, Amy. 1989. *The Joy Luck Club*. New York: Putnam.

Tong, Benjamin R. 1971. "The Ghetto of the Mind: Notes on the Historical Psychology of Chinese America." *Amerasia Journal* 1.3:1–31.

Tsiang, H. T. 1937. *And China Has Hands*. New York: Robert Speller.

Tsui, Kitty. 1983. *The Words of a Woman Who Breathes Fire*. San Francisco: Spinsters, Ink.

Wah, Fred. 1992. *Alley Alley Home Free*. Red Deer, Alta.: Red Deer College Press.

Walker, Alice. 1982. *The Color Purple*. New York: Harcourt Brace Jovanovich.

Wand, David Hsin Fu, ed. 1974. *Asian-American Heritage: An Anthology of Prose and Poetry*. New York: Washington Square Press.

Wang, L. Ling-Chi. 1976. "The Yee Version of Poems from the Chinese Immigration Station." *Asian American Review*, 117–26.

Wang, L. Ling-Chi, and Henry Yiheng Zhao, eds. Assisted by Carrie L. Waara. 1991. *Chinese American Poetry: An Anthology*. Foreword by Sucheng Chan. Santa Barbara: Asian American Voices. Distributed by Univ. of Washington Press.

Watanabe, Sylvia, and Carol Bruchac, eds. 1990. *Home to Stay: Asian American Women's Fiction*. Greenfield Center, NY: Greenfield Review Press.

Wei, Katherine, and Terry Quinn. 1984. *Second Daughter: Growing Up in China, 1930–1949*. Boston: Little, Brown.

Wenquan. 1982. "Chinatown Literature during the Last Ten Years." Trans. with an introduction by Marlon K. Hom. *Amerasia Journal* 9.2:75–100.

Westfall, Suzanne R. 1992. "Ping Chong's Terra In/Cognita: Monsters on Stage." In *Reading the Literatures of Asian America*, ed. Shirley Geok-lin Lim and Amy Ling, 359–73. Philadelphia: Temple Univ. Press.

White-Parks, Annette. 1995. *Sui Sin Far/Edith Eaton: A Literary Biography*. Urbana-Champagne: Univ. of Illinois Press.

Wong, Jade Snow. 1945/1989. *Fifth Chinese Daughter*. Rpt. with "Introduction to the 1989 Edition." Seattle: Univ. of Washington Press.

Wong, Nellie. 1986. *The Death of Long Steam Lady*. Los Angeles: West End Press.

Wong, Norman. 1994. *Cultural Revolution*. New York: Persea Books.

Wong, Sau-ling Cynthia. 1988. "Tales of Postwar Chinatown: Short Stories of *The Bud*." *Amerasia Journal* 14.2:61–79.

———. 1992. "Autobiography as Guided Chinatown Tour? Maxine Hong Kingston's *The Woman Warrior* and the Chinese-American Autobiographical Controversy." In *Multicultural Autobiography: American Lives*, ed. James Robert Payne, 249–79. Knoxville: Univ. of Tennessee Press.

———. 1993. *Reading Asian American Literature: From Necessity to Extravagance*. Princeton, NJ: Princeton Univ. Press.

———. 1995 " 'Sugar Sisterhood': Situating the Amy Tan Phenomenon." In *The Ethnic Canon: Histories, Institutions, and Interventions*, ed. David Palumbo-Liu, 174–210. Minneapolis: Univ. of Minnesota Press.

Wong, Shawn. 1979. *Homebase*. New York: I. Reed Books.

———. 1995. *American Knees*. New York: Simon and Schuster.

Wong, Su-ling [pseud.], with E. H. Cressy. 1952. *Daughter of Confucius: A Personal History*. New York: Farrar Straus.

Wong, Sunn Shelley. 1994. "Notes from Damaged Life: Asian American Literature and the Discourse of Wholeness." Ph.D. diss., University of California, Berkeley.

Wong-Chu, Jim. 1986. *Chinatown Ghosts*. Vancouver: Pulp Press.

Woo, Merle. 1986. *Yellow Woman Speaks*. Seattle: Radical Women Publications.

Wu, Tingfang. 1914. *America through the Spectacles of an Oriental Diplomat*. New York: Frederick S. Stokes.

Yau, John. 1989. *Radiant Silhouette: New and Selected Work 1974–1988*. Santa Rosa, CA: Black Sparrow Press.

Yep, Laurence. 1990. *Pay the Chinaman*. In *Between Worlds: Contemporary Asian-American Plays*, ed. Misha Berson, 180–96. New York: Theatre Communications Group.

———, ed. 1993. *American Dragons: Twenty-Five Asian American Voices*. New York: HarperCollins.

Yip, Yuen Chung. 1990. *The Tears of Chinese Immigrants*. Trans. and intro. by Sheng-Tai Chang. Dunvegan, Ont.: Cormorant Books.

Yung, Wing. 1909/1978. *My Life in China and America*. New York: Arno.

2

FILIPINO AMERICAN LITERATURE

N. V. M. GONZALEZ AND OSCAR V. CAMPOMANES

> Three generations of intellectuals were to go into the terrain, at times flamboyantly flashing their travel documents, but only to fail as transients or even as protracted sojourners owing to their inability to distinguish, it would seem, between travel and residence, between the merely naturalized and the native born.
>
> – N. V. M. Gonzalez (1979, 240)

Few efforts to specify and delineate Filipino American literature have been attempted (recent ones include Campomanes 1992a; Manguerra-Brainard 1993; San Juan 1993). Fewer still are extended explorations of what the term "Filipino American" means for a population that is heavily Philippine-born, predominantly female, and of diverse socioeconomic and ethnolinguistic profiles by the end of the 1980s (Cariño et al. 1990; Awanohara 1991). Many Filipino migrants and their second-generation offspring usually resist usage of the term, which tends to occlude the historical and power differentials engendered by the Philippine–American colonial experience (Gubatan 1990; San Juan 1991a, 125; Campomanes 1995). This ambivalence about nationality and colonialism has been expressed in various writings by migrant Filipino writers and intellectuals at different conjunctures (see, for example, Buaken 1948; S. P. Lopez 1966; N. V. M. Gonzalez 1976; Manguerra-Brainard 1991; Hagedorn 1993a, 185–7). Indeed, it is this "political impetus of the post-colonial" (Ashcroft, Griffiths, and Tiffin 1989, 83), or this historical engagement with the legacy of colonialism, that charges the Filipino (American) literary tradition with its constitutive tensions.

The colonial legacy is significantly embodied in an "indigenous" Philippine literature in English and in its convergences or contiguities with Filipino writings "nurtured on American shores" (Solberg 1983, 50). The following two-part account is presented in dialogic form to reflect the tentative or differing terms by which critics and practitioners historically construe these literary traditions and their areas of overlap. In the first part, N. V. M. Gonzalez – regarded both as a second-generation Filipino English writer (Alegre and Fernandez 1987) and as a "pioneer" or first-generation author in Filipino American literature (Hsu and Palubinskas 1972; Campomanes 1992a) – takes a broad view of Philippine cultural history as the determining frame for emergent writing by Filipino Americans. The imagination of this writing is described as "rhizomatous," and its genesis is posited as a Filipinization of America rather than as an Americanization of Filipino migrants. The sources of Filipino (American) writing are steeped in various Philippine literary traditions such as the folkloric and the vernacular, as well as those created in the colonial languages of Spanish and English.

It is the American legacy of English that figures, paradoxically, as both the deterrent and the medium of a "Filipino imagination" seeking to break out of colonial fetters. Here, colonization elicits expressions of a "cartographic impulse" (Eagleton et al. 1990, 77) from Filipino writers while dispersing them among sites of articulation that are always "some-where in motion" (Rutherford 1990, 13; see also N. V. M. Gonzalez 1990a). So whereas immigrant writers characteristically emplot America as the "promised land" of their narratives (Sollors 1980; 1986), Filipino writers usually chart and repossess a fictive "homeland" or an imagined Philippines for moorings in their exilic writings and peripatetic jour-neys. Residence in the United States becomes the productive space for displacement, suspension, and perspective for migrant Filipino writers (Campomanes 1992a, 51).

In the second part, Oscar Campomanes observes that there has been a "necessary and perplexing lack of discrimination between what was Fili-pino American and what was Filipino of the Philippines" in reckoning Filipino (American) histories and cultural productions (Solberg 1983, 56–7). This conceptual "confusion" is reshaped as a productive impetus in the debates over Filipino identifications and the writings that rework their expressions rather than as the disabling impasse or confusion that it may seem to observers. Indeed, it is read as symptomatic of the peculiar formations of Filipino English and Filipino American literatures/identi-ties, and of the need to address their historical specificities as well as conjunctions.

Forged by the amalgam of U.S. colonization and migratory move-ments, Filipino (American) formations resist being singularly absorbed into nationalizing rubrics like "ethnic" or "Asian American" and globalizing terms like "postcolonial" or "Third World." The categorical quandaries of Filipino migrants are understood both as instances of the "generalized condition of homelessness" (Said 1979, 18) or the cultural "disjunctures" (Appadurai 1990, 6) characteristic of late-twentieth-century population transfers, and as forms of being and becoming that are constrained and conditioned by nearly a century of Philippine–American (post)colonial encounters.

I PASSING THROUGH

N. V. M. GONZALEZ

> He just passed without having come.
> – Cesar Vallejo[1]

The bamboo and the *molave* (*vitez geniculata*) have served as sources of popular self-images of resilience and graceful endurance for Filipinos over the years. Avid seekers of metaphors for private and public experience have found them continually valuable (for classic examples, see Da Costa 1952 [1940]; Arguilla 1982 [1937], 180). The young and the old work in the clichés wherever and whenever possible, alert to the identity politics that Alex Haley's *Roots* (1976) had initiated. A peculiar poignancy informs such attempts in Filipino exilic communities, which may have to keep these images for some time yet. They are particularly helpful in providing a perspective on the literature that Filipinos are now writing for an American and international multicultural readership. How is it different from other Asian American literatures like the Chinese, Japanese, or Korean?

One difficulty is in determining what "Filipino American" means. One may even feel uncomfortable raising the question. Recent statements by Daniel J. Boorstin, former Librarian of Congress and Pulitzer Prize–winning historian, suggest that we give the matter more than passing attention. "I think," he is quoted in a magazine interview, "the notion of a hyphenated American – whether Polish-American, Italian-American or African-American – is un-American" (Szulc 1993, 5). The statement makes no reference to Asian immigrants in particular. The hyphen, moreover, may be conveniently regarded as a typographical convention, as easily omitted as insisted upon.

But this is not all; elsewhere in the interview, Boorstin is quoted as saying: "One of the symbols of the opportunities of America is the fact that our language is a borrowed language and that the sign of being a new American is speaking broken English – perhaps the only thoroughly American language. It is a sign of being a newcomer and a learner from afar." These concerns could lead one further to cultural identity issues, where assuming ingenious or convenient attitudes may be necessary. Edward Mattos could say (as late as 1965) that "The Filipino is one of the fortunate men of all time and place. He stands at that remarkable junction

between East and West, at that place where the twain would never meet"
(1).

That meeting ground, for Filipino intellectuals and a few Western
observers, resides in the literature, the practice of letters. And enviably so
in the United States, where, Philippine-born or not, the Filipino straddles,
perforce, two cultures and two histories. Indeed, the Filipino has acquired
the reputation of being the most Westernized – meaning Americanized –
of Asian peoples. Whether too superficial an impression or not, this is an
obvious simplification; to probe could be indelicate. Saul Bellow was once
introduced to "a writer from the Philippines" named Bienvenido Santos.
In *Memory's Fictions*, Santos's autobiography, he describes this meeting
with the American novelist who had just then won the Nobel Prize. "He
wanted to know if I wrote in English," Santos recalls, "but he was kind
enough not to ask why" (1993, 81).

Prior to their attainment of political independence from the United
States, Filipinos were understandably self-conscious about how they
stood in the eyes of the world. They were observed to have insisted "on
interpreting American democracy as giving them the right to leave the
kitchen and come into the living room," and on being recognized not as
strangers "who cannot be Americanized . . . but rather would-be Americans who refuse to remain strangers" (Catapusan 1972).[2]

If that sounds somewhat truculent, a stance half-defensive yet markedly assertive, perhaps the cause may be traceable to somewhere deep in
the past. There is a seldom-sounded bottom of history where forces
stultifying to the creative imagination have been at work; the Filipino has
had to endure them over a long stretch of time. On the practical side,
immigration has been one way of coping; writing in a language to which
one is not native, another. Under the yoke of colonial Spain for nearly
three centuries, the Filipino imagination could aspire to expression only
through orality (see N. V. M. Gonzalez 1979, 231–56). The native talent
hid in anonymity – if we give meaning, which we must, to Fr. Blancas de
San José's use of the Filipino's first-known poem in his *Memorial de la Vida
Cristiana en la Lingua Tagala*, published in 1605 (see N. V. M. Gonzalez
1979, 233). In that instance, the native imagination learned about the
virtue of self-abnegation. Fulfillment seemed possible only in folklore and
in the domain of metrical romances, those shards and fragments from
Europe reassembled for local use; imagination was afforded an experience in the use of the literary form. Language was found to work; the
vernacular could serve beyond pious supplications and the chores in the
yard.

An early harvest was in Tagalog poetry; this began with José de la Cruz
(Huseng Sisiw, 1746–1849) and Balagtas (Francisco Baltazar, 1788–
1862). From the point when printing was introduced into the country up

to this crop of poetry is a leap of over two hundred years. José Rizal (1861–96) does not figure on this horizon until the appearance of *Noli Mi Tangere* (1958 [1886]), that lodestar in Filipino letters.

Hiram Bingham, writing on Rizal in 1911, suggested what the past had been like and what it took for a *Noli Mi Tangere* and its author to emerge on the scene. Bingham describes how Rizal

> acquired great ability as a writer, [a] keen perception of truth and an unflinching realization of the defects of his people, and the unpleasant but essential fact that to have a better government they must deserve it. . . . In his famous novel, *Noli Mi Tangere* . . . he drew a masterly picture, not only of the life and immorality of the friars but also of the insolent Filipino chiefs or caciques, subservient to the powers, tyrannical to those below, superstitious, unprogressive and grasping. Caciquisim or "bossism," government by local aristocrats, was the prime feature of village life in the islands during the entire period of Spanish rule and existed long before their arrival. (398–9)

When the American conquest of the Philippines came to a close and a new era began, the colonial administration – the second in Philippine history – fielded a thousand teachers upon five hundred towns and villages throughout the archipelago. From them some twenty-five hundred Filipinos took instructions on modern schoolroom methods. Today, whatever else may have resulted from this American intervention, whether inspired by hegemonic reasons or otherwise, it is the English language that appears to have made a most unique contribution to the national culture.

The Commonwealth Period, roughly the years before Pearl Harbor, saw the emergence of considerable writing, works in English, in particular, attracting wide attention. "It is strange, but true," wrote A. V. H. Hartendorp, editor of *Philippine Magazine*,[3] "that Filipino literature in English is way ahead of literature in the vernacular insofar as artistic values are concerned" (1937, 18). It proved encouraging to come by so buoyant an outlook; regarding Filipinos and their borrowed language, Hartendorp further observed:

> The greatest gift that America has made to the Philippines is English; given English, everything else that America has brought would in time have come away. English has established direct contact between the Filipino and the most advanced peoples of the world; and through his own contribution to English literature the Filipino may hope to greatly enrich it by something unique and valuable, a stream of racial and cultural thought that is new even to English. (18)

Here was "a cultural windfall," in the words of Filipino critic Miguel Bernad. Of Philippine literature in general, though, he would say that it has been rather "inchoate." He contends that serious economic, linguistic, and cultural realities have been deterring Filipino writers in their progress toward maturity. "Properly nourished [the literature would grow] to something great, or at least something robust. But it must have deep roots: it may draw vitality from the soil, elegance from civilized art, and universality from Christendom" (1990, 382–7).

The economic realities of the 1920s and 1930s undoubtedly explain Filipino immigration to Hawai'i during this period, much in the same way as cultural climate explains the sending of *pensionados*, government-sponsored scholars, to American colleges and universities. At the same time, the colonial society found itself awash in cultural ferment, given the the sway and ambience of ample nationalism that Manuel Quezon (1878–1944) and his leadership created toward the imminent reality of political independence.

This nationalist resurgence withstood a second violent interruption, the Japanese Occupation. To the disbelief of the Japanese imperial command, the American colonization had rendered the Filipino psyche permanently seared, perhaps in a way comparable to how a branding iron leaves its mark on a hide. The Greater Southeast Asia Co-Prosperity Sphere could not compel the Filipino people brutally enough to turn anti-American, although the Japanese military and police did nearly everything short of herding them to the stockyard. To the ideologues of what might have been an Asian hegemony, it was incomprehensible that a people so scantily informed about their Asian-ness could be so stubbornly loyal to the United States. One reason for that loyalty, of course, was the English language and the literature that the Filipino imagination had discovered for itself.

Then, with the leap of barefoot fire-walkers over well-tended cinders, thousands of Filipinos had begun to leave the country, some joining the pioneer Filipino immigrants who had settled in Hawai'i during the early twenties, others relocating in the mainland or reuniting with family members already there. A good number came to the United States in the immediate aftermath of World War II by way of their service in the United States army and navy in the Pacific campaigns. Migration to the United States picked up in the late 1960s, as socioeconomic difficulties created by years of neocolonial dependency coincided with a political crisis that escalated in the imposition of dictatorial rule by Ferdinand Marcos in 1972. Many Filipinos could not have found a more compelling reason for escape: Marcos had installed a government that proclaimed itself the very harbinger of a "revolution from above," although what descended upon the country was an interminable play for power and wealth, with kitsch and camp for cover-up. If it was the best and worst of times for many, there were enough of the population who confirmed, through calculated resistance, where their cultural loyalties lay, bestirring themselves in the underground, unless stricken into inertia by fear of reprisal from the regime. Not a few were posted into the new bureaucracy and, from there, lofted themselves to new comforts and silence. Still others, unable to ingest the pablum and pap being offered at the lower and middle orders, risked detention and torture. How the Filipino imagination confronted these circumstances belongs to a study yet to be undertaken, but that this history was continually overwhelming and could beat such an imagination black and blue was to be, henceforth, a constant threat.

The hidden text of Filipino literature may well be a movement from a possibly Edenic past to a continually fallen state in the present; thus, the molave figure representing the strength of Filipino-ness, as the impetus toward creative expression rises from deep under layers of experience under empires and oppressions. What has been emerging as Filipino American literature is an egress through the cultural soil of East and West, that rhizomatous growth on an Americanized tropical soil and, later, on American earth itself.

The prescience of Philippine volcanos comes into play here. If 1900 was the year in which the United States resolved to conquer the Philippines, then Philippine American culture may be said to have been formally announced by the eruption of Taal Volcano (on Luzon island), on January nineteenth of that year, killing nearly one and a half times as many people as there were Yankees dispatched to the pioneer teacher-training outposts (Bernad 1990). Thus ensued ninety-two years of U.S. colonization, the last few months of that occupation awash in ceaseless discussions on the future of U.S. air force and naval bases in the country. But Mount Pinatubo, in the vicinity of these bases, said to be the abode of Apo Mallari – a deity eavesdropping! – awakened from a 650-year slumber in June 1991. The bilateral talks on the bases became moot thereafter; the air and naval installations of American neocolonial power had to go. Where diplomats had failed, Mount Pinatubo had succeeded, providing a closure in calendrical time to Philippine American culture.

Encouraged by issues on ethnicity that had engrossed college campuses, Asian American Studies assigned a special place to Carlos Bulosan. His best-known book, *America Is in the Heart* (1973 [1946]), subtitled "A Personal History," has continued to be widely discussed to this day, dealing as it does with a young Filipino's discovery of "America."[4] Not infrequently, it is referred to as an autobiography yet is often mistaken for a novel; likewise, it has been trashed by some as propaganda, and as readily exalted by others as a testament of faith.

Before the publication of Bulosan's book, however, a work of a different order had appeared: the collection of short stories *Footnote to Youth* (1933) by José García Villa. To date, Villa's importance in Filipino and American cultural relations has yet to be seriously addressed. To honor the author, Edward J. O'Brien dedicated to him one of his annual volumes of "Best Short Stories." Villa would provide, O'Brien hoped, "a new reading of the American scene." But Villa felt that he was more "suited to the medium of poetry," and *Have Come, Am Here* (1942) proved him right. Of a later collection, *Selected Poems and New* (1958), Dame Edith Sitwell wrote, "The best of these poems are among the most beautiful written in our time" (xiv).

> **From Poem 44, in *Selected Poems* (35–6):**
>
> God said, "I made a man
> Out of clay –
>   But so bright he, he spun
> Himself to brightest Day
> Till he was all shining gold
> And oh,
>   He was handsome to behold!
> But in his hands held he a bow
>
> *Aimed at me* who created
> Him. And I said,
>   'Wouldst murder me
> Who Am thy Fountainhead!'
>
> Then spoke he the man of gold:
> 'I will not
>   Murder thee! I do but
> Measure thee. Hold
>
> Thy peace.' And this I did.
> But I was curious
>   Of this so regal head.
> 'Give thy name!' – 'Sir! Genius.' "

Thus, if in the words of Dame Edith Sitwell "A poem can be all things to all men," (Villa 1958, xiv), then Fortune, as Fountainhead, has not dealt too shabbily with Archer. One might then wonder what it was that resided in that "regal head."

There are readers who are sensitive to some undertow of history, to the chill or boil of its waters. They know also about cultures breathless with promise and to which an artist's vision may bear witness. In introducing Villa's collection to the American public, O'Brien wrote:

> The individual viewpoint which he [Villa] has brought to the inter-
> pretation of American life, as well as the energy which these stories
> reveal, suggests that he might well give us a new reading of the
> American scene in novels of contemporary life. The circumstances of
> Mr. Villa's arrival in the United States after leaving a totally unre-
> lated civilization give him an altogether unique advantage in this
> respect. (Villa 1933, 5)[5]

Could that text be forthcoming? By 1933, this one rootstalk of the Filipino imagination had appeared: Villa's work placed him, in O'Brien's estimation, "among the half-dozen short story writers in America who count." Would others follow?

To his friend José de los Reyes, Bulosan would write on 25 August 1949: "I can't specifically tell you my plans for the future. But it is enough to tell you that I would like to repeat what Rizal has done for Philippine literature" (Bulosan 1960, 258). In a letter to de los Reyes dated 2 November 1949, Bulosan would further elaborate (1960, 259): "[Well, Joe, don't laugh! I have a secret dream of writing here (in America) a 1,500 page novel covering thirty-five years of Philippine history.][6] [T]he pressure for a novel about the Philippines at this stage of human civiliza-tion is demanding. And I am very sensitive to historical currents and cross-currents. I hope I am right."

Bienvenido Santos's *What the Hell For You Left Your Heart in San Francisco* (1989) could be the quintessential Filipino American novel to date, in our context. Not only is its setting American, but so are its characters and the attitudes and values that they cling to or pervert in the course of their lives. Here they are, treading water in the shallow pools of American consumer culture. Their aspirations and agonies are sensitively observed and recorded by a would-be popular magazine editor and part-time community-college instructor, who recognizes the malaise that has af-flicted them all, young and old alike. In the novel, it is among the young generation of students that the society's hapless state is most evident, specifically in how they shirk any serious encounter with books and how they prefer much that is pointless and frivolous. Santos allows his narra-tor to observe, in one of his many introspections: "How did I miss out on what my students were up to? . . . I felt no bond between us. I marked them out for what they were: just passing through. Perhaps in some way they had marked me out, too, for what I was: just passing through" (160–

70). Santos's earlier work, which began with *You Lovely People* (1955) up to and including his autobiography, *Memory's Fictions* (1993), identifies the Filipino talent that has undergone years of submersion in the subsoil of national culture and is now finding the opportunity of arrival and fulfillment on American terrain.

In such a writing as this, the themes of racial bias, nostalgia, and alienation find authentic expression, but the rendering must be understood not as ethnicized American or Western ideas. Nuances in the meanings of words are culture-bound, and exoticization is bane. Better that they be understood as ritual responses by the Filipino in full voice, as this voice is very early on and ever so often stifled, silenced, and thus forced to echo itself.

In this Santos has not been alone. Juan C. Dionisio has covered similar ground: the Filipino experience in the Alaska salmon factories, that hellhole Filipino laborers would rather not bring to mind until spring comes, and the promise of four months' pay.[7] This is the territory Dionisio has taken over; his stories about the erosion of values in Filipino life seem au courant no longer, although unfortunately all too central, to this day, in the culture of their source.

The Filipino is Asian, substantially Malay, in fact; Filipino literature, quite understandably, should be in a Philippine language. But through successive colonizations the Filipino has become an imagination engagé; at the advent of the nineteenth century it had found a destined track. Already, in the subcontinent half-a-journey to Europe away, his colleague the Anglo-Indian had discovered that track. In fraternal confidence, P. Mehta has described what he did with it: "All the Western art forms like the novel, biography, history, and the essay and the lyric, with their subdivisions, were moulds into which the spirit of awakened India poured itself" (1968, 11).

If Philippine letters today do not readily reveal influences from American and English literature, although comparativists may drop names like Ernest Hemingway, Sherwood Anderson, and William Faulkner now and again, the reason is not difficult to find. Rizal has dominated the field.

This is seen in both Juan C. Laya's *This Barangay* (1950) and Stevan Javellana's *Without Seeing the Dawn* (1947), two novels of the post–World War II period. In Javellana's choice of title is manifest his debt to Rizal; in Laya's fictional community, Rizal's keen search for social change. Both novels relived Rizal's preference for the traditional; and just as revealing is the choice of language by both authors, in this case English. Whether inevitable or not, the English replicates Rizal's Spanish; was this a sacrifice of potentially sizable readerships in Tagalog or Visayan? Did these two writers perhaps posit a future where apostasy to their vernaculars could be forgiven, or perhaps redeemed?

These are intriguing questions the answers to which can only be faintly glimpsed. Whatever those might be, it is continuity that the novels reveal. Had the commonwealth regime lasted a decade longer, more gratifying developments might have occurred, forging the link between past and present, the new writing building on what had been done in the vernacular, and the two currents joining the mainstream offering for a world audience.

In the generation of Villa and Bulosan, the Filipino discovered the United States as both an actual and a virtual cultural space. From Reagan's California to the eastern seaboard, how many thousands of their countrymen and their siblings would make the same discovery before the end of the twentieth century? And could they keep that hometown feeling strong, calling one another *Pinoy*, the name-tag of endearment of an increasingly diasporic people?

From the Pinoy communities transformed by currents of history into home would come the American-born, who, if later called upon to claim their Filipino-ness, would have to go rooting out their cultural heritage in its milieu. Hence the urgency for the literature of self-appraisal, the writing of which has begun. With the twenty-first century already on the horizon in a way no century has come within view, the age of the bamboo and the molave may well have arrived.

Carlos Bulosan anticipated this occasion in history in his perspicacious way. He wrote a poem on the subject (1942a, 25), with an uncommon eloquence:

> You did not give America to me, and never will.
> America is in the hearts of people that live in it.
> But it is worth the coming, the sacrifice, the idealism.
> Yes, it is worth all these – and the loneliness at night,
> The bitterness of prejudice, the sharp fangs of hunger,
> The terror of rootlessness. It is significant that I found
> You after the cold and filth in the long naked streets,
> After the screaming voices buried in the lost corridors
> That encompassed the shouting in the dark continent.
> But it is significant only that I found you in America.

Here, the persona sees himself as a visionary, an advantage that he renders in his next stanza; in the third, he reminds his countrymen about the space that current social realities may allow him in the United States. In the last stanza, his apostrophe has today's reader particularly in mind (25–6):

You did not make America for me, and never will.
You are a stranger to that land of mind and heart.
Where I travel dreaming of the future of the soul,
When the secured piety of one man is every man's
And none evolved from it, when the blood's desire
And the flesh's renascence are simple for every one,
And the center of heaven a legend for children's laughter,
And affinity starred, handshake a manifest of tenderness,
None may be severed from the joyous human bondage
That wheels history like a shocking nakedness
Of anger and fear and pity – all the living –

Bulosan gave the title "All the Living Fear," ending the poem with the reiterative line, "But it is significant only that I found you in America." It is a refrain that could be read today as a subtext in most writing under the signature of a Filipino or American-born Filipino.

But what an odd time, by and large, to exhibit that "regal head." For from Gore Vidal comes an advisory on "the decline of the idea of technical virtuosity," which has resulted in the culture enjoying "singers who sing no better than the average listener, actors who do not act yet are, in Andy Warhol's happy phrase, 'super-stars,' whose effects are too easily achieved, writers whose swift flow of words across the page is not submitted to the rigors of grammar or shaped by conscious thought. There is a Zenish sense of why bother?" (1993, 106).

True to its rhizomatous nature, the Filipino imagination may be expected to keep on testing the American soil for spots where more of its rootstalks can break through. Although there is no indication of a change in the cultural weather, roots in the nature of things are not so much a fact of life as rootedness itself.

II   LOOKING "HOMEWARD"

OSCAR V. CAMPOMANES

There is no Filipino literature.
— Arthur Stanley Riggs (1981 [1905], 1)

The identity of a Filipino today is of a person asking what *is* his identity.
— Nick Joaquin (1988, 244)

Connections between certain forms of nationalism (political or cultural) and the assertion of a distinctive literary tradition have historically authorized the idea of "national literatures" or canon formation and have provided the very bases for the practice of comparative literature and minority literary studies in the West, as well as the creation of postcolonial literatures and discourses (Said 1993, 43–61). Although it also enables other traditions or imagined orders of resemblances, the question of national identity – "the perpetual search for the determinants of a single, unified, and agreed meaning" (Ashcroft et al. 1989, 3) – haunts the category of Filipino American writing with singular persistence. Filipino American literature nonetheless resists any facile descriptions as a functionally coherent "tradition" even as, like other U.S. counterparts, it is constitutively determined by the principle of ethnicity and the national question. In a parallel vein, Filipino Americans have been observed to manifest a persistent disorganization and political formlessness as a "community" even as they are now predicted to become the largest Asian American/Pacific Islander group by the end of the millennium (see Espiritu 1992).

Marked by chronic and multiple displacements, Filipino American cultures/texts were and continue to be created under material, historical, and political conditions that are better described by the *(post)colonial* analogy of world literature rather than the "immigrant analogy" of U.S. multiculturalism.[8] Strikingly, however, U.S. and postcolonial discourses have not considered U.S. imperialist and Philippine American formations worthy of extensive study, and any semblance of U.S. Filipino cultural emergence in recent decades has been largely through the interventions of Asian and multicultural Americanists. To ask what domain Filipino American writing belongs to – Asian American literature or postcolonial discourse – thus imposes an irrelevant binarism. What demands scrutiny is why Filipino writing falls within, while exceeding, the discursive borders of both formations. Why does this body of texts resist *either* singular incorporations into a nation-based model that privileges the American mythography of immigration (San Juan 1991c, 545–9; Campomanes 1992a, 52–4, 72–4), *or* a transnational paradigm that excludes the United States from its articulations of the colonial and decolonizing moments (Ashcroft et al. 1989, 16–17, 32–3; Kaplan and Pease 1993, 17, 21)?

In what follows, this categorical indeterminacy is understood as itself a function and feature of the historical dilemmas and identity formations of U.S. Filipinos, and as a question often codified or explored (and at times elided or implied) in the available narratives. Peculiar Filipino experiences and displacements through U.S. colonial conquest (1902–40) and neocolonial dependency (1946–91) are examined to explain the politics and histories of Filipino American locations across a number of U.S. cultural terrains and institutional–representational regimes.

The numerous difficulties stalling the moments of Filipino American cultural emergence stem from competing narrations of U.S. and Filipino nation building that place Filipino Americans in an unusually difficult predicament of identity and community genesis. The distinctive experience of the Philippines as the only Asian-origin country subjected to a systematic and sustained U.S. experiment in formal colonial rule that had been historically deemed as "insignificant" or "exceptional" (see Welch 1979, 150–9) explains the "anomalousness" and instabilities of identity forms in Filipino American cultural texts.[9] That the possibility of Philippine nation building had been simultaneously constituted and repressed by multiple colonizations – Spain (1565–1895), the United States (1902–41), Japan (1941–5), and neocolonial dependency (1946–90s) – further complicates the anxieties over identity that drive, but sometimes paralyze, U.S. Filipino cultural politics and products.[10]

THE ROUTES OF U.S. FILIPINO ITINERANCY

The first characteristic, in fact, that confounds U.S. readers and critics when exploring Filipino American literature and identity formations is their oppositional but nearly unmappable amorphousness, their simultaneous colonial complicities and *postcolonial* differences with U.S. centered annexationist and "assimilationist" programs. This constitutional peculiarity of Filipino American literary forms and subjectivities is certainly counterpointed in its early phases – as is true of all postcolonial writing and cultures – by its paradoxical propensity (inculcated by colonial pedagogy) toward a "mimicry of the [imperial] centre proceeding from a desire not only to be accepted but to be adopted and absorbed" (Ashcroft et al. 1989, 6). To formulate such contractions of unassimilable amorphousness and colonial assimilation in Filipino (American) political and literary postcoloniality, however, is not to exhaust the complexity, diversity, and scope of its nomadic texts and expressions.

One need only think of the differential displacements of the "ambassadorial writers" Felipe Agoncillo, Sixto Lopez, and Galicano Apacible, who sought to dispel U.S. colonialist stereotypes of Filipinos at the turn of the century;[11] those who published their first literary efforts in English as *pensionado* or U.S. colonial government scholars in universities like California at Berkeley (from 1905 onward); subsequent sojourners who published volumes of lachrymose verse or platitudinous prose in order to prove Filipino competence in "colonial" American English, like Juan Salazar, Juan Collas, and Marcelo Gracía de Concepción in the 1910s–1920s, Greg San Diego and the brothers José and Teofilo del Castillo in the 1930s–1940s, or Manuel Buaken, Benny Feria, and Teresa Lucero Nelson in the 1940–1950s; those who apprenticed as Guggenheim, Rockefeller, and Fulbright creative writing fellows (1950s–1980s), and some of whom, like N. V. M. Gonzalez and Bienvenido Santos, eventually resided in the United States for most of their careers; second-generation "Flips" like Shirley Ancheta, Jeff Tagami, and Sam Tagatac, who announced the arrival of U.S. native, second-generation writing after the 1970s (Peter Bacho is this cohort's most visible figure); women writers like Ninotchka Rosca, Jessica Hagedorn, and Cecilia Manguerra-Brainard, whose "feminist" historical fiction aligned U.S. Filipino writing with the transformative publishing currents signified by U.S. minority women writers such as Maxine Hong Kingston and Toni Morrison; the Hawaiian Ilokano-language fictionists and playwrights who have maintained creative exchanges with Philippine Ilokano writers and their immigrant community since the 1970s; and such diasporic gay writers as John Silva and Martin Manalansan IV, who explore the sexual poetics of Filipino migrancy by the 1990s.

Many Filipino writers characteristically use and manifest various modes of ambivalence (into which they are pressed by historical circumstances) as sources of creative and oppositional energy, as generative questions of language and form/genre, and as obsessive thematics – modes such as exilic displacements, local subjectivities, Philippine-oriented nationalist imaginings, and U.S.-based postcoloniality or Filipino *American* reckonings with colonialism's legacies.

These ambiguities/discontinuities are demographically virtualized by the sheer fact of historic Filipino nomadism – its character as a "dispersed nationality" – as a consequence of territorial dispossession and multiple colonizations. What confronts the Filipino Americanist is an often unrecognizable "fusion of migration and exile: the scattering of a people, not yet a fully matured nation, to the ends of the earth, across the planet" (San Juan 1990, 40) under the coercive durations of colonial moments. In the U.S. Filipino case, a remarkably heterogeneous and unevenly formed community follows a differential three-waves history of arrivals: over 100,000 workers (mostly male) in the Pacific Coast states from the first decade of U.S. colonial rule to 1946 – as "American nationals" able to enter the United States without visas (including an elite group of *pensionados* who repatriated back to the Philippines after their U.S. cultural "apprenticeships"); 30,000 World War II veterans and their families (1946–64) – Filipinos could "anomalously" serve in the U.S. navy until the 1970s and obtain permanent residence on this basis; and a post-1965 profile of 782,000 skilled professionals and family reunification immigrants according to the 1980 Census (San Juan 1993, 148–9).[12]

All these conjunctural developments – some conceptual, others historical – significantly inhibit U.S. readers and critics from attending to the peculiar occlusions, characteristics, and contexts of Filipino American literary efforts and to the difficult conditions of their emergence. If these historical and categorical displacements are left unexamined, one is tempted to confirm the unstated impression that Filipino writers are few in number or congenitally unable to stand alongside their Asian American or minority and postcolonial confreres who have broken through U.S. and international publishing circuits in recent decades. Indeed, Filipino writing is represented in Asian American accounts and syllabi with little of the scope and plenitude demonstrated by critics for its Chinese and Japanese American equivalents.

U.S. Filipinos have not produced enough best-selling or retrievable bildungsromans and narratives of "becoming American," with all the troubled quests that such essentially developmentalist emplotments represent. Indeed, the massing of Asian American literatures as a "textual coalition" (Wong 1993, 9) around such U.S.-centric narrations has worked to delimit the field of Filipino American literature or the pool for its writers and texts. Hence, when asked to "sketch a literary background of Filipino American works" for a founding Asian American literary anthology in the early 1970s, three "Flip" writers were compelled to assert that no such account was possible and no such texts were recoverable (Peñaranda et al. 1974, 49).[13] It is as though Filipino writing needed to exhibit U.S.-specific geographical coordinates or recognizably "American" (immigrant or intergenerational) perspectives in order to be considered properly Asian *American* or to belong to the order of texts that this now conventional category secures.

Practiced by critics of multiethnic literatures, this operative parochialism glosses over much of U.S. Filipino writing that is largely diasporic/exilic and postcolonial in cast and oriented toward "Philippine" locales and reference points. Consequently, U.S. Filipino writing and Filipino Americans have become the unrepresentable of the Asian American or minority literary canons and cultural nations. For both to be decently representable within these constructs requires no less than the disruption or transformation of prevailing U.S. critical paradigms. However, this unrepresentability of Filipino Americans and their forms is just as attributable to the dizzying ambivalence of U.S. Filipino self-representations as it is to the *nationalizing* terms of U.S. minority identity and literary/critical constructions (Campomanes 1995).

Among the first to articulate this predicament of unrepresentability, and thus unassimilability, of Filipino cultures within U.S. nationality was Carlos Bulosan (1911–56), often claimed as the prototypical Asian/Filipino "immigrant" writer. In a 1941 letter to a friend, Bulosan recognized that "it is almost impossible for a Filipino writer to write like himself, to be part of the great American arena of writing, because he is always a Filipino, he is always a slave to his country's traditions and history." In a kind of a postscript, he declared, "I think I am forever an exile" (1960,

198). Then, the "great American arena of writing" for Bulosan meant a mélange of intellectual models from Walt Whitman and Sherwood Anderson to Richard Wright and Ernest Hemingway. But Bulosan's statement retains its expressive force in the context of continuing Filipino outsiderhood from a canon that has since absorbed minority and women writers.

Much of this canonical expansion derived its impetus from U.S. women's, ethnic, and social movements in the 1960s, and post–World War II national liberation struggles in the so-called Third World. Further pressures issued from major demographic, institutional, and cultural changes in the United States after such official or federal initiatives as the institution of civil rights legislation and immigration reform in the atmosphere of the tulmultuous 1960s (Novick 1988, 469–521; Chan 1991, 145–7; Mercer 1992). Here, then, since his death in 1956 and several decades later, was the opportunity for Bulosan to "belong," and to be counted as part of an "American arena of writing." Indeed, owing to the retrieval strategies and efforts of Frank Chin and the Combined Asian Resources Project (CARP) in the 1970s, an Asian American literary canon was established within which male writers like Bulosan and Chin himself were elevated as exemplars (Kim 1982, 174–213), followed by what Elaine Kim notes as the "golden age of Asian American cultural production" (Lim and Ling 1992, xi) frequently traceable to Maxine Hong Kingston's literary breakthroughs and publishing coups.

Still, even Bienvenido Santos, a surviving contemporary of Bulosan's who has partly benefited from these developments,[14] is unable to cast his identity and writing in an "American" mold. Asked in an interview if he saw himself as an "ethnic writer" or a "Filipino American," he responded thus: "I'm an Asian writer who writes in English. And we live in America[.] I want to be called a Filipino writer writing in English. A Filipino writer who has been in and out of this country, who has been more in than out of this country, perhaps. But Fil-American – I just don't get it; don't get it, you know" (Grow 1977, 18). Evidence for this chronic Filipino politics of "American" indeterminacy abounds, and perhaps such positionings are but unyielding attempts by U.S. Filipinos – whether they be sojourners, expatriates, or permanent residents and citizens – to "escape the pleasure-filled trap of hyphenation" (San Juan 1991a, 129). But what Santos and Bulosan seem to be saying is that this state of ambivalence (which is shared in large measure by those identified as Filipino Americans, perhaps because of their equivalent liminality in overdetermined U.S.–Philippines contexts),[15] is fraught with historical weight quite distinct from that characteristically experienced by American immigrants.

Such U.S. Filipino ambivalences are significantly attributable to the conflicting demands of "benevolent assimilation" and Filipino post-coloniality.[16] Writers like Bulosan paradoxically desired to be absorbed into the American canon even as they themselves limned the impossible terms which such an incorporation suggested. This form of nationaliza-tion required no less than a restitution, in one guise or another, of the logic of the United States–Philippines colonial relationship. Writers' al-most instinctive resistance to this agenda, evidenced in Santos's curious locutions in his statement of "what" he is as a writer, paradoxically show the force of this hegemonic prerequisite. Not even U.S. citizenship, the most literal form of this U.S. nationalization, can provide relief from the overweening legacies of the Filipino–American colonial encounter, as Santos himself discovered.[17] Although citizenship seemed to legitimize an Asian American space for his writing, Santos feared that it might have cut him off from a Philippine audience already caught in the throes of anti-American nationalist turmoil since the 1970s "First Quarter Storm" and suspicious of Filipinos like Santos and others who have gone "stateside."[18]

The material effects of these U.S. Filipino displacements have been historically real and are best demonstrable in the little-known underside of Villa's meteoric but ephemeral rise as literary "star."[19] Responding to the proposition, in a rare interview, that some critics considered him an "American poet," Villa denied this and cited the example of his nomina-tion for the Bollingen Prize, when he lost to Wallace Stevens on the grounds of "citizenship." He attributed this loss to one of the jurors, Oscar Williams, who "wouldn't include me in his anthologies because I wasn't American," even as the likes of W. H. Auden, Conrad Aiken, and Selden Rodman claimed him as an "American" talent. Pressed on the issue and asked if he considered himself Filipino, Villa replied: "Yes, I am Filipino, but an American resident" (Alegre and Fernandez 1993 [1984], 308).[20]

Filipino American literature, given the conditions of identity outlined above and elaborated below, is necessarily difficult to bound "nationally" and to periodize with certitude. Imagining the boundaries between the Philippine and the American nation spaces for Filipinos exceeds and does not coincide with geopolitical and nation-state borders or simple chro-nologies. Because of U.S. "benevolent assimilation," Americanization and "America" for Filipino migrants and their descendants assume remark-ably extended trajectories and mercurial expressions. The usual coordi-nates of departure (old country) and arrival (New World) do not exhaust the meanings of *Filipino* America for Filipino immigrants. Perhaps "Fili-pino *American*" can be pried loose from the conventional problematic of assimilative immigrant hyphenation and recharged with notions of Americanization and benevolent assimilation already imposed *in* the Phil-ippines by the U.S. colonial moment. As San Juan argues, "so long before the Filipino immigrant, tourist or visitor sets foot on the U.S. continent, she – her body and sensibility – has been prepared by the thoroughly Americanized culture of the homeland" (1991a, 117).

FILIPINO AMERICAN LITERARY/HISTORICAL DISPERSALS

In fact, to speak of a "Filipino American" literature is to imagine a discontinuous series of texts that assumes a semblance of coherence as a "tradition" in four formative moments: the republication of Carlos Bulosan's now classic *America Is in the Heart* (1946) by a university press in 1973; the contemporaneous emergence of "Flip" (one and a half- and second-generation) writers in the early 1970s; the international publishing breakthrough achieved by Ninotchka Rosca's *Monsoon Collection* (1982); and the phenomenal critical success of Jessica Hagedorn's *Dogeaters* in the 1990s. At each and every one of these junctures, what exactly comprised a "Filipino American" identity or similitude among these efforts merely seemed to assert self-evidence. What seemed to matter more was that such writers and writings represented an attempt by Filipinos to emerge onto some kind of scene in a U.S. context. Before and between these moments, what one finds are staggered and often unsuccessful attempts by Filipinos to break through the pall of invisibility that had historically shrouded anything Philippine-related in the U.S. American popular or historical memory and consciousness.[21]

This problem of literary periodicity and formlessness is immediately explicable in terms of a curious phenomenon: the inability – with the *few* exceptions cited above – of migrant and (post)colonial Filipino writers to achieve more visibility in the U.S. and international publishing worlds. This is no news to Filipino writers in English and other languages who have had extreme difficulty getting published outside of the Philippines, particularly in the United States. Many Filipino writers who – at various times and for differing durations – migrated to "America" in search of international recognition and a world audience have had mixed or little success.[22] Bienvenido Santos was lamenting as late as 1976 that, "in spite of our visibility and apparent good standing in the Philippine world of letters, American publishers persist in snubbing us [and] their book-keeping departments consider us commercial risks" (404).[23] Except for Bulosan and Hagedorn, there are no "major" or canonical U.S. Filipino writers to demarcate discrete stages of development, which, in turn, might crystallize stabilizing moments of generic and stylistic conventions across determinate periods. This curious publishing history of U.S. Filipino or even Filipino English and vernacular literatures, their highly contingent circulation and interruptible ability to gain effective currency in U.S. and world arenas, has remarkably analogous historical postulates across the board.

One periodizing quandary lies in the constitutive conflation of Filipino American writing with the Filipino English literary tradition coterminously formed by the U.S. colonization of the Philippines (the latter tradition's emergence is conventionally dated from 1925). Arguably, both traditions share antecedent figures in José García Villa (b. 1906), Bienvenido Santos (1911–96), N. V. M. Gonzalez (b. 1915), and Carlos Bulosan (1911–56), including the sojourning apprentices from the late colonial period up to the 1970s. As Sam Solberg notes, these writers found no meaningful difference between writing in the Philippines and in the United States (Solberg 1983, 50). Invoking their writing as the common bulwark of both traditions is a now familiar and habitual reflex as, taken together, their writings form a veritable corpus and mark significant trajectories in Filipino English and Filipino American literary histories. To either link or disarticulate these kindred literary formations, however, generates a host of problems. The notion of a shared "paternity" for both traditions reproduces the androcentric cast and anxieties of conventional literary-historical accounts.[24]

Even to claim Villa, Santos, Gonzalez, and Bulosan as the "pioneers" of a properly Filipino American writing tradition requires substantial qualification (Campomanes 1992a, 55–7). For example, Bulosan emerges as the privileged Filipino writer, whereas the other three occupy ambiguous, if mostly unacknowledged, slots in the kinship charts of Asian American literature.[25] Santos usually fares better than Villa and Gonzalez in Asian American literary studies, perhaps because of the recognizably "American" thematics of his stories and some of his novels (1976c, 1979a, 1979b, 1983b, 1987).[26] Inversely, the sainted status of Villa, Gonzalez, and Santos is unquestioned for Filipino English literary critics, whose exegetical work is neocolonially steeped in residual formalist and new-critical dogmas.[27] Thus was Bulosan routinely dismissed in the Philippines for his "counterfeit genius" or "derivative writing" up to his rediscovery by cultural workers in the United States in the 1970s and 1980s.[28] Tendentious critiques by Bulosan's Philippine contemporaries like the journalist I. P. Soliongco and by subsequent anthologists like Arturo Roseburg succeeded in relegating Bulosan to the status of a minor talent, in often harsh dismissals elaborated by Casper (1964), San Juan (1968), Bulaong (1966–7), Bernad (1975), Hizon (1982), and, most recently, Ticmpo (1991).[29]

The positions of such writers and the evaluation of their work thus alter markedly when pressed against sociocultural and ideological shifts in either a Philippines or United States context, or in their assymetrical interrelations. Raising this question also holds implications for women writers such as Ninotchka Rosca, Jessica Hagedorn, and Linda Ty-Casper and the places they inhabit within these trans-Pacific formations. The problem of categorization becomes further complicated if the Filipino American second-generation, gay/lesbian, and Hawaiian-Ilokano writers are gathered as discrete cohorts (Foronda 1978, 26; Campomanes 1992a, 54–7; Manalansan 1993). Using an equivalent "wave-theory" or simple periodizing schema (as in social-historical accounts) thus cannot adequately encompass the effects of various but related habitats on the submergence, emergence, and reception of these writers' oeuvres. What already strikes the critic is the oddly and commonly marginal status of all these writers in the world English and United States literary canons. The problem is epitomized in statements made by some Filipino English/ American writers themselves: Wilfrido Nolledo observes "that the Filipino writer, great or not, is sadly anonymous" (N. V. M. Gonzalez 1976, 416), and Bienvenido Santos likens certain Filipino writers (including himself) to "invisible stragglers" (1976b, 401).

N. V. M. Gonzalez, in an earlier essay, substantially anticipates Benedict Anderson's notion of "an immense subterranean shift" (1994, 108) in the loci and object of Filipino/Philippine quests for identity. Like Anderson, Gonzalez recognizes the twentieth-century Filipino "fusion of migrancy and exile" as a historic consequence of U.S. colonial dispossession and as the defining condition for the globally itinerant and indeterminate production of a Filipino nationality or national culture. Gonzalez, like Anderson, privileges the late-nineteenth-century Philippine nationalist martyr José Rizal as the paradigmatic figure for periodizing "three generations" of Filipino intellectuals or writers who, thereafter, hovered uneasily between transience and "protracted" sojourns "abroad."[30]

More important for Gonzalez, however, is that it was *in* the space of Rizal's *peripatetic* and *extended residence* in Spain and other parts of Europe that his classic novels of political satire and anticolonial critique (1887, 1891) – directed at the ill effects of centuries of Spanish theocratic rule over the Philippines – were conceived (see also Ileto 1982, 315).[31] Contrarily, whereas Rizal, out of this exilic experience, successfully reoriented Philippine Eurohispanic culture toward a vision of Filipino nationality and "mapped out a new geography for the literature of his country," subsequent writers have elaborated a perennial sense of displacement and experienced an intractable identity crisis. "With the advent of the American regime, a perturbed sensibility began to look about, anxious for indications of roots or beginnings, only to stumble into false starts and ludicrous posturings in hopes of pressing the Filipino experience into acceptable forms" (N. V. M. Gonzalez 1979, 240–1).

FILIPINO AMERICAN (UN)HOMINGS/NOMADISMS

History has always dismissed the nomads.
        – Gilles Deleuze and Félix Guattari (1987, 394)

What Gonzalez and Anderson observe as the U.S.-induced diasporic turn in Filipino nationalist questings and their literary expressions – from Filipino identifications with "Las Filipinas" to a "perturbed sensibility, anxious for indications of roots or beginnings" and profoundly obsessed about a *Filipino* "identity" – is, however, more descriptive of contemporary Filipino historical and sociological conditions than characteristic of U.S. Filipino literary postcoloniality. There are no easy correspondences between the historical/sociological condition and the cultural/literary text, nor should the reader look for them. Indeed, the sociological readings that Filipino American texts often automatically solicit can only succumb to their own self-delusions: namely, that Filipino texts, like all literary efforts emerging out of the colonial condition, are *colonially* dismissible as "nonliterary" or not "transcendentally universal" enough to escape their "ethnic-specific" conditions.[32]

In the following examination of some of the more "anomalous" but indicative texts of the U.S. Filipino "tradition," two sets of alternative critical possibilities emerge. First, current (postcolonial and multicultural) critiques/accounts of the despotic structures of nationalism and the nation-state might profit much from attending more closely to the Philippine and Filipino American historical predicaments and their multiple poetic (de)constructions. The so-called linguistic or poststructuralist turn of EuroAmerican thought – "the impetus toward decentring and pluralism" – is a position that "the situation of marginalized societies and cultures" might have "enabled them to [experience] much earlier and more directly," even differently, precisely through the effects of colonial-territorial *dispossession* and its abductive displacements (Ashcroft et al. 1989, 12). Second, the (post)structuralist notion that "language is a material practice and as such is determined by a complex weave of social conditions and experiences" might be better appreciated by seriously considering the linguistic and literary (*anti*)structures emerging out of colonial histories. That is, exactly "because the traversal of the texts by these conditions becomes so clear and crucial in post-colonial literatures, the ideals of art existing for its own sake or of literature appealing to some transcendent human experience are both rejected" (Ashcroft et al. 1989, 41).

Rather than potentially dismiss (in)coherent U.S. Filipino texts as a complex of "false starts and ludicrous posturings" born out of the "hopes of pressing the Filipino experience into acceptable forms," the question should be asked: which "forms" and "acceptable" to whom? Filipino cultural nationalists frequently rehearse enduring anxieties over the inability of any Filipino writer anywhere to produce "the great Filipino novel," over the confinement of Filipino literary achievements within such "small" forms as poetry and short fiction (see Santos 1967; N. V. M. Gonzalez 1966, 1993a; Galdon 1979). These anxieties are particularly acute over Filipino writing in the colonial languages of Spanish and English, sometimes resulting in precipitate dismissals of the adequacy or transformative utility of colonial linguistic legacies to the representation of "native" realities.

If "the imagination is the common denominator between the nation and the novel [because] a nation is comprised of individuals believing that they belong to one community [and] a novel calls on readers to imagine community" (Martinez-Sicat 1994, ix), is the Filipino difficulty with the novel then indicative of a "congenital" Filipino failure on both the imaginative and nation-building levels? Or are we actually confronted with unrecognizably different or alternative kinds of imagination and nationality in Filipino literatures and predicaments? What does it tell us that Filipino literary achievements, as observers note, have tended more toward the lyric than the epic, and more toward an economic poetics than an extended prose practice?[33] These kinds of binarist generic distinctions, of course, have their own problematic histories and cannot be imposed upon Filipino literatures or cultural forms without massive qualifications; yet it is precisely their perceivable intermixtures or alterations *between* Filipino (American) texts and conditions that demand more critical attention than they have received. If Filipinos seemed to have failed in the "epic" effort to forge a nation, and their intellectuals have only "lyrically" bewailed this miserable "failure," is it possible that this prevalent judgment can only be the result of the critic's own failure of "discriminating" imagination, and a function of residually (neo)colonial reading regimes?

This concluding section seeks to complicate Anderson's notion of contemporary Filipino diasporic dispersals as a "different transformation that began in a small way in the 1930s and has reached *flood-tide* today" (clearly an "epic" phenomenon), and Gonzalez's idea of this "dispersed nationality" as somehow having failed to produce, after Rizal, a new literary *geography* of its imagined communities (nation/s). What, by overlapping turns, will be called a Filipino "nomadology," "archipelagic poetics," and "aesthetics of economy," is teased out of an indicative sample of U.S. Filipino texts and writerly locales and experiences. In short, what are the Filipino literary or aesthetic (re)constructions of what Gonzalez himself characterizes as a historic response of "rhizomatous" Filipino outgrowths through the most inhospitable soils (through a "lahar of colonizations"; see N. V. M. Gonzalez 1992, quoted in Strobel 1993, 117), and what Nick Joaquin himself, alternatively but poetically, recognizes as a ceaseless process of "Philippine-*becoming* [not Filipino *being*]," in which "we don't grow like a seed [but] split like an amoeba" (1988, 245, 220)?[34]

If it is true that diasporic formation shifted Filipino nationalist questings from a land-based identification (Las Filipinas) to a deterritorialized privileging of "Filipino" identity, it is nonetheless the case – as anyone who inspects the available texts discovers – that figurations of exilic displacements, nostalgia for the old country, leave-taking, dispossession, and imagined "homecomings" are implicit and explicit refrains in Filipino American cultural products. Such tropes reimagine the home/land in various guises and thus repossess it in often poignantly symbolic attempts to reverse the sociological or historical condition of "identity crises" – a literary logic ensured by the inaugural moment of colonial-territorial dispossession that radically led to ceaseless wandering (exile) and migrancy in the first place.

The many nuances of this extra/territorial poetics – what Edward Said calls "the primacy of the geographical" or the "cartographic impulse" in postcolonial discourse and texts – surely survive this caricaturish rendition. It is only made to emphasize the frequently unappreciated fact of "a pressing need for the recovery of the land that, because of the presence of the colonizing outsider [and one's displacements abroad], is recoverable at first only through the imagination" (Eagleton et al. 1990, 77, 79). The impulse itself should not surprise readers who find it abundantly exemplified in the various elsewheres of postcolonial discourse. What is worth noting here for the Filipino case, especially in the following account, are the crucial differences and reversals in rhetorical objects *between* the Filipino historical condition and Filipino nomadic-imaginative forms. In short, the (dis)junctions between condition and text constitute a literary/ aesthetic problem, not an automatic invitation to facile sociological-historical exegeses. Indeed, it is conceivable in the Filipino case that the sociological-historical and literary/aesthetic are not mutually exclusive but mutually constitutive concerns; that one poetically *becomes* – while multiply qualifying – the other, but only *through* remarkably portable (inter)mediations that in themselves are *expressive* of the dizzying routes of Filipino itinerancy in the wake of colonial dislocations.

The brilliant story by Hawaiian Ilokano-language writer Pelagio Halaba (nom de plume: Val Amor), "Ti Langit ni Nana Sela" (A GrandMother's Horizons), provides an inexhaustible lode for what can be called the "aesthetics of economy" and "archipelagic poetics" of U.S. Filipino nations and narrations.[35] Halaba/Amor is part of the *Gunglo Dagiti Mannurat nga Ilokano iti Hawaii* (GUMIL, Association of Ilokano Writers in Hawaii), a community-based literary and cultural organization that has been in existence since 1971, has independently published several volumes of their writing (Saludes 1973; Saludes 1976; M. Albalos et al. 1981; Ponce et al. 1984), and has attracted nearly two hundred active members from a charter membership of seventeen within only a decade of its founding.[36] This group's literary credo and the oppositional exuberance of their creative styles or campaigns bear reiteration here (before we turn to the story), as they take remarkable exceptions to the often arrogantly prescriptive strains in "continental" criticism that seek to circumscribe what is to be recognized as "Filipino American writing."[37]

Unlike many postcolonial Filipino writers who operate in monadic terms, GUMIL members conceive of literature as a socially *nomadic*, and thus democratic, enterprise: compelling only if it derives its life and energy from – and is in active commerce with – the everyday world of Hawaiian Ilokanos. Organization members exult in the unusual history of the group itself. In the emphatic words of Mel Cadavona Agag, "it took a woman [Pacita Saludes] – not a man – in January 16, 1971" to achieve the feat of organizing and promoting Hawaii's Ilokano writers in well over half a century of Ilokano migration and settlement in the islands, and to overcome the initial skeptical resistance of a "nonliterary world" splintered among a multitude of Filipino social and fraternal organizations (Saludes 1973, 5).

Their decision to cultivate writing in the Ilokano language – and as widely as this could be managed, hence the free mix of old and young, men and women, neophyte and accomplished, immigrant or U.S.-born writers in their membership – forms part of this generous vision of a literature or culture come alive to its producers and "community" contexts.[38] A nearly exclusive emphasis of GUMIL on forms "accessible" to a largely working-class community – such as what they call the *drama* (usually one- or two-act plays almost like regenerated, transplanted, and mobile versions of the Filipino-Hispanic performance genres of the *zarzuela* and the *komedya*); the *sarita* ("talk" or story, not *short* story, even as the pieces are expected to achieve conventional brevity, because the emphasis is on the *telling*, not the genre); the *salaysay* (essay; also historical exposition); and the *nailadawan a pakasaritaan* ("imaged word/worded image" or photoessay; illustrated history) – is a crucial plank of this dynamic and socially engaged cultural *economy* envisioned by GUMIL members.[39]

Unlike the first-generation Filipino English/American or still expectant migratory writers, therefore, "homegrown" GUMIL artists do not have their sights set on New York's Publishers Row. Neither, apparently, could they care less if the language in which they create is one that few U.S. universities would consider legitimate enough (like Swahili or French) as "foreign-language" offerings.[40] This "independence" seems to offer a refreshing and creatively "local" qualifier upon the grand political events often ranged under the rubric "independence from the imperial centre" in postcolonial discourses. But the group's literary and language pedagogy, which was enunciated at the time of the group's formation to address what was perceived as an acute problem of "too many expatriot Filipinos ... failing to ensure that their children become proficient [in Ilokano]," has even more astonishing implications in terms of a historic process others have called "Ilokanization" (Foronda 1978).

In the Philippines, the somewhat anti-imperious notion of an "independent" cultural-linguistic "nation" called Ilocandia seems borne out by the transformation of Ilokano into a nomadic and transregional lingua franca (rivaling Tagalog's otherwise state-legislated sway) spoken and recognized as a language of commerce in frontier and contact regions inhabited by other groups such as the Igorots, Ibanags, Gaddangs, Isinais, and Pangasinanenses.[41] Ilocandia's fluid territorial boundaries encompass whatever parts of the country to which Ilocanos (driven by the harshness of their environment on the arid northern coasts) have migrated and settled – over ten Luzon provinces alone, plus parts of Mindanao and the Visayan islands.[42]

This alter-native "decentering," the installation of an imagined/shifting "center" other than "America" by which to orient one's dislocations, is the subject of Halaba/Amor's *sarita* (in Ponce et al. 1989), in the deceptively quotidian case of Nana Sela as an (im)migrant who maps her own affective geography or economy across seemingly insurmountable "national" boundaries. The extremely elegant and supple prose of this piece makes one recall such "classics" of the Philippine English short story as N. V. M. Gonzalez's "A Warm Hand" and "Bread of Salt" (reprinted in 1993b, 3–14, 96–106); Manuel Arguilla's "How My Brother Leon Brought Home a Wife," Estrella Alfon's "Magnificence," Aida Rivera Ford's "Love in the Cornhusks" (all reprinted in Francia 1993), Bienvenido Santos's "The Day the Dancers Came" (reprinted in 1979b, 113–128), or even the genius of the *dagli* (vignette, sketch) and the *maikling katha* (short literary composition) of the Tagalog tradition (N. V. M. Gonzalez 1979, 242–4). This *sarita*, in fact, thematizes and formalizes the power of the economic and poetic impulse for an unlikely nomad who feels "stranded," at the moment, on islandic Hawai'i. Nana Sela is a (grand)mother who, throughout the story, is gripped by an intense nostalgic longing (*iliw*) to return to her Philippine hometown (*purok*) after three years of sorely missing her eldest and youngest sons and their families, who remained behind when she moved to join her son Jim's immigrant household.

Nana Sela's predicament in this *sarita* resembles those of memorable Filipino (American) literary characters like Santos's "hurt men" or "old-timers" (the melancholic Alipio in "Immigration Blues," the nostalgic Fil in "The Day the Dancers Came," the lonely Celestino Fabia in "Scent of Apples" (1979b, 3–29, 113–28); or the dying Solomon King in *The Man Who (Thought He) Looked like Robert Taylor*; 1983b); Bulosan's sentimental Allos/Carlos/Carl, who covets the "wide American earth" yet yearns for the beautiful blue mountains of his Binalonan childhood (1973 [1946]); Gonzalez's unidentified *Lolo* (elder), whose unmitigated bachelorhood as a migrant California worker for "twenty, thirty" years makes him vulnerable to the marriage scams of the "Attorney-at-Law, Importer-Exporter of Brides" and confidence man Sopi ("The Tomato Game"; 1993b, 160–1); or those Filipino workers "without names" in Jeff Tagami's poignant poetry, "hunchbacked/From a lifetime of hauling irrigation pipes" and yet "Squeeze goat entrails clean,/Sticking their fingers/In places I think/Not possible" and, unflinchingly, "Drink the green bile/For long life" (1987, 15, 30).

Nana Sela, however, is also an entirely different and new creation. Although her "worded image" or "imaged word" in Halaba's *sarita* recalls the more familiar themes and representational styles associated with the iconic old-timers (*Manong*) of U.S. Filipino literature, she embodies a refreshing and startlingly contemporary departure from dominant emplotments of Filipino migration or exile. A partial transfer, like her son Jim, who first worked in Texas, then transferred to Hawai'i, Nana Sela should be a recognizable figure to post-1965 Filipino "family reunification" migrants: usually retirement-age parents brought over by their immigrant children, not only to "mind the house and the kids," but also, potentially, to petition the remaining family once the parents themselves become "U.S. citizens." Halaba's strategic choice of a "mother" and recent (im)migrant as the spinal figure for his remarkable contribution to Filipino "nomadology" creates startling effects, in light of the usually commemorative representations constructed by available texts around the "survivors of those who immigrated in the 1920s or even earlier, through the 1930s" (Santos 1982a, 89).

The iconic Pinoy (also "old-timer" and *Manong*) is probably as close to a "nationally" heroic figure spawned in a U.S. historical context as Rizal is for Filipinos in the Philippines' elsewheres, enabling a panoply of differing, at times identical, appropriations. Like Rizal, the Pinoy is lionized or privileged as a "martyr" by U.S. Filipinos; but, unlike Rizal in Philippine historiography, the old-timer's story remains largely unelaborated as a productive node in Asian/Filipino Americanist historical research even as these anonymous and inarticulate "pioneers" already assume many imagined lives in Filipino American cultural productions. Santos and Bulosan differently identify themselves as writers with the Manongs.[43] As a contemporary, Bulosan found an inexhaustible fount for his autobiographic poems, essays, stories, and epistles in the Pinoy's "epic" story of ceaseless struggles and displacements. As a distanced intellectual, Santos discovered the poetic distillate of the struggling exilic writer as a "straggler" – doomed into irrelevance for writing in the master's English – in the old-timer's plight as a "survivor [who] lives through years of hiding [and waits] until a miracle of change happens in the homeland, and in this [America], our other home" (1976b, 399, 404– 5).

Flip poets and second-generation writers anchor and identify their own multiple dislocations in the "epic" inability of these "founding fathers," owing to antimiscegenation and exclusivist laws, to "take root" on the very American soil that their cheaply waged labor made "fecund." Seen as a "lost generation," the Pinoy's looming extinction by the 1970s also unleashed a massive enterprise of remembrance in which still surviving old-timers became the object of frantic oral-historical researches undertaken by activists, writers, and second-generation youth before these bearers of a formative and inarticulate moment of U.S. Filipino history "died off" (for example, those collected by the Seattle Demonstration Project according to Cordova 1983; or, in the case of the migrant workers of the Alaska canning industries, the celebratory and elegiac photographic portraits of the 1987 Pioneer Alaskero Project and Exhibits).[44]

But, perhaps these "sociological-historical" forms of identity and difference in the aspects of a wholly indicative array of U.S. Filipino cultural products are less interesting than the more poetic U.S. Filipino "identities" and differentials that Halaba's *sarita* complicates for our understanding of the distinctiveness of Filipino literary economies (why the non-epic forms to capture a really "epic" re/formation of Filipino diasporic communities?). In what remains of this account, "identity" has to be understood not in the sense of a primordial, liberal selfhood (there are few Filipino bildungsromans, and not even in the conventional aspects that are critically recognized) but in the sense of nuanced resemblances among (in)coherent and differential U.S. Filipino narrations and nation/s.

The notion of the "economic" in "Ti Langit ni Nana Sela" does not derive its density from the social and historic stereotype of Ilokanos as inveterate tightwads; indeed, "dispelling degrading stereotypes" figures nowhere in the aesthetic economy of this *sarita*. In Nana Sela's story, the notion of the "economic" assumes highly poetic as well as historically resonant valences. For example, it manages to revalorize the excess of sentiment usually deemed endemic to nostalgic longings for the *heimat* or loved ones.⁴⁵ Nana Sela's affective economy or emotional calculus in this story does not emerge as a function of "culture" but of a concrete situation in which her affections and sense of place/displacement are shifted and decentered by what students of Filipino migrancy would recognize as a phenomenon of familial "binationalism" or "split households" (Denton and Villena-Denton 1986, 127; Salazar-Parreñas 1995).⁴⁶

Nana Sela's "identity problem" is how to establish an imaginative and mitigating *identity* between her Philippine "past" and her Hawaiian "present." But the *difference* between the locus of nostalgic desire (which is charged with memories) and the locus of conflict or isolation (which is charged with anxieties) does not heuristically exhaust her predicaments. To regroup a "household" which is split binationally between her sons/grandchildren in Ilocos and her immigrant son's family in Hawai'i requires that Nana Sela regularly shuttle back and forth – if not by actual travels, then by imagined returns.

What qualifies and confounds her desire to revisit home (*agbakasyon*) for the first time after three years is the forethought that she would quickly miss Jim, her daughter-in-law Tina, and their children once she is back in the Philippines (*Ammona na no makaawid idiay Filipinas, kailiwnanto dagitoy*). Identical to this anxiety is her unrelieved longing for the remaining sons and grandchildren, a feeling which remains so intense that she is only able to compare it to the "sleeplessness" of her very first night in the new land (16).

An inconsiderate writer would hew volumes of untrammeled emotion out of Nana Sela's desperate options and sentiments, but the genius of this story is precisely the point that nomadic (grand)mothers like Nana Sela cannot even afford sentimentality under such unenviable circumstances; and to theorize the resulting "aesthetics of economy" and nomadology of an "ordinary" *mater* adequately offers various devices and emplotments through an astonishing economy of nomadic and "archipelagic" images, which not only delivers the "dramatic" action in seven printed pages but allows us to recognize the "grandness" of an affectionate mother, her "epic" heroine-ism in poetic ("lyrical") terms.⁴⁷

The voice in which the *sarita* is told is split between Nana Sela's own (limited point of view) and an otherwise omniscient ("U.S.-based") narration. How this becomes homologous with the "social-historical" and literary event of a rent through the extended household which Nana Sela attempts to suture is evident enough; but the singular effect is of a filtering of the narrative action, its crises and resolutions, *through* Nana Sela's creative agency, as the omniscient voice refuses the reader any access to the other characters and, in fact, leaves them largely undeveloped. The effect is that of someone hearing Nana Sela's "unspoken" inner dialogues with herself – a someone who simultaneously *hails* the reader to verify or contrast Nana Sela's inner thoughts and feelings with her actual interactions with the developing events and the (other) undeveloped characters (a recruitment, in fact, that democratically turns readers into interpretive "poets").

The source of crisis or conflict in this *sarita*, a crisis which throughout threatens to mire Nana Sela in unrelieved nostalgia (deteriorating, midway through the narrative, to melancholic helplessness), is Jim's adamant refusal to let her go on a brief visit to the Philippines. Indeed, the story opens with a teary-eyed Nana Sela seeking solace in her regular ritual of attending Sunday mass, her chest "pierced" and pained (*masudsodak*) by her son's opposition to, and constant deferment of, her homecoming plans (13). This early image of Nana Sela as heavily overcome to the point of tears is the only one throughout the whole narrative (the story ends with a brief glimpse of Nana Sela's tearful happiness, but the "happy" resolution qualifies the tearfulness); from that point on, she struggles to supervene, while sympathetically trying to interpret the reasons for, her son's adamancy on the subject. "She knows the utter impossibility of appealing to her son's dispositions. If he says it's white, then white it is" (15).

Halaba/Amor uses two basic devices to condense, poetically, the tortuous but transformative process of Nana Sela's arrival at an effective affective economy, or a creatively economic geography, to reconcile Jim's opposition to her position/s. First, Halaba constructs a mathematical narrative structure ("numbers") around the classic metaphor/image of the nomad, the bird (*billit*), and such social-historical rituals that Filipinos would recognize as culturally resonant: Sunday Catholic mass and the spatially signifiable temporality of the calendrical year (the Ilokano *tawen*; the Tagalog *taon*). Second, he opens his *sarita* with the classic "recognition" scene or problematic of Filipino literature: the moment in which national/local/hybrid identity among or between "Filipinos" – or between Filipino repatriates and the Philippines they abandon/romanticize – is always, and ever, represented as a distinct (im)possibility in interactive situations.

Recall, for example, the pathos of the Chicago old-timer Fil's fumbling attempts to be recognized and "identified" as a fellow Filipino by the urbane "bamboo dancers" from the Philippines in Santos's "The Day the Dancers Came" (Campomanes 1992a, 60–2), or the Michigan farmer Celestino's successful and poignant attempt to establish commonality with the "first-class Filipino" in "Scent of Apples" (Santos 1979b, 21–3); the dance of recognitions and misrecognitions among Eliza, Anna, Adrian, and the various "native" and "foreign" revelers in the carnivalesque fiesta/revolution in Ninotchka Rosca's *State of War*, a choreography of conflict threatening to break through the surface of performative and Dionysian "community" (1988, 11–39); the bitter fail-ure of the Filipino American priest Ben Lucero, on his Philippine visit, to find an identity somewhere between his puritanical American Catholi-cism and tropical-baroque Filipino Catholic practices, in Peter Bacho's *Cebu*: a (non)identity that he blames upon a "superstition passing for religion, or his revulsion toward it" (1991, 95); the youthful *balikbayan* (returnee) Ruth who conciliates her "modern" immigrant ways with the "conservative" maternal solicitude of her spinster aunts (Skinner 1988, 71–6); Johnny Manalo's disenchanted romance with the Philippines he remembers and the corrupted, Marcos-ridden society he discovers upon returning after several years as an "illegal alien" in Boston (Ty-Casper 1986).[48]

In "A GrandMother's Horizons," the dialectic between this literary nomadology and the problematic of recognition or identity is tightly entwined in the opening church scene and in the inaugural moment before it, when Nana Sela glimpses a flock of migratory birds flying over the belfry, an image that she contrasts to her "incarceration" in Hawaii: "Better these birds for they are free to roam, she utters to herself" (13).[49]

> She heads for her usual spot in the pews. Barely does she warm her seat when an old woman comes along. A smile from the old woman somehow unknots the tautness in her breast. The woman sits right next to her. She strikes Nana Sela as an elder.
>
> Not a word is exchanged between them until the mass is over. They follow each other to the door.
>
> "*Manang*, are you Ilocana by any chance?" asks Nana Sela once they are outside the church.
>
> "Yes, *adik*, I am from Ilocos Norte," the old woman gladly throws Nana Sela a glance.
>
> "*I* am from Ilocos Sur," Nana Sela replies rather intimately. "Just exactly where do you live, *manang*?"
>
> "Our house is right behind the Westgate Shopping Center. And oh yes, by the way, *adik*, my name is Clara."

Here it is important that "Filipino" mutual recognition or identity is not only successful but also precarious: the untranslatability of the honorifics *manang* and *adik* signifies this precariousness and marks the interpretive limits of English from the point of view of the source language. *Manang* ("older sister") and *adi* or *ading* (neutral but gender-specific by context: "younger one") in the above exchange do not amount to a "hierarchy" but become terms of endearment between perfect strangers, whose first impulse is precisely to negotiate *(non)identity* (age difference; a possible ethnolinguistic misrecognition: "are you Ilokana, by any chance?"). These honorifics, usually reserved for use between Ilocano siblings or relatives, acquire a metaphorical charge when used for nonrelatives, and in the case of Nana Clara's affirmative reciprocation of Nana Sela's respectful recognition (*"Manang"*), *adi* or *ading*, in being cast as a possessive *adik* (*"my* younger sister"), emphasizes the women's "sisterhood" (identity) in functionally symbolic terms – an affectionate bridging of exilic distances on the level of everyday or ordinary exchanges.

But the literary qualifiers enabled by this ethnographic glossing are less interesting than the subsequent poetic uses into which the organizing image of the nomadic bird/*billit* and this inaugural problematic of recognition or identity are pressed and themselves become economic and nomadic "modular" frames for setting up Nana Sela's crises and conciliations. The natural image of the migratory "bird" punctuates the emplotment in *three* moments (including its inaugural visage and a final incarnation into those technological modes and spaces of transportability, the *eroplano*/airplane and the "airport"; 18). These three recurrences of the metaphor divide the *sarita* into *three* fairly even sections, which in turn demarcate *three* moments of identity/recognition (including the church scene) that anchor the *three dominggo*/Sundays containing the story's space in time. (Add to these symbolic syncopations of the number 3 the three years it has been from the story's conditional present since Nana Sela's arrival in Hawai'i.)

The women's mutual identity/recognition sets the ground for this tight numerical ("economic") series of identifications and qualifying differentials, which not only transforms Nana Sela's nostalgia into an economy of practical gestures but also reverses Jim's opposition to her desire for "repatriation." (By the story's end, Jim is compelled not only to make Nana Sela's "homecoming" a happy eventuality but also to desire it for himself – to confront unresolved conflicts from his Philippine past that are progressively revealed and recognized through Nana Sela's melancholic ruminations before the story's final conciliatory event.) Nana Clara not only proves to be an instant friend or "sister" but also embodies a contrapuntal narrative that intensifies and precipitates the story's action and the reader's "three-week" glimpse into the eventful crises and resolutions ("horizons") of a GrandMother's dislocated habitats.

Not only do the two women find out that they are practically neighbors and thus available to provide each other companionship and comfort (14); the differences in their situations, which intensify Nana Sela's nostalgia, are actually overcome by a decisive "identity" that explains the instantaneousness of their impulse for "community": both are unable to speak English, the linguistic determinant of their existential displacements and isolations (*agpadpada a di makasarita ti Ingles* [14]).

First, from the initial encounter, the story's action is demarcated by the succeeding Sundays when the women decide to attend mass together and discuss strategies or options for Nana Sela after Nana Clara learns about Jim's opposition to his mother's return. We, and Nana Sela, learn through this succession of encounters that Nana Clara is able to go "home" regularly with her immigrant family (*"Tinawenkam nga agaw-awid,"* kinuna ni Nana Clara [15]) and that their next trip is planned for December/Christmas, a culturally symbolic terminus to the Filipino Christian year (*tawen; taon*), a situational difference from Nana Sela's three-year "incarceration," which only heightens her longings and frustrations. This difference becomes doubly significant because the reader is told before the women's second Sunday reunion that Nana Sela anchors her hope for a Philippine trip on a December date: Christmas being a time for "rebirth" and the renewal of family ties (Filipino family reunions are typically organized around this merry season) and, in this case, of Nana Sela's comforting memory of the *piesta* (festivity) in her place of birth or hometown (*Kayatna ti agawid inton Disiembre ta piesta ti purokda* [15]).

When Nana Sela is offered the other's traveling company for a December homecoming, one of Jim's various excuses for deferring or obstructing her travel plans is revealed: that he will not allow her to go alone because her "ignorance" about the "complexities" of "modern-day travel" is indicated by her inability to speak English, the language of mobility and transit (16). Although Nana Clara's possible companionship on the trip presents a way out of this quandary, Nana Sela knows better: Jim will remain unmoved. This foreknowledge not only mires her in helpless longing (*Limmanlan ti iliwna*) but provides the occasion for the most powerful and integrative description of her plight in this *sarita*: "*Kimmarayo ti riknana.*/ Her nostalgia takes wing." Nana Sela's difference from, and identification with, the nomadic *billit* acquire their organizing and poetic purchase on the narrative's emplotments at this moment.

Second, "English" signifies not only these women's common isolation from the larger Hawaiian/American world but also their confinement within the sphere of the household ("domestic"). Their being stranded on islandic Hawai'i (like female Robinson Crusoes, except that they do not have Man Fridays) merely literalizes their acute sense of displacement and, in Nana Sela's case, a desire for a creative "homemaking" and "homecoming," a desire immensely enabled by the friendship of another whose similar linguistic "handicap" makes the problem of familial dispersal bearable. Hence, in the three Sundays that these GrandMothers explore their "identities," we learn of their nearly *identical* attempts and desire to mitigate their homelessness and to make Hawai'i more habitable through their shared set of references to some (in)accessible center across the Pacific ("Ilocandia"). Apart from the impulse for identity, such as their exchanges about the affection they feel for, and derive from, their grandchildren – with whom they babysit so that their own children can work and maximize their livelihoods ("division of labor," see pages 15 and 17) – the companionship itself (attending mass together) becomes the space for creative strategizing and mutual empowerment.

Nana Sela, for example, realizes more and more through her precipitating encounters with Nana Clara that she needs to understand, and thus generously forgive, her son's seemingly inexplicable decision; for the reasons behind Jim's opposition change in inflection as soon and as variously as the importunings she is able to impress upon it – on Nana Clara's proddings – produce certain kinds of crises and conciliations. Nana Sela is compelled to forge her own recognitions and identifications of Jim's position (under the impact of her increasing frustration with his steadfastness) so as to successfully unite her Hawaiian present with her Philippine memories (relentless anxiety with unrelieved nostalgia; symbolic homelessness with creative homemaking). When Nana Sela broaches Nana Clara's offer of companionship to Jim after the second Sunday, he shifts from the "English-only" position to a lame excuse that, if Nana Sela is only able to wait for the time to become more propitious in the coming year, her homecoming can become a happier occasion, with his family providing companionship on the journey. Nana Sela's sense of futility at such a reply is unsalved by her memory of Jim's repeated invocations of this reason over the past year (16).

The second identity/recognition "scene" occurs after the second and third Sundays, but this time from Nana Sela's end and toward Jim's own history of displacements. In an extended interior ("unspoken") monologue, Nana Sela generously reinterprets her son's dogmatism as a function of his "strength" to have ventured abroad and to have had the initiative to improve the life opportunities of Nana Sela's brood. (This is half anticipated by the first interior monologue after the first Sunday, when Nana Sela reflects upon Jim's differences from his brothers: he proved to be the smartest of her three children by excelling in school, moving to Manila, and supporting himself in college while earning an electrical engineering degree, then moving to Texas, and finally, to Hawai'i.) ("Nana Sela can still recall her son's uninterrupted remittances from abroad. His efforts gave their impoverished life a fresh start" [15].)[50]

This proves to be only partly mitigating; it is the *recognition* of her desires by her unconditionally sympathetic and affectionate daughter-in-law, Tina (in addition to the issue of the Hawaiian grandchildren's welfare, and Nana Clara's friendship), that allows Nana Sela to create her conciliations under these trying conditions of nostalgia and divided sentiments. Again, Nana Sela's second interior monologue, which enables her own "recognition" of Jim's stances after the third Sunday, is anticipated by her first monologue (revaluing Jim's absolutism as "strength") after the first Sunday, when the subject comes up in dinner conversation. Jim notices his mother's sagging appetite.

An observant Tina ventures that Nana Sela must be missing her Philippine sons and grandchildren again and castigates/urges Jim to let her travel home for a visit (*"Mailiw manen ni nanang ... No dikanto pay la ngamin palubosan nga agbakasyon"*). Perhaps to impress the urgency of Nana Sela's desires upon her impassive husband, Tina reminds him that Nana Sela is getting up there in age and probably wants to revisit the other brothers' families before the unthinkable moment snatches her away from all of them (*Mom, aya ti gasat ... yad-adayom, Apo*). Jim's flippant response, deferring the envisioned family trip and ribbing his mother that she must have a longer lease on life than Tina thinks, settles the subject at that point (15).

To Nana Clara's insistent queries about Jim's motivations and any progress on the homecoming question on the third and last Sunday we see the women together, Nana Sela is thus only able to proffer the same unpromising reports. This is the juncture at which Nana Sela verges on melancholic helplessness and the second moment of identity/recognition occurs. On that Sunday night, however, she overhears a bedtime argument between Jim and Tina (*agsinsinnupiat da Jim ken Tina iti kuartoda*), from which it finally dawns on her why Jim is refusing to let her go back and why she should begin to think of home as a mobile habitus. To Tina's importunings that he should just let Nana Sela go on the Philippine trip she so craves, Jim raises another issue: who will babysit the children in Nana Sela's absence? (*"Sino nga'd ti agawir kadagiti annakmo?"*). Unable to dispute Tina's reply that they can hire a babysitter, Jim mean-spiritedly introduces the matter of Nana Sela's traveling expenses. Undaunted, Tina reasons that it is incumbent upon him to assume them, given the savings they have made all this time (*"Ikkam a, kakaisuna nga adda met bassit urnongta"*). Jim complains about the "uneconomic" idea, arguing that no profit can be had from homecomings (*"Ania met ti maala ti agawid?"*) and that such expenses are probably best reserved for their pressing needs in Hawai'i.

When Tina appeals to Jim's empathy, his riposte sparks Nana Sela's own recognition of her son's real reason and her resulting self-undertanding in the interior monologue that follows, after also "respectfully" recognizing Tina's sympathetic identification with, and advocacy of, her desires (*Dinayaw ni Nana Sela ti panangikalintegan ti manugangna kenkuana*) – namely, that Jim would have been happy to see his youngest brother again after so long had the latter heeded his advice and treasured, not wasted, Jim's investments in him. Nana Sela, though identifying with Jim's position, also inwardly takes issue with its rigidities. Reading it as a vindictive act that hurts not only her youngest son but also her own feelings, Nana Sela, in perhaps the most indicative line in the story, concludes that Jim is suffering from a more radical problem: "*Nakurang ti pammati na iti iliw.*" / "He has little faith in the power of longing" (17). The next day, when a sudden development in which Jim has to travel to New York as his company's representative to a business conference sets the ground for the story's ending, Nana Sela experiences the epiphanies that not only render the conclusion moot but also allow her to reimagine the flux of her inhabitations between the separated branches of her "household." Having slept late, she resolves for the new day to actively deflect her persistent nostalgia (given the improbability of changing Jim's decision) by going through her usual ritual of housecleaning. "*Inkeddengna nga iturturednan ti iliwna.*" / "She decides to simply endure her intense nostalgia" (18).

It is in the acts of tending to her vegetable garden, however, that Nana Sela makes the poetic conjunctions and disjunctions of her ultimate crises and conciliations. "Loosening the soil" around her eggplant patch and "weeding around, as well as sprinkling water on, the loused leafings of her sweet potatoes" (*Rinukitna dagiti mulana a tarong[;] agparut kadagiti ruot sana pinugsitan dagiti inaplat a bulong ti kamote*), Nana Sela willfully divines a comforting identity between the old and new countries: *Sabagay, nakunana ti bagina, kas met la Filipinas ti Hawaii. Adu ti kapadpada a Filipino ken adu met ditoy dagiti natnateng sadiay.* / "After all, Hawaii is like the Philippines, she tells herself. Here, there are many fellow Filipinos, and vegetables from home also abound." The precariousness of this resolution, however, is brought back by the reappearance of a nomadic image as she turns to look at the sky: *Mailiwliwagna koman ti iliwna ngem idi tumangad, nakitana manen ti pangen dagiti billit a limmabas. Inapalanna ti wayawaya dagitoy.* / "But just as she successfully relieves her longings for home, she turns to regard the horizon and glimpses a flock of passing birds. How she envies their freedoms . . ." (18).

Three moments of these *habitual* fluctuations frame the final moment of identity/recognition, which now circles back to Nana Sela's displacements from Jim's own perspective. Early in the story, Nana Sela's desperation compels her to assure herself mentally that she means to return to Hawai'i after the brief visit, that the few days of such a homecoming would probably suffice to arm her with the will to withstand the foreseeably unstable separations and reunions with her Philippine/ American families (16). Later, as she cares for her Hawaiian grandchildren after the vegetable tending scene, Nana Sela compares the endearing memory of a young and demanding Jim with their utter dependence upon her caregiving, and makes her both doubt and desire the likelihood of an easy return (18). "But she really means to return, Nana Sela tells herself. Except that if she fails to do so, it will perhaps be for the best. The kids, then, can be spared the luxury of always having their way with her as they do now."

The third moment, which nearly shakes down Nana Sela's imaginative conciliations, occurs near the end of the story when Jim has flown to New York and she receives a letter from her youngest son imploring her to visit them in December in time for the birth of her new grandchild. In the letter her son also asks, and expresses some hope, for Jim's forgiveness. The "grandness" of this mother is brought to the reader in full force as Nana Sela generously reimagines and recognizes her youngest son's own longings, his transformation into a better person by his marriage, and his rightful need for the affection she is now showering on Jim's household (19).

When she accompanies Jim's family to the airport to send him off on his business trip, which is to last for over a week, Nana Sela's glimpse of the *eroplano* (mechanical "bird") instills in her a longing to board one for the homecoming she desires. What she has occasion to observe outside of her own plight, however, are Jim's anxieties over his separation from his children. The reader is told that this family separation is the first time it ever happened in Jim's experience (*Nalagip ni Nana Sela a damo ni Jim a panawan to pamiliana* [18]). Indeed, throughout the whole time that he is in New York, Jim makes daily long-distance calls to ask after the children and to express his intense longing for them. As Tina teases Jim, "So you know how to miss family, after all?" (*Sangkaulit ti nalaus nga iliwna. "Ammom met lat' mailiw aya?"* [19]).

When Jim finally returns, Nana Sela notices that he has lost some weight (*Imres ni Jim idi sumangpet*); Jim confesses that he was barely able to eat and sleep while he was away, as he worried endlessly over the children's well-being; he spends the first moments after his return hugging them again and again. During dinner that night, he acknowledges his newfound appreciation of Nana Sela's feelings about "home" as a result of the separation anxieties he endured in New York. He then surprises everyone with the announcement that they are proceeding with the long-deferred plan for the family to accompany Nana Sela on her Philippine trip. Now recognizing, and strongly *identifying* with, his mother's longings, Jim admits that being away from his family even for only a little over a week actually felt like a whole *year* to him ("*Nasurok la a makalawas a nayadayoak ngem kasla tawenen kaniak*"). More significantly, Jim now also articulates a longing to see his brothers and to reunite his family with theirs come Christmas, when the homecoming would be "appropriate" – an unexpected turnaround that makes Nana

Sela feel "like heaven" on hearing her son's comforting words (*Kasla langit ti yanna a nakangngeg kadagiti balikas ni Jim* [19]).

On an immediate level, this detailed descriptive translation of a Hawaiian-Ilokano *sarita* serves to illustrate that one text from the (U.S.) Filipino "heritage of smallness" alone can actually authorize extended exegetical possibilities. The "aesthetics of economy" that it presents mobilizes the "Filipino nomadology" and "archipelagic poetics" of U.S. Filipino writerly subjectivities, social-historical experiences, and their literary alterities or alterations. In the various decentering and pluralizing operations offered by both the "atypical" heroinic example and story of Nana Sela, and the "atypical" cultural-linguistic politics of the author, Pelagio Halaba, and the GUMIL-Hawaii writers, the critic/reader will find *economically* condensed, thematized, and typified the major (dis)organizing identities (resemblances) and differentials composing the characteristic preoccupations and forms of U.S. Filipino texts.

In a story written in Ilokano, rather than in English, one finds the iconic Old-Timer decentered by a GrandMother even as the exilic dis/placements of "archaic" Pinoy life are rehearsed *but* contemporized by the nomadology of a family-reunification "immigrant." By looking at a linguistically "atypical" rendition and context of U.S. Filipino indeterminacy and dispersal (Hawaiian Ilokano/Philippine Ilocandia), the "assertive independence" of Filipino English/American writers/writing from assimilative American-immigrant or exclusive Eurocentric-postcolonial traditions or critical models can be simultaneously qualified and enhanced. The GUMIL act of writing in the migratory "vernacular" itself holds tremendous implications for a Filipino (American) cultural politics and poetics other than that which passes through the institutions of "English." The colonial language of "English" clearly continues to produce material and symbolic dislocations for Filipinos (the inability of Nana Sela and Nana Clara to speak the master's language) and to retain its analogic powers in describing the "virtual and actual spaces" of Filipino American exilic texts and vistas (see N. V. M. Gonzalez, above; Campomanes 1992a, 58–62). If colonial-pedagogical English promised Filipino writers access to a cosmopolitan readership but hardly delivered on it, what does it mean when U.S. Filipino writers in the vernacular are pitching their literature to "other" audiences and contexts?[51]

The usually androcentric desire for "national" identity between or among Filipinos in the classic recognition scenes of Filipino (American) literature is here oscillated between a gendered, ethno-localizing imperative ("Are you *Ilocana* by any chance?") and an imagined community/nation decomposed into "archipelagic" and decentered locales (Filipinas as Ilocandia; America as Hawai'i).[52] If the continuous interruptions and reconstitutions of Filipino nationality and "nation building" by waves of colonizers and recent diasporic dispersals have resulted in political and literary patriarchies that are ever-destabilized (Filipino national leaders who possess no prestige in international politics or Filipino male writers who rarely acquire canonical status in world literature studies), what can shifting and decentered Filipino communities or literary nomadologies offer to a world increasingly disenchanted with, but continually gripped by, exclusive/monistic nationalisms and despotic nation-state structures? Nana Sela's location of a Philippines between the fluctuating borders of the two islandic territories of Ilocandia and Hawai'i is very much in keeping with the archipelagic poetics of Filipino diasporic writing and nostalgic discourses. Her extraterritorial poetics, which regroups a "split" household, can allegorically sustain the general problematic of what observers have noted as an increasing phenomenon of Filipino-American binationality, and what is characterized here as a "nomadology" produced by the "epic" dispersal of the Filipino nation/s.

Who can forget the oceanic vistas, the nomadic cultural forms, or the mobile settlements of swidden farmers celebrated in the fiction and literary essays of N. V. M. Gonzalez (1963, 1975, 1990a, 1993b), a writer whose turning to the "archipelagic" images of his Mindoro and Romblon Islander past was merely literalized by his "extended residence" across a variety of Philippine and California sites? Among the most memorable localizations of the Philippines in Filipino English literature are Manuel Arguilla's rustic Nagrebcan, the tropical-baroque institutions of Nick Joaquin's Manila, and Sinai Hamada's fog-kissed Baguio. In the sprawling historical novels of Ninotchka Rosca (1988, 1992) or the expansive serial novellas of Linda Ty-Casper, which rewrite Spanish and American colonial, and Filipino national-revolutionary or contemporary-political, narratives (1964, 1979, 1987b, and 1980a, 1985a, 1986), *Las Filipinas* is reimagined through the prism of the local and the locale: for Rosca, a Manila that resiliently rises through the devastations wrought by war after war; for Ty-Casper, a "Loyal and Ever-Noble City of Manila" wrapped in the "accumulated silences of centuries" or as the corrupted and conflicted imperium of dictatorial power that at once mobilizes and tyrannizes provincial politicos. The imaginary country to which Michelle Cruz Skinner returns, through young women characters, in *Balikbayan* (1988), is an Olongapo populated by American servicemen, prostitutes, and children in "oversized t-shirts." Even "Filipino America," in the poetry of Flip writers, is never the continent, but California in its most local lineaments: Pajaro, the streets of San Francisco, and a virtual "Big Sur" traversed and mapped by what Carlos Bulosan, in the powerful story "Be American," called "the unwritten law of nomad" (1983b, 56). Filipino (American) writers, it seems, have to negotiate and map their "communities" in the space of conflicting demands between "a national longing for form" (Brennan 1990) and a radically (anti)national predicament of "formless" dispersals.

Finally, the remarkably economic (anti)structure of Halaba's *sarita* offers a productive prototype for the aesthetics of economy, nomadalogy, and archipelagic poetics in Filipino (American) texts and contexts: a powerful fount of ripostes to hasty and problematic dismissals of Filipino literary and national formations by prevalent critical monisms. Leonard Casper, for example, castigates Bienvenido Santos for his "difficulty [in] organizing anything longer than a short story" or for the "failure [of the short-story collections of Santos] to find a sequence of patterned significance." From this salvo, Casper proceeds to criticize two of Santos's novels (B. Santos 1982b, 1983b) as failures which somehow illustrate that "Philippine nationalism continues to suffer from factionalism" (Casper 1986–7, 163, 166). The Filipino failure of novelistic and nationalistic imagination (Santos is merely a pretext) for Casper – what he calls its "confusion of genre" – is indicated by the repetitious or migratory incarnations of old-timer characters ("expatriate Pinoys") and emplotments between *You Lovely People* (1955) and *The Man Who (Thought He) Looked Like Robert Taylor*.

This "nomadic" narrative strategy is not peculiar to Santos, whose collection *Scent of Apples*, which contains some of the stories that Casper found "awkwardly" rewritten into the *Robert Taylor* novel as vignettes and even reprints or migrates stories from the 1967 collection, reads as a novel (like *You Lovely People*) because of the constancy among the stories in terms of characters and dramatic action. Recall the continuing and recurrent circulation or migration of certain Gonzalez stories across the earliest collections (1963, 1964a, 1977) up through the latest ones (1979, 1993). Cecilia Manguerra Brainard's *Woman with Horns* (1988), although a loose collection of pithy stories commonly set in a reimagined Cebu ("Ubec"), is readable as a novella that traces the cosedimentation of folklore and urbanity in a locale temporally framed by the early-1900s arrival of colonial Americans and the R-and-R invasions of U.S. troops seeking relief from the Vietnam War. What about the migratory transformation of the character sketches of Colonel Amor, Eliza, and Anna from a *Monsoon Collection* story (Rosca 1983, 129), "Earthquake Weather," into the terrifying torture-master (Loved One) and the pivotal heroines bearing the same names in *State of War* (1988)?[53]

Then, Carlos Bulosan is the guiltiest of these "easy shortcuts" through the unachievable accomplishment of the Filipino novel: his "personal history" (1946) not only breaks down miserably from the "epic" dislocations of the West Coast experience it formalistically mimed; Bulosan's own autobiographical personae, relatives, and peasant heroes (like *Apo*

Lacay) persistently reappear as characters and fragmentary narratives in his short stories, epistles, essays, and "novels" under various names, profiles, and guises. One has not even mentioned the migration of the popular-cinematic language, the maladjusted migrants and deviants, the kitschy sexuality and guerilla warfare of Jessica Hagedorn's *Pet Food and Tropical Apparitions* (1981), or the psychedelic idioms, the "dangerous musics," and the linguistic mannerisms of Hagedorn's early poetry (1975) *into* the episodic, decentered, palimpsest-like, and "confusing" spaces of Manila society, in *Dogeaters* (1990). Who cannot be better accused of the crime of "a certain abstract psychologism" in "failed" historical fiction (Lukács 1983 [1962], 81) than Linda Ty-Casper, whose pioneering historical novellas – perhaps merely expanded short stories seeking to form an "epic saga" in their seriality and scope from the 1750s Spanish Philippines to the tyrannical neocolonial regime of the Marcoses – clearly enabled the "historical" turn in Filipino women's writing? Is it noteworthy that her basic narrative device – in which "private events are not linked closely enough with the real life of the people [and] are too confined at their important points to the higher social regions" (Lukács 1983 [1962], 80) – nomadically crosscuts her interrogations of Spanish conquistador subjectivity (Ty-Casper 1963); of inchoate caciquism among the revolutionary and reactionary Viardo brothers (1979); of the American colonial missionism and disenchantment of the Rowbothams (1987b); and of the "hazards of distance" within Filipino petit bourgeois and provincial-cacique clans (1980a, 1985b) or between the repatriate Filipino and the ex-*patria* in *Wings of Stone* (1986)?

Perhaps this prevalent "economic" aesthetics (heritage of smallness) in U.S. Filipino writing merely compresses a multitude of narratives waiting to be elaborated on by historically informed readers. As Halaba's metered prose performance of the "economic" shows, the imaginative geographies of alter-native communities or commonalities in U.S. Filipino narrations are already powerfully suggested *and* mitigated by their archipelagic poetics and formal autocritiques through these deployments of nomadic forms and images that exceed both generic and "national" ambitions or constraints. The portability of Filipino literary identities and constructs already poeticizes – no matter how uneasily and variously – a "dispersed nationality" and the experience of multiple dislocations.

NOTES

1. The Spanish text, "Acaba de pasar sin haber venido," is quoted and translated thus by San Juan (1990, 36).
2. Catapusan attributes this observation to Bruno Lasker, whose *Filipino Immigration* (1931) is one of the earliest of the scholarly studies on the subject.

3. Of Hartendorp, Croghan has written: "The high quality of this magazine made it so popular that it became the most influential literary magazine in the country" (1975, 7).

4. This widely read and pioneering work has had several reprintings – the first in the Philippines by Alberto Florentino, and later, in the United States, by the University of Washington Press, in 1973.

5. In "About the Author" (Villa 1958, 236), an unsigned note (the publisher's?) reads: "Mr. Villa's early interest was in painting, but he turned to writing after the impact of reading Sherwood Anderson's *Winesburg, Ohio*. That book opened up for him the world of literature and of life itself."

6. The passage in brackets appears in a version of this letter reproduced by Sam Solberg for his course AA401 at the University of Washington; it does not appear in the edited version of the same letter in Feria's collection of Bulosan's correspondence (Bulosan 1960, 258–9).

7. See Dionisio's "A Summer in an Alaskan Cannery" (Hsu and Palubinskas 1972, 154–60); "Cannery Episode," originally published in *Philippine Magazine*, August 1936, 329 and 412, is forthcoming in my *Iba: The Filipino American Story*.

8. Throughout this chapter, postcoloniality in regard to the U.S. Filipino case is understood, both in the usual sense of independence struggles of colonized peoples or their "project of asserting difference from the imperial centre," and in the broad sense of "all the culture affected by the imperial process from the moment of colonization to the present day," including the pressures both exert on contemporary literatures (Ashcroft et al. 1989, 1–2, 4–5). According to this definition, the prophetic character of the *"post-colonial"* imagination does not necessarily stem from the developmentalist chronology of a period before and after political decolonization, as "the political impetus of the post-colonial begins well before the moment of independence" (83).

9. Edward Said observes that Palestinian national dispossession is extremely difficult to range against Jewish Zionism/Israel precisely because of its victimization by "the classic victims of oppression and persecution" (1994, 53). This condition provides an obverse analogy for contending Filipino *and* American "postcolonialities" (for more elaboration, see Campomanes 1995). Irreconcilable tensions obtain between the claim of the United States as the "originally postcolonial nation" and the unseeming possibility of a U.S. Filipino postcoloniality: it was exactly upon this "historical" antecedence that U.S. imperialist ideologues justified the taking of the Philippines at the turn of the century given the purported "racial unfitness" of Filipinos for "self-government." Evidently, Filipino postcoloniality is invisible and insensible to U.S. and international postcolonial discourse studies because of the compelling power of such exceptionalist arguments for U.S. empire- and nation-building enterprises. Indeed, Filipinos can hardly assert their postcolonial difference against the recognition granted to the United States as the originary model of postcoloniality (through its celebrated 1776 revolution against the British Empire) by international and U.S. postcolonial discourse analysts like Ashcroft et al. (1989, 16–17, 32–3) and Buell (1992). Recall that William Seward (Abraham Lincoln's secretary of state and of "Seward's Folly"

fame) once imperiously declared the story of American nation building "the most important secular event in the history of the human race" (quoted in LaFeber 1989, 5).

10. This Filipino "colonizability" leads to the recurrent claims that Filipinos are "a people without culture" (see Campomanes 1995).

11. On the notion of ambassadorial writing and its precedence in Asian American literary history, see Kim (1982, 23–57). The (U.S) Filipino "ambassadorial" writers Felipe Agoncillo and Sixto Lopez were literally ambassadors/envoys and propagandists sent by Emilio Aguinaldo's provisional revolutionary government to the Unites States to countervail racialist and reductive representations of Filipinos saturating U.S. mass media and official discourses (mostly between 1898 and 1902, the years of the Philippine-American War); and to seek U.S. and international diplomatic recognition of the Philippine revolutionary government and its rights of belligerency as a way of forestalling multiple imperialist ambitions in annexing the Philippines after the 1896–8 Philippine revolution practically spelled the collapse of the Spanish colonial state. These representatives were refused recognition everywhere (especially by William McKinley's government, on the grounds that there was no such thing as a Filipino nation). (Agoncillo 1899a, 1899b, 1900; Lopez, 1899, 1900, 1901). On Agoncillo's unrecognized diplomacy and its political effects/trajectories, see de la Costa (1977).

12. San Juan cites an approximate 1984 figure of 630,000 for the later cohort but does not identify his source; the 1980 census figure of 782,000 is derived from Awanohara and reconfigures the population as 70% Philippine-born and 60% female (1991, 40). An obvious exception to this periodization is the exceptional eighteenth-century Louisiana settlement of "Manilamen." An 1883 account described these former sailors, who deserted from the Spanish-Manila-Acapulco galleon trade and settled along the Louisiana bayous, as "alligator-hide hunters and fishermen" (Lawcock 1975, 720).

13. Nonetheless, these writers proceeded to appropriate a segment of a critical essay by Bienvenido Santos on the Philippine novel in English for their account of Filipino American literary developments. Moreover, they chose Carlos Bulosan and Santos (from five writers who left the Philippines and wrote "about" U.S. Filipinos) as the progenitors of the Filipino American "tradition," despite the fact these men's "sensibilities" were predominantly "Filipino" and nominally "American" (this *generational* assertion of differential nationalities merits more extensive critical attention than is possible here). "Flip" is a term used by Peñaranda et al. for U.S.-born or -raised Filipino Americans (Campomanes 1992a, 49–50, 73–4).

14. While Santos had been writing in the Philippines and United States and publishing his fiction in the Philippines and elsewhere for over thirty years, it was the 1979 publication of *Scent of Apples* by the University of Washington Press that, for the first time, made his writing widely available to an American readership. On Santos's inclusion in the 1970s CARP recovery program, see Kim 1982, 175.

15. We are "without names," so do the "Flip" (U.S.-born and/or -raised) writers similarly and jointly declare in a poetry collection (Ancheta et al. 1985). For

more indicative statements or instances, see Evangelista (1988, 50–3) and Campomanes (1992a, 49–50).

16. "Benevolent assimilation" is the official rubric in which the U.S. Philippine colonial project was cast by its premier architect, then President William McKinley in his 21 December 1898 instructions (after the yet unratified Treaty of Paris cession) to the U.S. Philippine occupation forces commanded by Maj. Gen. Elwell Otis. McKinley wanted the colonists to prove to Filipinos "that the mission of the United States is one of benevolent assimilation, substituting the mild sway of justice and right for arbitrary rule" (U.S. Adjutant General's Office, 1898–1902, 2: 858–9).

17. It has been claimed that Santos applied for U.S. citizenship in the early 1970s only as a political move, to protect himself from possible persecution by the Marcos regime as a consequence of his politically critical novel *The Praying Man* (censored as a book but eventually published in 1982 by a Philippine press), which the Manila magazine *Solidarity* serialized at the time (Casper 1986–7, 165).

18. See Lacaba (1982) for a firsthand account of late-1960s Philippine social unrest, particularly the first few months of 1971 ("FQS"), which were provoked by the severe economic crises and cumulative corruptions created by postindependence regimes, and which threatened to collapse the Philippines in revolutionary chaos, as politically mobilized youth, peasant, intellectual, and working-class movements led by a revitalized Communist Party of the Philippines launched strikes/demonstrations and confronted the Philippine police and constabulary in pitched and often bloody street battles. This was a moment invoked by Ferdinand Marcos, with U.S. government and CIA endorsement, to declare martial law and to inaugurate his despotic dictatorship. A most powerful novel that recollects and reimagines these moments and their historic consequences is Dalisay (1992). See also Gamalinda (1992) and Rosca (1992). Some "Flip" protest poetry flourished under the impact of these developments (e.g., Virginia Cerenio's "guerrilla children," "revolution," "hail mary," "the revolutionary," and "thoughts on pilipinas," 1989, 16–20, 46, 60; also, "Letter to Grandma," in Ancheta et al. 1985, 30–1). See Evangelista's discussion of second-generation Filipino American antidictatorship activism and creative writing (1988, 42–51). On U.S. Filipino women's writing that reckons with this conjuncture, see discussion below.

19. One writer astutely observes that "Villa was lionized somewhat for his poetry, immediately after World War II, precisely at the time when the Philippines had some historical resonance – MacArthur, Bataan and all that" (quoted in Gonzalez 1976, 415–16). This effect of a particular "representative" moment applies to Bulosan's short-lived publishing triumphs as well: recall his platitudinous wartime poetry (1943b), and his best-selling "village stories" (1944), which went through two reprintings (a rare accomplishment in a U.S. context for expectant Filipino writers of the time), were translated into several European languages, and were broadcast by the U.S. Office of War Information to all "fighting men and women" worldwide to boost their morale and to provide "comic relief" from wartime carnage. Bulosan, like Kingston in our time, was vilified by contemporary Philippine critics and writers for allegedly

"purveying" these "folkwise stories" – based on his peasant boyhood in Pangasinan – as representative of rural Filipino culture (a kind of bildungsroman, with the difference that it is a collection of short stories about "Life with Father," each of which can stand separately but which actually cohere as a fascinating "totality" or novelized narration). For a preliminary recuperation and account of the critical history of this other Bulosan writing, which Asian Americanists have not deemed incorporable into the canon, see Campomanes (1992b) and Tolentino (1986). For Bulosan's self-defense against his critics, see Bulosan (1979 [1946], 121–5, and 1983b [c. 1949]), and for equivalent literary codifications, Bulosan (1977).

20. To turn to the other side of national borders, Santos believes that he was not offered a residency by a famous university writing workshop in the Philippines because of his U.S. citizenship and the fact that he had written only in the English language (Alegre and Fernandez 1993 [1984], 224).

21. As Filipino writer and intellectual Nick Joaquin observes, "the Filipino-American dialogue [his term for the Philippine-American colonial encounter] has mainly been not between Filipinos and continental Americans (most of whom still sort of thought, like their ancestors in the 1890s, that we were canned goods) but between Filipinos and Americans *in* the Philippines" (1988, 199; emphasis added). The lofty turn-of-the-century ambition of the United States to turn the Philippines into its own India, "producing, if not diamonds, at least an American Kipling" amounted to a disenchantment with colonialism instead (Joaquin 1978, 44; 1988, 199). The Philippines proved to be costly and unprofitable from the outset, beginning with the bloody war of U.S. conquest and Filipino resistance (1899–1910s), which made the United States avoid similar colonial adventures thence (except for Vietnam) and seek global "spheres of influence" throughout the "American century" on the basis of its formidable economic clout (Campomanes 1995). Joaquin notes that one intriguing result is that even "the romance of the early American soldiers, teachers, and missionaries in the Philippines has been ignored by American literature," and that the Philippine-American " 'Empire Days,' a theme worthy of a Kipling or a Maugham, have become merely an ironic footnote to history" (1988, 45–6).

22. This migratory impetus was expressed in what N. V. M. Gonzalez has called "the Jones Law Syndrome." The Jones Law of 1916 was a colonial piece of legislation that deferred Philippine independence (yet again) by enforcing a continuing period of American tutelage in liberal democracy and "representative government." One result was that, after 1916, "the solicitation of foreign, and generally American, approval" became both a "national habit" and a matter of "national character" (Gonzalez 1976, 419). In the political realm, several lobbying teams were dispatched to Washington as generally circumscribed "independence missions" until the 1930s (Reyes-Churchill 1983), while in the literary-cultural realm, the likes of José García Villa headed for the mythic publishing capitals like New York from the 1930s onward. Philippine English (colonial) writers conventionally sought to work by (even to "indigenize") Anglo-American "scriptural models" in the move to join the exclusive circle of celebrity writers, but were dismissed by U.S. critics

like Sidney Hook, Donald Keene, Wallace Stegner, and John Leonard either as "minor" or "tropical" copycats of canonical Anglo-American literary exemplars (San Juan 1986, 29–30; 1988, 90–9).

23. N. V. M. Gonzalez (like Santos) was only able to publish a retrospective and definitive collection of his Philippine-canonical short fiction in the United States (1993b) after the same university press that gambled on Bulosan's recuperation responded to the slowly increasing critical demand for more U.S. Filipino writing enabled by the successful and multiple reprintings of Bulosan's *America*. (Santos had published intermittently in some international literary journals or anthologies, and Gonzalez's work had been translated into Russian and Malaysian, but it is noteworthy that much of their writing is available only from small Philippine publishers.) Even after Rosca's *Monsoon* (published in the United States by an Australian university press) met with widespread critical acclaim, inviting comparisons to Gabriel García Marquez, Rosca's novel *State of War* (1988) was turned down by eight major publishing houses before she could place it with Norton, partly on an editor's hunch that it would "do well, by word of mouth, citing the large Filipino communities on both coasts" (Mestrovic 1988, 91; see also Rosca 1989). Hagedorn's work could only be published by small underground presses until the convergence of Bulosan's and Rosca's breakthroughs allowed her to take Filipino international publishing aspirations to unimagined heights with *Dogeaters*. The Flip writers have yet to replicate these triumphs, but continue to be tokenistically published in a smattering of literary anthologies and journals.

24. Still more pressing as a question is the *specificity* of U.S.-native Filipino American writing against the overarching reach of its Filipino English counterpart. As the Filipino Chinese writer Paulino Lim Jr. puts it: "The American-born Filipino learns soon enough of a tradition of Philippine writing in English against which his work will be measured, even if his subject matter is American." For Lim, the Filipino American writer "might be astonished" to discover this heritage when seeking the "historical sense" that T. S. Eliot had deemed pivotal to a writer's formation. Others would have previously rebelled against this tradition or adopted "any strategy between denial and affirmation, not to mention retreat from creativity into suicidal silence" (1986, 73).

25. See Kim 1982, 32, 43 57, 91, 172–3, 199, and 258 (for Bulosan); 70, 265–72 (for Santos); 220 (for Gonzalez); 288 (for Villa). San Juan dismisses Santos, Gonzalez, and the Filipina writer Linda Ty-Casper "for the conciliatory and integrationist tendencies found in [their] works," as opposed to Bulosan's "radical project of solidarity of people of color against capital" (1993, 151); neither does he spare from condemnation Kim's effort to create strategic spaces for long-submerged Filipino writers within the admittedly limiting purviews of Asian American literature studies (145, 147).

26. It is noteworthy, however, that Tomas Santos felt he had to emphasize the thematic affinities of Santos's and Bulosan's writings to be able to place the former within the dominant Filipino/Asian American model (1976, 410). Yet a commentator laments that Santos "has been unjustly known only as the

chronicler of the Filipino exile in the United States" among Philippine readers and critical circles (Alegre and Fernandez 1993 [1984], 218).

27. This canonization of certain Filipino English writers according to a now debunked "American" critical orthodoxy is strongly evidenced in the pedagogical practices and choices of literature teachers in the Philippines. See the survey conducted by Valeros-Gruenberg (1986).

28. Arguments by Philippine critics for revaluing Bulosan's writings are put forth in Yabes (1952); D. S. Feria (1957, 1991); San Juan (1972); Evangelista (1985); and Tolentino (1986). For sympathetic treatments in the United States, see San Juan (1972); Campomanes and Gernes (1988); and Alquizola (1989, 1991).

29. The Ice-Age critics Bernad and Casper have recently expressed a readiness to reconsider their curt dismissals of Bulosan and to reappraise him as a "serious writer" (Bresnahan 1992, 3, 40), a reversal that recognizes the Bulosan revival in both the Philippines and the United States. San Juan's own turn-around is registered in his subsequently influential study of the astonishing range of Bulosan's achievement (1972) and in his efforts to recuperate and edit/publish Bulosan's previously unavailable or heretofore neglected texts (see Bulosan 1977, 1978, 1979, 1983a, 1983b, all posthumously published under San Juan's editorial direction).

30. Rizal's canonicity is the Filipino instantiation of the characteristic search for a "national genius" in the cultural nationalism of colonized peoples and their decolonizing intellectuals (Lloyd 1993, 88). For subsequent (post)colonial generations of Filipinos, this search for a figure who could represent and distill the genius of the "race" has been particularly obsessive and found its nearly unimpeachable anchor in Rizal (Anderson 1983, 32; 1994), who is said to embody the collective creativity of a people incessantly degraded by colonial discourses. Rizal also authorizes an immensely fascinating history of contradictory appropriations: he was the U.S colonial state's choice for a Filipino national hero (presumably for his "reformist" and "evolutionary" philosophy of Philippine social change, as opposed to the precipitate impulses of "plebeian" revolucionarios) and the postcolonial Philippine nation-state's official visage in its tokens and monuments (Ileto 1982, 315; Rafael 1990); a deity and miraculous ghost in the pantheon of peasant millenarian movements (Ileto 1982); an icon who graces the gatherings of Filipino immigrant fraternal organizations in the United States (Posadas and Guyotte 1992), and who finds a privileged place in the dazzling montage of empowering graphic and photographic images that glues together one of the first literary/cultural anthologies of Filipino American second-generation writers and activists, LIWANAG (Cachapero et al. 1975).

31. Rizal's canonical status in Philippine nationalisms was dramatically guaranteed at the very moment of his execution for treason by the Spanish colonial regime in December 1896, an event that is said to have catalyzed the 1896–8 Philippine revolution against Spain and the abortive independence struggle against the United States, the new and aspirant colonial power, from 1899 onward.

32. For a historical reformulation of regulatory and residual imperialist-

nationalist biases concerning the "Western universalism" of the literary or aesthetic, see Lloyd 1991.

33. From exchanges with N. V. M Gonzalez and the U.S. Filipino journalist and poet Luis Francia, who recently published a definitive anthology of Philippine English literature (1993).

34. On the dialectics between the rhizome/nomad and the process of "becoming," see Deleuze and Guattari (1987). I am grateful to John David Blanco for introducing me to the pleasures of their theoretics, but I derive my notions of Filipino nomadology/rhizomatics and "Philippine becoming" from Gonzalez (his account above) and Joaquin (1988), both of whom stunningly arrived at a somehow equivalent but remarkably Philippine-specific migratory poetics as a result of their own independent and iconoclastic investigations of Philippine cultural-historical "distillates."

35. Every translation is an interpretation and a negotiation. I am substantially accountable for the translations below, but Petronila Mabunga urged me to attend to the textured economy of the story's Ilokano and to avoid "English-dominated" thought-processes. The title is one example: roughly, it should be translated as "Nana Sela's Sky [or even Skies]" (alternatives include "Paradise" or "Heaven"). She argued that the central character of the story should be recognizable to all (grand)mothers in analogous situations everywhere, and so I should desist from using her "proper name" and emphasize the honorific "GrandMother" (*Nana/Inang*) instead. The words for *langit* (sky, paradise, heaven) do not have as much economic power as "horizons." A note about orthography: "Ilokano" is used to refer to the language; "Ilocano," to its speakers.

36. See also *Timek Dagiti Agtutubo/Voices of the Youth* (Filipino Association of University Women 1990), an unusual anthology conceived under the influence of this burst of Hawaiian Ilokano writing promoted by GUMIL and which collects precocious essays, poems, short stories, and meditations by Hawaiian Filipino Ilokano elementary and intermediate grade-schoolers. Of course, the pieces are in English, but it is noteworthy that many of them attempted to represent the Hawaiian-Ilokano-English pidgin of their immigrant and working-class parents and deploy it in often astonishing ways (similar to the dis/identifying romance with the iconic Pinoy/old-timer voice in Santos's short fiction and the poetry of Flip writers on the continent). Boundless thanks to Elsa E'der and Larry Padua for introducing me to this exciting strain of Filipino (American) writing and for the generous loan of the materials they gathered as Rockefeller Foundation Fellows in Hawai'i in 1992.

37. On "continental" Asian Americanist or multiculturalist criticism in respect to Hawaii's literatures, see Fujikane 1994. I learned immensely from Fujikane's brilliant readings of Hawaii's "archipelagic" differences from "mainland" critical monisms. For examples of "continentalist" and "prescriptive" critiques of Filipino (American) literature that are bound by "the perpetual search for the determinants of a single, unified, and agreed meaning," see Casper (1986–7) and San Juan (1993).

38. According to the linguist Lawrence Reid, Ilokano is spoken by over 90% of Hawaii's Filipino population, a result of the distinctive history of the Philip-

pine Ilokano provinces, with their largely peasant population, as the main pool for migrant Hawaiian/California plantation and Alaskan cannery laborers from 1903 onward. The Ilokos (Norte, Sur, and La Union) provinces – home to the third-largest Filipino ethnolinguistic group after the Cebuanos and Tagalogs – hug the arid and hilly northwestern coasts of Luzon island. Its barely arable land, bordered by the Cordillera Centrál mountain range, ensures a long and continuing tradition of migration throughout the Philippines, especially to nearby Luzon provinces and to places "abroad" like Hawai'i (Saludes 1976; Foronda 1978).

39. GUMIL organizes annual literary contests as well as regular writing/theater workshops, language classes, and writers' readings. Prize-winning entries and those produced in workshops then constitute the pool for their intermittent volumes and community performances. More important, however, is that these products are read and performed during community events such as picnics, national holidays, and even beauty contests.

40. Reid and Foronda tell us that Ilokano, one of over a hundred languages and vernaculars in the Philippines, is among "the most developed" of the Indonesian division of the 500-strong Austronesian/Malayo-Polynesian family, whose "spread from Madagascar in the West to Easter Island in the East" is equaled in number and expanse only by the Indo-European language tree (Saludes 1976–7, 188–9; Foronda 1978, 2); and that Ilokano, or sometimes Iluko, is "as fully developed in its syntax and rich in its lexicon as any of the classical European languages," according to Lawrence Reid, and that "existing dictionaries have only scraped the surface of the wealth of words that are available to the skilled orator or the proficient writer" (Saludes 1976–7, 190, 188).

41. For a ground-breaking account and transcription of the oral tradition that *survives* "abroad" and portrays lives specific to the situation of Bay Area Pangasinanense immigrants, see Siapno (1993). What inspired her project was "the fact that while much has been written about the political ideology of the writer Carlos Bulosan, who is considered to be the most powerful writer on the Filipino American immigrant experience, very little has been written to situate him in his own language group." She observes that "the disregard for Bulosan's local history" might be a function of the prevalence of criticism by "either nationalist or Marxist Tagalog speakers who are more interested in defining him as a 'Filipino' nationalist or Marxist labor union organizer, rather than as a prenationalist who very likely might have resented Manila-Tagalog cultural dominance." The most important fact for Siapno is that "Carlos Bulosan came from Binalonan, Pangasinan and spoke Ilokano and Pangasinan as his mother tongues" (35).

42. A very popular "joke" among other Filipinos, apart from the stereotype of Ilocano stinginess (*kuripot*), is that "there is no part of the world that is safe from Ilocanos." Indeed, GUMIL-Hawaii is merely one of several regional chapters of the "mother" organization de/centered in the various Ilokano provinces, and Saludes was a former GUMIL Philippines member herself before her migration to Hawai'i. Some GUMIL Philippine writers, like Manuel Diaz, for example, also write and publish in English. Even more interestingly,

it was GUMIL-Pangasinan that was instrumental in the official recognition by Binalonan (Bulosan's hometown) of Bulosan as its "most famous son" in 1983: the street on which the Bulosan house is found was renamed Carlos Bulosan Street, and a marker was established at its junction extolling Bulosan's literary achievements "abroad."

43. Tomas Santos establishes an interesting genealogical relationship between the two, in that Santos "lived in America during the early forties, at about the same time Bulosan's record of Pinoy life draws to a close [and so] Santos's writings may well be regarded as a continuation and development of the Pinoy story started by Bulosan" (1976, 410).

44. Bienvenido Santos was among the army of interviewers who fanned out and tracked down these survivors (Cordova 1983, 231). The impact of this experience on his self-identity as a writer can be seen in his various essays.

45. Critics like Leonard Casper stereotypically fault Filipinos with maudlin sentimentalism. Of the writers considered in this essay, Santos and Bulosan have been the most vulnerable to their charges, as their writing is presumably unable to contain or control this "cultural predisposition." I do not mean "economic" here, however, as expressing a desire for an Anglo-Saxonist "cultural predisposition" to repress emotion and express reserve but, as Halaba's story illustrates, as a politics and poetics of agentive negotiations by peoples faced with the starkest of options amidst strange and inhospitable environments.

46. "A move by part of the family to America will often mean that the extended family unit is, in some measure, binational" (Denton and Villena-Denton 1986, 97). These authors attribute this phenomenon to Filipino "familialism and clannishness" (again, the cultural-determinist argument) and not to the (post)colonial contexts of diasporic formation or even the various limits imposed upon "family reunification" – e.g., married sons and daughters or siblings of U.S. citizens are put on waiting lists that now take an entire lifetime to move for Filipinos.

47. In my own interpretive translation of this story, I experienced these mechanics and extreme difficulties of economic-nomadic movements between Ilokano and English. It is impossible to translate the story's elegant Ilokano passages into English without making them sound bombastic or excessive. Ilokano is such a preternaturally (I use this word advisedly) poetic language that even its more ordinary and quotidian forms of usage possess tremendous metaphorical charge.

48. In the cultural nationalist obsession over Filipino/American (mis)recognitions and (non)identities endemic to these usually catalytic scenes, Filipino American writing has much in common with the exilic tradition of Philippine colonial or second-language writing, that is, in its deployment of exile (or the perspective of outsiderhood nourished by years "abroad") as the space for reconstructing nationality and the "repatriate theme" – or the figure of the romantic returnee who attempts to *identify* his/her dispersed nationality with that of a nation-building project historically frustrated or made only partially imaginable by waves of foreign colonization and their aftermath (D. S. Feria 1991, 180; Burns 1992, 4; San Juan 1993, 150). In the Philippine

(post)colonial traditions, Rizal's *El Filibusterismo* (1891) and Juan C. Laya's *His Native Soil* (1940) are the scriptural texts; in Filipino (American) literary history, the most unusual is Bulosan (1977).

49. *Unegna* in Ilokano is "her 'inside' or 'inner self,'" but it is awkward to render *nakunana ti unegna* as "her inner self utters." Also, although the action of the story is rendered in the past tense, I chose to render my translations in the present tense; to replicate the Ilokano tense in English literally results in rather ungainly formulations. The economic character of the story seems best expressed in the English present tense.

50. *Dayta ti namaglupos ti biagda* literally translates into "It was his efforts that allowed their impoverished life to shed off its skin," but the resulting poetic meaning has to be displaced for the more prosaic but equivalent sense in English.

51. In this, the linguistic politics of U.S.-born/native Filipinos and writers becomes salient. Their characteristic creations of poetic "deviations" from "standard" Anglo-American English (the formation of "englishes" is a prevalent postcolonial act, according to Ashcroft et al. 1989, 38, 43–4, 51ff., 71ff.) are particularly striking given that English is their *first* language and not "received," as it was for postcolonial Filipino English confreres.

52. This male orientation of national "identities" is not surprising according to Aguilar (1988) because it is the male native who is chosen by colonial pedagogy as the representative and "ideal colonial subject," and who thus tends to obsess about his ascent to the patriarchal-representational status or power that the colonizer simultaneously promises and denies. Halaba's choice of a woman character and alter-native heroine, in this context, acquires mobile allegorical currencies well beyond its "local and islandic incarceration."

53. One can almost speculate that these are creative circumventions of the long-standing "publishing ban" on unfashionable Filipino writing effectively declared by U.S. exceptionalist colonialism or by market-conscious U.S. editors and presses. To cite only one instance, another version, under a different title, of Manguerra-Brainard's recently U.S.-published *When the Rainbow Goddess Wept* (1994) was published much earlier by New Day (Philippines).

■■■ WORKS CITED AND SELECTED BIBLIOGRAPHY

Filipino Writing

Abad, Gémino, et al., eds. 1991. *Flipside: Poems on America. Caracoa* 24. Special Issue. Manila: Philippine Literary Arts Council.

Agoncillo, Felipe. 1899a. *Memorials from Señor Felipe Agoncillo and the Constitution of the Provisional Philippine Government.* Boston: Anti-Imperialist League.

———. 1899b. "Are the Filipinos Civilized?" *Frank Leslie's Popular Monthly* 45, May, 75–85.

———. 1900. *To the American People.* Paris: Imprimerie Chaix.

Albalos, Edward. 1953. *Bartered Corn.* New York: Exposition Press.

Albalos, Mario, et al., eds. 1981. *GUMIL Hawaii iti Sangapulo a Tawen [GUMIL Hawaii in a decade]*. Honolulu: Gunglo Dagiti Mannurat nga Ilokano iti Hawaii [Association of Ilokano Writers in Hawai'i].

Ancheta, Shirley, et al., eds. 1985. *Without Names*. San Francisco: Kearny Street Workshop Press.

Angeles, Carlos. 1963. *A Stun of Jewels*. Manila: Alberto Florentino.

Arguilla, Manuel. 1982 [1932]. "A Son Is Born." In Lumbera and Nograles-Lumbera, 176–83.

Bacho, Peter. 1992. *Cebu*. Seattle: Univ. of Washington Press.

Bay Area Pilipino American Writers. 1985. *Without Names: A Collection of Poems*. San Francisco: Kearny Street Workshop Press.

Bergonio, Gemma. 1985. *"Mirror at Dawn" and Other Poems*. City of Industry, CA: L. A. C. Publishing.

Buaken, Manuel. 1948. *I Have Lived with the American People*. Caldwell, ID: Caxton.

Bulosan, Carlos. 1936. "A Letter." *Poetry* 47:292–3.

———, ed. 1942a. *Chorus for America: Six Philippine Poets*. Los Angeles: Wagon and Star.

———. 1942b. *Letter from America*. Prairie City, IL: J. A. Decker.

———. 1943a. "Freedom from Want." *Saturday Evening Post*, 6 March.

———. 1943b. *The Voice of Bataan*. New York: Coward, McCann.

———. 1944. *The Laughter of My Father*. New York: Harcourt, Brace.

———. 1960. *Sound of Falling Light: Letters in Exile*. Quezon City: Univ. of the Philippines Press.

———. 1973 [1946]. *America Is in the Heart: A Personal History*. Seattle: Univ. of Washington Press.

———. 1977. *The Power of the People*. Ontario: Tabloid Books.

———. 1978. *The Philippines Is in the Heart*. Quezon City, Philippines: New Day.

———. 1979. *Writings of Carlos Bulosan*. Special Issue of *Amerasia*. Asian American Studies Center, Univ. of California, Los Angeles.

———. 1983a. *Bulosan: An Introduction with Selections*. Ed. Epifanio San Juan Jr. Manila: National Book Store.

———. 1983b. *If You Want to Know What We Are: A Carlos Bulosan Reader*. Ed. Epifanio San Juan Jr. Minneapolis: West End.

———. 1990. *The Power of Money and Other Stories*. Quezon City, Philippines: Kalikasan Press.

———. 1991. *Now You Are Still and Other Poems*. Manila: Kalikasan Press.

Cachapero, Emily, et al., eds. 1975. *Liwanag: Literary and Graphic Representations by Filipinos in America*. San Francisco: Liwanag Publishing.

Caigoy, Faustino. 1974. *Bitter Sweet Chocolate Meat*. Los Angeles: Inner City Cultural Center.

Carunungan, Celso Al. 1960. *Like a Brave Man*. New York: Farrar.

Castro, Fernando. 1969. *Big White American*. New York: Vantage.

Cerenio, Virginia. 1989. *Trespassing Innocence*. San Francisco: Kearny Street Workshop Press.

Cuyugan, Tina, ed. 1992. *Forbidden Fruit: Women Write the Erotic*. Manila: Anvil Publishing.

Da Costa, R. Zulueta. 1952 [1940]. *Like the Molave and Collected Poems.* Manila: Carmelo and Bauermann.

Dalisay, Jose Y. 1992. *Killing Time in a Warm Place.* Manila: Anvil Publishing.

Dionisio, J. C. 1972. "A Summer in an Alaskan Salmon Cannery." In Hsu and Palubinskas, 154–60.

Feria, Benny. 1954. *Filipino Son.* Boston: Meador Press.

Filipino Association of University Women. 1990. *Timek Dagiti Agtutubo/Voices of the Youth.* Honolulu: n.p.

Francia, Luis, ed. 1993. *Brown River, White Ocean: An Anthology of Twentienth-Century Philippine Literature in English.* New Brunswick, NJ: Rutgers Univ. Press.

Gamalinda, Eric. 1992. *Empire of Memory.* Manila: Anvil Publishing.

Gonzalez, N. V. M. 1941. *The Winds of April.* Manila: Univ. of the Philippines Press.

———. 1947. *Seven Hills Away.* Denver: Alan Swallow; Manila: Halcyon House.

———. 1963. *Look Stranger, on This Island Now.* Manila: Benipayo Press.

———. 1964a. *Selected Stories.* Denver: Alan Swallow.

———. 1964b [1957]. *The Bamboo Dancers.* Denver: Alan Swallow.

———. 1975 [1956/63]. *A Season of Grace.* Manila: Bookmark.

———. 1977 [1954]. *"Children of the Ash-Covered Loam" and Other Stories.* Manila: Bookmark.

———. 1979. *Mindoro and Beyond: Twenty-One Stories.* Quezon City, Philippines: Univ. of the Philippines Press.

———. 1990a. *Kalutang: A Filipino in the World.* Manila: Kalikasan Press.

———. 1993b. *Bread of Salt and Other Stories.* Seattle: Univ. of Washington Press.

Hagedorn, Jessica Tarahata. 1975. *Dangerous Music: The Prose and Poetry of Jessica Hagedorn.* San Francisco: Momo's Press.

———. 1981. *Pet Food and Tropical Apparitions.* San Francisco: Momo's Press.

———. 1990. *Dogeaters.* New York: Pantheon.

———. 1993a. *Danger and Beauty.* New York: Penguin Books.

———, ed. 1993b. *Charlie Chan Is Dead: An Anthology of Contemporary Asian American Fiction.* New York: Penguin Books.

Javellana, Stevan. 1947. *Without Seeing the Dawn.* Boston: Little, Brown.

Laya, Juan C. 1940. *His Native Soil.* Manila: Univ. Publishing.

———. 1950. *This Barangay.* Manila: Inang Wika Publishing.

Laygo, Teresita, comp. 1978. *The Well of Time: Eighteen Short Stories from Philippine Contemporary Literature.* Los Angeles: Asian American Bilingual Center.

Lim, Paul Stephen. 1982. *Some Arrivals, But Mostly Departures.* Quezon City, Philippines: New Day.

Lim, Paulino Jr. 1988. *Passion Summer and Other Stories.* Quezon City, Philippines: New Day.

Lopez, Sixto K. 1899. "The Philippine Question from a Filipino Point of View." *Independent,* 14 December, 3333–40.

———. 1900. *The Tribes in the Philippines.* Boston: The New England Anti-Imperialist League.

———. 1901. *The Philippine Problem: A Proposition for a Solution.* New York: The Anti-Imperialist League of New York.

Manguerra-Brainard, Cecilia. 1988. *Woman with Horns and Other Stories*. Quezon City, Philippines: New Day.

———. 1991. *Philippine Woman in America*. Quezon City, Philippines: New Day.

———, ed. 1993. *Fiction by Filipinos in America*. Quezon City, Philippines: New Day.

———. 1994. *When the Rainbow Goddess Wept*. New York: Dutton.

Marin, Patricia, ed. 1953. *Love in Philippine Story and Verse*. Quezon City, Philippines: Bamboo Grove Association.

Morantte, P.C. 1982. *God Is in the Heart: Poetical and Symbolical Essays*. Quezon City, Philippines: New Day.

Murray, Sabina. 1990. *Slow Burn*. New York: Ballantine Books.

Navarro, Jovina, comp. 1974. *Diwang Pilipino: Philippine Consciousness*. Davis: Asian American Studies, Univ. of California.

———, comp. 1976. *Joaquin Legazpi: Poet, Artist, Community Worker*. El Verano, CA: Pilnachi Press.

———, comp. 1977. *Lahing Pilipino: A Pilipino American Anthology*. Davis: Mga Kapatid (Pilipino Student Association), Univ. of California.

Ponce, Francisco, et al., eds. 1984. *BIN-I: Antolohia Dagiti Nangabak a Drama ken Sarita 1980–1983 ken Dadduuma pay a Sinurat [HARVEST: An Anthology of Prizewinning Plays, Stories, and Other Writings, 1980–1983]*. Honolulu: Gunglo Dagiti Mannurat nga Ilokano iti Hawaii [Association of Ilokano Writers in Hawai'i].

——— et al., eds. 1989. *Dawa [Ears of Grain]*. Honolulu: Gunglo Dagiti Mannurat nga Ilokano iti Hawaii [Association of Ilokano Writers in Hawai'i].

Rizal, José. 1961 [1886]. *Noli Mi Tangere*. Trans. Leon Ma. Guerrero. London: Longmans.

———. 1968 [1891]. *The Subversive [El Filibusterismo]*. Trans. Leon Ma. Guerrero. New York: Norton.

Rosca, Ninotchka. 1970. *Bitter Country and Other Stories*. Quezon City, Philippines: Malaya Books.

———. 1983. *The Monsoon Collection*. Santa Lucia and New York: Univ. of Queensland Press.

———. 1987. *Endgame: The Fall of Marcos*. New York and Toronto: Franklin Watts.

———. 1988. *State of War*. New York: Norton.

———. 1992. *Twice-Blessed*. New York: Norton.

Salanga, A. N., and Esther Pacheco, eds. 1987 [1986]. *Versus: Philippine Protest Poetry, 1983–1986*. Seattle: Univ. of Washington Press.

Saludes, Patricia, ed. 1973. *Dagiti Pagwadan a Filipino iti Hawaii [Filipino Exemplars in Hawaii]*. Honolulu: Gunglo Dagiti Mannurat nga Ilokano iti Hawaii [Association of Ilokano Writers in Hawai'i].

———, ed. 1976. *Agtangkayagen [Arisen]*. Honolulu: Gunglo Dagiti Mannurat nga Ilokano iti Hawaii [Association of Ilokano Writers in Hawai'i].

San Diego, Greg. 1956. *Soliloquies in a Philippine Garden*. San Francisco: Pisani Publishing.

Santos, Bienvenido. 1956. *The Wounded Stag*. Manila: Capitol Publishing.

———. 1976a [1960]. *Brother, My Brother*. Manila: Bookmark.

———. 1976c [1955]. *You Lovely People*. Manila: Bookmark.

———. 1979a [1967]. *The Day the Dancers Came: Selected Prose Works*. Manila: Bookmark.

———. 1979b. *Scent of Apples: A Collection of Short Stories*. Seattle: Univ. of Washington Press.

———. 1982a. "Pilipino Old Timers: Fact and Fiction." *Amerasia* 9:89–98.

———. 1982b. *The Praying Man*. Quezon City, Philippines: New Day.

———. 1983a. *Distances in Time – Selected Poems*. Quezon City, Philippines: Ateneo de Manila Univ. Press, 1983.

———. 1983b. *The Man Who (Thought He) Looked Like Robert Taylor*. Quezon City, Philippines: New Day.

———. 1985. *Dwell in the Wilderness: Selected Short Stories (1931–1941)*. Quezon City, Philippines: New Day.

———. 1986a [1965]. *The Volcano*. Quezon City, Philippines: New Day.

———. 1986b [1965]. *Villa Magdalena*. Quezon City, Philippines: New Day.

———. 1987. *What the Hell For You Left Your Heart in San Francisco*. Quezon City, Philippines: New Day.

———. 1993. *Memory's Fictions*. Quezon City, Philippines: New Day.

Silva, John. 1992a. "The Romantic Vaquero." *Lavender Godzilla*, Fall Issue, 10–5.

———. 1992b. "Iyay." *Lavender Godzilla*, Spring Issue, 20–5, 30–4.

———. 1994. "Telling Dad." *Passport* 76 (April/May): 10–5.

Skinner, Michelle Cruz. 1988. *Balikbayan: A Filipino Homecoming*. Honolulu: Bess Press.

Tagami, Jeff. 1987. *October Light*. San Francisco: Kearny Street Workshop Press.

Ty-Casper, Linda. 1963. *The Transparent Sun and Other Stories*. Manila: Alberto Florentino.

———. 1964. *The Peninsulars*. Manila: Bookmark.

———. 1974. *The Secret Runner and Other Stories*. Manila: Alberto Florentino.

———. 1979. *The Three-Cornered Sun*. Quezon City, Philippines: New Day.

———. 1980a. *Dread Empire*. Hongkong: Heinemann.

———. 1981. *Hazards of Distance*. Quezon City, Philippines: New Day.

———. 1985a. *Awaiting Tresspass (A Pasión)*. New York and London: Readers International.

———. 1985b. *Fortress in the Plaza*. Quezon City, Philippines: New Day.

———. 1986. *Wings of Stone*. New York and London: Readers International.

———. 1987b. *Ten Thousand Seeds*. Quezon City, Philippines: Ateneo de Manila Univ. Press.

Villa, José García. 1933. *Footnote to Youth: Tales of the Philippines and Others*. New York: Scribner's.

———. 1939. *Many Voices: Selected Poems by José García Villa*. Manila: Philippine Book Guild.

———. 1942. *Have Come, Am Here*. New York: Viking.

———. 1948. *Seven Poems*. Cambridge, MA: Wake.

———. 1949. *Volume Two*. New York: New Directions.

———. 1958. *Selected Poems and New*. New York: McDowell, Oblensky.

———. 1962a. *Poems 55: The Best of José García Villa as Chosen by Himself*. Manila: Alberto Florentino.

———. 1962b. *Selected Stories*. Manila: Alberto Florentino.

————. 1973. *Makata 3: Poems in Praise of Love*. Manila: Alberto Florentino.

————. 1979. *Appasionata: Poems in Praise of Love*. New York: King and Cowen.

Villanueva, Marianne. 1991. *Ginseng and Other Tales from Manila*. Corvallis, OR: Calyx Books.

Yabes, Leopoldo, ed. 1975. *Philippine Short Stories 1925–1940*. Quezon City: Univ. of the Philippines Press.

————, ed. 1981. *Philippine Short Stories 1941–1955*. 2 vols. Quezon City: Univ. of the Philippines Press.

Philippine and Filipino American Criticism

Alegre, Edilberto, and Doreen Fernandez. 1993 [1984]. *Writers and Their Milieu: An Oral History of First Generation Writers in English*. Pt. 1. Manila: De La Salle Univ. Press.

————. 1987. *Writers and Their Milieu: An Oral History of Second Generation Writers in English*. Pt. 2. Manila: De La Salle Univ. Press.

Alquizola, Marilyn. 1989. "The Fictive Narrator of *America Is in the Heart*." In *Frontiers in Asian American Studies*, ed. Gail Nomura et al. Pullman: Washington State Univ. Press.

————. 1991. "Subversion or Affirmation: The Text and Subtext of *America Is in the Heart*." In *Asian Americans: Comparative and Global Perspectives*, ed. Shirley Hune et al. Pullman: Washington State Univ. Press.

Azurin, Arnold Molina. 1993. *Reinventing the Filipino: Critical Analyses of the Orthodox Views in Anthropology, History, Folklore, and Letters*. Quezon City: Univ. of the Philippines Press.

Bernad, Miguel. 1975. "Carlos Bulosan: The Issue of Honesty." *Manila Review* 5:103–7.

————. 1990. "Philippine Literature: Perpetually Inchoate." In *Philippine Contemporary Literature in English and Filipino*. 6th ed. Manila: Bookmark.

Bresnahan, Roger. 1992. *Angles of Vision: Conversation on Philippine Literature*. Quezon City, Philippines: New Day.

Bulaong, Grace. 1966–7. "Satire in Philippine Literature." *General Education Journal* 11:65–80.

Burns, Gerald. 1992. "The Repatriate Theme in Philippine Second-Language Fiction." *Philippine Studies* 40 (First Quarter): 3–34.

Campomanes, Oscar. 1992a. "Filipinos in the United States and Their Literature of Exile." In Lim and Ling, 49–76.

————. 1992b. "Laughter, Folk Culture, and Storytelling in Carlos Bulosan's Village Stories." *Verge* 5.1–2 (December): 100–8.

————. 1995. "The New Empire's Forgetful and Forgotten Citizens: Unrepresentability and Unassimilability in Filipino-American Postcolonialities." *Critical Mass* 2.2 (Spring): 145–200.

Campomanes, Oscar, and Todd Gernes. 1988. "Two Letters from America: Carlos Bulosan and the Act of Writing." *MELUS* 15.3 (Fall): 15–46.

Casper, Leonard. 1964. "Carlos Bulosan." *The Wounded Diamond*. Manila: Bookmark.

————, ed. 1966. *New Writing from the Philippines: A Critique and Anthology*. Syracuse, NY: Syracuse Univ. Press.

———. 1986–7. "Paperboat Novels: The Later Bienvenido N. Santos." *Amerasia Journal* 13.1:163–70.

Croghan, Richard, ed. 1975. *The Development of Philippine Literature in English (since 1900).* Quezon City, Philippines: Alemar-Phoenix.

David-Maramba, Asuncion, ed. 1982 [1965]. *Philippine Contemporary Literature in English and Pilipino.* Manila: Bookmark.

Evangelista, Susan Potter. 1985. *Carlos Bulosan and His Poetry: A Biography and Anthology.* Seattle: Univ. of Washington Press.

———. 1988. "Filipinos in America: Literature as History." *Philippine Studies* 36:36–53.

Feria, Dolores Stephens. 1957. "Carlos Bulosan: Gentle Genius." *Comment* 2:57–65.

———. 1991. *Red Pencil, Blue Pencil: Essays and Encounters.* Manila: Kalikasan Press.

Foronda, Marcelino, Jr. 1978. *Dallang: An Introduction to Ilokano Literature and Other Essays.* Honolulu: Univ. of Hawai'i Philippine Studies Program Working Paper 3.

Galdon, Joseph, ed. *Philippine Fiction.* Quezon City, Philippines: Ateneo de Manila Univ. Press.

Gonzalez, N. V. M. 1966. "The Filipino and the Novel." *Daedelus* 95:961–71.

———. 1976. "Drumming for the Captain." *World Literature Written in English* 15:415–21.

———. 1990b. *The Father and Maid: Essays on Filipino Life and Letters.* Quezon City: Univ. of the Philippines Press.

———. 1992. "Even as a Mountain Speaks." *Amerasia Journal* 18.2:55–67.

———. 1993a. "The Novel of Justice." *Journal of English Studies.*

———. n.d. "The Filipino American Story." Unpublished MS.

Grow, L. M. 1977. "The Harrowed and Hallowed Ground: An Interview with Bienvenido Santos." *Wichita State Univ. Bulletin* 113:3–22.

Harterndorp, A. V. H. 1937. "The Importance of Filipino Literature in English." *Philippine Magazine* 24.1.

Hidalgo, Cristina, and Priscelina Legasto, eds. 1993. *Philippine Post-Colonial Studies: Essays on Language and Literature.* Quezon City: Univ. of the Philippines Press.

Hizon, Ernesto. 1982. "A Critical Approach to Bulosan's 'The Philippines Is in the Heart.'" *Philippine Studies* 30:27–43.

Hosillos, Lucila. 1969. *Philippine-American Literary Relations, 1898–1941.* Quezon City, Philippines: Univ. of the Philippines Press.

Joaquin, Nick. 1978. "Red as in Revolution." In *Turn of the Century,* comp. Gilda Cordero Fernando and Nik Ricio, 22–47. Quezon City, Philippines: GCF Books.

———. 1988. *Culture and History: Occasional Notes on the Process of Philippine Becoming.* Manila: Solar Publishing.

Lim, Paulino Jr. 1986. "The Obscurity of a Learned Language: English and the Filipino American Writer." *Pilipinas* 11 (Fall).

Lumbera, Bienvenido. 1984. *Revaluation: Essays on Philippine Literature, Cinema, and Popular Culture.* Baguio City, Philippines: Index Press.

Lumbera, Bienvenido, and Cynthia Nograles Lumbera, eds. 1982. *Philippine Literature: A History and Anthology*. Manila: National Book Store.

Manalansan, Martin IV. 1993. "(Re)locating the Gay Filipino: Resistance, Postcolonialism, and Identity." *Journal of Homosexuality* 26:53–72.

Manuud, Antonio, ed. 1967. *Brown Heritage: Essays on Philippine Cultural Tradition and Literature*. Quezon City, Philippines: Ateneo do Manila Univ. Press.

Martinez-Sicat, Maria Teresa. 1994. *Imagining the Nation in Four Philippine Novels*. Quezon City: Univ. of the Philippines Press.

Mattos, Edward. 1965. "Invitation to the Arts." In *Readings in Philippine Arts and Letters*, ed. The Committee of the Humanities, U.S. Information Service. Quezon City, Philippines: Ken Incorporated.

Morantte, P. C. 1944. "Two Filipinos Abroad." *Books Abroad* 4 (Autumn): 323–7.

———. 1984. *Remembering Carlos Bulosan (His Heart Affair with America)*. Quezon City, Philippines: New Day.

Peñaranda, Oscar, et al. 1974. "An Introduction to Filipino American Literature." In *Aiiieeeee! An Anthology of Asian American Writers*, ed. Frank Chin et al. Washington, D.C.: Howard Univ. Press.

Rosca, Ninotchka. 1989. "The Arts and the Asian American Community: A Case of the Missing Audience." *Social Change*, November–December, 53–5.

San Juan, Epifanio Jr. 1968. "Philippine Literature in Crisis: An Interrogation." *St. Louis Quarterly* 6 (June): 155–70.

———. 1972. *Carlos Bulosan and the Imagination of the Class Struggle*. Quezon City: Univ. of the Philippines Press.

———. 1986. *Crisis in the Philippines*. South Hadley, MA: Bergin and Garvey.

———. 1988. *Ruptures, Schisms, Interventions*. Manila: De La Salle Univ. Press.

———. 1990. "Farewell, You Whose Homeland Is Forever Arriving as I Embark: Journal of a Filipino Exile." *Kultura* 3.1:34–41.

———. 1991a. "Mapping the Boundaries, Inscribing the Differences: The Filipino Writer in the U.S.A." *Journal of Ethnic Studies* 19.1 (Spring).

———. 1991b. "Beyond Identity Politics: The Predicament of the Asian American Writer in Late Capitalism." *American Literary History* 3.3:542–65.

———. 1991c. "The Cult of Ethnicity and the Fetish of Pluralism." *Cultural Critique* 18 (Spring): 215–29.

———. 1993. "Filipino Writing in the United States: Reclaiming Whose America?" *Philippine Studies* 41:141–66.

Santos, Bienvenido. 1967. "The Filipino and the Novel." In Manuud, 634–40.

———. 1976b. "The Personal Saga of a 'Straggler' in Philippine Literature." *World Literature Written in English* 15:398–405.

———. 1977. "The Filipino as Exile." *Greenfield Review* 6:47–55.

Santos, Tomas. 1976. "The Filipino Writer in America – Old and New." *World Literature Written in English* 15.2:406–14.

Siapno, Jacqueline. 1993. "Unrequited Love and Pre-Nationalist Sentiments in the Oral Traditions of Pangasinan Migrant Workers in California." *Asian America: Journal of Culture and the Arts* 2 (Winter): 33–54.

Solberg, Sam. 1983. "Introduction to Filipino American Literature." In *Aiiieeeee!*

An Anthology of Asian American Writers, ed. Frank Chin et al. Washington, D.C.: Howard Univ. Press.

Strobel, Lenny. 1993. "A Personal Story: On Becoming a Split Filipina Subject." *Amerasia Journal* 19.3:117–30.

Tiempo, Edilberto. 1991. "Carlos Bulosan Demystified: The Problem of Artistic Sensibility." *Solidarity* 130 (April–June): 33–43.

Tolentino, Delfin Jr. 1986. "Satire in Carlos Bulosan's 'The Laughter of My Father.'" *Philippine Studies* 34:452–61.

Ty-Casper, Linda. 1980b. "Philippine Literature: A Flesh Made of Fugitive Suns." *Philippine Studies* 28:59–73.

———. 1987a. "Philippine Women: A Room Shared." *Pilipinas* 9:27–33.

Valeros, Florentino, and Estrellita Valeros-Gruenberg, eds. 1987. *Filipino Writers in English: A Biographical and Bibliographical Directory.* Quezon City, Philippines: New Day.

Valeros-Gruenberg, Estrellita. 1989. "The Canon of Philippine Literature According to Teachers of Metro Manila." In *Manila: History, People and Culture,* ed. Wilfrido Villaconta et al. Manila: De La Salle Univ. Press.

Yabes, Leopoldo. 1952. "On Carlos Bulosan." *The Literary Apprentice,* Silver Jubilee Edition, 136–40.

Other Sources

Ade, George. 1985 [1899]. *Stories of Benevolent Assimilation,* ed. Perry Gianokos. Quezon City, Philippines: New Day.

Aguilar, Delia. 1988. *The Feminist Challenge.* Manila: Asian Social Institute.

Anderson, Benedict. 1983. *Imagined Communities: Reflections on the Origin and Spread of Nationalism.* London: Verso.

———. 1988. "Cacique Democracy in the Philippines: Origin and Dreams." *New Left Review* 169, May–June, 3–33.

———. 1994. "Hard to Imagine: A Puzzle in the History of Philippine Nationalism." In *Cultures and Texts: Representations of Philippine Society,* ed. Raul Pertierra and Eduardo Ugarte, 81–119. Quezon City: Univ. of the Philippines Press.

Appadurai, Arjun. 1990. "Disjuncture and Difference in the Global Cultural Economy." *Public Culture* 2.2:1–24.

Ashcroft, Bill, Gareth Griffiths, and Helen Tiffin. 1989. *The Empire Writes Back.* New York: Routledge.

Atkinson, Fred. 1902. *The Cost of War and Warfare from 1898 to 1902.* Brookline, MA: n.p.

Awanohara, Susumu. 1991. "Filipino Americans: High Growth, Low Profile." *Far Eastern Economic Review,* 7 February.

Bello, Walden, and John Gershman, eds. 1993. *Reexamining and Renewing the Philippine Progressive Vision.* Quezon City, Philippines: Forum on Philippine Alternatives.

Bemis, Samuel Flagg. 1965 [1936]. *A Diplomatic History of the United States.* 5th ed. New York: Holt, Rinehart and Winston.

Bingham, Hiram. 1910. "Philippines." In *The Encylopaedia Britannica.* 11th ed. Vol. 21. Cambridge: Cambridge Univ. Press.

Blauner, Robert. 1987. "Colonized and Immigrant Minorities." In *From Different Shores: Perspectives on Race and Ethnicity in America*, ed. Ronald Takaki, 149–60. Oxford and New York: Oxford Univ. Press.

Brands, H. W. 1992. *Bound to Empire: The United States and the Philippines*. New York: Oxford Univ. Press.

Brennan, Timothy. 1989. "Cosmopolitans and Celebrities." *Race and Class* 31.1:1–19.

———. 1990. "The National Longing for Form." In *Nation and Narration*, ed. Homi Babha, 44–70. New York: Routledge.

Brinton, Daniel. 1898. "The Peoples of the Philippines." *The American Anthropologist* 11 (October): 293–307.

Buell, Lawrence. 1992. "American Literary Emergence as a Postcolonial Phenomenon. *American Literary History* 2.2:411–42.

Campomanes, Oscar. 1994. "The Question of U.S. Imperialism and Asian American Studies East of California." *Building Blocks for Asian American Studies*, ed. Robert Lee and Lihbin Shiao, 1–30. Providence, RI: Brown University Asian American Studies Fund.

Cariño, Benjamin, James Fawcett, Robert Gardner, and Fred Arnold. 1990. *The New Filipino Immigrants to the United States: Increasing Diversity and Change*. Honolulu: East–West Hawai'i Center.

Catapusan, B. T. 1972. *The Filipino Social Adjustment in the United States*. San Francisco: R. & R. Associates.

Chan, Sucheng. 1991. *Asian Americans: An Interpretive History*. Boston: Twayne.

Chatterjee, Partha. 1993. *The Nation and Its Fragments*. Princeton, NJ: Princeton Univ. Press.

Cordova, Fred. 1983. *Filipinos: Forgotten Asian Americans*. Seattle: Demonstration Project for Asian Americans.

Daniels, Roger. 1977 [1962]. *The Politics of Prejudice*. Berkeley and Los Angeles: University of California Press.

De la Costa, Horacio, S. J. 1977. "Initial Contacts between American Officials and Filipino Revolutionary Leaders: A Problem in Diplomatic History." *Bulletin of the American Historical Collection* 5.1 (January): 7–26.

Deleuze, Gilles, and Félix Guattari. 1987. *A Thousand Plateaus*. Minneapolis: Univ. of Minnesota Press.

De la Rosa, Rolando, O. P. 1990. *Beginnings of the Filipino Dominicans*. Quezon City: Dominican Province of the Philippines.

Denton, Frank, and Victoria Villena-Denton. 1986. *Filipino Views of America: Warm Memories, Cold Realities*. Washington, D.C.: Asia Fellows.

Eagleton, Terry. 1983. *Literary Theory: An Introduction*. Minneapolis: Univ. of Minnesota Press.

———, et al. 1990. *Nationalism, Colonialism, and Literature*. Minneapolis: Univ. of Minnesota Press.

Espiritu, Yen Le. 1992. *Asian American Panethnicity: Bridging Identities and Institutions*. Philadelphia: Temple Univ. Press.

Fujikane, Candace. 1994. "Between Nationalisms: Hawaii's Local Nations and Its Troubled Paradise." *Critical Mass* 1.2:33–58.

Gates, Henry Louis. 1988. *The Signifying Monkey: A Theory of African American Literary Criticism.* New York: Oxford Univ. Press.

Gleeck, Lewis Jr. 1984. *The Manila Americans 1901–1934.* Manila: Carmelo and Bauermann.

Gonzalez, Andrew. 1980. *Language and Nationalism.* Quezon City, Philippines: Ateneo de Manila Univ. Press.

Gubatan, Gerald. 1990. "A Colonized Identity." *Gidra* 95.

Hayden, Joseph Ralston. 1942. *The Philippines: A Study in National Development.* New York: Macmillan.

Hill, David. 1899. "The War and the Extension of Civilization." *Forum,* February, 651–5.

Hsu, Kai-yu, and Helen Palubinskas, eds. 1972. *Asian American Authors.* Boston: Houghton Mifflin.

Hunt, Michael. 1987. *Ideology and U.S. Foreign Policy.* New Haven: Yale Univ. Press.

Ileto, Reynaldo. 1982. "Rizal and the Underside of Philippine History." In *Moral Order and the Question of Change: Essays on Southeast Asia,* ed. David Wyatt and Alexander Woodside, 274–337. New Haven: Yale Univ. Southeast Asia Studies.

JanMohamed, Abdul, and David Lloyd, eds. 1990. *The Nature and Context of Minority Discourse.* New York: Oxford Univ. Press.

Kaplan, Amy, and Donald Pease, eds. 1993. *Cultures of United States Imperialism.* Durham, NC: Duke Univ. Press.

Karnow, Stanley. 1989. *In Our Image: America's Empire in the Philippines.* New York: Random House.

Kennan, George. 1951. *American Diplomacy 1900–1950.* Chicago: Univ. of Chicago Press.

Kennedy, Philip Wayne. 1962. "The Concept of Racial Superiority and United States Imperialism, 1890–1910." Ph.D. diss., St. Louis University.

Kim, Elaine. 1982. *Asian American Literature: An Introduction to the Writings and Their Social Context.* Philadelphia: Temple Univ. Press.

Lacaba, Jose. 1982. *Days of Disquiet, Nights of Rage: The First Quarter Storm and Related Events.* Manila, Philippines: Salinlahi Publ.

LaFeber, Walter. 1989. *The American Age.* New York: W. W. Norton.

Lasker, Bruno. 1931. *Filipino Immigration to the Continental United States and Hawaii.* Chicago: Univ. of Chicago Press.

Lawcock, Lawrence. 1975. "Filipino Students in the United States and the Philippine Independence Movement, 1900–1935." Ph.D. diss., University of California, Berkeley.

Lim, Shirley Geok-lin, and Amy Ling, eds. 1992. *Reading the Literatures of Asian America.* Philadelphia: Temple Univ. Press.

Lloyd, David. 1991. "Race under Representation." *Oxford Literary Review* 13.1–2:62–94.

———. 1993. *Anomalous States: Irish Writing and the Post-Colonial Moment.* Durham, NC: Duke Univ. Press.

Lopez, S. P. 1966. "The Colonial Relationship." In *The United States and the Philippines,* ed. Frank Golay, 7–31. Englewood Cliffs, NJ: Prentice-Hall.

Lowe, Lisa 1994. "Unfaithful to the Original: The Subject of *Dictée.*" In *Writing Self, Writing Nation,* ed. Elaine Kim and Norma Alarcón, 35–72. Berkeley: Third Woman Press.

Lukács, Georg. 1983 [1962]. *The Historical Novel.* Lincoln: Univ. of Nebraska Press.

May, Glenn. 1987. *A Past Recovered: Essays on Philippine History and Historiography.* Quezon City, Philippines: New Day.

———. 1991. *Battle for Batangas.* New Haven: Yale Univ. Press.

Mehta, P. 1968. *Indo-Anglian Fiction: An Assessment.* n.p. Prakash Book Depot.

Mercer, Kobena. 1992. "'1968': Periodizing Politics and Identity." In *Cultural Studies,* ed. Larry Grossberg et al., 424–49. New York: Routledge.

Mestrovic, Marta. 1988. "Ninotchka Rosca." *Publishers Weekly,* 6 May.

Miller, Stuart Creighton. 1982. *"Benevolent Assimilation": The American Conquest of the Philippines.* New Haven: Yale Univ. Press.

Natividad, Larry David. 1993. "What Is Correct? Filipino or Pilipino?" *Journal on Pilipino American Issues* (Spring), 6–8.

Novick, Peter. 1988. *That Noble Dream: The "Objectivity Question" and the American Historical Profession.* New York: Cambridge Univ. Press.

Omi, Michael, and Howard Winant. 1986. *Racial Formation in the United States from the 1960s to the 1980s.* New York: Routledge.

Paredes, Ruby. 1989. *Philippine Colonial Democracy.* Quezon City, Philippines: Ateneo de Manila Univ. Press.

Paz, Octavio. 1985 [1961]. *The Labyrinth of Solitude and Other Writings.* Trans. Lysander Kemp et al. New York: Grove Weidenfeld.

Perkins, Whitney. 1962. *Denial of Empire: The U.S. and its Dependencies.* Leyden, Netherlands: A. W. Sythoff.

Pier, Arthur. 1950. *American Apostles to the Philippines.* Boston: Beacon.

Posadas, Barbara, and Roland Guyotte. 1992. "José Rizal and the Changing Nature of Identity in Chicago." Unpublished MS.

Pratt, Mary Louise. 1992. *Imperial Eyes.* New York: Routledge.

Rafael, Vicente. 1984. "Language, Identity, and Gender in Rizal's *Noli.*" *Review of Indonesian and Malaysian Affairs* 18:110–40.

———. 1990. "Nationalism, Imagery, and the Filipino Intelligentsia of the Nineteenth Century." *Critical Inquiry* 16.3 (Spring): 591–611.

———. 1991. "White Love: Surveillance and Nationalist Resistance in the U.S. Colonization of the Philippines." Dartmouth Conference on the Cultures of U.S. Imperialism. Revised in Kaplan and Pease, 185–218.

Reyes-Churchill, Bernadita. 1983. *The Philippine Independence Missions to the United States, 1919–1934.* Manila: National Historical Commission.

Riggs, Arthur Stanley. 1981 [1905]. *The Filipino Drama.* Manila: Intramuros Administration.

Rosaldo, Renato. 1989. *Culture and Truth: The Remaking of Social Analysis.* Boston: Beacon Press.

Rutherford, Jonathan, ed. 1990. *Identity, Community, Culture, Difference.* London: Lawrence and Wishhart.

Said, Edward. 1979. "Zionism from the Standpoint of Its Victims." *Social Text* 1:7–58.

————. 1993. *Culture and Imperialism*. New York: Knopf.

————. 1994. *The Pen and the Sword: Conversations with David Barsamian*. Monroe, ME: Common Courage Press.

Salazar-Parreñas, Rhacel. 1995. " 'Split Households Means Strong Families': The Strategy of Split-Household Formation in Contemporary Filipino Migration to the U.S." Unpublished MS.

Schirmer, Boone, and Stephen Shalom. 1987. *The Philippines Reader*. Boston: West End Press.

Schumacher, John, S. J. 1991. *The Making of a Nation: Essays on Nineteenth-Century Filipino Nationalism*. Quezon City, Philippines: Ateneo de Manila Univ. Press.

Scott, William Henry. 1994. *Barangay: Sixteenth Century Philippine Culture and Society*. Quezon City, Philippines: Ateneo de Manila Univ. Press.

Shalom, Stephen. 1981. *The United States and the Philippines: A Study of Neocolonialism*. Philadelphia: Institute for the Study of Human Issues.

Sollors, Werner. 1980. "Literature and Ethnicity." In *Harvard Encyclopedia of American Ethnic Groups*, ed. Stephan Thernstrom, 647–65. Cambridge, MA: Harvard Univ. Press.

————. 1986. *Beyond Ethnicity: Consent and Descent in American Culture*. Oxford: Oxford Univ. Press.

Spivak, Gayatri Chakravorty. 1988. "Can the Subaltern Speak?" In *Marxism and the Interpretation of Culture*, ed. Lawrence Grossberg and Cary Nelson. Urbana-Champaign: Univ. of Illinois Press.

Sullivan, Rodney. 1991. *Exemplar of Americanism: The Philippine Career of Dean Worcester*. Ann Arbor, MI: Center for South and Southeast Asian Studies.

Szulc, Tad. 1993. "The Greatest Danger We Face [Interview with Daniel Boorstin]." *Parade*, 25 July.

U.S. War Department. 1910. *Annual Reports, Vol. 4*. Washington, D.C.: Government Printing Office.

Vidal, Gore. 1993. "French Letters: Theories of the Novel." In *United States*. New York: Random House.

Welch, Richard. 1979. *Response to Imperialism: The United States and the Philippine-American War, 1899–1902*. Chapel Hill: Univ. of North Carolina Press.

Wilentz, Sean. 1990. "American Exceptionalism." In *Encyclopedia of the American Left*, ed. Mari Jo Buhle et al. New York and London: Garland.

Williams, William Appleman. 1973 [1955]. "The Frontier Thesis and American Foreign Policy." *History as a Way of Learning*. New York: Franklin Watts.

————. 1990. *Empire as a Way of Life*. New York: Oxford Univ. Press.

Wong, Sau-ling. 1993. *Reading Asian American Literature*. Princeton, NJ: Princeton Univ. Press.

Worcester, Dean. 1914. *The Philippines Past and Present*. New York: Macmillan.

Young, Marilyn. 1972. "The Quest for Empire." In *American-East Asian Relations*, ed. Ernest May and James Thomson. Cambridge, MA: Harvard Univ. Press.

3

JAPANESE AMERICAN LITERATURE

STAN YOGI

In a 1949 editorial, the nisei journalist Larry Tajiri commented, "Although Nisei writing has been published in one form or another, in their own newspapers and magazines, for nearly a quarter of a century, Japanese Americans have yet to develop a literature of their own." After making this pronouncement, Tajiri, in the same editorial, went on to chronicle the vibrant literary life of nisei in the prewar years, thereby undercutting his own assessment.

The immediate postwar years found many mainland Japanese Americans scrambling to rebuild their lives after the traumas of internment. Japanese American writers who might have seriously considered literary careers before the war now found themselves confronting basic economic necessities and a society that still regarded anything Japanese with suspicion, if not hostility.

Tajiri's statement, fortunately, was not the final word on Japanese American literature. Three generations of Japanese American authors have written and continue to write poems, stories, novels, memoirs, and plays that explore and record Japanese American experiences and perspectives. Read broadly, the body of Japanese American literature can be interpreted as an ongoing construction of identity at numerous levels: individual, collective, political, cultural, and generational. Throughout various historical periods, Japanese American authors have grappled with major issues of their times and in the process have examined the boundaries of ethnicity and nationality, often arriving at increasingly complex and sometimes antagonistic definitions of Japanese American identity.

Generational identity has been central to "nikkei," the term used to refer to people of Japanese ancestry living in North and South America. Japanese Americans have developed distinct terms for each generation: "issei" refers to immigrants who arrived in Hawai'i and the U.S. mainland between 1885 and 1924, "nisei" to second-generation Japanese Americans, and "sansei" to the third generation.

After the imposition of the 1882 Chinese Exclusion Act that barred immigration of Chinese laborers into the United States, and after the lifting of internal Japanese edicts restricting emigration, young Japanese male laborers began settling in Hawai'i and the western United States in 1885. Initially an almost exclusively male population who worked in agricultural, mining, and railroad jobs, the Japanese in the United States were the only Asian American community in the early twentieth century to develop families. Federal laws prevented the immigration of Chinese and Filipino women, but Japanese women were allowed into the country.[1] Because of this, stable Japanese American communities formed in Hawai'i, California, Oregon, and Washington prior to World War II.

Historical and political factors such as alien land laws prohibiting Japanese ownership of land and the 1921 Supreme Court decision in *Ozawa v. U.S.* denying Japanese naturalization rights contributed to a sense of generational identity among issei. The internment during World War II of over 110,000 Japanese Americans in concentration camps affected the issei but perhaps had its most profound impact on the nisei, most of whom were born between 1910 and 1940 and were adolescents or young adults during the war years. Simultaneously influenced by their parents' Japanese values and the "American" ideas of their peers, nisei negotiated between two cultures, but ultimately considered themselves American. Consequently, the mass internment raised fundamental questions for them regarding race relations and the definition of nationality.

Although most sansei were not yet born at the time of internment, the event has marked the third generation psychically, mainly through the silence issei and nisei maintained about the complexities and traumas of the war years. Many sansei were also affected by the various social movements of the 1960s and 1970s and sought to recover the history of their parents and to shape a self-conscious Japanese American culture. Although more heterogeneous than the issei and nisei, sansei nonetheless retain and transform Japanese American culture.

ISSEI WRITING IN ENGLISH

Japanese American literature in English has been written primarily by nisei and sansei authors. Although most issei were relatively well-educated, the demands of their daily lives left little time for them to master the English language, let alone time to write. Issei did, however, compose poems (haiku, tanka, and senryu) and other literary works, many of which appeared in Japanese-language newspapers in major cities in Hawai'i and along the West Coast.

The few issei who did write in English are unique and do not reflect the concerns of the majority, who, for the most part, were plantation workers and small-business owners in Hawai'i, and farmers, small-business owners, or domestics on the West Coast.[2] The most flamboyant of early Japanese American writers in English is Carl Sadakichi Hartmann. Born of a German father and a Japanese mother, Hartmann was well known as an artist, art critic, writer, and aesthetician at the turn of the century. He introduced avant-garde European writers and artists as well as Japanese art and literature to American audiences. According to Kenneth Rexroth, Hartmann may have been the first author to compose haiku in English (Hartmann 1971, ix). A noted figure in the Greenwich Village cultural milieu of the fin de siècle, Hartmann consciously cultivated an identity as the "king of Bohemia" and influenced many noted artists and writers of his time.

Author of four novels about life in Japan, Etsu Sugimoto first came to the American public's attention with the publication of her autobiographical novel, *A Daughter of the Samurai* (1925). Raised in the aristocratic class of Japan, Sugimoto received a thorough education in the English language and Western culture. She saw herself as a cultural ambassador between Japan and the United States, a role that many nisei were to assume in the prewar years. Her novels present a romantic view of Japanese culture and customs that Sugimoto saw disappearing due to Japan's rapid modernization. Sugimoto's novels indicate that she was secure with an identity as a Japanese who could explain the ways of her people to her adopted American compatriots (Kim 1982, 27).

Unlike Hartmann, who was busy creating an identity as a bohemian artist, and Sugimoto, who saw herself as an aristocratic bridge between countries, the poet Bunichi Kagawa wrestled with an identity as a Japanese American. Of all issei writers in English, Kagawa had the closest link with Japanese American communities and wrote poems that appeared in their newspapers. In the 1920s, he had immigrated to join his father in the Los Altos area of northern California, where he was befriended by the poet and Stanford professor Yvor Winters and his wife, the writer Janet Lewis. That Kagawa was interested in the question of identity is evident in his 1930 volume of poetry *Hidden Flame*. The opening section of the book is titled "Identity," and the title poem conveys an austere sense of isolation and self-reflection that characterizes many of the other poems in the book.

During the war, Kagawa was interned in the Tule Lake camp, where he was involved in the publication of a Japanese-language literary magazine entitled *Tessaku*. Before the war, however, Kagawa was in contact with nisei writers and for a short time was married to Chiye Mori, a nisei who was one of the more prolific young writers among a vibrant group of nisei literati.

ESTABLISHING AN IDENTITY:
PREWAR NISEI WRITING

Beginning in the late 1920s, a number of nisei began writing poems and stories for the English-language sections of Japanese American newspapers on the West Coast. Iwao Kawakami, English-language editor of the San Francisco newspaper *The New World–Sun*, inaugurated an English-language section in 1929 called "For the Thinking Japanese Young People" and made several pleas for nisei to engage in creative writing. Kawakami, himself a poet whose works appeared in *The New World–Sun*, was interested in literature and culture, and wrote editorials that frequently explored cultural matters of the time. In one of his early editorials, for example, he praised James Joyce's *Ulysses* and defended the book against censorship. Conscious of the uniqueness of nisei life, Kawakami encouraged budding nisei literary talents by initiating a story and essay contest, from which a story and essay club among his young nisei readers developed.

Another influential figure among early nisei writers was the journalist Larry Tajiri. Born in Long Beach, California, Tajiri became assistant editor of the Los Angeles newspaper *Kashu Mainichi*. In 1932, he introduced a weekly literary column, and during his tenure *Kashu Mainichi* became a leading publisher of nisei literature. Until the outbreak of the war, *The New World–Sun*, *Kashu Mainichi*, and other community newspapers continued to publish an increasingly sophisticated group of nisei writers.

Examples of work appearing in these papers reveal the cultural and literary influences on young nisei. In 1932, for example, *Kashu Mainichi* began to publish translations of noted Japanese literature along with the original Japanese text. An editorial commenting on this series explained that these works would be helpful to nisei attending Japanese-language schools and that the "ultimate activities of the second generation is [*sic*] in America and the mission of these schools should be the development of training to be able to assimilate the culture of Japan and to distribute that understanding in America" (8 May 1932, Los Angeles). The inclusion of these works indicates that nisei were perceived as a cultural bridge between the United States and Japan. This role, however, would take on political dimensions that put nisei in difficult positions when Japan became increasingly aggressive in Asia and tensions flared between the United States and Japan.

Although some nisei saw themselves as instructing their fellow citizens in Japanese culture, works written by young nisei authors for the community press reveal that the cultural conversation flowed in two directions. Poems such as Toyo Suyemoto's "Improvident" reflect the influence of Western literary traditions:

Through starless hours I stumbled down a road
Lost in the night and blowing mist and fear –
I fled strange urgings where the moonlight showed
A brief, white calm. I was afraid of near
Familiarities that shadows wrought
To awesome forms. With proud despair I went,
Resigned to flight, till suddenly I thought

And knew myself at fault, improvident.
The lone heart had been haunted with a dream
Of beauty gone, life desolately burned
Out in the dark, and through this disesteem
I foundered on the way I once had learned.
Only the dread remained, only the cool
Winds mocked, half pityingly: Fool – poor fool!

(c. 1935, 6)

Following the strict rhythmic pattern and rhyme scheme of an English sonnet, Suyemoto in this poem does not allude to anything in theme or imagery that is particularly Japanese American. Other works by nisei – highly formal verse, extravagant love poems, murder mysteries, stories in which protagonists are indistinguishable from other Americans except for their Japanese names – reflect not only the popular literary forms of the period, but also a nisei desire to claim those traditions as their own.

Nisei literature of the 1930s and early 1940s also reveals the growing concern of the second generation about international tensions, domestic race relations, and self-awareness as a distinct ethnic group. Chiye Mori's 1932 poem "Japanese American" was one of the first nisei works to explore explicitly the intersection between personal identity and international politics. Mori compares Japanese Americans to "clay pigeons traveling swiftly and aimlessly / On the electric wire of international hate / Helpless targets in the shooting gallery of political discord / Drilled by the clattering shells / That rip toward us from both sides" (1932, 2). She lays out in definite terms the frustration and politically precarious position of the nisei. The political critique of both the United States and Japan was bold for a young nisei.

Other nisei writers were interested in politics, particularly in cross-cultural relations within the United States, and in building bridges between nisei and other American ethnic groups. A leading figure among this group of nisei was Mary Oyama, who wrote in various forms for the Japanese American press all along the West Coast. Oyama was a strong voice among nisei who attempted to forge a nisei identity as second-generation Americans. She looked to other ethnic Americans for models and corresponded with well-known writers of the time such as William

Saroyan and Louis Adamic, who were concerned that various American ethnic groups voice their stories. Oyama was a cofounder of the League of Nisei Artists and Writers, a group modeled upon the League of American Writers. The nisei group was "devoted to literary and artistic endeavors and . . . organized for the purpose of promoting individual and collaborative creative activity, of stimulating a critical outlook on matters of life, art and broad problems of society" (1939, n.p.).

Taro Katayama's short story "Haru" explores internal conflicts resulting from cultural rather than political tensions. Perhaps the most moving and sophisticated of the prewar short stories, "Haru" chronicles the emotional turmoil of a young nisei who agrees to an arranged marriage. Because most nisei fiction of the prewar era was written by adolescents and tended to be somewhat underdeveloped, "Haru" is remarkable for its psychological insight and control of style and plot. The first two sentences of the story lay out the basic premise of the tale: "The realities of her world were those that were forced upon her by the unalterable fact of her being what she was. Haru was the daughter of a poor Japanese farmer in [the] western United States, and therein lay the beginning and the seeming end of her whole existence" (1933, 7). Katayama shows how economic, cultural, and psychological factors force the protagonist, Haru, to marry a man she finds repulsive. Tensions between issei and nisei because of arranged marriages had been the subject of other short stories, but Katayama's sensitive treatment of the subject moves far beyond any prewar nisei fiction.

"Haru" first appeared in *Reimei*, one of several small literary magazines that nisei developed in the prewar period. Inaugurated in 1931 by a Salt Lake City nisei club of the same name, *Reimei* was edited by Yasuo Sasaki, a prolific young writer of the period whose works appeared in many of the newspapers of the time and who went on to publish two books of poetry, *Ascension* (1968) and *Village Scene/Village Herd* (1986). *Leaves* was a modest mimeographed pamphlet published by a group of Los Angeles writers led by Mary Oyama, who hosted literary salons for young nisei writers. *Gyo-Sho: A Magazine of Nisei Literature*, published circa 1935 by the English Club of Cornell College in Mount Vernon, Iowa, reiterated the cultural-bridge role for nisei. The foreword to the sole issue of the magazine stated: "The Nisei [are] an interstitial cultural group [that] will bridge the chasm between the cultures of the East and the West" (5). There was enough interest in nisei writers for the October 1940 issue of *Current Life*, another nisei magazine that featured literature, to include an article entitled "Who's Who in the Nisei Literary World" that informally catalogued twenty-four leading nisei writers.

Perhaps the best-known Japanese American author to prewar audiences was Toshio Mori, who developed largely outside the circle of nisei literati. In the 1930s, Mori's stories appeared in journals such as *New Directions in Poetry and Prose*, *The Clipper*, and *Common Ground*, which also published works by authors such as Gertrude Stein, Langston Hughes, and William Saroyan. A collection of Mori's stories entitled *Yokohama, California* was originally slated for publication in 1942. The war, however, postponed the appearance of the book, and it was not published until 1949.

Modeled on James Joyce's *Dubliners* and Sherwood Anderson's *Winesburg, Ohio, Yokohama, California* is a series of stories about the Japanese American inhabitants of a fictional town situated across the bay from San Francisco in the late 1930s. Mori focuses on the seemingly mundane and reveals the profound in daily life. Although little plot action occurs in his stories, the psychological and emotional resonances are rich. "Tomorrow and Today," for example, deals with the quotidian existence of a plain nisei woman, Hatsuye, who is eclipsed by her prettier younger sister. Hatsuye is content with her lot, managing the family household and indulging in an innocent infatuation with Clark Gable, until her sister, in the heat of an argument, announces: "You are ugly, Hatsuye! You're so ugly no man will look at you" (1949, 164). The declaration wounds Hatsuye, but she recovers with a tempered sense of hope, accepting that "she is no beauty but . . . hopeful that she is not all ugliness to others" (Mori 1949, 165). One of the final paragraphs of the story captures the underlying message and overall timbre of *Yokohama, California*: "When one has been around the neighborhood a while, the routine is familiar and is not emphasized. It appears dull and colorless. But in this routine there is breath-taking suspense that is alive and enormous, although the outcome and prospect of it is a pretty obvious thing. Although [Hatsuye's] hope may be unfilled, there is no reason why she cannot be a lover of Clark Gable" (1949, 165–6). This passage highlights Mori's appreciation of the ways in which the smallest incidentals of daily life carry significant meaning. Although "Tomorrow and Today" could have degenerated into maudlin sentimentalism, Mori is careful to infuse his characters, even the most self-deluded, with dignity and respect.

All of the characters in *Yokohama, California* are Japanese American, and the narrative voice speaks with confidence to a familiar community. However, because many of the stories tap into rich emotional veins and refer to the mass American culture of the late 1930s, Mori claims new literary ground for Japanese Americans. His writing does not exoticize nikkei, but rather situates them in a broader social context.

Mori also portrays distinctive Japanese American characteristics. Stories dealing with issei, for instance, refer back to a heritage in Japan. Yet, even more subtly, Mori records Japanese American norms and cultural expressions. This sense is perhaps best exemplified in "The Woman Who Makes Swell Doughnuts," a portrait of an issei woman and the story that would have originally opened the collection. Although she has given birth to six children and worked for forty years, the title character does not depend on others to care for her. On the contrary, she cares for others, frying her wonderful doughnuts for the narrator and looking after her family and community. The woman who makes swell doughnuts becomes a metaphor for overarching values among Japanese Americans: sensitivity and obligation. These values are seen in various cultural phenomena such as *giri* (indebtedness), *on* (obligation), and *enryo* (reserve, constraint), which are based in empathy and interdependence.[3]

Two stories added to the 1949 version of *Yokohama, California* deal with the war and its effects on Japanese Americans. Both involve issei women who speak forcefully in favor of the United States. In "Slant-Eyed Americans," for example, an issei woman comments to a nisei man: "America is right. She cannot fail. Her principles will stand the test of time and tyranny" (1949, 132). Although some issei did fully support America during the war, others were ambivalent. Works written in concentration camps by nisei explore the ambiguities of identity.

IDENTITY IN QUESTION: INTERNMENT LITERATURE

The war and subsequent internment profoundly altered the lives of Japanese Americans living along the West Coast. Communities such as that depicted in *Yokohama, California* were shattered, and identities and loyalties called into question. The wholesale internment of over 110,000 nikkei without trial or hearing raised serious questions for Japanese Americans, especially the nisei. For some, it resulted in a fierce embracing of a thoroughly "American" identity. For others, it led to bitter disillusionment over what were perceived to be the empty rhetorical promises of American equality and justice. Others fell between these two extremes, as Japanese Americans attempted to cope with the traumas of forced removal from their homes and internment in desolate camps scattered throughout the United States.

These struggles were mirrored in camp literature. Three camps published English-language magazines: *Tulean Dispatch* (Tule Lake, California), *The Pen* (Rowher, Arkansas), and *Trek* (Topaz, Utah). Of these three, *Trek* offers the broadest array of talents and perspectives. Originally edited by Jim Yamada, a budding writer and Berkeley student, and Mine Okubo, an artist who later wrote the illustrated memoir *Citizen 13660* (Okubo 1946) about camp life, *Trek* was published three times. (A fourth issue of the camp magazine was entitled *All Aboard* and edited by Toshio Mori.)

Each issue opens with a lead article on the state of camp life, followed by stories, poems, articles on the geography and history of the Topaz region, and a women's column entitled "A la Mode."

Although only three issues were produced, each one reflects tensions between "optimistic" and "critical" perspectives. "Optimistic" writing is characterized by admonitions not to be bitter and to believe in America. The leading writer of this group is Toshio Mori. In "Topaz, Station," a sketch Mori wrote for the first issue of *Trek*, the narrator comments that Japanese Americans are interned in Topaz "to continue living, a station . . . a stopping-off place on the way to progress as good Americans for a better America" (Mori 1942, 24). Mori echoes the motto of the Japanese American Citizens League (JACL): "Better Americans in a Greater America." Mori's allusion is not only an optimistic statement but also a political one, given the complex and bitter tensions that developed around the JACL. At the time of the war, the JACL advocated cooperation with the government as a sign of loyalty. Because of this, the JACL was targeted as an opportunistic organization suspected of betraying fellow Japanese Americans, particularly issei. In some camps, JACL spokespeople were beaten and threatened.

Because camp publications were censored by government authorities, overt criticism of the internment was rare. Consequently, writers had to mask their criticisms. Susan Schweik offers a fascinating analysis of Toyo Suyemoto's wartime poems as examples of "resistance and critique embedded within the forms and diction of poems which appear apolitical" (Schweik 1991, 186). Suyemoto was one of the most prolific and talented of prewar nisei writers, and her poems, which appeared in the same issues of *Trek* as Toshio Mori's stories, on the surface at least, seem to be innocent commentaries about nature – poems that would easily pass the eyes of camp censors. "Gain" is an example:

> I sought to seed the barren earth
> And make wild beauty take
> firm root, but how could I have known
> The waiting long would shake
>
> Me inwardly, until I dared
> Not say what would be gain
> From such untimely planting, or
> What flower worth the pain?

> (1942, 7)

Given the context in which the poem appeared, Suyemoto's nature imagery takes on powerful metaphorical significance. The "barren earth" referred to can be interpreted as not only the desert of Topaz, Utah, but also what a nisei peering from behind a barbed-wire fence in 1942 might consider to be the desert of American society. The long wait for "wild beauty" to take root can refer to an acceptance of Japanese Americans within American society as well as within the confines of camp. Read as an extended metaphor, the poem can be an expression of the costs the internment had already inflicted on Japanese Americans.

IDENTITY IN FLUX: POSTWAR NISEI LITERATURE

In 1968, the respected nisei writer Hisaye Yamamoto commented that "a writer proceeds from a compulsion to communicate a vision and he cannot afford to bother with what people in general think of him. We Nisei, discreet, circumspect, care very much what others think of us, and there has been more than one who has fallen by the wayside in the effort to reconcile his inner vision with outer appearance" (Yamamoto 1976, 126–7).

Yamamoto's observation codifies the postwar psychology of many mainland nisei. After being the targets of intense racism and hostility, many nikkei were eager to blend in and not be noticed. In an effort to rebuild their lives, many sought to merge into the American mainstream, to forget about the traumas of internment, and in some cases to escape from nikkei communities and heritage.

Despite this context, nisei continued to write. The Christmas/New Year holiday issues of Japanese American newspapers such as *Rafu Shimpo* in Los Angeles, *Hokubei Mainichi* in San Francisco, and the JACL's national paper *Pacific Citizen* remained forums for nisei authors. While not as prolific as in their more innocent prewar years, they still wrote for these papers, as well as nisei magazines such as *Scene* and *Bandwagon*, albeit not necessarily with the same gusto and ambition as they had in the 1930s.

A few nisei writers, however, produced notable works in the immediate postwar years and throughout the 1950s. Perhaps because Japanese Americans in Hawai'i, for the most part, did not experience the traumas of internment and constituted a large portion of the islands' population, it might have been easier for Hawaiian nisei to explore Japanese American history and identity in the immediate postwar years. In the 1950s and 1960s, three novels written by Hawaiian nisei dealt with issei history and intergenerational issues: Shelley Ota's *Upon Their Shoulders* (1951), Margaret Harada's *The Sun Shines on the Immigrant* (1960), and Kazuo Miyamoto's *Hawaii: End of the Rainbow* (1964).

Stephen H. Sumida has explained that each novel evidences a differing attitude toward history. *Upon Their Shoulders*, which focuses on the trials of the issei immigrant Taro Sumida and his family both in Japan and in

Hawai'i, adopts what Sumida calls a "karmic attitude" regarding history. Writing in the assimilationist period of Japanese American history, Ota implies that nikkei cannot escape their history, which is bound to recur in new manifestations (Sumida 1991, 207–14).

The Sun Shines on the Immigrant, however, suggests a different perspective. The novel's protagonist, Yoshio Mori, climbs the entrepreneurial ladder from poor immigrant to comfortable businessman. The novel makes no attempt to tie Mori's rise to a broader Japanese American community and ends curiously just before World War II, leaving the postwar reader with a sense of disillusionment, knowing the history that follows the novel's end (Sumida 1991, 214–16).

Miyamoto's *Hawaii: End of the Rainbow* is grounded in history, based in part on the author's journals written while he served as a physician in mainland concentration camps, where he himself was imprisoned for eleven months. The novel is epic in its detail, chronicling the lives of two issei as well as the experiences of Hawaiian Japanese Americans interned during the war. Unlike *The Sun Shines on the Immigrant*, Miyamoto's novel insists on addressing a traumatic episode in collective Japanese American history.

Of mainland nisei authors writing in the immediate postwar period, Hisaye Yamamoto is one of the best known. In the 1930s, she began writing acerbic columns for the Japanese American press, and in the early 1950s her finely crafted stories depicting prewar Japanese American life began receiving national attention. Yamamoto started publishing her essays and stories in national journals in 1948 and was awarded a John Hay Whitney Foundation Opportunity Fellowship in 1950. *"Seventeen Syllables" and Other Stories*, a collection of her work, was published in 1988.

Yamamoto's stories often explore tensions between issei men and issei women, and also the relationships between nisei and issei, especially the bonds between mothers and daughters. Two of her stories, "Seventeen Syllables" (1949) and "Yoneko's Earthquake" (1951), exemplify Yamamoto's sensitive treatment of theme as well as her oblique narrative style. Ostensibly a story about the sexual awakening of an adolescent nisei, "Seventeen Syllables" is also a story of the young woman's mother and her thwarted aspirations as a poet. "Yoneko's Earthquake" chronicles the infatuation of a young nisei girl with a Filipino hired hand, while also revealing the disturbing ramifications of her mother's relationship with the same man. Yamamoto structures both stories to develop constant links between the mothers and daughters, and these parallels underscore the legacy of disruption and pain passed from generation to generation. In "Seventeen Syllables," for example, Rosie Hayashi, the young protagonist, discovers her sexuality, but her awakening is complicated by troubling revelations about her mother's romantic past. Similarly, in "Yoneko's Earthquake," young Yoneko's innocent crush mirrors her mother's more serious affair with the hired worker.

Yamamoto was one of the few nisei to address internment in the immediate postwar years. "The Legend of Miss Sasagawara" (1951) is her haunting tale of a nisei ballet dancer considered insane by her fellow internees. Initially intrigued by the aging dancer, the internees soon hold her suspect because of her aloof and puzzling behavior. Deceptively simple in its presentation, the story is layered with implicit allusions to the suspicions hurled at Japanese Americans during the war. Miss Sasagawara becomes a symbol of all Japanese Americans who, especially during the war, were thought to be disloyal and consequently were interned. Thus, in its exploration of intracommunity tensions, the story also mirrors broader societal conflicts.

Monica Sone's autobiography, *Nisei Daughter* (1953), is another literary work depicting the internment in the immediate postwar years. The book spans Sone's life, from her childhood in Seattle's Japanese American community, where her family ran a hotel, to her internment in Minidoka and her eventual resettlement in a small liberal arts college. *Nisei Daughter* provides insight into the development of a nisei identity. Early in the book, Sone comments on the duality of her childhood: "Nihon Gakko [Japanese school] was so different from grammar school I found myself switching my personality back and forth daily like a chameleon. At Bailey Gatzert School, I was a jumping, screaming, roustabout Yankee, but at the stroke of three when the school bell rang and doors burst open every-where . . . I suddenly became a modest, faltering, earnest little Japanese girl with a small, timid voice" (22).

Sone goes on to chronicle the prewar discrimination and prejudice issei and nisei encountered in employment and housing. The book ends, however, on a hopeful note. After visiting her parents in Minidoka during one of her Christmas holidays from college, Sone recalls, "I was going back into [America's] main stream, still with my Oriental eyes, but with an entirely different outlook, for now I felt more like a whole person instead of a sadly split personality. The Japanese and the American parts of me were now blended into one" (238). Sone's positive outlook is not surprising, in part because of the period in which the book was published – an era when many Japanese Americans were attempting to assimilate into the mainstream of American life.

Not all postwar literary accounts, however, resolved the question of Japanese American identity so neatly. John Okada's *No-No Boy*, although not about the internment, is a powerful depiction of its aftermath. When first published in 1957, the novel received little attention and was more or less rejected by Japanese Americans. While troubling, this reaction is understandable considering that the book is a painful and disturbing portrait of postwar Japanese American life. The book was rescued from obscurity by young Asian American writers and critics in the 1970s, and it has subsequently been canonized as a classic of Asian American literature. Okada, unfortunately, died before his novel was rediscovered.

Set in Seattle at the war's end, *No-No Boy* is a bildungsroman that focuses on the struggle of a twenty-five-year-old nisei, Ichiro Yamada, to accept his wartime actions. The double negative of the title refers to two questions that internees over the age of seventeen were required to answer. One asked men if they would serve in the military. The other demanded unqualified allegiance to the United States. The government permitted only yes or no answers, denying internees the opportunity to voice their complex reactions to these questions. For answering "no" to both questions and for refusing to be drafted into the army, Ichiro spends two years in prison.

No-No Boy depicts Ichiro's attempt to reclaim an identity as an American as he also tries to understand why he answered "no" to the questions. In the process, he must confront an antagonistic and fragmented nikkei community. Just as Japanese Americans were forced to answer either "yes" or "no" to the loyalty questions during the war, so the postwar community faced similar binary choices. Through Ichiro's journey to reestablish an identity, Okada explores the gray area between polarized definitions of "Japanese" and "American," individuality and community, assimilation and cultural maintenance.

Tragically, issei and nisei characters throughout the novel find few ways to reconcile their Japanese roots with their American experience to forge a unique American identity: Japanese American. The war left deep and lasting wounds on individuals and communities, and it would take decades before Japanese Americans could discuss the effects of the war publicly.

Beginning in the mid-1970s, Japanese Americans and Japanese Canadians began to explore the possibility of obtaining monetary redress for their wartime experiences. The process encouraged many nisei to think and speak about their internment (in the United States) and forced migration (in Canada and the United States) and break decades-long silences about those years. Not surprisingly, nisei began writing about internment and dislocation. One of the first creative treatments focusing specifically on internment was Jeanne Wakatsuki Houston and James Houston's *Farewell to Manzanar* (1973), a memoir that captures the details of camp life and its effects in adjusting to postwar society. In 1982, Yoshiko Uchida, a well-known author of books for young adults, published *Desert Exile*, an autobiography of her life during the war.

The most critically acclaimed novel dealing with nikkei during World War II was not written by an American but a Canadian, Joy Kogawa. Her poetic and haunting novel *Obasan* (1981) attests to the traumas endured by Japanese Canadians during the war. Set in 1972, *Obasan* focuses on the war's effects as discovered and remembered by a middle-aged sansei woman, Naomi Nakane. The death of Naomi's uncle, Isamu, with whom she lived as a child, spurs her confrontation with family history, and by extension the history of Japanese Canadians. Prior to the war, Naomi's family was secure and well-established in Vancouver. The onset of the war, however, brings about a series of events that results in the virtual disintegration of the family: Naomi's father and grandparents are separated from the rest of the family; Naomi's mother is trapped in Japan where she is tending an ailing relative; Naomi, her brother Stephen, and their Aunt Aya (the *obasan* or aunt of the title) are forced to move to Slocan, a ghost town in the country's interior. After reestablishing a life in Slocan, the family is forced to move once again to Alberta, where they live in even worse deprivation.

In addition to providing a powerful and moving account of Japanese Canadian lives during the war, *Obasan* explores the multiple layers of silence and speech. Naomi's two aunts, Aya Obasan and Aunt Emily, come to symbolize each notion. Naomi comments on them: "How different my two aunts are. One lives in sound, the other in stone. Obasan's language remains deeply underground but Aunt Emily, BA, MA, is a word warrior" (Kogawa 1982, 32). The symbolism of silence and articulation is multilayered and more complex than this quotation implies. Kogawa explores the varying natures of silence, its oppressiveness as the mechanism of secrets but also its symbolism as a sign of strength and courage. Similarly, through Aunt Emily and official Canadian decrees, Kogawa reveals how speech can be liberating but also the source of profound pain (Cheung 1993, 126–67).

In the 1960s, 1970s, and 1980s, other notable nisei writers emerged. Milton Murayama's landmark novel, *All I Asking For Is My Body*, was originally published in 1959 but did not receive wide recognition until the 1970s. The story of a Japanese American family living on a Hawaiian sugar plantation in the late 1930s and early 1940s, the novel depicts plantation and family politics. The narrator, Kiyoshi Oyama, is a young nisei who recounts the tension between his parents and his older brother, Tosh, as the family struggles to repay a large debt. Through the antagonistic dynamic that develops between issei and nisei, Murayama explores the complex interaction between traditional Japanese values of family loyalty and the exploitative and racially stratified plantation system. In Tosh, Murayama creates a character that rebels against personal limitations (imposed by his family) and, less explicitly, against political oppression (as symbolized by the plantation). Throughout the book, Murayama clearly delineates the racial hierarchy of the plantation and the strategies of dividing workers to prevent a sense of solidarity.

All I Asking For Is My Body is also one of the first literary works by a nikkei to incorporate "pidgin English" or the Hawaiian Creole English that has developed on the Islands. Though the narrative of the story is written in standard English, much of the dialogue is written in "pidgin." Like writers who have legitimized regional dialects and black English in literature, Murayama pioneered the use of "pidgin English" as a literary language.

The nisei playwright and short-story writer Wakako Yamauchi began writing seriously in the 1950s but, like Murayama, did not receive recognition until the 1970s. Better known as a playwright than as a short-story writer, Yamauchi has adapted several of her stories for the stage. The best known of her plays is *And the Soul Shall Dance*, based upon a story of the same name. The memoir of a nisei woman, the story captures many of the themes recurrent in Yamauchi's work: the ambiguities of gender relationships, tensions between issei and nisei, and the confining lives of issei, especially women, who seek escape in various ways. The narrator, raised in a desolate desert farming community, recounts her fascination with a neighbor, Mrs. Oka, an aloof, disturbed issei. The story describes Mrs. Oka's unconventional behavior, which both frightens and intrigues the narrator, and unfolds the history of Mrs. Oka's troubled life.

Like Yamamoto, Yamauchi often explores issei lives through the perspective of nisei narrators and, as in *And the Soul Shall Dance*, depicts with sympathy the unconventional behavior of issei women. By viewing issei women's drunkenness, adultery, and abandonment of family through a nisei lens, Yamauchi recovers and recounts the history of women rebelling against strict norms. She creates strong women characters who pursue their desires, often in defiance of societal standards.

Mitsuye Yamada is a writer who crosses generational boundaries. Born in Japan, she is technically an issei but grew up among nisei peers. Her poems, which deal with explicit feminist and antiracist concerns, reflect the perspective of sansei activists. Yamada's first collection, *Camp Notes* (1976), brings together works she wrote while interned in Minidoka (or soon thereafter) and poems written in the 1970s. The book is notable for its straightforward irony and depth of perception. Raw emotion filtered through an ironic lens characterizes Yamada's early work. Many of her poems temper indignation over injustice with poignant details.

In her second book, *Desert Run* (1988), Yamada returns to many of the themes and emotional landscapes of *Camp Notes*. A poem such as "The Club" combines her concern over both sexism and racism. The opening stanza lays out the poem's major premise:

> He beat me with the hem of a kimono
> worn by a Japanese woman
> this prized
> painted
> wooden statue
> carved to perfection
> in Japan or maybe Hong Kong.
>
> (1988, 76)

The poem explores the violent implications of the sexual stereotypes assigned to Asian women (as represented by the Japanese doll with which the speaker is beaten) and implies that the very standards of femininity represented by the stereotype can be a destructive force for women who do not live up to it. In addressing issues of feminism, racism, human-rights abuses around the world, and Japanese American identity, Yamada melds personal and political concerns, and in so doing bears a strong affinity with sansei activist writers.

EXPANDING IDENTITIES: SANSEI ACTIVIST WRITING

The late 1960s and early 1970s were years of self-conscious "Asian American" literary production. Sansei authors were often at the center of these efforts, expanding the boundaries of Japanese American culture and identity. Influenced by the progressive and radical politics of the times, these writers often linked their literary work to overtly political agendas: many likened the battles for independence of colonies throughout the world with the struggles of people of color in the United States.

Sansei writers also sought to recover the traditions and literature of issei and nisei. The poets Lawson Inada and Janice Mirikitani were leading figures in the recovery of issei and nisei literature. Inada was one of the coeditors of the influential anthology *Aiiieeeee!* (1974), and Mirikitani was the lead editor for the collection *Ayumi* (1980), an anthology of issei, nisei, and sansei writing and visual art. The discovery of previous generations of literary Japanese Americans provided sansei activist writers with a stronger appreciation of history and allowed them to write with a greater sense of community identity.

These sansei authors also recognized the politics of literature and rejected traditional literary forms in favor of styles forged from their own experiences or those of other people of color in the United States as well as internationally. Many sansei women, affected by the feminist movement of the 1970s, wrote with a consciousness of gender and its implications. Beginning in the late 1960s and continuing through the early 1980s, numerous sansei wrote with an aesthetic and political sensibility grounded in the social movements of the era. Their works appear in community-based Asian American journals and anthologies. Inada and Mirikitani capture, in different ways, the spirit and tone of this group of writers.

In Lawson Inada's poem "For E.H.W." the speaker comments, "There's a lot more of me/where I'm from, where I'm/continually being born." These lines could serve as an epigraph to Inada's ground-breaking book *Before the War: Poems as They Happened* (1971). The book is a melange of styles, themes, and influences, and foreshadows postmodern Japanese American writing of the 1980s and 1990s. *Before the War* is the first collection of poetry by a Japanese American to be released by a major publisher, and appeared the same year as Daniel Okimoto's autobiography, *American in Disguise*, which some Asian American activists criticized as a reflection of ethnic self-contempt. Although a master of traditional Western poetic language and tropes, Inada claims colloquial language as the stuff of poetry and fuses powerful emotion with contemporary idioms. Jazz has been a major influence on Inada, and the rhythms, figures, and strategies of music flow in his poetry. Throughout his work, he insists on the aural nature of verse. These qualities reappear in his 1992 collection, *Legends from Camp*.

At times, Inada writes in an overt political posture, as in 'Projected Scenario of a Performance To Be Given before the U.N.," in which the speaker berates a U.N. audience and warns of the Asian world majority coming to power. But in his poem "From Our Album" politics are expressed more subtly. "From Our Album" is a series of shattering portraits of life in an internment camp. These lines from the poem reveal a jarring mixture of innocence and violence:

> Because there was little else to do,
> they led us to the artillery range
> for shells, all that we gathered,
> and let us dig among dunes
> for slugs, when they were through
>
> Because there was little else to do,
> one of them chased a stray
> with his tail between his legs
> and shot him through the head.

(1971, 17)

These stanzas are as powerful, if not more so, as a polemic against internment, because they viscerally describe the daily violence witnessed by (and threatening) the child whose experiences with soldiers watching the internees the poem depicts.

Like Lawson Inada, Janice Mirikitani writes of difficult topics with a powerful resonance that distinguishes her work from that of previous generations of Japanese American writers. Her two books, *Awake in the River* (1978) and *Shedding Silence* (1987), reveal a sensibility that is deeply concerned about connections between the personal and the political. At times, she writes with the bold force of a manifesto, as in these lines from "Japs":

> if you're too dark
> they will kill you.
> if you're too swift
> they will cripple you.
> if you're too strong
> they will buy you.
> if you're too beautiful
> they will rape you.
>
> (1978, np)

Mirikitani's rhetoric, however, is not without substance and introspection, and her artistic style, as these lines indicate, is rich in the rhythms and tones of oral traditions. Her poems connect the experiences of oppressed people throughout the world with those of Japanese Americans, particularly the issei and nisei generations, as in these stanzas from "Attack the Water":

> My first flash
> on the newsprint/face
> she could have been
> Obachan[4]
> back then/just after
> the camps
> when the land/dried/up
> . . . .
> Vietnamese woman
> her face etched old
> by newsprint/war
> mother/grandmother
> she has bared them all.
>
> (1978, np)

The connections (among countries, races, and genders) that infuse Mirikitani's work are based in political beliefs and actions that are themselves grounded in her work as a community activist with the poor and disempowered in San Francisco.

Although Mirikitani writes with the conviction that poems can make a political difference, she also recognizes the limitations of poetry. The speaker in "Jungle Rot and Open Arms," for example, after hearing the horrors of a Vietnam veteran's experiences, confesses:

> i stood amidst
> his wreckage
> and wept for myself.
>
> so where is my
> *political education*? my
> *rhetoric answers* to everything? my
> *theory into practice*? my
> *intensification of life in art*?
>
> (1978, np)

This kind of self-reflection sets Mirikitani's work apart from that of other activist writers of the era. She writes with the force of a street-corner preacher but also with the reflection of a philosopher.

IDENTITY IN LOCATION: SANSEI WRITERS OF PLACE

Sansei writing in the 1980s and 1990s has channeled into a number of different streams, with authors oftentimes building on the bases provided by activist writers of the 1970s. One subset of contemporary sansei literature is characterized by a sense of rootedness in a particular geographic locale. Sansei who write from an identification with place recall nisei writing of the prewar era, especially the work of Toshio Mori. Many of these sansei, however, write with a sense of urgency, to capture Japanese American communities that are either disappearing or changing in dramatic ways.

This motivation is clear in *Talking to the Dead* (1992), a collection of stories by the Hawaiian sansei, Sylvia Watanabe. When discussing her impulse to write, Watanabe has commented, "I first began writing because I wanted to record a way of life which I loved and which seemed in danger of dying away. . . . I wanted to save my parents' and grandparents' stories" (1992, np).

Like *Yokohama, California*, the stories in *Talking to the Dead* take place in a single geographic location: a small rural Hawaiian village. Many of the stories deal with characters who are on the verge of changes that possibly could be irrevocable. These characters confront shifting relationships and mores brought on, in part, by modernization. These themes come together in the title story, "Talking to the Dead." Yuri Shimabukuro, the protagonist of the story, apprentices herself to Auntie Talking to the Dead, the village's mortician, who is well-versed in traditional lore, not modern science. Unfortunately, Yuri cannot stomach the work, but she nevertheless stays with Auntie Talking to the Dead and learns everything she can about the old ways. Yuri's relationship with Auntie becomes a metaphor for differing attitudes toward progress and personal loyalty. Unlike Yuri, Auntie's own son, Clinton, is in competition with his mother, promoting his modern mortuary that advertises "Lifelike Artistic Techniques and Stringent Standards of Sanitation." Through the depiction of Yuri's loyalty to her mentor, Watanabe honors traditions associated with a particular place and community.

Like Sylvia Watanabe, several sansei writers depict what those who are born and raised in Hawai'i refer to as the "local" culture of the islands. Local culture exists in contradistinction to the tourist culture of Hawai'i and captures a mix of people and traditions. For many contemporary local Japanese American writers, *Bamboo Ridge: The Hawaii Writer's Quarterly* has served as a venue for publication. Initiated in 1978, the journal has consistently featured the voices of Hawaii's Asian American literary community, and many of its contributors convene regularly in study groups to discuss literature and Asian American culture in Hawai'i.

Juliet Kono, a sansei writer, is involved with the Bamboo Ridge group, and her collection of poems, *Hilo Rains* (1988), is intricately linked to a particular place – Hilo and the surrounding area. Place is so pervasive in *Hilo Rains* that it almost becomes a persona in the book. The three parts of the collection explore the three generations of Kono's family and record the emotional history of familial relations. Kono weaves together memories and complex emotion in a spare and dignified style. She strongly identifies with Hilo and is concerned that an appreciation of this particular locale and its significance in family history be perpetuated for and by future generations.

A sense of place is central to many of the poems in Garrett Kaoru Hongo's two collections, *Yellow Light* (1982) and *The River of Heaven* (1988), winner of the Lamont Poetry Selection award for 1987. Like Watanabe and Kono, Hongo writes of Hawai'i, where he was born, but also of other Japanese American communities in southern California, where he spent part of his youth. In elegant verse, which sometimes has the spirit of earlier activist poems, Hongo often uses a particular place as the basis for deeper reflections and connections.

These lines from "The Pier," Hongo's elegy to his father, are telling: "I think splendor must be something of what we all want / somehow, respite from privation and a world / of diminishment, a small drama so strange / it exiles the common yet thrills us with our own stories" (1988, 62). Hongo's poems elevate the "common" to poetry and remind us of the power of "our own stories." Meditations on his father's death in "The Pier" lead Hongo to fluid juxtapositions that connect his father, Southeast Asian immigrants, and his own immigrant grandparents, linkages that cross generational, regional, and ethnic lines. This desire for connection is echoed in "The Legend," a poem that describes the random shooting death of an Asian American man in Chicago. After recounting the shooting, the speaker comments:

> Tonight, I read about Descartes'
> grand courage to doubt everything
> except his own miraculous existence
> and I feel so distinct
> from the wounded man lying on the concrete
> I feel ashamed.
>
> Let the night sky cover him as he dies.
> Let the weaver girl cross the bridge of heaven
> and take up his cold hands.
>
> (1988, 67)

Although the speaker admits to feeling a certain distance from the dead man, in the next stanza he rejects the solipsism of Descartes. By invoking the legend of the weaver girl, an astrological myth in which a celestial couple is allowed to unite only once a year, Hongo calls for connections in a profound way.

In the stories of David Mas Masumoto, a connection with place is grounded in an understanding of family history in a particular region: the Japanese American farming communities of the lower San Joaquin valley of California. "Fire Dance," the opening story of his collection *Silent Strength* (1984), dramatically lays out the cultural geography of the small valley town of Del Rey in 1938. The town is literally divided by the railroad tracks, with the immigrant Japanese community on one side and the more prosperous European American community on the other. On the night of the *obon* (festival of the dead) celebration, a suspicious fire breaks out on the Japanese side of town. The white residents merely look on without helping as the Japanese American community struggles to contain the fire. It is not until the fire spreads to their side of town that the European American townspeople act. Masumoto's stories subtly reveal the intricate history of ethnic relations in the valley and the early struggles of Japanese Americans in that area.

Although a nisei, the anthropologist Akemi Kikumura writes with a sansei sensibility about the Central Valley of California, where she was raised. In two books, *Through Harsh Winters: The Life of a Japanese Immigrant Woman* (1981) and *Promises Kept: The Life of an Issei Man* (1991), she writes of her parents and their lives in Japan and in California. Both books are based on oral history interviews and combine anthropological techniques with dramatic narrative structures to reveal the rural life of Japanese Americans.

R. A. Sasaki, in her collection *"The Loom" and Other Stories* (1991), writes about Japanese Americans in postwar San Francisco. Linked together by recurring characters, the stories depict baby-boom-age sansei who were raised in the Richmond District of San Francisco during the 1950s and 1960s. Sasaki's stories explore the varying ways in which sansei maintain and transform ethnic identity and search for cultural stability.

Two sansei playwrights capture the intricacies of Japanese American communities. Throughout the 1980s, Philip Kan Gotanda's plays explored the complexities of Japanese American families. Though not grounded in a particular geographic locale, his plays do find their basis in the dynamics of West Coast Japanese American communities. *Song for a Nisei Fisherman* is a paean to a nisei man, in which fishing becomes a metaphor for the varying stages of the man's development. *The Wash* (1990) and *Fish Head Soup* explore intergenerational conflicts within Japanese American families.

The Canadian sansei Rick Shiomi has written plays in various styles and has captured the spirit of Canada's nikkei community. *Yellow Fever* and *Once Is Not Enough* follow the adventures of Japanese Canadian detective Sam Shikaze as he investigates racial tension and witnesses the rebuilding of the Japanese Canadian community in Vancouver. *Uncle Tadao* explores the effects of the war on a Japanese Canadian family and the efforts of Japanese Canadians to obtain monetary compensation for their wartime treatment. Sometimes mixing drama, mystery, and comedy within the same play, Shiomi's style at times hints at the array of postmodern Japanese American writing.

A DIVERSITY OF IDENTITIES: POSTMODERN JAPANESE AMERICAN LITERATURE

Perhaps because the activist writers of the 1970s forged a political and cultural identity as Japanese Americans, postactivist writers can take for granted the validity of writing about their experiences as ethnic

Americans. Although writing from a sense of Japanese American experience and history, postmodern Japanese American writers explore other identities and sympathies that may have little or no overt connection with Japanese American culture or communities. These authors may write from a variety of identities and places or with a sense of rootlessness that characterizes postmodernism in general.

In his book of poetry, *After We Lost Our Way* (1989), winner of a National Poetry Series award, and his memoir, *Turning Japanese* (1991), David Mura, like Hongo, is concerned with connecting his emotions and experiences with those of others with whom he, on the surface, has little in common: an atom bomb survivor, a South African informer, or a Vietnamese immigrant. This ability to identify with the "other" is perhaps best exemplified in a bold series of eleven poems about Pier Paolo Pasolini that is central to *After We Lost Our Way*. In these poems, Mura explores the life of the gay communist filmmaker and writer, sometimes writing in the voice of Pasolini. Mura conveys a postmodern sense of juxtaposition and fluid identity that moves beyond anything geographically or ethnically based.

The novels of Cynthia Kadohata provide another shading to postmodern Japanese American writing. Although the characters in *The Floating World* (1989) and *In the Heart of the Valley of Love* (1992) may have a less fluid sense of identity than that suggested by the eclectic array of Mura's poems, her works convey a sense of rootlessness and randomness. Narrated by a precocious adolescent, *The Floating World* is a picaresque novel chronicling the experiences of Olivia Osaka, her mother and stepfather, three younger brothers, and an irascible grandmother as they travel throughout the United States in the 1950s and 1960s. Kadohata's hypnotic, spare prose style and her cinematic narrative structure enhance the jarring, sometimes surreal situations that fill the book. The junction between the leanness of the writing and the magic of the story results in a consistent feeling of slight disorientation that suggests the work of Gabriel García Marquez and other writers of the magic realist style. Because the nikkei characters that populate *The Floating World* are unconventional, the novel points to the diversity of Japanese American experiences. Kadohata's characters, who engage in premarital sex, behave cruelly and crudely, and speak eloquently, often defy impressions of Japanese Americans as a "model minority." Through her convincing characterizations, Kadohata subtly explodes that myth and reminds readers that there is no one monolithic Japanese American experience.

The playwright Velina Hasu Houston examines the complexities of cross-cultural and cross-racial identities. The daughter of a Japanese woman who married an African American soldier at the end of World War II, Houston gives a voice to postwar Japanese immigrant women (referred to as "war brides") who were often isolated in marriages with American GIs. *Asa Ga Kimashita* depicts the romance between a Japanese woman and an African American in occupied Japan. *Tea* expands upon the theme of cross-cultural identity and explores the lives of four Japanese American "war brides" who gather together after a fifth commits suicide.

Moving beyond the geographic boundaries of the United States and Canada, Karen Tei Yamashita has set her two novels, *Through the Arc of the Rain Forest* (1990) and *Brazil Maru* (1992), in Brazil, the country with the largest Japanese diaspora population. Yamashita lived for ten years in Brazil, where she studied the Japanese community that developed there. *Brazil Maru*, told from the perspective of five characters, is a *Rashamon*-like account of a Japanese commune in Brazil. Although the use of multiple narrators in *Brazil-Maru* hints at postmodernism, *Through the Arc of the Rain Forest* is more indicative of a postmodernist style. A dazzling mixture of magic realism, satire, and futuristic fiction, the novel explores the folly of environmental ruin for short-term gain and the vain attempt to substitute material comfort for spiritual well-being. Through the book's narrator, Yamashita boldly maps out the surreal world of the novel: a small, silver sphere that inexplicably rotates inches from the forehead of one of the novel's heroes, Kazumasa Ishimaru, a Japanese immigrant who amasses a fortune from Brazilian lotteries. *Through the Arc of the Rain Forest* is noteworthy in the history of Japanese American literature because it marks a movement away from the treatment of specifically Japanese American characters toward a stunning blend of genres and characters.

Japanese American identity has been and continues to be complex and multifaceted. The neat demarcations of this chapter are meant merely as guideposts, not as definitive statements on the identities of either individual writers or groups of writers. The interplay among history, politics, and culture has influenced Japanese American identities over time, and the development of distinct nikkei identities has been recorded by three generations of Japanese American authors who have, despite Larry Tajiri's 1949 judgment, created a literature of their own.

■■■■ NOTES

1. Koreans were then under Japanese rule and thus were counted, for immigration purposes, as "Japanese." Few Korean women immigrated in the early twentieth century.
2. I confine my discussion to authors who remained in the United States. Thus, Yone Noguchi, author of at least eight volumes of poetry in English and two

epistolary novels about Japanese domestics in the United States, is not treated here. Noguchi eventually returned to Japan, where he spent the rest of his life.
3. For a full discussion of these concepts, see Harry H. L. Kitano, *Japanese Americans: The Evolution of a Subculture* (Englewood Cliffs, NJ: Prentice-Hall, 1976).
4. An affectionate term for "grandmother."

WORKS CITED

Aiiieeeee!: An Anthology of Asian-American Writers. 1974/1983. Ed. Frank Chin, Jeffrey Paul Chan, Lawson Fusao Inada, Shawn Wong. Washington, D.C.: Howard Univ. Press.
All Aboard. 1944. Topaz, UT: Central Utah Relocation Center.
Ayumi: A Japanese American Anthology. 1980. Ed. Janice Mirikitani. San Francisco: Japanese American Anthology Committee.
Bamboo Ridge: The Hawaii Writers' Quarterly. 1978–. Honolulu: Bamboo Ridge Press.
Bandwagon (magazine). 1949–50. New York.
Cheung, King-Kok. 1993. *Articulate Silences: Hisaye Yamamoto, Maxine Hong Kingston, Joy Kogawa.* Ithaca, NY: Cornell Univ. Press.
Current Life (magazine). October 1940–January 1942. San Francisco.
Editorial. *Kashu Mainichi* (8 May 1932):2.
Gotanda, Philip Kan. 1990. "The Wash." In *Between Worlds: Contemporary Asian-American Plays*, ed. Misha Berson, 30–73. New York: Theatre Communications.
Gyo-Sho: A Magazine of Nisei Literature. c. 1935. Mt. Vernon, IA: Cornell College.
Harada, Margaret. 1960. *The Sun Shines on the Immigrant.* New York: Vantage.
Hartmann, Sadakichi. 1971. *White Chrysanthemums: Literary Fragments and Pronouncements.* Ed. George Knox and Harry Lawton. New York: Herder.
Hokubei Mainichi. San Francisco.
Hongo, Garrett Kaoru. 1982. *Yellow Light.* Middletown, CT: Wesleyan Univ. Press.
———. 1988. *The River of Heaven.* New York: Knopf.
Houston, Jeanne Wakatsuki, and James Houston. 1973. *Farewell to Manzanar.* Boston: Houghton Mifflin.
Houston, Velina Hasu. 1993. "Asa Ga Kimashita" [Morning has broken]. In *The Politics of Life: Four Plays by Asian American Women*, ed. Velina Hasu Houston. Philadelphia: Temple Univ. Press.
Inada, Lawson Fusao. 1971. *Before the War: Poems As They Happened.* New York: Morrow.
———. 1993. *Legends from Camp.* St. Paul, MN: Coffee House Press.
Kadohata, Cynthia. 1989. *The Floating World.* New York: Viking.
———. 1992. *In the Heart of the Valley of Love.* New York: Viking.
Kagawa, Bunichi. 1930. *Hidden Flame.* Stanford, CA: Half Moon Press.
Katayama, Taro. 1933. "Haru." *Reimei*, n.s. 1.3:7–18.
Kikumura, Akemi. 1981. *Through Harsh Winters: The Life of a Japanese Immigrant Woman.* Novato, CA: Chandler and Sharp.
———. 1991. *Promises Kept: The Life of an Issei Man.* Novato, CA: Chandler and Sharp.

Kim, Elaine H. 1982. *Asian American Literature: An Introduction to the Writings and Their Social Context*. Philadelphia: Temple Univ. Press.

Kogawa, Joy. 1982. *Obasan*. Boston: David R. Godine.

Kono, Juliet. 1988. *Hilo Rains*. Honolulu: Bamboo Ridge Press.

League of Nisei Artists and Writers. 1939. Typescript.

Leaves. c. 1932. Los Angeles.

Masumoto, David Mas. 1984. *Silent Strength*. n.p.: New Currents International.

Mirikitani, Janice. 1978. *Awake in the River*. San Francisco: Isthmus Press.

———. 1987. *Shedding Silence*. Berkeley: Celestial Arts.

Miyamoto, Kazuo. 1964. *Hawaii: End of the Rainbow*. Rutland, VT: Bridgeway Press, Charles E. Tuttle.

Mori, Chiye. 1932. "Japanese American." *Kashu Mainichi* 6 Nov. 1932:2.

Mori, Toshio. 1942. "Topaz Station." *Trek*, December 1942, 24ff.

———. 1949/1985. *Yokohama, California*. Intro. by William Saroyan. Caldwell, ID: Caxton. Intro. by Lawson Fusao Inada. Seattle: Univ. of Washington Press.

Mura, David. 1989. *After We Lost Our Way*. New York: Dutton.

———. 1991. *Turning Japanese: Memoirs of a Sansei*. New York: Atlantic Monthly Press.

Murayama, Milton. 1959/1975. *All I Asking For Is My Body*. San Francisco: Supa Press.

Okada, John. 1957/1979. *No-No Boy*. Rutland, VT: Charles E. Tuttle. Intro. by Lawson Fusao Inada. Afterword by Frank Chin. Seattle: Univ. of Washington Press.

Okimoto, Daniel. 1971. *American in Disguise*. New York: Walter-Weatherhill.

Okubo, Mine. 1946/1983. *Citizen 13660*. New York: Columbia Univ. Press. Preface by author. Seattle: Univ. of Washington Press.

Ota, Shelley Ayame Nishimura. 1951. *Upon Their Shoulders*. New York: Exposition Press.

Pacific Citizen. 1930–. Los Angeles.

The Pen. 6 Nov. 1943. Rowher, AK.

Rafu Shimpo. 1903–. Los Angeles.

Reimei. 1931–3. Salt Lake City: Reimei Club.

Sasaki, R. A. 1991. *"The Loom" and Other Stories*. Saint Paul, MN: Greywolf Press.

Sasaki, Yasuo. 1968. *Ascension*. Pasadena: Balconet Press.

———. 1986. *Village Scene/Village Herd*. Cincinnati and Berkeley: Balconet Press.

Scene. c. 1952–5. Place of publication varied.

Schweik, Susan. 1991. *A Gulf So Deeply Cut: American Women Poets and the Second World War*. Madison: Univ. of Wisconsin Press.

Shiomi, R. A. 1982. *Yellow Fever*. In *West Coast Plays* 13–14:1–44. Los Angeles: California Theatre Council.

Sone, Monica. 1953. *Nisei Daughter*. Boston: Little, Brown.

Sugimoto, Etsu Inagaki. 1925. *A Daughter of the Samurai*. Garden City, NY: Doubleday.

Sumida, Stephen H. 1991. *And the View from the Shore: Literary Traditions of Hawai'i*. Seattle: Univ. of Washington Press.

Suyemoto, Toyo. c. 1935. "Improvident." In *Gyo-Sho: A Magazine of Nisei Literature*. Mt. Vernon, IA: Cornell College.

————. 1942. "Gain." *Trek*, December 1942, 7.

Tajiri, Larry. 1949. "Nisei U.S.A.: Notes on Nisei Writing." *Pacific Citizen* 9 April 1949.

Trek. 1943–4. Topaz: Cental Utah Relocation Center.

Tulean Dispatch Magazine. 1942–3. Newell, CA: *Daily Tulean Dispatch*.

Uchida, Yoshiko. 1982. *Desert Exile: The Uprooting of a Japanese American Family*. Seattle: Univ. of Washington Press.

Watanabe, Sylvia. 1992. *Talking to the Dead*. New York: Doubleday.

Yamada, Mitsuye. 1976. *"Camp Notes" and Other Poems*. San Lorenzo, CA: Shameless Hussy Press.

————. 1988. *Desert Run: Poems and Stories*. Latham, NY: Kitchen Table, Women of Color Press.

Yamamoto, Hisaye. 1976. "Writing." *Amerasia Journal* 3.2:126–33.

————. 1988. *"Seventeen Syllables" and Other Stories*. Latham, NY: Kitchen Table, Women of Color Press.

Yamashita, Karen Tei. 1990. *Through the Arc of the Rain Forest*. Minneapolis: Coffee House Press.

————. 1992. *Brazil Maru*. Minneapolis: Coffee House Press.

Yamauchi, Wakako. 1974/1983. "And the Soul Shall Dance." In *Aiiieeeee!: An Anthology of Asian-American Writers*, ed. Frank Chin, Jeffrey Paul Chan, Lawson Fusao Inada, Shawn Wong, 193–200. Washington, D.C.: Howard Univ. Press.

————. 1982/90. *And the Soul Shall Dance*. In *West Coast Plays* 11–12:117–64. Reprinted in *Between Worlds: Contemporary Asian-American Plays*, ed. Misha Berson, 128–74. New York: Theatre Communications.

■■■■ **SELECTED BIBLIOGRAPHY**

Anthologies/Journals/Magazines

Fusion '83: A Japanese American Anthology. 1984. Ed. James K. Okutsu. San Francisco: Asian American Studies Dept., San Francisco State Univ.

Fusion-San. 1986. Ed. James K. Okutsu. San Francisco: Asian American Studies Dept., San Francisco State Univ.

Fusion Too: A Japanese American Anthology. 1985. Ed. James K. Okutsu. San Francisco: Asian American Studies Dept., San Francisco State Univ.

The Hawk's Well: A Collection of Japanese American Art and Literature. 1986. San Jose, CA: Asian American Art Projects.

Paper Doors: An Anthology of Japanese-Canadian Poetry. 1981. Toronto: Coach House.

Yoisho: An Anthology of the Japantown Arts and Media Workshop. 1983. San Francisco: Japantown Art and Media Workshop.

Prose

Hartmann, [Carl] Sadakichi. 1908. *Schopenhauer in the Air: Twelve Stories*. Rochester, NY: Stylus Publishing.

————. 1915. *Permanent Peace: Is It a Dream?* New York: G. Bruno.

Hongo, Bob Nobuyuki. 1958. *Hey, Pineapple!* Tokyo: Hokuseido Press.

Hongo, Garrett. 1995. *Volcano: A Memoir of Hawai'i.* New York: Knopf.

Houston, Jeanne Wakatsuki. 1985. *Beyond Manzanar: Views of Asian American Womanhood.* Santa Barbara, CA: Capra Press.

Jelsma, Clara Mitsuko. 1981. *Teapot Tales.* Honolulu: Bamboo Ridge Press.

Kanazawa, Tooru. 1989. *Sushi and Sourdough.* Seattle: Univ. of Washington Press.

Masumoto, David Mas. 1995. *Epitaph for a Peach: Four Seasons on My Family Farm.* San Francisco: Harper San Francisco.

Miyakawa, Edward. 1979. *Tule Lake.* Waldport, OR: House by the Sea.

Miyamoto, Kazuo. 1957. *A Nisei Discovers Japan.* Tokyo: Japan Times Press.

Mori, Kyoko. 1993. *Shizuko's Daughter.* New York: Henry Holt.

———. 1995. *The Dream of Water: A Memoir.* New York: Henry Holt.

Mori, Toshio. 1979a. *"The Chauvinist" and Other Stories.* Intro. Hisaye Yamamoto. Los Angeles: Asian American Studies Center, Univ. of California.

———. 1979b. *Woman from Hiroshima.* San Francisco: Isthmus Press.

Nunes, Susan. 1982. *"A Small Obligation" and Other Stories.* Special issue of *Bamboo Ridge: The Hawaii Writer's Quarterly* 16.

Saiki, Patsy Sumie. 1977. *Sachie: A Daughter of Hawaii.* Honolulu: Kisaku.

Shirota, Jon. 1965. *Lucky Come Hawaii.* New York: Bantam.

———. 1972. *Pineapple White.* Los Angeles: Ohara Publications.

Sugimoto, Etsu Inagaki. 1932/1968. *A Daughter of the Narikin.* Garden City, NY: Doubleday; Rutland, VT: Charles E. Tuttle.

———. 1935. *A Daughter of the Nohfu.* Garden City, NY: Doubleday.

———. 1940. *Grandmother O Kyo.* New York: Doubleday.

Tamagawa, Kathleen Eldridge. 1932. *Holy Prayers in a Horse's Ear.* New York: Ray Long and Richard R. Smith.

Uchida, Yoshiko. 1987. *Picture Bride: A Novel.* Flagstaff, AZ: Northland Press.

Yamauchi, Wakako. 1994. *Songs My Mother Taught Me.* New York: Feminist Press.

Yashima, Taro [Jun Atushi Iwamatsu]. 1943. *The New Sun.* New York: Henry Holt.

———. 1947. *Horizon Is Calling.* New York: Henry Holt.

Poetry

Ai. 1973. *Cruelty.* Boston: Houghton Mifflin.

———. 1979. *Killing Floor.* Boston: Houghton Mifflin.

———. 1981. *Conversations: For Robert Lowell.* Saint Paul, MN. Printed at the Toothpaste Press for Bookslinger.

———. 1986. *Sin: Poems.* Boston: Houghton Mifflin.

———. 1987. *Cruelty/Killing Floor.* Foreword by Carolyn Forche. New York: Thunder's Mouth Press.

Foster, Sesshu. 1987. *Angry Days.* Los Angeles: West End Press.

Furuta, Soichi. 1980. *To Breathe.* Westbury, NY: Edition Heliodor.

Hahn, Kimiko. 1989. *Air Pocket.* Brooklyn, NY: Hanging Loose Press.

———. 1992. *Earshot.* Brooklyn, NY: Hanging Loose Press.

Hartman, Yuki. 1970. *A One of Me.* Fenesis, NY: Grasp Press.

———. 1976. *Hot Footsteps.* New York: Telephone Books.

———. 1980. *Red Rice: Poems.* Putnam Valley, NY: Swollen Magpie.

———. 1984. *Ping.* New York: Kulchar Foundation.

Hartmann, [Carl] Sadakichi. 1913/1916. *My Rubáiyyát*. St. Louis, MO: Mangan Printing. New York: G. Bruno.
——. 1915. *Tanka and Haiku: 14 Japanese Rhythms*. New York: G. Bruno.
——. 1925. *Naked Ghosts: Four Poems*. South Pasadena, CA: Fantasia.
Ikeda, Patricia Y. 1978. *House of Wood, House of Salt*. Cleveland, OH: Cleveland State Univ. Press.
Imura, Ernest Sakayuki. 1976. *Sunrise-Sunset: A Continuous Cycle of Living*. New York: Vantage.
Kakugawa, Frances. 1970. *Sand Grains*. San Antonio, TX: Naylor.
——. 1971. *Winter Ginger Blossom*. San Antonio, TX: Naylor.
——. 1976a. *Golden Spike*. San Antonio, TX: Naylor.
——. 1976b. *Path of Butterflies*. San Antonio, TX: Naylor.
Kaneko, Lonny. 1986. *Coming Home from Camp*. Waldron Island, WA: Brooding Heron Press.
Kiyooka, Roy. 1964. *Kyoto Airs*. Vancouver: Periwinkle Press.
——. 1967. *Nevertheless These Eyes*. Toronto: Coach House.
——. 1975. *Transcanada Letters*. Vancouver: Talonbooks.
——. 1977. *The Fountainebleau Dream Machine: 18 Frames from a Book of Rhetoric*. Toronto: Coach House.
——. 1982. *Wheels*. Toronto: Coach House.
Kogawa, Joy. 1968. *The Splintered Moon*. Fredericton, N.B.: Fiddlehead Poetry Books.
——. 1974. *A Choice of Dreams*. Toronto: McClelland & Steward.
——. 1977. *Jerico Road*. Toronto: McClelland & Steward.
——. 1985. *Woman in the Woods*. Tucson, AZ: Mosaic Press.
Kudaka, Geraldine. 1979. *Numerous Avalanches at the Point of Intersection*. Greenfield Center, NY: Greenfield Review Press.
Matsueda, Pat. 1985. *The Fishcatcher*. Honolulu: Petronium Press.
Mitsui, James [Masao]. 1974. *Journal of the Sun*. Port Townsend, WA: Copper Canyon Press.
——. 1975. *Crossing the Phantom River*. Port Townsend, WA: Graywolf Press.
——. 1985. *After the Long Train*. Minneapolis: Bieler Press.
Mori, Kyoko. 1994. *Fallout*. Chicago: Tia Chucha Press.
Mura, David. 1995. *The Colors of Desire*. New York: Anchor Books.
Noda, Barbara. 1979. *Strawberries*. Berkeley: Shameless Hussy Press.
Oka, Francis Naohiko. 1970. *Poems: Memorial Edition*. San Francisco: City Lights.
Sakaki, Nanao. 1966. *Bellyfulls*. Eugene, OR: Toad Press.
——. 1983. *Real Play: Poetry and Drama*. San Juan Pueblo, NM: Tooth of Time Books.
Shikatani, Gerry. 1973. *Barking of Dog*. Toronto: Missing Link Press.
——. 1975. *Haliburton*. Toronto: Missing Link Press.
——. 1978. *Ship Sands Island*. Toronto: Ganglia Press.
——. 1985. *A Sparrow's Food*. Toronto: Coach House.
Tanaka, Ronald. 1981. *The Shino Suite*. Greenfield Center, NY: Greenfield Review Press.
Tsuda, Margaret. 1972. *Cry Love Aloud*. New York: Poetica Press.
——. 1976. *Urban River*. Newark, NJ: Discovery Books.

Yasuda, Kenneth [under pseud. Shosun]. 1947. *A Pepper-Pod: Classic Japanese Poems together with Original Haiku*. Foreword by John Gould Fletcher. New York: Knopf.

Drama

Gotanda, Philip Kan. 1983. *The Dream of Kitamura*. In *West Coast Plays* 15–16:191–223.

———. 1995. *Fish Head Soup and Other Plays*. Seattle: Univ. of Washington Press.

Hartmann, [Carl] Sadakichi. 1971. *Buddha, Confucius, Christ: Three Prophetic Plays*. Ed. Harry Lawton and George Knox. New York: Herder.

Secondary Sources

Cheung, King-Kok. 1991. "Double-Telling: Intertextual Silence in Hisaye Yamamoto's Fiction." *American Literary History* 3.2:277–93.

———. 1991–2. "Thrice Muted Tale: Interplay of Art and Politics in Hisaye Yamamoto's 'The Legend of Miss Sasagawara.'" *MELUS* 17.3:109–25.

Chua, Cheng Lok. 1992. "Witnessing the Japanese Canadian Experience in World War II: Processual Structure, Symbolism, and Irony in Joy Kogawa's *Obasan*." In Lim and Ling, 97–108.

Crow, Charles. 1984. "Home and Transcendence in Los Angeles Fiction." In *Los Angeles in Fiction: A Collection of Original Essays*, ed. David Fine, 189–205. Albuquerque: Univ. of New Mexico Press.

———. 1986. "The *Issei* Father in the Fiction of Hisaye Yamamoto." In *Opening Up Literary Criticism: Essays on American Prose and Poetry*, ed. Leo Truchlar, 34–40. Salzburg: Verlag Wolfgang Neugebauer.

Fujita, Gayle Kimi. 1985. "'To attend the sound of stone': The Sensibility of Silence in *Obasan*." *MELUS* 12.3:33–42.

———. 1986. "The 'Ceremonial Self' in Japanese American Literature." Ph.D. diss., Brown Univ.

Gottlieb, Erika. 1986. "The Riddle of Concentric Worlds in *Obasan*." *Canadian Literature* 109:34–53.

Inada, Lawson Fusao. 1976. "The Vision of America in John Okada's *No-No Boy*." In *Ethnic Literatures since 1776: The Many Voices of America*, ed. Wolodymyr T. Zyla and Wendell M. Aycock, 275–87. Lubbock, TX: Texas Tech. Univ.

———. 1982. "Of Place and Displacement: The Range of Japanese American Literature." In *Three American Literatures: Essays in Chicano, Native American, and Asian American Literature for Teachers of American Literature*, ed. Houston A. Baker, Jr., intro. by Walter J. Ong.

Lim, Shirley Geok-lin. 1990. "Japanese American Women's Life Stories: Maternality in Monica Sone's *Nisei Daughter* and Joy Kogawa's *Obasan*." *Feminist Studies* 16.2:289–311.

Lim, Shirley Geok-lin, and Amy Ling, eds. 1992. *Reading the Literatures of Asian America*. Philadelphia: Temple Univ. Press.

McDonald, Dorothy Ritsuko. 1979. "After Imprisonment: Ichiro's Search for Redemption in *No-No Boy*." *MELUS* 6.3:19–26.

McDonald, Dorothy Ritsuko, and Katharine Newman. 1980. "Relocation and

Dislocation: The Writings of Hisaye Yamamoto and Wakako Yamauchi."
MELUS 7.3:21–38.

Matsumoto, Valerie. 1987. "Desperately Seeing 'Dierdre': Gender Roles,
Multicultural Relations, and Nisei Women Writers of the 1930s." *Frontiers*
12.1:19–32.

St. Andrews, B. A. 1986. "Reclaiming a Canadian Heritage: Kogawa's *Obasan*."
International Fiction Review 13.1:29–31.

Sato, Gayle K. Fujita. 1992. "Momotaro's Exile: John Okada's *No-No Boy*." In Lim
and Ling, 239–58.

Schweik, Susan. 1989. "The Pre-Poetics of Internment: The Case of Toyo
Suyemoto." *American Literary History* 1.1:89–109.

Sumida, Stephen H. 1989. "Japanese American Moral Dilemmas in John Okada's
No-No Boy and Milton Murayama's *All I Asking for Is My Body*." In *Frontiers of
Asian American Studies: Writing, Research, and Commentary*, ed. Gail M.
Nomura, Russell Endo, Stephen H. Sumida, and Russell C. Leong, 222–33.
Pullman: Washington State Univ. Press.

Willis, Gary. 1987. "Speaking the Silence: Joy Kogawa's *Obasan*." *Studies in Canadian Literature* 12.2:239–49.

Wilson, Rob. 1981. "The Languages of Confinement and Liberation in Milton
Murayama's *All I Asking for Is My Body*." In *Writers of Hawaii: A Focus on Our
Literary Heritage*, ed. Eric Chock and Jody Manabe, 62–5. Honolulu: Hawaii
Committee for the Humanities and the Hawaii Foundation for the Arts.

Yogi, Stan. 1989. "Legacies Revealed: Uncovering Buried Plots in the Stories of
Hisaye Yamamoto." *Studies in American Fiction* 17.2:169–81.

———. 1992. "Rebels and Heroines: Subversive Narratives in the Stories of
Wakako Yamauchi and Hisaye Yamamoto." In Lim and Ling, 131–50.

4

KOREAN AMERICAN LITERATURE

ELAINE H. KIM

Published works written in English by Korean Americans are relatively few and were mostly brought to press after 1980. In terms of place and period, Korean American writers emerge from several distinctly identifiable groups: foreign students and political exiles who came to the United States between the early part of the century and the mid-1960s; children and grandchildren of immigrants to Hawai'i between 1903 and 1905, when sugar planters launched an intense though short-lived campaign to recruit Korean plantation labor; children of immigrant farm and cannery workers in California and on the Pacific Coast in the early decades of this century; and children of the post-1968 immigrants, whose presence in America was made possible by changes in U.S. immigration quotas in 1965.

Almost entirely missing from this modest array of inscriptions are writings, either originally in English or translated from Korean, by the early laboring immigrants themselves, by more recent Korean-speaking immigrant workers and small-business operators, or by the tens of thousands of women who immigrated as wives of U.S. servicemen.[1] Many Korean American viewpoints are represented only through the filtering memories of an English-speaking descendant or the modifying lens of a writer's class privilege. The voices of the "mainstream" or majority of Korean Americans have thus been faint and mediated. Of course, the phenomenon of the privileged few speaking for the many is in no way unique to Korean Americans. Racial minority immigrants in the United States are often spoken for by English-speaking people from both their own group and the dominant culture. Further, given the context of power and race relations, questions of the authenticity and representativeness of Korean American inscriptions have assumed particular significance – in the dominant culture, where Koreans are often viewed as "all alike," and in the ethnic community as part of an essentialist defense.

The perspectives of the immigrants' English-speaking children should not be dismissed out of hand as just an outcome of the privileging of English over Korean. Fascination almost to the point of obsession with the immigrants' stories is shared by many English-speaking Asian American writers, but at the same time the storyteller is usually much more than a mere ethnographer or ethnic informant. I have noticed that many readers of Jeanne Wakatsuki Houston's *Farewell to Manzanar* and Amy Tan's *The Joy Luck Club* are so eager to explore the more exotic experiences of the issei father or the China-born mothers that they pay little heed to the daughters' subjectivities. Readers of Asian American works like Maxine Hong Kingston's *The Woman Warrior* or Jessica Hagedorn's *Dogeaters* should pay as close attention to the "viewer" as to the "view," noticing exactly where and when she/he enters.

Korean Americans share space not only with Koreans on other continents and with other Asian Americans, but also with other Americans of color and other ethnic groups that were constituted through immigration to a new land.[2] At the same time, Korean Americans are as unique as other groups, because their experiences are all rooted in specific historical and sociopolitical circumstances. Although Korean American literature is not wholly determined by these circumstances, it emerges from the dialectical interplay between social forces and cultural production, which continually alters its boundaries and contours. The resulting shifts and reconfigurations are particularly dramatic currently, because of rapid growth and change in Korean American communities stemming from shifting sociopolitical circumstances in the United States, Korea, and the world, especially during the last twenty-five years. Thus, Korean American cultural expressions, which have been comparatively few until now, can be expected to grow quickly and become increasingly heterogeneous, just like the population itself, especially as the children of post-1965 Korean immigrants to the United States grow into their artistry. No doubt we can also expect the accelerated breakdown of the old East/West, American/Korean, and immigrant foreigner/(civilized) citizen binaries that circumscribed the reading of many early Korean American writers.

Historically, Korean Americans, like other Asian Americans, were materially and discursively excluded from the mainstream of U.S. American life, denied subjectivity, and defined according to the degree of threat they were thought to pose to the dominant culture at particular points in time (see Kim, 1986). The earliest Korean American writing emerged from the context of a century and a half of persistent and deeply rooted racist inscriptions of Asians in both official and mass culture as grotesquely alien "others." Pressed to demonstrate the falseness of these representations, early Korean and other Asian American writers often attempted to present the "true story," sometimes by showing how Asian Americans could become successfully "Westernized" or "Americanized." For writers who had to fight even to establish themselves as discursive subjects, dealing with subtleties, hybridities, paradoxes, and layers must have seemed impossibly luxurious.

Although Korean American writing emerges from conditions shared by other Asian American groups, it is also rooted in the particularities of Korean American social history. The size of the Korean American population was until recently only a fraction of that of the severely restricted Chinese and Japanese populations.[3] Thus, unlike these other Asian American groups, Korean American communities have been dominated by successive groups of immigrants, which helps explain the relatively small number of published Korean American writings in English until quite recently.[4] The double impact of U.S. racial discrimination and Japan's colonization of Korea effectively limited the growth of Korean American communities for six decades. Political and economic development of Korean American communities was also impeded by the "double colonization" of Korean immigrants, who could not look to their homeland as a source of merchandise for trade or for diplomatic assistance as other immigrants in the United States traditionally did, with varying degrees of success. Long after the Japanese occupation was formally ended in 1945, Korean American writing continued to express the particular anguish of the exile deprived even of the sustaining illusion of a triumphant return "home" after a life of toil in a country where she/he felt hated. Korean American writers from New Il-han, Younghill Kang, and Richard Kim to Ronyoung Kim, Theresa Hak Kyung Cha, and Sook Nyul Choi grapple in different ways with the effects of Japanese colonization on Koreans and Korean Americans. Only now, half a century after World War II, has this concern begun to become muted in Korean American writing, which can be expected to address an ever-increasing array of other themes.

I

The early Korean American literary voice is largely autobiographical and speaks primarily from the perspectives of members of an elite class of educated, nonlaboring immigrants.[5] The best known of these early writers is Younghill Kang (1903–72), a pioneer of Korean American writing.[6] Kang arrived in the United States in 1921, just three years prior to the enactment of laws that excluded Korean immigrants for more than three decades. Thus, he was one of a very small number of Korean intellectuals who settled in America before the quotas were revised in 1965. The protagonist in both of Kang's novels, Chung-pa (meaning "blue wave" and possibly even "green [young?] hill") Han, is imprisoned briefly by the Japanese after his peripheral participation in the widespread *Sam Il Oondong*.[7] This experience only reinforces his desire to flee his country. Wishing to "escape death and torture if possible and come to America," Han concludes that the "ancient . . . spiritual planet that had been [his] father's home," old Korea, with its "curved lines, its brilliant colors, its haunting music, its own magic of being" was becoming a wasteland unable to sustain its young. "In loathing of death," Han is pulled as if by "natural gravity" toward the younger, more vital cultures of the West.

As a pioneer Korean writer in English, Kang came to represent Korea and Koreans to Western readers, for whom he was both purveyor of the unfamiliar in terms of a faraway Oriental nation and reinforcer of the familiar in terms of popular notions about backward peoples yearning for the light of the West. Whereas Kang's first novel describes the narrator's life in Korea before his emigration to the West, the second is a narrative about the lives of exiled Korean intellectuals in the urban United States during the 1920s and 1930s. Kang himself considered the second book more important than the first, "more mature in style and technique" as well as more highly developed in content. "*The Grass Roof* may be said to have been written in the mood of the Everlasting Nay of Carlyle; *East Goes West* may be compared to the mood of the Everlasting Yea" (Kunitz 1955, 744).[8] However, *The Grass Roof* attracted more critical attention. Reviewers may have preferred the more exotic earlier book, which is set entirely in Korea, because *East Goes West* presents an unflattering view of the underside of American life from the perspectives of people locked out by the color bar. Even so, despite its stories of rejection, brutality, loneliness, and hunger, many reviewers of *East Goes West* read the book as an Asian American "success story," perhaps because the stories are often presented humorously and because the protagonist, Chung-pa Han, never relinquishes his hope of one day finding acceptance in American life. This reading, in my view, misses the deftness with which Kang satirizes both the misguided optimism and naiveté of his characters and the arrogance and ignorance of the Americans who reject them.[9]

East Goes West brushes U.S. history against the grain to reveal moments in the lives of those otherwise invisible to U.S. American readers – in this case, Korean exiles in the 1920s and 1930s. Their work, their aspirations, and their absolute exclusion from American social and intellectual life are the subject. Instead of taking the reader on an immigrant's journey from penniless foreigner to successful citizen, Kang's book calls into question U.S. American nationalist narratives of progress, equality, assimilation, and upward mobility with his portrait of Korean immigrants' endless wandering. The three major characters fail to achieve their

American dream. Park, the patriot, is stranded in America, working as a domestic servant and dreaming of an impossible return to his colonized homeland. Jum, the gadfly, tries to be American in his stylish clothes that he wears to Harlem nightclubs, but in the end admits, "I have not failed; I have only not succeeded." Kim, the aristocrat in exile, fails to gain access to American high culture and commits suicide when the American woman he loves is forcibly separated from him by her parents. The narrator, Han, finds no entry into American life: reading Shakespeare in unheated rooms, he can think only of food, and the young American woman he so eagerly hopes to befriend moves away, leaving no forwarding address. Hoping to impress his new employers with his Western learning, Han scrambles to pick up scattered volumes of secondhand English classics as he struggles with his suitcases. The Americans, however, are interested in him only as a docile servant. Far from being impressed by his erudition, they simply fear that the books might be contaminated with "Oriental" germs. *East Goes West* ends with Han's dream of being locked in a dark cellar with some blacks, as torch-bearing white men are about to set them all on fire. His only hope is a Buddhist interpretation of the dream: that he will be reincarnated to a better life.

Originally interested in science, Kang reportedly felt compelled to write because he could not find what he wanted to be said expressed anywhere. Two generations later, another young Korean intellectual who immigrated to the United States and earned a name for himself as a writer of novels in English felt compelled to write for similar reasons.

Richard E(un Kook) Kim was born in Kang's native place, Hamheung, in northern Korea in 1932.[10] The grandson of a Christian minister and the son of a landowner, Kim fled south with his family before the Korean War. He had just begun studying at Seoul National University when the war broke out. He escaped to Inchon, where he hid until he was able to join the U.N. forces. From 1950 to 1954, he served in the South Korean military. Kim's sensibilities were no doubt shaped by the four years he spent, between the ages of eighteen and twenty-two, immersed in the extraordinary circumstances of a war that burned its indelible mark into the memories of millions of Koreans.

Partly for relief from those circumstances, Kim accepted an opportunity to go to the United States in 1954 to study at Middlebury College, fully intending to return to Korea to live and work, perhaps even in the military, which he believed would play a critical role in Korea's political and economic future.[11] It was at Middlebury, studying history and political philosophy, that he began to wonder, "Where do *I* come in?" (Engle 1954, 35). A few years later, as a student in the University of Iowa writing program, he wrote his first novel, *The Martyred* (1964).

Set in the North Korean capital of Pyongyang during the Korean conflict, *The Martyred* explores the human conscience and the meanings of evil, suffering, and truth. The narrator, Captain Lee, has been sent by Colonel Chang of South Korean Army Intelligence to investigate the deaths of twelve Christian ministers reportedly killed by the Communists. Suspecting that one of the two surviving ministers, Reverend Shin, betrayed the others, Chang hopes to obtain a confession that will clear Shin's conscience and then present all of the ministers as martyrs, thus discrediting the Communists and shoring up the Korean Christians' support for the war effort. It turns out that the other ministers died "like dogs," pleading for mercy. Shin was spared because he was the only one of the ministers who did not grovel and recant his faith. Instead of telling the truth, however, Shin confesses that he betrayed the others to save his own life. The believers forgive him and flock to hear his sermons. Although he does not believe in God or in justice, Shin passionately preaches illusion because of his love for others whose weakness renders them unable to bear the truth – that there might be nothing beyond "death, inexorable death."

Kim's affinities with Western existentialist thinkers and with writers of unembellished prose, along with his choice of theme in the Cold War days before the full-blown United States involvement in Vietnam, may have helped to assure his success in the West in the early 1960s.[12] Few first novels have met with the critical success of *The Martyred*, which remained on the nation's best-seller lists for twenty consecutive weeks and was translated into ten languages. The book remains the only work by an Asian American ever nominated for a Nobel Prize for literature. Stories about the young immigrant from Korea appeared in *Newsweek* and *Life* magazines.[13] Literally overnight, Richard Kim became one of the best-known Koreans in the West, which in turn assured his fame in South Korea as well.[14] Pearl Buck, whom Younghill Kang suggested had eclipsed him three decades earlier, wrote a promotional statement for Richard Kim.

While the issues dealt with in *The Martyred* brought Kim critical and popular success in 1964, his second novel, *The Innocent* (1968), was panned. It focuses on the events surrounding a military coup d'état in South Korea. The characters are all male army officers who learn the dangers of soft-hearted emotionalism and discover that at times one is forced to do evil deeds in order to be truly moral. The book was published at the height of popular resistance to the U.S. involvement in the Vietnam War. Few critics found convincing the portrayal of South Korean military men as decent, moral leaders struggling to save their country from corruption and communism. The primary defenders of the book were rightists, who asserted that the book was "garotted, clubbed, shot in the back of the head, drawn, quartered and pushed over a high cliff" by the liberal book-review establishment because of its negative depiction of soft-headed liberalism and because it presents "a disturbing essay on the Asian mind and spirit" at the very moment when U.S. intellectuals were grop-ing to make sense of the actions of the South Vietnamese military (Nichols 1969, 183).

Kim contends that *The Innocent* was written not for Americans but for South Korean readers. "I wanted to show that you have to be prepared to die for your cause. You may have to kill people, but in the end you will have to pay; when you destroy others, you have to be prepared to be destroyed yourself," he has said.

> In a poor and backward country like Korea was at the time, the military may be the only instrument or institution of modernization. I had a lot of affection for the military. Almost everyone in the country was in it. Country boys learned how to drive cars and operate machinery in the military. The military had a certain role to play, and I wanted to be part of that. There was no other organiza-tion that could have matched the military in terms of organizational skills, discipline, and expertise. But military leaders, it turns out, were not prepared to sacrifice themselves. Power corrupts. They could not resist the accoutrements of power. (interview, 17 October 1993)

Despite the author's insistence that *The Innocent* was not about the 1962 military coup but rather about universal human problems and ethical and moral issues, many South Korean readers saw the book and its author as siding with the military, which was becoming more and more notorious for its excesses, abuses, and brutal repression of citizens. Certainly the South Korean officials enjoyed representing Kim as a friend of the mili-tary government.

Kim's third book, *Lost Names: Scenes from a Korean Boyhood*, was published in 1970. The title refers to the Japanese practice of requiring Koreans to cast off their Korean names and adopt Japanese ones. The book is an autobiographical narrative about Kim's boyhood years in Korea during the Japanese occupation, with emphasis on the anti-Japanese activities of son and father. When *Lost Names* was translated into Korean, it was given the title *Bbaekun Irum* (Forcibly seized or Confiscated names) instead of the name Kim preferred, *Iloborin Irum* (Lost names).

> Koreans have lost so much. Things have been taken away, but we have also lost things ourselves. In Korea, we are always exhorted to rail against the bad guys who take things away. But did we do

something dumb ourselves that feeds into our loss? In *Lost Names*, there are Japanese atrocities; but there are also Korean collaborators. My grandfather used to say that he shed no tears over the demise of the Korean royalty because they were rotten through and through; he just felt sorry that it had to be Japanese and not Koreans who got rid of them. (interview, 17 October 1993)

Perhaps discouraged by what seemed to be U.S. readers' lack of interest in Korea and Koreans, and by Korean readers' desire for a "good guy versus bad guy" theme, Kim has turned in recent years to translation and South Korean television documentary work.[15] In Korea in 1989, he published a book of photographs and text, *In Search of "Lost" Koreans in China and Russia*. Rather than writing fiction about Korean Americans, from whom he feels estranged because he has never actively participated in Korean American community affairs, or about contemporary Korea, which he believes is the task of young writers "in it right now," Kim wants to focus on another place, another time: "I never intended to be a writer; I wanted to be a student of history. I am obsessed with the past, with all the things we have lost. I want to remember them, to record them, to think about them."[16]

During the past half-century, a succession of first-generation Korean intellectuals immigrated to the United States, beginning with a small number of political exiles who arrived shortly after Japan's annexation of Korea and continuing with several thousand foreign students who arrived after the exclusion of laboring immigrants from Asia in 1924, and increasing greatly when U.S. immigration policies strongly favored educated Asian immigrant professionals and technicians in the early to mid-1970s. Korean immigrant intellectuals have produced relatively few literary works in English. Korean American writings in Korean can be found in three issues of the journal *Jip'yongsun* (Horizon), which were published between 1973 and 1976, and the *Miju Hankuk Munihyophoe* (Koreans in America literary association)–sponsored journal, *Mijumunhak* (Korean American literature), which produced four issues between 1981 and 1985. Homeland political debates caused tensions among the editors of the two journals. *Mijumunhak* received support from the government of the South Korean president, military strongman Chun Doo Hwan, who came to power in 1980 with the bloody suppression of widespread citizens' demand for democratic elections and constitutional reforms. Saying that they wished for a clear separation between the realms of literature and "politics," those who had produced *Jip'yongsun* did not work with the editors of *Mijumunhak*. Several more recent attempts to bring forth Korean American writings in Korean include two volumes of *Chaemi Si-in Jakp'umjip* (Collected Korean American poetry, 1989 and

1990), published by the Los Angeles–based Korean Poets Association of America, and a 1988 issue of *Munhaksegye* (The literary realm 1, no. 1, Spring 1988), which also includes some poetry and short stories in English.

According to poet Ch'oe Yun-hong, Korean American literature could extend the reach of Korean literature were it not for Koreans' lack of sympathy for or interest in Korean Americans (Y. Ch'oe 1989, 64). Some scholars of Korean literature think that *iminmunhak* (Korean immigrant literature) about life in the United States should be written in English. Thus, it could be thought of as Korean, U.S. American, and "world" literature. They believe that Korean immigrant literature should attempt to win sympathy and understanding from non-Koreans. Further, it should be written by writers who live in the "dirt" of the United States and can thus actually feel and not just imagine being "dirty" from U.S. life. "It would not be *iminmunhak* if it just depicts a love affair with America," they contend (T. Ch'oe et al. 1989, 4–44).

Asserting that the harshness of the immigrants' lives in the United States has intensified their "desire for poetry," Ch'oe Yun-hong argues that immigrant writing ought to address "the 800,000 Korean Americans who are lonely and facing many hardships" and should therefore be "warm and soft, like a mother's hand, not so abstract as easy to read, imparting a sense of peace." Separating the "emotional" or "artistic" aspects of literature from the "sociological," Ch'oe asserts that the immigrants cannot be "literary" because their lives are too stressful and filled with suffering, adding that if they could really write about their immigrant lives, they would win the Pulitzer Prize (Y. Ch'oe 1989, 64). Indeed, Korean immigrant writers in English are few and tend to be not recent immigrants but people who came to the United States as students and have lived in this country for decades. Their work generally focuses not on immigrant life but on memories of Korea, which casts its long shadow over their lives in the West.

One fairly recent Korean immigrant writer in English is Ty (T'ae Young) Pak. *Guilt Payment*, his collection of short stories, was published in Hawai'i in 1983. Born in Korea in 1938, Ty Pak earned a degree in law at Seoul National University and worked as a journalist for *The Korean Republic* and *The Korea Times* before coming to the United States as a foreign student in 1965. He completed a Ph.D. in English at Bowling Green State University and began teaching English at the University of Hawai'i in 1970. In the late 1980s, Pak left Hawai'i to try his hand at small business on the mainland.

The most compelling stories in *Guilt Payment* highlight the incongruity of the immigrant's Korean American life with his Korean past. In the title story, the narrator is a middle-aged college teacher living an ostensibly ordinary life in Honolulu. From looking at or talking with him, no one, not even his own daughter, would be able to imagine what he has been through – no one, that is, except fellow Korean immigrants of a similar age. The immigrant father, now safely ensconced in a middle-class suburb, is tyrannized by his petulant daughter, who wants him to pay for an expensive musical education in Italy. She invokes her dead mother, which triggers his memories of the war. The father recalls the terror and violence of his past experiences, remembering vividly how he wanted to run away and save himself when his baby daughter's crying threatened to disclose his hiding place to enemy soldiers. His wife, who refused to leave the baby, was killed, but both he and the baby survived to live in another world, in another era. Now the howling baby has grown into a spoiled and demanding daughter who has no idea what makes her father give in.

Younghill Kang's world is an immigrant "bachelor society" and Richard Kim's is an exclusively male military world. Like Kim and many other men of that generation in Korea, Pak's view of the world may have been deeply affected by his war experiences. The stories in *Guilt Payment* are mostly male-centered war and adventure stories. Pak's female characters are often described as seductive objects of male desire. Many are cast as female avengers, returning now, perhaps, to exact a price for male insensitivity and selfishness; portrayed as shrieking shrews, shamans possessed by spirits, and frightening vampires. In story after story, Pak imagines the woman's body raped, tortured, maimed, and mutilated. The wife in "Guilt Payment" dies with the jagged end of a beam "rammed through her chest" (17). In "Possession Sickness," George's wife, Moonhee, is unable to pass stool for a week, so that "[h]er clammy skin oozed and stank" (24). After she is possessed by spirits, a crowd gathers to spit and throw stones at her, knocking her to the ground, bleeding. In "A Second Chance," the protagonist embraces a casual lover so hard that her bones "crackle" as she moans "in pained delight" (117). Faced with a woman offering her body in exchange for her husband's freedom, this man thinks of her as "inert and yielding, like a lump of mud." Then he recalls "the body of a woman he'd seen near Hwachon with a stick driven up her vagina, half submerged in a swampy rice paddy and festooned with a ring of floating feces" (122). Though some readers might find Pak's action-oriented stories exciting, others might find the vividness of the accounts compromised by their various manifestations of misogyny.

In contrast with Korean male writers, many of whom accept the subordination of women as natural and even desirable, is immigrant woman writer Sook Nyul Choi. Younghill Kang's work suggests the effects Japanese colonization had on Koreans and Korean Americans. The sensibilities of Richard Kim and Ty Pak were no doubt forged by their experiences of both Japanese occupation and the Korean War. But these immigrant male writers make little or no mention of the fate of women under Japanese rule, and their war stories either omit women or objectify them as prostitutes and victims.[17] Choi's characters are women who are able successfully to survive the privations of foreign occupation and the turbulence of war without husbands, fathers, brothers, and sons, from whom they are separated by political upheaval and war.

Born in Pyongyang in northern Korea, Choi (b. 1937) experienced the Japanese occupation as a child and refugee life as an adolescent during the Korean War. She came to the United States as a student in 1968. After graduating from Manhattanville College, she taught social studies, English, and art in New York public schools for almost twenty years. Her two novels for children and adolescents, *Year of Impossible Goodbyes* (1991) and *Echoes of the White Giraffe* (1993), are both set entirely in Korea. "Having lived through this turbulent period of Korean history, I wanted to share my experiences," Choi has written. "So little is known about my homeland, its rich culture and its sad history. My love for my native country and for my adopted country prompted me to write this book to share some of my experiences and foster greater understanding."[18] At the same time, Choi's books are addressed to Korean Americans like her two U.S.-born, second-generation daughters, so that they may understand who their parents are and where they came from.[19]

Year of Impossible Goodbyes, which is set in northern Korea near the end of World War II, when the Japanese colonizers were intensifying their exploitation of Korean resources and labor as part of their war effort, focuses specifically on the lives of women. Ten-year-old Sookan lives with her mother, her aunts, her grandfather, and her younger brother. The adult male members of the family are fighting in the resistance movement or imprisoned in Japanese labor camps. The females, the young, and the old have been mobilized into war material production at factories set up in their own homes by the Japanese. Near the beginning of the novel, Sookan witnesses in horror the Japanese loading young Korean women workers into trucks that will carry them to the front, where they will be forced to serve the Japanese soldiers as prostitutes.[20] Sookan experiences the cruelty and racism of Japanese colonial schoolteachers. When the war ends with Japan's surrender, Korea is divided in half by the superpowers, and instead of tasting freedom Sookan sees northern Korea overrun with Russian soldiers. Delivered from Japanese exploitation, Sookan's family finds itself face to face with Russian and Korean Communists, whom Choi depicts as cold and sinister. The novel ends with the family's dramatic escape to southern Korea, thanks to the courage of her relatives, especially Aunt Tiger.

Echoes of the White Giraffe takes place five years later. Sookan, now fifteen, is living as a refugee in Pusan during the Korean War. Still separated from the men in the family, she and her mother live in a shack on a hill with throngs of other refugees from Seoul. Refugee life and young love are depicted from a teenage girl's point of view. Sookan befriends Junho, a young man from her church, at an age deemed inappropriate according to Korean middle-class mores at the time. She is obliged to give Junho up when the family returns to Seoul. Sookan had been dreaming about going to America anyway, and Junho would have limited and restricted her. Junho thinks that "America is too far to go" (65).

Noting that the men discuss work, school, and international events while her mother joyously "rushe[s] back and forth from the kitchen, constantly bringing more hot food, tea, and warm rice wine," Sookan decides that she cannot be satisfied with family life and traditional female roles. Sookan asks herself why she "always felt so empty, restless, and incomplete." "What was I searching for? I didn't know exactly, but I felt I had to go away to find something that would fill the emptiness inside me" (115–16).

Choi suggests that Sookan is compelled to leave because she understands too well the limitations facing her and other women in Korean society, even though they exhibit extraordinary courage and strength during times of political upheaval. For Sookan, fulfillment, resolution, and completion are not possible in Korea. The novel ends with her taking the government test for study abroad in a room full of men, some of whom glare at her, insulted that a female "dared to be there." Even after she passes the examination and finds her name "amidst the long list of men's names," her brothers are so surprised that they call the Ministry of Education to make sure that there has been no mistake. "I knew that [everyone] had hoped I would give up, join my friends at Ewha [women's] University, and then join the convent to be with my sister," she ruminates. Sookan runs away from these limitations, and the book ends with her aboard a plane en route to America.

In both of Choi's novels, America is seen as a promise or a promised land. In *Year of Impossible Goodbyes*, the family members anxiously await the Americans, whom they expect will deliver them from Japanese oppression. Listening to recordings of "Clementine," "Swanee River," and "Home on the Range," Sookan imagines America vaguely as the place where she will no longer feel empty, restless, and incomplete.

II

Whereas Sook Nyul Choi's novels shed light on how a contemporary immigrant parent such as herself might have emerged from Korean history, the daughters of early, mostly working-class Korean immigrants in Hawai'i and on the mainland have begun in recent years to imagine their parents' lives in fictional and nonfictional accounts as well as in oral histories collected by researchers in recent years (see Sunoo 1982). But, after all, the promised land hoped for in Choi's novels is not what these second-generation Korean American women writers describe.

Margaret K. Pai's *The Dreams of Two* Yi-Min (immigrants) (1989), traces five decades in the history of the author's family in Hawai'i. In this first-person narrative, Pai (b. 1914) tells the story of her picture-bride mother and her inventor–small-business owner father, who migrated in 1912 and 1905, respectively. The book details the mother's participation in the movement for Korean independence from Japanese colonial rule, the father's attempts to succeed in his own business, first as a furniture maker and later as a manufacturer of bamboo draperies, and the subtly strained relations between them as they struggle to establish their livelihood and raise their children in their adopted land. The parents' tale is told with sympathy and respect, and Pai's depictions of community life are richly detailed. Her own voice is muted and her psychic identity remains mostly in shadow. Although it is presented chronologically, Pai's tale is not a simple developmental narrative celebrating the seamless integration of the immigrant into the fabric of American life: at the end of the book, the parents' beloved homeland, no longer occupied by the Japanese, is divided in half as a Cold War battleground, and the father's dream of bequeathing a successful business to his children literally goes up in smoke shortly after his death.

Quiet Odyssey: A Pioneer Korean Woman in America (1990) is supposed to be an autobiographical account of the life of Mary Paik Lee, who immigrated to America with her family in 1905, when she was five years old. The family's "odyssey" takes them from Hawai'i to California and then all over California's rugged agricultural and mining country in search of a livelihood during times of relentless poverty and race discrimination. The "odyssey" is "quiet," not because Paik Lee is given to excessive restraint, but because the experiences and viewpoints of poverty-stricken Asian immigrants in early-twentieth-century America have remained on the periphery of most American people's consciousness. The narrative focuses primarily on her early life, through the 1920s.

Paik Lee gives us a vivid sense of her personality, especially her fierce loyalty to her family, the intense satisfaction she derived from hard work, and her appreciation of the subtlest details of nature's beauty. Militantly antiracist, she insists on being heard and understood, recounting with almost palpable glee the lessons in history she delivers to supposedly educated bigots. For her, each lesson seems to function as a kind of private revenge. When she discovers that her employer, a school official, has been embezzling school funds for his private use, she is exultant. He had worked her like a slave, feeding her only a slice of bread so thin that she could see the outline of a tree outside the window when she held it up to the light.

Although *Quiet Odyssey* is a book by a woman, the writer focuses only on men: her father, her brothers, her husband, and her sons. Her mother is barely mentioned, her sisters are dismissed, and most of the worst racists in the book are white women. Though perhaps regrettable, this is not surprising, given that "Korean identity" has been traditionally defined as male-centered, and that racism, rather than sexism, is viewed by many women of color as the fiercer and more dangerous source of material and psychic violence. *Quiet Odyssey* insists on using the family story to criticize the society at large. The point of both *The Dreams of Two Yi-Min* and *Quiet Odyssey* was apparently not to express the writers' individuality but rather to provide testimony of the families' experiences that would bring them into visibility, while also providing a social commentary about what America and American life has been to some of those otherwise missing from the master narratives. Such a commentary would move far beyond ethnographic, transparent descriptions of Korean American life to reach into U.S. society as a whole.

On the dust jacket of her 1987 novel, *Clay Walls*, Ronyoung Kim (1926–89), also known as Gloria Hahn,[21] wrote, "A whole generation of Korean immigrants and their American-born children could have lived and died in the United States without anyone knowing they had been here. I could not let that happen." In *Clay Walls*, Kim presents a daughter's perspectives on her immigrant parents' changing and often conflicting notions about what being Korean in California meant in the decades between the two world wars. The book purveys a sense of the nationalist spirit that made possible the psychic survival of the early Korean immigrants to the United States in their daily struggles with poverty and racism (see E. Kim 1993 for a further discussion of nationalism). Of particular interest to today's readers is the portrayal of the mother's mostly successful efforts to carve out a self-determined identity in America as a woman and as a Korean nationalist. Kim hints that this negotiation is possible because Haesu can take advantage of the interstitial position she occupies as a woman of aristocratic Korean background in what is, to her, her husband, and her ethnic community, a new land. The book also illustrates how successfully the immigrants passed on their fierce resistance to cultural extinction to their children, who did not directly experience Japanese colonialism because they were born in America. Divided into three sections, the novel focuses first on Haesu, the immigrant woman; then on Chun, her husband; and finally on Faye, their daughter. By arranging the book in sections representing the mother, the father, and the daughter separately, Kim is able to bring the immigrant parents almost into dialogue with their American-born daughter; the daughter speaks *with* the parents instead of *for* them.[22] Moreover, her identity is not subordinated to that of her immigrant parents.

III

In the work of second-generation women writers, Pai, Paik Lee, and Kim call dominant narratives about U.S. American national identity into question. Emerging young Korean American writers and artists in the 1990s are continuing the legacy in different ways. Though acutely conscious of the insinuation of their forebears' lives into their own, they were born after the war, and their work emerges from their hybridity, heterogeneity, and multiple positions as raced and gendered Korean American subjects in the West.

The Korean American's ideas about what "America" and "American" mean vary according to where she/he lives. People in South Korea sometimes observe how different the various descriptions of Korean American life are, depending on whether it is being lived in Los Angeles, New York City, Dallas, or Chicago. Further, Korean American writers in Hawai'i are distinct from their "mainland" counterparts, undoubtedly because in Hawai'i, as nowhere else in America, it has been possible for Asian Americans to claim to be both Asian and American.

The increasing hybridity and heterogeneity of Korean and Asian American identities, especially in Hawai'i and among the children and grandchildren of pre-1965 immigrants, challenge old categories and notions of who can be called a Korean American writer. For many, what matters is only the wish to be so called, "Korean American" being but one of many facets of identity. Alison Kim describes herself as "a Chinese Korean born in Hawai'i and raised in California . . . a Virgo with a Scorpio moon and Virgo rising, an activist, a lesbian, a writer, and an artist" (Lim and Tsutakawa 1989, 266). Hawaii's Nora Okja Cobb is working on *Miscegenation*, a new anthology of writers of "women of part Asian ancestry struggling to define the language and characterizations surrounding multi-racial and ethnic identities" (flyer).

The voices of the several thousand laborers who immigrated to Hawai'i at the turn of the century are represented in a small but very heterogeneous body of writings by their grandchildren. The grandson of Korean immigrants, Gary Pak (b. 1952) was born in Honolulu, attended college in New England (Boston University), and returned to live and work in Hawai'i. Relying on the pictures evoked by his relatives' stories, Pak is currently at work on *A Ricepaper Airplane*, a novel about an outspoken Korean immigrant union leader in Hawai'i at the turn of the century.[23] What interests Pak is not necessarily Korean nationalism itself but bringing to light the hidden, the forgotten, and the derogated, whether it be

Asian labor leadership, Korean history, or the pidgin spoken in Hawai'i. When, in "Catching a Big Ulua," the father tells the son facts little known in the West, such as that Koreans invented the submarine and the printing press, he adds, "You go college, but a lot of things dey no tell you about in college."

For Pak and other Korean American writers in Hawai'i, ethnic heritage is to be cherished. At the same time, it is not the only identity a person possesses: "I am a writer, a father of three, a husband, a son, a teacher, a soccer coach, a resident of Kaneohe. I am all of these. When I go to California, people say that I am Asian American or Korean American. I don't mind this, because I *am* Asian American and Korean American. It would only bother me if being labelled that way were a put-down or a way to exclude me" (telephone interview, 8 October 1993).[24]

The characters in Pak's collection of short stories, *The Watcher of Waipuna* (1992), belong to many different ethnic groups. They are not defined exclusively or even primarily by their ethnicity. At the same time, their ethnicity describes them. The narratives are infused with reminders of Hawaii's blended "talk-story" traditions, incorporating elements of the supernatural, spirited dialogues in pidgin, and vivid adventures told from a child's viewpoint. But at the heart of the book lurk sinister suggestions of atrocities wrought by racism and greed, often seen opaquely by children. In "The Trial of Goro Fukushima," a Japanese laborer is accused of murdering a white woman; unable to speak for himself in English, he dies at the hands of a lynch mob, betrayed by the church. There is no "trial" for Goro Fukushima except his own state of pain and anguish. In "A Toast for Rosita," the gay part–native Hawaiian protagonist loses his battle to prevent the government from taking over the land to build a freeway and dies of a drug overdose. But despite the undeniability of darkness, Pak insists on the slender but luminous possibility that wrongs of the past may be righted and wrongs of the present halted. In "The Watcher of Waipuna," Gilbert Sanchez's insanity, as well as his good heart, saves the land from the developers. And although one of his sisters succumbs to greed, the other cannot bring herself to cheat her brother. In the end, she sacrifices what seems to be a golden opportunity because she will not step on Gilbert to get ahead. Pak has commented on this story, "In Hawaii, the community is just so big; things will come back to you. But even if you are bad, you can have another chance. People have been abused by the rich, and they have survived because they have soul, because of their good heart" (telephone interview, 8 October 1993).

Since the mid-1980s, Pak and other local writers have been meeting to read and critique each other's work. "Writers from Hawaii feel like locals," Pak contends. "I am part of a community. Here, we do not have to look for our identity because we live it."

One of the members of the writers' group is poet Cathy Song (b. 1955). Born in Honolulu, Song returned to live in Hawai'i after graduating from Wellesley College and receiving a master's degree in creative writing at Boston University. *Picture Bride*, her first book, won the 1982 Yale Series of Younger Poets competition. Her second volume, *Frameless Windows, Squares of Light*, was published in 1988. Like Pak, Song cherishes and writes about her Chinese and Korean heritage and her roots in Hawai'i. But she has said that she does not want to be read only through the lens of race and ethnicity, calling herself "a poet who happens to be Asian American" (Nomaguchi, 9).[25] Worried that her work was being regarded as "leaning too heavily on 'the Asian-American theme,'" Song said in an interview, "I'll have to try not to write about the Asian-American theme. . . . it is a way of exploring the past. . . . But I write about other things, too."

Song's intensely personal poems recall childhood memories of a much-loved sister or father, a glimpse back at a classmate from long ago, or a baby son in an intense childhood moment. Savoring remembered and imagined small moments of everyday life, like the mournful notes of the widower's bamboo flute in the night and the fragrance of "sun-warm" laundry, Song traverses a landscape of kinship and generational ties, creating a family album filled with fragmentary glimpses of the past. The pictures often suggest subtly layered tensions between containment and expression, between pain and heroism, between artistry and freedom. The past is "still and distant," containing "great mystery," like the poet's aging Korean immigrant grandfather, whom she tries to imagine as a young man meeting his picture bride on the docks decades ago. Perhaps

> . . . his young man's eyes scanned
> the cargo of brides
> who bowed before the grim life held out to them;
> sucking in their breath
> at the vision of their own faces
> caught like orange blossoms
> in the sad hands of laborers
>
> ("Living Near the Water," *Frameless Windows,
> Squares of Light*, 15)

The poet herself is "descended from that moment of regret."

Many of the poems in *Picture Bride* contain images of almost suffocating restriction: sunless rooms; a pressing against mesh screens like barbed wire; a mother who sleeps in tight blankets and peers almost fearfully through a gray curtain of rain, fencing her children's playground with her skirt hems, keeping them "under cover" within the "safe circumference" of the house. There are women "handcuffed" to China by jade bracelets or "squinting" in hot, still rooms, like Japanese dolls "encased in glass boxes/displayed like shrines," their legs tucked under them, their world the piece of cloth they hold in their seamstress hands. Although Song's Korean and Chinese family and ethnicity provide inspiration and material for her poetry, she seems to feel restricted by them as an artist. To become an artist, she must leave home; she can return to her ethnicity and family only by rendering them as voiceless though aesthetically beautiful images.

Hawai'i-born, third-generation Korean American writer Willyce Kim (b. 1946) now lives and works in California, where her two wittily erotic mystery-adventure novels, *Dancer Dawkins and the California Kid* (1985) and *Dead Heat* (1988) are set. Kim has also published two books of poetry, *Eating Artichokes* (1972) and *Under the Rolling Sky* (1976). The main characters of *Dancer Dawkins* and *Dead Heat* are young lesbians who rescue their friends from danger. They are assisted by a middle-aged Korean woman from Hawai'i and her dog, Killer Shep, whose humanlike – and feminist – thoughts Kim transmits to the reader. "Ta Jan the Korean" has reinvented and renamed herself: born in O'ahu as the descendant of a Korean immigrant worker and a picture bride, she is baptized Penelope Frances Lee, a name she detests, because, she says, all this ancient Greek namesake ever did was wait and "weave, weave, weave." At the height of the hippie movement, she heads for San Francisco with a suitcase full of marijuana and renames herself Ta Jan. Now she operates an all-night diner called The Golden Goose, where she serves omelets, salads, curries, bagels with lox and cream cheese, and Lili'uokalani Coolers, as well as drinks named after Martina Navratilova and desserts named after Gertrude Stein.

Agreeing with Pak and Song that Korean heritage is just one of many facets of her identity, Kim also notes that she created Ta Jan the Korean because she wanted a character that could be recognized specifically as Korean American: "When I was a child, I remember that Koreans were sometimes classified as 'others' or lumped with Chinese or Japanese. I wanted Ta Jan to stand out as a Korean and not just a generic Asian American" (interview, 22 October 1993).

IV

Until a decade ago, most published Korean American writers were male. Today, it is the women writers who are proliferating, not only because of general heightened interest in women's writings among readers in the United States, but also because the ratio of Korean American females to males was not balanced until after immigration quotas were changed in 1965. Whereas nine out of ten of the immigrants to Hawai'i at the turn of the century were men, now more women are immigrating to the United States from Korea than men.

Thus the preponderance of Korean American writers today are women; furthermore, many of them are feminists. Moreover, other boundaries are being stretched and traversed in previously unimaginable ways. Whereas earlier Asian American communities and cultural expression were shaped by legal exclusion and containment, contemporary Asian American experiences grow from the internationalization of the world's political economies and cultures. Yesterday's young Korean American might have labored beside his migrant farm-worker parents in segregated rural California, like *Quiet Odyssey*'s Mary Paik Lee, or hung around the fringes of an urban Chinatown, like the narrator of Younghill Kang's *East Goes West*. Today's young Korean American, on the other hand, probably watched "The Wonderful World of Disney" on television in Seoul as a child and today rents Korean-language videos at a Los Angeles mini-mall store. Those videos might feature Korean performers imitating Hammer (formerly known as M. C. Hammer) on Korean late shows hosted in the style of David Letterman. Unlike in the days in which Richard Kim was in Iowa writing *The Martyred*, now transportation and communication between the United States and South Korea is no longer daunting. Four decades ago, when Kim first immigrated to the United States, telephones were rare and transmission unclear in Korea, and a letter could take two weeks to go between Iowa City and Seoul; today, both cities are almost equally accessible by telephone or fax. Formerly distinct boundaries between South Korea and the United States have become increasingly blurred.

Many of the daughters of these immigrants belong to what some Korean Americans call the "1.5 generation," a term coined in the late 1970s and early 1980s to denote those who were born in Korea and speak Korean but were educated primarily in the United States. Although some of the work of these writers is informed by the kinds of national consciousness forged under colonial rule and civil war in the parents' and grandparents' generations, a key element for the younger writers is their experience of America, which involves the interplay of racial, ethnic, female, and colonial subjectivities.

Important among this generation of Korean American women writers is the late Theresa Hak Kyung Cha (1951–82), whose influential *DICTEE* (1982) and other written and visual art work has expanded the boundaries of Korean American literature by insisting on both heterogeneity and a specifically Korean ethnic identity (see Kim and Alarcón 1993). Producer, director, performer, creator of video and film productions, installations, performances, and published texts, Cha immigrated to the United States with her family when she was eleven years old. While a student of art in the mid-1970s, she studied French film theory and produced a number of performance art pieces, utilizing videos that emphasize the splice to challenge the illusion of seamlessness. She hoped that by revealing the process of making video art she could point out the interdependent relationships between the film, the filmmaker, and the viewer. In her films and videos, French, Korean, and English often overlap, with words sometimes spoken in two languages simultaneously to express her layered and multiple identities as well as the layers of silence imposed by colonial "dictations." The subject of *DICTEE* disrupts the dictation by refusing to reproduce what is being dictated exactly, thereby revealing the constructed nature of the hierarchical system that insists on reproduction.

Attracted by Cha's deployment of concepts such as multiplicity and indeterminacy, some poststructuralist critics have written about *DICTEE* without considering the importance of her Korean American identity to the text. *DICTEE* is a subversive book about a specific set of excluded experiences. Indeed, it undermines popularly accepted notions of genre and of history and questions common assumptions about time, place, origins, identity. By questioning the notion of progress from fragmentation to wholeness or from immigrant to citizen, Cha challenges the United States nationalist narrative. And by bringing Korea and Koreans into view after the damage done by Japanese colonization has been glossed over by history, she creates a space for justice as well as for difference.

> To the other nations who are not witnesses, who are not subject to the same oppressions, they cannot know. Unfathomable the words, the terminology: enemy, atrocities, conquest, betrayal, invasion, destruction. They exist only in the larger perception of History's recording, that affirmed, admittedly and unmistakably, one enemy nation has disregarded the humanity of another. Not physical enough. Not to the very flesh and bone, to the core, to the mark, to the point where it is necessary to intervene, even if to invent anew, expressions, for *this* experience, for this *outcome*, that does not cease to continue. (32)

Cha's work has attracted and influenced the work of Korean American writers like Walter Lew (b. 1955) and Myung Mi Kim (b. 1957). For *Excerpts from: ΔIKTE for DICTEE (1982)* (1992), Lew arranges what he calls a "critical college . . . of proximal texts and structures," such as pages from comic books about Korean historical figures, images and writing about archaeological sites like those referred to in *DICTEE*, and film theory text. Lew's objective is to create art that resonates with, rather than interprets, Cha's work.

Myung Mi Kim's volume of poetry, *Under Flag* (1991), explores the unmoored, disjunctive splinteredness of Korean American women's identities. "A singular story connects to a collective story," she has said, "but not to just one rendition. There is no time, no chronology; as life is, memory is – fragmented, not part of a trajectory that can be tracked or named" (interview, 20 May 1992). The poems in *Under Flag* explore the immigrant's loss of homeland and the Korean American's encounters with racism and experiences with the loss of language. Transfer of meaning, whether linguistic or cultural, is impossible when the given content becomes alien and estranged in the act of translation, and Korean American identity is not planted in any one place but multiple and shifting.

In the poem "Food, Shelter, Clothing," Kim traces the Korean immigrant experience:

> They had oared to cross the ocean
> And where had they come to
> These bearers of a homeland
> Those landing amphibious (under cover of night)
> In a gangplank thud and amplification take
> Spot of ground.
> . . . .
> How little space they take up given the land's reach
> All those whose feet had resounded
> Smear fear tyranny of attack
> Already the villages already the cities receding.
>
> (22–3)

Kim draws an ironic parallel between the Korean immigrants' "landing amphibious (under cover of night)" and the U.S. military landing in Korea. Unlike the U.S. "invaders," however, the immigrants walk a "gangplank," taking up only a "little space" in the vastness of the United States, a limited and restricted "spot of ground" where they will live tyrannized by fear of "smear" and attack. Korea becomes the "homeland" when they leave home.[26]

Visual artist and cultural critic Yong Soon Min (b. 1953) was Cha's art department classmate at the University of California at Berkeley in the mid-1970s. Like Kim and Cha, Min refuses to place politics and aesthetics in opposition. She explores the Korean American woman artist's multiple subjectivities, although her work more directly addresses a variety of contemporary political issues. Essays, prints, installations, and video art works are informed by her participation in the *minjung* (folk or common people's) art movement, the Asian American movement against racism and injustice, and her interest in the affinities between Koreans/Korean Americans and the Third World diasporas. Min designed *Voices Stirring* (Hong and Kim 1992), a new anthology of Korean American writing, which continues to call into question the meaning of "American" in the late twentieth century with a sampling of poetry and prose by young women writers who explore various facets of Korean American identity in the 1990s, including Joo-Hyun Kang, Diana Song, Mi Ok Bruining, Lisa Simmons, and Marie G. Lee.

An essayist and writer of fiction for adolescents and young adults, Lee (b. 1964) addresses the issue of how young Korean Americans struggle to find a place for themselves in a society that is ignorant of their cultural roots. Although each of Lee's works focuses on different kinds of Korean American experiences, all of them address the ways in which Korean Americans struggle against their entrapment in false dualisms – between "white" and "nonwhite," between Korea and America, between "foreign" and "native." Her first novel, *Finding My Voice* (1992), is set in the U.S. American Midwest, where Lee herself grew up. The protagonist is Ellen Sung, a Korean American high school student who learns during the course of the novel how to deal with racism and how to understand where her parents' views and values come from. Lee's second novel, *If It Hadn't Been for Yoon Jun* (1993), is about a seventh-grader, Alice, who was adopted as an infant by a white family and has been successfully crafting her identity as an all-American teenager, despite the disagreements between her father, who wants her to learn about her Korean roots, and her mother, who prefers that she ignore them. Alice's self-concept and desire for her peers' acceptance are brought to a crisis when a "strange, quiet" Korean immigrant student enrolls at her school.

There are elements of the bildungsroman in both of Lee's novels, which, like so many works of young adult fiction, seem intent on reassuring members of the older generation that in the end youth will refuse to capitulate to peer pressure and will learn to appreciate their elders. But on the evidence of her short essay, "We Koreans Need an Al Sharpton," Lee is no simple teller of corny tales for teenaged "squares." She writes at a specific moment in history when young Korean Americans are contesting a paradigm of U.S. American identity and race relations that allows for their existence only as statements about African or European American experiences. Her third novel, *Saying Goodbye* (1993), is a sequel to *Finding My Voice*. *Saying Goodbye* follows Ellen Sung to college, where she finds herself torn between her politically involved African American roommate and her Korean American boyfriend, whose father's market was destroyed during the 1992 civil disaster in Los Angeles. This very specific Korean American attempt to create a "third space" cannot be contained in the "promise of happiness" formula for young adult fiction any more than Korean American personal narratives can be interpreted only as developmental.

Currently, one of the most fruitful places to look for new Korean American writing is in Asian American and Korean American college student publications. The population is relatively new and comparatively young, and Korean Americans comprise a percentage of college students disproportionate to their total numbers.[27] In some ways reminiscent of the Japanese American nisei literary journals that emerged from the internment camps during World War II, these occasional journals have appeared on such campuses as Northwestern University, the University of California at Berkeley, and Harvard University. The essays, short stories, and poetry published in these journals are sometimes unevenly written or overblown. But beautiful writing and new perspectives also emerge from the pages of these publications.

Many contemporary Korean American college students are the sons and daughters of Korean immigrant shop owners. Their views of their parents' lives contrast sharply with popular media stereotypes of Korean American merchants' lives. In Shin Yung Oh's "Two Lives for One," which was published in the spring 1992 University of Chicago Korean American magazine, *Kil Mok* (Corner), Christine, a college student, helps out at her parents' dry-cleaning shop. Sorting through the reeking, soiled clothing, she daydreams about going to a movie with a friend, until she realizes that she can never enjoy herself knowing that her parents do not have "the privilege of such an escape." Christine understands that her parents' two lives are being sacrificed for her one life. Their sixty-hour workweek is punctuated by the humiliating treatment they receive each day from condescending, well-heeled customers. She feels compelled to repay her parents for having "purchased my future with their lives" – lives that have been reduced to "nothing more than eating and sleeping so that they could clean other people's clothes." After the ranting customers leave the store, family members vent their frustration and anger upon each other: "Heaves and sighs and grunts and glares . . . hidden tears . . . and stifled screams exchanged in our little store, prevented from seeping out of our limited enclosure."

Christine realizes that she is invisible, both to her parents and to the customers, who represent both her parents' oppression and their only hope for liberation. At times, because she speaks English without an accent and wears a Gap shirt and Calvin Klein jeans, the customers mistake her for one of them and ask her to side with them against her parents. Christine is torn between her hatred for the well-to-do customers, who regard her limited-English-speaking parents as subhuman, and her parents' desire that she become like them. They want her to

live just like the customers who walk into our store day after day
. . . and give us these patronizing looks. . . . Live just like our customers who smile and ask if "the little woman" can help them carry the
clothes out to their car because they just had a manicure done and
don't want to risk damaging their decorated nails. Live just like our
customers who make a point of telling us that they are lawyers, and
that they will not hesitate to take us to court if we don't pay for the
damage that was done to their shirts. (18)

Christine's immigrant parents cannot know that they are pushing her
away from them and toward a world that hates them, a "world that had
no understanding of the lives we led."

If Korean immigrant merchants are known to most people in the
United States only as cartoonlike stereotypes, Korean immigrant wage
workers are completely invisible. Despite popular misconceptions, the
Korean American community is not and has never been homogeneous,
whether in terms of religious preference, sexual orientation, social class
status, or other ways. Even among Korean American college students,
differences abound: the young woman in the Gap shirt and Calvin Klein
jeans who speaks fluent English could be the daughter of a wealthy
engineer, a dry-cleaning shop owner, or a janitor. Ju Hui "Judy" Han
provides a glimpse of the strata in a poem in *KAWA, A Zine By & About
Korean American Women with Attitudes* (1993): "who says koreans own
liquor stores / some koreans own / other koreans," she writes. She wants
to ask a fellow student:

> . . . do you know my dad pays
> for your tuition your car your computer with
> his minimum wage you may be
> the storeowner's son but I am
> the storekeeper's daughter
>
> (40–1)

These student writings give us a glimpse of some of the circumstances
young Korean Americans must grapple with if they want to be writers.
But they are fortunate to have inherited the unexpected legacy of a writer
like Theresa Hak Kyung Cha, who left behind not transparent autobiographical musings on identity but poetry about the philosophical question
of what constitutes a self.

Korean American writers will have to cross some boundaries and
maintain others as they struggle to create a new, hybrid culture from
jumbled elements of U.S. and Korean life. Meanwhile, the heretofore

small body of work by these writers gives us a tantalizing glimpse into the kinds of Korean American literature we can look forward to in the twenty-first century, when what has been missing will surely burst forth to populate the pages of U.S. American literature with surprises, great beauty, and new meanings.

■■■■ AFTERNOTE

Indeed, in the brief period between the completion of this chapter in late 1993 and the copyediting only two years later, Sook Nyul Choi published two more books for young readers, *Halmoni and the Picnic* (Boston: Houghton Mifflin, 1993) and *Gathering of Pearls* (Boston: Houghton Mifflin, 1994), Heinz Insu Fenkl published "Surgical Mercy," an excerpt from his forthcoming novel *Mimosa Sector*, in *Muae: A Journal of Transcultural Production* 1 (1995): 15–29; and Myung Mi Kim published a new volume of poetry, *The Bounty* (Minneapolis: Chax Press, 1996). In 1994, Hyun-Yi Kang edited an interesting collection of essays, fiction, and poetry by mostly young Korean American writers titled *Writing Away Here* (Oakland, CA: Korean American Arts Festival Committee). Work by a number of Korean American poets and fiction writers appears in six new issues of *The Asian Pacific American Journal* that appeared over a two-year period, as well as in *Moonrabbit Review*, a new Colorado-based journal of Asian American poetry and prose. In 1995, Sung Rno's play, *Cleveland Raining*, was produced in several cities across the country, and a moving and beautifully written first novel, *Native Speaker* (New York: G. P. Putnam's Sons), was published by Chang-rae Lee to rave reviews.

■■■■ ACKNOWLEDGMENTS

I want to thank Sunwoo Lee, Eui-Young Yu, and Laura Hyun-Yi Kang for their helpful translations and suggestions.

■■■■ NOTES

1. Wives of U.S. servicemen and adopted children constitute a major component of the Korean American population. A significant proportion of Korean American immigration can be traced to a sponsoring female relative who was married to a U.S. serviceman, although most immigrants prefer not to draw attention to this fact because of their social class prejudices. Likewise, many middle-class Korean immigrants are reluctant to accept as fellow Korean Americans the thousands of Korean children who were adopted into American families between the Korean War and the 1988 Olympics, after which the South Korean government, embarrassed by publicity about adoptions, took steps to limit them. This reluctance is rooted in traditional patriarchal attitudes. In South Korea, where paternity and patrilineality still determine

social power, adoptions outside the clan are rare. And because social identity is passed on by fathers, even the child of a widowed mother is socially disadvantaged, particularly in terms of marriageability. Adopted Korean Americans' self-inscriptions have begun to appear in print recently; the work of Mi Ok Bruining is a case in point.

2. Koreans in the United States share much in common with South Asian Americans, who established small communities in Yuba City and elsewhere on the West Coast before India was declared a "barred zone" from which immigrants were excluded. As among Korean Americans, the small earlier settlement is overshadowed by hundreds of thousands of newcomers from the postcolonial homeland's urban centers. Like South Asians, who were colonized by the British, Korean Americans emerge from what might be called a history of "double colonization" and emigration to, or exile in, the colonial centers.

3. Unlike the much larger Japanese American population, which was about half U.S.-born by the 1930s (thanks to the picture-bride immigration allowed by the Gentlemen's Agreement), Korean America did not produce a significant group of second-generation writers until recent years. Like other Asians, Koreans were prohibited by law from immigrating or becoming naturalized U.S. citizens after 1924. But Korean emigration had already been severely curtailed by 1905, when Japan made Korea a protectorate, dismantling the Korean military, governmental, and diplomatic institutions and harnessing Korean labor to Japanese militarism and industrialization efforts. After 1905, Koreans in the United States fell under the jurisdiction of Japanese consulates.

   Between 1905 and 1924, about 11,000 "picture brides" and fewer than a thousand political exiles who came by way of China or Europe entered the United States. Between the end of World War II and the beginning of the Korean War, a small number of students and servants immigrated under the sponsorship of U.S. missionaries and military personnel. Between 1951 and 1964, about 6,300 orphans and 6,500 wives of U.S. servicemen were brought into the country. During that period, about 6,000 foreign students enrolled at U.S. colleges and universities, many of whom later become permanent residents or U.S. citizens when the laws were changed in 1965. Thus, the community remained small, and indeed more Koreans left than entered the country during the period between 1924 and 1950.

4. Yun-hong Ch'oe, who posits that first-generation Korean immigrant literature is "Korean" as opposed to "American" or "Korean American" literature, contends that the development of Korean American literature has been hampered because the second generation, which is the group that looks at U.S. American life and how racism shapes identity, has not yet sufficiently "come of age."

5. See my chapter on early Asian immigrant writers in *Asian American Literature: An Introduction to the Writings and Their Social Context* (Philadelphia: Temple University Press, 1982), pp. 23–43, for a discussion of several Chinese immigrant writers and of Kang.

   New Il-han's *When I Was a Boy in Korea* (1928) was one of the last of a series of books by young immigrants from various countries. It describes Korean traditional holidays, food, housing, silkworm culture, and sports. The book was an attempt to win sympathy for Korea and Koreans through the presentation of "positive" cultural images. Born in P'yongan Province in northern Korea, New (b. 1894 or 1895) came to the United States in 1904. He graduated in business from the University of Michigan in 1919 and established La Choy, a successful food company that concentrates on products for cooking Chinese-type foods at home. He founded the Yuhan (named after New, which is the anglicized version of the Korean name "Yu") Corporation in Korea in 1926. At the end of World War II, he returned to Korea for good, becoming the chair of Yuhan, now a major South Korean corporation. New used his considerable wealth for philanthropic purposes, such as establishing technical schools for working-class young men. He died in Korea in 1971.

Another autobiographical account is Park No-Yong's *Chinaman's Chance* (1940), which is set in China, Europe, and the United States. Born in Manchuria to Korean parents, Park entered the United States with a Chinese passport and considered himself Chinese. Induk Pahk who, like New, returned to Korea to live and work, wrote *September Monkey* (1954), a Christian autobiography chronicling Korean customs, expressing gratitude for the kindness of American missionaries and admiration for U.S. American culture, and testifying to her Christian faith. Another woman's narrative is Taiwon Koh's *The Bitter Fruit of Kom-pawi* (1959), which tells the story of the author's escape from communism to the United States. One recent autobiography is Peter Hyun's *Mansei* (1986), which chronicles Hyun's boyhood life in Korea and China, ending with his arrival in Hawai'i at the age of seventeen in 1924. While contemporary readers might find interesting and exciting the writer's reminiscences of his personal experiences during a particularly eventful period in Asian history, some might be distracted by such anachronistic elements as Hyun's unquestioning acceptance of male dominance as natural and desirable.

6. Born in Hamkyong Province in northern Korea, Kang was educated at first in the Confucian tradition and later at Christian schools, which were established all over Korea by missionaries from North America. Describing himself as "self-educated," he read English and American classics voraciously, attending classes at Harvard and Boston universities while working at various jobs to support himself. Between 1924 and 1927, Kang wrote in Korean or Japanese, and in 1928 he began writing in English with the help of his Wellesley-educated American wife, Frances Keeley. He found work as an editor at the *Encyclopaedia Britannica* and at the Metropolitan Museum of Art's Department of Far Eastern Art in New York. He also obtained a position as a lecturer in the English department at New York University, where he befriended Thomas Wolfe. At the time, Kang was working on *The Grass Roof*. Wolfe read four chapters of the book and then took it to his own editor at Charles Scribner's Sons, which published it in 1931. Translated into French, German, and other languages, *The Grass Roof* won the Prix Halperine Kaminsky in 1937. Between 1933 and 1935, Kang went to a Germany and Italy on a Guggenheim Award in Creative Literature. In 1937, Scribner's published *East Goes West*.

Kang lived in genteel poverty with his wife and three children in a Long Island farmhouse overflowing with books. Always in demand as a visiting lecturer, he was unable to obtain a stable teaching position. Instead, he traveled from one speaking engagement to another in an old Buick, astonishing Rotary Club audiences with his recitations of Hamlet's soliloquy or his lectures on Korea. He is said to have commented that it was his great misfortune that Pearl Buck's Pulitzer Prize–winning novel about China, *The Good Earth*, was published in the same year as *The Grass Roof*, eclipsing his own tale of Asia.

Kang also published translations of Korean literature, such as *Meditations of the Lover* and *Murder in the Royal Palace*, and a children's book based on the first part of *The Grass Roof* (*The Happy Grove*, 1933), as well as a number of book reviews on Asian culture in the *New York Times*. For a brief period after World War II, Kang served as chief of publications under the U.S. occupation forces. An avowed opponent of the First Republic's U.S-backed rightist president, Syngman Rhee, Kang returned to the United States to live after Rhee assumed power. He received the Louis S. Weiss Memorial Prize in 1953, which cited him as "poet, writer, and teacher," and was awarded an honorary doctorate in literature from Korea University in 1970, when he was a guest of the 37th P.E.N. Congress. Kang donated 5,000 books to Korea University. Hospitalized in New York for postoperative hemorrhaging after a massive stroke, Kang died in 1972.

7. *Sam Il Oondong* was a series of massive peaceful demonstrations protesting Japan's colonization of Korea that began in Korea on March 19, 1919, and lasted for several months, during which thousands of Koreans were killed and imprisoned.

8. A lover of poetry, Kang is said to have recited it late into the night. John Kyhan Lee notes that whereas Kang quotes poetry frequently in *The Grass Roof*, by the time of *East Goes West*, the narrator declares he wants neither dreams nor poetry, suggesting his feeling that in America, unlike in Korea, there is no place for poetry (1990).

9. I notice that some reviewers in the 1930s who applauded Kang's portrayal of Koreans even when it seemed to ridicule them were offended by any but the most positive descriptions of Westerners and the West. For example, one reviewer of *The Grass Roof*, a self-proclaimed "lover of the East," appreciates the way Kang "explains scenes [of Korea] only half understood before." She is less enthusiastic, however, about his rendering of the West and Westerners: "Mr. Kang does not, I think, give a full account of American missionaries. Doubtless these are blundering human beings, just like the rest of us. He accuses them of lack of education, yet he longed ardently to come to their country for the kind of education they receive. He was desperately eager to receive the benefit of their escort to America. . . . Mr. Kang is, however, on sure ground when he gives us Korea and Koreans. His book is a real contribution to literature and to our understanding of his countrymen and women" (Hosie, 707). Another reviewer for *The Saturday Review* finds Kang's "observations on American civilization" in *East Goes West* disappointing and banal: "a department store is an unpleasant place to work in, New England is austere

but agreeable, Boston cold (spiritually), American life is centered on movement and romantic love is a disturbing experience, particularly for Orientals,
who do not know it at home . . . the book [is] . . . only a disappointment
when one approaches it with the preconception that it should be profound or
original or both" (*Saturday Review of Literature*, Sept. 18, 1937, p. 15).

10. Persecuted as landowning Christians, the Kim family fled south before the
Korean War. Kim had just begun studying at Seoul National University when
the war broke out. He escaped to Inchon, where he hid until he was able to
join the U.N. forces. He served at first in the ROK marines and later in the
ROK army. Although he never graduated from Middlebury, Kim earned
master's degrees at Johns Hopkins, Harvard, and the State University of Iowa.

11. In a 1964 interview, Kim is quoted as saying: "I sensed the future power the
army would have in Korea and wanted to stay" (1964, 126).

12. *The Martyred* was inspired by and dedicated to Albert Camus. Parallels between it and Camus's *The Plague* are numerous. Like Camus, Kim grapples
with questions such as the human urge toward order and unity, as promised
by traditional Christian faith, in a universe devoid of meaning and morality.
The deft exploration of existential crisis and the chaste prose style of *The
Martyred* were enthusiastically praised by American critics and reviewers,
who compared him favorably with Conrad, Bellow, and Unamuno.

13. Thinking back on that period now, Kim says: "When *The Martyred* attracted all
that attention, I learned about the writing game in this country – about
agents, publicists, public relations people, talk shows. It was flattering and
seductive, but it was also scary and unpleasant" (17 October 1993 interview).

14. Kim was vilified in his homeland, however, for what was considered his
unflattering depiction to the world of Korean Christians. During that intensely anti-Communist period in South Korea, a group of Korean clergy
even petitioned the government to ban the Korean film version of *The
Martyred* for "defamation of the national spirit," an offense that could aid the
"enemy" (North Korea). According to James Wade, the book could not be
attacked because of its international success, but the clergy thought that if the
film were condemned, the book would also be deemed unacceptable, especially as it was an almost literal adaptation ["Author Richard Kim Looks
Homeward," *Korea Journal* 5, no. 8 (Aug. 1, 1965): 53]. In the end, neither
the book nor the film was banned, and in South Korea Kim continues to
enjoy the reputation of being the Korean writer who has achieved the
greatest degree of international recognition.

15. During the 1980s, he translated six books into Korean, including Bronowski's
The Ascent of Man, Hemingway's *The Garden of Eden*, and Bellow's *More Die of
Heartbreak*. He also worked as a reporter and narrator for Korean Broadcasting in Seoul, most recently focusing on documentaries on Koreans in China
and Russia.

16. 17 October 1993 interview.

17. It should be noted that in Korea in Kang's time, as well as for those born in
the 1930s like Kim and Pak, males were segregated from females after the age
of seven, after which they did not play, study, or even eat together; they did
not even use the same clothes hangers. Thus it is to be expected that Korean

immigrant writers would find it difficult to write about the lives and experiences of the opposite sex.

18. Dust jacket, *Year of Impossible Goodbyes*, 1991.

19. Most of the immigrants experienced either the Korean War of both the colonization and the war, and about half of the Koreans in the United States can trace their family origins to northern Korea. Many Korean Americans were separated from family members when Korea was partitioned in 1948. Because *kohyang* or "native place" has been traditionally one of the most important identity markers for Koreans, people who have already left their home villages presumably find it easier to migrate abroad, as they are in a sense already in exile.

20. Recently, the *jungshindae*, or official conscription of thousands, perhaps tens of thousands, of Korean girls as young as nine years old as wartime prostitutes (called "comfort women" by the Japanese), has become an issue around which Korean feminists have rallied to demand acknowledgment and reparations from the Japanese government.

21. Born in Los Angeles, Kim grew up in the tiny Korean ethnic community that was the geographical starting point for what has now become Los Angeles Koreatown. Like many other American-born Korean children in Los Angeles during the pre–World War II era, she attended Korean language school, where she also learned about Korean history, especially the Korean struggle against Japanese colonial rule. Kim's father, Kim Lhrong Sun, like the father in *Clay Walls*, was an immigrant laborer who died when his daughter was only twelve. Her mother, Haeran (Helen) Kim, was in many ways like the mother in *Clay Walls*. Educated and spirited, the widowed woman raised her four sons and two daughters by taking in sewing, while participating actively in the overseas movement for Korean independence. Kim's mother published poems and essays in a Korean-language newspaper and hosted weekly meetings of a group of mostly male Korean leftists who engaged in lengthy discussions of Marxism. As a young woman, Kim helped her mother make neckties to sell to local department stores. During World War II, she worked at a Disney Studios assembly plant, dipping puppet dolls' feet into black paint, until she obtained a higher-wage drill-press job. At nineteen she married, and by 1956 she had given birth to three daughters and a son. When she was almost fifty, she earned a B.A. at San Francisco State University, but shortly thereafter she was diagnosed with breast cancer. Ronyoung Kim was planning to write about the daughters and sons of the early Korean immigrants when she died in 1989.

22. I am grateful to Laura Hyun Yi Kang for pointing out this narrative strategy.

23. Excerpts from this novel in progress have been published in *Chaminade Literary Review* and *Amerasia Journal*.

24. Pak remarks that he knows his family's history and considers his ethnic heritage important as a source of pride and self-definition, but not as something to be used to exclude others. His relatives by marriage include Samoans, Filipinos, *haoles*, Hawaiians, Chinese, Japanese, and Portuguese – people who look different but belong to the same family.

25. Though Shirley Geok-lin Lim characterizes Song as a poet of immense talent,

she finds fault with her references to such "ethnic coloristic effects" as jade, tofu, wonton skins, buddhas, sour plums, and Maj-Jongg, suggesting that these "predictable mannerisms" might be "strained, mechanical, and unconvincing" concessions to an orientalist creative writing instructor (Lim and Tsutakawa, 237–8). Indeed, the critic who chose Song's manuscript from among 625 other submissions to the Yale competition seems to have been susceptible to the popular stereotypes of Asians and Asian Americans. In his foreword to *Picture Bride*, Richard Hugo invokes two notions highly popular in the West – that of "China's systematic repression of women" and the Enlightenment idea of progress from East to West – and is captivated by the "relentless desire for escape" he finds in Song's poetry. He reads Song as having an "oriental sensibility," "a sensibility strengthened by patience that is centuries old, ancestral, tribal, a gift passed down" (x), as coming from a "background" that engenders or necessitates passivity. Hugo may also have accepted the stereotype of Asian Americans as a "model minority" that (unlike unnamed other people of color) "need not rave or struggle" because they have "discovered how hard work" can "pay off": "If we accept Cathy Song's background as it comes through the poem 'Leaving' and through bits and pieces of other poems, we may sense the origin of, and even the necessity for, her passive/receptive sensibility. She need not rave or struggle. She has learned the strength of quiet resolve. As a poet, she has discovered how hard work and the long act of writing and rewriting pay off if one remains passionately committed" (xiii–xiv).

26. An informative reading of the poetry of Cathy Song and Myung Mi Kim is contained in L. Kang (1992).

27. As indicated previously, the preponderance of Korean immigrants to the United States arrived after 1968. They were mostly adults with small children. The children of this newest wave of Korean immigrants began to reach college age in the late 1980s. Moreover, college attendance has been high among Korean children raised in the United States, even among the children of earlier laboring immigrants. Indeed, according to the 1980 census, 54.8% of Korean Americans twenty to twenty-one years old were enrolled in school, as compared with only 33.3% of whites.

■■■ WORKS CITED

"Author Richard Kim Looks Homeward." 1965. *Korea Journal* 5, no. 8 (August 1). *Honolulu Star-Bulletin*, March, 1983.

Cha, Theresa Hak Kyung. 1982. *DICTEE*. New York: Tanam Press.

Ch'oe, T'ae-ung, et al. 1989. "Hankukmuntan 43 Nyunkwa Iminmunhak" [43 years of Korean literature and immigrant literature]. *Yoksa Bip'an* [Modern praxis] 8 (Spring): 4–44.

Ch'oe Yun-hong. 1989. "Mikuk Sok-e Hankukmunhak" [Korean literature in America]. *Yoksa Bip'an* [Modern praxis] 9 (Fall): 59–66.

Choi, Sook Nyul. 1991. *Year of Impossible Goodbyes*. Boston: Houghton Mifflin.

———. 1993. *Echoes of the White Giraffe*. Boston: Houghton Mifflin.

Engle, Paul. 1954. "The Story of Kim." *New York Times Book Review*, Feb. 16, 35.

Hong, Maria, and David D. Kim, eds. 1992. *Voices Stirring: An Anthology of Korean American Writing/The Asian Pacific American Journal* 1.2.

Hosie, Lady. 1931. Review of Younghill Kang's *The Grass Roof. Saturday Review of Literature*, April 4, 707.

Kang, Younghill. 1931. *The Grass Roof*. New York: Charles Scribner's Sons.

———. 1937. *East Goes West: The Making of an Oriental Yankee*. New York: Charles Scribner's Sons.

Kang, L. Hyun-Yi. 1992. "(De)formed Languages and (Re)formed Voices: Four Asian American Women Poets." Paper presented at the MELUS conference, Berkeley, California.

KAWA: A Zine By & About Korean American Women with Attitudes. 1993. Univ. of California at Berkeley student publication.

Kim, Elaine H. 1982. *Asian American Literature: An Introduction to the Writings and Their Social Context*. Philadelphia: Temple Univ. Press.

———. 1986. "Asian Americans and American Pop Culture." In *Dictionary of Asian American History*, ed. Robert H. Kim, 99–114. New York: Greenwood Press.

———. 1993, "Home Is Where the *Han* Is: A Korean American Perspective on the Los Angeles Upheavals." In *Reading Rodney King, Reading Urban Uprising*, ed. Robert Gooding-Williams, 215–35. New York: Routledge.

Kim, Elaine H., and Norma Alarcón, eds. 1994. *Writing Self, Writing Nation: Four Essays on Theresa Hak Kyung Cha's DICTEE*. Berkeley: Third Woman Press.

Kim, Myung Mi. 1991. *Under Flag*. Berkeley: Kelsey St. Press.

Kim, Richard. 1964. *The Martyred*. New York: George Braziller.

———. 1964. "Best-selling Korean." *Life* 56:125–7.

———. 1968. *The Innocent*. Boston: Houghton Mifflin.

———. 1970a. *Lost Names: Scenes from a Korean Boyhood*. New York: Praeger.

———. 1989. *In Search of "Lost" Koreans in China and Russia*. Seoul: Eulyoo Publishing Company.

Kim, Ronyoung. 1987. *Clay Walls*. Sag Harbor, NY: The Permanent Press.

Kim, Willyce. 1972. *Eating Artichokes*. Oakland: Women's Press Collective.

———. 1976. *Under the Rolling Sky*. n.p.: Maude Gonne Press.

———. 1985. *Dancer Dawkins and the California Kid*. Boston: Alyson Publications, Inc.

———. 1988. *Dead Heat*. Boston: Alyson Publications, Inc.

Koh, Taiwon. 1959. *The Bitter Fruit of Kom-Pawi*. Philadelphia: The John C. Winston Company.

Kunitz, Stanley, ed. 1955. *Twentieth Century Authors*. New York: H. W. Wilson.

Lee, John Kyhan. 1990. "The Notion of 'Self' in Korean American Literature: A Socio-Historical Perspective." Ph.D. diss., University of Connecticut.

Lee, Marie G. 1991. "We Koreans Need an Al Sharpton." *The New York Times*, 12 December.

———. 1992. *Finding My Voice*. Boston: Houghton Mifflin.

———. 1993. *If It Hadn't Been for Yoon Jun*. Boston: Houghton Mifflin.

———. 1994. *Saying Goodbye*. Boston: Houghton Mifflin.

Lee, Mary Paik. 1990. *Quiet Odyssey: A Pioneer Korean Woman in America*. Seattle: Univ. of Washington Press.

Lew, Walter. 1992. *Excerpts from ΔIKTE for DICTEE*. Seoul: Yeul Eum Sa.

Lim, Shirley Geok-lin, and Mayumi Tsutakawa, eds. 1989. *The Forbidden Stitch: An Asian American Women's Anthology*. Corvallis, OR: Calyx Books.

Nichols, Christopher. 1969. "The Tough and the Tender." *National Review*, 25 February, 183.

Nomaguchi, Debbie Murakami. 1984. "Cathy Song: 'I'm a Poet Who Happens to Be Asian American.'" *International Examiner*, May 2, 9.

Oh, Shin Yung. 1992. "Two Lives for One." *Kil Mok* 3 (Spring). Univ. of Chicago Korean American student literary magazine.

"Oriental Yankee." 1941. *Common Ground* 1:59–63.

Pahk, Induk. 1954. *September Monkey*. New York: Harper.

Pai, Margaret K. 1989. *The Dreams of Two Yi-Min*. Honolulu: Univ. of Hawai'i Press.

Pak, Gary. 1988. "From *A Ricepaper Airplane*." *Chaminade Literary Review* 2:104–13.

———. 1989. "Excerpt from *A Ricepaper Airplane*." *Chaminade Literary Review* 5:159–76.

———. 1992a. "A Ricepaper Airplane." *Amerasia Journal* 18.3:17–31.

———. 1992b. *The Watcher of Waipuna and Other Stories*. Honolulu: Bamboo Ridge Press.

Pak, Ty. 1983. *Guilt Payment*. Honolulu: Bamboo Ridge Press.

Park, No-yong. 1940. *Chinaman's Chance: An Autobiography*. Boston: Meador.

Review of Young-Hill Kang's *East Goes West*. 1937. *Saturday Review of Literature* 16, no. 21 (18 September): 15.

Song, Cathy. 1983. *Picture Bride*. New Haven: Yale Univ. Press.

———. 1988. *Frameless Windows, Squares of Light*. New York: W. W. Norton and Company.

Yoon, Esther. 1984. "Vanishing Point." *Hawaii Review* 16:61–3.

■■■ SELECTED BIBLIOGRAPHY

Bruining, Anne Mi Ok. 1990. "To Omoni in Korea." In *Making Face, Making Soul*, ed. Gloria Anzaldúa, 153–5. San Francisco: Aunt Lute Foundation Books.

———. 1992. "Challenging the Lies of International Adoption by White Lesbians and Gays." *Color Life!* 28 June, 22–3.

Cha, Theresa Hak Kyung, ed. 1980. *Cinematographic Apparatus: Selected Writings*. New York: Tanam Press.

———. 1982. *DICTEE*. New York: Tanam Press.

Cheung, King-Kok, and Stan Yogi. 1988. *Asian American Literature: An Annotated Bibliography*. New York: Modern Language Association of America.

Ch'oe, T'ae-ung, et al. 1989. "Hankukmuntan 43 Nyunkwa Iminmunhak" [43 years of Korean literature and immigrant literature]. *Yoksa Bip'an* [Modern praxis] 8 (Spring): 4–44.

Ch'oe, Yun-hong. 1989. "Mikuk Sok-e Hankukmunhak" [Korean literature in America]. *Yoksa Bip'an* [Modern praxis] 9 (Fall): 59–66.

Choi, Sook Nyul. 1991. *Year of Impossible Goodbyes*. Boston: Houghton Mifflin.

———. 1993. *Echoes of the White Giraffe*. Boston: Houghton Mifflin.

Choy, Bong-youn. 1979. *Koreans in America*. Chicago: Nelson Hall.

Cobb, Nora Okja. 1990. "Sessions." In *Making Face, Making Soul,* ed. Gloria Anzaldúa, 120–3. San Francisco: Aunt Lute Foundation Books.

Hong, Kyung Won. 1991. "But for You I Would Have Nothing." *Burning Cane/ Amerasia Journal* 17.2:99–102.

Hong, Maria, and David D. Kim, eds. 1992. *Voices Stirring: An Anthology of Korean American Writing/The Asian Pacific American Journal* 1.2.

Hyun, Peter. 1981. *Darkness at Dawn: A North Korean Diary.* Seoul: Hanjin Publishing Company.

———. 1986. *Mansei! The Making of a Korean American.* Honolulu: Univ. of Hawai'i Press.

Kang, Younghill. 1931. *The Grass Roof.* New York: Charles Scribner's Sons.

———. 1937. *East Goes West: The Making of an Oriental Yankee.* New York: Charles Scribner's Sons.

———. 1941. "Oriental Yankee." *Common Ground* 1:59–63.

KAWA: A Zine By & About Korean American Women with Attitudes. 1993. Univ. of California at Berkeley student publication.

Kennel, Nancy Lee. "Mirrors." *Gathering Ground* 105:43–4.

Kim, Alison. 1989. "Sewing Woman." In *The Forbidden Stitch: An Asian American Women's Anthology,* ed. Shirley Geok-Lin Lim and Mayumi Tsutakawa, 203. Corvallis, OR: Calyx Books.

Kim, Chungmi. 1982. *Chungmi: Selected Poems.* Los Angeles: Korean Pioneer Press.

Kim, Elaine H. 1982. *Asian American Literature: An Introduction to the Writings and Their Social Context.* Philadelphia: Temple Univ. Press.

———. 1986. "Asian Americans and American Pop Culture." In *Dictionary of Asian American History,* ed. Robert H. Kim, 99–114. New York: Greenwood Press.

———. 1993. "Home Is Where the *Han* Is: A Korean American Perspective on the Los Angeles Upheavals." In *Reading Rodney King, Reading Urban Uprising,* ed. Robert Gooding-Williams, 215–35. New York: Routledge.

Kim, Elaine H., and Norma Alarcón, eds. 1994. *Writing Self, Writing Nation: Four Essays on Theresa Hak Kyung Cha's DICTEE.* Berkeley: Third Woman Press.

Kim, Elizabeth M. 1981. "Detours Down Highway 99." *Quilt* 2:103–10.

Kim, Illsoo. 1981.*The New Urban Immigrants: The Korean Community in New York.* Princeton, NJ: Princeton University Press.

Kim, Kichung. 1973. "A Homecoming." *Bridge* 2.6:113–25.

———. 1988. "America, America." *San Jose Studies,* 113–25.

Kim, Leigh. 1982. "Da Kine." *Echoes from Gold Mountain* 3:96–106.

Kim, Myung Mi. 1989. "A Rose of Sharon." In *The Forbidden Stitch: An Asian American Women's Anthology,* ed. Shirley Geok-Lin Lim and Mayumi Tsutakawa, 20. Corvallis, OR: Calyx Books.

———. 1991. *Under Flag.* Berkeley: Kelsey St. Press.

Kim, Richard. 1964a. *The Martyred.* New York: George Braziller.

———. 1964b. "Best-selling Korean." *Life* 56:125–6.

———. 1968. *The Innocent.* Boston: Houghton Mifflin.

———. 1970a. *Lost Names: Scenes from a Korean Boyhood.* New York: Praeger.

———. 1970b. "Notes from Underground." *Korean Quarterly* 12.3:24–7.

———. 1989. *In Search of "Lost" Koreans in China and Russia.* Seoul: Eulyoo Publishing Company.

Kim, Ronyoung. 1987. *Clay Walls.* Sag Harbor, NY: Permanent Press.

Kim, Willyce. 1972. *Eating Artichokes*. Oakland: Women's Press Collective.
———. 1976. *Under the Rolling Sky*. n.p.: Maude Gonne Press.
———. 1985. *Dancer Dawkins and the California Kid*. Boston: Alyson Publications, Inc.
———. 1988. *Dead Heat*. Boston: Alyson Publications, Inc.
Kim, Yong Ik. 1965. "From Our Rostrum." *The Writer* 78:44–51.
Ko, Song-won [Ko Won]. 1974. *The Turn of Zero*. Merrick, NY: Cross Cultural Communications.
———. 1984. *With Birds of Paradise*. Los Angeles: Azalea Press.
Koh, Taiwon. 1959. *The Bitter Fruit of Kom-Pawi*. Philadelphia: The John C. Winston Company.
Ku, Robert Ji-Song. 1991. "Leda." *Burning Cane/Amerasia Journal* 17.2:99–102.
Lee, John Kyhan. 1991. "The Notion of 'Self' in Korean American Literature: A Socio-Historical Perspective." Ph.D. diss., University of Connecticut.
Lee, Marie G. 1991. "My Two Dads." *Brown Alumni Monthly* (April), 55, 56.
———. 1991. "We Koreans Need an Al Sharpton." *The New York Times*, 12 December.
———. 1992. *Finding My Voice*. Boston: Houghton Mifflin.
———. 1993. *If It Hadn't Been for Yoon Jun*. Boston: Houghton Mifflin.
———. 1993. "Talking Back to Stereotypes: Asian Women and Caucasian Men." *Colors* 2.3:6–8.
———. 1994. *Saying Goodbye*. Boston: Houghton Mifflin.
Lee, Mary Paik. 1990. *Quiet Odyssey: A Pioneer Korean Woman in America*. Seattle: Univ. of Washington Press.
Lew, Walter. 1992. *Excerpts from* DIKTK *for* DICTÉE. Seoul: Yeul Eum Sa.
Lim, Shirley Geok-lin, and Mayumi Tsutakawa, eds. 1989. *The Forbidden Stitch: An Asian American Women's Anthology*. Corvallis, OR: Calyx Books.
Min, Yong Soon. 1988. "Whirl War." *New Observations* 62.
———. 1990. "Territorial Waters: Mapping Asian American Cultural Identity." *New Asia: The Portable Lower East Side* 7.2.
———. 1991. "Comparing the Contemporary Experiences of Asian American, South Korean, and Cuban Artists." In *Asian Americans: Comparative and Global Perspectives*, ed. Shirley Hune et al. Pullman: Washington State University Press.
New, Il-han. 1928. *When I Was a Boy in Korea*. Boston: Lothrop.
Oh, Shin Yung. 1992. "Two Lives for One." *Kil Mok* 3 (Spring). Univ. of Chicago Korean American student literary magazine.
Pahk, Induk. 1954. *September Monkey*. New York: Harper.
———. 1965. *The Hour of the Tiger*. New York: Harper.
———. 1977. *The Cock Still Crows*. New York: Vantage.
Pai, Margaret K. 1989. *The Dreams of Two Yi-Min*. Honolulu: University of Hawaii Press.
Pak, Gary. 1988. "From *A Ricepaper Airplane*." *Chaminade Literary Review* 2:104–13.
———. 1989. "Excerpt from *A Ricepaper Airplane*." *Chaminade Literary Review* 5:159–76.
———. 1990. "Catching a Big Ulua." *Bamboo Ridge* 47:17–27.

————. 1992a. "A Ricepaper Airplane." *Amerasia Journal* 18.3:17–31.

————. 1992b. *The Watcher of Waipuna and Other Stories.* Honolulu: Bamboo Ridge Press.

Pak, Ty. 1983. *Guilt Payment.* Honolulu: Bamboo Ridge Press.

Park, No-yong. 1934. *An Oriental View of American Civilization.* Boston: Hale, Cushman & Hunt.

————. 1937. *Retreat of the West.* Boston: Hale, Cushman & Hunt.

————. 1940. *Chinaman's Chance: An Autobiography.* Boston: Meador Publishing.

Song, Cathy. 1976. "Beginnings (for Bok Pil)." *Hawaii Review* 6:55–65.

————. 1983a. "Living Near the Water." *Amerasia Journal* 10.2:105–7.

————. 1983b. *Picture Bride.* New Haven: Yale Univ. Press.

————. 1988. *Frameless Windows, Squares of Light.* New York: W. W. Norton and Company.

Sunoo, Sonia. 1982. *Korea Kaleidoscope.* Davis, CA: Korean Oral History Project, Sierra Mission Area, United Presbyterian Church U.S.A.

Yoon, Esther. 1984. "Vanishing Point." *Hawaii Review* 16:61–3.

5
SOUTH ASIAN AMERICAN LITERATURE

KETU H. KATRAK

Where did a language go once it was forgotten, I wondered. I often forgot Malayalam, at least little bits of it, but on my child-hood returns to Kerala, from Khartoum, it always revived, the deep buried roots stirring again. . . . After all, as a child it was my first spoken tongue. . . . In Manhattan, I am a fissured thing, a body crossed by fault lines. Where is my past? What is my past to me, here, now, at the edge of Broadway? Is America a place without memory?

– Meena Alexander, "Transit Lounge"

call me a poet
    dear editor
they call this my alien language . . .
I have my hopes
    hopes which assume shapes
    in alien territories

– Agha Shahid Ali, "Dear Editor"

South Asian American writers in English are among the newest voices in a multiethnic Asian America. Writers of South Asian origin are either first-, second-, or third-generation immigrants from India, Pakistan, Sri Lanka, Bangladesh; some have also journeyed here via Kenya and Uganda, or Trinidad and Guyana, areas where the long arm of British colonization "invited" a predominantly merchant class into East Africa, and a mainly indentured laboring class into the West Indies. Today, new forms of colonization dictated by the geopolitical and geoeconomic realities of a capitalist "new world order" continue to necessitate migrations and relocations from South Asia into North America. Writers from South Asian nations (themselves often invented as nations by the British) encompass a multiplicity of ethnicities, religions, languages, and cultures. Hence the category "South Asian American" does not indicate a monolithic whole, but rather a collection of differences that are often more compelling and significant than any similarities.

The use of the category South Asian American indicates the need for such ethnic demarcations within the climate of a peculiarly North American (United States and Canada) multiculturalism, replete with state policies, immigration quotas, and academic curricular battlefields. Amid this clamor, one must remember to listen to the struggling voices of the actual lived realities of peoples of color struggling to make a "home" within mainstream hegemonies, institutional or on the streets. Even within the same ethnic group there is multiplicity rather than homogeneity, and this is often the hardest fact for any mainstream to recognize. The "internal conflicts" among peoples of South Asian origins have much longer historical and geographical origins than our more recent location in the United States or Canada. As Saloni Mathur points out with regard to Canada, ethnic groups are not "internally consistent" as required by the state. There is no monolithic South Asian ethnicity as "required by the needs of multiculturalism." Within multiculturalism, there is room for usually only one variety of one ethnicity, not a complex plurality. Such a need for homogeneity is "closely connected," notes Mathur, "to state power and regulation. . . . The problem, in part, with the doctrine of pluralism as it has been politically employed by the Canadian government is its paternalistic insistence on the notion of diversity, when its underlying agenda has always been unity" (Mathur 1992, 2–5).

The multiplicity of differences among South Asians is linked by common histories of British colonization that they share with writers from other ex-colonies in Africa and the Caribbean. I include in the concept of colonization both physical and metaphoric parameters. The imposition and institutionalization of the English language as crucial components of cultural imperialism have left a legacy of writers using the English language even as they grapple with what Trinidadian-Canadian Marlene Nourbese Philip calls "this anguish that is English" (1989, 11). In a now commonplace phrase, the empire writes back, and often in a distinctive English that Philip describes as "Kinglish and Queenglish" (11).

It is important to note that in this analysis of writers one is leaving out whole populations of South Asians who came to the Pacific coast of the United States and Canada between 1904 and 1924, mainly male farmers originally from Punjab. This class often did not speak English, and their experiences of racism, of living through the Asian Exclusion League of 1905, and the California Alien Land Act of 1913 that barred aliens from owning land and that was not repealed until 1948, constitute part of an important historical bedrock for a study of immigrants of the post-1960s. As Sucheta Mazumdar notes:

Citizenship through naturalization was denied to all Asians from 1924 until 1943, when over the next ten years the laws were changed on a country-by-country basis. After 1943, with the exception of war brides and family members of U.S. citizens, immigration was permitted only on a quota system which allowed between 100 and 150 Asians annually from each country.... The 1952 McCarran-Walter Act enabled Asians to acquire citizenship through naturalization.... Between 1943 and 1965 when the quota system was in effect, 50 percent of the quota was reserved for professionals. (*Making Waves*, 1989, 4, 13)

Facilitated by immigration policies, South Asian immigrants since the 1960s belong predominantly to a professional class, the educated elite who benefited from an English colonial education in South Asia and came here equipped with educational skills and fluency in English. Contemporary South Asian American writers belong primarily to this middle and upper class: Indo-American Agha Shahid Ali, Meena Alexander, Bharati Mukherjee, Vikram Seth, Pakistani American Sara Suleri, Javaid Qazi, Indo-Canadian Rohinton Mistry, Uma Parameswaran, Sri Lankan Canadian Michael Ondaatje, and Indo-Guyanese Canadian Cyril Dabydeen, among others. Asian Indians who have come to America since 1965 have "created a new community," note Kitano and Daniels, "one that has few connections in ethnicity, in class, in occupation, or in location with the majority of its early 20th-century predecessors" (1988, 96). The 1980 census was the first to use the designation "Asian Indian" and "to put the figures of the 1980s into perspective, about every tenth Asian American was either an immigrant from India or the offspring of such a person" (98). The 1980s also witnessed migrations of a working class that, for instance, in New York runs newsstands in subways. Another such labor force is located in the motel business: "two fifths of all the motels in the Interstate 75 'between Detroit and Atlanta,' note Kitano and Daniels, are owned and operated by Asian Indians" (101). Popularly known as "Patel motels," they are managed mainly by a Gujarati community that arrived here at times via Kenya and Uganda, often after disastrous ousters by dictators like Idi Amin.

In this chapter I will deal with South Asian writers in English, omitting writers in languages such as Punjabi, Urdu, Bengali, and Sinhala, among others. The losses of that exclusion must be recognized, particularly of Punjabi literature, the earliest by South Asians. One advantage of studying only English-language writers is a cohesiveness of language, literary forms, and thematic concerns such as ethnicity, loss of homeland, uses of memory and indigenous folklore as sustaining mechanisms in alien environments, reconciliation, and hope in creating new spaces of belonging.

I shall undertake a theoretical discussion of the dialectic connection between ethnicity and location; between multiple identities and transforming geographies; and between being at "home" within one's body, one's native or adoptive home, and the English language. Writers' identities as immigrant/citizen/exile/expatriate are negotiated along issues of race, gender, class, language, and – crucially, in our contemporary time – geography. In a discussion of ethnicity, it is important to analyze how geography intersects with geopolitics and geoeconomics within a contemporary capitalist new world order. Economic and political forces that necessitate migrations and relocations often transform homes into alien homes. How do writers contend with this new geography in their search for home and belonging? Writers' ethnic affiliations as defined within immigrant spaces can overdetermine their political sympathies between their native and adoptive homes. Ethnicities are transformed, celebrated, or erased in terms of location. In other words, the pressures on ethnicity are experienced and expressed in a climate that paradoxically both propagates and devalues multiculturalism.

LOCATION AND THE LITERARY MARKETPLACE

Marginal cultural productions are capitalized on in today's marketplace. A complex process leads to marginalization. When marginality is utilized as a selling tactic, such modes of production have serious implications for writers and critics, introducing the dangers of a commerce that can change the very terms of what is written and can dictate what themes will sell. The marketplace is a key conditioning factor in producing and consolidating marginality. The commercialization of "multiculturalism," of "third worldism," as items for sale in the marketplace has serious consequences for the creative artist/worker.

For writers in particular, their ethnicities are evoked as either desirable or undesirable commodities by a literary marketplace that blows hot or cold for reasons that have very little to do with the quality of the work produced. When a marketplace is eager to consume marginal cultural products, and when the game of inclusion and exclusion is played without the players always knowing the rules – who is considered marginal, and when – such forces have serious repercussions on the possibilities and losses of cultural production. The market traffics in a desire that is racialized and gendered. Meena Alexander, an Indo-American writer who lives in New York, astutely discusses how writers have to be vigilant and resist commercializing factors in the literary marketplace:

> This new emerging art, without even knowing what we are buying in and are bought in, consists of images magnified, bartered in the

high places of capitalist chic . . . one of the things that is incumbent upon us as artists is to create works which, even as they take this phase within the social world, are in some way recalcitrant to it. The power of the media is so enormous. The public language in relation to which our work stands is extremely important. And it is painful because there is an extraordinary intimacy about the work which we are sharing with the public world. (1992a, 26–7)

My own position as a native of India who teaches Third World literatures in the United States reveals some aspects of loss and gain embedded within a colonial history and geography. *What* one can say *where* requires mechanisms of self-censorship, often dictated by self-preservation. When I pursued my B.A. and M.A. in India, we followed a tradition-bound syllabus of English literature. It was not until I came to the United States to work on a doctorate that I explored writers from other Third World areas whose cultures and experiences are closer to mine than those of the English male canon. My study of Asian American writers, rich with personal discoveries and intellectual illuminations, has been possible partly because of my geographic location here, which has serious repercussions in terms of my intellectual production, uses of particular languages, theories, and the addressing of certain audiences. This situation is not only a trajectory of colonial and postcolonial history and educational systems but, equally significantly, of "human geographies," to use Edward Soja's phrase (1989, 6).

A KALEIDOSCOPE OF SOUTH ASIAN VOICES IN NORTH AMERICAN LOCALES

Hyphenated American Identities

This is a study of selected writers of South Asian origin, writers who have been productive over the years. One can demarcate a post-1970s, and an earlier generation of writers of the 1950s and 1960s, some of whom were published in the P. Lal series in Calcutta, India. Among the earlier writers are Zulfikar Ghose from Pakistan, and A. K. Ramanujan, Deb Kumar Das, B. Rajan, and Peter Nazareth of Indian (Goan) origin (via Uganda).

Zulfikar Ghose, who is from pre-Partition India and Pakistan, lived in Britain from 1952 to 1969 and then moved to the United States, where he is a professor at the University of Texas, Austin. He is the author of four volumes of poetry, ten novels, two books of criticism, and an autobiography. In his poem, "One Chooses a Language," Ghose explores the dilemmas of people with many languages who write in English:

The English alphabet dangled its A
for Apple when I was eight in Bombay.
I stuttered and chewed almonds for a cure.
My tongue, rejecting a vernacular
for a new language, resisted utterance.
Alone, I imitated the accents
of English soldiers.

(1967, 5)

In an interview with M. G. Vassanji, Ghose discussed issues of rootless-ness, migrations, and identity formations. He has personally lived through the horrors of Partition when his family was uprooted from Bombay, where his father's "identity as a Muslim was creating difficulties for him," and instead of moving to Karachi, "which [his father] knew nothing about," the family emigrated to Britain. The title of Ghose's first volume of poetry, *The Loss of India* (1964), encapsulates "enormous per-sonal despair," loss, and rejection. He notes, "Indian secularism is a myth . . . I could not live in India because I am a Muslim; and I cannot live in Pakistan because I have no interest in being a Muslim." In this 1986 interview Ghose stated that he had not been back for nearly twenty-five years, "because I might once again be rejected – once again experience the loss of India. . . . Home is in my mind, my imagination. Home is the English language and what I can do with it" (1986, 17). This sense of not belonging to any one place informs Ghose's work, particularly his novels, which are fantastic inventions and, though often set in Latin American cities, could be located anywhere. He enjoys experimenting "with new forms, new uses of language, rather than being a chronicler of [his] time – I am not interested in my time in the sociological sense. . . . Actually, I never had a heritage . . . [that] I am supposed to be guilty of having broken with" (Interview with Vassanji, 1986, 20). Nor did he have a Muslim education; his father changed his name from the Muslim "Ghaus" to the Hindu "Ghose." Despite the accusation that Ghose is trying "to escape from the East," the imagery and landscape of his novels reveal superimpositions of memory and nostalgia about India.

India-born A. K. Ramanujan, poet, scholar, and translator, worked at the University of Chicago until his recent death in 1993. He is the author of fifteen books that include poetry in English and Kannada. Ramanujan presents a body of work that is most significant in demonstrating the value of the oral tradition in the Indian context. *Speaking of Siva* (1973) was nominated for a National Book Award. In his poems, "the family," as Parthasarathy notes, "is one of the central metaphors with which he thinks" (quoted in Lall 1983, 51). As the epigraph (taken from a Classical Tamil Anthology) for *Relations*, his volume of poems, states, "living /

among relatives/binds the feet." The intricate workings of the Hindu joint family system are explored with biting irony and an objective distance that simultaneously present sympathetic portrayals of wife, mother, father, aunts, and cousins. The persona weaves in and out of family events and memories that are often disputed, as in "Love Poem for a Wife. 1":

> Really what keeps us apart
> at the end of years is unshared
> childhood . . .
> Only two weeks ago, in Chicago,
> you and brother James started
> one of your old drag-out fights
> about where the bathroom was
> in the backyard . . .
>> Sister-in-law
>> and I were blank cut-outs
>> fitted to our respective
>> slots in a room
> really nowhere.

The preoccupation with family history is balanced by a situating of his poetic psyche in his adoptive home of Chicago, and often the poems bring the Indian and Chicagoan landscapes together, as in "Chicago Zen":

> Watch your step. Sight may strike you
> blind in unexpected places.
>> The traffic light turns orange
>> on 57th and Dorchester, and you stumble,
> you fall into a vision of forest fires,
> enter a frothing Himalayan river,
>> rapid, silent.

(1986, 83)

Ramanujan's poetic voice is balanced delicately between his past and his present. He retains a strong sense of being part of a rich Indian tradition, along with the texture of his adoptive home and its landscape.

Peter Nazareth, located at the University of Iowa's International Writers Program, deals with writers from India, the African diaspora, and Latin America in his critical work *The Third World Writer: His Social Responsibility* (1978). He debates whether the "Third World" has a geographical and historical identity. And he discusses accountability for the production of various Third World dictators and the responsibility of writers in the task of decolonization. Nazareth's novel, *In a Brown Mantle* (1972), is followed by a sequel of sorts in "Rosie's Theme," a short story (*Callaloo*, 2 [1978]). A family journeys through five generations in places like Goa, Malaysia, Africa, Canada, and the United States. Rosie adapts to different worlds: "We can live anywhere . . . make a start anywhere and win for ourselves."

Hyphenated-Canadian Identities

Himani Bannerjee, born in 1942 in what is now Bangladesh but was then still part of pre-Partition India, is a poet and an engaged theorist about issues of race and multiculturalism in the Canadian context. She has published two volumes of poems: *A Separate Sky* (1982) and *Doing Time* (1986), and a children's novel, *Coloured Pictures* (1991). As a note on the back cover of *Doing Time* states, Bannerjee believes that "you cannot change the world with art alone, nor can you do without it." When asked in an interview with Arun Mukherjee about "what it means to be ethnic and what ethnicity has to do with being a 'visible minority,'" Bannerjee responded:

> It means that we are not considered to be Canadians. We are "immigrant women.' . . . People's memories of the places they have come from persist with them. So this spill of memory has to be contained, and the dominant group contains this spill through various means. . . . Multiculturalism to me is a way of managing seepage of persistent subjectivity of people that come from other parts of the world. . . . On the one hand, you have the multicultural ossificatory imperative. On the other, you have the state and the dominant media with their assimilative imperative. . . . I think it is very important that we don't allow this "other-ization" of ourselves. (1990, 146, 148)

Other noteworthy Indo-Canadian writers are Saros Cowasjee, Rohinton Mistry, and Uma Parameswaran. Cowasjee, who worked as assistant editor for *The Times of India*, Bombay, moved to Canada in 1963. He has published novels, critical studies, and short stories. As editor of *Stories from the Raj* (1982) and *When the British Left: Stories on the Partitioning of India* (1987), he explores a changing history from the perspectives of Britishers and Indians, a time of change, a crumbling empire. Rohinton Mistry has published short stories over the years and came to prominence with *Swimming Lessons and Other Stories from Firozsha Baag* (1989). Most recently, he won a Commonwealth Regional Prize for *Such a Long Journey* (1991).

Uma Parameswaran, poet, playwright, and critic, is among the only Indo-Canadian writers who has ventured into drama in English. Her play, *Rootless But Green Are the Boulevard Trees* (1985), is set in her adoptive home of Winnipeg. An immigrant Indian family faces familiar generational conflicts between parents and children, who often inhabit different worlds. Both parents live "with blinkers night and day" and refuse to face what their children must in the mainstream society. Jyoti appeals to her mother, "We need to know, mom, we've got to know more about our parents" (92). Vithal's comment on race and assimilation expresses a biting separatism:

> They've never wanted us and now we are a threat. Serve us right for wanting to try to be one of them. We have to stay separate from them and stay together within and we've got to show them that we have as much right to be here as the pissed-off whites who've bullied their way into this country these last three hundred years. (100)

Among Indians who emigrated to the United States and Canada via the Caribbean are Indo-Trinidadian-American Ismith Khan, author of novels such as *The Jumbie Bird* and *The Obeah Man*,[1] Indo-Guyanese-Canadian Frank Birbalsingh, and Cyril Dabydeen. Dabydeen has published poetry collections, *Elephants Make Good Stepladders* (1982) and *Distances* (1989). His novel *The Wizard Swami* (1985) is described by compatriot Birbalsingh as "a signal achievement . . . one of few novels dealing with Indo-Guyanese experience and written by an insider" (1986, 78).[2]

Sri Lankan Canadian writers of note are poet Rienzi Crusz (*Elephant and Ice, Singing Against the Wind*) and Michael Ondaatje, poet and novelist. Ondaatje's talent as both has been recognized by The Governor-General's Literary Award and, in 1992, the prestigious Booker Prize for his latest novel, *The English Patient*. He is also the author of six volumes of poetry. His novels include *Running in the Family* (1982), a magnificent, surrealist rendition of family members (who remind one of G. V. Desani's *My Family and Other Animals*), amply and marvelously fictionalized. Ondaatje's *In the Skin of a Lion* (1987), unlike most ethnic novels, does not probe the history of his own ethnic group but researches the lives of Macedonian immigrants, "the un-historical stories" of ordinary folk not recorded in history books. This laboring class came to Toronto in the early 1900s and constructed several important bridges and viaducts in the city. Ondaatje acknowledges his Sri Lankan Canadian identity, but does not regard being "Sri Lankan in Canada" as his single theme. "I go to writing," he notes in an interview, "to discover as many aspects of myself and the world around me as I can. . . . [In *In the Skin of a Lion*] I wanted to step away from a private story into a public one, a social one – although obviously much of the emotion that the migrants feel in the book has a personal source" (1990, 198, 199). The novel plays with anti-hero Patrick's own sense of un-belonging although he is native Canadian. Ondaatje is a dazzling writer whose creative consciousness transforms any theme into magical wordplays. He has also made two documentary films.

Certain journals that have provided space for South Asian American writers are: *Fuse Magazine, Fireweed: A Feminist Journal, Asianadian, Tiger Lily*, and *The Toronto South Asian Review*. The latter, under the able editorship of Indo-Canadian M. G. Vassanji (born in Kenya, educated in Tanzania and the Unites States), has been an important forum since 1982 in publishing writers of occasional poems, short stories, critical pieces, to those of volumes of poetry or novels. Some noteworthy names that have reappeared over the years in this journal are Indo-Americans Lalita Gandbhir and Roshni Rustomji; Pakistani American Javaid Qazi; and Sri Lankan Canadians Asoka Weerasinghe and Suwanda Sugunasiri.

In the 1950s and 1960s, it was much more difficult for South Asian American writers to be recognized within an ethnic category than it might be today. Such ethnic visibility in terms of employment, publication, and daily life is advantageous and problematic, as is represented by a contemporary generation of South Asian writers who openly engage with issues of ethnicity, location, and racism within mainstream institutions.

ETHNIC IDENTITIES AND TRANSFORMING GEOGRAPHIES

But everybody needs a home so at least you can have some place to leave which is where most other folks will say you must be coming from.

June Jordan

Relocations are often marked by violence, what Meena Alexander, in her discussion of Asian American aesthetics, calls "an aesthetics of dislocation." She explains, "In India, no one would ask me if I were Asian American or Asian. Here we are part of a minority, and the vision of being "unselved" comes into our consciousness. It is from this consciousness that I create my work of art. Because of this dialectical element there is a "violence" involved for me even in the production of the work of art" (1992a, 26).

In a study of literary works and the parameters of the literary imagination, the *simultaneity of geography* – namely, the possibility of living here in body and elsewhere in mind and imagination – provides significant frameworks for a historical analysis of contemporary South Asian writers, and indeed writers of Asian, African, and Caribbean diasporas. This simultaneity, this sort of mind–body experience, may be somewhat generalizable in literary study. However, I would argue that the simultaneity is of a specific kind for writers with a colonial history whose socioeconomic, intellectual, and cultural conditions require migrations and displacements, for writers who express themselves in English.

The temporal trajectory of history, of events unfolding in time, places necessary boundaries around the past, present, and future. When one adds a spatial dimension, for instance, migrations, into this temporal unfolding, the intersection of geography with history opens up new areas for imaginative exploration – returning home through the imagination, re-creating home in narrative, creating a simultaneous present of being both here and there. As Jamaica Kincaid remarked in an interview, "I don't know how to be there [Antigua], but I don't know how to be without there" (cited in Kennedy 1990, 89). Kincaid's view is reflected in the work of other diaspora writers who imaginatively challenge the linearity of time and the specificity of space by juxtaposing their here and now with their histories and past geographies.

Within the complex and troubling historical times in which we live a new geography permeates the globe. Displacement of large numbers of people by necessity or by "choice" continues apace in a world where the concept of "home" has derived new parameters. Matters of "choice" in terms of location often turn out to be necessitated by the geopolitical and geoeconomic realities of the world today. Geography importantly inscribes contemporary history. In their very uneasy habitation within borderlands of different ethnicities, languages, and cultures, recent migrations of ethnic peoples provide significant clues for historical analysis.

Geoeconomic national borders are redrawn under financial dictates of bodies such as the IMF and the World Bank in a capitalist "new world order" that has unleashed, in Neil Smith's words, "all kinds of satanic geographies on the third world."[3] As capital travels and establishes new controls over physical spaces, its effects pervade silently, like an undetected cancer, into the bodies of vast populations. Forced relocations are part of a contemporary geography drearily full of dry statistics that must be humanized.[4]

No doubt, the history underpinning these geographic terrorisms is very important. In his provocative text *Postmodern Geographies: The Reassertion of Space in Critical Social Theory* (1989), Edward Soja argues convincingly for "a flexible and balanced critical theory that re-entwines the making of history with the social production of space, with the construction and configuration of human geographies. New possibilities are being generated from this creative commingling, possibilities for a *simultaneously* historical and geographical materialism" (11). Soja's analysis of "the historical geography of capital . . . [the] changing mosaics of uneven regional development within the capitalist state, and the various reconfigurations of an international spatial division of labor" illuminates the geopolitics of migrations. Spatial factors such as geographic migrations are important to analyze, because, as Soja argues, "space can be made to hide consequences from us." And since "relations of power and discipline are inscribed into the apparent innocent spatiality of social life," we need to analyze "how human geographies become filled with politics and ideology" (6). In my study of South Asian American writers, Soja's discussion of "the *spatialization of history* . . . the structuring of a historical geography" is enabling and provocative, especially when one recognizes that within any external lived reality there is always a set of social relations and that "space is fundamental in any exercise of power" (18).

IDENTITIES DEFINED AND DEFIED BY LOCALES

Kashmir shrinks into my mailbox,
my home a neat four by six inches.
        I always loved neatness. Now I hold
        the half-inch Himalayas in my hand.
This is home. And this is the closest
I'll ever be to home.
                Agha Shahid Ali, "Postcard from Kashmir" (1987, 1)

The poetic voice of Agha Shahid Ali is one of the most significant contemporary voices among South Asian poets. Agha has published five volumes of poetry. His self-description as "triple exile" from Kashmir, India, to New Delhi, and then to the United States, traces a journey of loss that has been extremely enabling in his creative universe. Agha's poems explore and contain the anguish of displacement and exile through memories, history, and the Urdu poetic tradition that he evokes from his 1979 collection *In Memory of Begum Akhtar* to his very fine translations of Faiz Ahmed Faiz in *The Rebel's Silhouette*. Agha journeys from Begum Akhtar's voice of loss to the revolutionary love ideals of Faiz, "the poet who redefined the cruel Beloved as Revolution," notes Lawrence Needham in a fine assessment of Agha's work. Needham contends that "from Faiz, perhaps, Agha increasingly assumes in his poetry the role of witness, and in Faiz, perhaps, he discovers a model for employing tradition in startling and original ways" (1992, 67). In *A Nostalgist's Map of America* (1991), Agha realizes a unique amalgam of indigenous influences along with a mature situating of his own voice and place in his exile home of the United States. Along with a nurturing, often painful, bagful of the bones of memory from other homes and distant locales, Agha re-creates an imaginative simultaneity of place and time, of history and geography. The very loss of "home" inspires in Agha's poems a very strongly felt sense of space and location – acutely observed geographical locations that exist in history and return to life through his imaginative re-creation, as in the tactile and poignant poem "The Dacca Gauzes":

> Those transparent Dacca gauzes
> known as woven air, running
> water, evening dew:
>> a dead art now, dead over
>> a hundred years. "No one
>> now knows," my grandmother says,
> "what it was to wear
> or touch that cloth."

> (1987, 15)

Although the grandmother had worn that fine gauze once, the poem is more a lament about the murder of that art at the hands of the colonizers: "In history we learned: the hands / of weavers were amputated, / the looms / of Bengal silenced, / and the cotton shipped raw / by the British to England."

Further, this history is astutely personalized: "History of little use to her, / my grandmother just says / how the muslins of today / seem so coarse." In the poem's closing stanza, the grandmother re-creates that lost time and place, and retrieves in imagination an irretrievable loss: "one morning, she says, the air / was dew-starched: she pulled / it absently through her ring."

Loss is not felt simply as a result of geographical dislocation. Agha's poems explore other kinds of loss associated with community and religion that are influenced by historical factors and changes, such as the skeptical voice in "Note Autobiographical – 2":

> My voice cracked on Ghalib
> as dreams of God crumbled for me:
>> Our servant, his shoes
>> stolen at the mosque,
>> turned deaf to the muezzin's call ...
> my tongue forgot the texture of prayer.

> (1979, 21)

A commingling of geographies enables Agha to take accountability for the past and present. His poetic voice performs a poignant balancing act between drawing upon memory and re-creating a past without romanticizing it, and residing simultaneously in the present. It is through his clearly felt and imagistic re-creation of actual spaces that he is able to set up a dialogue, even a dialectic movement between past and present. The various geographies of his journeyings in different spaces – "Autumn in Srinagar," "A Lost Memory of Delhi," "I Dream It Is Afternoon When I Return to Delhi," "Another Desert" – enable him to situate himself within a unique personal and diasporic history. History and geography commingle as a way of coping with loss, as in his poem "Snow on the Desert" (Agha 1991, 100). The Arizona desert that "was a sea once" evokes a memory of Begum Akhtar singing one night in New Delhi when the lights went out. That voice, time, place, and the poet's physical presence in the once-ocean-now-desert of Arizona encapsulates "a time / to recollect / every shadow, everything the earth was losing, / a time to think of everything the earth / and I had lost, of all / that I would lose / of all that I was losing."

Another writer who interweaves history and geography remarkably in her work is Sara Suleri from Pakistan, the author of the acclaimed autobiographical narrative, *Meatless Days* (1989). Suleri, a professor at Yale University, also has a vast scholarly output, her latest text being *The Rhetoric of English India* (1992). She combines a theorist's acuteness with a unique feminist awareness in her evocations of family members in *Meatless Days*. This is a nontraditional, nonlinear life story, equally about Pakistani politics, her family's roles and responsibilities in the fortunes of changing regimes, as it is about acutely drawn portraits of family members: her siblings; her grandmother Dadi, who "went scuttling through the day in the posture of a shrimp"; her Welsh mother, her journalist father, who when he took to prayer embodied "Islam's departure from Pakistan . . . the great romance between religion and the populace, the embrace that engendered Pakistan was done." Suleri's is a cerebrally recounted story, including assertions such as "the third world is locatable only as a discourse of convenience" (20). Often, one has to search for the emotionality that creeps up like delicate mist from between the lines, such as the horror and loss of Bhutto's hanging, which made "Pakistan feel unreliable, particularly to itself. Its landscape learned a new secretiveness" (18). Suleri's rich text moves blithely amid different geographies and histories – Pakistan, England, the United States, moving from the 1947 creation of Pakistan to contemporary reunions with family members, or re-memoryings of dead family members, unfolding in Suleri's adoptive home of New Haven.

"THE BARBED WIRE IS TAKEN INTO THE HEART"

For me, in the United States, the barbed wire is taken into the heart, and the art of an Asian American grapples with the disorder in society, with violence. And in our writing we need to evoke a chaos, a power equal to the injustices that surround us.

Meena Alexander, "Is There an
Asian American Aesthetics?"

Meena Alexander, a poet and one of the finest thinkers of Asian American aesthetics, has published several volumes of poetry and been widely anthologized in journals. Hers is certainly one of the finest poetic voices among South Asian American poets. She has also written a novel, *Nampally Road* (1991a), and a memoir, *Fault Lines* (1993). Born in India, Alexander was taken to Sudan at the age of five. She returned to her grandparents' home in India each summer. Since 1980 she has lived and worked in New York City. As she puts it in *The Storm* (1989), her five-part poem, relocations are part of a gendered violence: "Displacement, violence, but also the poise of a ritualised order are all parts of the feminine world" (iii).

Alexander's work voices a deep concern for the survival of the female imagination in different spaces. History, memory, and myth interact as she re-creates strongly felt images of her childhood in Kerala. Her poetic voice seeks an accountability to a history of migration and dislocation as it affects so many ordinary people, whose anonymous stories are evoked in "The Travellers":

> Consider us crawling forward . . .
> small stoppages in unknown places
> where the soul sleeps:
> Bahrain, Dubai, London, New York,
> names thicken and crack
> as fate is cut and chopped
> into boarding passes . . .
> Migrant workers stripped
> of mop and dirty bucket . . .
> night nurses raising their dowry
> dollar by slow dollar,
> tired chowkidars ekeing their pennies out
> in a cold country.

(1989, 9, 10)

In her essay, "Transit Lounge" (1991b), Alexander records a scene at Bombay Airport where she witnesses about thirty men whose names, written in Hindi, hang from their necks on name-tags along with destinations like Kuwait, Abu Dhabi, and other Middle Eastern destinations. She notes the economic necessities of these relocations: "There were whole families in India, dependent on the money these men would send home" (638). With deep sensitivity that recognizes these men "did not know how to speak Arabic or English," Alexander travels back in memory to her own childhood when those "two languages [had] surrounded" her in Khartoum. Her memory of learning Arabic from her friend Haadia's uncle, Abdullah Tayib, the famous Sudanese poet, is suffused by this urgency to learn how to name oneself. "Unless you learn, who will speak your name? . . . I think it is the pain of no one knowing my name that drives me to write. That and the sense that I am living a place where I have no history. Where all I am is surface and what is not reducible to a crude postcard dangled round the neck" (640).

Alexander's work poignantly explores the anguish of finding a name and the struggle to belong to a place. "We are our outsides," she notes in "Transit Lounge," as she observes a homeless man with his "habitat of cardboard," an image that evokes the need for a home of a different kind for the poet. As she "peoples that underground passage [at the subway stop] with cousins I have not seen for decades, ancient aunts from Kerala, bonded workers on their way to the Persian Gulf, all of us migrants and even those settled in ancestral lands, jolted by time," her prose spans time and space, and evokes the imaginative possibility of living simultaneously here in body and in several elsewheres in mind and imagery.

Alexander explores the need to re-create a past, to use it as a healing bedrock for the onslaughts of life in the present. Similar to the necessity of re-memorying lived spaces of her childhood, Alexander recognizes the significance of family history. Poems and prose are part of Alexander's *House of a Thousand Doors* (1988). In "Text from the Middle Earth," the two voices make "distances heave" as physical and psychic journeyings unravel through the female generations of grandmother, mother, daughter: "Thinking on my mother. / What kept her from harm shall keep me . . . I must trust to this voice to make a place. . . . The sea of this middle earth is always green. . . . In the middle where I am, there is no beginning." Alexander re-creates her grandmothers: Kanda, whom she never knew, and Mariamma, whom she did. Kanda "was the political grandmother," remarks Alexander, and Mariamma was house-bound, "her life, in all its pent up power, was lived within the rim of the domestic."

Often in Alexander's poems, the continuity of history is through the line of the female body, as though memory were ensconced in the cells, muscles, bones. In "Grandmother's Mirror," the voice records: "I swore never to forget . . . our childhoods . . . our dates inscribed inside / like welts on grandmother's palm." The history is kept intact, wordlessly inside the body and given voice by the poet. The pain of loss and recovery is located also within the female body itself, as opposed to Agha Shahid Ali's more external resolution through history and myth. Along with the family and the natural world, Alexander creates an archetypal identification with a spirit of femaleness that spans time and space: "lines of women from the field below" come to help the poet-person deliver her child. In the final prose piece, "House of Mirrors," this continuity is reasserted: "Again and again the child is born, each time in this very spot, each time she has a woman's body. . . . Might it be said, after so many births, that she has a female soul?" (119)

In "Grandmother's Letters" Alexander wonders whether her grandmother Kanda was like her and "invent[ed] a great deal." The letters that Alexander re-creates are written by Kanda to her husband, who is imprisoned by the British. "Unlock the bars with your gaze, deceive the distances. . . . Let the distances uphold you" – a wisdom that also touches a chord in a condition of exile and the need to conquer distances psychically. The poet in the present also deciphers meanings between lines written from a time in history when her grandmother "was struggling to spell out feelings that lay outside the ordinary territory of her days" (26).

In Alexander's *Night-Scene, The Garden* (1992b), the "mother's face" and "a fragrance most maternal" revive memories of the grandmother and the poet-narrator herself at age seven, then move into "No Man's Land" and the fierce attempt at claiming a heritage, a land, and a language:

> My back against barbed wire . . .
> No man's land
> no woman's either . . .
> I stand in the middle
> of my life . . .
> Come ferocious alphabets of flesh
> Splinter and raze my page
> That out of the dumb
> and bleeding part of me
> I may claim
> my heritage.
>
> (1992b, 26, 29)

In her essay "Is There an Asian American Aesthetics?" Alexander warns against "play[ing] endlessly in the post-modernist fashion" with our ethnicity as it "is located in our bodies." For Alexander, art is "always political, even if it is most abstract, even if it is a simple visual image of a leaf falling from a tree." In her work, she powerfully wrenches the English language into expressions of a complex, deeply felt resonance that place her within her ancestral history as well as her present immigrant locale.

ETHNICITIES CELEBRATED OR ERASED IN TERMS OF LOCATIONS

Although it is important to recognize the importance of "Indianness," of claiming one's heritage, the concept needs new definitions within immigrant locales. Meena Alexander links her heritage with that of other Asian Americans in her negotiation of past and present:

> I want to find a way that we can make a durable and usable past that is not just nostalgic but exists in the present. The present for me is the present of "multiple anchorages." It is these multiple anchorages that an ethnicity of Asian American provides for me, learning from Japanese Americans, Chinese Americans, African Americans, Indian Americans, and everyone juggling, jostling, shifting, and sliding the symbols that come out of my own mind. (1992a, 27)

Unlike Alexander's blending of past with present, which retains its specificity in terms of class and education, it is deeply problematic when cultural groups such as the National Federation of Indian Associations (NFIA) present a monolithic cultural identity of all Indians in the United States irrespective of class, religion, and education. This drive for homogeneity seeks to re-create a "national" unity within immigrant spaces. In a fine essay, "Woman, Nation and Identity in the Indian Immigrant Community,"[5] Annaya Bhattacharjee recounts how, at a Divali (Hindu New Year) celebration event in New York City, the NFIA put Indian culture on display as timeless and universally applicable to all Indians. Only acceptable representations of culture (*mehndi*, food, arts and crafts) were allowed. The activist group Sakhi, which deals with South Asian women and domestic violence, was denied permission "to stage a play that would highlight select aspects of . . . women's roles in Indian society . . . on the grounds that the topics were too political and ha[ve] no place in this exclusively cultural display. . . . The organizers deliberately excluded the participation of feminist, or gay/lesbian, or working-class organizations" (9). Group members of Sakhi were forced to "restrict [their] activities to an area outside the grounds of the main event. This marginal location mirrored the recognition of abuse against women in the

Indian community." Sakhi's challenge of the stereotyped ideal images of Indian womanhood drawn from mythology was percieved as a "betrayal" of all that this model represents – Indian "nation, culture, tradition, family" (10).

Bhattacharjee analyzes how a community's need to preserve a national homogeneity, often sited in their cultural traditions, places an additional burden on women. In attempts at cultural preservation throughout history, women have been regarded as the *guardians of tradition*, particularly against a foreign colonizer during nationalist liberation struggles. Now, in this different kind of colonized space, immigrant Indians must demystify a "mythical 'Indian' identity" unchanged by history and location. For a woman to leave an abusive space of battering and move out of the heterosexual, patriarchal family is tantamount to betraying a "nationalist" ideal.

Ironically, as Bhattacharjee points out, "the terms of cultural preservation are set by the dominant power." For example, in the United States, Indians, along with other Asian communities, are regarded as "a model minority, exemplifying high educational status and financial success" (11). She points out the contradiction in the very phrase "model minority." In its desire to belong inside an "American dream," the Indian bourgeois community "actively engages in the politics of minority status and representation within the U.S. These activities, dictated over limited resources for people of color, as well as by a rivalry over an imaginary standard of acceptance into the 'majority,' succeeds in making 'race' into a number game and a policy issue for Indians rather than an area of radical social change and action" (12).

"BROKEN IDENTITIES AND DISCARDED LANGUAGES"

Literary artists envision different types of negotiations in terms of their personal identities, histories, and geographies. Bharati Mukherjee might be considered the quintessential immigrant-turned-citizen who now embraces being an "American citizen" with a troubling and insistent fierceness. Her personal essay discusses the advantages of moving from a racist Canada into the United States where she feels more culturally integrated. Mukherjee lived from 1966 to 1980 in Canada, where she was treated as an outsider and adopted an "expatriate" identity and state of mind. She describes her move to United States as "a movement away from the aloofness of expatriation, to the exuberance of immigration." Mukherjee bitterly records her Canadian experience where she was frequently taken for a prostitute or shoplifter, frequently assumed to be a domestic, praised by astonished auditors that I didn't have a "sing-song" accent. The society itself, or important elements in that society, routinely made crippling assumptions about me, and about my "kind." In the United States, however, I see myself in those same outcasts . . . in professors, domestics, high school students, illegal busboys in ethnic restaurants. (1985, 2–3)

Mukherjee's adoption of an immigrant as opposed to an expatriate identity has been profoundly enabling for her writing. In her own words, she has "joined imaginative forces with an anonymous, driven underclass of semi-assimilated Indians with sentimental attachments to a distant homeland but no real desire for permanent return." Further, Mukherjee does not see her "Indianness" as an isolated configuration that can only be at "home" with other Indian people: "instead of seeing my Indianness as a fragile identity to be preserved against obliteration (or worse, a 'visible' disfigurement to be hidden), I see it now as a set of fluid identities to be celebrated." Mukherjee takes this further and relates her personal identity to that of her identity as a writer; she "sees [herself] as an American writer in the tradition of other American writers whose parents or grandparents had passed through Ellis Island."

Mukherjee's novels *The Wife* (1975) and *The Tiger's Daughter* (1971) trace a trajectory of a kind of upper-class female protagonist, socialized within a Brahmin (the highest caste) religious and social code, equipped with an English-language education. By the time Mukherjee publishes *Jasmine* (1989), she has become an American citizen. Her village protagonist, Jyoti, leaves behind the stranglehold of traditional customs such as dowry and *sati* – all presented with an objective, distant narrative voice – and embraces the myth of becoming an individualistic American, prepared to forge her own path and destroy what stands in her way: "There are no harmless, compassionate ways to remake oneself. We must murder who we were so we can rebirth ourselves in the image of dreams" (25). In her struggle to remake herself, Jasmine does not resist several renamings by others, and moves fluidly among new identities thrust upon her. Kali is her only act of self-naming when she murders her rapist, Half-Face. (The novel presents a disturbing ideology of violence as part of remaking oneself in American culture.) Jasmine is intent upon murdering her past as the only way to make a new life. She is described accurately by Karin, Bud's ex-wife, as "a tornado," as one who wreaks havoc and takes no accountability. In *Jasmine*, the adopted Vietnamese Du provides a striking contrast to the protagonist, who regards her own transformation as "genetic," Du's as "hyphenated." He has more agency than she does in terms of directing his young life, when he connects with his Vietnamese sister.

Mukherjee's earlier novels, *The Wife* and *The Tiger's Daughter*, present female protagonists who undergo disillusionments with marriage and struggle between identities as defined within their upper-class home environments in Calcutta, and their movements into an impersonal America where they must face loneliness and redefinitions of their ethnicities. In *The Wife*, Dimple Dasgupta remains isolated and on the margins of American life, unable to connect with an alien culture. Her predicament is similar to that of newly brought-over wives, sometimes by husbands who travel home for a couple of weeks, "interview" several prospective brides, and select one – there are plenty of bright-eyed women who wish to come to America. Their knowledge of America, often based on Hollywood films, does not include the realities of homeless people, poverty, and loneliness. "Losing" one's family's control also entails losing their warmth and love. Dimple becomes suicidal, thinks about where to die – in Calcutta or in New York. The novel concludes with her stuck in her indecisiveness. Mukherjee does not allow her protagonist much interaction with the "natives." Dimple remains in the claustrophobic apartment space or with other Indians. America hardly exists except as a backdrop, a physical location where she finds herself geographically. Her mental space is in turmoil – not really at home anywhere, she desperately needs help but is unable even to accept or articulate her needs.

In *The Tiger's Daughter*, Mukherjee depicts Tara, an upper-class Bengali woman who comes to the United States for an undergraduate degree at Vassar. Tara marries an American, and the novel traces her conflicts of identity and belonging as she returns "home," familiar and strange, gets to know the "David [her husband] of aerogrammes . . . a figure standing in shadows, or a foreigner with an accent on television. 'I miss you very much. But I understand you have to work this out. I just hope you get it over with quickly. . . . Remember the unseen dangers of India. Tell your parents to cable me if you get sick'" (63). "A foreignness of spirit" takes over Tara's consciousness as she struggles between a sense of exile both in her childhood "home" and in the newly acquired "home" of the United States. Mukherjee's explorations of the personal dimensions of female identity and belonging within marriage, an integral part of traditional Indian socialization for females, now resonates in a new key, as Tara's husband belongs "elsewhere" and so her home "should" be with him, even though that space is not yet "home."

Mukherjee is more successful as a short-story writer than as a novelist. Her first collection, *Darkness* (1985), documents the struggles of newly arrived South Asians, their experiences of alienation and racism as they try to find their "place" in American society. Their personal and professional lives within mainstream America often entail severe psychological costs. Mukherjee blasts the myth of the immigrant's desire to "return home" – a dream that she/he necessarily clings to, often as a way of coping in an alien world.

In her latest collection of stories, *The Middleman and Other Stories* (1988), Mukherjee "has vastly enlarged her geographical and social range," remarks Jonathan Raban in *The New York Times Book Review* (19 June 1988). In a more confident voice than in the earlier works, Mukherjee writes in the same breath about "Polish jokes and Patel jokes." According to Raban, she "hijacks the whole tradition of Jewish-American writing and flies it off to a destination undreamed of by its original practitioners. Her characters . . . see the surfaces of America with the bug-eyed hangover clarity of the greenhorn afloat in a gaudy new world. Yet they're not tired, huddled or even poor: they own motels, work scams, teach in colleges, breeze through on private funds. Their diaspora is a haphazard, pepperpot dispersal."

What Raban does not note, in typically *New York Times* reviewer manner, is Mukherjee's own upper-class background and the classist and elitist tone she adopts toward her characters. She overtly endorses the melting-pot concept and regards American society as the most welcoming of any in the world toward the "other." Even when racism is part of her exploration and critique, there is no attempt to place it within a larger political system of exploitation in the United States. Mukherjee gets a lot of mileage out of contrasting her own experiences in Canada, which were more overtly racist than in the United States, and endorses this society as "safer" for peoples of color than almost any other in the world. In an interview she remarked:

> In the U.S. I feel I am allowed to see myself as an American. It's a self-transformation. Canadians resisted my vigorous attempts to see myself as a Canadian. They exclude, America includes. And everywhere else, in Europe, France, Germany, Switzerland, the newcomer is a guest worker. . . . To be a Swede, a German, a Frenchman is a quality of soul and mind that takes hundreds of generations. (cited in Monagan 1988, 1E)

Mukherjee ignores the fact that to peoples of color of lower class and educational background than hers America is not always welcoming. Also, according to her use of racial categorization, France and Germany may have longer histories of white supremacy than the United States does. And simply to assert that because all Americans do come from elsewhere they are all equal is naive. One need only consider African

Americans and the shameful history of slavery, or the nightmare of Japanese American internment camps, and so on. These stories constitute the "soul" of America. The power mechanisms that lie behind such systemic methods of oppressing particular racial groups remain ultimately marginal in Mukherjee's work. Although she renders her immigrant characters sympathetically, in that sense departing from a Naipaul-esque disdain for colored peoples, her refusal to engage with what lies behind racism and oppression enables her to receive similar types of applause from a Western readership and the critical establishment.

In conclusion, South Asian writers have made their immigrant, expatriate spaces in North America extremely productive for their creative work. Through a mist of loss, through the anguish of lost homelands that become, in Salman Rushdie's words, "imaginary homelands," writers revisit these geographies most powerfully through their imaginations. They re-create their familial, social, cultural, political histories and locate them in their present spaces, giving them "a local habitation and a name." They work through complex negotiations of identity and belonging, juggling new words and new worlds. Their variously cadenced voices remind readers of the very different ethnicities to which South Asian American writers belong. Their work reveals the intersections of history and geography, of past and present. They provide new, imaginative ways of returning home through the imagination and of sustaining the human spirit that is capable of inhabiting different spaces simultaneously.

■■■■ NOTES

1. For a detailed discussion of Khan's novels, see my essay in *The Dictionary of Literary Biography* 125 (1993): 48–53.
2. Frank Birbalsingh 1986. Review of *The Wizard Swami*, in *Toronto South Asian Review* 4.3 (Spring): 78. Birbalsingh, author of *Passion and Exile: Essays in Caribbean Literature* (1988), teaches at York University and is an important critic of Indo-Caribbean-Canadian literatures. His text, *Indo-Westindian Cricket*, was one of a series that commemorated the 150th anniversary of Indians in the Caribbean.
3. Neil Smith, "Political Geographies of the New World Order," presentation at the "Rethinking Marxism" Conference. University of Massachusetts, Amherst, November 1992.
4. Recently, there were over one million homeless in Bosnia; 400 Palestinians were held in exilic no-man's-land; and citizens made refugees such as the 60,000 Muslims fleeing riot-torn Bombay during the terrifying January 1993 pogrom against them. The recent horrors in India vivify the importance of geography and location – real and symbolic – as categories of analysis for "third world" literatures. The controversy has been brewing for the past several

years over the issue of site, the location of Ram Janmabhoomi (the birthplace of the Hindu god Ram), at precisely the spot where a 500-year old mosque, Babri Masjid, stood in Ayodhya, India. The Hindu fundamentalist political lobby, spearheaded by the Bharatiya Janata Party (BJP), has been stirring discontent by propagating a theory that has been discredited by every eminent historian of ancient India, Romila Thapar among others. The BJP's inflammatory proposition – namely, to tear down the mosque and build a Hindu temple at precisely that site – has proven to be a recipe for disaster. The political fueling of religious differences – "Hindustan for Hindus" – has struck terror into the minority Muslim citizens of India, who have suffered loss of homes, businesses, and lives in the Babri Masjid riots and aftermath since 1993.

5. Annaya Bhattacharjee, "Woman, Nation and Identity in the Indian Immigrant Community," *SAMAR* [South Asian Magazine for Action and Reflection] 1 (Winter 1992): 6–12.

■ WORKS CITED AND SELECTED BIBLIOGRAPHY

Agha, Shahid Ali. 1972. *Bone-Sculpture: Poems* Calcutta: Writer's Workshop.
———. 1979. *In Memory of Begum Akhtar*. Calcutta: Writers Workshop.
———. 1987. *The Half-Inch Himalayas*. Middletown, CT: Wesleyan University Press.
———. 1991a. *A Nostalgist's Map of America*. New York: Norton.
———, trans. 1991b. *The Rebel's Silhouette*, by Faiz Ahmed Faiz. Salt Lake City: Peregrine Smith Books.
———. 1992. *The Beloved Witness: Selected Poems*. New Delhi: Penguin India.
Alexander, Meena. 1977. *I Root My Name*. Calcutta: United Writers.
———. 1978. *Without Place*. Calcutta: Writers Workshop.
———. 1988. *House of a Thousand Doors: Poems and Prose Pieces*. Washington D.C.: Three Continents Press.
———. 1989. *The Storm: A Poem in Five Parts*. New York: Red Dust.
———. 1991a. *Nampally Road: A Novel*. San Francisco: Mercury House.
———. 1991b. "Transit Lounge." *Michigan Quarterly Review* 30.4 (Fall): 636–46.
———. 1992a. "Is There an Asian American Aesthetics?" *Samar* 1:26–7.
———. 1992b. *Night-Scene, The Garden*. New York: Red Dust.
———. 1993. *Fault Lines: A Memoir*. New York: Feminist Press.
Asian Women United of California, eds. 1989. *Making Waves: An Anthology of Writings by and about Asian American Women*. Boston: Beacon Press.
Bannerjee, Himani. 1982. *A Separate Sky*. Toronto: Domestic Bliss.
———. 1986. *Doing Time*. Toronto: Sister Vision Press.
———. 1990. "The Other Family, and Interview with Arun Mukherjee." In *Other Solitudes: Canadian Multicultural Fictions*, ed. Linda Hutcheon and Marion Richmond, 141–52. Toronto: Oxford Univ. Press.
———. 1991. *Coloured Pictures*. Toronto: Sister Vision Press.
Birbalsingh, Frank. 1986. Review of Cyril Dabydeen's *The Wizard Swami*. In *The Toronto South Asian Review* 4.3(Spring):78.

―――. 1988. *Passion and Exile: Essays on Caribbean Literature*. London: Hansib.

―――. ed. & intro. 1989. *Indenture and Exile: The Indo-Caribbean Experience*. Toronto: TSAR Publications.

Cheung, King-Kok, and Stan Yogi, eds. 1988. *Asian American Literature: An Annotated Bibliography*. New York: Modern Language Association.

Dabydeen, Cyril. 1982. *Elephants Make Good Stepladders: Poems*. London, Ont.: Third Eye.

―――. 1989. *Coastland: New and Selected Poems 1973–1989*. Oakville, Ont.: Mosaic Press.

Gandbhir, Lalita. 1986. "Amba." *Toronto South Asian Review* 4 (Spring): 44–52.

―――. 1988–9. "Free and Equal." *Massachusetts Review* (Special Issue, "Desh-Videsh: South Asian Expatriate Writing and Art"), guest-ed. Ketu H. Katrak and R. Radhakrishnan, 29.4 (Winter): 733–41.

Ghose, Zulfikar. 1964. *The Loss of India*. London: Routledge & Kegan Paul.

―――. 1965. *Confessions of a Native-Alien*. London: Routledge & Kegan Paul.

―――. 1967a. *Jets from Orange: Poems*. London: Macmillan.

―――. 1967b. *The Murder of Aziz Khan*. London: Macmillan.

―――. 1972. *The Incredible Brazilian*. New York: Holt, Rinehart & Winston.

―――. 1986. Interview with M. G. Vassanji. In *Toronto South Asian Review* 4.3 (Spring): 14–21.

―――. 1984. *A Memory of Asia: New and Selected Poems*. Austin, TX: Curbstone Publishing Co.

―――. 1991. *Selected Poems*. Karachi and New York: Oxford Univ. Press.

―――. 1992. *The Triple Mirror of the Self*. London: Bloomsbury.

Grewal, Shabnam et al., eds. 1988. *Charting the Journey: Writings by Black and Third World Women*. London: Sheba Feminist Publishers.

Hutcheon, Linda, and Marion Richmond, eds. 1990. *Other Solitudes: Canadian Multicultural Fictions*. Toronto: Oxford Univ. Press.

Katrak, Ketu H., and R. Radhakrishnan, ed. 1988–9. "Desh-Videsh: South Asian Expatriate Writing and Art." *The Massachusetts Review* 29.4 (Winter).

Kennedy, Louise. 1990. "A Writer Retraces Her Steps: Jamaica Kincaid Finds Herself in Her Words." *The Boston Globe*, Nov. 7, 89.

Kitano, H. L., and Roger Daniels. 1988. *Asian Americans: Emerging Minorities*. Englewood Cliffs, NJ: Prentice-Hall.

Lall, E. N. 1983. *The Poetry of Encounter: Three Indo-Anglian Poets*. New Delhi: Sterling.

Lim, Shirley Geok-lin, and Mayumi Tsutakawa, eds. 1989. *The Forbidden Stitch: An Asian American Women's Anthology*. Corvallis, OR: Calyx Books.

Mathur, Saloni. 1992. "Broadcasting Difference." *Samar* [South Asian Magazine for Action and Reflection] 1:2 (Winter): 5.

Mazumdar, Sucheta. 1989. "A Woman-Centered Perspective on Asian American History." In Asian Women United of California, 1–22.

Mistry, Rohinton. 1989. *Swimming Lessons and Other Stories from Firozsha Baag*. Boston: Houghton Mifflin.

―――. 1991. *Such a Long Journey*. New York: Random House.

Monagan, George. 1988. "Crossroads of Culture Inspires Words of Indian Expatriate." *Star Tribune* (Minneapolis), September,10:1E.

Mukherjee, Bharati. 1971. *The Tiger's Daughter.* Boston: Houghton Mifflin.

———. 1975/1977. *Wife.* Harmondsworth: Penguin.

———. 1985. *Darkness.* Markham, Ont.: Penguin.

———. 1988. *The Middleman and Other Stories.* New York: Grove.

———. 1989. *Jasmine.* New York: Grove.

———. 1993. *The Holder of the World.* New York: Fawcett.

Nazareth, Peter. 1972/1981. *In a Brown Mantle.* Nairobi: East African Literature Bureau.

———. 1978. *The Third World Writer: His Social Responsibility.* Nairobi: Kenya Literature Bureau.

———. 1984. *The General Is Up: A Novel.* Calcutta: P. Lal.

Needham, Lawrence. 1992. "'The Sorrows of a Broken Time': Agha Shahid Ali and the Poetry of Loss and Recovery." In *Reworlding: The Literature of the Indian Diaspora,* ed. Emmanuel S. Nelson, 63–76. New York, Westport, London: Greenwood Press.

Nelson, Emmanuel S., ed. 1992. *Reworlding: The Literature of the Indian Diaspora.* New York, Westport, and London: Greenwood Press.

Ondaatje, Michael. 1970. *The Collected Works of Billy the Kid: Left Handed Poems.* Toronto: Anansi.

———. 1976. *Coming Through Slaughter.* New York: Norton.

———. 1979. *There's a Trick with a Knife I'm Learning to Do: Poems 1963–1978.* New York: Norton.

———. 1982. *Running in the Family.* New York: Norton.

———. 1985. *Secular Love: Poems.* New York: Norton

———. 1987. *In the Skin of a Lion.* Toronto: McClelland & Stewart/New York: Random House.

———. 1990. "The Bridge." Interview. In *Other Solitudes: Canadian Multicultural Fictions,* ed. Linda Hutcheon and Marion Richmond, 179–202. Toronto: Oxford Univ. Press.

———. 1992. *The English Patient.* Toronto: McClelland & Stewart/New York: Vintage International.

Parameswaran, Uma. 1985. *Rootless But Green Are the Boulevard Trees. Toronto South Asian Review* 4.1 (Summer): 62–103.

Philip, Marlene Nourbese. 1989. *She Tries Her Tongue: Her Silence Softly Breaks.* Charlottetown: Ragweed Press.

Ramanujan, A. K. 1966. *The Striders.* London: Oxford Univ. Press.

———. 1985. *Poems of Love and War: From the Eight Anthologies and the Ten Long Poems of Classical Tamil.* New York: Columbia Univ. Press.

———. 1986. *Second Sight.* Delhi and New York: Oxford Univ. Press.

———. 1971. *Relations: Poems.* London and New York: Oxford Univ. Press.

———, trans. 1973. *Speaking of Siva.* Harmondsworth: Penguin.

———. 1976. *Selected Poems.* Delhi and New York: Oxford Univ. Press.

Rustomjee, Roshni. 1988–9. "Expatriates, Immigrants, and Literature: Three South Asian Women Writers." *Massachusetts Review* 29.4:655–65.

Soja, Edward. 1989. *Postmodern Geographies: The Reassertion of Space in Critical Social Theory.* London and New York: Verso.

Suleri, Sara. 1989. *Meatless Days.* Chicago & London: Univ. of Chicago Press.

———. 1992. *The Rhetoric of English India.* Chicago & London: Univ. of Chicago Press.

Vassanji, M. G., ed. 1985. *A Meeting of Streams: South Asian Canadian Literature.* Toronto: TSAR Publications.

———. 1989. *The Gunny Sack.* Portsmouth: Heinemann.

———. 1991. *No New Land: A Novel.* Toronto: McClelland & Stewart.

6

VIETNAMESE AMERICAN LITERATURE

MONIQUE T. D. TRƯƠNG

Scholars and students of the art of telling the story of the past periodically engage in discussions on the ways of writing history, and among the changing fashions and philosophies, the one clear certainty is that the past changes with the times. And the past changes not so much because the returns aren't in, but because the living insist, as we must, on making our way to the historical stage where we further insist on reshaping the past according to our lights and the age's needs.

— Marco A. Portales (1984, 97)

I said I did this not for them
but for our ancestors.
Inside I was sad
feeling myself on a desert
knowing my customs will die with me.

— Tran Thi Nga (Larsen and Nga 1987, 264)

Layers upon layers of contradictions, like the sediments of not so distant eras, form the loose and porous body of works defined here as Vietnamese American literature from 1975 to 1990. Emerging out of a social and historical moment of military conflict, Vietnamese American literature speaks of death and other irreconcilable losses and longs always for peace – peace of mind. Death and peace are not the subjects of their contradiction. It is life and peace: one does not guarantee the other. Life as a refuge-seeker and a peace-seeker has placed us in a United States battle zone of historical revisionism, racial tensions, and ideological maneuverings. Playing out a grotesque but unfortunately applicable metaphor, Vietnamese American lives and their textual reincarnations have provided the newest arsenals for this national infighting.

I

For the majority of Americans, Vietnam as a self-defined country never existed, and Vietnam, North and South, as countries defined by military conflict did not exist until the U.S. involvement in the haze of the mid-1960s.[1] This U.S.-centric conceptualization of Vietnam also carries over to its people. The Vietnamese and Vietnamese American population within the United States prior to the fall of Saigon in 1975 commanded little public interest. Consequently, their existence is rarely, if ever, documented and discussed in conjunction with the numerous studies and analyses of the Vietnamese American community.[2]

Providing a rare glimpse, historian Ronald Takaki observes, "Twenty-five years ago, in 1964, there were only 603 Vietnamese living in the United States. They were students, language teachers, and diplomats" (1989, 448). The United States, considered a mecca of higher learning for so many people of the Third World, had been a cherished place of exile for Vietnamese students, scholars, and researchers for many years prior to 1975. Some may have chosen to remain, legally or illegally, in the United States, and for those already here in 1975 remaining was no longer a choice but a necessity. Therefore, for the purpose of this analysis and as a suggested corrective guideline for further studies, the term "Vietnamese Americans" refers to Americans of Vietnamese descent, including immigrants who may have arrived prior to 1975, refugees who started arriving in 1975, those who entered the United States as immigrants, starting in 1979 through the Orderly Departure Program, as well as the subsequent generations who have been and will be born in the United States.

The temporal scope of the analysis, therefore, commences not with the actual year of literary emergence but with 1975, a year that stands as a popular signifier for the fictional "initial" entrance and incorporation of people of Vietnamese descent as a racial ethnic group into the social fiber of the United States. The gesture and its subsequent exclusions of literature appearing prior to 1975 can be seen as a compliance to socially imposed and erroneous conceptions about Vietnamese Americans and their arrival (as opposed to arrivals) in the United States as refugees, and thus as a people defined exclusively by the military conflict that forced their resettlement. It also can be seen as a necessary and crucial adoption and recognition of the socially constructed "fictions" surrounding Vietnamese Americans in order to understand fully the conception, production, and reception of their literature into the context at hand.

In an effort to diminish oversights and dismissals of the "literary voice" of first-generation refugees or immigrants, the working definition of Vietnamese American literature in this analysis includes transcribed oral her/histories, folklore, song lyrics, and any other orally communicated narratives, as well as the more traditionally acceptable forms of literature such as autobiographies, poetry, epistles, essays, and other forms of nonfiction and fiction.

Elaine Kim's *Asian American Literature: An Introduction to the Writings and Their Social Context* limits her analysis of Asian American literature to only those texts written in English. She, however, emphasizes that non-English texts are and should be considered within the scope of Asian American literature.[3] Kim does, in fact, discuss and analyze poetry written on, or rather carved into, the walls of the Angel Island detention center by first-generation Chinese immigrants from the period between 1910 and 1940, as well as the haiku, tanka, and senryu written by issei prior to World War II for poetry circles or for publication in Japanese-language, community-based newspapers. In both instances, the poems in question have had to be rediscovered, collected, and translated by those scholars generations later who are in search of a culturally unique and specific Asian American literary history. To avoid the risk of similar periods of cultural and social amnesia and those ensuing excavation efforts, the definition of Vietnamese American literature suggested here includes transcription of orally communicated narratives and written texts in any and all languages to be deemed applicable and creatively relevant by the storyteller(s) and not by monolingual critics or theorists.[4]

Although there are now a number of well-publicized Vietnamese American autobiographical efforts, such as *When Heaven and Earth Changed Places* (1989) and *Child of War, Woman of Peace* (1993), both by Le Ly Hayslip and cowritten respectively with Jay Wurts and James Hayslip, this analysis chooses to take a number of necessary steps backward to encompass Vietnamese American transcribed oral her/histories. The analysis to follow recognizes their value as foundational Vietnamese American texts that have direct and relevant implications for the development of Vietnamese American literary voices. Beginning with transcribed oral her/histories will ideally serve as an (academic) field-fallowing gesture that can then act as an inroad for the development of a socially and historically informed discursive language necessary for further analysis and close readings of Vietnamese American texts. A close reading of *Shallow Graves* by Wendy Wilder Larsen and Tran Thi Nga will then follow to serve as an example of this discourse at work.

II

The United States in April of 1975 experienced the most immediate and extensive influx of refugees in its history, with over 86,000 South Vietnamese arriving within a span of a few days. "The refugee . . . is not an actor or reactor but is the object of attitudes and behavioral reactions of the receiving country or other authorities," writes William T. Liu, sociologist and author of *Transition to Nowhere*, an analysis of Vietnamese refugee resettlement (1979, 9). Within days of their arrival, concrete and extremely expedient structures were already forming for the refugees' recognition and incorporation as a permanent racial ethnic component of the United States. According to Liu, in May of that same year a proposal was drafted by the Asian American Mental Health Research Center's National Community Advisory Board for research and the "monitoring of the adjustment" of this community, especially for its comparative value within an analysis of the continuum of Asian American experiences (Liu 1979, preface, 1). As part of the research, Liu and his staff extensively interviewed and surveyed a number of randomly chosen family groups from among the Vietnamese refugee population detained at Camp Pendleton in California.

Employing the data generated from this original research project to inform his own analysis, entitled *Vietnamese Americans: Patterns of Resettlement and Socioeconomic Adaptation in the United States*, sociologist Darrel Montero suggests, "[T]he original Vietnamese respondents in our sample should be re-interviewed annually, thus ensuring that this rich and unique sample of Vietnamese is not lost to professional and lay audiences" (1979, 72). Over the next few years, Montero's call for a continued cultivation of an interviewer/respondent relationship with the Vietnamese American community received quite a few "responses." The responses came not just in the form of sociological studies but in decidedly literary projects with respective editors, who often spent years interviewing, collecting, translating, and editing the oral her/histories of Vietnamese Americans. These transcribed life stories most often found themselves showcased and confined within a larger "organizing" text that attempted to incorporate and employ the Vietnamese American voices/texts for the construction and facilitation of narrative goals extending far beyond the respondents' original speech/narrative act.

For example, *American Mosaic* (1980) includes interviews with several Vietnamese Americans, including the former Premier Nguyen Cao Ky. Edited by Joan Morrison and Charlotte Fox Zabusky, it is an attempt to reenvision the American melting pot in terms of the less assimilationist imagery of a colorful and complex mosaic. The editors interviewed, tape-recorded, and transcribed stories of "immigration" from both white ethnics and racial ethnics. Before each individual's transcribed voice/text, the editors included a short explanatory paragraph with information such as the respondent's country of origin, date of arrival in the United States, and a personalized vignette with facts deemed pertinent to the contextualizing of the text to follow.

The paragraph serving as a prologue for Thien Vinh's text states that he is from Vietnam and has been in the United States for "only" six months. The editors also write, "His teenage daughters were learning to drive, the younger ones were taking piano lessons, and the fifteen-year-old boy had earned enough from his newspaper route to buy a ten-speed bicycle" (427). The "only" before their six months in the United States is not merely a commentary upon a relative temporal duration. The editor's "only" stands in opposition to their description of "every" thing and of "all" the material possessions that Vinh's family had acquired (read "achieved") in their half-year as Americans. Morrison and Zabusky's framing of Thien Vinh's narrative fits seamlessly into a matrix of current (mis)conceptions about Asian Americans as the "model minority." In *Strangers from a Different Shore*, Takaki emphasizes that the model-minority myth not only denies the diversity in the Asian American community but also transforms Asian Americans into easy targets for misdirected racial tensions, especially within the economically depressed climate of the 1980s. Takaki writes, "Asian Americans also find themselves pitted against and resented by other racial minorities and even whites. If Asian Americans can make it on their own, pundits are asking, why can't poor blacks and whites on welfare?" (478). It is necessary to recognize that Vietnamese American oral her/histories exist within a complex social web that ensnares not only the remnants of the Vietnamese Conflict but also the present-day experiences of other Asian Americans.

Another editorial decision placed the Vietnamese American voices/texts in a section entitled "Immigration: A Continuing Process" where they serve as reinforcements for a metanarrative identified earlier in Morrison and Zabusky's text. While acknowledging the obvious social and historical differences of each ethnic and racial ethnic group's arrival in the United States, the editors maintain, "[W]e share a common heritage: in the background of every American is a farewell to the familiar, a long voyage, and a fresh start in a strange country" (xv). Morrison and Zabusky are not only the editors but also the "authors" of *American Mosaic*. Employing the various voices/texts as if each text itself represented one word, or rather a signifier, of an immigration experience, Morrison and Zabusky "wrote" a complex sentence that expresses and celebrates the proverbial "American Dream." The metaphors, like the voices, have changed and modified with each successive social and historical moment, but the metanarrative celebrating America's diversity remains the same. As the Vietnamese American voices/texts are included for what they say and not necessarily how they say it, an analysis of their poetics would prove rather futile. It is an analysis and close reading of the organizing texts and their textual manipulations, translations, and mediations of Vietnamese American voices/text that will prove to be more applicable and revealing in terms of the emergence and development of a "literary voice."

While Morrison and Zabusky's usage of Vietnamese American voices/texts delivers an elegiac vision of the United States as the New World, Al Santoli's *To Bear Any Burden* (1985) amasses voices for the vindication of the past. The text is subtitled *The Vietnam War and Its Aftermath in the Words of Americans and Southeast Asians*. Over a period of three years, Santoli, with assistance from a host of translators, interviewed people in the United States, Europe, and Asia. He claims, "I have chosen these people because I was deeply touched by the depth of their experience on the front lines of the Indochina conflict. Even though some were on the opposing side of the war, they share a common humanity that transcends their differences" (xix). Santoli's title, in itself, already establishes an inherent basis for these differences in terms of a polemic with "Americans" at one end and "Southeast Asians" at the other. It is crucial to note that while "Americans" immediately denotes one ("our") side of the war/conflict, the term "Southeast Asians" is constructed here as a signifier of both sides, South Vietnam and North Vietnam, as well as the Cambodians who were on neither side per se of the Vietnamese Conflict. Santoli's polemic reorganization reflects his text's internal ideological structure, which aligns the U.S. military involvement in Vietnam with the defense of democracy and the Southeast Asian "collective" (as constructed by Santoli) experience with the victimization of innocents by communism. Santoli's primary textual emphasis, however, depends upon a final regrouping and reshuffling on his part that allows all of his respondents to share common ground. He writes, "We who remember invite you to look back with us, behind the veil of myth and rhetoric" (xx).

This process of looking back that Santoli calls a journeying "through the dark night of memory" controls and dictates the overall construction of narrative meaning in *To Bear Any Burden* (xix). He initiates a process of inquiry that inherently propels each of his respondents back into a specific social and historical moment and their respective responses, without the benefit of contextualization with the present, then acts as a semipermanent fixer of their voices within an overdetermined and mythically constructed past. Santoli, in fact, organizes each voice/text entry so that the respondents are first identified and defined by their role in the Vietnamese Conflict and then by the duration of their active fulfillment of that role. For example, Santoli identifies a South Vietnamese respondent as the "Commandant" as opposed to the more accurate "former Commandant." It is not until the end of the text that Santoli allows his respondents to retrace, to resume, and, for some, to reconcile their present and even more binding identities with their more textually developed past.

In a section entitled "Biographies," Santoli provides a curt and rather unsatisfying blurb on each respondent, detailing place of birth, present country of residence, occupation, and family. The Americans can "travel" rather effortlessly and seamlessly from their former identities to their present ones, but the "Southeast Asian" respondents' journey is complicated by changes in nationalities and "sides." For example, Santoli intersperses both South Vietnamese and North Vietnamese respondents' voices/texts throughout *To Bear Any Burden*. Especially for those who now reside in the United States, their present status as refugees and as Vietnamese Americans plays a minuscule part within the organizing epic that Santoli has constructed for and with them. Within his text, they remain foremost Southeast Asians, and, depending on the respondent, they are initially contextualized as either a citizen of South Vietnam or a Việt Cộng. Santoli, for example, offers Nguyen Cong Hoan, identified as "Representative, National Assembly Socialist Republic of Vietnam, Ho Chi Minh City-Hanoi, 1976–1977," as the concluding Southeast Asian voice/text (332). Nguyen, who now resides in California, states:

> Today, it's ironic to live in America, whose presence in my country I opposed for so many years. When I first arrived, I went to Washington and talked with congressmen. They had their own concerns and did not want to think about Vietnam. So I came to California to take care of my family, working in an electronics firm. . . . Even though I now live well, I only think and dream to someday go back home. (332–3)

Exercising his editorial and essentially his authorial control, Santoli subdivided each individual's oral history into fragments, organized them within a roughly chronological time frame, and then assigned a title to each entry. Nguyen's concluding installation received the title "The Dream." Blatantly symbolic, this title immediately recalls the classic theme of the immigrant's American Dream, and yet the content of Nguyen's transcribed text does not outline or conform with its traditional themes. Nguyen's version stipulates a return to the homeland and an unwillingness to accept the United States as his home. "The Dream," in fact, appears to have been included and textually organized by Santoli as the Southeast Asian version of "Full Circle," an entry that immediately follows. The final voice/text entry in *To Bear Any Burden*, this entry is identified as Ken Moorefield's, an American military and foreign service officer. When he returned to Southeast Asia briefly in 1983 to film the refugee experience, Moorefield claimed, "I'd come full circle" (335). By placing these two entries back to back, Santoli attempts to suggest an analogous and thematic correlation between these two men and their desires to return to Southeast Asia. Instead, he succeeds in juxtaposing two very different "returns," with Southeast Asia as the geographic common ground. For Moorefield, his 1983 return offered him an opportunity to assist the people of Vietnam, Laos, and Cambodia without the use of military force. The filming of their experiences, he hoped, would foster international attention and aid. Moorefield's return can easily be interpreted as a purely humanitarian gesture. Nguyen's desired return to Vietnam, on the other hand, is loaded with implications of recalcitrant loyalties and of questionable ties to the mother country – ties that, according to the American melting pot or mosaic, must be displaced by the new arrival's commitment and devotion to the United States. Santoli may have attempted to conclude his text with two symbolic life circles/ cycles, but instead he succeeded in presenting a highly problematic representation of the Vietnamese American voice.

According to historian Takaki, Nguyen's desire to return to his homeland is not an isolated one. Takaki writes that during the early 1980s a number of fiercely patriotic former members of the South Vietnamese military services often expressed a desire to return and to regain their homeland through military force (452). Takaki's example, however, refers to Vietnamese Americans who were South Vietnamese and not to those, like Nguyen, whose allegiance had belonged to the Northern forces. The difference, in Vietnam as well as now in the United States, is a strong and crucial dividing line among people of Vietnamese descent. Vietnamese Americans do not blur the dividers, and few would consider themselves in a collective with Nguyen.[5] Again, the critique cannot be directed toward Nguyen, for it is only because of Santoli's placement and his employment of the respondent's entry that it becomes infused with the textual power to conclude, to represent a false Southeast Asian category, and to signify beyond his own personal experiences.

Santoli's use of Nguyen's voice/text as a mouthpiece to support his own underlying theme is a misguided and extravagant act of representation. In the United States, the fear of the "unassimilable" Asian immigrant has bolstered acts of institutionalized racism, from the Immigration Act of 1924 to the internment of Japanese Americans during World War II (Kim 1982, 9). Ultimately, it is not a question of assimilation and adaptation but one of the Asian American's overall capacity for trustworthiness, loyalty, and patriotism to the United States. This lingering doubt and distrust fueled the social rejection that allowed for the internment of Japanese Americans during World War II. Japanese Americans embodied an underlying fear on the part of Americans that an enemy front was coexisting inside the geographic boundaries of the United States.

For Vietnamese Americans, this question of loyalties and, more specifically, sides has been a recurring and life-threatening issue since the arrival of U.S. forces in South Vietnam. One of Santoli's respondents, in fact, speaks of this persistent layer of ambiguity. In an entry entitled "Counterterror," General Lu Mong Lan, "Commandant, Command and General Staff College, Dalat, 1966–1967," states:

> It is very important to distinguish the friendly people from the enemy. Each month, when I was corps commander, I issued a map of my area to all American and Korean units. And I used to assign one Popular Forces or Regional Forces leader to the U.S. 4th Infantry Division in Pleiku to accompany each American unit on operations. It was impossible for Americans to distinguish among our people: "How can we tell these Vietnamese apart? They all wear black pajamas. If they wear white, does this mean that they are on our side?" And if they killed somebody thinking he was VC, a hamlet chief might come to see me crying, "He was my nephew. And he was Anti-Communist." (154)

Notice that although both Korean and American forces are mentioned, only the American forces were assigned guides to help them distinguish between the enemy and the ally. The echo of American racism against Asians and Asian Americans can be heard throughout Lu Mong Lan's account. "They all wear black pajamas" stands as the more specific social-historical version of "they all look alike," a phrase commonly heard in the United States in conjunction with people of Asian descent. Santoli, as a veteran and the interviewer, has obviously come into contact with this theme of misidentification. His symbolic usage of Nguyen's voice/text as the concluding Southeast Asian voice "heard" in his text directly calls into question this issue of enemy versus ally – except that now the questions are raised within the parameter of the United States and the loyalties of its Vietnamese American community.

In a 1986 issue of *The Journal of American History*, George C. Herring's "Vietnam Remembered" emphasizes: "Of all the books [out of seven texts reviewed], Santoli's *To Bear Any Burden* is the most blatantly revisionist. . . . The purpose of his book is thus to reaffirm the rightness of the war as a cause and by showing how a war that could have been won was lost to help the nation learn how to use its power more wisely" (161). Herring's analysis of the revisionist nature of Santoli's text also has rather disturbing implications for the Vietnamese American voice/text and its role as a cooperative and/or collaborative text. In his introduction, Santoli indicates that he has chosen forty-eight respondents out of an unspecified number of personal interviews collected over a period of three years. His editorial decisions appear to have been directly motivated by the content of the voice/text as well as the former identity of the respondent. Herring emphasizes, "His [Santoli's] forty-eight interviewees were chosen with . . . [a] larger goal in mind" (161). In "Counterterror," for example, the former general follows up his discussion of mistaken-loyalty killings with a well-timed declaration of empathy. General Lu Mong Lan states:

> The Americans would get completely confused. For example, I understand what could have happened to Lieutenant Calley at My Lai. . . . I know all the tactics the VC used to harass you. And the population is used as a shield by them. This is a deliberate tactic. They had used it for many years, but the Americans had no understanding of this. And in Calley's case, it broke him under the pressure. (Santoli 154–5)

The My Lai massacre becomes just another case of communist "Counterterror"-ism, with the Vietnamese people and Lieutenant Calley as the unfortunate victims. Santoli cannot be accused of altering Lu Mong Lan's words, but the accusation does stand that he has showcased the former general's statement for his own revisionist goals. Like the editors of *American Mosaic*, Santoli could claim that he was simply providing the forum for these divergent voices to come together, and that it is ultimately their stories and not his that are being told. The editors of these organizing texts of transcribed oral her/histories, however, do hold in their hands the power of exclusion. Santoli fashioned an organizing text that only includes voices/texts which support his conceptualization of the Vietnamese Conflict. He therefore created a forum in which his viewpoints are in the overwhelming majority, as well as one in which all voices/texts complement and support each other's assertions. The construction of a self-fulfilling epistemological circle lends an aura of clear-cut factuality to a collection that otherwise could easily be acknowledged as an assemblage of arbitrary and selective remembrances of individuals, not of a collective.

Whereas it has only been possible to engage discursively with the end products of the previous organizing texts, James A. Freeman's *Hearts of Sorrow: Vietnamese-American Lives* (1989) provides its own explicit analysis of the interviewer/respondent relationship and therefore makes possible a revealing encounter with the theoretical underpinnings of the relationship itself.[6] Freeman's text showcases fourteen transcribed oral her/histories from respondents ranging in age from sixteen to eighty. The accounts were fragmented and then recomposed around five chapters, each with a specific narrative theme. The first chapter is entitled "Vietnam: Childhood, Youth, and Character" and the fifth, "America: Heartache Beneath Success." Freeman introduces each chapter with a brief discussion of its narrative goals and guiding motivations. For example, the prologue to the first chapter declares: "Of particular significance was the way in which the narrators drew on their childhood experiences to understand their responses to war and to domination by the Communists, and their adjustments in America" (27). Applying a second coat of textual "primer," Freeman precedes each of his respondents' accounts with a descriptive introductory passage, which sometimes rivals the length of the transcribed accounts. Although Freeman's organizing format does not challenge the precedents set by editors like Morrison, Zabusky, and Santoli, his academic grounding in anthropology forces him to acknowledge and to assume a more self-conscious if not critical perspective upon the interviewer/respondent process.

Known primarily for his studies of the Untouchables of India, Freeman emphasizes that he has applied his previously developed "perspective" and "style of research" to his fieldwork with Vietnamese Americans (429). For Freeman, the Untouchables were an "invisible people" who had little agency to speak and communicate with others about their condition until he engaged them in an interviewer/respondent relationship. He claims that prior research has continuously overlooked and denied the Untouchable's voice as a descriptive agent in favor of the more authoritative anthropologist's voice. Freeman claims he found an analogous situation in the Vietnamese American community in Santa Clara County, California. He writes, "I heard increasing complaints that most [media] reporting about them remained erroneous, misleading, and demeaning" (10). According to Freeman, Vietnamese Americans have silently faced and withstood "misconceptions" and "accusations" that they are abusers of welfare, undeserving receivers of special governmental treatment, and usurpers of jobs from other Americans. Freeman emphasizes that the Santa Clara community felt especially "dismayed" by America's understanding, or rather misunderstanding, of the Vietnamese Conflict. Freeman declares, "Because of these complaints, I designed this book, in which Vietnamese-American people could express themselves in their own terms about subjects they considered important and wanted other Americans to hear" (10).

Freeman would argue that his textual forums, first for the Indian Untouchables and now for Vietnamese Americans, are his contributions to their human-rights struggles. His final chapter, entitled "Implications for Biography," however, alludes to a less altruistic, more self-gratifying attitude. Freeman states: "In asking people to tell me the story of their lives, I was not observing a pre-existing social reality. Neither the Indian Untouchables nor the Vietnamese rural woman whom I interviewed had any idea what a life story was, and certainly neither would have related theirs had I not prompted them" (431).

Freeman's grouping together of Vietnamese Americans and the Indian Untouchables had heretofore been an understandable academic gesture, but as he persists in his discussion the gesture becomes increasingly ironic, if not socially and historically ludicrous. All of his emphasis on the diversity of the Vietnamese American community pales and dissipates next to this construction of misleading parallels and a false system of referentials between these two distinct groups. For Freeman, it is obviously an implied condition of illiteracy that binds together the Indian Untouchable and the "Vietnamese rural woman" presented here as a prototypical Vietnamese American respondent. Illiteracy is not a universal condition of the Vietnamese American community at large nor of the fourteen respondents whose transcribed oral histories appear in Freeman's text. Illiteracy, for that matter, is not even a condition of the Vietnamese rural woman in question. According to her own transcribed accounts, she can both read and write (64). For Freeman, it is not illiteracy, therefore, which binds his two objects of study, but specifically illiteracy in the English language. Even if she is illiterate, the "Vietnamese rural woman," like her foremothers, does have access to an oral tradition and therefore a history. If not strictly a personal/individual "life story" in a Western/Eurocentric tradition, it is nonetheless a history of her life in relation to her ancestors. It is a story told while rocking her babies to sleep. It is a story that she tells her daughters before they leave her house for those of their husbands. It is a story that literary theorist Trinh T. Minh-ha would characterize as "a gift." Referring to the narrative structure of an oral society, Trinh writes, "[A]n empty gift which anybody can lay claim to by filling it to taste, yet can never truly possess. A gift built on multiplicity. One that stays inexhaustible within its own limits. Its departures and arrivals. Its quietness" (1989, 2). Hinting at such a story, the "Vietnamese rural woman" relates: "The elder sister was considered a mirror for the younger ones to follow. This was taught to us just by talking . . ." (Freeman 1989, 65).

Freeman, however, needs to establish a context of collective "illiteracy" in order to support his primary theoretical argument. He emphasizes, "My interviews involved the creation of a whole new body of data that previously did not exist" (431). Although Freeman recognizes that the interviewers or, to use his terminology, the "investigators" or "researchers-interpreters," play an active and decisive role in the development of transcribed oral histories, he ultimately does not focus upon their mediation but rather upon their creation of the respondents' voices/texts. He writes, "These life stories of Vietnamese Americans came into being, not as an integral or historical part of the cultures of the narrators, but because an American outside investigator provoked and guided their creation" (431). Freeman's claim that the communication of one's life story is outside of the "cultures" of Vietnamese Americans is simply socially and historically inaccurate. As William T. Liu's research for the Asian American Health Research Center clearly indicates, the Vietnamese refugee community has been engaged in an interviewer/respondent relationship from the first days of its arrival in the United States. As a result of a program of relocation that considered the widespread dispersal of the Vietnamese refugee population as one of its primary goals, Vietnamese refugees became members of small towns and cities all over the United States. Upon their arrival, especially in these close-knit and otherwise homogeneous communities, they have had to tell their life stories to inquisitive newspaper reporters, to eyewitness television news crews, and to their interested and invested individual, group, or church sponsors. The answering of questions and the continual recontextualization of their past lives with their present have been necessary, high-demand components expediting the reception and acceptance of the Vietnamese refugees into the United States.

Freeman's oddly aggressive vocabulary, with its terms such as "investigator" and "provoked," signals a rather unexpected move on his part to usurp authorial control and agency from his respondents. Such a move is unexpected, for Freeman had earlier on distanced himself from that school of anthropology which denies and ignores the voices of their subjects of study. Yet his insistence on the researcher-interpreter's role as creator aligns him once again within this traditional discourse. He states, "[W]e recognize that the investigator's role in the creation of a collaborative biography is not an interference with the data, but rather an integral part of it, indeed *is* the data" (432–3). Freeman, in fact, refers to his respondents' transcribed oral histories not as autobiographies but as "collaborative biographies." The respondents no longer occupy the position of active tellers/authors of their own her/histories. They are, instead, the collaborating subjects of stories that are told and authored *for* them by their researcher-interpreter and biographer.

Freeman's paradigm is a suggestive rereading of the interviewer/respondent relationship. His blatant divestment of authorial control from his respondents, although disturbing in its conceptualization, does represent an alternative perspective upon the act of cowriting and its ultimate textual creation. Whereas the previous organizing texts depended and thrived upon the "authority" and/or "authenticity" of the Vietnamese American voices/texts to bolster their own textual arguments and goals, Freeman's paradigm suggests the possibility of a more contentious relationship, with interviewer openly vying with respondent for authorial recognition.

III

Shallow Graves: Two Women in Vietnam, by Wendy Wilder Larsen and Tran Thi Nga (1986), is a Vietnamese American text whose analysis and close reading reveal murky shadows of Freeman's expanded if not distorted reenvisioning of the interviewer/respondent relationship. The text more appropriately should be referred to as an American–Vietnamese American collaboration, for it includes poems "composed" by both women. Further attempts to classify it become rather complicated and muddled, for whereas the first third of the text includes poems written by Larsen, the remaining two-thirds includes poems attributed to Tran but are in fact the coproducts of Tran and Larsen. According to Larsen, their act of coauthorship began as weekly and sometimes biweekly sessions during which Tran told her life story to Larsen. Working with and from these tape-recorded sessions, Larsen claims, "I transformed her [Tran's] memories into narrative verse trying to stay as close to her voice as possible" (foreword).

Although an adage warns against judging a book by its cover, *Shallow Graves's* front cover offers a more than accurate indicator of its content. A black-and-white photograph of Larsen and Tran adorns the front cover of the Perennial Library's 1987 paperback edition. With one hand underneath her chin in the classic position of Rodin's *The Thinker*, Larsen stares contemplatively and intently at Tran, whose own eyes do not meet Larsen's but instead are focused on a point somewhere outside of the photograph. Serving as an absurdly accurate "diagram" of the power relationship at work inside the covers, the photograph captures the American researcher-interpreter observing her Vietnamese American respondent. It also exemplifies the organizing text's unabashed (dis)regard for Tran, who is constructed as object rather than subject of her own life story. Also appearing on the front cover is an endorsement by Frances Fitzgerald, author of *Fire in the Lake*. Fitzgerald declares, "*Shallow Graves* is a haunting book. Wendy Larsen speaks for herself – the American in Vietnam – and for Tran Thi Nga – a woman whose life is an epic intertwined with two wars. . . . She [Larsen] speaks for all those who, metaphorically, lie in shallow graves, unable to forget the war, unable to resolve it for themselves."

Fitzgerald's assertion is only partially and figuratively true, for Larsen does not actually speak for Tran in terms of performing a straightforward act of biographical writing. Her "transformation," or rather her imposition of a poetic form onto Tran's spoken narrative, is, however, an act that assumes and absorbs an incredible amount of her respondent's authorial control. Notice that Larsen does not claim she has translated Tran's story but, rather, that she has "transformed" it. It is obvious from what Larsen writes in her foreword as well as in Tran's "narrative verses" that this Vietnamese American woman respondent is highly literate in English. A recipient of a scholarship to study Social Administration at Swansea University in South Wales and a former bookkeeper in an American press office in Saigon (the office of Larsen's husband, and thus their initial connection), Tran's command of English should have proved more than sufficient as a means to communicate effectively her life story to Larsen. Larsen, in fact, appears to have accomplished little more than a superfluous, self-motivated act of textual reorganization. At the end of her foreword, she states that she had written quite a number of poems about her own experiences in South Vietnam prior to her collaboration with Tran. This body of work constitutes the "American in Vietnam" section of *Shallow Graves*. The transformation of Tran's oral history into narrative verses appears to have been motivated precisely by these preexisting works by Larsen and her desire to create for them an accompanying and complementary body of verse rather than by any compelling "poetic" impetus within Tran's own narrative or speech act.

Larsen justifies the "transformation" by conjuring up images of cultural determinism. To justify her poetic interventions, she begins her foreword with an anthropological musing about a Vietnamese oral tradition dating back to the fifteenth century. Larsen likens herself to a singer, "a blind person," who traveled from village to village offering renditions of truyện, or verse novels. She writes, "I feel like the performer of Tran Thi Nga's story as well as my own" (foreword). Freeman's self-congratulatory assertion of his creation of "an entirely new body of data" – namely, collaborative biographies – immediately comes to mind. Larsen, the interviewer in this instance, has assumed the active role not as creator but as performer of the respondent's narrative. For all his bravado, Freeman at least had the foresight to prepare for his own inevitable exit. In "Implications for Biographies," he writes that his position as creator is tenuous and temporary, stating, "I served . . . as a transitional mediator between two cultures; in coming years, Vietnamese-American writers can be expected to express themselves eloquently without the need for cultural translators" (435). Tran, with her proven English skills, appears to be an ideal candidate for such a nonmediated literary project. Ironically, her voice/text was nonetheless, transformed and translated, not on the level of language, but on the level of a textual language of representation.

Admittedly, proficiency in a language does not necessarily imply or guarantee an "eloquent" written expression, but it should at least guarantee one's ability and agency to speak for oneself. Fitzgerald's rather sweeping assertion that Larsen speaks for herself as well as for Tran is troubling, for women of color who engage in feminist discourse have emphasized and demanded that white women feminists stop speaking *for* them. The issue is not one of semantics but rather of the ideological positioning of the preposition *for*, which assumes a lack of voice and critical language on the part of women of color. In *Shallow Graves*, there is also an assumed absence of a viable as well as appropriately aesthetic language of textual self-representation.

As an organizing text, *Shallow Graves* commences with the customary, interviewer-provided foreword – a contextualizing framework for the Vietnamese American voice/text to follow. Entitled "Ba Larsen's Story," the section includes Larsen's poems as well as essays, personal letters, and various other textual artifacts from her one year spent in South Vietnam. As she herself acknowledges, the Vietnamese word bà translates as "Mrs." or "lady" and functions as a "sign of respect" (20). It is interesting to note that Tran's poems are entitled simply "Nga's Story." The conspicuous absence of this "sign of respect" in front of Tran's given name is a concrete textual indicator of an obvious power imbalance that existed and continues to exist between these two women and between their respective narratives.

Providing a rather revealing glimpse of their relationship as it was constructed in South Vietnam, Tran describes her attempts to fulfill Larsen's wish for a "souvenir" in a poem entitled "The Noodle Cart." Tran recounts:

> My boss's wife was educated.
> She taught English literature at the university.
> She called the office and asked questions,
> . . . . . .
> One day she asked me to find a noodle cart
> to take home to the United States.
> She was my boss's wife.
> Of course I would do it. (220)

Revealing the bare components of their relationship, Tran renames Larsen "my boss's wife" in accordance with her primary societal relationship to the American woman. For Tran, their association was first and foremost a business transaction that ensured job security, economic stability, and employer goodwill.

Larsen, on the other hand, portrays Tran's relationship with her as a movement from "guide" to "friend" (foreword). Larsen's terminology fluctuates throughout her poems, and for the most part the label she chooses depends on the land mass that her perspective is grounded in at that moment. Simply stated, in South Vietnam Tran is Larsen's "guide" and in the United States Tran is Larsen's "friend." Arguably, Larsen may have intended the shift from "guide" to "friend" to illustrate the deepening nature of Tran's relationship with her as it moved from economically interested service provider to narrative-sharing confidante. However, Larsen is unwilling or unable to acknowledge the economic interest that initially defined their relationship. For Larsen, the word "guide" is simply constructed as a signifier for cultural insider and benevolent holder and sharer of local knowledge. The economic underpinning of their relationship drops cleanly out of Larsen's social equation. This move proves to be narratively strategic, for it allows Larsen to create a more balanced juxtaposition of their respective narratives. For example, in "Reunion," the concluding poem of the section entitled "Ba Larsen's Story," Larsen suggests that a rather clean role reversal had taken place now that Tran was a refugee and a newcomer to the United States. In short, Larsen now saw herself in the role of the cultural "guide." The poem, which casts their first meeting in the United States in terms of Larsen's "reunion" with Tran, not in terms of Tran's separation from her homeland, commences with the following image: "Mrs. Nga is coming toward me / on the Avenue of the Americas." In the next stanza she follows up with "I remember my first walk in Saigon / asking everyone I met for directions" (101). Further transfixed by the notion that she and Tran had exchanged roles, Larsen concludes the poem with her response to Tran's lament regarding her teenage son. Larsen writes: "Remembering her advice to me in Vietnam, / I say 'give me a week' / hoping I'll come up with something / to bring peace to her American household" (102).

Accepting for the large part Larsen's fiction of an equitable relationship, and therefore the existence of a reversible and interchangeable set of roles for herself and Tran, Richard Eder, a reviewer for the *Los Angeles Times Book Review*, characterized *Shallow Graves* as a narrative informed by two instances of "complementing displacement[s]" (1986, 3). Although conceding the undeniable differences between Larsen's one-year sojourn in South Vietnam and Tran's lifelong search for refuge in the United States, Eder writes, "The two displacements were not symmetrical. Larsen's was temporary and by choice; Nga's was permanent and unavoidable. Asymmetrically, then, like bow and violin, they draw out a grave and elegiac theme of our times" (3). Whether they complement each other or not, Eder's metaphor of the bow and violin illustrates, presumably with unintentional irony, the discrepant power dynamics at work in Larsen and Tran's act of cowriting. Larsen is the active, narrative-generating bow while Tran is the passive instrument used for the narrative's creation and production.

IV

Liu's assertion again comes to mind: "The refugee . . . is not an actor or reactor but is the object of attitudes and behavioral reactions of the receiving country or other authorities" (1979, 9). The United States, the receiving country, has never fully recovered from its initial involvement in Vietnam. That involvement has been officially classified as the "Vietnamese Conflict" by the Library of Congress, implying that the United States does not lose wars but conflicts are apparently permissible losses. Justification and resolution for both the initial involvement and the ultimate defeat remain a high and persistent societal priority. Daily telecasts of a media "war" into the homes of the United States had created a high-impact and emotionally unresolved phenomenon. Emerging in the past decade, the ground swell of literature about the Vietnam era has only begun to explore the hidden corners and the silent victims of a televised war/conflict. Edward Eckert claims, in "The Vietnam War: A Selective Bibliography": "Vietnam may have been the first war the United States lost, but if popularity is measured by the number of books published, it ranks third – surpassed only by World War II and the Civil War" (1986, 51). The term "obsession" would seem a more appropriate stand-in for what Eckert suggests as popularity. Not only have political figures, scholars, soldiers, nurses, and reporters written nonfiction and fiction about the Vietnam era, but in 1986, with the publishing of Bobby Ann Mason's fictional work *In Country*, the generation who knew of Vietnam only through media-generated images also found a literary voice.[7] As in an oil slick, the failure to confine the flow (of images) results in a permanent alteration of the affected environment. Television coverage undermined an unwritten rule of selected U.S. military involvement: exile and confine activities to someone else's shores. This tactic had always spared the majority of the U.S. population the psychological trauma of seeing and living with disintegration, chaos, and death on a daily basis. Yes, the viewers always had the choice to turn down the volume or turn off the set, but with every returning veteran and every successive wave of Vietnamese refugees and immigrants the reminders could no longer be easily and effortlessly ignored.

The U.S. collective consciousness switched off and into automatic. If the flow of images could not be stopped, the presentation and representation of them needed to be altered and manipulated to meet what Marco A. Portales calls "the age's needs." What better place to rethink, reexamine, and reenvision a media war than in its most effective medium to date. No longer dealing with the "facts" of the Vietnamese Conflict, the discussion moved from the television screen's evening news onto the Hollywood silver screen, a medium known for its stylized and fictionalized accounts of history from the fall of Rome to the siege of Iwo Jima.[8]

The United States, now seemingly close to the verge of a fabled resolution of the Vietnamese Conflict, if only a filmic one, finds itself ill at ease to complete the task by itself. As Hollywood attempts to provide the film equivalent of group therapy, it looks to texts by Vietnamese Americans, especially autobiographical accounts, which promise to deliver the narratives, perspectives, and voices necessary for the framing of the conflict from the Vietnamese point of view.[9] At the writing of this analysis, Oliver Stone has released *Heaven and Earth*, the final film in his "Vietnam trilogy."[10] His acquisition of the film rights to Le Ly Hayslip's autobiographies, *When Heaven and Earth Changed Places* (1989) and *Child of War, Woman of Peace* (1993), cowritten respectively with Jay Wurts and James Hayslip, has transformed Hayslip's narratives into fragments of American popular culture and in the process has codified them into a definitive Vietnamese American perspective of the Vietnamese Conflict. The burden of representation hangs and weighs upon these texts, which had previously been received as compelling but nonetheless benign gestures of healing and resolution.[11] David K. Shipler, a reviewer for the *New York Times Book Review*, appears to have predicted this inevitable transformation and "translation" of Hayslip's *When Heaven and Earth Changed Places* from textual to filmic representation. Concluding his review entitled "A Child's Tour of Duty," Shipler writes rather wistfully, "If Hollywood has the courage to turn this book into a movie, then we Americans might finally have a chance to come to terms with the tragedy of Vietnam" (1989, 37). The headline of Shipler's review had already begun this process of transmutation by framing and reducing a Vietnamese American woman's life experiences to fit a trope of U.S. military involvement. For Shipler, the text's raison d'être is clear and one-sided: to serve as a medium for America's resolution of the Vietnamese Conflict.

CODA

Since I completed the first "final draft" of this chapter, the publishing world has issued the first examples of Vietnamese American autobiographies that are noncollaborative in nature: Jade Ngọc Quang Huỳnh's *South Wind Changing* (1994) and Nguyễn Qúi Đức's *Where the Ashes Are* (1994).[12] Freed, at least on the surface, from the tension of coauthorship and the uneasiness of submerged textual collaboration and manipulation, these texts offer a much longed for and tempting invitation to engage with the poetics of two distinct Vietnamese American literary voices. It is an invitation that deserves a greater engagement than what is to follow. More like a quick glance that reveals intriguing glimpses of white lingering beneath the hair's surface, the following is a gathering of discursive strands that await further analysis and development.

Published in the same year and written from the perspective of two Vietnamese American men who came to the United States in their late teens and early twenties as refugees, Huỳnh's and Nguyễn's texts invite comparison. The surface similarities, however, cannot begin to articulate both the overlapping and the singular mechanics of narration that incite their texts. Within the confines of this chapter, I offer a few words about their areas of overlap, for it is these areas which reveal the authors' common positions as survivor and storyteller.

The intertwining of the two – survivor and storyteller – exacts a heavy toll, for the authors are entrusted with, often laden down by, and thus must tell the stories of those Vietnamese who are, literally or figuratively, unable to recount their own narratives. As their respective texts demonstrate, it is only after the authors have served their role as messenger and facilitator that they may begin the act of self-narration. Huỳnh, who devotes the majority of his narrative to his imprisonment in "reeducation camps" and his attempts to escape communist-unified Vietnam, crafts a harrowing metaphor of this narrative strategy. After describing how he found a letter on the corpse of a fellow camp prisoner, Huỳnh includes what appears to be the text (or a reconstructed, remembered version) of this letter in translated form. Addressed to the prisoner's wife, the letter begins:

> What will I say to you now? I don't know if this letter will reach you or not. It would be easy for me to say I'm sorry, but this was unbearable. I couldn't hold onto my life any more, any longer. I had to run. If they shoot me, I will die faster than by being tortured here. I know I hold the love for you and our children, but what can I do . . . ? Will you understand me? (89)

From family photographs and other documents also found on the prisoner's body, Huỳnh concludes that the man was a former South Vietnamese soldier. In a move reminiscent of the guilt of survivors before him, Huỳnh equates the prisoner's death with an act of "honor and duty," which he contrasts with the lack of "patriotism" in his own life (90). Huỳnh writes: "I felt I wanted to prove something to myself at this moment – do something for this family. I would hide the nylon bag which I had just opened. I promised myself I would take it back to his family if I could get out of this place. I prayed that his spirit would help me escape safely so that I could bring his message to his family" (90).

While the remainder of Huỳnh's text is not so pointedly punctuated by the found narratives of others, his text is nonetheless pockmarked throughout with the rapid successions of questions reminiscent of the soldier's letter. The strings of questions are reminiscent in both form and function, for they often signal junctures in Huỳnh's text where he has seemingly lost his narrative to another. For example, describing his encounter with an old woman employed at a Việt Cộng hospital, Huỳnh writes:

> I wondered what would have happened if I had tried to walk away and gotten caught by the comrades. . . . Would she have been happy to see me grieving while I was dying? Wouldn't she? What would happen if I was her son, she the mother who had given birth to me, but she hadn't seen her son for years, and now we had crossed each other's paths? I didn't know. . . ." (171)

Huỳnh, in fact, often ends his strings of questions with a form of "I don't know." When faced with another individual, one perhaps with a narrative he feels to be more compelling or more deserving than his own, such as the soldier who dies in captivity while longing for his family or the old woman who has perhaps lost a son in the maze of war-driven migration, Huỳnh responds by sowing the seeds of their narratives that he carries with him. Unable to germinate and bring them to life in another manner, he resorts to strewing them chaotically throughout his own autobiography. This strategy of employing a series of questions to suggest a narrative is ultimately unsuccessful, because the strings of questions cannot sustain his or anyone else's narrative. We as readers are left with an author with a compelling story but whose narrative force is dissipated and often blocked by the enormity of his posture as survivor and storyteller.

Suggestive of another variation on the dual role as survivor and storyteller, the subtitle of Nguyễn's *Where the Ashes Are: The Odyssey of a Vietnamese Family* appropriately reveals that his text is both an autobiography and a family biography. Once prominent in South Vietnam, Nguyễn's family was well enough placed socially and economically that they were able to send two of his older siblings to study in the United States prior to the end of the war. Nguyễn's brother and sister, who remained in the United States after the fall of Saigon, eventually helped to ease his and his parents' subsequent arrival. Nguyễn's text, however, reveals little about these siblings. Instead, it focuses selectively on members of his family who were initially unable to escape war-torn Vietnam. His narrative voice, in fact, is most tender and expressive when speaking of the only member of his immediate family who did not escape to the United States, an older sister who suffered from bouts of mental illness and died of medical complications in communist-unified Vietnam.

Even in his self-proclaimed posture as family biographer, Nguyễn's embrace of his role as survivor and storyteller weighs less heavily on his text than Huỳnh's, and overall it is the better crafted and edited of the two autobiographies. Nguyễn is a correspondent and commentator for National Public Radio and perhaps has had more opportunities to practice his narrative skills, though another equally significant reason for the ease and unimpeded flow of his narrative may lie in the valuable resource provided by his father's own autobiographical text, entitled *Ánh Sáng và Bóng Tối* (Light and darkness) (1990). A Vietnamese-language text published by a small Vietnamese American publishing house, the memoir of Nguyễn Văn Đãi details the twelve years of his life during which he held the dubious honor of being the highest South Vietnamese government official to be held captive by the Việt Cộng. Too valuable to let die or to let go, Nguyễn's father was shuttled unmercifully from one prison camp to another even after the Việt Cộng had defeated the South Vietnamese/U.S. forces.

For three of his twelve chapters, Nguyễn freely borrows from his father's memoir as well as several of his poems to retell, with considerable skill, his father's experience of captivity and forced migration. Though he sometimes included English translations of passages from his father's memoir, Nguyễn reserves this narrative strategy for junctures within his text when his own narrative skills were ill-equipped to enable him to proceed alone. For example, in a passage describing his father's forced march out of the city of Huế as a newly captured prisoner, Nguyễn strategically defers to his father's own powerful description:

> The town seemed covered by a film of ash. There was something unnatural about a street so devoid of people. . . . We crossed a bridge over a small river where a lone Việt Cộng soldier stood guard laconically and headed toward the hills of Nam Giao. Gazing at the leaves trembling in the late afternoon wind, the deserted streets of the dead town, and the murky water flowing through the river, I thought of life's bitter upheavals. . . . It was getting dark, and in the gloomy moments when daylight was giving way to blackness, a wintry feeling and a sense of doom penetrated my body. (45–6)

In the three chapters devoted to his father's captivity, Nguyễn, in essence, employs a narrative strategy akin to Huỳnh's inclusion of the dead soldier's letter. For even though his father has engaged in his own narrative act via his memoir and his poems, Nguyễn's inclusion of them within his text breathes new life into them. Nguyễn's *Where the Ashes Are* serves as a medium for his father's works, in short, helping them to cross the chasm created by language and limited distribution.

Nguyễn, in his own words, is "indebted" to his father's memoir for the substantive clarity of the three chapters in question, but, to his credit, Nguyễn makes the narrative his own by accentuating it with some of the most compelling writing to be found in all of *Where the Ashes Are*. For example, although it is his father's narrative voice that marches the reader out of Huế and into captivity, it is Nguyễn's own eloquent refrain that guides the reader as she accompanies Nguyễn Văn Đãi home to the city of his youth. Nguyễn writes:

> When he turned up the street toward town, a peach-colored building came into view. He slowed his steps. The paint had faded unevenly, and [the] trim around the windows and balconies was brown with dust that must have taken years to accumulate. The green shutters, also faded, were closed. . . . The colors overwhelmed him. He remembered the summers of his youth, the high school close by where he had once been a student, and a teacher, and where he had first met my mother. . . . Switching his bundle to the other arm, he glanced back at the guest house one last time. His moist eyes recognized in the faded paint the color of home, and of freedom. (194)

Huỳnh's and Nguyễn's texts also yield another area of overlap, with which I shall conclude, for it is a stark and fitting reminder that the act of writing is a political one, literally as well as figuratively. Although autobiography as confession is hardly a novel equation or a controversy-free one within the field of Asian American literature, these two Vietnamese American texts contribute their own social and historical context to this trope. Huỳnh's focus on his own "reeducation" camp experience and Nguyễn's on his father's prison camp ordeal both populate their respective texts with grim metaphors of writing, especially autobiographical writing, as acts of punishment, confession, and redemption. Deconstructing the role of the writing act within the mechanics of "reeducation," Nguyễn writes, "Nightly interrogation sessions were always followed by the writing of the daily reports. The inmates were separated while they wrote. . . . No matter how one explained it, a discrepancy between two reports would be the subject of repeated, long-drawn-out cross-examinations. . . . At such moments the Việt Cộng would throw seeds of doubt into the inmates' minds, thus beginning the process of reeducation" (56).

Remembering one of many exhortations by his captors to confess to his own sins against the state, Huỳnh writes, "[Comrade Son] started his speech as if he was a general: 'This is the time for you to do something to pay us back, to prove your sincerity to our people. If you don't, you may stay here forever. Make your decision. I want you to write down your family history, your background and whether you feel guilty or innocent. I want the truth'" (85). Huỳnh's passage highlights the bitter nature of the psychological torment that accompanied each decree to write and confess. The torment came in the guise of the elusive promise of freedom dangled enticingly, and falsely, before each prisoner who yearned to write his own ticket home. For those first Vietnamese Americans who engaged in the collaborative narrative act, it was this same promise of freedom – not from the physical confines of a prison camp but from the psychological isolation of displacement and exile – which coaxed forth their narratives. Because the same impossible narrative requirements and demands for truth, guilt, and innocence were submerged beneath the methodology and ideology of the respective editors of the organizing text and cowriters of their narratives, it is a promise that has remained unfulfilled.

■ NOTES

1. It is significant to note that the word "Vietnam" in the United States context has been whittled down to nothing more than a signifier of a military conflict, and specifically an American, not a North and South Vietnamese, military conflict: Vietnam = war/conflict; Vietnam veteran = U.S. soldier; Vietnam era = a time period of U.S. military involvement and therefore heightened consciousness about Vietnam; Vietnam film = films dealing with the U.S. involvement in Vietnam; Vietnam literature = texts about this U.S. involvement. Although the "Vietnamese Conflict" is the official U.S. government term, the majority of Americans still employ the more widely accepted designation, the "Vietnam War." The vocabulary that emerged from the preceding American military involvement in Korea does not reflect this same syntactic exclusion and denial of the indigenous people, conflict, and country. For example, whereas the "Korean" component of "Korean War" is an adjective that describes as well as denotes possession, "Vietnam" is a proper noun that only lends specificity and context to the war in question. The unstated, understood agency of possession belongs to the United States: the United States' Vietnam War.

2. Writing in 1979, four years after the arrival of the first wave of Vietnamese refugees, sociologist Darrel Montero, in *Vietnamese Americans: Patterns of Resettlement and Socioeconomic Adaptation in the United States,* claimed, "Moreover, they [Vietnamese refugees] had no indigenous ethnic community within the United States to give them emotional and material support" (65).

3. Informing this analysis of Vietnamese American literature is Elaine Kim's discussion and definition of Asian American literature (1982).

4. This analysis, however, does not contain those texts written in Vietnamese. Those Vietnamese American authors now writing and publishing Vietnamese-language texts are of a generation schooled in a vocabulary, a literary

tradition, and an aesthetic that is uniquely and primarily Vietnamese. Their texts unfortunately cannot be adequately grasped or analyzed by a student who has only recently begun a program of study and research on the Vietnamese literary tradition. For an example of scholarship that does focus on Vietnamese-language texts, see Qui-Phiet Tran's "Exile and Home in Contemporary Vietnamese American Writing" (1993).

5. Refer to the afterword of David Chanoff and Doan Van Toai's *Portrait of the Enemy* for a discussion of this antipathy within the Vietnamese American community (1986).

6. Freeman's usage of a hyphenated "Vietnamese-American" is not a universally accepted convention in the field of ethnic studies. The hyphen indicates a possibility for bifurcation of the self into the Vietnamese half and the American half. Rejecting this notion of a clear-cut cultural divide existing within one's identity, this analysis has chosen to use the nonhyphenated alternative.

7. For another example of the self-styled narratives of this stateside generation, see issues of *Viet Nam Generation: A Journal of Recent History and Contemporary Issues*.

8. According to film historian Julian Smith, Hollywood has been finding Vietnam rather handy as an exotic backdrop for its films, especially "Communist aggression" films, since the late forties. Smith comments, "Hollywood couldn't seem to wait to get involved" (1975, 105). Tracing the postwar/ conflict developments, film historian Brock Garland writes, "In the early 1980's, fanned by the flames of a resurgent patriotism that accompanied Ronald Reagan to the Presidency, Hollywood came up with a new twist – while America may have lost the war in Vietnam, it could win on the movie screen" (1987, 7).

9. The following morsel of film-industry history serves as fair warning that, though Hollywood may covet Vietnamese American texts/voices to satisfy its cinema verité impulses, the narrator's identity is second to the ideological content of his narrative. In 1967, three years after the Tonkin Gulf Resolution, Hollywood was offered an opportunity to produce a film representing the war/conflict from the "other" side. According to Julian Smith, Vinh Noan, Director of the Motion Picture Center of the Republic of Vietnam's Ministry of Information, came to Hollywood with a script he had written entitled "A Night of Terror." "[The] film [was] about the war as seen from the point of view of villagers who must choose between turning a group of helpless Americans (including a blond newswoman) over to the Vietcong or fighting to save them. It was a rather novel approach, suggesting *Americans* needed the South Vietnamese. There were no takers." (Smith 1975, 14)

10. The previous two installments of the trilogy are *Platoon* (1986) and *Born on the Fourth of July* (1989).

11. For examples of their reception by the popular press, refer to the reviews by David K. Shipler and Lynne Bundesen.

12. The reader will note that some of the Vietnamese names in this chapter and in the Works Cited and Selected Bibliography appear with diacritics while others do not. The apparent inconsistency reflects my decision to print the names as they originally appeared in the respective texts. In general, this

means that most of the names of the early authors/respondents do not appear here with diacritics. Although it would have been possible for me to "reinsert" them, I chose not to because I believe it is important to "document" the authors/respondents own choice(s) or lack thereof with respect to the usage and inclusion of diacritics in their names. The absence of diacritics may signal a number of important issues, including lack of control, editorial or otherwise, over one's text and textual representation; the desire to "Americanize" one's name (possibly a Vietnamese American take on the truncation/mutation of names as a way to deemphasize one's ethnicity and foreignness); or the development of a Vietnamese American idiom. By the same token, the more recent instances of authors using diacritics may represent a desire for essentialist authenticity or the emergence of a viable and expedient emblem of ethnic pride and identification.

■■■■ WORKS CITED AND SELECTED BIBLIOGRAPHY

Adair, Gilbert. 1989. *Hollywood's Vietnam*. London: Heinemann.

Bundesen, Lynne. 1989. "Vietnam: One Woman's Story." Review of *When Heaven and Earth Changed Places*, by Le Ly Hayslip. *Los Angeles Times Book Review*, 25 June, 4.

Cao, Lan. 1994. "The Details Are Vietnamese, the Vision, Guilty American." Review of *Heaven and Earth*, directed by Oliver Stone. *New York Times*, 23 January, 13, 22.

Chanoff, David, and Doan Van Toai, eds. 1986. *Portrait of the Enemy*. New York: Random House.

Dinh, Thuy. 1991. "Of Luggage and Shoes." *Amerasia Journal* 17.1:159–63.

Dorais, Louis-Jacques, Lise Pilon-Lê, and Nguyễn Huy. 1987. *Exile in a Cold Land: A Vietnamese Community in Canada*. New Haven: Council on Southeast Asia Studies, Yale Center for International and Area Studies.

Duffy, Dan, and Kalí Tal, eds. *Viet Nam Generation: A Journal of Recent History and Contemporary Issues*, 1–4.

Dũng, Đinh Tiến. 1994. "Mỹ Sơn" [The Sacred Valley]. *The Việt Nam Forum* 14:287–8.

Dũng, Đỗ Trí. 1994. "Going Home." *The Việt Nam Forum* 14:253–61.

Eckert, Edward. 1986. "The Vietnam War: A Selective Bibliography." *Choice Magazine* 24.9:51–2.

Eder, Richard. 1986. "Shallow Graves." Review of *Shallow Graves*, by Wendy Wilder Larson and Tran Thi Nga. *Los Angeles Times Book Review*, 20 April, 3.

Fields, Rick. 1987. *Taking Refuge in L.A.: Life in a Vietnamese Buddhist Temple*. New York: Aperture Foundation.

Freeman, James A. 1989. *Hearts of Sorrow: Vietnamese-American Lives*. Stanford, CA: Stanford University Press.

Garland, Brock. 1987. *War Movies*. New York: Facts on File Publications.

Gordon, Elizabeth. 1990. "On the Other Side of the War." In *Home to Stay*, ed. Sylvia Watanabe and Carol Bruchac, 48–51. Greenfield Center, NY: Greenfield Review Press.

Haines, David W. 1989. *Refugees as Immigrants: Cambodians, Laotians and Vietnamese in America.* Totowa, NJ: Rowman & Littlefield.

Hayslip, Le Ly, with Jay Wurts. 1989. *When Heaven and Earth Changed Places.* New York: Doubleday.

———, with James Hayslip. 1993. *Child of War, Woman of Peace.* New York: Doubleday.

Herring, George C. 1986. "Vietnam Remembered." *The Journal of American History* 73:152–64.

Ho, Khanh. 1993. "Bittermelons." *Amerasia Journal* 19.3:151–3.

Howard, Katsuyo K., comp. 1990. *Passages: An Anthology of the Southeast Asian Refugee Experience.* Fresno: California State Univ., Southeast Asian Services.

Huỳnh, Jade Ngọc Quang. 1994. *South Wind Changing.* Saint Paul, MN: Gray Wolf Press.

Karnow, Stanley. 1986. *Vietnam: A History.* New York: Penguin Books.

Kim, Elaine. 1982. *Asian American Literature: An Introduction to the Writings and Their Social Context.* Philadelphia: Temple Univ. Press.

Lam, Andrew Q. 1994a. "My Vietnam, My America." *The Việt Nam Forum* 14:268–72.

———. 1994b. "Dark Wood and Shadows." *The Việt Nam Forum* 14:273–84.

Lâm, Maivân Clech. 1992. "Resisting Inside/Outside Classism." *forward motion* 11.3:59–63.

Larsen, Wendy Wilder, and Tran Thi Nga. 1987. *Shallow Graves: Two Women and Vietnam.* New York: Perennial Library.

Le, Phi-Oanh. 1991. "Palace Walls." *Amerasia Journal* 17.2:27–35.

Liu, William T. 1979. *Transition to Nowhere.* Nashville, TN: Charter House.

Luu, Khoi T. [Luu' Trưởng Khôi]. 1994. "A Heart of Sorrow? Exposing the Lighter Side of the Vietnamese American Experience." *The Việt Nam Forum* 14:321–32.

Montero, Darrel. 1979. *Vietnamese Americans: Patterns of Resettlement and Socioeconomic Adaptation in the United States.* Boulder, CO: Westview Press.

Morrison, Joan, and Charlotte Fox Zabusky, eds. 1980. *American Mosaic.* New York: E. P. Dutton.

Nguyễn, Chúng. 1994. "Power from the Heart: A Trip to Việt Nam." *The Việt Nam Forum* 14:262–7.

Nguyễn, Dung. 1994. "Rising from the Ashes: A Tale Told Through the Voice of Memory." *The Việt Nam Forum* 14:333–7.

Nguyen, Huong Giang. 1988. "A Vietnamese Lesbian Speaks." In *IKON Second Series #9: Without Ceremony,* ed. Asian Women United Journal Collective, 60–3. New York: IKON Inc.

Nguyen, Minh D. 1994. "The Monster in the Toilet Bowl." *The Việt Nam Forum* 14:338–55.

Nguyễn, Qúi Đức. 1994. *Where the Ashes Are.* Reading, MA: Addison-Wesley.

Nguyễn, Thị Thu-Lâm, with Edith Kreisler and Sandra Christenson. 1989. *Fallen Leaves: Memoirs of a Vietnamese Woman from 1940–1975.* New Haven: Council on Southeast Asia Studies, Yale Center for International and Area Studies.

Nguyen, Thi Tuyet Mai. 1994. *The Rubber Tree: Memoir of a Vietnamese Woman Who Was an Anti-French Guerilla, a Publisher, and a Peace Activist.* Ed. Monique Senderowicz. Jefferson, NC: McFarland.

Nguyễn, Văn Đài. 1990. *Ánh Sáng và Bóng Tối* [Light and darkness]. Westminster, CA: Văn Nghệ.

Nguyễn, Việt Thanh. 1994. "Untitled." *The Việt Nam Forum* 14:303–4.

Nguyen-Hong-Nhiem, Lucy Halpern, and Joel Martin Halpern, eds. 1989. *The Far East Comes Near.* Amherst: Univ. of Massachusetts Press.

Phan, Don T. 1991. "The Tradition That Was Grandmother." *Amerasia Journal* 17.1:7–11.

Phan, Ngân Hà. 1994. "Flashbacks of Emptiness." *The Việt Nam Forum* 14:307–11.

Portales, Marco A. 1984. "Literary History, a 'Usable Past,' and Space." MELUS 11.1:97–102.

Rutledge, Paul James. 1992. *The Vietnamese Experience in America.* Bloomington: Indiana Univ. Press.

Santoli, Al, ed. 1985. *To Bear Any Burden: The Vietnam War and Its Aftermath in the Words of Americans and Southeast Asians.* New York: E. P. Dutton.

Shipler, David K. 1989. "A Child's Tour of Duty." Review of *When Heaven and Earth Changed Places,* by Le Ly Hayslip. *New York Times Book Review,* 25 June, 1, 37.

Smith, Julian. 1975. *Looking Away: Hollywood and Vietnam.* New York: Charles Scribner's Sons.

Takaki, Ronald. 1989. *Strangers from a Different Shore: A History of Asian Americans.* Boston: Little, Brown.

Tenhula, John. 1991. *Voices from Southeast Asia.* New York: Holmes & Meier.

Tran, Qui-Phiet. 1989. "Exiles in the Land of the Free: Vietnamese Artists and Writers in America, 1975 to the Present," *Journal of American Studies Association of Texas* 20:101–10.

———. 1993. "Exile and Home in Contemporary Vietnamese American Writing." *Amerasia Journal* 19.3:71–83.

Trinh T. Minh-ha. 1989. *Woman, Native, Other.* Bloomington: Indiana Univ. Press.

———. 1991. *When the Moon Waxes Red.* New York: Routledge.

———. 1992. *Framer Framed.* New York: Routledge.

Trương, Monique T. D. 1991a. "Kelly." *Amerasia Journal* 17.2:41–8.

———. 1991b. "Teacher, I Am Sitting in Silence Not in Ignorance." *New York Asian News* 1.2:18.

———. 1994. "April–May, 1975." *The Việt Nam Forum* 14:292–6.

Uba, George. 1993. "Friend and Foe: De-Collaborating Wendy Wilder Larsen and Tran Thi Nga's *Shallow Graves.*" *Journal of American Culture* 16.3:63–70.

PART TWO

7

JOURNALISTIC REPRESENTATIONS OF ASIAN AMERICANS AND LITERARY RESPONSES, 1910–1920

RACHEL C. LEE

Give me your tired, your poor,
Your huddled masses yearning to breathe free,
The wretched refuse of your teeming shore,
Send these, the homeless, tempest-tost to me:
I lift my lamp beside the golden door.

> – Poem engraved on the base of the Statue of Liberty

America likes to couch itself in grand-scale symbols of racial tolerance: the Statue of Liberty, the melting pot drama, the mantra "liberty and justice for all" – these all beckon to immigrants. Yet America's more mundane symbolic venues – newspapers and magazines – define the country, not for all, but for some.

Nowhere is this more apparent than in the editorial stance toward Asian immigrants and settlers in popular magazines of the 1910s.[1] These periodicals, claiming to be the mouthpieces of popular opinion, depicted Asians as unfit for America's prospective society. The first part of this chapter examines these journals' distinct characterizations of Asians as less evolved, as a mass of undifferentiated difference, as unclean, and, finally, as unknowable. Except for the last of these traits, journals appropriated scientific rhetoric (notably, from the discourses of evolution and sanitation) in order to portray Asians as an element that, in the proper progress of man, should not be (re)assimilated into the fabric of Western humanity. In addition to these identifiable characteristics, these magazines assigned Asians an "unknowable" quality, designed to dichotomize the East and the West. The East was everything that the West was not. This negative definition allowed for contradictions in editorial and political policy, contradictions that furthered the domestic exclusion and foreign colonization of Asian subjects.

Concurrent with these publications were short stories and novels written by and about Asian Americans. The second part of this chapter

examines these literary works, many of which appeared in popular maga-
zines prior to republication in book collections. Centering their works on
Asian characters, four writers – Sax Rohmer (Arthur Sarsfield Ward),
Onoto Watanna (Winnifred Eaton), Paz Marquez Benitez, and Sui Sin Far
(Edith Eaton, also elder sister to Winnifred) – responded directly to the
images of Asians produced in the popular press. Although similar in this
respect, these authors differed in the degree to which they challenged an
Orientalist depiction of Asia as the West's mere contour. From Sax
Rohmer, who capitalizes on the fearful and unknowable characterization
of Asians, to Sui Sin Far, who wrote sympathetically from her Chinese
American characters' point of view, these writers' works are presented
here in an order of increasing ideological challenge to the popular press's
encouragement of Asian exclusion and colonization. Though meant as a
presentation of the spectrum of responses, the sections on the four writers
can be read individually as windows onto each author's works and his or
her particular relation to journalistic orientalism and the concomitant
commerce in Asiatic bodies.

THE PERIL OF THE UNKNOWN

On 1 January 1910, *Collier's* ran two pieces, one heralding the
"arrival of Japan" as "nothing less than the miraculous creation of another *Western power*" (17, emphasis added) and the other, entitled "The
Awakening of China," detailing the country's nine-year term of probation
in preparation for a constitutional government (14).[2] The language of
both articles draws a time-line of evolution, where having "arrived" or
being on time (as Japan has) means Westernization, and where being late
signals backwardness and stagnation.

Asian "satellite" nations like the Philippines fared even worse in this
time-line created by the magazines. While the debate over Philippine
independence raged in the popular press, features such as Dean C.
Worcester's "Field Sports among the Wild Men of Luzon" and "The
Non-Christian Peoples of the Philippine Islands" (*National Geographic*,
March 1911 and November 1913) portrayed Filipinos as a variegated
(hence disunited) people, unable to curb their native inhabitants' pen-
chant for head-hunting, let alone govern themselves. The 1913 article
underscores the evolutionary backwardness of the Philippine native
"Negritos," "probably the lowest type of human beings known [who]
have been described as 'not far above the anthropoid apes'" (1180).
Implicitly sanctioning America's policy of colonial "tutelage," the article
depicts the Western administrator bestowing his civilized institutions (of
education, industrial training, sports, and sanitation) upon the less
evolved "wild men."

On the domestic front, Joshua Wanhope, writing for the *Masses* (June 1912), reported the Socialist party's exclusion of Asiatic labor from its ranks because Asiatics "were so far behind the peoples of Europe in the plan of evolution that they were not readily assimilable" (12). Ignoring the role of education in labor activism, the party contended that the mental and psychological "plane" of Asiatic peoples made them irredeemably different (in a separate Darwinian category) from European labor. The party's appeal to "evolutionary development," though seemingly focused on progress and change, denied its subjects any potential for growth. Asiatic peoples could not *develop* class consciousness precisely because of the limits of their assigned stage of *development*. Clearly, the argument acts as a strategy of containment, which masks its purpose in pseudoscientific language.

This evolutionary discourse that slotted Asian nations into developmental stages also amassed all Asians into a near-primate stage, with only the Anglo-American as the fully developed human. Other races remained either "anthropoid apes" or "children" who needed to be "spanked regularly" (*Philippines Free Press*, 1 June 1912, 2). Thus, editorials of this era often conflated a single Asian nation with "the East in general," reflecting a propensity to see Asian nations as a political bloc and pointing to the way in which journalistic prose applied the "character" of any one Asian nation to all Asian nations. For instance, "the yellow peril" during this decade served as a general reference to all Asiatic peoples and their perceived threat to American labor and real-estate markets. Wanhope recorded the Socialist party's majority stance against that mass of Asiatic immigration, concluding that Chinese, Japanese, Hindus, Malays, and the peoples generally of eastern Asia "would most likely serve the ruling classes of this country as solid, unassimilable, racial wedges for the purpose of splitting the modern labor movement" (12).

This tendency to lump all Asians under one racial category enabled various journalists to take single instances of culturally "foreign" behavior and apply them to another national group so as to compile an amalgamated image of "the Asian race" (which functioned less as a physiological category than as a discursive trope for the Other). This amalgamated image, in turn, served Anglo writers who wished to stir up negative public sentiment toward a specific Asian group. For example, in his feature "Japan in California" (*Collier's*, 17 June 1913), Peter McFarlane, in support of the Alien Land Law,[3] condemned the members of a Japanese farming community in Florin by calling them "Oriental" and proclaiming their "unclean" habits and morals. McFarlane deemed the Japanese "unclean" because "There are no lace curtains at the windows, only shades. ... There are no cows or calves, not even a fowl [in the barnyard], for these Japanese of Florin are tillers of the soil pure and simple" (6).

"Unclean" becomes synonymous with nonconformity to American tastes in home decoration and husbandry. McFarlane additionally called the aspirations of the Japanese "sordid" because they "are *not our* ambitions ... *not our* satisfactions, with morals that *to us* are no morals..." (6, emphasis added). In McFarlane's rhetoric, "sordid" simply translates into "not like us." One sees the discourse of "uncleanliness" appropriating scientific terminology in order to make "cultural difference" a dirty word.

This focus on the supposed unhygienic nature of the Japanese appeals to the racist fear of infection. This fear was particularly acute with regard to the Chinese, who became "medical scapegoats" in the San Francisco community from 1870 to 1905.[4] In 1911, photographic coverage of the plague epidemic in Manchuria only compounded the associations of Chinese with unhygienic approaches to disease. Filipinos, especially the aboriginal population, were likewise being portrayed as "naturally dirty" or "filthy." For instance, *National Geographic*'s coverage of mountain provinces in 1913 described American governors converting malaria-ridden, "ill-kept, foul-smelling *rancherias*" into sanitary towns.

Besides portraying them as carriers of disease, the journals furthered the stereotype of Asians as "stoic" and "inscrutable." Reporting on the continuing "Plague in Manchuria," *Collier's* captioned one photograph of an infected man: "With the remarkable fatalism of the Chinese he is facing the inevitable with the calmness of indifference. In thirty-six hours he was dead" (15). Ironically, the photographic medium helped *Collier's* to construct the Chinese "character." In trying to make news of photographs that did not necessarily lend themselves to spectacle, *Collier's* captioned the pictures so that the reader could behold in a frame of neutrality the phenomenon of "indifference at death." Because of the American emphasis on emotional display, "inscrutability" became almost a criminal trait – evidence of inhumanity. Blaming the object of knowledge for its impermeability, the caption transformed the observer's inability to read someone's facial expression into a projected fault of the observed.

The "inscrutable" label also bespeaks an uneasiness with the implicit limits to which Asians can be "known" (placed in familiar categories) and then assimilated (adjusted socially and politically so as to develop not only familiarity but similarity). Although the ostensible object of orientalist studies is to create a verifiable body of knowledge about the East, its underlying objective is to secure boundaries for the West, precisely by delimiting what the West *is not*. Having set up ontological boundaries between East and West (defining the East essentially as "not us"), the magazines' orientalist discourse rationalized diverse – even contradictory – political, economic, and social policies toward Asians. On the one hand, the "not us" definition allowed Americans to ignore their brotherly duties toward Asian immigrants in their midst; on the other hand, it dissociated the Filipino cry for independence from a similar American one in 1776, thereby permitting U.S. retention of the Philippines as a colonial possession. In the end, the "not us" association led to a driving out of Asian Americans at home and an Americanizing of Asians abroad.

The seemingly contradictory policies toward Asians can be read more productively as signs of a flexible power exercised by orientalist discourse. This flexibility is also observable within these journals' own textual spaces. Although editorial prose condemned Asians as probable sites of infection, at the same time advertisements capitalized on the allure of the Orient to sell products. Almost every issue of *Collier's* from 1910 to 1915 carries an advertisement for tours to the East as well as ads for American-made products such as Massatta Talcum Powder, which lent one the "True Oriental Odor" (see Figure 1), and Jap-A-Lac varnish.

The advertisement for Jap-A-Lac that ran on 4 March 1911 is particularly revealing of stereotypes of black, white, and Asian women (see Figure 2). Accompanying the sales pitch is an illustration of an aproned black woman facing her white mistress. At the bottom of the ad is the spectacle of a kimonoed Japanese girl kneeling atop a varnish container, winking and holding a freshly dipped brush. Most protected from the gaze of the consumer is the white woman, who, partially turned away from the viewer, remains least identifiable. The black woman, on the other hand, nearly faces the plane of the picture, exposed to both the onlooker and her white counterpart. However, that she is a black woman is not visually unequivocal; it is only through the prose supplement where she speaks of her "last missus" that one perceives her characterization as black. In contrast, the Japanese girl acts as a visual emblem. Her costume, hair, and slanted eyes all identify her as the "Jap" of the product name. Although both the black and Asian figures are subordinate to the larger image of white women's household advantages, they are pitched in the advertisement in contrasting ways. The black "girl" actively sells the product by detailing her last mistress's refurbishing success. The mute but winking Japanese girl becomes the genie in the bottle – the unknown element that distinguishes this varnish from other brands. The marketing value of this silent figure lies precisely in her potential as spectacle and in her identifiable exoticism.

How, then, does one account for the potential of such Asian emblems to sell domestic goods at the very time when "negative" images of Asians were circulating in these same journals? In one case, the *American* ran an article on "Mr. Ishiboshi: My Japanese Servant and Friend" column-stripped between Jap-a-lac varnish and Iver Johnson Revolver ads. The

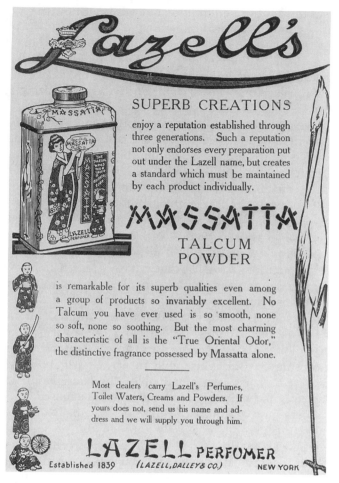

Figure 1. In addition to articles and editorials expressing antipathy toward Asians, *Collier's* printed advertisements that capitalized on the allure of the Orient. This ad for Massatta Talcum Powder appeared on 8 April 1911.

feature describes a newlywed wife's relation to her husband's houseboy, whom she compares to a well-loved dog (August 1913, 71). Clearly, magazines felt no sense of incongruity in circulating ads that promoted desire for a commodified Asiatic body yet printing articles and editorials that voiced loathing for Asian peoples.

More suggestively, might the threatening portraits of Asians found in journalistic texts have assisted the commercial interests of advertisers? While negative images of the Orient encouraged an American readership

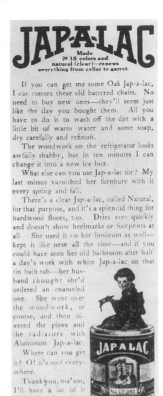

Please, Ma'am, Have You Any Jap-a-lac?
I Can't Keep House Without It—

I'm very particular about my kitchen and with no disrespect to the girl who was before me — you'll excuse me for saying it — it's about time yours was fixed up.

The pantry shelves need a coat of Jap-a-lac badly. It will not only make them look nicer, but being like enamel they're cleaned so much easier.

And the table needs coats of white Jap-a-lac, too. It costs less than oilcloth and don't need constant recovering. When a girl has a nice, bright, sanitary kitchen, she takes so much more pride in it; besides I like a kitchen fit to receive company in.

JAP·A·LAC
Made in 18 colors and natural (clear)—renews everything from cellar to garret.

If you can get me some Oak Jap-a-lac, I can restore these old battered chairs. No need to buy new ones—they'll seem just like the day you bought them. All you have to do is to wash off the dirt with a little bit of warm water and some soap, dry carefully and refinish.

The woodwork on the refrigerator looks awfully shabby, but in ten minutes I can change it into a new ice box.

What else can you use Jap-a-lac for? My last missus varnished her furniture with it every spring and fall.

There's a clear Jap-a-lac, called Natural, for that purpose, and it's a splendid thing for hardwood floors, too. Dries very quickly and doesn't show heelmarks or footprints at all. She used it on her linoleum as well—kept it like new all the time—and if you could have seen her old bathroom after half a day's work with white Jap-a-lac on that tin bath tub—her husband thought she'd ordered an enameled one. She went over the woodwork, of course, and then silvered the pipes and the radiators with Aluminum Jap-a-lac.

Where can you get it? O! it's sold everywhere.

Thank you, ma'am, I'll have a lot of it sent up right away.

The Glidden Varnish Company
Cleveland, O.   Toronto, Ont.

IN ANSWERING THIS ADVERTISEMENT PLEASE MENTION COLLIER'S

Figure 2. Glidden regularly promoted Jap-a-lac in the pages of *Collier's*. This ad appeared on 4 March 1911.

to be wary of Asian peoples, the commodification of the Orient into a saleable product abated this sense of vulnerability promoted in editorial copy. By purchasing the product (or employing an Oriental houseboy), an American consumer could figuratively "own" a part of the East, thereby defusing its threat. Packaging the Asian as a commodity enacts a "domestication of the exotic," as Edward Said phrases it, wherein the previously unknown becomes familiarized by its identification with a previous experience (for example, talcum powder, varnish) (Said 1978, 59–60). The commodity, by its quintessential knowability (laid out in the advertising pitch), enables the consumer to overcome this bit of the "unknown." One might also conjecture that the larger the perceived threat constructed by the journalistic prose, the greater the audience's desire to conquer the unknown through consumption. Negative portraits of the Orient, rather than discouraging purchase, might fuel the popularity of Asiatic goods. Thus, fear of Asians promoted by journalistic copy resulted not only in vociferous protest against social integration with Asians but also in readerly pleasure at seeing and consuming Asiatic commodities.

LITERARY RESPONSES

Overlapping these practices in the popular press were literary representations of Asians that replicated, critically as well as uncritically, the various types of Asian portraiture circulating in these magazines. The works of Sax Rohmer (1883–1959), Onoto Watanna (1875–1954), Paz Marquez Benitez (1894–1983), and Sui Sin Far (1865–1914)[5] provide a window onto the literary trade that often reinforced images of Asians as recalcitrant children needing punishment but in rare instances countered the notion of Asians as inscrutable aliens.

The Riddle of China, Sax Rohmer's Dr. Fu-Manchu

Speaking about the most prominent images of Asians in Anglo-American literature, Elaine Kim details how the U.S. State Department in the 1930s received a crank threat from the "President of Si-Fan," causing the FBI to consult Rohmer about that imaginary organization whose prime agent was the equally fictitious Dr. Fu-Manchu (Kim 1982, 4). The anecdote attests to the far-reaching effects of Rohmer's fiction.[6] In the FBI response, one has an instance of fabrication infringing upon "reality" and of representation and simulacra providing the substance of a national security concern. This confusion between fact and fiction lies at the structural core of Rohmer's Fu-Manchu pieces. Possible fictions circulate as facts, deceiving both detective and reader alike. While certain narratives are revealed during the course of the detective story as "red herrings" or unreliable discourses, others, though certainly as highly constructed, become privileged as "facts."

"The Green Mist" installment, published on 29 April 1913 in *Collier's* and later reissued as chapter 10 of *The Insidious Dr. Fu-Manchu*, epitomizes this blurring of fact and fiction. The two detectives, Nayland Smith and Dr. Petrie, must sort through a mass of sensory data to figure out how the orientalist scholar Sir Lionel Barton has been murdered. Put simply, the two investigators must separate fact (verifiable events) from fiction (false leads). On one level, then, the episode is about the process of detection itself, teaching the audience how to read – decipher – the mysterious East.

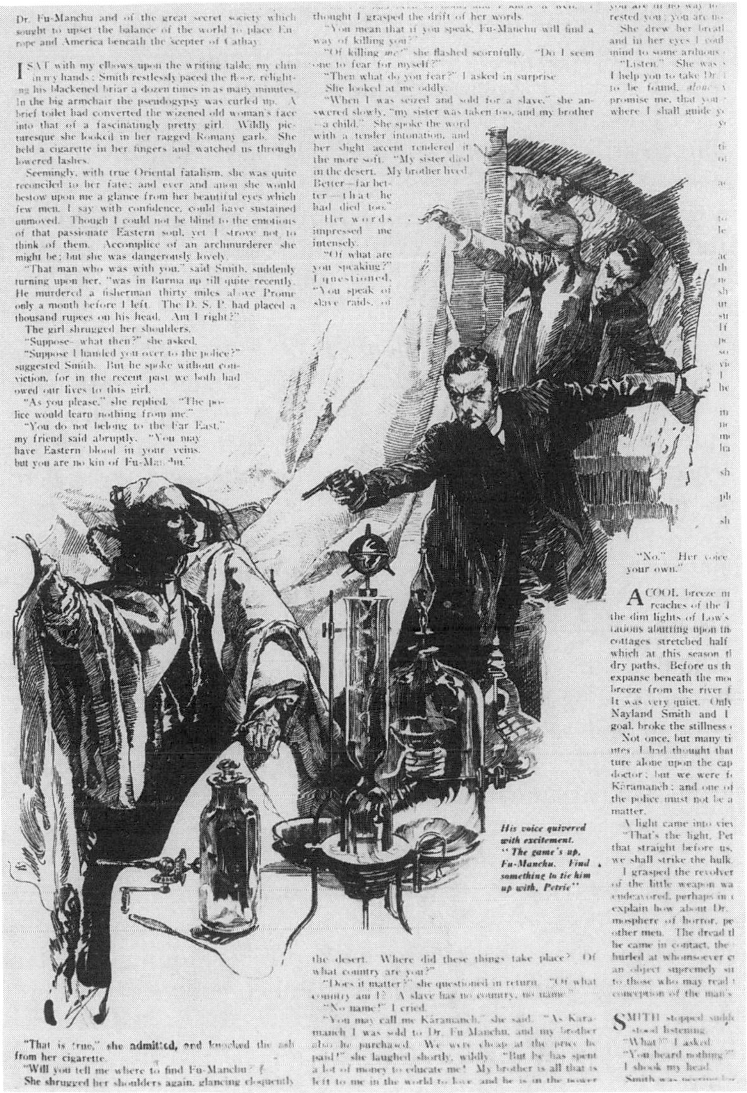

Dr. Fu-Manchu and of the great secret society which sought to upset the balance of the world to place Europe and America beneath the scepter of Cathay.

I SAT with my elbows upon the writing table, my chin in my hands; Smith restlessly paced the floor, relighting his blackened briar a dozen times in as many minutes. In the big armchair the pseudogypsy was curled up. A brief toilet had converted the wizened old woman's face into that of a fascinatingly pretty girl. Wildly picturesque she looked in her ragged Romany garb. She held a cigarette in her fingers and watched us through lowered lashes.

Seemingly, with true Oriental fatalism, she was quite reconciled to her fate; and ever and anon she would bestow upon me a glance from her beautiful eyes which few men, I say with confidence, could have sustained unmoved. Though I could not be blind to the emotions of that passionate Eastern soul, yet I strove not to think of them. Accomplice of an archmurderer she might be; but she was dangerously lovely.

"That man who was with you," said Smith, suddenly turning upon her, "was in Burma up till quite recently. He murdered a fisherman thirty miles above Prome only a month before I left. The D. S. P. had placed a thousand rupees on his head. Am I right?"

The girl shrugged her shoulders.

"Suppose—what then?" she asked.

"Suppose I handed you over to the police?" suggested Smith. But he spoke without conviction, for in the recent past we both had owed our lives to this girl.

"As you please," she replied. "The police would learn nothing from me."

"You do not belong to the Far East," my friend said abruptly. "You may have Eastern blood in your veins, but you are no kin of Fu-Manchu."

"That is true," she admitted, and knocked the ash from her cigarette.

"Will you tell me where to find Fu-Manchu?"

She shrugged her shoulders again, glancing eloquently

thought I grasped the drift of her words.

"You mean that if you speak, Fu-Manchu will find a way of killing you?"

"Of killing *me*!" she flashed scornfully. "Do I seem one to fear for myself?"

"Then what do you fear?" I asked in surprise.

She looked at me oddly.

"When I was seized and sold for a slave," she answered slowly, "my sister was taken too, and my brother—a child." She spoke the word with a tender intonation, and her slight accent rendered it the more soft. "My sister died in the desert. My brother lived. Better—far better—that he had died too."

Her words impressed me intensely.

"Of what are you speaking?" I questioned. "You speak of slave raids, of the desert. Where did these things take place? Of what country are you?"

"Does it matter?" she questioned in return. "Of what country am I? A slave has no country, no name."

"No name!" I cried.

"You may call me Káramaneh," she said. "As Káramaneh I was sold to Dr. Fu Manchu, and my brother also he purchased. We were cheap at the price he paid!" she laughed shortly, wildly. "But he has spent a lot of money to educate me! My brother is all that is left to me in the world to love and he is in the power

His voice quivered with excitement. "The game's up, Fu-Manchu. Find something to tie him up with, Petrie"

Figure 3. In the *Collier's* Fu-Manchu installments, exotic illustrations embellished the text. This one, drawn by J. C. Coll, appeared on 26 April 1913.

The chapter begins with Dr. Petrie perusing four newspaper items about the Chinese. Journalistic images form the fabric of Rohmer's fiction, re-presenting the "character" of the Chinese for an audience already primed to these newspaper accounts (see Figure 3). The first clipping reports the Hawaiian Chinese practice of infanticide; the second details a Chinese assassin's attempt on the Hong Kong governor; the third covers an incident wherein Chinese soldiers and villagers set fire to a Russian's house; and the fourth documents Fu-Manchu's success in preventing "Parson Dan" of the Boxer Rebellion from returning to China (121–4).

After "reading" the first item regarding infanticide, the narrator Dr. Petrie muses: "Is it any matter for wonder that such a people had produced a Fu-Manchu? I pasted the cutting into a scrap-book, determined that, if I lived to publish my account of those days, I would quote it therein as casting a sidelight upon Chinese character" (122). This exclamation frames the successive press clippings as documents constructing a monolithic "Chinese character." It is of no account that the first article comments on self-directed violence, the second on oppressor-directed violence, and the third on victim-directed violence. For Dr. Petrie, all the items point to Chinese cruelty.

These journalistic "facts" disseminate false "knowledge" about the Chinese. Such fabrication, however, comprises the central device of the Fu-Manchu pieces. Rohmer's stories only pretend to seek answers to the "riddle of China." Under such pretense they intensify the puzzling and "inscrutable" characterizations of the Chinese and their exemplar, Fu-Manchu. Lending readers the illusory experience of thinking themselves engaged in finding out who Fu-Manchu (and by extension China) really is, Rohmer's short fiction actually displaces responsibility for an actual dialogue with Asian culture.

In essence, Rohmer's episodes present a fictional miniversion of Asian exclusion wherein the narrator constructs Fu-Manchu as the ultimate "unknown," who must be either penetrated or killed off. The two sleuths must halt the invasion of elements from outside an Anglocentric epistemology. Thus, Smith and Petrie do battle by hunting Fu-Manchu and transforming mysterious (read "exotic") phenomena into scientific "facts" (147).

The detectives suspect that Sir Barton has been killed because he burrowed too deeply into the secrets of India, Tibet, and China (125, 129). As evidence of his orientalist might, Barton has assimilated Eastern characteristics – he employs a Bedouin groom and a Chinese body-servant; his Finchley-based apartments are "topsy-turvy" with Oriental plunder (126). It is amid this Asian "loot" that Barton's dead body is found. Smith and Petrie sort through the disorderly apartments, which are not only furnished haphazardly but also arrayed with objects from a separate (Oriental) order. The whole apparatus of Sir Barton's orientalist mission, then, comprises the "disorderliness" the sleuths must exclude in their discovery process. Not surprisingly, the story's central exotic item –

the Egyptian sarcophagus – emerges as the narrative point of disorder, the "red herring." In this equation of disorder with an Eastern burial item (which metonymically evokes Eastern belief systems) one sees a cultural valence to the "order" that Smith and Petrie seek to restore. Theirs is an ideological, Western "science" that eradicates symptoms of Eastern "superstition."

Although masked as an engagement with the East, "The Green Mist" is really about the power and talent of the British. The success of Smith and Petrie's investigation reinforces the notion of "clean British efficiency" reasoning through the sneaky ways of the Chinese (138). Ironically, nothing is discovered about the Orient in the detection process; the two sleuths come no closer to "knowing" the East. Rather, the investigation – as well as Rohmer's pieces on Fu-Manchu – produces the "Oriental unknown," that which must be excluded and simultaneously that which propels the story. By way of analogy, then, Smith and Petrie exclude the Oriental element from a Western geographic and textual terrain, even as their creator, Rohmer, appropriates the exotic to generate interest in his stories. This curious production of nonknowledge issues forth the commodity, Fu-Manchu.

While holding titular privilege in Rohmer's works, Fu-Manchu remains essentially a cypher; his larger-than-life characterization, his monumental genius, are mere straw-man constructions which, rather than establishing his real puissance, act as a foil for the two protagonists. According to William Aydelotte, the "criminal" in any detective fiction functions as a deeply gratifying scapegoat, his charm lying in his ultimate conquerableness. Any strength which the narrative attributes to this criminal "though great, is futile, only sham strength. His position is actually unreal, for he has no place nor meaning in an ordered world" (Aydelotte 1976, 72).

Nayland Smith's first characterization of Fu-Manchu illustrates this "sham" or empty construction: "Imagine a person, tall, lean and feline, high-shouldered, with a brow like Shakespeare and a face like Satan. . . . Invest him with all the cruel cunning of an entire Eastern race. . . . Imagine that awful being, and you have a mental picture of Dr. Fu-Manchu, the yellow peril incarnate in one man" (25–6). The listener's projected horror produces the character Fu-Manchu. His only constant feature through various people's "imagining" is his "inscrutability" – his puzzling essence. Rather than being an "objective" portrait of the enemy, the description provided by Nayland Smith relies upon the listener's subjective baggage.

The horror that seems to be embodied in Dr. Fu-Manchu reveals itself ironically as the horror of Western orientalist strategies, their self-generated fears that enable the horrible use of Asian bodies for acts of self-definition. That is, focusing only superficially on the East, "The Green Mist" promotes the notion of a British "efficiency" defined by the capture and elimination of Oriental bodies. Exclusion of Asians becomes the very essence of the British character. Thus Rohmer's thirteen Fu-Manchu books helped to justify the many violences in America directed toward Asians (economic discrimination, political disenfranchisement, physical assault, social segregation, and exclusion from immigration) by framing that violence as a necessary means to preserve the integrity of Western character.

Western Professors and Japanese Pupils in Onoto Watanna's *Tama*

Whereas Rohmer's pieces advocate domestic exclusion of Asians, Onoto Watanna's 1910 romance, *Tama*, portrays the Japanese as children who learn well the stern lesson of the West. By birth a Chinese Eurasian, Watanna reinvented herself as a Japanese noblewoman born in Nagasaki and published several "Japanese" novels featuring exotic settings and romantic plots (Ling 1990, 25). Though exploiting exotic stereotypes of the East, *Tama* nevertheless broaches issues of colonization, Japanese–American relations, and interracial intimacy.

Tama's setting, the village of Fukui during the earliest stages of the Meiji restoration (c. 1868), proves a poignant political landscape. Virtually free of foreign contact, Fukui provides a microcosm for the intrusion of Western force, power, and value systems on isolationist Japan. Supporting Western "enlightenment," Watanna portrays the American professor, O-Tojin-San ("Honorable Mr. Foreigner"), as opening this small province to Western science and reason. Tojin-san uses Tama, the mysterious, blind fox-woman, to teach his imperialist lesson.

The Fukui villagers distrust the eponymous heroine, a half-white, half-Japanese woman with long golden tresses. Never having seen a blond-haired individual, the villagers perceive Tama as a spirit-woman exiled from the Japanese community because of her miscegenated birth. Tama's presence on the Shiro grounds occasions Tojin-san's reformation of the superstitious villagers into knowledgeable thinkers. First, the American derides their belief in Tama's supernatural origins:

> "Your excellency disbelieves our legend of the fox-woman?" [the Daimio's high officer] queried courteously.
>
> "Legends," said the Tojin-san slowly, "belong to literature, and are tales to charm and beguile adults and deceive children. In the West we no longer heed them." (28)

When this "slow" attempt at didacticism fails, Tojin-san reprimands his listener:

> "It seems to me an amazing thing that to-day when you are frankly hoping to join the nations of enlightenment, you still give yourselves up to . . . a legend fit for children only. For my part, I intend to sweep from my house vigorously the absurd belief I find actually seated on my hearth-stone." (34)

Tojin-san implies that the Japanese people's arrested development is manifest in their "childish" legends. His attack on indigenous folklore and cultural belief comprises the first step of his lesson plan.

The Jo-i (foreign-haters) represent another hurdle to Tojin-san's tutelage. Watanna mentions the international reasons behind the Jo-i's race hatred: "the punishments, the indemnities, the humiliations forced upon the [Japanese] government by the foreigners, but added to the hatred and malice of the Jo-i" (14–15). These "humiliations" refer to the several treaties, beginning in 1854, that "wrested privileges from Japan similar to those acquired by European nations in China," such as cash indemnities, an open-door policy to Christian missionaries, and extraterritoriality making Westerners immune to national laws; as well as the violent displays of power that reminded Japan of what "could befall their country should it refuse to abide by these treaties" (Chan 1991, 9). These forcible "reminders" included the 1863 naval bombardment of Kagoshima and the 1864 destruction of Japanese cannons used to block the passage of ships through the Straits of Shimonoseki.

Watanna also portrays the domestic crisis accompanying Japan's change from a feudal to an industrial economy. A large proportion of the Jo-i are ex-samurai warriors or *ronin* who "now found themselves without aristocratic employment, and, too proud to turn to trade . . . wandered about the provinces, voicing their discontent of the order of things" (50). The narrator not only naturalizes the West's imperialist incursions as "the order of things," but also makes clear that the *ronin*'s discontent born of unemployment lies at their own feet for being "too proud." Only those who humbly concede the wisdom of the Western father will succeed in this new "order of things."

Several confrontations between Tojin-san and the angry *ronin* dramatize the Western father's struggle with his Japanese recalcitrant sons. Repeatedly, the *ronin* demand that Tojin-san release the "fox-woman" from his protection. In one instance, Tojin-san's student, Junzo, tries to persuade the teacher to leave "this foul witch of the mountains" and resume his place in the community. The American professor responds by asserting his racial obligation:

GENJIRO KATAOKA, '10.

Figure 4. The spectacle of Tama's hair – rendered yellow-gold in the tinted frontispiece – helped construct the heroine as "white." (From Onoto Watanna's *Tama*.)

"I am a white man," said the Tojin-san slowly, in a deadly voice. . . . "As such I protect, not abandon, the women of my race. It will not be well for Fukui if harm comes to either me, your guest and teacher, or to her, whom I choose to befriend." (128)

Tojin-san defends his association with Tama by asserting himself as "a white man," thereby appealing to codes of chivalry and race affiliation. His statement also rhetorically constructs Tama as "white," thus effacing her Asian half (see Figure 4). Although persecuted in Fukui, Tama emerges as the recipient of white privilege.

In Tojin-san's avowal to "protect . . . the women of [his] race," imperialist might becomes discursively constructed as a knightly armament with which to save the beautiful heroine. In other words, the romantic plot sanctions imperialist force as a means to achieve the lovers' happy ending. Throughout the narrative, Watanna manipulates the interest generated by her romance plot to undermine potential critiques of imperialism. For instance, because the *ronin* represent the primary threat to the romantic heroine (hence the romantic plot), their justifiable protest against Western intrusion becomes narratively undermined. The cowardly fashion in which they scapegoat Tama overshadows their legitimate grievances.

Triumphing over the Jo-i's militarism is the American professor and his Japanese disciples. The narrative dramatizes the theme of educational victory by depicting an ex-samurai assailing the American professor with a sword. Tojin-san's "great white fists" flash faster than the steel, and, bare-handed, he defeats his attacker (148). Preventing further assaults from the assembled *ronin*, Tojin-san's Japanese students, properly enlightened by him, surround their teacher's residence, thereby protecting him from harm.

Having portrayed the American "cure" for Japanese ignorance, the narrator displays the Japanese people's gratitude. In a final romantic twist, Watanna depicts Tojin-san's reluctance to be seen by Tama (after her operation to remove the cataracts from her eyes) because of his pockmarked visage. His superficial rejection of Tama allows her to express her loyalty to her Western "father," teacher, and lover. Her return to Tojin-san upon "enlightenment" demonstrates Japanese loyalty to the Western father, as it also reassures the audience of the Japanese pupil's successful indoctrination to notions of white superiority.

Tama/*Tama* thus reflects "the successful operation of the stereotype" where "the subject race itself embodies and perpetuates the white supremacist vision of reality" (Chin et al. 1991, 10). Following this operation, the subject race poses "no threat to white supremacy," as Tama and Japan pose no threat by the novel's conclusion. While Watanna promotes the Japanese as "sympathetic" characters (model adherents to Western ideals), her worldview never leaves that imperialist "order of things." Though not depicting Asians as frightful criminals, she nevertheless fuels the childlike stereotype of the Japanese that quells American fears of the Orient.

Paz Marquez Benitez and Pastoral Resistance

In contrast to Watanna's fiction of Japanese gratitude for Western tutelage, Paz Marquez Benitez, herself a colonial subject, pens a more subdued and allegorical response to Americanization.[7] Although not publishing in stateside journals, Benitez was tangibly affected by the composite image of Asians as less-developed, diseased, and unknowable, because this image "justified" America's initial retention of the Philippines and policy of "benevolent assimilation."

Numerous critics have praised Benitez's artistry, but not her political themes.[8] I shall illuminate her stories of disillusionment in the context of Filipino thwarted independence and the people's loss of political idealism when forced to settle for American tutelage. Instead of hailing progress – conceived as the ability to assimilate Western knowledge – "Dead Stars" (1925) evokes the pastoral and casts a critical light on the American administration's hurried development of the islands.

"Dead Stars" presents the dilemma of Alfredo Salazar, a young man who must choose between two women, Julia, "a smooth rich brown" woman (43) whose vitality excites him, and Esperanza, a woman of "light and clear . . . complexion" to whom he is engaged. Marquez portrays Julia as the less Westernized Filipina: she comes from a Laguna town near the mountains, where "there is nothing to see – little crooked streets, *yunut* roofs with ferns growing on them, and sometimes squashes" (47). For Alfredo, much of Julia's appeal lies in her local color and sense of "home" – a place "so far from [the city]," where "there isn't even one American . . . !" (49, 47).

Julia's residence in Laguna also discreetly alludes to national politics. During the first decade of American "protectorship," the Laguna province abounded in "'outlawry' [which] in those days meant primarily Katipunan [a revolutionary, religious society] and other proindependence movements" (Ileto 1979, 192). Laguna remained the likely center of revolutionary activity because of its association with the Filipino nationalist José Rizal. Thus Alfredo's personal attraction to Julia reverberates with political significance. Laguna symbolizes the dream of independence.

Preventing Alfredo from making a home with Julia is his previous "hasty" engagement to Esperanza: "'Hurry, hurry, or you will miss it,' someone had seemed to urge in his ears. So he had avidly seized on the shadow of love" (41). Anxious to rush into the future, Alfredo mistook progress for happiness and contracted himself to the mere shadow of love. Yet hindsight cannot reverse his actions. To sever his engagement would entail taking back his word – an unthinkable breach of honor.[9]

Thus Alfredo describes himself as having reached a point beyond his control – "a point where a thing escapes us and rushes downward of its own weight, dragging us along. Then it is foolish to ask whether one will or will not, because it no longer depends on him" (52–3). This nay-saying of human will, though essential to Benitez's tragic construction, dooms her characters to a state of already lost innocence and thwarted desire. Any moments of possible happiness or freedom exist only in the past, making inevitable a narrative reliance upon the pastoral, wherein the writer looks "back to a happier place, to a lost 'organic' moment" (Fischer 1986, 113).

Rather than encouraging rebellion, the pastoral mode induces resignation. Alfredo describes himself in his marriage as "not unhappy. . . . He felt no rebellion: only the calm of capitulation to what he recognized as irresistible forces of circumstance and of character. . . . From his capacity of complete detachment he derived a strange solace. The essential himself . . . would, he reflected, always be free and alone" (56). Benitez redefines freedom here not politically but internally and figuratively. Freedom recedes into the past and into the hills, the site of Julia Salas's "home town."

To extend the political allegory, then, because Philippine locales (cities, plantations, even formerly remote hills) were rapidly being transformed in accordance with the new American policy of infrastructural development, the fictional space of Julia Salas's timeless town emerges as the only site uncorrupted by foreign influence.[10] The Laguna town becomes the cultural repository for pre-American memories: "How peaceful the town was! Here and there a little *tienda* was still open. . . . An occasional couple sauntered by, the woman's *chinelas* making scraping sounds. From a distance came the shrill voices of children playing games on the street – *tubigan* perhaps, or 'hawk-and-chicken'" (57–8). Spanish and Tagalog references abound, emphasizing the pristine quality of the community. Yet such an "untainted" site has already become "lost" within the narrative's textual space.[11] That is, Alfredo's visit to the village symbolizes the civic realm's encroachment on the pastoral locale. (He comes to elicit testimony from an old woman who lives in the hills.) Thus, while *National Geographic*'s ethnographic accounts were preserving Luzon tribesmen as the "lowest type of human beings known," Benitez portrays the village community as the site of an already lost innocence and peace. In the end, Alfredo cannot find an authentic moment in the lake town, as the pastoral recedes further and further into the past (and into the jungle).

Benitez concludes her narrative with a portrait of Alfredo filled with a "vast homesickness for some immutable refuge of the heart . . . where live on in unchanging freshness, the dear, dead loves of vanished youth" (59). Though one can read Alfredo's yearning for his former vitality as a specific longing for Julia Salas, one cannot ignore the larger panorama of Philippine upheaval that frames Benitez's writing. Alfredo's great "home-sickness" evokes a broader Filipino cultural estrangement. Her use of the pastoral and her themes of lost youth and lost authenticity remain literary metaphors for cultural alienation, a product of American colonial practices. However, Benitez glosses over colonial specificity by tracing her characters' sense of cultural loss to an innate aspect of the human condition.

"Its Wavering Image": Sui Sin Far's Reflections on Journalistic Reflections

Of the four authors examined, Sui Sin Far, who herself published in numerous journals of the era, wrote most directly about the problems of journalistic intrusion, biculturalism, production of knowledge, and commerce in exotica.[12] Her short story "Its Wavering Image" (1912) critiques the circulation of "knowledge" about Asian immigrants in the press.

In this piece, a Eurasian woman, Pan, falls in love with a white journalist, Mark Carson, who uses her as a liaison to the Chinatown community. He writes an exposé of some of their most sacred customs and asks Pan to declare herself "a white woman," presumably so they may continue their romance. Sui uses this narrative to tackle the issue of how to write about Asians without exposing them to a critical white gaze. Not merely her character Mark Carson, but Sui herself displays Asian immigrants to the reading public at large. Just as Carson is sent to the Chinatown community to find a story, so does the author herself "benefit" from a readerly voraciousness for things Asian.

In her autobiographical "Leaves from the Mental Portfolio of an Eurasian," Sui gives two accounts of her Asian half as prey to white spectatorship, one in which an old man calls the six-year-old Sui away from a childhood party and "surveys [her] critically," and the other in which young French and English Canadians amuse themselves by pinching her and plying her with questions: "what we eat and drink, how we go to sleep . . . if we sit on chairs or squat on floors" (126–7). Sui portrays the meanest aspect of cultural "curiosity" – its propensity to objectify as it scrutinizes. Rather than showing admiration, this wanting to "know" about the Chinese constitutes a palpable form of violence. Through their "gazes" and interrogation, the white inquisitors simultaneously overcome the fear of difference in their midst and indulge in their pleasure at perusing things "strange."

"Its Wavering Image" discovers its protagonist, Pan, in much the same position as Sui. The narrative describes her as "always turn[ing] from whites," feeling in their presence "strange and constrained, shrinking from their curious scrutiny as she would from the sharp edge of a sword" (85–6). The journalist, Mark Carson, becomes both the perpetrator of white scrutiny and the wielder of another type of "sword" – the pen with which he lays bare the Chinatown community. Initially, he directs his curiosity toward Pan, asking "What was she? Chinese or white?" His city editor answers, "She is an unusually bright girl, and could tell more stories about the Chinese than any other person in this city – if she would" (86). Following the city editor's suggestion, Carson targets the Eurasian girl as his entry-point into Chinatown's secrets. Describing Carson as "a man who would sell his soul for a story" (86), the narrator subtly satirizes the then popular portrait of crusading, trust-breaking journalists. Will Irwin's series on "The American Newspaper" (*Collier's*, 1911) remains a famous example of such articles, wherein the reporter ostensibly defies old-time traditions and any corporate entity that seeks to keep its doors closed.

Carson's professional mission soon turns personal. He teaches his unknowing informant, Pan, a "lesson" about assimilation to white ideals and the problems of interracial romance in the present society. In effect, he negates her bicultural heritage by insisting that "you have got to decide what you will be – Chinese or white? You cannot be both" (90). Choosing for her, Carson tries to persuade the Eurasian woman to renounce the Chinatown community by enlisting notions of social segregation: "'Pan,' he cried, 'you do not belong here. You are white – white'"(89). Carson argues for Pan's separation from Chinatown, first proclaiming her racial difference and then asserting, "You have no right to be here" (89). Thus he casts her both as a victim of a subculture that desires racial homogeneity within its ranks and as a potential intruder upon that otherwise homogeneous space. According to Carson's rhetoric, it is not Pan's duty to stay with her father's people. Instead, she is violating this community's racial pact by her mere presence.

In addition to proclaiming Pan's racial difference from the Asian community, Carson attempts to distinguish her "real self" from her presumably daily self that communes with the Chinese: "'But they do not understand you,' he went on. 'Your *real self* is alien to them. What interest have they in *the books you read – the thoughts you think*?'" (89). Appealing to notions of the higher life, the young journalist asserts the primacy of intellectual pursuits over social or familial obligations. In addition, he implicitly associates this intellectual life with Western culture and learning. Rather than positing a universal "real self" that would transcend culture and environment, Carson constructs for Pan a specific racial and ideological self that primarily serves his own interests.

In exclaiming "How beautiful above! How unbeautiful below!" (89),

Carson also imbues his dualism with a hierarchy. His contemplative sessions with Pan's "real self" remain above and separate from the motley-thronged streets. His privileging of this separate space excludes the Chinese from his perceptual horizon even as he wishes to mold them into a journalistic stock image.

Pan responds to Carson's reasoning by proposing a different sort of affiliation. She realizes that as a bicultural subject her thoughts are being informed by Western values. Yet, despite the dissimilarity of her perspective from those of other Asian immigrants, Pan still sees herself as part of the community. Emerging from this dialogue, then, is a definition of human connection and communal relationship predicated not merely upon intellectual empathy or racial homogeneity. The author, here as in her other stories, tackles the question of what binds together any cultural group despite their generational, class, racial, and gender differences.

Carson's serenade to Pan, by contrast, instructs her in his race separatism by harkening to its binary oppositions. He sings her the central conceit of the story: " 'The moon and its broken reflection, /And its shadows shall appear, /As the symbol of love in heaven, /*And its wavering image here*' " (90, emphasis added). Carson's song refers to the moon and its watery reflection in the river. It also alludes to the Platonic and aesthetic division between ideal, "beautiful" forms, and worldly, "unbeautiful" appearances. Chinatown's street-life, like the "broken reflection" below, corresponds to this lesser world of ugly appearances. By aligning this Asian American community with mere appearances, the journalist also defuses its threat.

By contrast, Carson's balcony serenade to Pan approximates his ideal world. Only Pan's stubborn affiliation with the Chinese mars his ideal. For Carson, then, Pan must do the following to complete his portrait of ideal love: renounce the Chinese, identify herself as white, and pass out of Chinatown into the arms of her journalist teacher and lover. (Perhaps the similarities here between Carson's version of love and Tojin-san's version in *Tama* are not merely coincidental.) Love, as conceived of by Carson, requires the wholesale conversion of Pan to his interests.

By publishing his exposé, thus rendering her the "betrayer" of the community, Carson attempts to extricate Pan from Chinese society (making her white by default). Pan exclaims, upon seeing the article, " 'Betrayed! Betrayed! Betrayed to be a betrayer!' . . . Was it unconsciously dealt – that cruel blow? Ah, well did he know that the sword which pierced her through others, would carry with it to her own heart, the pain of all those others" (91–2). By making her a "powerful" betrayer, Carson hopes Pan will take the role of victimizer upon herself; and, as Pan's words indicate, though she is the victim of her lover's stratagem, she herself has been a "betrayer" – the sword which pierces through others. Her exclamation perhaps reflects upon Sui's own awareness both of the facility with which journalistic demands could lure one to trade upon one's nationality and of her precarious position as a writer revealing the lives and character of Asian peoples.

Carson accomplishes his discursive exploitation first by educating Pan, or assimilating her to his beliefs and his loyalty, second by plundering her for information, and third by exporting and trading on her as a (re)source. These three phases mimic the process of colonization and highlight how cultural assimilation through "education" acts as a first step to knowledge production and trade. Furthermore, the colonization metaphor underscores the way in which orientalist discourse, whether in journals or novels, acts in conjunction with the "sword" to further the exploitation of less powerful peoples.

Pan's final response to Carson's admittedly "harsh" lesson is to reassert her collective affiliation to "those who loved her" – the Chinese. She examines the various symbols with which Carson has taught her his hierarchical dualism and reverses their significance. That is, she looks into the sky and sees the moon as "Its Wavering Image" (92). Rather than the privileged original, high above the Chinatown streets, Pan sees "the beautiful" and "the ideal" as themselves simulacra – images only with a value determined by the perspective of the observer. Correspondingly, Carson's wooing of her also turns out to be a simulated liaison. Love, according to Carson, can occur only between the racially homogeneous.

Despite the fact that Pan objects to Carson's notion of racial homogeneity, she is unable to discover a satisfying alternative. Though Sui suggests the possibility of interracial intimacy in the relationship of Pan's parents, Pan's mother never appears in the story, having died before the narrative begins. Even in the stories in which Sui does represent interracial marriages, the author emphasizes social complications (see "Her Chinese Husband"). At the story's conclusion, Pan becomes resolutely "a Chinese woman," her white half effaced. This ending suggests that, because of the present state of affairs, the Eurasian must choose in accordance with the journalist's imperative: "Chinese or white? You cannot be both." Yet Sui perhaps recognizes a bicultural "ideal" of coexistence not reflected in those "wavering images" of race essentialism and race integrity prevailing in the contemporary literature. It is this "ideal" toward which Sui's own stories strive even as they depict the necessary negotiations one's "real self" must conduct with present circumstances.

CONCLUSION

American magazines of the 1910s encouraged only the still lives of Asians. Rather than promoting interactions with living peoples, magazines championed a nonthreatening dynamic wherein Asians could be reproduced as commodities that might be gazed upon and finally owned. Emphasizing Asian peoples' cultural difference, periodicals at once justified America's ban on Asiatic immigration and rationalized the United States's exploitation of Asian peoples and their habitats abroad.

Sax Rohmer, Onoto Watanna, Paz Marquez Benitez, and Sui Sin Far responded to this journalistic milieu. Echoing the magazines' race separatism, Sax Rohmer depicts the "yellow" cause in opposition to "white" existence. His fiction fosters racial antagonism and advocates the eradication of the "unknown" as embodied in the Asian Other. Onoto Watanna, on the other hand, emphasizes the possibility of a racial bridge, especially in Japan's potential to be like "Tojin-san" – the great America foreigner. Watanna, however, premises this harmony on Asian subservience. Her portrait of Asians indoctrinated with ideas of white superiority pacified Western fears of Japanese imperialism and power. Paz Marquez Benitez, likewise, evades critiquing colonial tutelage and progressivism by employing a nostalgic, pastoral mode. Yet she does not fantasize her colonial situation into a triumphant "love story." Even though her circumstances were restricted by colonial policies that discouraged nationalism and independence, Benitez subtly criticizes American intrusion. More direct in her responses than her literary contemporaries, Sui Sin Far focuses upon the domestic repercussions of all this international imaging. She emphasizes not only global coexistence but intranational toleration. In her stories, racial homogeneity as a societal philosophy poses an especially acute problem for the biracial subject. Attuned to the influence of broader theories of race on interpersonal dynamics, Sui comments upon journalistic intrusion and the way in which publishers packaged Asians for "trade."

Constituted under the gaze of an Anglo-American community, the three works written by authors of Asian descent represent survivalist texts. This corpus of early Asian American fiction comprises a foundation of Asian American literature as it also expands our definition of literary experience to include that expressed by the colonized and those limited by power relations unfavorable to them. Yet mapping the journalistic creation of a mythic "Asia" should suggest more than the regulatory power of the literary market in which these writers published their works. The discursive institution of the press remains a fruitful site for both past and present voices of resistance to review critically America's promised freedoms.

■■■ ACKNOWLEDGMENTS

I thank Mary Pat Brady, Sonia Saldívar-Hull, and Valerie Smith for reading drafts of this chapter, and Martha Banta for inspiring this project. My special gratitude goes to King-Kok Cheung, whose personal support and critical comments were invaluable in bringing this essay from draft to final version.

■■■ NOTES

1. This chapter draws predominantly from images of Japanese, Chinese, and Filipinos in the magazines, though I have also surveyed representations of Indians, Koreans, and Thai (Siamese). As I argue later, American journals of this era extended characteristics of specific nationalities to Asian peoples in general. Thus, depictions of individual nations bear not only on that specific nationality but on the "character" of Asians and Asian immigrants in general. My research focused primarily on *Collier's*, self-proclaimedly "the last surviving muckraker" magazine, with a circulation over half a million by 1912 (Mott 1957, 462). I also looked at the Socialist magazine the *Masses* (1910–7), the Manila-based *Philippines Free Press*, and scattered pieces in the *Outlook, Good Housekeeping*, the *Independent*, and the *American*. Related studies include Wu's extensive coverage of Chinese Americans in fiction from 1850 to 1940 (1982); Chung's brief survey of Chinese Americans in popular periodical fiction from 1920 to 1940 (1976); and Moy's examination of the Chinese as "staged" spectacles from the nineteenth century to the present (1993).
2. These articles exemplify the ways in which Japan and China, as two Asian superpowers, were constantly being compared and contrasted in American magazines. In "Leaves from the Mental Portfolio of an Eurasian," Sui Sin Far comments on Americans' low esteem for the Chinese, their higher regard for the Japanese, and the resulting temptation of Chinese Eurasians to "pass as Japanese" (1909, 131).
3. In 1913, California passed the Alien Land Law, which prohibited "'aliens ineligible [for] citizenship' from buying land or leasing it for longer than three years" (Chan 1991, 195).
4. Joan Trauner contends that medical scapegoatism was particular to the Chinese: "increasingly, the fear was expressed that the Chinese were carriers of alien disease that would ultimately cause the physiological decay of the American nation" (1978, 76). However, as previously noted, journalistic discourse tended to conflate the various Asiatic races. McFarlane's depiction of the Japanese as "unclean" might be an instance of associative transference.
5. For biographical information and a survey of Rohmer's work, see Briney 1970. For a historical analysis of Fu-Manchu's function in Chinese American fiction, see Wu 1982. See Ling 1990 and 1992 for a survey of Watanna's life and works; Alegre and Fernandez 1984 for a biographical sketch of Paz Marquez Benitez; Ling 1990 and Yin 1991 for biographical information and

critical analyses of Sui's works. See also Ling 1992 for a discussion of pseu-
donyms as acts of "self-creation" (307), given the preponderance of aliases
among these writers.

6. Rohmer published fifty-eight book-length works. The first series of Fu-
   Manchu stories appeared in the British periodical *Story-Teller* and in *Collier's* in
   1913. The serial was republished in book format in America under the title
   The Insidious Dr. Fu-Manchu, to which all citations refer.

7. As an American colonial subject, Benitez offers an intriguing perspective on
   journalistic images of Asians and their relation to imperialism.

8. See Santillan-Castrence 1967, Hosillos 1969, and Yabes 1977 for critical
   surveys of this "apprentice period" of Filipino writing in English (1900–25).

9. In "Dead Stars," Benitez repeats the theme and political allegory of "forced
   marriage" that she began in "The Siren of 34 Real" (1917). In this earlier
   work, she again used a "domestic tale" to craft a political critique of American
   colonialism. The U.S. extortion of a contract against the will of the Philippines
   emerges allegorically in these two pieces as the story of young Filipino men
   forced into undesirable marriages.

10. See Chapter 2 on Gonzalez and Campomanes's characterization of "nostalgia
    for the old country" and "recovery of the land" as themes through which
    Filipino writers contest colonial and territorial dispossession.

11. As the presence of Spanish references suggests, sites "untainted" by American
    colonial influence are still overdetermined by the history of Spanish imperi-
    alism. No place of purely native memory exists in Benitez's story.

12. Sui's short stories appeared in the *Independent, Century, Hampton's, Out West,
    Ladies' Home Journal, Good Housekeeping, Gentlewoman, New York Evening Post,
    New England, Overland, Sunset*, and *Western*, among others (Ling 1990, 28).

■■■ WORKS CITED

Alegre, Edilberto N., and Doreen G. Fernandez. 1984. *The Writer and His Milieu: An
    Oral History of First Generation Writers in English*. Manila: De La Salle Univ.
    Press.

Aydelotte, William O. 1976. "The Detective Story as a Historical Source." In
    Dimensions of Detective Fiction, ed. Larry N. Landrum, Pat Browne, and Ray B.
    Browne, 68–82. Bowling Green, OH: Bowling Green State Univ. Popular
    Press.

Briney, Robert E. 1970. "Sax Rohmer: An Informal Survey." In *The Mystery
    Writer's Art*, ed. Francis M. Nevins Jr., 42–77. Bowling Green, OH: Bowling
    Green State Univ. Popular Press.

Chan, Sucheng. 1991. *Asian Americans: An Interpretive History*. Boston: Twayne.

Chin, Frank, Jeffrey Paul Chan, Lawson Fusao Inada, and Shawn Wong. 1974/
    1991. *Aiiieeeee! An Anthology of Asian-American Writers*. New York:
    Mentor.

Chung, Sue Fawn. 1976. "From Fu Manchu, Evil Genius, to James Lee Wong,
    Popular Hero: A Study of the Chinese-American in Popular Periodical
    Fiction from 1920 to 1940." *Journal of Popular Culture* 10:3:534–47.

Fischer, Michael M. J. 1986. "Ethnicity and the Post-Modern Arts of Memory." In *Writing Culture: The Poetics and Politics of Ethnography*, ed. James Clifford and George E. Marcus, 194–233. Berkeley and Los Angeles: Univ. of California Press.

Hosillos, Lucila V. 1969. *Philippine-American Literary Relations 1898–1941*. Quezon City: Univ. of the Philippines Press.

Ileto, Reynaldo Clemeña. 1979. *Pasyon and Revolution: Popular Movements in the Philippines, 1840–1910*. Quezon City, Philippines: Ateneo de Manila Univ. Press.

Kim, Elaine H. 1982. *Asian American Literature: An Introduction to the Writings and Their Social Context*. Philadelphia: Temple Univ. Press.

Ling, Amy. 1990. *Between Worlds: Women Writers of Chinese Ancestry*. Elmsford, NY: Pergamon Press.

———. 1992. "Creating One's Self: The Eaton Sisters." In *Reading the Literatures of Asian America*, ed. Shirley Geok-lin Lim and Amy Ling, 305–18. Philadelphia: Temple Univ. Press.

Marquez, Paz. 1917. "The Siren of 34 Real." *The Philippine Review* (July): 38–40.

———. 1925/1956. "Dead Stars." In *Philippine Prose and Poetry*, 4:39–59. Manila: Bureau of Printing.

Mott, Frank Luther. 1957. "Collier's." In *A History of American Magazines 1885–1905*, 4:453–79. Cambridge, MA: Harvard Univ. Press.

Moy, James. 1993. *Marginal Sights: Staging the Chinese in America*. Iowa City: Univ. of Iowa Press.

Rohmer, Sax [Arthur Sarsfield Ward]. 1913. *The Insidious Fu-Manchu*. New York: McBride, Nast.

Said, Edward S. 1978/1979. *Orientalism*. New York: Vintage.

Santillan-Castrence, P. 1967. "The Period of Apprenticeship." In *Brown Heritage: Essays on Philippine Cultural Tradition and Literature*, ed. Antonio G. Manuud, 546–74. Quezon City, Philippines: Ateneo de Manila Univ. Press.

Sui Sin Far [Edith Eaton]. 1909. "Leaves from the Mental Portfolio of an Eurasian." *Independent* 21 (January 21): 125–32.

———. 1912. "Its Wavering Image." In *Mrs. Spring Fragrance*, 85–95. Chicago: A. C. McClurg.

Trauner, Joan. 1978. "The Chinese as Medical Scapegoats in San Francisco 1870–1905." *California History* 57:70–87.

Watanna, Onoto [Winnifred Eaton]. 1910. *Tama*. New York: Harper and Brothers.

Wu, William F. 1982. *The Yellow Peril: Chinese Americans in American Fiction*. Hamden, CT: Archon Books.

Yabes, Leopoldo Y. 1977. "Pioneering in the Filipino Short Story in English (1925–1940)." In *Philippine Writings*, ed. A. G. Hufana, 370–89. Manila: Regal Publishing.

Yin, Xiao-Huang. 1991. "Between the East and West: Sui Sin Far – the First Chinese-American Woman Writer." *Arizona Quarterly* 47 (Winter): 49–84.

8

POSTCOLONIALISM, NATIONALISM, AND THE EMERGENCE OF ASIAN/PACIFIC AMERICAN LITERATURES

STEPHEN H. SUMIDA

When I was drafting this chapter, I had the opportunity to discuss with Davianna Pomaika'i McGregor, a historian of Native Hawaiian and ethnic studies, my questions about examining the emergence of Hawaii's literatures as a postcolonial historical and cultural phenomenon. *"Post-colonial?"* she said. Her eyebrows leaped up. "Since when?"[1]

Applied to American literary histories, the term "postcolonial" makes an imperfect but, in some ways, useful lens. In "minority" American literatures generally – and because they are often still considered "minority" ones, continuing to struggle for equality – an incongruity of "postcolonial" models arises from this: for peoples of racial minority groups of the United States there has not been a point of "liberation" from colonialism in the political, *inter*national sense that the British colonies became "liberated," gained independence and nationhood, whether in North America or, say, in South Asia. It is arguable that in minority American literatures generally, political and cultural issues are being played out in ways that resemble dynamics of race, class, and gender in postcolonial nations engaged in processes of creating new national narratives out of their old and their recent indigenous, colonial, and current postcolonial histories and languages. Rather than establishing a similarity, however, a comparison between postcolonial literary phenomena and various ways in which Asian/Pacific American literatures have been "emerging" brings into view, as well as into question, certain distinctions among Asian/Pacific American and other "minority" literatures of the United States.[2]

From the point of view of indigenous peoples of the United States, colonialism did not end in 1776 and with the Declaration of Independence. The colonizers remained in charge under the new dispensation. The language in which a national literature of the United States emerged was primarily English. The transition from British colony to independent nation did not result in a rejection of English – for the most part the rebels' native tongue, after all – and a return to an indigenous language and culture predating the arrival of colonists, though such a construct (and adoption of a Native American language) for the new nation was once and again proposed by colonizers. The colonization of the indigenous peoples – and the notion that they are subjects (namely, subjected to) rather than agents of changes – continues despite the fact that, importantly, American culture has been and is alive with changes effected not only by the arrivals of peoples, ideas, and arts from around the world but by influences of indigenous cultures, and with changes necessitated or inspired by the very lands, waters, and skies that comprise the United States.[3] Agents of American cultural changes are not exclusively European colonizers; but these changes are not exactly "postcolonial" because they are still largely claimed and owned by the colonizers themselves.

In Asian/Pacific American literary history, questions regarding post-colonialism ought first of all to be applied thus to Hawai'i, a state of the union that has, however, capitalized on an exceptionalism which aims to give the impression that Hawai'i and its cultures are, in appeal to some recess of the yearner's desire, most *naturally* untouched by whatever colonialist grip the rest of the United States may have on the Islands. I find it important to begin this discussion with thoughts about Native Hawaiian history, because of how it simultaneously affects the development and characteristics of the Asian American literature of Hawai'i and exposes some assumptions about class and national values in the Asian American literature of immigration, whether of Hawai'i or of the continental United States.[4] In a colonialist view, 1778 and the first arrival of the British Captain James Cook signify the beginning of the colonization of Hawai'i by Europeans. But a different view, a view from the shore, though recognizing the fact that Cook interacted with changes historically under way in his time, would place 1778 within a long struggle waged by and among native Hawaiians to unify and gain political control over the entire chain of islands of Hawai'i (Sumida 1991, 7–19, 160–2). This warfare culminated, not in some kind of Native Hawaiian defeat at the hands and brains of superior Europeans led by one who arrived by accident in Hawai'i, but in the successful conquest and unification of the Islands, completed in the mid-1790s, by Kamehameha I, first monarch of the Kingdom of Hawai'i. Hawaiian sovereignty under a unified monarchy lasted almost a full century, during which many Europeans and Americans, with their colonialist views of taking over the realm, might have thought and acted as if Hawai'i were their "colony" and did fight over whose it was. But it was Native Hawaiians who ruled. When, in the late twentieth century, assertions of and opposition against Hawaiian sovereignty are voiced, it is to this history that the partisans allude – indeed to this already powerfully mythical time when Native Hawaiians consolidated political, national agency for themselves, among themselves, and by themselves.

Nonetheless, outside would-be colonialist influences were certainly strong enough that Hawai'i, even under the monarchy, struggled with such forces. Hawaiian arts such as the *mele* (poetry) and *hula* (dances), including *mele ma'i* celebrating the genitals of royal ones and other honored persons, were suppressed by Christian missionaries and some of their converts (Elbert and Mahoe 1970, 6). Although genital chants may seem an extreme form of art in our (postmissionary) minds, the genre had not been extreme in pre-Christian Hawai'i; and the suppression of arts and culture extended to historical chants, for Hawaiian history was pagan history, to be wrested from the convert entering the new life of Christianity.[5] Whatever his own strategies of sometimes opposing, sometimes courting the support of Americans in the realm, in the 1870s and 1880s the elected king, David Kalākaua, instituted what became known as a "Hawaiian Renaissance" of native arts and sciences. The fact that there was a recognized "renaissance" clearly suggests that Kalākaua sought through it to supply something he felt lacking but needed for the life of the land. The "reborn" Hawaiian culture emerged in opposition to the European imports and influences in eclectic and sometimes secret ways. Here was an assertion of Hawaiian nationalism even while in principle as well as in practical rule it was the Native Hawaiians themselves who were still in power.

The need for the sovereign nation to proclaim a renaissance and a cultural nationhood in Kalākaua's reign foretold the change that soon followed. His successor, Queen Lili'uokalani, who has the reputation of being one of the greatest Native Hawaiian poets and songwriters and is still widely known for her lyrics today, was overthrown by American businessmen, backed by U.S. naval power, in January 1893.[6] President Grover Cleveland declared this takeover illegal when the businessmen offered the United States the opportunity to annex Hawai'i immediately. The illegal takeover is the occasion that marks in Hawaiian history the beginning – not the end – of the American colonial period. Immediately after the overthrow of the queen and monarchy, Ellen Wright Prendergast, an attendant of Lili'uokalani, composed the mele, "Kaulana nā Pua." Though its words, in the Hawaiian language, were little understood through much of the next century, this song has become one of the most familiar-sounding expressions today of protest against colonization (Elbert and Mahoe 1970, 62–4; Sumida 1991, 62–3, 109, 1992, 218–19). This mele was at first considered sacred, not to be accompanied by a hula. It was a document in an underground movement. The very music of the song seems happy (as in the former vice president Dan Quayle's saluting

American Samoans by calling them "happy campers") to anyone who does not understand its language. Merely hearing the tune, who would suspect "Kaulana nā Pua" of being subversive?

Kaulana nā pua a'o Hawai'i	Famous are the children of Hawai'i
Kūpa'a mahope o ka 'āina	Ever loyal to the land
Hiki mai ka 'elele o ka loko 'ino	When the evil-hearted messenger comes
Palapala 'ānunu me ka pākaha.	With his greedy document of extortion.[7]

The song's statement of protest and its invocation of indigenous, heroic traditions and values springing directly from a precontact history of self-sufficiency of the island culture – an experience centered on the cultivation of the land and of families, the work and the rule of sustaining the life of the land – became "masked" from the ignorant. This already, in about February 1893, was assuredly a colonized Hawai'i with a poetry and discourse crafted for that new status. This too is the colonial period some of the two hundred thousand indigenous Hawaiians see themselves living in today, as evidenced by sovereignty movements currently under way.[8]

Simultaneously energizing and confusing arguments over cultural and historical relations in Hawai'i, however, is the convergence today of the Native Hawaiian renaissance with a "Local" cultural upwelling that includes a large measure of diversely Asian American participation. Whether of indigenous or immigrant descent, most "Locals" of Hawai'i are quick to note the irony when a tourist refers to the "States" and implies that Hawai'i is not one. Asian Americans in this Local society also generally assume identification with the national, political, and economic label "American," as well as their specific ethnicities within Local, heterogeneous culture. Historically, these Asian American peoples were imported under contract, amounting to indentured servitude, to work on the sugar plantations in Hawai'i. As laborers, and in particular as non-white laborers, they were at best promoted to the ranks of subalterns, not colonialists like the sugar planters, missionaries, big capitalists, and military leaders. Today when those who are Asian American Locals – people like myself, third- or fourth-generation descendants of imported laborers – voice ethnically specific and collectively Local identities and unity through a recognized body of fiction, poetry, and drama, it appears in a sense that a postcolonial, nationalist movement is under way, under an implicit assumption that we have been liberated (supposedly by American opportunities) from colonialist and class oppression and are in the process of forging a new national identity through politics, economic strides, and the raising of our own voices. But this construct, based as it is on assumptions about *immigrant* histories and dreams, again leaves out the Native Hawaiian. Further, the idea that the emergence of a Local culture in Hawai'i is evidence of a kind of nationalism, not primarily Native Hawaiian but heterogeneous, obscures the fact that the Asian American Locals, too, despite their numbers in the population, are still inheritors of a colonial history they have not escaped, a history shaped greatly by nineteenth-century notions of white superiority and therefore white rule. The nation of Hawaii's peoples is still the United States, where Asian Americans are assuredly not the majority.

In Hawaii's Local literature today there is, however, a language of agency, of self-determination. It is Hawai'i Creole English, or what Locals popularly call "pidgin." If there were an emergence of a postcolonial literature of Hawai'i today, one of its languages would be this pidgin. Here is a sample from Lois-Ann Yamanakas, a poem called "Parts" (that is, body parts):

"The Face"

Stop muttering
under your breath
before I pound
your face.
Want me
to punch
your face in?
You cannot run away
from me.
Try.
I catch you
and give you
double lickens.
Now get
your ass
in your room
and fold
all the laundry.
Then I'm gonna
teach you
how to iron
your father's shirts.
Go. The laundry

is on your bed.
Hurry up.

"The Eye"

I

found this letter
in you panty drawer.
Did you write
all these evil things?
Looks like your
handwriting.
Like me read this
to Joy and her mother?

Like me call them up
come over for lunch
right now?
What you mean,
no, wait?
So you did
write it.

I

cannot believe
that so much evil
can live
in one person.
You are a evil child.
You are filthy.
You are a hypocrite.
Stay in your room.
Forever.
[*Sister Stew* (1991), 27–28]

If Hawaiʻi *were* a postcolonial site, how apt would Yamanaka's poem be, with its blunt and nuanced, parodic verbal assaults against the daughter's body and her sexuality? This treatment courses through the mother from a history of being virtually owned, bodily, by the plantation boss and of being suppressed by fears of sinning and looking bad, where an individual's looks and behavior could have consequences for the entire community if the boss decided so.[9] The poem would aptly be postcolonialist, too, because it exposes how we inherit colonialism even when we may think we are and should be free of it, and the poem critiques what it exposes: the pecking order, the downhill course of the sewage ditch, or the abuse of the subordinate runs headlong down the hierarchies exposed in Ota's *Upon Their Shoulders* (1951), Lum's "Primo Doesn't Take Back Bottles Anymore" (1972) and "Beer Can Hat," Murayama's "I'll Crack Your Head *Kotsun*" and all throughout his *All I Asking for Is My Body* (1975) to Yamanaka's "Parts." In this lineage Yamanaka's speaker also inherits an identification with a social class, a labor class. It is an identification which in this case opposes and transcends colonial standards, gendered constructs of how boys and men might talk pidgin, "bad English," whereas girls and women are supposed to "talk nice" and become schoolteachers, middle-class, haolefied (whitewashed), and accepting of being colonized.

Yamanaka's "pidgin" language *is* Local identity in one of its many forms, whether in daily life or in the poem, and therefore in its treatments of otherwise widespread themes. The primacy of the voice of one person speaking to others, in Hawaii's Local literature, is expressed through the poem's genre: it is a dramatic monologue, a valuable device among Hawaii's contemporary poets, including Cathy Song, who, writing in so-called standard English, may be said moreover to demonstrate that poetic traditions of Hawai'i are by no means confined to Hawai'i Creole.

Another language of a postcolonial Hawai'i, if there were ever to be such a place, would be Native Hawaiian, the prime language of Hawai'i. Put Hawai'i Creole and Hawaiian together in the linguistic identity of a hypothetical postcolonial nation, and we have *the* tongues native to Hawai'i. If in an instant you could take away all other languages, including English, that native speakers have brought from outside Hawai'i, then certain Local writers and most of the population would still have their own tongues of Hawai'i to exercise cultural agency in the literary arts and talking story.

The same may not yet be said of Asian American cultures of the American continent. Frank Chin grumbles about the failure thus far of West Coast Asian Americans to create a language that can be sustained and put to every conceivable linguistic use even if the speaking of English, Spanish, Black English, and a variety of Asian tongues were to vanish.[10] Beyond the immigrant generation, Asian Americans of the mainland generally write in English. Native Hawaiian and pidgin being quite different matters, in Hawai'i and elsewhere in the Pacific a similar phenomenon is occurring in the emergence of a new growth in "traditional" indigenous literatures, this outgrowth being Pacific Island literatures written by indigenous peoples but in the languages of the colonizers.[11] On some of these islands, now nations, we can truly speak of the emergence of a postcolonial literature in English, just as there is a strong Anglophone, postcolonial literature in India. Regarding Chin's observation about the confinement of Asian American writers to the language that has dominated them, there is something to be learned from African American literature and the arts of subversion or of strategic, ostensible accommodations to domination through artistry in the English language. And as Chin has been insisting for some years now, verbal strategies and the creation of Asian American discourses of agency as resistance can be derived from abundant methods found in "heroic" Chinese and Japanese stories about social, sometimes interethnic, oppression and social justice, as well as from the early history of the Chinese American laborer and adventurer classes.

But whereas in Hawai'i the literary uses of pidgin and native Hawaiian languages may allow a writer to be expressive in what are perceived to be his or her own terms, in virtually monolingual Asian American literature of the continent assertions of cultural identity, I think, tend to be made by way of opposition or resistance that in a sense depends upon, and unavoidably reifies, the racial, cultural, and nationalistic constructs of a perceived "majority" American culture, the adversary when it assumes and asserts domination. Thus, in any number of works we find a central conflict or tension addressed, though in significantly different ways, between what it is to be "Asian" and what it is to be "American," or what it is to be stereotyped as one or the other or both.[12] This occurs, for instance, in works by Frank Chin, Maxine Hong Kingston, and Amy Tan, to name only three out of a century-long history of Asian American writers. Some, like Tan, simply assume an intercultural conflict and the opposing sides to be "real." This is a well-established, highly problematic tradition in continental Asian American literatures. Others, like Chin and Kingston, in their different ways deconstruct the sides, and therefore the conflict, and show them to be profoundly "unreal" yet a virulent basis for racist actions. Still, in Kingston's *Woman Warrior* and *Tripmaster Monkey*, and in Chin's *Donald Duk*, the protagonists have to approach a radically different understanding by first exhausting old, ultimately pointless questions about their identities as supposedly being alien, in contrast or opposition to the identities of others by race, culture, and language – pointless in part because, except for immigrants among them, the protagonists do not possess or *own* any Asian "race," "culture," or "language" apart from American orientalist constructs of these concepts, and in part because their questions of ethnic and racial identity are "American," ones asked in distinctly twentieth-century American contemporary and historical contexts. "Asian" cultural elements that immigrants transmit to younger Asian American generations are selectively remembered, reduced to serve the needs and purposes of the immigrant trying to deal with life, security, and the upbringing of Asian American youngsters in a land that lacks the full support of the culture the immigrant has left. Yet both the immigrants and the American-born characters have to deal with the construct of the former as supposedly a full-blown representation of an Asian land, culture, and people. By comparison, in Yamanaka's "Parts," the poem's speaker and daughter have other concerns than cultural identity on their minds, and they have these concerns with no need for self-consciousness about the language they speak and its difference from "standard" English (except that Yamanaka is highly conscious of her linguistic choices in writing the poem).

This is to suggest that Asian American literature of the continental United States, too, has been emerging not exactly as a postcolonial phenomenon. It is indeed a "minority" literature in a troubling sense, sometimes and perhaps at its best an oppositional literature in an American culture that "colonizes" Asian Americans within America's own borders. When Asian American literature *is* postcolonial, it is about another nation and is written in languages taken from those of the former colonizers. Thus Jessica Hagedorn's *Dogeaters* and Ninotchka Rosca's *State of War* are novels about the Philippines, the setting also for parts of Peter Bacho's *Cebu* and of Michele Cruz Skinner's *Balikbayan*, after the nation was granted independence from the United States in 1946. N. V. M. Gonzalez's works (for instance, his short story "The Popcorn Man," about a Filipino who teaches English composition to American soldiers on an installation resembling the former Clark United States Air Force Base) are "postcolonial," drenched in references to things, ideas, and terms of a combined four centuries of Spanish and American rule and the author's consciousness of taking part in the creation of a national literature. A similar observation may be made of Meena Alexander's novel, *Nampally Road*, sparked by the rape of a woman by police in a station house in Hyderabad during the Emergency of the 1970s in India.

Indeed, about the immigrant's refusal to see that in America he is no longer in Asia, no longer of a national majority group, George Leong recites a poem with the refrain, "Are you a Chinese? Or are you a Chinaman?"[13] A Chinese American speaker (a "Chinaman") addresses an immigrant who still considers himself "Chinese":

> Do you have a flag? Do you have an army?
> Are you a Chinese? Or are you a Chinaman?
> Do you have one billion people? Are you a nation?
> Are you a Chinese? Or are you a Chinaman?

In other words, the immigrant is now a "Chinaman" like the poem's speaker, a subject of a nation in which he is not of a majority that matters in ways he might wish. This awareness is seen, in Leong's poem, to be a necessary first step toward any possibility of the Chinaman's becoming empowered, not fractured from a meaningful historical identity and not rendered bone by bone into one more soul exploited, an "individual" who emerges from divisiveness rather than a fulfilled selfhood.

Some writers seem to me to be most aware that Asian America is not a "nation" and that the nation they are most determined to affect, indeed transform, is the United States, in a vision which *includes* Asian America, in order that fresh immigrants and nativists of long standing alike might perhaps understand that being "American" ought not be restricted by race. That is, even sometimes-so-called Asian American cultural nationalists seek not sovereignty but recognition of Asian Americans' historical rights *in America*.

Whether or not it, like a movement for Native Hawaiian sovereignty, can also be called "nationalist," this continental Asian American drive for recognition of these voices in American literature signifies the emergence of a literature out from under an Anglo-American colonialism. It is a burgeoning literature full of self-consciousness about individual and collective identities, still bearing marks of exploitation by and through inequalities of gender and race, even after class and class differences seem to have ceased to be an issue for now because of a predominance in it of middle-class assumptions and dreams. This would mean that the "nation" assumed in Asian American literature is an *ideal* of "America" – precisely as in Carlos Bulosan's classic Filipino American, migrant-labor novel of exile, *America Is in the Heart* – and it is an "America" where power or potentiality, citizenship, and equality are democratic rights not determined by race, gender, age, and other attributes that are ordinarily outside anyone's choice. I do not think Asian American literature is alone among "minority" literatures in assuming this cluster of ideals, a yet unrealized postcolonial "nation" to which, with their visions, certain authors of this and other literatures already belong.

But this affirmation of "America," occurring even in works of Asian American literature most critical of acts of the United States, such as John Okada's *No-No Boy*, when combined with historical circumstances, also tends to set Asian American literature and communities apart from other "minority" literatures and communities in a way that has been divisive and should not be: among America's peoples of color, it is mainly Asian Americans who are generally distinguished by their having come to the United States by choosing to subject themselves to American rule and by passing the legacies of this choice down to the American-born generations. In this context, the idea that Asian American literature is emerging as a "postcolonial," revolutionary or postrevolutionary phenomenon is inconceivable, for given a (mis)reading of the evidence, is it not the Asian's will and nature to be colonized, as the immigrant American by choice, despite the fact that David Henry Hwang tries to destroy this idea of the naturally yielding Asian in his *M. Butterfly*? All the more, then, to counteract this misreading, we have to understand how the "America" envisioned in some works of Asian American literature is not America as it is, but a utopian "postcolonial America" that may be seen, through fictions, as emerging from an actual, still colonial America. It used to be a prevalent stereotype about Asians in America that the opposite was the case – that Asians came willingly, but only to return home to Asia rich. That stereotype was used to condemn Asian immigrants, settlers, for not truly being committed and responsible to this land and for being unassimilable in any case. Now, however, the *settlement* of Asians in America and the growing awareness that these peoples are here to stay are sometimes taken as signs that they are sellouts, mimicking Europeans, the other racial group who supposedly followed the myth of the American Dream to these shores.

Even while opposing such generalizations, Asian American literature has gone quite far to promote identification with America, or with a better America. And this brings me back to particulars of the beginning of this chapter, to the questions that need to be addressed concerning indigenous peoples, expressly in connection with constructs of Asian American literature. How can the ideas of a "better America" be reconciled with concepts of postcolonial agency and its foundation – as I have been treating it in this instance – upon a liberation from colonization? In the main, whether in Hawai'i or on the continent, is Asian American literature of the coming decades to support or perhaps improve the nation, the United States, at the expense of others colonized? Occasionally I have received responses to my comments about Asian American and Native Hawaiian relations that isolate these concerns out there in the middle of the Pacific – literally isolated incidents peripheral to Asian American concerns. My point, however, is that these concerns apply throughout America when the question asked of me and my colleagues about *post*colonialism stir up questions about the nation or nations implicit or assumed in Asian American and other ethnic literary studies nationwide. The inquiry prompting this discussion of postcolonialism and ethnic literatures brings certain bases and contours of Asian American literature into prominence, and I find myself repeating a question. What liberation from colonialism – for anyone, from whatever sites of oppression – is there when indigenous peoples of these lands are still colonized?

■■■■ NOTES

1. Conversation with McGregor, October 1992. The original version of this chapter was presented at the annual convention of the American Studies

Association, Costa Mesa, California, November 1992, in the session titled "American Literary History as a Postcolonial Phenomenon." For a critique of the ongoing colonization of Hawai'i by the United States, see Trask 1993.

2. The term "Asian/Pacific American" configures many differing ethnic groups into a political entity, a conceptualized coalition. Political agendas of constituent groups in the category continually merge and diverge, changing the category, so that currently, what two decades ago was envisioned – hopefully – to be an alliance of Asian Americans and Pacific Islanders does not hold. My discussion reflects this divergence and certain comparisons it opens among Native Hawaiian, Hawaii's Asian American, and continental Asian American literatures. For a treatment of the development of the panethnic concept "Asian American," see Espiritu 1992.

3. These changes, both distinctive to and resulting from the social and natural environments of American settings (of time, place, history) have often been considered central to defining and promoting America and the United States' strength and position in the world, under theories and practices of "American exceptionalism" especially in the four decades of the Cold War. The concept of "exceptionalism" in this sense, although not for purposes of promoting the power of the American nation in the world, may be basic to current images of Hawai'i and of Asian Americans, the former promoted as a special destination and the latter characterized as a model minority.

4. For another case where the category of an Asian American "literature of immigration" is critiqued, see Campomanes (1992), who, against the predominance of this category, contrasts a Filipino American "literature of exile." Also, Rafael (1993) details some of the colonial cultural and hegemonic strategies the United States employed in taking over the Philippines from which the "old-timers" departed.

5. Hawaiian historical and genealogical chants narrate and record some aspects of culture that pass on the empowering knowledge of descent, which both identifies particular individuals, each standing in unique relation to others, and narrates those relationships tieing individuals, by acts and events, to one another. In the twentieth century, it was a genre of seemingly ahistorical love lyric that selectively came to symbolize Hawai'i in a tourist's ears. This is one of the aspects of what I call a suppression of narrative, historical chants.

6. See Lili'uokalani, *Hawaii's Story by Hawaii's Queen*. See also John Dominis Holt's drama, *Kaulana Na Pua* (1974), and his historically based long poem, *Hanai* (1986); and Aldyth Morris's drama, *Lili'uokalani* (1993), for treatments of the life and illegal overthrow of Hawaii's last monarch.

7. When orally delivering this paper, I presented "Kaulana nā Pua" by first playing some stanzas of Genoa Keawe's singing of it with her group at the Waimea Music Festival. Her performance, its vocal exuberance, its pitches, instrumentals, tempo, and style (called "chalangalang" in echo of the lively strumming of the ukulele) epitomize the presentation of "Kaulana nā Pua" in the subversive guise of a party song. I next read translated stanzas, one of which I quote here, of lyrics that many in my audience found quite unexpected.

8. The United States Census Bureau recorded 211,014 Native Hawaiians in

1990. The figure includes "pure Hawaiians" and "part Hawaiians" who identified themselves as Hawaiian in the census. In that census the total population of Hawai'i was 1,108,229.

9. In her novel, Ota narrates the plantation owner's rape of a Japanese housemaid, chosen for her duties and victimization because of her looks (46). Theories and rationalizations of physique and physical abilities in connection with race supported the selection of laborers imported to Hawai'i and its plantations.

10. Chin's comments about the value of Hawaii's pidgin and Creole occur for me in a long-standing conversation with him, speaking with Hawai'i Creole writers such as Milton Murayama and Darrell H. Y. Lum in mind, going back to 1976.

11. See Hamasaki, whose thesis and literary activities offer materials and analyses related to postcolonial studies of Pacific Island literatures, distinct from immigrant-based approaches.

12. For comparisons that highlight, by contrast, a concern with this dual "Asian American" identity, consider the popular novel, *Kitchen*, by Banana Yoshimoto, a Japanese woman – that is, a member of the racial and ethnic majority group in her nation. In *Kitchen* here is no emphasis on matters of racial and ethnic hierarchies or resistance against them. The fact that the characters cook and eat foods of different international derivations does not signify that their identities are fragmented. See, too, Sara Suleri's autobiography, *Meatless Days* (1989), for what is simultaneously a high degree of consciousness of constructs of race and ethnicity and a high awareness and questioning of how her multiplicity of identities relates to the postcolonial forging of a new nation, Pakistan.

13. I have never been able to find the poem in print, so I paraphrase it from where I have heard it, on the soundtrack of *Dupont Guy: The Schiz of Grant Avenue*, a film by Curtis Choy about Chinatown in San Francisco.

■ WORKS CITED

Alexander, Meena. 1991. *Nampally Road*. San Francisco: Mercury House.

Bacho, Peter. 1991. *Cebu*. Seattle: Univ. of Washington Press.

Bulosan, Carlos. 1946/1973. *America Is in the Heart*. Seattle: Univ. of Washington Press.

Campomanes, Oscar V. 1992. "Filipinos in the United States and Their Literature of Exile." In *Reading the Literatures of Asian America*, ed. Shirley Geok-lin Lim and Amy Ling, 49–78. Philadelphia: Temple Univ. Press.

Chin, Frank. 1991. *Donald Duk*. Minneapolis: Coffee House Press.

Choy, Curtis. 1976. *Dupont Guy: The Schiz of Grant Avenue*. Film. Oakland: Chonk Moonhunter.

Elbert, Samuel H., and Noelani Mahoe, eds. 1970. *Nā Mele o Hawai'i Nei: 101 Hawaiian Songs*. Honolulu: Univ. Hawai'i Press.

Espiritu, Yen Le. 1992. *Asian American Panethnicity: Bridging Institutions and Identities*. Philadelphia: Temple Univ. Press.

Gonzalez, N. V. M. 1993. "The Popcorn Man." In *The Bread of Salt and Other Stories*, 136–50. Seattle: Univ. of Washington Press.

Hagedorn, Jessica. 1990. *Dogeaters*. New York: Pantheon Books.

Hamasaki, Richard. 1989. "Singing in Their Genealogical Trees: The Emergence of Contemporary Hawaiian Poetry in English – Dana Naone Hall, Wayne Kaumuali'i Westlake, Joseph P. Balaz." M. A. thesis, Univ. of Hawai'i at Mānoa.

Holt, John Dominis. 1974. *Kaulana Na Pua, Famous Are the Flowers: Queen Liliuokalani and the Throne of Hawaii: A Play in Three Acts*. Honolulu: Topgallant Publishing.

———. 1986. *Hanai: A Poem for Queen Liliuokalani*. Honolulu: Topgallant Publishing.

Hwang, David Henry. 1988. *M. Butterfly*. New York: Penguin.

Kingston, Maxine Hong. 1976. *The Woman Warrior: Memoirs of a Girlhood among Ghosts*. New York: Knopf.

———. 1989. *Tripmaster Monkey: His Fake Book*. New York: Knopf.

Leong, George. 1976. ["Are You a Chinese, or Are You a Chinaman?"] Text from film by Curtis Choy, *Dupont Guy: The Schiz of Grant Avenue*. Oakland, CA: Chonk Moonhunter.

Lili'uokalani. 1898/1986. *Hawaii's Story by Hawaii's Queen*. Tokyo: Charles E. Tuttle.

Lum, Darrell H. Y. 1972/1986. "Primo Doesn't Take Back Bottles Anymore." Reprinted in *The Best of Bamboo Ridge: The Hawaii Writers' Quarterly*, ed. Eric Chock and Darrell H. Y. Lum, 184–8. Honolulu: Bamboo Ridge Press.

———. 1980/1986. "Beer Can Hat." Reprinted in *The Best of Bamboo Ridge: The Hawaii Writers' Quarterly*, ed. Eric Chock and Darrell H. Y. Lum, 175–83. Honolulu: Bamboo Ridge Press.

Morris, Aldyth. 1993. *Lili'uokalani*. Honolulu: Univ. of Hawai'i Press.

Murayama, Milton. 1975/1988. *All I Asking for Is My Body*. Honolulu: Univ. of Hawai'i Press.

Okada, John. 1957/1979. *No-No Boy*. Seattle: Univ. of Washington Press.

Ota, Shelley Ayame Nishimura. 1951. *Upon Their Shoulders*. New York: Exposition Press.

Rafael, Vicente L. 1993. "White Love: Surveillance and Nationalist Resistance in the U.S. Colonization of the Philippines." In *Cultures of United States Imperialism*, ed. Amy Kaplan and Donald E. Pease, 185–218. Durham, NC: Duke Univ. Press.

Rosca, Ninotchka. 1988. *State of War*. New York: Simon and Schuster.

Prendergast, Helen Wright. 1893/1970. "Kaulana na Pua." In *Nā Mele o Hawai'i Nei: 101 Hawaiian Songs*, ed. Samuel H. Elbert and Noelani Mahoe, 62–4. Honolulu: Univ. of Hawai'i Press.

Skinner, Michelle Cruz. 1988. *Balikbayan: A Filipino Homecoming*. Honolulu: Bess Press.

Song, Cathy. 1983. *Picture Bride*. New Haven: Yale Univ. Press.

Suleri, Sara. 1989. *Meatless Days*. Chicago: Univ. of Chicago Press.

Sumida, Stephen H. 1991. *And the View from the Shore: Literary Traditions of Hawai'i*. Seattle: Univ. of Washington Press.

————. 1992. "Sense of Place, History, and the Concept of the 'Local' in Hawaii's Asian/Pacific Literatures." In *Reading the Literatures of Asian America*, ed. Shirley Geok-lin Lim and Amy Ling, 215–37. Philadelphia: Temple Univ. Press.

Tan, Amy. 1989. *The Joy Luck Club*. New York: Putnam.

Trask, Haunani-Kay. 1993. *From a Native Daughter: Colonialism and Sovereignty in Hawai'i*. Monroe, ME: Common Courage Press.

Yamanaka, Lois-Ann. 1991. "Parts." In *Sister Stew: Fiction and Poetry by Women*, ed. Juliet S. Kono and Cathy Song, 26–33. Honolulu: Bamboo Ridge Press.

Yoshimoto, Banana. 1988/1994. *Kitchen*. Trans. Megan Backus. New York: Washington Square Press.

9

IMMIGRATION AND DIASPORA

SHIRLEY GEOK-LIN LIM

I

Many U.S. feminist and ethnic critics question the patriarchal, Eurocentric interpretations of texts, but they seldom interrogate the national-identity parameters in these interpretations. Instead, they attempt to enlarge that American identity, appropriating myths and characteristics that construct more permeable, flexible, and plurally enclosing borders. U.S. literary tradition has been until recently constructed on works produced by "white, middle-class, male[s], of Anglo-Saxon derivation or at least from an ancestry which had settled in this country before the big waves of immigration which began around the middle of the nineteenth century" (Baym 1985, 69); in these works, "America as a nation must be the ultimate subject . . . setting America off from other people and the country from other nations" (67). With the Civil Rights Movement in the 1950s and 1960s, some Asian American critics, taking their cue from Black Arts Movement figures such as Ishmael Reed, criticized Asian American texts that represent Asian Americans as the model minority – successfully assimilated, law-abiding, and Anglo-identified citizens (Chin et al. 1974). This "assimilationist" tradition, they contended, imposes ethnic-based restrictions on the production of self-representations and is gender-biased, resulting in the stereotyping of Asian American males as effeminate and in the skewed success of Asian American women writers. John Okada's *No-No Boy* (1957), Louis Chu's *Eat a Bowl of Tea* (1961), Shawn Wong's *Homebase* (1979), and Frank Chin's *Donald Duk* (1991) could be seen to represent the male-identified "American-born sensibility" that these critics privilege. In contrast to this cultural nationalist position, other critics explicate Asian American works as situated in and reflecting the tensions between their Asian descent and the Anglo-conformed world that discriminates against them and assumes that the Asian American imagination is cathected in cultural conflict "between worlds." "Whether recent immigrants or American-born, Chinese in the United States find themselves caught between two worlds. Their facial features proclaim one fact – their Asian ethnicity but by education, choice, or birth they are American" (Ling 1990, 20).

Opposing these American, even if multiculturally identified critical positions, other critics have bracketed a group of "cosmopolitan" writers who "present their own Third World identities as a mark of distinction in a world supposedly exempt from national belonging" (Brennan 1989, 2). The term suggests an elite "of perennial immigration, valorized by a rhetoric of wandering, and rife with allusions to the all-seeing eye of the nomadic sensibility" (ibid.). The concerns of these "cosmopolitan" writers are not specific to nation-states and often overlap with those of writers who have moved out of their country of origin to resettle in Western urban centers. The term "metropolitan" underlines their absorption into Western publishing markets.

This essay proposes to deal with two categories in Asian American literature that problematize the reifications of U.S. canonical and U.S. minority literature *and* cosmopolitan, metropolitan literature – that is, with writing categorized as immigrant and diasporic, produced by writers who are either first-generation Americans or who mark themselves with a non-U.S. culture and society. Works viewed as diasporic are usually excluded from a U.S.-based grouping for extraliterary, ideological, and political reasons. Although immigrant and diasporic writings overlap with literatures considered minority, cosmopolitan, or metropolitan, they are often seen as falling outside U.S. canonical work.

Ethnic scholars have become receptive to reading Asian American writing as immigrant writing (Sucheta Mazumdar points out that Asian American Studies has existed for a long time as a subfield of immigration history [1991, 29]). But the shift from "writing produced by U.S. writers of Asian descent" to "writing produced by members of a diasporic group" (the Chinese, South Asian, or Filipino diasporas, for example) carries ideological, political, and institutional consequences that have been addressed by a number of critics and writers. Lisa Lowe marks Asian American heterogeneity, hybridity, and multiplicity as condensing around generational, class, and language stratifications, which she argues are not "exclusively hierarchical and familial" but also "horizontal" (1991, 26), that is, operative between subjectivities within similar generations, classes, and ethnic communities. Lowe constructs her argument for recognition of the shifting and unstable marks of Asian American differences around "the terms of debate about nationalism and assimilation" (33) to take into account the "uneven development, nonequivalence, and cultural heterogeneities" (41) between and within the recent immigrants. Sau-ling Wong cautions against an uncritical adoption of a diasporic perspective because it vacates the position on the domestic American scene that Asian Americans hold to create their own panethnic solidarity and identity with other people of color, an abdication that also leads to Asian American literature being subsumed under the global metanarratives of postmodernism (paper presented in 1993). In urging the formation of a strategic essentialist Asian American cultural nationalism unified under U.S. history, many Asian American critics ironically repeat the call of U.S. nationalists for a shared unified American identity in response to the threat of fragmentation posed by minority interest groups. Thus, even as the oppositional concept of "minority discourses" – covering feminist, ethnic, and gay literature – has begun to receive institutional support, the category of diaspora writing generally has been ignored.

Part of the reason may be hegemonizing dynamics acting within minority discourses, dynamics that these very discourses are supposed to be deconstructing. U.S. minority groups seldom see their interests as being in common with those of new incoming groups or, worse, with groups who speak for concerns outside U.S. borders: their gains in academia have been too recent and too small, and the fear of diffusion of purpose and rewards is understandable. However, if "viewing American race relations from an international perspective [provides] an important corrective to the parochial and ahistorical outlook of our national consciousness" (Blauner 1982, 518), then, in an international perspective, paradigms of diaspora will tend to overlap, destabilize, or supersede paradigms of immigration.

II

Although it is true that, except for Native Americans, all Americans are descended from immigrant populations and are members of diasporas, Asian American immigration history manifests distinctive differences from that of other groups. These differences, attributable to historical legislative racism against Asians (Weglyn 1976; Chan 1991), have been continuously foregrounded and thematized in Asian American literary productions. Articulated through tensions between cultural reciprocity and resistance, themes and subjects in Asian American literature play on issues of identity that encompass non-Western cultural configurations and heterogeneous Asian communities. One must read Asian American immigrant autobiographies as both within and expanding beyond the autobiographical tradition that James Craig Holte defined as "a central part of the American literary tradition" illustrating "the American question [as] a question of self" (1982, 250).

Immigrant non-English texts – for example, the poems translated in *Songs of Gold Mountain* (1987) and *Island* (1991) – generally offer propositions of cultural incommensurability and mourning, juxtaposed with propositions of desire for an Other figured as a sexualized object or as U.S. material culture. Except for a few nonethnic-marked texts by writers such as José García Villa (1949) and Diana Chang (1974), second-generation English-language works – often autobiographical – generally rework themes of generational and cross-cultural conflicts that negotiate between foreign and native-born communities. A social and regional present/presence constructed on U.S. memory and history, such as we find in William Faulkner's or Flannery O'Connor's fiction, or even in the work of second-generation writers such as Grace Paley or Philip Roth, is seldom represented in Asian American writing. Instead, the individual who is articulated in poem or scene or narrative is often constructed in relation to at least two national cultures, two homelands, two origins. Mitsuye Yamada, for example, articulates this double-consciousness in her poem "Guilty on Both Counts," in which the Japanese American narrator, on a visit to Japan, is rudely treated by a survivor of the Hiroshima holocaust and ruefully notes that in the United States she is also held responsible for the infamous 1941 attack on Pearl Harbor (1988, 20–3). Conflict, often privatized and psychologized in U.S. mainstream literature or embedded in U.S. cultural history, is socialized in the context of Asian and U.S. cultural values that are enacted as immigrant memory and history.

Immigrant memory and history function as major narrative strategies that infuse genres as diverse as poetry, drama, and fiction with an ethnographic discourse (Fischer 1986). As William Boelhower theorizes, memory is integrally related to the ethnicization of the subject through specific genealogical projects and strategies of ethnic semiosis (1987). Family, home, community, origin, loss, dislocation, relocation, racial differences, cross-cultural resistance, second-generation Americanization and assimilation, identity destabilization and reformulation, as in many other American ethnic texts, are common trajectories in Asian American literature. Even third-generation (sansei) Japanese American writers like Garrett Hongo (see "Bon: Dance for the Dead") and David Mura (for example, "A Nisei Picnic," in Bruchac 1983, 207) position their subjects in relation to family and community through immigrant memory and history, which inevitably entail histories of an Asian homeland, of U.S. immigration, and of cultural loss and change.

This immigrant logos – insisting on a time before U.S. entry and on cultures separate from U.S. Anglo-identity – may be explained by the fact that Asian Americans are chiefly a recent immigrant group. Until 1965, Asians formed a very small percentage of the U.S. population. Filipino sailors had settled in Mexico and parts of Louisiana during the Manila galleon trade between Mexico and the Philippines, both colonies of Spain;

but the major Asian immigration began only in 1848, with the discovery of gold in California. Drawn by a combination of push–pull factors – famine, civil unrest, and poverty in China; labor opportunities in the gold mines, Hawaiian plantations, and railroads in the American West (Cheng and Bonacich 1984) – Chinese immigration rose dramatically between 1860 and 1880. Like the nineteenth-century immigrants from Europe, many Chinese eventually returned to their villages; 47 percent of the 330,000 Chinese immigrants who came to the United States between 1850 and 1882 returned to China (Takaki 1990, 116). But, unlike their European counterparts, a series of exclusion acts, beginning in 1882 and culminating in the severest legislation against immigration from Asian populations east of the Barred Zone in 1924, prevented these Chinese immigrants from returning to the United States. Other discriminatory legislation against landownership, naturalization, "miscegenation," and the entry of Chinese women further discouraged Chinese American settlement. Between 1882 and 1943, when all the Chinese exclusion acts were repealed, the Chinese American population barely increased from 0.02 percent to 0.05 percent of the U.S. population.

Indeed, the Asian American demographic explosion after the 1965 revised immigrant laws is closely related to the development of the interdisciplinary nexus of Asian American Studies, which "focused on the migration and subsequent settlement experiences of various Asian groups to the United States." As Evelyn Hu-Dehart points out, "Only recently has the field made a move toward recognizing the importance of the Asian diaspora throughout the Americas and the world" (1991, 7). Paralleling the research emphasis on immigrant history, literary scholars have generally concentrated on the immigrant thematics sounded in archival as well as contemporary Asian American writing. Though the subject of race relations is primary in Asian American writing, as it is in other ethnic literatures, the intersection of race with immigrant and other-national histories is to a greater extent less visible in this writing than in the other ethnic literatures.

The convergence of race with national identity is demonstrated in contemporary global politics that continue to cast immigrants as a racial problem. According to the 1991 United Nations Population Fund, about seventy million people now work legally or illegally in countries of which they are not native-born citizens. Their numbers grow annually by two million refugees and immigrants. Whereas the United States is a primary destination for immigrants from Asia and Central America, high birth-rates in North Africa and other parts of the developing world also lead to immigration pressures on Europe (Meisler 1992, A9). Although these immigrants are needed to work in jobs that nationals no longer desire, they are unwanted because they are perceived as "strangers" and "aliens."

This phenomenon of internal colonialism, critiqued in Milton Murayama's tragifarcical novel of Japanese-Hawaiian plantation families, *All I Asking For Is My Body* (1975), carries cultural consequences: as people move from their natal territories, notions of individual and group identity, grounded in ideas of geographical location as a national homeland and of segregated racial purity, become contested and weakened. The literatures being produced today by immigrant populations *and* by nationalists reflect, address, express, and reconstruct the late-twentieth-century preoccupation with and interrogation of concepts of "identity," "home," and "nation," whether through recuperating ideals of tribal origin and community, through reinscribing the modern invention of nationalism as a political strategy for social organization, or through negotiating the unstable territory of the minority subject or destabilized psyche through a cosmopolitan elite attached to an ideology of the autonomous subject.

III

Critical awareness of the cooperation or absence of cooperation between birthplace and identity is crucially missing in literary canons that categorize by national distinctions. At the heart of critical consciousness, Edward Said argues in "Secular Criticism" (1986, 605–22), is the cooperation between filiation and affiliation. He defines filiation as chiefly natal, natural, situated in the capacity to produce or generate children; but because men are alienated from all the products of human labor, including children, filiation is fraught with difficulties and ultimately impossible. The pressure to produce new and different ways of conceiving human relationships results in alternatives provided "by institutions, associations, and communities whose social existence was not in fact guaranteed by biology but by affiliation." In the dialectic between natal relations and social relations, Said interposes "a worldly self-situating, a sensitive response to the dominant culture – that the individual consciousness is not naturally and easily a mere child of the culture, but a historical and social actor in it" (1986, 613). Such critical awareness must "trouble the quasi-religious authority of being comfortably at home, at home among one's people, supported by known powers and acceptable values, protected against the outside world" (614).

We find this "worldly self-situating" in much of the extant Chinese-language writing recently translated into English. The poems found on the walls of the Angel Island detention barracks where Chinese immigrants were held for interrogation before admission into California directly treat themes of protest against U.S. immigration policies and testify to the outrage, humiliation, fear, and feelings of vengeance that these detainees harbored (Lai, Lim, and Yung 1991). Countering the nineteenth-century stereotype of Chinese immigrants as illiterate, degenerate coolies (S. C. Miller 1969), many poems express a consciousness of human rights and ideals of social justice and patriotism:

> I beat my breast when I think of China and cry bitterly like
>   Ruan Ji.[1]
> Our country's wealth is being drained by foreigners,
> causing us to suffer national humiliations.
> My fellow countrymen, have foresight, plan to be resolute,
> And vow to conquer the U.S. and avenge previous wrongs!
>
> (Lai, Lim, and Yung 1991, 92)

The undifferentiated gap between immigrant status and diaspora identity is evident in such non-English "mother-tongued" text, in the ways in which the subjects of the poems name themselves, and in their cultural di/stance toward U.S. society and culture. "I am a member of the Huang clan from Xiangcheng," one Angel Island detainee proclaims; while another laments that "the [Western] powers still have not yet recognized *our* China" (emphasis added, 86). The Cantonese poems published in U.S. Chinatown newspapers at the beginning of the twentieth century and translated in *Songs of Gold Mountain* (Hom 1987) exhibit more extreme oscillating markers that offer alternative affiliations. Unlike the *Angel Island* poems, however, many of these folk poems site the conflicting and contradictory social values on Asian American women's bodies. Although some of these Gold Mountain songs celebrate the liberating effects of Westernization on Chinese women ("Following the practice of Western countries, / I am free to make my marriage choice. / . . . . I have found a good husband on my own" [223]), others condemn these same effects as threatening unbounded female sexuality: "What a batch of lousy broads, / All without proper upbringing. / . . . . Alas, their dissipation is shameful to *our* China" [emphasis added, 225]). Any discussion of Asian American immigrant and diaspora writing must take into account such non-English productions, a body of texts usually delimited as archival, but which make emphatic the shifting relations between diasporic and immigrant social formations (see Hom 1984 for an example of this recuperative move).

In contrast, the tensions between filiation and affiliation demonstrated in Chinese-language first-generation literature are redacted in the naive reproductions of assimilationist narratives of second-generation Chinese American writing in English. Pardee Lowe's *Father and Glorious Descendent* (1943) and Jade Snow Wong's *Fifth Chinese Daughter* (1945) construct Chinese American lives as progressing from immigrant to U.S. national identity. Although both autobiographies have been critiqued for their alleged appeal to ideals of American-defined democracy and citizenship and consequent refutation of Asian cultural origin, they also suggest some of the tensions that have historically rejected Asians as unassimilable immigrants; and Wong's autobiography recuperates a strong patriarchal figure in the Confucian father whom the daughter struggles to persuade of her value (Lim 1992a).

Claims to full U.S. national-cultural designation, moreover, are claims to a privileged norm. As Said points out, these claims carry with them "a formidable battery of other distinctions between ours and theirs, between proper and improper, European and non-European, higher and lower" (Said 1986, 612). Reviews of Wong's and Lowe's works that insist on their "American" qualities collapse the diasporic subject into the amnesiac condition of the "new American," a tabula rasa on whom is inscribed an ethnic-cleansed national identity. These reviews repeat orthodox myths regarding immigrant abdication of memory in the face of the cultural and material superiority of the intaking state.

The differences between Asian American literature – past and present – and other American minority literatures can be understood differently in the framework offered by the diaspora paradigm. In contrast to reductive notions of the immigrant as someone without history prior to entry into the Western state, recent critical theories recognize the historical discontinuities and the psychological violence visited on individuals through the tragic course of wars, famine, and economic dislocations, and the resulting contradictory constructions of social identity that disallow any racial or national essentializing of the subject.

Said's binarism of filiation and affiliation, therefore, should logically be elaborated to incorporate the histories and notions of exile and the diaspora. Immigration, which is the condition of being outside the natal order, has usually been constructed in assimilative narratives as proceeding toward integration into the "ideas, the values, and the systematic totalizing world-view validated" by an affiliative order (Said 1986, 616). When the relationship between affiliative identity (socialized self) and filiative place (homeland) is reified, the resulting condensation of signification underlines national canonical categories and, arguably, also produces the conditions of exile and diaspora. The exilic experience, like that of immigration, is the condition of voluntary or involuntary separation from one's place of birth; but, unlike immigration, this physical separation is offset by continued bonds to the lost homeland, together with nonintegration into the affiliative order in which the exilic subject is contingently placed. Literatures of exile have become increasingly evident as wars, famines, and natural disasters result in more and more involuntary dislocations of large groups of people.

Diaspora, as imagined in a work like Hualing Nieh's *Mulberry and Peach: Two Women of China* (1981), denotes a condition of being deprived of the affiliation of nation, not temporally situated on its way toward another totality, but fragmented, demonstrating provisionality and exigency as immediate, unmediated presences. The discourse of diaspora is that of disarticulation of identity from natal and national resources, and includes the exilic imagination but is not restricted to it. To this category, I would also assign the literature of the transnational, the minoritism of a Kafka, for example, as Deleuze and Guattari reconfigure his work, that deterritorialization of language and imagination exhibited in works attending "the decomposition and fall of the Empire" (1983, 25), when a work turns away from the dream of fulfilling "a major language function" and uses its polylingualism instead to "find its point of non-culture and underdevelopment." Many works written from the position of the ex-colonial or postcolonial attempt acts of deterritorialization and reterritorialization: Diana Chang's novel *The Frontiers of Love* (1956), set in World War II Shanghai, literally and figuratively constructs a political space in which nationalities are militarily and philosophically contested, to critique both "native" and "colonial" historical and cultural hegemony.

IV

The contemporary debate surrounding a text's national identity is no longer simply one of admitting immigrant voices into a national canon, or even of replacing a centripetal monocultural construct with a rhizomic decentered paradigm (Deleuze and Guattari 1981). Technological innovations in the twentieth century – for example, the transistor, satellite television, microchips, fiber optics, and jet propulsion – have resulted in the emergence of global cultures in which events taking place in once remote places of the earth are acknowledged as directly affecting peoples far away. The shift from the discourse of immigration to the discourse of diasporas is one example of the dynamics of an evolving global technology capable of transmitting information simultaneously through mass media to geographically separate yet culturally related peoples.

This global culture must be distinguished from the globalization of cultures, the changes taking place within separate societies in response to increasingly transnational forces, such as the multinational and corporate nature of the publishing industry, or of most late capitalist industries for that matter. Even without the migrations of refugees and immigrants that break down the historically recent state constructions of nationality as social identity, the new technologies of travel, media, and industry subvert these constructions and lead to renewed state efforts to control, and patrol, their physical and cultural borders. These technologies, increasing in global reach and affect, relate and commingle cultures once separated by tribal, racial, and national distinctiveness, which are thus threatened by their loss in ability to protect themselves from uncontrollable change or unwanted influence from "alien" cultures.

Benedict Anderson, in his study of nationalism, points to the entry of print capitalism or print language as laying the bases for national consciousness (1983, 46). However, as publishing becomes absorbed into the circulation of late-twentieth-century international corporate capital, it now arguably lays the basis for a transnational consciousness that undermines national consciousness. Much diaspora literature that rethematizes Western cultural hegemony has become a highly marketable product. One can read in the privileging of the diasporic imagination in Jessica Hagedorn's *Dogeaters* (1990) the convergence of capitalism and print technology to create the possibility of a new form of imagined community, but a community/nation that is Western metropolitan-based rather than non-Western national. It is not only the choice of the English language and of Western publishers that has consequences for the community the texts purport to represent. The axis of diplomatic history in which the interpretive community is situated, a situation that is historically contingent and provisional, also affects the community constructed in the text and the kinds of community addressed by the text.

The literature produced by "metropolitan" writers across borders is thus open to contradictory interpretations. One reading situates diasporic writing as interrupting or challenging the hegemony of metropolitan cultures (for example, L. Lowe 1991). Another reading interprets the popular publication and reception of texts produced by writers who are situated outside their natal borders – especially those works that can be taken to illustrate Western notions of Asian corruption or Western practices of postmodernism – as pointing to the dispersal of their strangeness, and finally to the naturalization/nationalization of the alien (see Lim 1992b). The transformation of the non-natal – of U.S. space and time – through interpretative affiliations marks writing produced by writers of Asian descent as American in intention.

The tradition of writing by transnationals of multiple diasporas resists such nationalistic appropriation. Han Suyin's multivolume autobiography (1965, 1966, 1968) and Edward W. Said's critical work (1978, 79) are prime examples of this tradition, in which the West is one agent in a diplomatic axis, with China or the Middle East as the other agent. Commenting on the momentous changes in U.S. attitudes after Nixon's historic visit to China in 1972, Michael Hunt points out, "The history of U.S. dealings with China neatly illustrates how likely Americans . . . are to ignore diversity in the world and instead reduce cultures radically differ-ent . . . to familiar, easily manageable terms. There is a danger in putting great national power at the service of such a flawed and essentially ethnocentric vision. . . . If more harmonious cross-cultural and interstate relations is an ideal worth pursuing, then Americans must rein in the fatal tendency to project our tendencies beyond our borders" (Hunt 1983, 313). This axial positioning opens up problematics of affiliation that suggest a different history of the individual imagination as modulated by at least two cultural systems, each undermining and reconfiguring the other in a dynamic of intranationalism that is the ground of diplomatic history. Such works construct a confrontational relation between place and identity and compose a tradition of "global literature" complexly differentiated from the tradition of nationally bounded and divided iden-tities that has conventionally organized our understanding of "world literature." These global traditions, read together, indicate a recent mul-tifaceted cultural phenomenon, produced within the borders of the met-ropolitan state, by migrant and diasporic intellectuals – a phenomenon different in kind from immigrant writing.

To give an example of the nonaffiliative and affiliative traditions in Chinese American women's literature, when Diana Chang's novel *The Frontiers of Love* (1956) and Lin Tai-yi's *The Eavesdropper* (1958) appeared, they were not reviewed as American productions but as writings by diasporic Chinese writers. Like the author, the protagonist in Chang's novel, Sylvia Chen, is the daughter of an American mother and Chinese father; but because the action takes place in World War II Shanghai, reviewers approached the novel as being of "the Far East." Similarly, although half of *The Eavesdropper* treats the protagonist's, Shutung's, immigrant experiences in the United States, reviewers focused on its Chinese sections (Martin 1959; Payne 1959). Written by China-born Lin, now resident in Washington, D.C., *The Eavesdropper*, on the one hand, attempts an act of deterritorialization, locating itself through a critique of Chinese and American historical and cultural hegemony; Shutung's point-of-view is one of resistance to U.S. civilization, which is presented as seductively easy to penetrate. The novels by second-generation writers (for instance, Amy Tan's *The Joy Luck Club* [1989] and *The Kitchen God's Wife* [1991] and Gish Jen's *Typical American* [1991]), on the other hand, share a common set of assimilationary themes. These novels, beginning with an ex-filiative position, plot the acculturation of their Asian pro-tagonists into a U.S. society represented as desirable, fetishistically possessable, and offering utopianist possibilities. They exhibit many of the marks of affiliation that symbolically reknit American sociopolitical hege-mony. Read together, they indicate a different, although multifaceted, tradition of literature, written and published within the borders of the

United States, produced by Asian women of the diaspora, a tradition that includes such disparate works as Jade Snow Wong's *Fifth Chinese Daughter* (1945) and *No Chinese Stranger* (1975); Anna Chennault's *A Thousand Springs* (1962); Maxine Hong Kingston's *The Woman Warrior* (1976), *China Men* (1980), and *Tripmaster Monkey* (1989); Monica Sone's *Nisei Daughter* (1953); and Bharati Mukherjee's *Wife* (1975) and *Jasmine* (1989).

In contemporary geopolitics, the West is identified with international corporate capital. In the diasporic imagination of Lin Tai-yi's *The Eaves-dropper*, the loss of vital native place and the removal of exilic themes attendant on this loss can be said to be filled in by an a-filiative sensibility in which the material/territorial world inflates or deflates to subdue and to reattach the individual psyche into a social world now without traditional place or national boundaries. In contrast, the subject of Gish Jen's immigrant fiction, *Typical American,* suggests that assimilation into this corporate world is innocent, natural, inevitable, or valuable; in the progression from "origin" to metropolitan inhabitant, the natal "home" is constructed as less than already past – it is always already absent. The void of origin prepares the reader for the construction of the metropolis as material vitality, and for the resolution in favor of an international culture based on capital.

Unsurprisingly, Kingson's, Tan's, and Jen's novels (unlike Lin's and Chang's works) published in rapid succession between 1989 and 1991 have been well received as contributions to the emerging body of U.S. minority writing. Like those canonical critics Nina Baym analyzed for us, reviewers look for the "American" qualities in these novels. Jen herself, arguing that to read her novel "solely through an Asian-American prism is 'to use just one lens,'" insists "this book is about America" (Mehren 1991, E2). The protagonist, Ralph, develops in the Chinese American assimilation narrative seen in Pardee Lowe's and Jade Snow Wong's books. Jen's *Typical American* begins with a protagonist who leaves Shanghai for the United States in the throes of the Nationalist defeat. An engineering student, Yifeng (renamed Ralph) Cheng's first experience in the United States is falling in love with a Caucasian secretary. In the space of two pages, the novel imagines Yifeng's assimilation into the American socioeconomic world. The hegemonic cultural force that dislodges the individual from an original community is naturalized and at the same time given the inexorable mechanic force of a giant clock (32). In the progression from China origin to United States indigenous, China is represented as a void, thus preparing the reader for the construction of the United States as material vitality, possessing everything: "He missed his home, missed having a place that was home. . . . He might gild it, but in truth it was lacking. . . . Something, everything."

Ralph marries, gains tenure, and ventures into the capitalist mechanism of the United States with obsessive energy. Much of *Typical American* describes the Changs' upward mobility, a near vertiginous climb accompanied by an accelerated appetite for material accumulation. The melodrama in the last third of the novel, however, exposes that immigrant vision of an America of endless invention, filled with the possibility of containing everything and satisfying every desire, as a cultural fantasy. In a diasporic move, Ralph, on his way to visit his sister, who has just emerged from a coma, unexpectedly finds himself on that border that destabilizes national-grounded identities: "It seemed to him at that moment, as he stood waiting, trapped in his coat, that a man was as doomed here as he was in China. . . . He was not what he had made up his mind to be" (296). The promise of American capital, which is the promise of progressive improvement, of change and accumulation, is set against the limits of human ability: "A man was the sum of his limits; freedom only made him see how much so. America was no America" (296). This "bleak understanding" strips the immigrant of the naturalizing totality of American culture, which has composed a fiction of seamless yet contradictory values: progressive social mobility and community cohesiveness, increasing wealth and intensifying consumer patterns, hyperindividualism and strong family bonds.

Jen's novel interrogates even as it reinscribes American bourgeois narratives of capital competition and individual psychic struggle and survival. Still, as A. G. Mojtabi, a recent immigrant, suggests, contradictions bedevil the reading of *Typical American* as a wholly U.S. work: "Were there no contending forces? No dim remembrances of Confucianist harmonies or Buddhist detachment . . . [to raise] a little point–counterpoint?" The novel's gaze on the "foreign" Chinese is constituted by an American Other, the narrator, who is represented through extraliterary means – publisher's publicity, book blurbs, and reviews – as authorially identified and as immigrant U.S. citizen. This problematic gaze elides the absent half of the equation, the lacuna of the other half of the world, in the thematic totalization of capital as the sole motive in the narrative.

A different phenomenon partly accounts for the way in which Amy Tan's second novel has been mediated and sold to the American public. In contrast to the 1950s reception of Chang's and Lin's novels, *The Kitchen God's Wife*, whose action is set chiefly in wartime China, has been received as a U.S. text. Arguably, this "Third World" imagined in *The Kitchen's God's Wife*, as Spivak explains in a different context, is the site of "raw" material that is "monstrosity" – the socially monstrous phenomena of concubinage, abandoned daughters, arranged marriages, patriarchal abuse, and so forth – produced "for the surplus-value of spectacle, entertainment, and spiritual enrichment for the 'First World'" (84). China, after all, "has been for the past several decades a spectacle for the West . . . an overdetermined event" (Chow 1991, 83). In *The Kitchen God's Wife*, it is not the novel's apparent content, its Third World materials, but its affiliative grid, the insertion of American ideological positions, including those of Western feminism, ethnic identity, and class, that affects its reception. Critics, however, must be careful to distinguish between what is national fantasy and what bears traces of Asian identity formation in the works by second-generation Asian Americans produced within U.S. borders. Uncritical acceptance of all Asian American writing as accurate representations of China, India, or the Philippines must itself be contextualized critically, as a mode of appropriating these "Orients" for American national purposes.

Kingston repeatedly asserts that in her books she is claiming America for Chinese Americans, a proposition that can be restated to mean claiming Chinese Americans for America. The double movement of appropriation is marked in the critical reception of her work, chiefly praised for making accessible to American readers the strange world of Chinese living in the United States. The accessibility works more in one direction than the other. Americans of Chinese ancestry, or even Chinese living in the United States, do not find that *The Woman Warrior* has made the United States more accessible to them, or that the book helps them to negotiate the dominant culture and to appropriate it for their needs. The book's popular reception in the universities suggests that it is the dominant culture which is incorporating Kingston's version of the Chinese into its transcultural psyche.

Rather than breaking, interrupting, or challenging the hegemony of U.S. mainstream culture, the popular adoption of selected Asian American texts – illustrating, for example, Western feminist notions of Asian patriarchal modes, or Western literary ideas of the postmodernism – points to the dispersal of their strangeness, and finally to the Americanization of Asia (Lim 1993). The transformation of the natal country, China, in the reception of *The Woman Warrior*, through the interpretative affiliations that make it the national text it is today (read under the grids of U.S. feminism, U.S. immigrant history, U.S. ethnographic community, U.S. literary experimentation, and so forth), underlines its power as a text of assimilation. As Edward Said elaborates, the affiliative order "surreptitiously duplicates the closed and tightly knit family structure that secures generational hierarchical relationships to one another. Affiliation then becomes in effect a literary form of re-representation, by which what is ours is good, and therefore deserves incorporation and inclusion in our programs of humanistic study, and what is not ours in this ultimately provincial sense is simply left out" (1986, 617).

V

Until the 1980s, Asian American literary criticism focused chiefly on Chinese American and Japanese American writers, but it is now also exhibiting shifting positions and sensitivities around the status of U.S. identity. These disavowals and fixities of identity, as seen in the sharply divided reactions among Asian American critics to the popularity of Kingston's and Tan's novels, for example, complicate critical theories and evaluations and keep them fluid. The 1970s' critique of the conflation of Asian American with Asian and Asian immigrant identity, and the enunciation of a U.S. identity not composed of Asian cultural elements, had severely delimited the terms for cultural belonging for smaller and more recent immigrant groups such as South and Southeast Asians and Filipinos (Penaranda et al. 1974). The historical specificities in the experiences of heterogeneous Asian immigrant groups inevitably call into question and destabilize the construction of a monolithic U.S.-identified Asian American identity.

Writing by South Asian immigrants or "Indo-American" writing (Tapping 1992, 288) exhibits similar dialectical relations between the U.S. and an Asian homeland or point of origin as in the Chinese American texts, but the best known of such Indo-American writing tends toward diasporic versions of identity that exceed the notion of exile (see Mehta 1972, 79, 82, 85; Suleri 1989; Seth 1986). Bharati Mukherjee goes further than many Asian American writers in her assimilationary position. After her naturalization in February 1988, she addressed an audience of New Yorkers from the front page of the *New York Times Book Review*, stating, "I am one of you now" (1988b). Arguing that the immigrant writer is situated without history prior to her U.S. entry, her construction assumes that mastery by people of color of and in the United States is simple and given, that it works one way, with the immigrant writing the great epic. Mukherjee openly embraces a twenty-first-century version of assimilation, advocating historical amnesia, "arising from nowhere and disappearing into a cloud" (1989, 214), and reprivileging the myth of America as the unhindered and sovereign individual, "greedy with wants and reckless with hope" (214), reinscribing a manifest destiny on the American landscape.

Mukherjee distinguishes between exiled Asians, whose works she dismisses as "too often hokey concoctions composed of family memory and brief visits to ancestral villages," and U.S. immigrants, whom she idealizes as "masters of America in ways I can never be" (1988b, 28) – a retrograde notion that sociologists such as Oscar Handlin had criticized as early as 1951. As an outsider, Mukherjee claims to have an advantage over the incompetent, blind, putative insider-immigrant and so is able to appropriate "some of the richest materials ever conferred on a writer." She represents herself as an avowed writer of American affiliation: "I mean [my fiction] to be about assimilation. My stories centre on a new breed and generation of North American pioneers. I am fascinated by people who have enough gumption, energy, ambition, to pull up their roots. . . . My stories are about conquest, and not about loss" (Hancock 1987). Though she acknowledges "cashing in on the other legacy of the colonial writer," this colonialist duality is truncated into the here and now of American opportunity, with "third world material" represented in her schema as "the fugitive attraction of something dead."

Mukherjee's career, from India as an Anglophone daughter of Westernized and upper-middle-class Brahmins, via a university education in the United States, marriage with a white Canadian, to a university position in Toronto, and finally immigration to the United States in her forties, underlines one formation of American identity, in which a pre-U.S. history becomes degraded as "nostalgia" and "sentimentality" lacking effective cultural power (Wickramagamage 1992). Her rejection of Indian cultural vestiges has been praised as evidence of the continued vitality of American national ideals, permitting the triumphant location of her work in the tradition of American immigration epics next to "the best of our [American] writers" (Mukherjee 1988a). Problematically, however, her self-representation as immigrant success ignores the history and present existence of other immigrants – the illegals, refugees, poor, and working class – immigrants who – ironically – are heavily represented in her fictions (see *Darkness* [1985] and *The Middleman and Other Stories* [1988a]), suggesting a disjunctive and strategic commodification of these figures in her texts.

Mukherjee's novel *Jasmine* (1989) reformulates the American romance, depicting the development of an autonomous subject who enters the new world and successfully negotiates the dangers posed by the instability of capital (Jasmine's midwestern banker-lover is paralyzed by an aggrieved debtor-farmer's bullet; her young neighbor, under the stress of banking loans and reinvestment, hangs himself) to a happily-ever-after conclusion with her true love, a university professor, and his affectionate daughter. The assimilation narrative in *Jasmine* reproduces the hegemonic epic of the United States as the nation of limitless opportunity, freedom, and triumphant individualism, repeating a master narrative of individual autonomy, economic competition, and race-assimilation that masks the convergence of the discourse of nationalism with that of racism and sexism (Balibar and Wallerstein 1991, 37) in U.S. cultural productions.

In sharp contrast to Mukherjee's renewed assimilationist position,

Oscar Campomanes, surveying Pilipino American literature, argues that "The orientation toward the Philippines prevents prevailing notions of Asian American literature from reducing Filipino writing in the United States to just another variant of the immigrant epic, even if this in itself must be seen as an ever-present and partial possibility as time passes and Philippine-American relations change" (1992, 55). While seeing Filipino American experiences as part of a larger diaspora, Campomanes reads all Filipino American writing as postcolonial and neocolonial produced discourse within an exilic tradition. The exilic interpretation, of course, comes from a specific critique of the continuing relation between a resisting subaltern culture and a U.S. imperial culture. Campomanes's exilic paradigm emphasizes a historically oppositional construction of identity that can be validated only outside of U.S. borders (in the Philippines) and which is different in kind from the constructions of ethnic and minority identities that seek empowerment within U.S. borders.

The exilic paradigm maps bodies of literature and brings to consciousness the more complex problems of identity politics that an insistence on "an American-born sensibility" excludes. But it does not fully account for all the dynamics of the diasporic cultures that produce Asian American literature, including the Filipino diaspora. The work of Bienvenido Santos, for example, demonstrates a richer relational problematic within the subject of the writing and between that subject and national affiliation thematics than can be suggested in the trope of exile.

In his collection of short stories, *Scent of Apples* (1979), and in novels such as *The Man Who (Thought He) Looked Like Robert Taylor* (1983) and *What the Hell For You Left Your Heart in San Francisco* (1987), Santos constructs the experiences of the Pinoy or first-generation Filipino American as an existentialist condition. Viewed by Americans as "alien" ("I look like nobody," the protagonist says to the young American woman who mistakes him for a Mexican [1983, 140]), Santos's protagonists appear to elaborate on the theme of the outsider that Bulosan had vividly portrayed in *America Is in the Heart* (1946). Exile is an explicit motif running through his fictions: "The way of the exile was a series of passing through, a habit of roads, and the highways were so easy and inviting" (1983, 157). As with the Pinoy characters in "Manila House" and "The Day the Dancers came" (Santos 1979), Solomon King lives *in* America but is not *of* America: "Home was always a bit of the faraway land of their birth. No matter how long they stayed in America, they were still Filipinos" (1983, 12). Neither expatriate nor immigrant, these characters are like the transients they observe, befriend, or eventually become, shifting inhabitants without a fixed address. Shaped by intimate Filipino village communities and extended kinship systems, they attempt to reproduce these social relations in a culture that is urban, distant, and individual. Aliens in the United States, U.S. culture is also alien to them. Nostalgia, homesickness in the original Greek sense, is the prevailing sentiment in Santos's fiction.

In *The Man Who (Thought He) Looked Like Robert Taylor*, Sol, who has tied his life to his dimly acknowledged American double, the actor Robert Taylor, finds himself an old man, alone in the United States; his "vacation" from Chicago to San Francisco, retracing his youthful wanderings, metaphorizes his preparation for death, which itself is metaphorized as a return to his Filipino social roots. Two contrasting dreams summarize the novel's theme of the transplanted Filipino. In the first dream Sol, the brown man, sees the White House, "barbed wire around it, familiar like the board now swinging in the wind with the words . . . OFF LIMITS, NO TRESPASSING, U.S. PROPERTY" (156). In the concluding dream, Sol's mother offers him a candy bar from his childhood sweetheart "To sweeten his way" (173). The first dream suggests a history of U.S. imperialism and racism that has raised political and psychological barriers to the Filipino's entry into U.S. identity; the second refigures the nostalgia for a childhood home that keeps him psychically enmeshed in a past that is no longer available except through death.

However, although Santos categorized his position as that of the exile, Sol's alienation in the United States does not arise from his desire to return to the Philippines. In fact, the novel carefully maps a counter-desire to remain in the United States despite the awkwardnesses of cultural differences: "As soon as Sol received his green card . . . he knew that for him there was no more going back to the Philippines. . . . Now there was one thing he had to do, master the English language as a way out of the many difficulties that plagued the lives of his countrymen in America" (48). Sol's many failed relations with white American women function as a trope for his failed relation in the United States. Sexual desire and satisfaction stop short of marriage and a stable family life, a plot that hinges on the miscegenation laws that the novel only barely suggests and that had historically prevented Filipino male immigrants from full assimilation into U.S. society. The tragedy of Sol's life, his unsatisfied longing for a child as seen in the incident with Blanche and her son Jerry (148), becomes more than mere psychological dysfunction in the context of American racist legislations. In contrast to Sol's lonely aging, Alipio and Noli, who marry Filipino women, are portrayed as contented old men, settlers in a materially comfortable United States.

Rather than a novel of exilic longing for a homeland, *The Man Who (Thought He) Looked Like Robert Taylor* is chiefly a critique of desire as it operates in and is operated upon expatriate Filipinos in U.S. culture. The fiction of Sol's relations with white women – relations that fail to move beyond the level of the sexual to the social – narrativizes the problematics of cultural desire of the Filipino in America. Desire in the novel is not unidirectional, exilic desire; it is also desire for the United States, assimilationary desire. That this assimilationary desire, gendered as male and raced as brown, is frustrated, unsatisfied, and dysfunctional in no way obverts its counter, nonexilic reach. Sol's absence of and longing for familial paternity in the United States, as well as his regressive nostalgia for an idealized familial childhood in the Philippines, recalls the paradigm of "between worlds" that critics like Amy Ling have foregrounded in their interpretations. But, chiefly, the novel's siting of desire in brown men for white women – Filipinos for the United States – reconstitutes the metanarratives of domination–subordination relations that underlie the cultural production of differences in U.S. discourses of race and gender.

The contesting notions of the American-born sensibility (Chin et al. 1974), the between-worlds dilemma (Ling), the immigrant/assimilation narrative (Mukherjee), and the exilic paradigm (Campomanes) together demonstrate the historically shifting, heterogeneous processes of identity-formation and identity-politics thematics in the works of first-generation and second-generation Asian American writers. Indeed, the intersecting discontinuous trajectories of immigrant and diasporic constructions of race, class, and gender identities call into question any hegemonizing theoretization or orthodoxics, suggesting instead that these works need to be interpreted as *individually negotiating* the contestations and the coop-erations of the filiative and the affiliative in the historicized context of the subjects' particular diasporic/ethnic cultures.

■■■■■ **NOTE**

1. "Ruan Ji (A.D. 210–63), a scholar during the period of the Three Kingdoms (A.D. 220–80), was a person who enjoyed drinking and visiting mountains and streams. Often when he reached the end of the road, he would cry bitterly before turning back" (Lai et al. 1991, 66).

■■■■■ **SELECTED BIBLIOGRAPHY**

Anderson, Benedict. 1983. *Imagined Communities: Reflections on the Origin and Spread of Nationalism.* London: Verso.

Balibar, Etienne, and Immanuel Wallerstein. 1991. *Race, Nation, Class: Ambiguous Identities.* London: Verso.

Baym, Nina. 1985. "Melodramas of Beset Manhood: How Theories of American Fiction Exclude Women Authors." In *The New Feminist Criticism*, ed. Elaine Showalter, 63–80. New York: Pantheon Books.

Blauner, Robert. 1972. *Racial Oppression in America.* New York: Harper & Row.

———. 1982. "Colonized and Immigrant Minorities." In *Classes, Power and Conflict*, ed. Anthony Giddens and David Held, 501–19. Berkeley and Los Angeles: Univ. of California Press.

Boelhower, William. 1982. "The Brave New World of Immigrant Autobiography." *MELUS* 9.2:5–23.

———. 1987. *Through a Glass Darkly: Ethnic Semiosis in American Literature.* New York: Oxford Univ. Press.

Brennan, Tim. 1989. "Cosmopolitans and Celebrities." *Race and Class* 31.1:1–19.

Bruchac, Joseph, ed. 1983. *Breaking Silence: An Anthology of Contemporary Asian American Poets.* New York: Greenfield Review Press.

Bulosan, Carlos. 1946/1973. *America Is in the Heart.* Seattle: Univ. of Washington Press.

Campomanes, Oscar V. 1992. "Filipinos in the United States and Their Literature of Exile." In Lim and Ling, 49–78.

Chan, Sucheng, ed. 1991. *Entry Denied: Exclusion and the Chinese Community in America, 1882–1943.* Philadelphia: Temple Univ. Press.

Chang, Diana. 1956/1994. *The Frontiers of Love.* Seattle: Univ. of Washington Press.

———. 1974. *Eye to Eye.* New York: Harper & Row.

Cheng, Lucie, and Edna Bonacich, eds. 1984. *Labor Immigration under Capitalism: Asian Workers in the United States before World War II.* Berkeley and Los Angeles: Univ. of California Press.

Chennault, Anna. 1962. *A Thousand Springs: A Biography of a Marriage.* New York: Paul S. Eriksson.

Chin, Frank. 1991. *Donald Duk.* Minneapolis: Coffee House Press,

Chin, Frank, Jeffery Paul Chan, Lawson Fusao Inada, and Shawn Wong, eds. 1974. *Aiiieeeee! An Anthology of Asian-American Writers.* Washington, D.C.: Howard Univ. Press.

Chow, Rey. 1991. "Violence in the Other Country: China as Crisis, Spectacle, and Woman." In *Third World Women and the Politics of Feminism,* ed. Chandra Talpade Mohanty, Ann Russo, and Lourdes Torres, 81–100. Bloomington: Indiana Univ. Press.

Chu, Louis. 1961/1979. *Eat a Bowl of Tea.* Seattle: Univ. of Washington Press.

Chuang Hua. 1986. *Crossings.* Boston: Northeastern Univ. Press.

Deleuze, Gilles, and Felix Guattari. 1981. "Rhizome." Trans. P. Fox and P. Ratton. *Ideology and Culture* 8:49–71.

———. 1983. "What Is a Minor Literature?" *Mississippi Review* 11.3:13–33.

Fischer, Michael M. J. 1986. "Ethnicity and the Post-Modern Arts of Memory." In *Writing Cultures: The Poetics and Politics of Ethnography,* ed. James Clifford and George E. Marcus, 194–233. Berkeley and Los Angeles: Univ. of California Press.

Hagedorn, Jessica. 1990. *Dogeaters.* New York: Pantheon.

Han Suyin. 1965. *The Crippled Tree.* London: Jonathan Cape.

———. 1966. *A Mortal Flower.* London: Jonathan Cape.

———. 1968. *Birdless Summer.* London: Jonathan Cape.

Hancock, Geoff. 1987. Interview with Bharati Mukherjee. *Canadian Fiction Magazine* 59:30–44.

Handlin, Oscar. 1951. *The Uprooted: The Epic Story of the Great Migrations That Make the American People.* Boston: Little, Brown.

Holte, James Craig. 1982. "The Representative Voice: Autobiography and the Immigrant Experience." *MELUS* 9.2:25–46.

Hom, Marlon K. 1984. "A Case of Mutual Exclusion: Portrayals by Immigrant and American-born Chinese of Each Other in Literature." *Amerasia Journal* 11.2:29–45.

———. 1987. *Songs of Gold Mountain: Cantonese Rhymes from San Francisco Chinatown*. Berkeley and Los Angeles: Univ. of California Press.

Hongo, Garrett. 1988. *The River of Heaven*. New York: Knopf.

Hu-Dehart, Evelyn. 1991. "From Area Studies to Ethnic Studies: The Study of the Chinese Diaspora." In Hune et al., 5–16.

Hune, Shirley, et al. 1991. *Asian American Comparative and Global Perspectives*. Pullman: Washington State Univ. Press.

Hunt, Michael. 1983. *The Making of a Special Relationship: The U.S. and China to 1914*. New York: Columbia Univ. Press.

Jen, Gish. 1991. *Typical American*. Boston: Houghton Mifflin.

Katrak, Ketu H., and R. Radhakrishnan, eds. 1988. "Desh-Videsh: South Asian Expatriate Writers and Artists." *Massachusetts Review* (Special issue) 29.4.

Kingston, Maxine Hong. 1976. *The Woman Warrior: Memoirs of a Girlhood among Ghosts*. New York: Knopf.

———. 1980. *China Men*. New York: Knopf.

———. 1989. *Tripmaster Monkey: His Fake Book*. New York: Knopf.

Kramer, Jane. 1976. "On Being Chinese in China and America." Review of *The Woman Warrior* by Maxine Hong Kingston. *New York Times Book Review*, 7 November, 1 ff.

Lai, Him Mark, Genny Lim, and Judy Yung, eds. 1991. *Island: Poetry and History of Chinese Immigrants on Angel Island, 1910 1940*. Seattle: Univ. of Washington Press.

Lim, Shirley Geok-lin. 1992a. "Chinese-American Women's Life-Stories: Jade Snow Wong's *Fifth Chinese Daughter* and Maxine Hong Kingston's *The Woman Warrior*." In *American Women's Autobiography: Fea(s)ts of Memory*, ed. Margo Culley, 252–67. Madison: Univ. of Wisconsin Press.

———. 1992b. "When the West Is One: Undoing and Re-doing the Hegemony of U.S. Culture in Diasporic Writing by Chinese American Women." *Cahiers Charles V*, no. 14, 129–39. Paris.

———. 1993. "The Americanization of Asia: Discourses of Transformation in Asian American Literature." *Humanities Journal*, 31–8.

———. 1994. "Who Do We Name When We Say 'Diaspora'?: Race, National Identity, and the Subject of the Subject in Timothy Mo's Novels." In *Writing South/East Asia in English: Against the Grain*, 91–104. London: Skoob Books.

Lim, Shirley Geok-lin, and Amy Ling, eds. 1992. *Reading the Literatures of Asian America*. Philadelphia: Temple Univ. Press.

Lin, Tai-yi. 1958. *The Eavesdropper*. Cleveland, OH: World Publishing.

Ling, Amy. 1990. *Between Worlds: Women Writers of Chinese Ancestry*. New York: Pergamon.

Lowe, Lisa. 1991. "Heterogeneity, Hybridity, Multiplicity: Marking Asian American Difference." *Diaspora* 1.1:24–44.

Lowe, Pardee. 1943. *Father and Glorious Descendant*. Boston: Little, Brown.

Martin, S. E. 1959. Review of *The Eavesdropper. New York Herald Tribune,* 15 February, 5.

Mazumdar, Sucheta. 1991. "Asian American Studies and Asian Studies: Rethinking Roots." In Hune et al., 29–44.

Mehren, Elizabeth. 1991. "Dodging Literary Labels." *Los Angeles Times,* 29 April, E1–2.

Mehta, Ved. *Daddyji/Mamaji.* 1972/1984. London: Picador/Pan Books.

———. *Vedi.* 1982/1985. London: Picador/Pan Books.

———. *The Light Between the Streams.* 1984/1985. London: Picador/Pan Books.

Meisler, Stanley. 1992. " 'Rising Wind of Migration' Foreseen." *Los Angeles Times,* 30 April, A9.

Miller, Judith. 1991. "Strangers at the Gate." *New York Times Magazine,* 15 September, 32–7, 49, 80, 86.

Miller, Stuart Creighton. 1969. *The Unwelcome Immigrant: The American Image of the Chinese 1785–1882.* Berkeley and Los Angeles: Univ. of California Press.

Mojtabai, A. G. 1991. " 'The Complete Other Side of the World.' " *New York Times Book Review,* 31 March, 9–10.

Mukherjee, Bharati. 1971. *The Tiger's Daughter.* Boston: Houghton Mifflin.

———. 1975. *Wife.* New York: Fawcett Crest.

———. 1985. *Darkness.* New York: Fawcett Crest.

———. 1988a. *The Middleman and Other Stories.* New York: Fawcett Crest.

———. 1988b. "Immigrant Writing: Give Us Your Maximalists!" *New York Times Book Review,* 28 August, 1, 27, 28.

———. 1989. *Jasmine.* New York: Fawcett Crest.

Mukherjee, Bharati, and Clark Blaise. 1986. *Days and Nights in Calcutta.* New York: Penguin.

Mura, David. 1991. *Turning Japanese.* Boston: Atlantic.

Murayama, Milton. 1975/1988. *All I Asking For Is My Body.* Honolulu: Univ. of Hawai'i Press.

Nieh, Hualing. 1981/1988. *Mulberry and Peach: Two Women of China.* Trans. Jane Parish Yang and Linda Lappin. Boston: Beacon Press.

Okada, John. *No-No Boy.* 1957/1981. Seattle: Univ. of Washington Press.

Payne, Robert. 1959. "Shutung's Shrines." *Saturday Review,* 28 February, 42:20–1.

Penaranda, Oscar, et al. 1974. "An Introduction to Filipino American Literature." In Chin et al., 37–54.

Said, Edward W. 1978. *Orientalism.* New York: Pantheon.

———. 1979/1992. *The Question of Palestine.* New York: Vintage.

———. 1986. "Secular Criticism." In *Critical Theory since 1965,* ed. Hazard Adams and Leroy Searle, 605–22. Tallahassee: Florida State Univ. Press.

Santos, Bienvenido N. 1979. *Scent of Apples.* Seattle: Univ. of Washington Press.

———. 1983. *The Man Who (Thought He) Looked Like Robert Taylor.* Quezon City, Philippines: New Day Publishers.

———. 1987. *What the Hell For You Left Your Heart in San Francisco.* Quezon City, Philippines: New Day Publishers.

Seth, Vikram. 1986. *The Golden Gate.* New York: Random House.

Sollors, Werner. 1986. *Beyond Ethnicity: Consent and Descent in American Culture.* New York: Oxford Univ. Press.

———. 1988. "Immigrants and Other Americans." In *The Columbia Literary History of the United States*, ed. Emory Elliott et al. New York: Columbia Univ. Press

Sone, Monica. 1953. *Nisei Daughter*. Boston: Little, Brown.

Spivak, Gayatri Chakravorty. 1987. *In Other Worlds: Essays in Cultural Politics*. New York and London: Methuen.

Suleri, Sara. 1989. *Meatless Days*. Chicago: Univ. of Chicago Press.

Takaki, Ronald. 1990. *Strangers from a Different Shore: A History of Asian Americans*. New York: Penguin.

Tan, Amy. 1989. *The Joy Luck Club*. New York: Putnam.

———. 1991. *The Kitchen God's Wife*. New York: Putnam.

Tapping, Craig. 1992. "South Asia Writes North America: Prose Fictions and Autobiographies from the Indian Diaspora." In Lim and Ling, 285–301.

Villa, José García. *Poems*. 1949. New York: New Directions.

Weglyn, Michi. 1976. *Years of Infamy: The Untold Story of America's Concentration Camps*. New York: William Morrow.

Wickramagamage, Carmen. 1992. "Relocation as Positive Act: The Immigrant Experience in Bharati Mukherjee's Novels." *Diaspora* 2.2:171–200.

Wong, Jade Snow. 1945/1989. *Fifth Chinese Daughter*. Seattle: Univ. of Washington Press.

———. *No Chinese Stranger*. 1975. New York: Harper & Row.

Wong, Sau-ling C. 1989. "What's in a Name? Defining Chinese American Literature of the Immigrant Generation." In *Frontiers of Asian American Studies: Writing, Research, and Commentary*, ed. Gail M. Nomura et al., 159–67. Pullman: Washington State Univ. Press.

———. 1991. "Immigrant Autobiography: Some Questions of Definition and Approach." In *American Autobiography: Retrospect and Prospect*, ed. Paul John Eakin, 142–61. Madison: Univ. of Wisconsin Press.

———. 1993a. *Reading Asian American Literature: From Necessity to Extravagance*. Princeton, NJ: Princeton Univ. Press.

———. 1993b. "Going Diasporic? Concepts and Constituencies in Asian American Literature." Paper delivered at Univ. of California, Santa Barbara.

Wong, Shawn. 1979. *Homebase*. New York: I. Reed Books.

Yamada, Mitsuye. 1988. *Desert Run*. Latham, NY: Kitchen Table/Women of Color Press.

10

IDENTITY CRISIS AND GENDER POLITICS: REAPPROPRIATING ASIAN AMERICAN MASCULINITY

JINQI LING

This chapter explores three ongoing issues of gender that arise from the problematics of Asian American literary discourse since the mid-1970s: the "emasculation" of the Asian American man; the politics of simultaneous articulations of gendered subjectivities; and gender transgression as a representational strategy for disrupting hierarchical assumptions about heterosexual relationships. My inquiry is prompted, in part by the unabated controversy in Asian American literary circles over the implications of these issues, and in part by current efforts to rearticulate gender both within and outside of Asian American communities, which provide fresh insights into the nature of the controversy and point toward directions that the interrogation of gender in Asian American literature may take in the future. For present purposes, my inquiry will focus on Asian American writers who reappropriate masculinity in ways that both resist a phallocentric economy and go beyond forms of feminism unable to evaluate the meaning of patriarchy outside the framework of male/female oppositions. I shall illustrate my analysis by examining a range of Asian American literary texts as sites of specific forms of entanglement of racial ideology, social power, and sexual politics. Less directly, I also hope to use these texts to show that gender politics of one location can neither fully represent the results of events under other circumstances nor ultimately resolve the tensions between the necessity of staking out positions through localized articulations of difference and the need to fashion collective strategies for more comprehensive social change. But a careful deployment of gender politics may enable us to deal with such tensions constructively and, as Stuart Hall phrases it, "to move from one detotalized or deconstructed problematic to the gains of another" (1992, 290).

To draw a trajectory of how the issue of gender figures in Asian American literature historically, it is useful to identify two stages of gender exploration in Asian American literary practice, despite the fact that a history of such exploration rarely follows a linear and coherent line of development. Most Asian American writing did not feature explicit critiques of sexism as a social and political issue before the advent of the civil rights and feminist movements of the late 1960s and early 1970s. In this period, a tentative yet persistent search for the meaning of gender is reflected in literary works by both women and men. Since the mid-1970s, the issue of gender has become a consciously employed identity politics in Asian American literature, which has not only produced an unprecedented number and variety of gender-specific writings, especially by women, but has also inspired hybrid projects that distinguished or valorized Asian American men's and women's subjectivities.[1] In much of this latter period, however, gender has been viewed mainly as a women's issue, as if men can make full sense of their experience outside the social matrix of gender and, conversely, as if women's articulation naturally constitutes their subjectivity irrespective of other historical considerations. Such a dichotomy between a male defense of patriarchy and a feminist defense of women reaches a point of crisis in the community's debate over Maxine Hong Kingston's autobiography, *The Woman Warrior* (1976).[2] In the meantime, the agony of the debate has led Asian American writers and critics to wrestle with the meaning of gender, making it increasingly a more contested, self-reflexive, and politically engaged category for understanding Asian American men's and women's identities in contexts of differential power and of concrete historical experiences.[3] The analysis that follows attempts to contribute to this broadening discourse on gender in Asian American literary criticism.

I

The "emasculation" of the Asian American man has long been a vexatious issue to the community. Used as a metaphorical expression of outrage over the humiliations historically suffered by Asian men in America, the term nevertheless evokes a scenario in which being a woman necessarily implies an inferior social existence, to be both feared and repudiated. The phallocentrism inherent in using the term to describe Asian American men's plight has been pointed out by critics who are rightly concerned about the usage's complicity with patriarchal prejudices and its further marginalization of women. As much as I share such a critique of the term's defects, I find that most of these arguments favor linguistic or philosophical interpretations of the term and fail to examine its usage within specific social and political formations. Such neglect, I shall argue, not only risks decontextualizing Asian American men's deeply felt historical injustices toward them but also obscures the connection between a full account of the term's figurative history and its social components, and a more effective critique of masculine essence.

To investigate the meaning of Asian American men's sufferings troped on their "emasculation," it is necessary to distinguish the term from what is often taken as its semantic substitute, "feminization"; for the equation between the two is perceived mainly within a symbolic rather than a social framework. This symbolic equation reinforces the view of Asian American males' sexuality as being simple and coherent, and prevents more revealing investigation of the trope's meaning, not only in terms of the image it evokes, but also in terms of the material condition of its construction.[4] For example, despite the fact that Asian men are often viewed collectively in the West as lacking sexual rigor, they are not infrequently seen, in the process of their immigration to the United States, as having the potential to threaten white people sexually. This second perception was partially responsible for the instituting of various antimiscegenation laws against Asians in the United States since the nineteenth century and for such physical violence against Asian men as the 1931 Watsonville riot, in which white men attacked and killed Filipino males because the latter were able to attract white women at a local dance hall.[5] Within this context, the rhetorical orientation of "feminization" clearly does not overlap seamlessly with that of "emasculation" in the same historical time and cultural space. Rather, the two terms appear to occupy related yet different layers of a socially produced configuration, in which "emasculation" more fully suggests the overall social consequence of the displacement of Asian men's subject position, whereas "feminization" constitutes but one specific form of Asian men's racial gendering in America, as differing from (not opposed to) another form to which they are sometimes subject – the perception of them as sex fiends. Both these forms of cultural racism toward Asian men in America contribute to their social and political "emasculation" in a context of patriarchal capitalism.

The "feminization" of Asian men in the West has long and complex historical and cultural roots, but the phenomenon itself is intimately associated with the rise of modern Western colonialism, the predominantly male Asian labor immigration to North America, and the various attendant racial ideologies. In such contexts, the traditional Western concept of masculinity – which values men as embodiments of civilization, rationality, and aggressiveness and devalues women as embodiments of primitiveness, emotion, and passivity (Spelman 1982) – was extended to account for the West's sense of economic and political superiority over Asia by projecting the latter as a diametrically opposed feminine Other.[6] Illustrating the West's self-serving application of the traditional gender divide is one dimension of David Henry Hwang's complexly positioned play, *M. Butterfly* (1986).[7] In the play, Hwang offers an ironic portrayal of René Gallimard, a French diplomat to Beijing during the 1960s and 1970s, who has a twenty-year love affair with a Beijing opera singer, Song Liling, without knowing that Song is a man. Gallimard's fascination with Song's perceived femininity is ironically contrasted with his nervous relationships with two Western women, Isabelle and Renée, whose "uninhibited" expression of sexual desires reveals the illusory nature of the West's self-constitution as a stable and unified male subject. Gallimard's sense of potency toward Song derives from a stereotypically constructed "modest" Asian woman, a stereotype that Song, as a spy working for the Chinese government, utilizes to the fullest extent. Implicitly, Hwang takes Gallimard's selective and willful blindness toward Song's sexual identity as symptomatic of the Western prejudice of treating not only Asia but also Asian men as "feminine" and desirous of accommodating to the needs of the "masculine" Western powers. The depth of such cultural prejudice is revealed dramatically in the play when Song undresses in front of Gallimard in order to force him to see what he has refused to recognize, and when Gallimard stubbornly refuses to let go of his culturally constructed "Chinese woman" by declaring that he prefers to choose "fantasy" over "reality" (90). Hwang thus vividly shows, in a deliberately anachronistic fashion, the determining role that race plays in the West's definition of the sexuality of Asian men, and the extent to which the sexual fantasy thus created serves, in turn, both to reproduce the West's self-amplifying desire and to justify its power relationship with Asia. Hence Song comments:

> The West thinks of itself as masculine – big guns, big industry, big money – so the East is feminine – weak, delicate, poor . . . but good at art, and full of inscrutable wisdom – the feminine mystique.
> Her mouth says no, but her eyes say yes. The West believes the East, deep down, *wants* to be dominated – because a woman can't think for herself. (83)

The West's willful "feminization" of Asian men, viewed in this context, is premised on its awareness of its power relationship with the East, as well as on its tacit assumption that powerless Asians will not challenge the established West–East hierarchy and are therefore harmless. An often cited contemporary variation of such "feminization" of Asians in America is the mass media's projection of their collective image as a model minority, a term that distinguished Asian Americans from blacks, Hispanics, and Native Americans during the political ferment of the 1960s because the latter's back-talking militancy is typically viewed as a sign of male potency.

Asian men's sexuality takes on different characteristics as the power relationships and historical circumstances in which these men find themselves alter or change. In Carlos Bulosan's autobiography, *America Is in the Heart* (1946), the portrayal of white men's construction of Filipino male immigrants as "brown monkeys" who lust for white women reveals the structural malleability of Asian men's racial gendering in the West (144).[8] This violent yet contemptuous production of Asian men's sexuality, however, needs to be understood in the context of Filipino immigrants' legal status in America within the time frame of Bulosan's autobiography. During the 1920s and the first three years of the thirties, Filipinos, as U.S. nationals, were the only Asians who could enter and travel in the United States with relative freedom. Filipino men could maintain limited contact with white women through taxi-dance halls, brothels, and even occasional marriages, because of the sporadic recognition of their racial origin as Malay rather than Mongolian. Yet such contact could quickly give rise to political hysteria. In one scene that Bulosan describes, white detectives break into the apartment where Alonzo, a Filipino student, lives with a white woman, beat him up before sending him to prison, and warn the woman not to see Filipinos again (135). Underlying this violent disruption is the fear that Filipino males may think and act as if they were "white."

"White male" is a category that symbolizes the exclusive right not only to possess white women but also to abuse them, as Bulosan indicates in his representations of the "ravished girl" on the freight train and the sick and overworked prostitute, Marian (113, 209–18). The invention of Filipino males' threatening sexuality is thus bound up with white men's concern about securing their social power, a concern brought to the point of crisis by Filipino workers' participation in the labor movement. White men take extreme measures to maintain racial hierarchy: they use Helen, a white woman and an undercover strikebreaker, as bait to win the trust of an all-male Filipino union organization so that she can destroy its activities from within. The subsequent defeat of a Filipino farmers' strike as a result of Helen's deployment of various womanly "strateg[ies]" is immediately followed by Carlos's violent physical castration by a white man who pinned him down to the ground, "grabbed [his] testicles with left hand and smashed them with right fist" (202, 208). Constructed either as a defenseless victim or as the forbidden fruit, the white woman thus functions as an ideological sign simultaneously encoded with the white patriarchal culture's sense of crisis and its readiness to suppress Filipino men's struggle for equality. Meanwhile, the contingent portrayal of the Filipino male as a sex fiend – one that derives from the dominant cultural myth of Asian femininity but acquires its shape from mainstream society's unintentional allowing Filipino males limited access to America's sociocultural discourse in the 1920s and 1930s – requires that he be seen as less masculine and less human so that his violent subjugation can appear to be not only natural but also justifiable.

The racial gendering of the Asian/Asian American man reflected in Hwang's and Bulosan's texts thus illustrates not only the institutional need to "emasculate" Asian males in the process of their incorporation into American society, but also the dependence of such "emasculation" on the ideological norm of male domination over women. When Asian American men are economically and politically subordinate, they are seen as feminine and incapable of living up to Western definitions of masculinity; when they struggle against odds to secure limited social space for themselves or contend for some degree of equality with the cultural establishment, they are immediately regarded as "bastardized" males whose criminal libido has to be controlled.[9] In either case, traditional assumptions of masculinity and femininity are appropriated to rationalize Asian American men's economic, cultural, or political subjugation.[10] Viewed in this light, Asian American men's "emasculation" as a concept metaphor is not only problematic but also revealing: it shows how the compounding of their sexual identity on the basis of their race perpetuates the hierarchical gender divide both socially and epistemologically, and how continued devaluation of women in these terms naturalizes, in turn, using "emasculation" as a basic strategy for articulating Asian American men's plight while entrapping such articulation in an endless repetition of the oppressor's logic. The interventionary value of a metaphorical use of "emasculation" lies, therefore, not in its establishing an accusing position, but in its initiating a critical process capable not only of disclosing how race, gender, and class are entwined in the construction of Asian American men's sexuality but also of disengaging the metaphor's critical energy from its habitual semiotic situation.

In light of this observation, we can better understand both the ideological thrust and the attendant problems of the gender politics reflected in Frank Chin's evocation of Asian American manhood in his first play, *The Chickencoop Chinaman* (1981), a work that interrogates the historical and cultural consequences of the "emasculation" of the Asian American man. The plot of Chin's play revolves around a Chinese American filmmaker, Tam Lum, who seeks in myths about a black boxer a metaphorical substitute for a heroic Asian American history: the central character undergoes a comicotragic reenactment of the author's own perception of Asian America's alienation from its actual but largely effaced heroic past. One central factor in Tam's search is his disdain for his own father, whom he identifies as "an old dishwasher" who wears underpants in the bath for fear that "old toothless goofy white ladies" would peek at his body through the keyhole (16–17). The broader cultural and rhetorical contexts of Chin's parody of this image of a self-contemptuous and paranoid Chinaman indicate deliberate authorial irony at work, while the subtext of this image evokes issues of potency, reinforced by a comment from a Eurasian woman, Lee, on her Chinese American husband that he "wasn't a man" (18). Significantly, it is Charley Popcorn, a black father figure and trainer of boxers, who gives Tam a different story about the filmmaker's father, a man who in fact loves boxing and maintains a fierce sense of dignity.

The empowerment of the Chinese American father, as well as of Chinese American masculinity, through the voice of this black boxing trainer provides insights into the meaning of Chin's dramatization of Tam's search for a father figure: Tam implicitly avoids accepting his own father or recognizing the strength and dignity underlying his behavior; he appears deeply ambivalent about his own children; and his filmmaking evades directly addressing his own plight as a Chinese American man in order to celebrate the "warrior" heritage passed down by a black father-trainer. The tortured, voluble Tam thus highlights Chin's struggle against the historical and cultural falsification and distortion of Asian manhood in America, which leaves little social space within which his interlocutor in the play, Tam, can contend. More significantly, Tam's agony under-scores the connection that Chin sees between the lack of a male-oriented Asian American heroic tradition and the invisibility of Asian American cultural expression. As Chin problematically describes it, "Without a language of his own . . . [the Asian American] no longer is man" (Chin et al. 1974, xlviii). Thus, Tam's struggle symbolizes the difficult emergence of the Asian American artist who is self-conscious about the historical and cultural limitations of his position. For Chin, the crisis in masculinity is bound up not only with the Asian American man's socially inflicted "emasculation" but also with the crisis in language facing the artist; his ultimate hero therefore becomes not only the idolized ancestral Chinese American male who built North America's railroads but also the emerging Asian American artist, who must not only envision and connect with an Asian American heroic tradition but also fight to make his voice effective in the present. In this way, Chin's celebration of Asian American mascu-linity in *The Chickencoop Chinaman* does promise a historical understanding of the "emasculation" of Asian American men, while allowing the play-wright to argue dramatically for the moral importance of fashioning an "authentic" Asian American manhood.

As critics have pointed out, Chin's male inscription of gender is limited either to a mere resistance to the externally imposed cultural image or to a search for a prediscursive Asian American male subject (Cheung 1990, 216–18; Kim 1990a, 75–9; Lowe 1991, 33–4; Wong 1992, 125–6). As a result, even though Chin's construction of male subjectivity polemically invades mainstream readers' evaluative systems with a demand for recognition of Asian American men's historical agency, his construction necessarily loses a considerable degree of its force as a radical critique. On the one hand, Chin's angry reversal of stereotypical representations of Asian American men is resisted by the dominant patriarchal discourse, which characteristically ignores traits of "heroism" possessed by Asian American men and prohibits Asian American men from full participation in the social hierarchy of masculinity.[11] On the other hand, his legitimation of "Asian American cultural integrity" through effectively ignoring women minimizes rather than enhances the representation of the depth and the scope of Asian America's crisis (Chin et al. 1974, xxxviii). Furthermore, his institution of such "cultural identity" based on American birth, speaking English, and masculine ethos conceals rather than accentuates the emerging multiple agendas and the changing ethnic composition of the Asian American communities.[12] Thus, Chin's frontal assault on the cultural establishment by reifying Asian American masculinity has become both an obstacle to and a catalyst for Asian American women's articulations of their differences on their own terms. Paradoxically, his negation of the exclusionary dominant culture has promoted an oppositional consciousness in which Asian American women opt, in turn, to negate his reproduction and entrenchment of male domination within the community; and his insistence on recovering Asian American manhood in combating a unidimensionally perceived racism has become a site of dialectical resistance. Viewed in this light, the appearance of Maxine Hong Kingston's 1976 autobiography, *The Woman Warrior*,[13] can be seen as much as a manifestation of the author's strategically activated cultural disruption and historical reconstruction as of her positioning regarding the gender dynamics into which her autobiography entered.

II

To some extent, the publication of *The Woman Warrior* can be seen as a self-inscription of Chinese American women's sensibilities both in mainstream culture and in the discourse represented by Chin's Asian American masculinity. As we have seen, Chin's artist-figure struggles to maintain an Asian American "cultural integrity" and to recover Asian American history as a product of the demythologizing strategies of his angry, satiric, and often self-referential discourse. Kingston's heroine, on the other hand, engages in an imaginative reconstruction of the lives of Chinese American women in a symbolic realm that the female narrator/subject of her autobiography seeks to enter through language. Kingston's heroine thus constitutes an implicit commentary both upon Chin's vision of the Asian American artist – which fails to take into account the full range of domination that faces Asian American writers who are not male – and upon Chin's vision of Asian American history that leaves little room for a full understanding of Chinese/Asian American women's experiences.

The response to Kingston's narrative intervention has been by no means unambiguous. The literary establishment generally embraces *The Woman Warrior* even while some Asian American scholars feel themselves "sold out" by the autobiography. Feminist critics across cultures often enthusiastically endorse the book for its explicit critiques of sexism, whereas detractors of the text argue that it achieves its success mainly through bashing Chinese men and through reproducing mainstream culture's prejudices against Asian Americans as a collective (Tong 1977, 20).

Most discussions of the controversy have so far focused on the treatment of gender and emphasized, undoubtedly very correctly, the unwillingness of some Asian American scholars to acknowledge the social impact of feminism, as well as Chinese American women's urgent need to voice their concerns in their own terms. This unwillingness has been confirmed by Chin's recent refusal to acknowledge unequal gender relationship as an inherent feature of traditional Chinese culture by drawing counterevidence from a Chinese fairy tale (1991a, 7–8).[14] In my view, a greater contextualization of this controversy reveals important ideological complications that have been neglected in prior analyses of the publication and reception of Kingston's 1976 book. Admittedly, it is simplistic to see the literary establishment's misappropriation and adoption of *The Woman Warrior* for its own purposes as an unambiguous reflection of some motivated urge for assimilation on the part of Kingston. It is equally problematic, I shall argue, to regard the Asian American community's negative responses to the autobiography's canonization as merely sexist reactions against Asian American women's artistic freedom. Rather, we need to understand these varying responses also as illustrations of how the articulation of Chinese American women's oppression is intertwined with that of Chinese American men, and how *specific* contextual constraints on the writing, the production, and the reception of *The Woman Warrior* reflect problems that confront a woman writer of color, culturally and historically.

Chin's aversion to *The Woman Warrior*, as critics point out, arises from his failure to see the entanglement of the socioeconomic oppression of Asian men in America with their cultural oppression in terms of sexism. When Asian American women seek to expose antifemale prejudices in their own ethnic community, he and others, not illogically, feel "betrayed" by attacks that appear to line up with the stances of the majority culture (Cheung 1990, 234–6; Kim 1990a, 75–9). As previously noted, from the mid-1950s until the publication of *The Woman Warrior* in 1976, most writings by Chinese American women writers did not feature open critiques of racism and sexism in American society. The overtly oppositional literature produced by such Chinese American male writers as Chin in the early 1970s strategically raised Asian America's angry voice publicly, a development of Asian American cultural sensibility congruent with and partly shaped by the black protest and counterculture movements of the era. If this sensibility was at a fledgling or, in the words of the editors of *Aiiieeeee!*, a "delicate" stage (Chin et al. 1974, ix), it was also little informed by feminist politics. With the publication of *The Woman Warrior*, Kingston virtually started a revolution within a revolution. Shortly after the formation of a narrowly defined counterhegemonic Asian American literary discourse represented by Chin and other editors of *Aiiieeeee!*, Kingston's Chinese American feminist discourse defiantly branched out from the largely community-based Asian American literary revival and drew support from the mainstream feminist movement. This formative moment created a ripe context for perceived betrayal. More significantly, it reveals the contextual constraints on these two sets of oppressed yet mutually interactive discourses within a restrictive cross-cultural space of representation.

As a product of this historical moment, Kingston's articulation of oppressed Chinese American women's voices in their male-dominated community could scarcely have been free from reactive impulses, and it was understandably done without a full control of how it might intersect with the social construction of gender and sexual orientation at a time when the social history of Chinese American women's oppression in America was largely ignored. In fact, Kingston was sensitive to the cultural risk and the multivalent nature of her injection of a Chinese American woman's voice into an Asian American literary discourse characterized by a male ethos. Immediately after the publication of *The Woman Warrior*, she realized that her book "was one of only heroines. Men are minor characters. It seems an unbalanced view of the world" (Taylor 1976, B1). On another occasion, Kingston reflected that, although she intended to write about women's and men's experiences as an "interlocking story," because of her fear that the men's story was "anti-female and would undercut the feminist viewpoint," she decided to write about women's issues "separately" in *The Woman Warrior* – her "selfish book" (Kim 1982, 207–8). Kingston's concerns here obviously were not unique to Asian American women but could be shared by other women writers of color in an era when women's claim on the ethnic community's interests, as Elaine Kim persuasively argues, became "inseparable from the[ir] claim on female self and subjectivity," and when women's "interpret[ation of] their own experiences as women" could hardly be made without simultaneously "airing the 'dirty laundry'" (1990a, 78, 81).

It is against the historical background of such an emotionally and ideologically charged moment of cultural emergence that we can better understand, for example, Kingston's rhetorical reference in *The Woman Warrior* to "the female *I*" as an interchangeable word in Chinese culture for "slave" (47). As a strategy to differentiate and enhance Chinese American women's condition, this rhetoric offered an image that is both coherent in meaning and easily recognizable to many women readers of the 1970s; at the same time, it produced meanings that obscured how the racial element in Chinese American women's social oppression was inextricably bound up with Chinese American men's, hence occasioning the well-known rupture of her autobiography's discourse from various Asian American voices. In this sense, the conflict between Chin's valorization of Asian American manhood and Kingston's inscription of the Chinese American woman warrior becomes highly illustrative of what Mae Henderson calls the "discursive dilemma" of the simultaneity of oppression and articulation of ethnic writers of both sexes (1989, 24–30), a dilemma characterized by the discourses' specific contextual usage of cultural symbols, by different degrees of dependence on reversal, and by imprecise use of terminology. In fact, Chin admits, when looking back at the era, that "rhetoric(s) counted for a lot . . . [but they] were no substitutes for real knowledge" (1991b, 3). Similarly, Kingston embraces images associated with "war" in writing *The Woman Warrior* despite her well-known stance against violent solutions to controversies. Apparently, the Asian American "man" and "woman" that are constructed with an explicit purpose of disrupting the dominant culture remain problematic in their implicit suggestion of gender opposition as a permanent feature of Asian American social relations.

Clearly, *The Woman Warrior*'s rupture of its alliance with some Asian American scholars, along with its disruption of racism and patriarchal domination, is historically contingent. On the one hand, it reflects the collision of interests within the ethnic community as an inevitable part of the complex and unpredictable process of articulating various historically submerged concerns; on the other, it calls into question romanticized views of individual Asian American writers' utterances at any given moment of cultural emergence as capable of historical transcendence or ideological self-fulfillment. The particular problem for Kingston quickly becomes, one might speculate, how to carry out the task of articulating Asian American women's concerns and still locate common ground with Asian American men's interests. Can an Asian American feminist discourse transform and strengthen rather than weaken an evolving Asian American cultural identity that embraces both men's and women's concerns? More generally, Asian American feminist discourse is faced with the need to determine where its interests overlap or contradict the interests of mainstream feminism, and how its inscription of Asian American feminist sensibility affects its relationship with both the Asian American community and the predominantly Euro-American mainstream culture.

From this perspective, Kingston's second work, *China Men* (1980),[15] can be viewed not only as the author's recognition of the need for postdisruption reassessment of changing situations, but also as her dynamic response to existing and newly risen cross-cultural polemics involving the reception of *The Woman Warrior*. Kingston's positioning in *China Men* thus constitutes a reassertion of her authorial voice through a dialogue with Chinese/Asian American feminists, with Chinese/Asian American men, and with a mainstream literary establishment that tended to interpret works by ethnic writers stereotypically.

Kingston's renegotiation of gender relations in *China Men* involves two main strategies: first, her female protagonist's effort to reconnect to the Chinese American men's world through recognizing their contribution to the economic and social development of North America; and second, her simultaneous deconstructing and problematizing of available versions of Chinese American history and history making. The key development in Kingston's narrative treatment of the ambiguous history of Chinese men in America is her interrogation of the "ideal" male artist-figure produced by the problematic of Chinese history and the female narrator's immediate family heritage. Of the various such figures described in *China Men* (Tang Ao, the "ghostmate" artisan, Tu Tzu-Chun, and so on), the most significant to the narrator is her father, BaBa, a "born" scholar with hands "made for holding pens," whose poetic voice is omitted by the Chinese examination process and whose knowledge is unappreciated by disrespectful students at a village school in Guangdong (16). BaBa's initial frustration is followed by the multiple trials he has to undergo in the United States as a self-proclaimed scholar: to be nailed inside a stuffy crate on a smuggler's ship to New York; alternately in the narrative, to be detained at the Immigration Station on Angel Island in San Francisco Bay, his genitals probed, his eyelids pulled with a hook, and his mouth forced open for examination. It is at the Immigration Station that BaBa recognizes the end of his career as a scholar: the walls of the detention room are covered with poems written by educated immigrants like himself, poems that protest the jailing of new immigrants, unfair laws, and a Chinese emperor too weak to protect them. The failure of the father/scholar figure in *China Men* is a significant episode in Kingston's historicizing of her female narrator's family heritage: he represents the silencing of the poetic voice of those who fail because their aspirations and the world they must face are so disjointed. In her own narrative assumption of the artist role, the narrator implicitly strives to break that silence.

BaBa's passing of the American Immigration examination through the "skill of his deceit" precedes as troubled a life in America as his failure to pass the Imperial Examinations had in China (60). Eventually, he loses a laundry and a house in New York City; his savings are drained away; his friends desert him; and his land in China is confiscated by the Chinese Communists. These experiences make him a "disheartened man," who sulks in alcoholic quiescence during the day and screams in his sleep (247). Although BaBa's silencing is unproductively broken at home in abusive behavior toward his wife and daughter, he, like the Chinese poet Kao Chi, has also left them a more positive legacy. The latter was "famous for poems to his wife and daughter written upon leaving for the capital; he owned a small piece of land where he grew enough to eat without working too hard so he would write poems." The narrator thinks of her own father's planting of "luffa and grapevines," of vegetables and fruit trees, as a parallel: if he is a poet in exile, he nevertheless is planting "trees that take years to fruit" (255) – and his daughter's own work must become part of that fruit. BaBa's angry silences, while leaving the daughter out of his world, also fill her with an urge to understand him. The daughter's awareness of her father's voicelessness defines a key negotiating stance that Kingston employs to reconnect to the men's world, a world that she had obviously distanced herself from in writing about Chinese American women's issues in *The Woman Warrior*. Implicitly, in taking up the role of writer she also takes up the frustrations and pain her own father suffered.

In *China Men*, the daughter reconnects to other father figures besides BaBa. More than a simple recognition of the "emasculation" issues raised by various Asian American male scholars, Kingston's narrative strategy is highly deliberated, debated, and negotiated. A case in point is her description of her grandfather Ah Goong's metaphorical breaking of silence while working on the Transcontinental Railroad. One day, while riding a basket being lowered like a "plummet" into a valley that needs to be cleared for the base of a trestle (132), Ah Goong is suddenly seized by "sexual desire," masturbates, and "squirted out into space," murmuring, "I am fucking the world" (133). Allegorically, Ah Goong's explosive yet vain expression of his socially suppressed sexual energy parallels the thwarted creativity Bak Goong experiences in being forbidden to talk on a Hawaiian sugar plantation. The narrator, by "speaking" the "forbidden" – the never directly transmitted memory – is taking up the role of the artist unrealized by her male ancestors: symbolically, in speaking the "forbidden," the narrator is "fertilizing" the world with words.

Such are men's "secrets," secrets of their spiritually vulnerable and disenchanted sufferings, that the narrator (re)enters into history to give an inside narrative to an external, and more accessible, narrative of their experiences – their loss of ears and toes during blizzards or the destruction of their flesh during dynamite accidents (136–7). After such sacrifices, the narrator implies, it was especially humiliating that China men were dismissed once the Transcontinental Railroad was completed, only to be excluded subsequently from other forms of labor. Kingston's perception of Asian American masculine heroism is clearly not a simple one. She celebrates what Chinese workingmen achieved for the United States (rather than seeing them as totally exploited victims). At the same time, she also points out the often devastating effects of their social isolation and their painful and violent experiences in American society. The fact that the exclusion proposals could make it through Congress and into federal law in the 1880s indicates that Chinese immigrants' "coming to claim America" in the second half of the nineteenth century cannot be told as a story of an unambiguous heroic success against overwhelming odds (149). Kingston's treatment, when read against an idealized vision of Asian American history that would presumably offer various incarnations of Guan Gong, implies that such a vision cannot change the fate of the fathers in *China Men*. They bear physical and psychological scars from their struggles, scars that their successors, according to the daughter-narrator of *China Men*, must recognize and understand.

III

The negotiating position taken by Kingston in writing *China Men* underscores the ideologically interdependent relationship among gender, race, class, and other historical experiences. It also indicates the irreducibility of complex, multilayered, and variously entangled Asian American identities to convenient categorizations. Kingston's disturbing critique of patriarchy in *The Woman Warrior* and her constructive reconfiguration of gender relations in *China Men* clearly show that articulation of the subjectivities of Asian American women and men cannot be understood as an ideological given or as an explicitly triumphal or recuperative endeavor. Rather, such subjectivities have to emerge from complex and contested processes of differentiation and renegotiation of discourses. External and internal constraints and changing combinations of interests or identities may frequently defer such subjectivities from being clearly and fully realized. In this sense, the kind of disruption-negotiation that Kingston attempts is not an ahistorical exercise of goodwill but requires that the negotiating parties move toward and at least mutually acknowledge their respective power positions. This means that an "essentialist" position, as respectively taken by Chin and Kingston in their early articulations, may at times be strategically necessary; for the adoption of such positions is directed as much at attempting to win accommodation from those within the community who take exclusionary approaches to the canon formation of Asian American literature as it is at asserting the existence of Asian American cultural sensibilities that the dominant culture refuses to acknowledge.

Recent narrative strategies in Asian American literature that explore the mediational ground between male and female identities suggest the range of discursive positions that have emerged since the 1970s. To illustrate how such strategies can open possibilities for gender politics in Asian American literature, my subsequent discussion will focus on relevant aspects in Wendy Law-Yone's novel, *The Coffin Tree* (1987), and Jessica Hagedorn's novel, *Dogeaters* (1990). In both works, gender ambiguity or gender transgression serves the ideological purpose of eliding the rigidity of cultural strictures on sexual differences and becomes a potential site for historical understanding of the inherent problems of the hierarchical fixation of gender binarism.

The strategy of gender ambiguity plays a unique role in Law-Yone's *The Coffin Tree*, a novel that deals with the immigration experience of two young Burmese to America. The novel features a difficult quest for knowledge by the female protagonist/narrator, whose experience of gender is profoundly shaped by her social status in Burma and later in the United States. In Law-Yone's treatment of this quest, the birth of the narrator, which coincides with the death of her mother, and the death of her half-brother, which precedes the narrator's spiritual rebirth, are two crucial textual junctures in the novel's subversion of the historical exclusion of its protagonist/narrator from the possession and production of knowledge. As will be seen, this subversion hinges on the narrator's and, secondarily, her half-brother's ambiguous gender identities.

Early in the novel, we find the narrator fleeing with Shan (her half-brother) from an agrarian and war-torn Burma to a postindustrial United States, thanks to arrangements made by her father, the ousted commander of the Burmese rebel army. Shocked at the racial discrimination, precarious existence, and profound sense of alienation that she experiences in her adopted country, the narrator is mentally drawn back to her family history in Burma for a sense of reassurance. But that history turns out to be not only "unsorted" but also inaccessible (44–6). The narrator's sense of being severed from her past points back toward the first significant textual juncture in the novel – her emotional pain of separation from the mother who dies while giving her birth. The simultaneous death and birth can be understood metaphorically as both a historical erasure of the mother's creative authority and an unrecognized maternal legitimation of the narrator's desire for a potential reclamation of that authority.[16] The gender-specific meaning of both the narrator's historical separation from the past and her biological separation from her mother is reinforced by a Catholic schoolteacher, Mother Immaculata, who silences the narrator as an eleven-year-old girl for composing a letter to an imaginary lover (93–4). In addition, the narrator's historically "non-pregnant" memory is ironically contrasted to that of her imaginative half-brother, Shan, a contrast that symbolically illustrates patriarchal ideology's preference for male speaking agents in the realm of artistic creation.

A condition that ironically spurs the narrator's desire to know and to create involves her isolation in the family because of her disruptive, quasi-"gargoyle" looks (142) – lusterless hair, squared-tipped fingers, dark skin, broad face, and an Easter Island head with half-moon shadows under her eyes (14, 143) – which sharply contrast with her mother's delicate features as recalled by her grandmother. Images of the mother's beauty are sustained through hearsay and dreams, whereas the narrator's failure to measure up to patriarchal definitions of acceptable appearance for women is punished on a daily basis with scolding by the grandmother and taunts by the servants (8). As a result, the protagonist develops a "self-loathing" and gradually shrinks from her womanhood (13, 31). What enables the narrator's sexual ambiguity to become a means of transcendence of the familial, social, and cultural barriers that bar her from creativity is Shan's simultaneous crisis in his own gender identity. In Burma, at the age of eighteen, the young man revolts against his childhood nurse Nankee's sexual advances; later, in the United States, he interprets an encounter with racial discrimination by American male coworkers as being collectively "raped" (113, 73). Viewed in the broad context of the novel, the dysfunctional gender identities of both half-siblings reflect their social and emotional displacement. In Shan's case, the father's abusive attitude toward his presumably unmanly deficiency of stuttering (108), real or imagined, has clearly driven the young man toward a "feminine scale" of behavior, as well as toward closer ties with his sexually ambivalent sister (49). Whereas Shan is still able to project his suppressed desire for male domination onto his "slavish" friend Danson, who plays his "whipping boy" at games (118), he becomes real allies only with his half-sister (16). The relationship provides them with a condition free from gender expectations. More significantly, it allows the narrator to share the "arcane and forbidden skills" used by boys in play as well as Shan's anarchic creativity (116–17), which marks the young man as the surviving twin of the potentially insane woman with whom his violent father consorts.

The second important textual juncture involves Shan's mental and physical collapse in America, which symbolizes the narrator's separation from male creativity and the simultaneous transmission of male authority over history making to the charge of the female. This process of separation and transmission, though coincidental with the narrator's desire to end her own life because of having lost her brother's "sustaining friendship to offer comfort" (154), is reinforced by her deep yearning "to be reunited with Mother" (145). Symbolically, the narrator wants to become Mother herself so that she can be in a position to (pro)create a woman's version of history long forbidden by patriarchal gender binarism. After an unsuccessful suicide attempt and a subsequent brief confinement in a mental asylum, where the narrator ironically witnesses instances of rationality and creativity rather than passive abandonment to insanity, she feels "born again" (190); she becomes her own creator as a woman and as an artist who is finally able to "sit at . . . [her] table . . . and *labor* over these pages" (195; emphasis added). Thus, Law-Yone creatively uses gender ambiguity both as a point for her female narrator's entry into history making and as a means of her transcendence of the boundaries separating men from women, creativity from body, clear-mindedness from insanity, and history from myth.

In many ways, Hagedorn's *Dogeaters*, which focuses on events in the Philippines rather than on those in the United States, signifies both a departure from and an extension of earlier representations of Filipino American experience reflected in *America Is in the Heart*. This new development in the portrayal of Asian American experiences reflects profound changes in West–East relations since World War II: the increasing political, military, and economic presence of the United States in the Pacific region; continuing Western colonialism in Third World Asian countries during the process of these countries' decolonization; and the contemporary Asian diaspora as an inseparable part of the globalization of America's economic and cultural influence. Hagedorn's novel shows connections between the post–World War II Philippines and Asian America in such a sociocultural context. In particular, *Dogeaters* portrays the tensions between the Philippines' attempt to claim its postcolonial political subjectivity and its having to deal with both the legacy and the continuing power of imperialism, and to live and speak in severely limited postcolonial space.

Such tensions are dramatized through Hagedorn's portrayal of the sexual orientation of the male protagonist of the novel, Joey Sands, a gay nightclub dancer in Manila. The context in which Joey finds himself a sexual deviant is the Philippines of the mid-1950s, where Western cultural invasion, consumerism, and domestic political strife permeate every sector of the Filipino social life. Under Western influence, female beauty comes to be defined by fictitious movie images, and women's social value is measured primarily in terms of their resemblance to such images.

Hence, Madame Alacran, the wife of the King of Coconuts, has painstakingly "reconciled her life and past to suit her taste" for such role models as "Dietrich, Vicomtesse Jacqueline de Ribes, Nefertiti, and Grace Kelly" by programmatically having herself "manicured and oiled, massaged and exercised, pampered like some high-strung, inbred animal" (20). Such internalized objectification of women, moreover, is both demanded by and in the service of modern Filipino social institutions. In the novel, these social institutions are collectively symbolized, first, by the imposing department store, SPORTEX, where women employees work hard at getting thin or get fired for "having dirty nails" (160) and, second, by the mannerist generals who take turns conquering the "flagrant sexuality and magnificent body" of a local movie star, Lolita, and display her "used panties" as trophies of masculine aggressiveness and virility (171, 176).

Against this background of fetishism of Western standards of femininity and masculinity, Joey's sexual identity as a gay man takes on special meaning and constitutes a locus in which the political consequences of Western cultural imperialism can be evaluated and critiqued. Specifically, Joey's social identity as gay – which gives him Teiresias-like access to both sexes' perspectives and experiences – enables him to avoid the moral and social obligations prescribed by established heterosexual behavior. Hence, he "do[es]n't have to work at being sexy" like Lolita (44), nor does he have to entertain illusions about the physical appearance of his sexual partner, as does Romero, who unleashes his "insatiable lust" onto the plain, bony, and gold-toothed Trinidad by fantasizing about being atop the "torrid siren Lolita Luna, ecstatic beneath his own pumping body" (53). Joey's relative freedom from heterosexual constraints, however, does not land him outside the social matrix of male/female binarism: he is attractive to other men mainly because of his effeminacy, and he remains an object of male sexual domination. The critical potential of Joey's sexual orientation thus lies not in the fact of his being homosexual but in the gender consciousness that he has gained from his firsthand experience with sexism and male domination from the perspective of a gay man, a consciousness that is in turn shaped by his family history and class status.

As the son of a Filipino woman and an African American soldier stationed at Subic Bay after World War II, Joey is thin, short, and possesses racial features that allow him no place on the scale of acceptable masculinity in Filipino society. At the same time, saddened by his uncle's revelation that his mother was a prostitute who drowned herself after having been "disgraced and abandoned" (42), Joey has been acquainted almost from childhood with the consequences of sexual oppression of lower-class women. These material conditions of his early life constitute an important clue not only to the political implications of his sexual orientation but also to the vengeance he takes on a society that marks him as the son of a "legendary whore" (205); the painful legacy of his mother's sufferings from men's sexual exploitation marks Joey's sexual marginality as a subversive ideological critique of the sexism being perpetuated in Filipino society through the "legacy of colonialism" (100). In this sense, Joey's sexual identity becomes firmly grounded in a historical realm and endowed with an explicit purpose. He says: "I'm dressed, fed, and high. I can take it or leave it, break hearts wherever I go" (45). As "Mister Heartbreak" (34), Joey thus sees the homosexual activities in which he participates as opportunities to "take advantage of the situation" (44), to "keep . . . things slightly off-balance," and to "make a point" (37).

Ironically, Joey's two male sexual partners in the novel – Neil, a middle-aged American serviceman, and Rainer, a German film director in his forties – are both Western men touring the Philippines, who, in their eagerness to fulfill their sexual fantasies through Joey, provide occasions for their own moral defeat. The following exchange between Neil and Joey constitutes one such example:

> "Call me Neil," he said, his eyes fixed on me in that bad, funny way of his. . . . "NEIL. What kind of name is that?" I loved making fun of him.
>
> "Good sport," he'd laugh with me, jabbing at his own chest with one of his large hands.
>
> I spit on the floor in contempt. "Man, you don't have to talk to me like I don't know any thing! *Puwede ba* – good sport," I mimic, rolling my eyes. "What do you think of this? The Lone Ranger and Tonto?"
>
> I sulk, looking away from him. Scan the room for a pretty face. Make him feel real bad.
>
> Embarrassed, he looks lost. "Joey, I'm sorry." He means it. I like that best. I could make him do anything.
>
> I keep at it for just a little while longer. "Man, I'm no savage." When he looks like he's going to cry, I stop. (73)

The context of this exchange between the two involves Neil's desire to please the "little pretty black boy" so that he can start an affair with him and Joey's purposeful subversion of the discourse initiated by Neil by introducing images of the Lone Ranger and Tonto – a symbolic scenario of racial domination. The irony of the parallel lies in contrastive effects immediately recognizable to both. Joey, presumably the dark-skinned, subservient prostitute, in fact can make the desire-driven Neil "do anything" for him. Neil, ostensibly the masterly white patron, appears devoid of the dignity and courage that marks the Lone Ranger as a hero in American popular culture; indeed, with his drooping face and eyes (72–

3), Neil is "unmasked" in a gesture that recalls Chin's *Chickencoop Chinaman* and exposes him as an old, sad-looking, bumbling racist, a beggar of favors from the colonized. By creating such a politicized moment in the sexual marketplace, Joey pointedly exposes the sexist and racist attitudes that confound the relationship Neil seeks.

Joey's verbal taunt at Neil's smugness precedes his open revulsion at Rainer's hypocrisy about homosexuality and ludicrous sentimentalism toward the person who comes within his reach only as a sexual commodity. Rainer fears being seen by Filipino servants while he is engaged with Joey; that is, he fears public exposure of what had been a privately indulged sexual deviancy in Germany even in what for him is the "safety" of the exotic social arena of the Philippines. The result is obviously ironic: on the one hand, Rainer is unconsciously made to act, under the public gaze of Manila, as if he were a "criminal" (147), implicitly revealing his internalization of the regulatory assumptions of homophobia; on the other hand, his profuse expressions of love for Joey on private occasions are met with the latter's disdain, neglect, and abuse – finally, Joey steals from him. Underlying Joey's responses to these two Western men's sexual demands are both his explicit rejection of the persistence and controlling authority of hierarchical assumptions about heterosexuality – assumptions now masquerading in a homosexual relationship – and his critique of the West's arrogance toward and commodification of Filipinos. Joey's revulsion at Rainer's hypocrisy, as well as the latter's imposition on him of a subordination that threatens to deprive him of his social mobility, is vividly evoked in Joey's comment on shitting. He tells Rainer: "Sometimes I shit, Rainer. Sometimes I shit all day long. I wonder where all my shit is coming from, especially when I don't eat. I don't eat for days. How can I shit? It's scary at first. Then it feels good. Good shit cleans my system. I get rid of everything" (145).

Only by expelling Rainer's "crazy shit" (148) from within his system can Joey disrupt the external cultural norms imposed upon his body. Joey's implicit expulsion of Rainer's hypocrisy and immorality parallels his pissing, toward the end of the novel, on his uncle's treasured collection of foreign magazines featuring glossy pictures of naked white women. In both these acts, Joey's symbolic rejection of rigid cultural and social constructs of his identity constitutes a radical problematization of gender as a static category, keeps gender both disruptively and constructively mobile, and, above all, makes homosexuality a site to comment on the mutually exclusive sexual identifications imposed by the traditional gender divide.

The broadening of discourse on gender in Asian American literature clearly goes beyond the range of works sampled here. My limited goal has been to illustrate the view that the meaning of gender evolves from one historical contingency to another, and that gender politics often shifts to recognize the limitations of what it achieves and to facilitate the emergence of new forms of agency. More specifically, gender politics has functioned in Asian American literary practice to expose and to negotiate tensions across a wide range of power imbalance, as well as to challenge self-ghettoizing tendencies in nonreflexive articulations of identities. Given the historical complexity of gender construction and articulation, any analysis of gender politics in Asian American literature needs to go beyond a simple delineation of gender roles, to recognize both the urgency for social change while acknowledging continuing social power, and to assess at what stakes, for what purposes, and from what power positions specific forms of gender subjectivity are conceived and mobilized. Thus, King-Kok Cheung has urged us to see gender identity as a self-conscious construct and to use gender politics in ways that truly expand the possibilities of critique in Asian American literary discourse (1990, 246). If self-consciously employed and self-critical, gender politics will allow Asian Americans of all sexual orientations not only to uncover the social inequalities from which they suffer but also to relate to one another in recognition of the complexities of their experiences and differences, as well as of their shared goal of constructing a truly democratic world.

■■■■■ ACKNOWLEDGMENTS

Research for this chapter was facilitated by an Academic Senate grant and a grant from the Asian American Studies Center, UCLA. I would like to offer my special thanks to King-Kok Cheung for her encouragement, astute readings of various drafts of this chapter, and advice on revision. Earlier versions have benefited from critical commentary by Jenny Sharpe, Shu-mei Shih, Russell Leong, and Alexander Hammond.

■■■■■ NOTES

1. Several book-length studies examine various aspects of gender in Asian American literature from its beginning to its present: Kim, *Asian American Literature* (1982); Trinh, *Woman, Native, Other* (1989); Asian Woman United of California, ed., *Making Waves* (1989); Ling, *Between Worlds* (1990); Wong, *From Necessity to Extravagance* (1993); Cheung, *Articulate Silences* (1993); The Women of South Asian Descent Collective, ed., *Our Feet Walk the Sky* (1993); Cheung, ed., *Seventeen Syllables/Hisaye Yamamoto* (1994); Kim and Alarcón, eds., *Writing Self, Writing Nation* (1994); Grewal and Kaplan, eds., *Scattered Hegemonies* (1994), chaps. 4, 5, 10, 11; and White-Parks, *Sui Sin Far* (1995).
2. The debate also involves such interrelated issues as canonization, the genre of

autobiography, marketplace, and contexts of language signification. These issues need to be addressed under different topics.

3. Such efforts include, for example, Kim, "'Such Opposite Creatures'" (1990a); Cheung, "The Woman Warrior versus The Chinaman Pacific" (1990); Lowe, "Heterogeneity, Hybridity, Multiplicity" (1991); Wong, "Ethnicizing Gender" (1992); Lim, "Assaying the Gold" (1993); and Okihiro, "Recentering Women" (1994, 64–92).

4. Fung, for instance, contests the monolithic stereotype of the desexed "Oriental" man by offering perspectives on competing and contradictory sexual associations based on nationality (1991, 146–7, 161).

5. Antimiscegenation laws against Asians, though motivated by racial prejudice, were implicitly aimed at the male population of early Asian immigrants, whose sexuality – whether constructed as passive/languorous or as primitive/kinky – was seen as repulsive and dangerous. For a brief description of the Watsonville riot (designated alternatively as taking place in 1929), see Takaki (1989, 327–8).

6. The myth of Asian sexuality places women on an ultrafeminine scale where they are often seen as desirable sexual partners willing to serve and please. For further discussions of the topic, see Kim (1990b, 167) and Tajima (1989, 309–14). Historically, Western stereotyping of Asians – often designated as "Orientals" – is mainly concerned with people in East Asia. South Asians – people in India, Pakistan, Sri Lanka, and Bangladesh – are not represented. My use of "East" or "Asia" here refers to areas that include such countries as China, Japan, and Korea.

7. For discussions of other aspects of Hwang's play, see Kondo (1990), Garber (1992), Pao (1992), and Eng (1994).

8. I am grateful to Gregory Sarris for his comments on Filipino male experience in the United States, which helped me to formulate my analysis. Takaki discusses similar aspects of *America Is in the Heart* in a somewhat different context (1989, 343–9).

9. Although the representation of Filipino males as sex fiends during the 1920s and 1930s bears some similarity to that of blacks as rapists, there are differences in the actual versions of Filipino men's and black men's sexuality. I am grateful to Jenny Sharpe for bringing to my attention Sinha's observation about the late-nineteenth-century British portrayal of Bengali males as rapists through the Age of Consent Act. Sinha argues that such a concept of the Bengali male's sexuality does not place him on a par with Victorian manliness but, rather, turns him into its bastardized or incomplete form (see Sinha 1987, 229–30). The perception of Filipino men's sexuality, in this sense, is more similar to that of Bengali males rather than to that of blacks. For an incisive discussion of the misconception of black sexuality in contemporary American culture, see West (1993, 81–91); for a study of the discursive production of rape in colonial discourse, see Sharpe (1993).

10. My analysis of the relationship among notions of emasculation, manhood, and patriarchy has benefited from the critical insights of Hooks (1990, 57–77), Smith (1990, 272–6), and Yarborough (1990, 174).

11. Yarborough points out, regarding nineteenth-century African American male

writers' quest for black manhood, that the "warlike" features which signify heroism for whites were often seen as qualities of inferiority when applied to blacks (1990, 169). This observation obviously applies to similar quests by Asian American writers in the 1970s. Cheung suggests that, instead of subscribing to Western patriarchal prescriptions for manhood and to the Western association of male self-restraint with passivity and femininity, Asian American writers and critics need to investigate alternative meanings of men's "silence" in specific ideological and historical formations (1990, 244–5; 1993).

12. See Chin et al. (1974, ix, xxii, xlviii). It should be noted, however, that Chin's position toward "Asian American cultural integrity" is more complex than it appears. For example, despite his narrow definition of the concept, he also argues that "between the writer's actual birth and birth of the sensibility, we have used the birth of the sensibility as the measure of being an Asian American," and that "the universality of the belief that correct English is the only language of American truth had made language an instrument of cultural imperialism"(1974, ix, xxxvii). The contradiction between Chin's pronouncements, as well as the different oppositional symbols he emphasizes at various stages of his writing career, suggests that more factors are involved in the constitution of the playwright's evolving position (including the recent hardening of his stance toward issues of gender and authenticity). The complexity of Chin's position, which he complains that "I daresay they will not take . . . on its own terms" (1991b, 4), should be investigated, particularly in light of its connections with specific social and political processes and conditions.

13. For assessments of *The Woman Warrior*, see, for example, Wong (1988), Schueller (1989), and Cheung (1993, 78–100). For a useful reference book for teaching *The Woman Warrior*, see Lim (1991).

14. See Ling (1990, 1–6) and Okihiro (1994, 68–74) for historical perspectives on male social status in traditional Chinese society.

15. For studies of other aspects of gender in *China Men*, see Rabine (1987), Goellnicht (1992), and Cheung (1993, 100–25).

16. My discussion of the subversive use of childbirth in Law-Yone's novel draws on the critical insights of Susan Friedman and Trinh Minh-ha. Both critics suggest that in a patriarchal society, where men are associated with mind and creativity and women with body and procreativity, the metaphor of childbirth can be used to challenge the binary oppositions of patriarchal ideology and to validate women's artistic efforts by unifying mental and physical labor into (pro)creativity. See Friedman (1989, 73–4) and Trinh (1989, 36–9).

■■■■ WORKS CITED

Asian Woman United of California, ed. 1989. *Making Waves: An Anthology of Writings by and about Asian American Women*. Boston: Beacon.

Bulosan, Carlos. 1946/1977. *America Is in the Heart: A Personal History*. Seattle: Univ. of Seattle Press.

Cheung, King-Kok. 1990. "The Woman Warrior versus the Chinaman Pacific: Must a Chinese American Critic Choose between Feminism and Heroism?" In *Conflicts in Feminism*, ed. Marianne Hirsch and Evelyn Fox Keller, 234–51. New York: Routledge.

———. 1993. *Articulate Silences: Hisaye Yamamoto, Maxine Hong Kingston, Joy Kogawa*. Ithaca, NY: Cornell Univ. Press.

———, ed. 1994. *"Seventeen Syllables."* New Brunswick, NJ: Rutgers Univ. Press.

Chin, Frank. 1981. *The Chickencoop Chinaman and the Year of the Dragon*. Seattle: Univ. of Washington Press.

———. 1991a. "Come All Ye Asian American Writers of the Real and the Fake." In *The Big Aiiieeeee! An Anthology of Chinese American and Japanese American Literature*, ed. Jeffery Chan et al., 1–92. New York: Meridian.

———. 1991b. "Frank Chin: His Own Voice." Interview by Frank Abe. *The Bloomsbury Review*, September, 3–4.

Chin, Frank, et al., eds. 1974. *Aiiieeeee! An Anthology of Asian-American Writers*. Washington, DC: Howard Univ. Press.

Eng, David. 1994. "In the Shadows of a Diva: The Commitment of Homosexuality in David Henry Hwang's *M. Butterfly*." *Amerasia Journal* 20.1:93–116.

Friedman, Susan Stanford. 1989. "Creativity and the Childbirth Metaphor: Gender Difference in Literary Discourse." In *Speaking of Gender*, ed. Elaine Showalter, 73–100. New York: Routledge.

Fung, Richard. 1991. "Looking for My Penis: The Eroticized Asian in Gay Video Porn." In *How Do I Look? Queer Film and Video*, ed. Bad Object-Choices, 145–68. Seattle: Bay.

Garber, Marjorie. 1992. "The Occidental Tourist: *M. Butterfly* and the Scandal of Transvestitism." In *Nationalism and Sexualities*, ed. Andrew Parker et al., 121–46. New York: Routledge.

Goellnicht, Donald C. 1992. "Tang Ao in America: Male Subject Positions in *China Men*." In *Reading the Literatures of Asian America*, ed. Shirley Geok-lin Lim and Amy Ling, 191–212. Philadelphia: Temple Univ. Press.

Grewal, Indepal, and Caren Kaplan, eds. 1994. *Scattered Hegemonies*. Minneapolis: Univ. of Minnesota Press.

Hagedorn, Jessica. 1990. *Dogeaters*. New York: Penguin.

Hall, Stuart. 1992. "Cultural Studies and Its Theoretical Legacies." In *Cultural Studies*, ed. Lawrence Grossberg et al., 277–94. New York: Routledge.

Henderson, Mae Gwendolyn. 1989. "Speaking in Tongues: Dialogics, Dialectics, and the Black Women Writer's Literary Tradition." In *Changing Our Own Words: Essays on Criticism, Theory, and Writing by Black Women*, ed. Cheryl A. Wall, 16–37. New Brunswick, NJ: Rutgers Univ. Press.

hooks, bell. 1990. *Yearning: Race, Gender, and Cultural Politics*. Boston: South End.

Hwang, David Henry. 1986. *M. Butterfly*. New York: Penguin.

Kim, Elaine H. 1982. *Asian American Literature: An Introduction to the Writings and Their Social Context*. Philadelphia: Temple Univ. Press.

———. 1990a. "'Such Opposite Creatures': Men and Women in Asian American Literature." *Michigan Quarterly Review* 29.1:68–93.

———. 1990b. "Defining Asian American Realities through Literature." In *The*

Nature and Context of Minority Discourse, ed. Abdul R. JanMohamed and David Lloyd, 146–70. New York: Oxford Univ. Press.

Kim, Elaine H., and Norma Alarcón, eds. 1994. *Writing Self, Writing Nation: A Collection of Essays on DICTÉE by Theresa Hak Kyung Cha.* Berkeley: Third Woman.

Kingston, Maxine Hong. 1976. *The Woman Warrior: Memoirs of a Girlhood among Ghosts.* New York: Knopf.

———. 1980. *China Men.* New York: Knopf.

Kondo, Dorinne K. 1990. "*M. Butterfly.* Orientalism, Gender, and a Critique of Essentialist Identity." *Cultural Critique* (Fall):5–29.

Law-Yone, Wendy. 1987. *The Coffin Tree.* Boston: Beacon.

Lim, Shirley Geok-lin. 1993. "Assaying the Gold: Or, Contesting the Ground of Asian American Literature." *New Literary History* 24.1:147–69.

———, ed. 1991. *Approaches to Teaching Kingston's "The Woman Warrior."* New York: Modern Language Association.

Ling, Amy. 1990. *Between Worlds: Women Writers of Chinese Ancestry.* New York: Pergamon.

Lowe, Lisa. 1991. "Heterogeneity, Hybridity, Multiplicity: Marking Asian American Differences." *Diaspora* 1.1:24–44.

Okihiro, Gary Y. 1994. "Recentering Women." In *Margins and Mainstreams: Asians in American History and Culture,* 64–92. Seattle: Univ. of Washington Press.

Pao, Angela. 1992. "The Critic and the Butterfly: Sociocultural Contexts and Reception of David Henry Hwang's *M. Butterfly.*" *Amerasia Journal* 18.3:1–16.

Rabine, Leslie E. 1987. "No Lost Paradise: Social Gender and Symbolic Gender in the Writings of Maxine Hong Kingston." *Signs* 12.3:471–92.

Schueller, Malini. 1989. "Questioning Race and Gender Definitions: Dialogic Subversions in *The Woman Warrior.*" *Criticism* 31.4:421–37.

Sharpe, Jenny. 1993. *Allegories of Empire: The Figure of Woman in the Colonial Text.* Minneapolis: Univ. of Minnesota Press.

Sinha, Mrinalini. 1987. "Gender and Imperialism: Colonial Policy and the Ideology of Moral Imperialism in Late Nineteenth-Century Bengal." In *Changing Men: New Directions in Research on Men and Masculinity,* ed. Michael S. Kimmel, 217–31. London: Sage.

Smith, Valerie. 1990. "Split Affinities: The Case of Interracial Rape." In *Conflicts in Feminism,* ed. Marianne Hirsch and Evelyn Fox Keller, 271–87. New York: Routledge.

Spelman, Elizabeth V. 1982. "Woman as Body: Ancient and Contemporary Views." *Feminist Studies* 8.1:109–31.

Tajima, Renée E. 1989. "Lotus Blossoms Don't Bleed: Images of Asian Women." In *Making Waves: An Anthology of Writings by and about Asian American Women,* ed. Asian Woman United of California, 308–17. Boston: Beacon.

Takaki, Ronald. 1989. *Strangers from a Different Shore: A History of Asian Americans.* New York: Penguin.

Taylor, Lois. 1976. Review of *The Woman Warrior. Honolulu Star-Bulletin,* 1 September, B1.

Tong, Benjamin R. 1977. "Critics of Admirer Sees Dumb Racist." *San Francisco Journal*, 11 May, 20.

Trinh, T. Minh-ha. 1989. *Woman, Native, Other: Writing Postcoloniality and Feminism*. Bloomington: Indiana Univ. Press.

West, Cornel. 1993. *Race Matters*. Boston: Beacon.

White-Parks, Annette. 1995. *Sui Sin Far: A Literary Biography*. Champaign: Univ. of Illinois Press.

The Women of South Asian Descent Collective, ed. 1993. *Our Feet Walk the Sky: The Women of South Asian Diaspora*. San Francisco: Aunt Lute Books.

Wong, Sau-ling Cynthia. 1988. "Necessity and Extravagance in Maxine Hong Kingston's *The Woman Warrior*: Art and Ethnic Experience." *MELUS* 15.1:3–26.

———. 1992. "Ethnicizing Gender: An Exploration of Sexuality as Sign in Chinese American Immigrant Literature." In *Reading the Literatures of Asian America*, ed., Shirley Geok-lin Lim and Amy Ling, 111–29, Philadelphia: Temple Univ. Press.

———. 1993. *From Necessity to Extravagance: Contexts and Intertexts in Asian American Literature*. Princeton, NJ: Princeton Univ. Press.

Yarborough, Richard. 1990. "Race, Violence, and Manhood: The Masculine Ideal in Frederick Douglass's 'The Heroic Slave.'" In *Frederick Douglass: New Literary and Historical Essays*, ed. Eric Sundquist, 166–88. New York: Cambridge Univ. Press.

11

BLURRING BOUNDARIES: ASIAN AMERICAN LITERATURE AS THEORY

DONALD C. GOELLNICHT

I

> For most ethnic peoples, the path by which they arrive at the con-
> sciousness of their prescribed "otherness" is not the convoluted one
> of theory, but the simple accident of birth. (Rey Chow 1991, xvi)

The opening bind: how, as a privileged academic, to think and write
about the imbrication of critical theory and Asian American literature
without adopting the imperialist position of the subjugator, the "Voice of
Knowledge"/Power employing theory as a weapon with which to control
the "other" through definition and analysis, and with which to claim
more intellectual territory for my own advantage?[1] The double bind:
how, as a white male academic, to achieve this task? The Asian American
critic at least simultaneously fills the supposedly paradoxical subject positions of privileged academic and ethnic "other" in America, positions so
complex and shifting that they deconstruct the simple victimizer–victim
binary and enable the critic to see from both "inside" and "outside" (terms
to which I shall return in order to complicate them). The triple bind: how
to enter a discourse that uses metaphors like "double bind," "triple bind,"
"inside" and "outside" – metaphors usually associated with the subject
positions of those "marginalized" by gender, race, and class – without
sounding like I wish to cast myself as victim or subaltern, an absurd
proposition that would make a mockery of those groups who are genu-
inely oppressed?

   I must begin by admitting that I cannot escape these binds, cannot
escape the subject positions I find myself occupying due in large part to
the accident of birth, which has facilitated my achieving the position from
which I now write. In raising the issue of "descent" here, however, I do
not wish to venture into a full-scale discussion of what has come to be
called the "ethnicity school" debate,[2] except to say that I find problematic

Werner Sollors's privileging of "consent" (legal, constitutional, contractual rights) over "descent" (ethnic, racial, cultural, national, familial origin) as the important factor in American culture; nor can I accept his warnings against the interpretation of texts by means of "biological insiderism" ("the belief that only ethnic insiders are entitled to criticize literature from a given 'ethnic tradition'" [1986a, 275; see also 1986b, 13]). Such an approach, Sollors claims, results in the fragmentation of American Studies. But to lament the loss of "universalism" to "pure pluralism" in American Studies seems to me to indicate a perverse blindness to the asymmetrical nature of existing power relations within society and the academy: "insiderism" is an experiential rather than a biologically determined position, and to acknowledge the significance of such a position is to acknowledge the unequal distribution of power within American culture, in which the mainstream has used and continues to use race as a mark or sign of differential rights and powers at the same time as it has based its ideology on the claims of equal rights and individual freedoms.

Although a full discussion of these issues would be far too complex for the space available here, I wish to stress that my perspective, that of a white, male, naturalized Canadian who immigrated from a "Third World" country, Trinidad, where I belonged to a privileged minority, makes my views different both from those of the traditional "dominant" culture and from those of Asian Americans. To assert that my position is not entirely aligned with that of the "mainstream" is not to deny, however, that I enjoy the privileges of white, patriarchal culture; but as my example illustrates, the "dominant culture" is far from monolithic. I would suggest, in fact, that the concept of the "mainstream" as monolith is a strategy employed to maintain the power of those who see themselves as members of that mainstream; such "unity" forms the foundation for the myth of universalism.

But if the dominant culture is not homogeneous, neither is the group known as Asian Americans, a term E. San Juan calls "an artificial hypostasis of unstable elements" (543). As King-Kok Cheung points out, "Asian American sensibilities vary in accordance with nationality, birthplace, age, social background, and individual endowment" (1993, 21).[3] Even within a group from a single national or ethnic origin positions vary: the wealthy and highly educated professionals and entrepreneurs immigrating at present from Hong Kong to North America have different backgrounds and experiences from those of earlier waves of Chinese immigrants. Thus the binds of "outsiderism" are not simply untied for Asian American critics as the configurations of hybridity change; nor, I should stress, is it clear what is "inside" and what is "outside" for an Asian American, who always exists in a state that W. E. B. DuBois, describing

African Americans, long ago called "double consciousness," and that we might expand to "multiple consciousness." Rather than thinking in binary terms of inside/outside, we should perhaps think of hybrid positions as a web of multiply intersecting and shifting strands in which the precise location of the subject is extremely difficult to map. Maxine Hong Kingston brilliantly articulates the shifting positionality of the self as subject-in-the-making when she asks: "Chinese-Americans, when you try to understand what things in you are Chinese, how do you separate what is peculiar to childhood, to poverty, insanities, one family, your mother who marked your growing with stories, from what is Chinese? What is Chinese tradition and what is the movies?" (1976, 6). There is, then, no "pure"/"essential"/"authentic" Chinese American self, no "biological inside" against which she can be measured and found wanting. She teaches us that subject positions are not the result of essential determinants but are culturally produced (in relation to other positions) and socially learned, a complex and continuous process that Kingston explores through her writing.

To return to my suspended question: how, then, to minimize the effects of positions of privilege and thus to subvert/disrupt/displace existing power relations within the literary and academic spheres? How does one employ theory positively, to "elucidat[e] the significances of ethnicity," rather than "pathologically, as symptomatic of the mutual implications between modernity and imperialism" (Chow 1991, xvi)? One way, I believe, is to read Asian American texts as theoretically informed and informing rather than as transparently referential human documents over which we place a grid of sophisticated Euro-American theory in order to extract meaning. This theory-as-grid model repeats the colonizing or imperialistic strategy of containment and domination of the "other" as inferior and dependent (on external theory to construct meaning), the very strategy we must seek to escape if Asian American literature is to speak to us in its own theoretically informed voice. To borrow an uncannily prescient image from Joy Kogawa's *Obasan*, we (academics interested in exploring theoretical issues in "ethnic" texts) must cease to be Grand Inquisitors interrogating Asian American texts and must learn to listen, must listen to learn:

> The Grand Inquisitor was carnivorous and full of murder. His demand to know was both a judgement and a refusal to hear. The more he questioned her, the more he was her accuser and murderer. The more he killed her, the deeper her silence became. What the Grand Inquisitor has never learned is that the avenues of speech are the avenues of silence. To hear my mother, to attend her speech, to

attend the sound of stone, he must first become silent. (Kogawa 1987, 228)

Trinh Minh-ha makes a strikingly similar point about the imperialistic potential of theory, although, paradoxically, she expresses it in the discourse to which we in the academy have become more attuned: "Indeed, theory no longer is theoretical when it loses sight of its own conditional nature, takes no risk in speculation, and circulates as a form of administrative inquisition. Theory oppresses, when it wills or perpetuates existing power relations, when it presents itself as a means to exert authority – the Voice of Knowledge" (1989, 42). This is not to say that theory does not also have a threatening or subversive potential capable of exposing oppressive ideologies, of deconstructing violent hierarchies, and of bringing about paradigm shifts; but we must always remain on guard against its totalizing tendencies (even as it theorizes difference), its own mystification-in-the-name-of-demystification, its authoritarian control of the "other" whereby *it* dissects, analyses, and classifies like Schoolteacher in Toni Morrison's *Beloved*.

To view Asian American literary texts as theoretically informed and informing enables us to escape the binary opposition described by Valerie Smith whereby the creative texts of women of color are made to work for white theorists/critics in that those texts become the praxis, the "material ground" that embodies and thus proves the white critics' abstract theories (1989, 45); it is also to appropriate to Asian American texts the power usually reserved for European texts. We frequently discard the arbitrary division between "theory" and "creative writing" when dealing with texts by writers like Hélène Cixous, Julia Kristeva, Luce Irigaray, and Monique Wittig, to the extent that what would traditionally be called "creative writing" becomes "theory"; but we do not usually extend the privilege of writing a more personalized and narrative form of theory to non-European writers.[4] Thus, texts by writers like Maxine Hong Kingston and Joy Kogawa are classified as autobiography or fiction, or autobiographical fiction, but rarely as theoretical fictions or fictionalized theory, autobiographical theory or theoretical autobiography, a topic I shall return to in a minute. I would stress now, however, that I offer these alternative categories, not in order to decide on one over the others, but to draw out the arbitrary and ideologically grounded nature of taxonomic classifications, which seek to contain texts through maintaining generic – and genetic – purity.

According to this approach, as I describe it in deliberately exaggerated form, "theory" is what metropolitan Europeans and Americans at the center of academic power write. We would do well, however, to remember Barbara Christian's claim that "people of color have always theorized – but in forms quite different from the Western form of abstract logic. And I am inclined to say that our theorizing . . . is often in narrative forms, in the stories we create, in riddles and proverbs, in the play with language" (1989, 226). Christian's notion of theory as inherent to certain forms of ethnic literature may allow us to escape the bind predicated on a binary, hierarchized division between theory and creative narrative. It also allows us to acknowledge that Asian American theory is indigenous to the literature, and so it must take account of the Asian American literary tradition rather than being a tool of domination that polices and mines the literary texts. In this respect we can learn a great deal from work already done in the area of African American literature and criticism/theory. As Henry Louis Gates Jr. has observed: "The challenge of black literary criticism is to derive principles of literary criticism from the black tradition itself, as defined in the idiom of critical theory but also in the idiom which constitutes the 'language of blackness.' . . . The sign of the successful negotiation of this precipice of indenture, of slavish imitation, is that the black critical essay refers to two contexts, two traditions – the Western and the black" (1984, 8). To explore black cultural difference, critics must redefine "theory" – which is not color-blind or neutral – by turning to the black vernacular tradition for models (Gates 1989, 28). We must pledge to undertake a similar task in relation to Asian American, and other "marginalized" and "minoritarian," literatures and theories.[5]

To take account of the Asian American literary tradition – or, more correctly, a number of traditions – and the theoretical concerns that grow out of that tradition is, of course, impossible within the scope of this chapter. Choices, then, are necessary – choices made with the knowledge that they inevitably skew the conclusions that will emerge: a different set of texts would produce different results. I have selected for consideration here four texts by Asian American women writers: *The Woman Warrior* (1976) by Maxine Hong Kingston, a native Chinese American; *Obasan* (1981) by Joy Kogawa, a native Japanese Canadian; *Dictée* (1982) by Theresa Hak Kyung Cha, a naturalized Korean American; and *Woman, Native, Other* (1989) by Trinh T. Minh-ha, a naturalized Vietnamese American. I selected these texts not because they constitute a general poetics of Asian American women's writing, nor because they are "representative" of their respective ethnic groups,[6] but because they focus in different ways on the issues I wish to examine: genre and gender, history and language, issues that have necessitated for these writers negotiations between "dominant" and "minority" cultures, between "masculine" and "feminine" positions, between "truth" and "fiction," between "Asian" and "American" selves. Of course, these issues do not divide neatly into the binary oppositions I have listed here, nor are they discrete; rather, they are interwoven to such an extent that it is virtually impossible to disentangle them completely, although for the purposes of presenting a linear argument, I shall attempt to do so.[7]

II

> The difficulty of getting by external gatekeepers, and particularly the unconscious assimilation of the "universality" of writing, cripples the normal growth of an ethnic literature. Cultural hegemony maintains itself not so much by imposing white writing upon the minority but by soliciting white writing from the objectified minority. (David Leiwei Li 1991, 214)

I want to begin my discussion of genre with a basic question: how and by whom are classificatory labels attached to books? This question is itself revealing of power relations in the fields of publishing, cataloguing, and criticism, areas still haunted by ghosts of colonial imperialism. The best example of this situation is Alfred A. Knopf's decision, about which Kingston had little say (see S. C. Wong 1992, 249), to publish *The Woman Warrior* as "autobiography," which in turn resulted in a Library of Congress subject classification of "United States – Biography." These labels are difficult to justify on traditional generic grounds: there is no single autobiographical "I" in *The Woman Warrior*, Maxine (the unnamed narrator) appearing sometimes in the first person, sometimes in the third, and with other first-person narrators telling their stories. Nor is there a central biographical figure, but instead a series of female figures from Kingston's family who form a composite or communal (auto)biographical subject that both is and is not Kingston herself. In addition to drawing on family history, most of which the narrator invents from bare bones given her by her mother, Kingston also makes extensive use of Chinese myths and legends, which she revises for her own purposes of self-fashioning. The text, then, has few of the conventions we have come to expect in "traditional" (that is, white, Western, male) autobiography, which is linear, chronological, progressive, and individualist.[8]

The only apparent reason for Knopf's decision to classify this text as autobiography seems to have been the previous success of Chinese American autobiographies, notably Pardee Lowe's *Father and Glorious Descendant*, published in 1943, and Jade Snow Wong's *Fifth Chinese Daughter*, originally published in 1945 and in a revised version in 1950. Appearing at a time when there was intense focus in America on Asia as theater of war, but when China was an ally of the United States (before the Communist takeover in 1949), these autobiographies enjoyed considerable success. As Elaine Kim points out in her detailed contextualizing of

these texts, "[b]oth writers express accommodation to rather than challenge of distortions about Chinese Americans and, by placing the blame
for whatever difficulties they faced upon themselves, their families, their
communities, or their race, promote the image of Chinese Americans as
the model minority" (1982, 61). Pandering to a white readership, Jade
Snow Wong defined her Chinese American identity through "whatever
was most exotic, interesting, and non-threatening to the white society
that was her reference point" (Kim 1982, 66), strategies that Kingston
completely reverses, even though her white publishers chose to ignore
that radical inversion of generic expectations when it came to marketing
her book to a predominantly mainstream audience.

Kingston herself insists, and proclaims in her subtitle, that her text fits
into the genre of memoirs: "When I write most deeply, fly the highest,
reach the furthest, I write like a diarist – that is, my audience is
myself. . . . I do not slow down to give boring exposition, which is information that is available in encyclopedias, history books, sociology, anthropology, mythology. (After all, I am not writing history or sociology,
but a 'memoir' like Proust . . . 'a form which [as Diane Johnson says]
. . . can neither [be] dismiss[ed] as fiction nor quarrel[ed] with as fact'"
(1982, 64). Exploring this avenue, Lee Quinby has recently pointed out
how *The Woman Warrior* follows the conventions of memoirs, which differ
significantly from those of autobiography; she concludes: "[u]nlike the
subjectivity of autobiography, which is presumed to be unitary and continuous over time, memoirs (particularly in their collective form) construct a subjectivity that is multiple and discontinuous. . . . In relation to
autobiography, then, memoirs function as countermemory" (1992, 299).
Compelling and illuminating as Quinby's argument is, I take issue with it
at a number of points. In particular, her insistence on reading the text as
memoir and not autobiography reveals a strong desire to stabilize generic
boundaries, when it seems to me that one of the most powerful and
productive aspects of life-writing by marginalized peoples is its ability to
challenge, destabilize, and subvert traditional generic conventions. True,
Kingston herself has proclaimed her book a memoir, but an appeal to
authorial intention seems strange from a critic as committed to Foucault
as Quinby is.

More interesting than any attempt to fix the generic boundaries of
Kingston's text is the effect texts like hers have had on the theorizing of
autobiography. Ironically, the overall result of Knopf's "misclassification"
has not been the measuring of Kingston's text by the standards of traditional, Eurocentric, male autobiography in order to find it wanting and
thus to dismiss it. Rather, the opposite has happened: *The Woman Warrior*
has had a profound and lasting effect on our definition of what constitutes the genre of autobiography, especially ethnic and women's autobi-

ography, which is now routinely identified as stressing group or community identity and as being written in a nonlinear, fluid, fragmented style. Another way of putting this is that *The Woman Warrior* has become an important theoretical text in bringing about a paradigm shift in (auto)biographical study, one that not only has changed the way we view contemporary autobiographies but also has assisted in the recuperation and revaluation of autobiographical writings from the past. The case is most forcefully put by Sidonie Smith, who, in her *Poetics of Women's Autobiography*, claims that "no single work captures so powerfully the relationship of gender to genre in twentieth-century autobiography as Maxine Hong Kingston's *Woman Warrior*. . . . [A]n autobiography about women's autobiographical storytelling, . . . it exemplifies the potential for works from the marginalized to challenge the ideology of individualism and with it the ideology of gender. . . . Using autobiography to create identity, [Kingston] breaks down the hegemony of formal 'autobiography'" (1987, 150–1).[9] Kingston has succeeded brilliantly at overcoming what David Leiwei Li calls the soliciting of "white writing from the objectified minority" that is clearly in evidence throughout much of early Asian American literature, which attempted to describe – usually in apologetic and euphemistic terms – Asian American cultural practices to a "mainstream" white audience by paradoxically marking difference as exotica while appealing to notions of universal humanity. But Kingston has ignored those constraints, has in fact recovered from the missteps of mainstream publishers to produce a radical and transforming work. As she says slyly, "I had to develop a whole new literary form to accommodate living with my mother" (quoted in Loke 1989, 50). Almost all critics now agree that Kingston's text is highly fictional – a rather ironic position, given its publication as autobiography and its subsequent winning of the National Book Critics Circle award for the best book of nonfiction published in 1976.

Kogawa's text has been taken as rather easier than Kingston's to classify because it follows the conventions of novelistic fiction, even though much of the third-person narrative is based on her own experiences of the evacuation, internment, and dispersal of Japanese Canadians during World War II, and thus qualifies as autobiographical fiction. Here too, however, the fictional narrative is combined with traditional source material for the writing of history – news accounts, "documents and letters from the files of Muriel Kitagawa,[10] Grace Tucker, T. Buck Suzuki and Gordon Nakayama," and a lengthy "[e]xcerpt from the memorandum sent by the Co-Operative Committee on Japanese Canadians to the House and Senate of Canada, April 1946" (1981, 248) – and the tone of the work swings radically from the soaring lyricism of what amounts to prose poems to the apparently neutral reportage of documentary history.

The result is not an organically whole, seamless, realistic novel, but a disruptive, or polyphonous, generic mixture that I have elsewhere identified as an example of "historiographic metafiction," a phrase I borrow from Linda Hutcheon. Hutcheon uses the term to describe "novels which are both intensely self-reflexive and yet lay claim to historical events and personages"; as a mode it incorporates fiction, history, and theory: "its theoretical self-awareness of history and fiction as human constructs (historio*graphic meta*fiction) is made the grounds for its rethinking and reworking of the forms and contents of the past" (1987, 12). As this definition implies, Hutcheon identifies a blurring of generic boundaries between fiction, history, and theory as a hallmark of such texts, and it is precisely such generic crossings that we find in the four texts under discussion.[11]

Of the four, Cha's *Dictée* has proved the most stubbornly resistant to conventional classification. The hard-cover edition I am using gives no Library of Congress cataloguing categories, and its publication by a small, noncommercial press (Tanam, which has since gone out of business) makes the task more difficult. Further, Cha's text is resolutely derivative (a term I do not use in a derogatory sense) at the same time that it is supremely original. It draws together quotations from, among others, Sappho, "The Autobiography of St. Therese of Lisieux, *Story of a Soul*: A New Translation from the Original Manuscripts by John Clarke," the "Petition from the Koreans of Hawaii to President Roosevelt," and French-language academic exercises; borrows biographical material from "the journals of Hyung Soon Huo"; narrates the life of Korean hero Yu Guan Soon; uses photographs, calligraphy, diagrams, maps, and other visual media ("documents, proof, evidence" [Cha 1982, 56]); reproduces, in script, rough drafts of parts of the text; and imitates film scripts in some sections (see Lew 1992, 92). This list is by no means exhaustive, but it gives a sense of the generic variety and pastiche quality of *Dictée*, which has been described by Michael Stephens as a "novel" (1986, 188); as "a recitative, and perhaps it is best understood, not as fiction, not as philosophy, not as religious meditation – all of which it is to various degrees – but as song" (191); and as "a fiction, a prose, a daring and poetic work, brilliantly original, full of charged idiomatic utterance, as well as being vanguard, even deeply philosophical, in its thought" (196). Susan Wolf claims that here "many of the issues of film, history, and autobiography merge in a fully developed way. *Dictée* is a book that cannot be categorized; Cha intricately combines several different writing styles, different voices, and different kinds of information" (Wolf 1986, 13). Later, I shall discuss the implications of this generic transgression; what I wish to stress here is that Cha's work could be classified as "theory," although theory that performs many of the issues it raises so that it becomes a form of praxis rather than mere abstraction or speculation, as the best theory inevitably does. (Here it is worth noting that Cha herself was a performance artist.)

The fourth text, Trinh's *Woman, Native, Other*, may seem at first glance to be totally outside the bounds of this grouping. Widely accepted as a significant contribution to the fields of feminist and postcolonial theory, and cultural and ethnic studies, this text/author package very much fits the mold of published academic products: Trinh was at the time of publication an associate professor of cinema at San Francisco State University; the book is published by Indiana University Press with the classificatory labels "Cultural Studies" and "Feminist Studies" on the back cover, and it exhibits the usual apparatus of academic texts (chapter and subchapter divisions, numerous quotations, endnotes, selected bibliography, and index, all used "straight" rather than parodically); and the discourse is to a large extent that of an academic immersed in contemporary critical theory. Yet there are important ways in which Trinh not only discusses in the abstract the necessity of subverting the academic discourse of the intellectual industry, but in which her text enacts such subversion by transgressing the boundaries of its genre. For one thing, she self-consciously frames her discussion of postcoloniality and feminism as a narrative, a personal story she feels compelled to tell and that she attempts to fit into the age-old tradition of women's storytelling, which she interprets as a form of building historical consciousness within a living female tradition. Thus, in the opening section, "The Story Began Long Ago . . . ," Trinh enters the discourse of oral storytelling (insofar as that is possible in a written text) and blurs the distinctions between herself as narrator and the world she narrates, subject and object: "The story began long ago . . . it is old. Older than my body, my mother's, my grandmother's. As old as my me, Old Spontaneous me, the world" (1989, 1). In this way, she attempts to enter the world she is about to deal with – the world of women, "natives," "others" as an equal rather than as the imperializing force of Theory. This opening also subtly enacts her own narrative method as she describes the narrative techniques of villagers in many parts of the world: "Never does one open the discussion by coming right to the heart of the matter. For the heart of the matter is always somewhere else than where it is supposed to be. To allow it to emerge, people approach it indirectly by postponing until it matures, by letting it come when it is ready to come" (1). Such a message "explains" the delay caused by this opening narrative, which diverts us momentarily from "the heart of the matter," the "theory" that is the center of this text; but it also calls into question the very concept of theory as being of central importance: if "the heart of the matter is always somewhere else than where it is supposed to be," then surely the theoretical center of this text both is and is not its heart. This "marginal" introduction surely has as much claim to being the heart of the matter. In autorepresentational fashion, Trinh problematizes – perhaps even subverts from within – her own and all academic projects that would attempt to "explain" Third World peoples through analysis and dissection.

The "body" of Trinh's text is a dense, at times abstract, discourse on issues central to postcolonial and feminist study: language and writing, nativism and anthropology, difference, and storytelling. But throughout, Trinh disrupts the confident, settled nature of academic discourse with a number of strategies. She keeps returning to illustrative stories from which no overt conclusions are drawn; she re-visions language through creative use of hyphens and virgules; and, perhaps most disruptively, she intersperses her text with still photographs from her films (as well as a critic and theorist, Trinh is a filmmaker, a poet, and a composer). These photos interact with the written text in complex ways. At their most basic, they illustrate the text, giving "weight" and "substance" (as far as that is possible in a two-dimensional image, itself a re-presentation of the material world) to abstract or metaphorical concepts described in language. For example, the first set of photos (4) is of an Indian (South Asian) woman sewing with a long thread, a set of images illustrative of the metaphor (used not only by Trinh, but also by Kogawa and Kingston) of storytelling as an act of threading narrative elements together, of spinning and weaving a useful garment. In this way Trinh "concretizes" the metaphor at the same time as she attempts to align her work of storytelling (an act of cultural production) with the work of Third World women, who produce items of material culture that are both functional and aesthetic. This point is driven home in the next set of photos (14), in which the production of clay pots, palm fans, and building decorations is presented along with a quotation from Nikki Giovanni: "Poetry is the culture of a people. We are poets even when we don't write poems." Through this gesture of solidarity, this celebration of women's work and play, Trinh attempts to subvert the elitist position of academic theory and to present herself as engaged in ordinary, daily activities that are an integral part of the liberation struggle. "Mind work and mind play," she asserts, are not in any way superior to other expressive forms.

At the very moment when these photos concretize the written text, however, Trinh – in a postmodern move typical of those found in the other texts being considered here – does not allow us to forget that her whole text is language, sign systems, re-presentation; and language is never transparently referential. To emphasize the paradoxical nature of these pictures – they are and are not windows on the world – Trinh sandwiches images together, sometimes presenting a collage (25) and sometimes the equivalent of a film strip (24), but always reminding us that these are constructed images from another medium, fragments selected and ordered for a particular purpose, fictions in themselves, whose frames of blank space draw attention to their constructedness and fictionality. The multiple images of these women also draw to our attention their multiple subjectivities. At the same time, though, the stills are exactly what their name implies, and what Trinh describes in her text: "words, fragments, and lines that I love for no sound [a pun on "valid" and "silent"] reason; blanks, lapses, and silences that settle in the gaps of fresh air as soon as the inked space smells stuffy" (25). The images and the writing become, then, mirrors, "the machinery of endless reflexivity" (26) (not to mention self-reflexivity), at the same time as they transport us beyond the "stuffy" "inked space" of theory. The text simultaneously installs and subverts its own authority, presenting itself as constructed fiction at the very moment it gestures beyond the closed world of the text to link with the material world.

What should be obvious from this brief account is that Trinh's "theory" is not the usual abstraction we have come to expect; instead, it shares a number of elements in common with the more "creative" texts I am examining in this grouping. What I am suggesting, then, is that genres are not compartmentalized boxes; rather, they exist as points on a continuum, constantly merging, blending, shifting, like racial or gendered positions, never fixed or pure. All of these texts illustrate graphically that no text exists entirely within a single discourse system, but operates within and between a variety of discourses that overlap and intersect. All of these texts pose, to greater or lesser degrees, postmodern challenges to traditional generic boundaries, opting instead for a technique of pastiche that utilizes and juxtaposes a host of generic conventions and discourses, even a variety of media. In their problematizing mixtures of history and fiction, (auto)biography and myth, lyrics and diaries, legends and prosaic dailiness, photographs and words, they reject all forms of univocality. Such an approach is not, of course, unique to Asian American literature; the use of meta-texts and para-texts has become the norm of postmodernist art. What particularly interests me is how such methods of transgressive pastiche might be used for political and theoretical purposes by "minority" women writers. How are these techniques and strategies – these new conventions – used to foreground theoretical questions and to engage us, as readers, in political struggle?

There cannot be a single answer to this broad question, but a starting point might be to suggest that, by employing neglected, marginalized, and feminized genres like diaries, memoirs, letters, and photographic stills, these texts form an important part of the feminist challenge to the traditional, patriarchal hierarchies of genre. In employing multiple narrative modes and discourses, they also mount powerful challenges to the masculinist, Western notion of a unified self and posit the self as a split, multiple, and discontinuous subject, as has been recognized by many critics. Perhaps most important, however, is the way these texts problematize the act of reconstructing history by interlacing it with the production of fiction. In examining the issues that surround the transformation of empirical events into historical text and complicating these issues by drawing parallels between how history and fiction are made, they expose and explore crucial questions for those silenced "minority" groups that have all too often been denied access to the textual production of either history or fiction. Further, these texts are doubly revealing because their narrative positions are those of doubly marginalized subjects: Asian American women.

III

> I am weary of starting from scratch each time I speak or write, as if there were no history behind us, of hearing that among the women of color, Asian women are the least political, or the least oppressed, or the most polite. (Mitsuye Yamada 1981, 71)

Like the return of the repressed, history, or more correctly histories, both public and personal, have recently been reinscribed in the discourse of literary criticism/theory, from which they were banished to the wilderness by the dominance of the New Criticism and other formalist approaches, as well as by structuralism and certain forms of deconstruction. Histories, however, have never been absent for long from "minority" discourses, which have almost always insisted on the presence of the past in the formation of identity or ethnic subjectivity, even though – or *because* – that past has frequently been ignored or silenced by the dominant culture.

The plea by Asian American writers for an approach to their texts as culturally and historically specific is not new, then; the example quoted above is from the late seventies, and in a recent collection of essays on Asian American literature Stephen Sumida has argued vigorously that "literary theories based heavily on linguistics, when these theories are ahistorical, are insufficient and often misleading when applied to Hawaii's literatures. One must also closely read, interpret, and question Hawaii's past and contemporary histories and historiographies in order simply to make a start at interpreting and judging" (1992, 230). Sumida's model of placing literary texts in their historical, geographical, social, and cultural context brilliantly illuminates "local" literatures, texts produced initially for local consumption by an audience that shares the same values and knowledge as the writer. When such texts are read outside of this local context, they become open to ethnocentric misinterpretations, a term I use to indicate not openly hostile interpretations by arrogant readers who see themselves as "superior" to the culture encoded in the text, but interpretations that are ignorant of the text's cultural context and of their own culturally coded and historically specific perspectives. To avoid such misreadings, elaborate contextualizing is necessary for the "outside"/ uninformed reader.

There is, however, another model of reading that does not displace or supersede Sumida's text–context model, but which emerges from recent postmodern Asian American texts that are not so decidedly "local" in nature and that appeal consciously to a wider reading audience.[12] The four books I am examining fall into this category; Kingston's and Kogawa's have succeeded in finding places in the canons of American and Canadian literature. These texts are, of course, produced in culturally and historically specific moments that register particular significances;[13] but as highly self-reflexive and autorepresentational fictions, they also seek to interrogate, revise, and theorize history, to explore the whole concept of historiography (and its relation to autobiography) by examining the complex interconnection of history and language. Like all fiction they are historically mediated forms, but they also mediate history, questioning and affecting our understanding of the past and how that past is conveyed through language, is textualized as history. They perform what Rey Chow considers the "positive" role of theory, "the programmatic acts of funda-mentally reconceptualizing the past" (1991, xvi) and thus shaping the future. They enact the threatening potential of theory to expose the workings of ideology, to uncover the matrices of established power rela-tions, and to challenge traditional canons and official histories. These texts problematize not only the text–context division but also the theory–narrative fiction division; they recount and interrogate, are shaped by and shape, history and theory.

It seems to me that here too we might learn some lessons from the different phases through which African American criticism has passed. In the 1960s, with the advent of Black Studies programs at many American universities, African American literature was treated as simple historical or sociological documentation, an approach that implied it had not achieved the privileged status of "art." In the mid- and late-1970s, how-ever, with the "reconstruction of instruction" project, there was a shift toward the examination of the "blackness" of texts through their use of language. Political and ideological concerns were deliberately subordi-nated to formalist or "literary" issues.[14] This strict text-based phase has also passed, so the most recent theory provides us with intricate close readings that also attend to the rich social text; in other words, the division between history/ideology/politics, on the one hand, and language/form/text, on the other, has been exposed as too simple – some might say fallacious. What we should be examining in/through Asian American and other "minority" literatures is not history *or* language, but history *and* language, which is precisely the complex relationship explored in texts like Kingston's, Kogawa's, Cha's, and Trinh's.

It is not always easy, or strategically advantageous, to admit to the complexity of the relationship between history and language. Because Asian Americans have for so long been a silenced (rather than a silent) minority, the temptation obviously exists simply to produce a counterhistory that would contradict the "official" version disseminated by the dominant culture. After all, to have one's voice heard, one's history read, after decades of silencing is a major achievement. Kingston herself points out the need to inscribe such a counterhistory, made up of erased aspects of the "official" version, in her description of the genesis of "The Laws" section of her second (auto)biographical fiction, *China Men:* "The mainstream culture doesn't know the history of Chinese-Americans, which has been written and written well. The ignorance makes a tension for me, and in the new book [*China Men*] I just couldn't take it any more. So all of a sudden, right in the middle of the stories, plunk – there is an eight-page section of pure history" (Pfaff 1980, 26). As I have argued elsewhere, the tension Kingston experiences here registers her resistance to writing "pure history," a factual account of the discrimination leveled against the Chinese who came to America that stands out as anomalous in her dialogical or polyphonous narrative, with its multivalent truths. Yet there is also a sense in which "The Laws" is ironic: by imitating the monological voice of authorizing History – the history imposed by the dominant culture that made the laws – this section uncovers both the dullness of this voice and its deafness to other, competing voices, those of the minorities suffering legalized discrimination (Goellnicht 1992, 196–7).

In fact, the necessity of recuperating the past for survival in the present and growth in the future is a compelling impulse in all four texts: for "minorities" written out of "official" history, recorded memory is not a luxury, an academic exercise, but the very proof of existence: "we were/ are here." Again and again in these texts, the act of re-membering, of putting fragments back together, of reclaiming the body (of flesh, history, and memory) is presented as essential for survival. Words must flow if "minority" individuals and cultures are to survive and to find voice. It is therefore no accident that both *Obasan* and *Dictée* open with compelling descriptions of speech straining to be born out of silence, to give voice to identity: "Beneath the grass the speaking dreams and beneath the dreams is a sensate sea. The speech that frees comes forth from that amniotic deep. To attend its voice, I can hear it say, is to embrace its absence. But

I fail the task. The word is stone. . . . Unless the stone bursts with telling, unless the seed flowers with speech, there is in my life no living word" (Kogawa, *Obasan*; cf. Cha, *Dictée* 3, 5).

But while recognizing the importance of uttering the past for the construction of identity, many Asian American texts have simultaneously been acutely cognizant of the difficulty of knowing the past through language, which is never a neutral container of factual information, but always an ideologically loaded tool whose workings need to be explored and explicated. The task is especially important because language is constitutive of the subject (which can therefore never be unified or whole, but is always already disseminated and discontinuous) and has been used by dominant cultures to produce compliant subjects. All of these authors are haunted by the knowledge that the discourse of history has worked to support the position of the dominant culture, whether that culture is white North America or Imperial Japan (the colonizing power in the Korea depicted by Cha). In either case, the dominant/colonizing culture used language to manufacture consent and acquiescence, to mask material and physical conditions, to police and censor thoughts. Thus, as Cha points out:

> The enemy becomes abstract. The relationship becomes abstract. The nation the enemy the name becomes larger than its own identity. . . . Japan has become the sign. The alphabet. The vocabulary. To *this* enemy people. . . . To the other nations who are not witnesses, who are not subject to the same oppressions, they cannot know. Unfathomable the words, the terminology: enemy, atrocities, conquest, betrayal, invasion, destruction. They exist only in the larger perception of History's recording, that affirmed, admittedly and unmistakably, one enemy nation has disregarded the humanity of another. (1982, 32)

Language is the powerful tool, the sign system, used by the colonizer to subject, control, discipline, and punish occupied Korea through the imposition of Japanese as the official language of the occupied territory. And as well as the Japanese occupiers, there were European imperialists who also used language to dominate and oppress, as the French translation exercises – imitations of the school exercises faced by a child – that form a significant portion of the text, indicate. The translation exercises include such statements as "Paris is not only the capital of France, it is the capital of the world" (15). Similarly, the quotations from the Roman Catholic catechism demonstrate how European religion performs a disciplinary function through its claim to panoptic vision and linguistic superiority: "*Everything is visible to God. Thought as visible as word as act. . . . God is every-*

where. . . . God who has made me in His own likeness. . . . Acquiesce, to the correspondence. Acquiesce, to the messenger. Acquiesce, to and for the complot in the Hieratic tongue. Theirs. Into Their tongue, the counter-script, my confession in Theirs. Into Theirs. To scribe to make hear the words, to make sound the words, the words, the words made flesh" (17–18).

Yet, for Cha, language, despite its tremendous potential for control, is never powerful enough to convey the reality of material conditions, "the volume of blood, the physical substance blood as measure, that rests as record, as document." Words fail to move the international community because they are "[n]ot physical enough. Not to the very flesh and bone" (32). Thus, "[t]o the others [foreign countries], these accounts are about (one more) distant land, like (any other) distant land" (33). All Cha as narrator can do is begin her text with a prayer adopted from Sappho, another powerful woman writer: "May I write words more naked than flesh, stronger than bone, more resilient than sinew, sensitive than nerve." At the same moment as she recognizes the impossibility of this task – for language can never totally capture life – the narrator, like her precursor from Lesbos, still hopes to convey her knowledge and under-standing, for that is the best that language can and should do. She hopes that her words will enter the dialogical fray as another telling voice, powerful enough to combat that of the dominant culture.

Kogawa, too, through her narrator, Naomi Nakane, expresses a great deal of ambivalence about the relationship between language and history, not only because of the manipulative power of language to create differ-ent versions of "truth," but also because of the impossibility of language ever conveying absolute truth, signifier and signified being irrevocably split. Kogawa thematizes the ability of language to "disguise any crime" (1981, 34) through the observations of Naomi's maternal aunt, Emily Kato, who is acutely aware of the fascist use made of words and names by the Canadian government and press during and after World War II. In this discourse, the Vancouver collection center for Japanese Canadians becomes the Pool, the area along the West Coast from which Japanese Canadians were banished becomes "the protected area," and the prisons in the remote areas of British Columbia to which Japanese Canadians were sent become "Interior Housing Projects." Emily rails against the "power of print" (36) that shapes, rather than merely reflects, reality for both the victimizers and the victims, its manipulation resulting in empiri-cal, concrete actions by the government and white majority against the Japanese Canadian minority.

The power of language to construct reality for a whole society proves especially threatening to a disenfranchised racial minority, which does not have access to the media or other avenues of power and speech. To combat this disadvantage, Emily becomes "a word warrior," adopting language as her own weapon, which she turns against the dominant culture when she, in her words, "write[s] the vision and make[s] it plain" (32). She urges Naomi to do the same, but Naomi is too aware of the impossibility of such a task, of the ambiguities and distortions in language, to embrace speech and writing so unequivocally. As she says, "For her [Emily], the vision is the truth as she lives it. . . . The truth for me is more murky, shadowy and grey" (32), always provisional and partial, never clear and absolute. That Naomi maintains the self-consciousness to recognize the uncertainties in epistemology is her abiding strength: she knows that history is not fixed, but discursive, a "form of saying" that is always in a state of flux. So aware of this is she that at times she doubts the efficacy of Emily's words to represent reality or effect change: "what good they do, I do not know – those little black typewritten words – . . . They do not touch us where we are planted here in Alberta. . . . The words are not made flesh. Trains do not carry us home" (189). But Naomi is also vividly aware that not to have access to language amounts to an inability to shape recorded history, so that the minority is condemned to the history formed for it by the dominant culture. To remain silent in the face of oppression, as Uncle and Obasan have done, is to be "rendered voiceless, stripped of car, radio, camera and every means of communication" (111); it is to erase oneself from the map of history, to become invisible. Naomi thus ventures into her version of history, but always with the understanding that it is partial, incomplete, provisional. She recognizes that in shaping history through narrative one must remain self-consciously aware of the manipulative power of language so as to avoid making absolute truth-claims for one's vision. The self and the history one constructs through language thus remain dynamic and dialogical, a disruptive excess capable of contesting any univocal claims to History.[15]

Cha, too, hopes to combat the violence and propaganda of the West – of her adopted country, the United States – which, in claiming the Lacanian position of the Father, the one who names and thus determines symbolic reality, has violated her mother country, Korea, by severing her in two, "under the title of liberators who have conveniently named the severance, Civil War. Cold War. Stalemate" (1982, 81). Through this act of naming by the Father/America, SHE/Korea/the mother has been projected as split, divided against herself – "SHE opposes Her" (87) – the site of self-division imposed by imperial powers as language splits the mother. Yet this divided body of the mother culture, which is shaped by language, simultaneously manages to escape total entrapment in language, material culture always managing to exceed the boundaries of any particular discourse: "From its memory dust escapes the particles still material still respiration move" (87). Cha's text itself is intent on offering an alternative discourse to the dominant one, on evoking Korea *"From another epic another history. From the missing narrative. From the multitude of narratives. Missing. From the chronicles. For another telling for other recitations"* (81). She is self-conscious enough about the limitations of her own history and her own discursive field to know that this will be "another telling" rather than "THE telling," but it is necessary as a groping toward a truth that always already eludes and exceeds language.

I want to close this section on history and language by returning to Trinh's theoretico-narrative text, which concisely summarizes a great deal of what I have been trying to say. Trinh comments that "historical analysis is nothing other than the reconstruction and redistribution of a pretended order of things, the interpretation or even transformation of documents given and frozen into monuments. The re-writing of history is therefore an endless task, one to which feminist scholars have devoted much of their energy" (1989, 84). The onus, she points out, is on all of us to help deliver the multiple facets of humanity's story, which is greater than history and which crosses all disciplinary and generic boundaries:

> The story depends upon every one of us to come into being. It needs us all, needs our remembering, understanding, and creating what we have heard together to keep on coming into being. The story of a people. Of us, peoples. Story, history, literature (or religion, philoso-phy, natural science, ethics) – all in one. They call it the tool of primitive man, the simplest vehicle of truth. . . . On the one hand, each society has its own politics of truth; on the other hand, being truthful is being in the in-between of all regimes of truth. (119–21)

Trinh enunciates a message all these texts expound to varying degrees; not a retreat to a traditional notion of "universalism" (which was vested interest masquerading as universal truth), but a call for as many texts as possible to come into being, so that out of the dialogue of voices, the disruptive excess of heteroglossia, may emerge some form of harmonious tension.

It is no accident, I think, that the three other texts discussed above conclude by staging scenes of harmoniously negotiated tension that ex-emplify or enact dialogism. *The Woman Warrior* ends with Maxine nego-tiating a balance between her mother and her newly independent self through the story of Ts'ai Yen, "a story my mother told me . . . recently, when I told her I also talk-story. The beginning is hers, the ending mine" (1976, 240). The voices of mother and daughter, of Han and "barbarian," merge and mingle here, but neither dominates or assimilates the other; instead, they enter into dialogue, seeking identity through mutual difference, through the heterogeneity and hybridity of multiple, shifting subject positions. Similarly, Kogawa's novel closes with an epiphany of "water and stone dancing. It's a quiet ballet, soundless as breath" (1981, 247). The scene brings together and holds in harmoniously negotiated tension the "stone" of silence and the "stream" of language that have run throughout the novel, affirming that both are necessary and valuable for life. Cha's text also ends with a scene depicting a harmonious moment between mother and child that takes place at "early dusk or dawn when light is muted" (1982, 179), a between-stage. As the child is lifted to the window by the mother, she sees the "[t]rees [that] adhere to silence in attendance to the view to come," but she also requests the unleashing of "ropes tied to weights of stones . . . to break stillness bells fall a peal to sky." Mother and child, silence and sound, reticence and celebration, stillness and movement exist simultaneously, mutually supporting and contending with each other, like *yin* and *yang* in the Taoist Way.

Ultimately, I trust that these texts lift me up to the window, acting as agents that enable me to see – even if it is through a glass darkly – and that assist my voice, the voice of a white male critic from an-other world, to enter into dialogue with theirs. As Maxine, the narrator of *The Woman Warrior*, says about the life story of her no-name aunt, "[u]nless I see her life branching into mine, she gives me no ancestral help" (1976, 10). But Maxine also comes to recognize that "branching into" does not entail her domination of the aunt's stories. She, like me, must learn to listen if these stories are to become ones that "translate well" (243).

ACKNOWLEDGMENTS

I wish to thank King-Kok Cheung for her enabling criticism and enduring patience. I am perpetually grateful to Susan Chang-Hong and to our children, Sophie and Julian, my immediate community, who keep me honest and who have informed this chapter in more ways than they could ever know.

NOTES

1. To pose this question, of course, exposes academic hubris, the same hubris that underpins the concept of a survey or mapping of the field, as if one individual who is embedded in the field could attain the spec(tac)ular position outside/above the discursive field from which to survey the whole. This chapter, then, does not pretend to be a survey. I should also acknowledge here that I was goaded into my opening questions by Karin Aguilar-San Juan's challenge to my "right" as a white male academic to speak about texts by Asian American women (see Aguilar-San Juan 1991, 187–8).
2. On the "ethnicity school" debate, see Cheung 1993, 20–1; Fox-Genovese

1990; Lauter 1991; Sollors 1986a, 1986b, 1990; Wald 1987; S. C. Wong 1993, 14–15.

3. The most detailed and sophisticated theorizing of Asian American subjectivity as heterogeneous, hybrid, and multiple is by Lisa Lowe, who, like San Juan, argues against the notion of a fixed or essentialized "identity" or "nation." She states: "Taking seriously the heterogeneities among Asian Americans in California, we must conclude that the grouping 'Asian American' is not a natural or static category; it is a socially constructed unity, a situationally specific position that we assume for political reasons. It is 'strategic' in Gayatri Spivak's sense of a 'strategic use of a positive essentialism in a scrupulously visible political interest'" (1991, 39; see also S. C. Wong 1993, 6). The one danger I see in the stress on difference within and among ethnic groups, on multiply intersecting factors forming the ethnic subject, and on fluid or shifting positionality is that the dominant group may come to see all groups as "different but equal" ("We're all different, so what's the difference?"), a concept supported by official, state-sponsored "multiculturalism," which deliberately obscures differential relations of power within and among groups, and thus serves to keep the "dominant" group dominant. To fall into that trap would be totally self-defeating: "difference" would become a new universalism.

4. Texts like Wittig's *Les Guérillères* and *The Lesbian Body*, Cixous's plays, and Kristeva's *About Chinese Women* are considered to be both theoretically and artistically significant, examples of *écriture féminine*, a disruptive excess that breaks the generic boundaries imposed by masculine discourse; some "theoretical" texts, like Kristeva's "Stabat Mater," Irigaray's "The Looking Glass, from the Other Side" and "When Our Lips Speak Together" (both in *This Sex Which Is Not One*), and Cixous's "The Laugh of the Medusa," use self-consciously creative/artistic or lyrical/poetic discourse in order to undermine the masculinist notion of theory as speculative abstraction. For discussions of how Kingston's work compares to French feminist "theory," in particular how her concerns extend beyond those of French feminism, see Rabine 1987 and Goellnicht 1991.

5. The dual cultural heritage of Asian Americans is an issue that has caused a good deal of debate. Frank Chin and Jeffery Paul Chan warned in the early 1970s that "[t]he concept of the dual personality successfully deprives the Chinese-American of all authority over language and thus a means of codifying, communicating and legitimizing his experience. Because he is a foreigner, English is not his native tongue. Because he was born in the U.S., Chinese is not his native tongue" (1972, 76). Yet Chin's self-promotion as a Chinatown Cowboy stressed a dual heritage, and more recently he has championed a return to the "heroic" traditions of Asian literature as a means of fostering cultural assurance (see Chin 1991) at the same time as he insists on his Americanness. Maxine Hong Kingston argues for a dual – but not equally weighted – cultural heritage: "[W]e ought to leave out the hyphen in 'Chinese-American,' because the hyphen gives the word on either side equal weight, as if linking two nouns. . . . Without the hyphen, 'Chinese' is an adjective and 'American' a noun; a Chinese American is a type of American"

(1982, 60). For a more rigorous critique of the positive aspects of dual heritage, "the comforting illusion of a stabilized schizophrenia ('both/and,' that image most exploited by ideology)," see David Palumbo-Liu 1990. Much recent criticism of Asian American literature has focused on dual heritage or plural heritage/hybridity as a form of dialogism or polyphony that is a source of strength rather than weakness (see Cheung 1993, 15–23).

6. The notion of representativeness is itself an imperialistic one whereby a mainstream audience assumes it can learn about an ethnic group by reading a single text, treating literature as ethnography. In an interview with Arturo Islas, Kingston insists that her fictions do not "represent the race" and that "each artist has a unique voice" (Islas 1983, 11; see also Kingston 1982, 63). Ironically, while a number of white readers have insisted on viewing Kingston's text as "representative," a number of important Asian American critics – most notably Frank Chin and his group of coeditors – have faulted it for not being "representative" enough, for not providing an "accurate" or "authentic" picture of Asian American life. Both sets of readers fall into the trap of reading autobiography as ethnography, whereby "[t]he individual's life serves the function of conveying anthropological information" (S. C. Wong 1992, 262). See also Cheung 1990 for another comprehensive and convincing response to Kingston's critics.

7. There are other reasons for selecting texts by these four writers. Kingston and Kogawa come from a slightly older generation of writers, whose works do not engage Continental critical theory in the direct way that the works of Cha and Trinh do. Cha and Trinh were both graduate students at Berkeley in the late 1970s, when semiotic, feminist, and poststructuralist theories were on the rise; both have worked in other media, notably film and video, which have been heavily theorized.

8. In what is considered a seminal essay on the theory of autobiography, Georges Gusdorf claims that autobiography is "a solidly established literary genre, its history traceable in a series of masterpieces from the *Confessions* of St. Augustine to Gide's *Si le grain ne meurt*" (1980, 28). Gusdorf's canon consists entirely of texts by European men; he claims, in fact, that autobiography "expresses a concern peculiar to Western man" (29). Needless to say, Gusdorf's theoretical model is extremely narrow and would by no means include all autobiographical writings by Western men, which are far more various than he allows; I think, for example, of Coleridge's *Biographia Literaria*, a dialogical text that consists of a pastiche of genres. On Kingston's breaking of the autobiographical mold and her subversion of the expectations of a white audience, see S. C. Wong 1992. See also S. C. Wong 1991 on Kingston's adaptation, revision, and expansion of traditional Chinese sources.

9. Kingston's text features prominently in numerous recent works – both single-author texts and collections of essays – theorizing ethnic and women's autobiography, whether as an example of plural or communal subjectivity, of a poststructuralist split or divided subjectivity, of an ambivalent recuperation of the mother, of a search for voice, etc. Examples include essays by Cheung (1988), Demetrakopoulos (1980), Eakin (1985), Friedman (1988), Frye (1988), Gilead (1988), Goellnicht (1991), Homsher (1979), Hunt (1985),

Juhasz (1979, 1985), Li (1988), Lim (1992), Miller (1983), Quinby (1992), Rabine (1987), Shirley K. Rose (1987), Schenck (1988), Sidonie Smith (1987), Wang (1985), and S. C. Wong (1988, 1992).

10. See Kitagawa's *This Is My Own* (1985).

11. See Goellnicht 1989 for a more detailed discussion. Manina Jones has also used Hutcheon's theory of historiographic metafiction to read *Obasan*, which she labels "a simultaneously literary, historical, and theoretical work" (1990, 214). King-Kok Cheung applies Hutcheon's term to the works of Kogawa, Kingston, and Yamamoto (1993, 13; see also 152).

12. Sumida agrees with Wing Tek Lum's assertion that "in Hawaii today poetry is generally characterized by a 'concreteness' of description, imagery, and allusion. Local poets . . . eschew self-consciously crafted postmodernist constructions and deconstructions of thoughts, emotions, perceptions, and associational designs" (Sumida 1992, 229). In describing postmodern Asian American Literature as less "local," I want to stress that I am not attempting to establish a violent hierarchy in which Hawai'i figures as a simpler society than the metropolitan mainland; such a view would completely ignore the complex racial and cultural diversity of Hawaiian society and its literatures. Nor do I wish to imply that postmodern Asian American literature, by appealing to a wider audience, escapes the possibility of falling victim to ethnocentric misinterpretation; Kingston's "Cultural Mis-readings" gives the lie to such a view.

13. Kingston's *The Woman Warrior* (1976) and *China Men* (1980) were published a century after the California constitution restricting the rights of Chinese and just before the centennial of the first Chinese Exclusion Act (1882). In 1978, equal treatment of American immigrants from all countries was initiated, and the 1980 census confirmed Kingston's prediction that it would "show a million or more" persons of Chinese ancestry to be living in the United States. Kingston hopes to shape the future treatment of Chinese Americans by narrating a heroic past. Similarly, Kogawa's text is intricately entangled with the quest for reparations by Japanese Canadians and had profound influence on public opinion in Canada. When, in late 1988, the Canadian government finalized a negotiated compensation settlement with the Japanese Canadian community, Ed Broadbent, then leader of the New Democratic Party, read parts of *Obasan* in the House of Commons.

14. On the development of the "reconstruction of instruction" project, see *Minority Language and Literature*, ed. Dexter Fisher (1977), *Afro-American Literature: The Reconstruction of Instruction*, ed. Dexter Fisher and Robert Stepto (1979), and *English Literature: Opening Up the Canon*, ed. Leslie Fiedler and Houston Baker (1981).

15. This discussion of Kogawa's treatment of language and history is adapted from a longer version I presented earlier (1989, 290–5). On this subject, see also Cheung 1993, 11–14, 133–9, and Jones 1990; on the broader question of language/speech and silence in the novel, see also Fujita 1985, Gottlieb 1986, Lim 1990, Magnusson 1988, M. R. Rose 1988, and Willis 1987. Fujita and Cheung achieve the most culturally sensitive discussions of silence in *Obasan*.

■■■■ **WORKS CITED**

Aguilar-San Juan, Karin. 1991. "Exploding Myths, Creating Consciousness: Some First Steps Toward Pan-Asian Unity." In *Piece of My Heart: A Lesbian of Colour Anthology*, ed. Makeda Silvera. Toronto: Sister Vision Press.

Blinde, Patricia Lin. 1979. "The Icicle in the Desert: Perspective and Form in the Works of Two Chinese-American Women Writers." *MELUS* 6.3:51–71.

Cha, Theresa Hak Kyung. 1982. *Dictée*. New York: Tanam.

Cheung, King-Kok. 1988. "'Don't Tell': Imposed Silences in *The Color Purple and The Woman Warrior*." *PMLA* 103.2:162–74.

———. 1990. "The Woman Warrior versus The Chinaman Pacific: Must a Chinese American Critic Choose between Feminism and Heroism?" In *Conflicts in Feminism*, ed. Marianne Hirsch and Evelyn Fox Keller, 234–51. New York: Routledge.

———. 1993. *Articulate Silences: Hisaye Yamamoto, Maxine Hong Kingston, Joy Kogawa*. Ithaca, NY: Cornell Univ. Press.

Chin, Frank. 1991. "Come All Ye Asian American Writers of the Real and the Fake." In *The Big Aiiieeeee!: An Anthology of Chinese American and Japanese American Literature*, ed. Jeffery Paul Chan, Frank Chin, Lawson Fusao Inada, and Shawn Wong, 1–92. New York: Meridian.

Chin, Frank, and Jeffery Paul Chan. 1972. "Racist Love." In *Seeing Through Shuck*, ed. Richard Kostelanetz, 65–79. New York: Ballantine.

Chow, Rey. 1991. *Woman and Chinese Modernity: The Politics of Reading between West and East*. Minneapolis: Univ. of Minnesota Press.

Christian, Barbara. 1989. "The Race for Theory." In *Gender and Theory: Dialogues on Feminist Criticism*, ed. Linda Kauffman, 225–37. Oxford: Basil Blackwell.

Cixous, Hélène. 1976. "The Laugh of the Medusa." Trans. Keith Cohen and Paula Cohen. *Signs* 1.4:875–93.

Demetrakopoulos, Stephanie A. 1980. "The Metaphysics of Matrilinearism in Women's Autobiography." In *Women's Autobiography: Essays in Criticism*, ed. Estelle C. Jelinek. Bloomington: Univ. of Indiana Press.

Du Bois, W. E. B. 1903. *The Souls of Black Folk: Essays and Sketches*. Greenwich, CT: Crest, 1965.

Eakin, Paul John. 1985. *Fictions in Autobiography: Studies in the Art of Self-Invention*. Princeton, NJ: Princeton Univ. Press.

Fiedler, Leslie, and Houston A. Baker Jr., eds. 1981. *English Literature: Opening Up the Canon*. Baltimore: Johns Hopkins Univ. Press.

Fisher, Dexter, ed. 1977. *Minority Language and Literature: Retrospective and Perspective*. New York: Modern Language Association.

Fisher, Dexter, and Robert B. Stepto, eds. 1979. *Afro-American Literature: The Reconstruction of Instruction*. New York: Modern Language Association.

Fox-Genovese, Elizabeth. 1990. "Between Individualism and Fragmentation: American Culture and the New Literary Studies of Race and Gender." *American Quarterly* 42.1:7–34.

Friedman, Susan Stanford. 1988. "Women's Autobiographical Selves: Theory and Practice." In *The Private Self: Theory and Practice of Women's Autobiographical*

Writings, ed. Shari Benstock, 34–62. Chapel Hill: Univ. of North Carolina Press.

Frye, Joanne S. 1988. "*The Woman Warrior:* Claiming Narrative Power, Recreating Female Selfhood." In *Faith of a (Woman) Writer*, ed. Alice Kessler-Harris and William McBrien, 293–301. New York: Greenwood Press.

Fujita, Gayle K. 1985. " 'To Attend the Sound of Stone': The Sensibility of Silence in *Obasan.*" *MELUS* 12.3:33–42.

Gates, Henry Louis Jr. 1984. "Criticism in the Jungle." In *Black Literature and Literary Theory*, ed. Henry Louis Gates Jr., 1–24. New York: Methuen.

———. 1989. "Canon-Formation and the Afro-American Tradition." In *Afro-American Literary Study in the 1990s*, ed. Houston A. Baker Jr. and Patricia Redmond, 14–39. Chicago: Univ. of Chicago Press.

Gilead, Sarah. 1988. "Emigrant Selves: Narrative Strategies in Three Women's Autobiographies." *Criticism* 30.1:43–62.

Goellnicht, Donald C. 1989. "Minority History as Metafiction: Joy Kogawa's *Obasan.*" *Tulsa Studies in Women's Literature* 8.2:287–306.

———. 1991. "Father Land and/or Mother Tongue: The Divided Female Subject in Kogawa's *Obasan* and Hong Kingston's *The Woman Warrior.*" In *Redefining Autobiography in Twentieth-Century Women's Fiction*, ed. Janice Morgan and Colette T. Hall, 119–34. New York: Garland.

———. 1992. "Tang Ao in America: Male Subject Positions in *China Men.*" In *Reading the Literatures of Asian America*, ed. Shirley Geok-lin Lim and Amy Ling, 191–212. Philadelphia: Temple Univ. Press.

Gottlieb, Erica. 1986. "The Riddle of Concentric Worlds in *Obasan.*" *Canadian Literature* 109 (Summer): 34–53.

Gusdorf, Georges. 1980. "Conditions and Limits of Autobiography," trans. James Olney. In *Autobiography: Essays Theoretical and Critical*, ed. James Olney, 28–48. Princeton, NJ: Princeton Univ. Press.

Homsher, Deborah. 1979. "*The Woman Warrior*, by Maxine Hong Kingston: A Bridging of Autobiography and Fiction." *Iowa Review* 10.4:93–8.

Hunt, Linda. 1985. " 'I Could Not Figure Out What Was My Village': Gender Vs. Ethnicity in Maxine Hong Kingston's *The Woman Warrior.*" *MELUS* 12.3:5–12.

Hutcheon, Linda. 1987. "Beginning to Theorize Postmodernism." *Textual Practice* 1.1:10–31.

Irigaray, Luce. 1977/1985. *This Sex Which Is Not One*. Trans. Catherine Porter with Carolyn Burke. Ithaca, NY: Cornell Univ. Press.

Islas, Arturo. 1983. "Maxine Hong Kingston." In *Women Writers of the West Coast: Speaking of Their Lives and Careers*, ed. Marilyn Yalom, 11–19. Santa Barbara, CA: Capra.

Jones, Manina. 1990. "The Avenues of Speech and Silence: Telling Difference in Joy Kogawa's *Obasan.*" In *Theory between the Disciplines: Authority/Vision/Politics*, ed. Martin Kreiswirth and Mark A. Cheetham, 213–29. Ann Arbor: Univ. of Michigan Press.

Juhasz, Suzanne. 1979. "Towards a Theory of Form in Feminist Autobiography: Kate Millet's *Flying* and *Sita*; Maxine Hong Kingston's *The Woman Warrior.*" *International Journal of Women's Studies* 2.2:62–75.

————. 1985. "Maxine Hong Kingston: Narrative Technique and Female Identity." In *Contemporary American Women Writers: Narrative Strategies*, ed. Catherine Rainwater and William J. Scheick, 173–89. Lexington: Univ. of Kentucky Press.

Kim, Elaine H. 1982. *Asian American Literature: An Introduction to the Writings and Their Social Context*. Philadelphia: Temple Univ. Press.

Kingston, Maxine Hong. 1976. *The Woman Warrior: Memoirs of a Girlhood among Ghosts*. New York: Vintage, 1977.

————. 1980. *China Men*. New York: Knopf.

————. 1982. "Cultural Mis-readings by American Reviewers." In *Asian and Western Writers in Dialogue: New Cultural Identities*, ed. Guy Amirthanayagam, 55–65. London: Macmillan.

Kitagawa, Muriel. 1985. *This Is My Own: Letters to Wes and Other Writings on Japanese Canadians, 1941–1948*, ed. Roy Miki. Vancouver, B.C.: Talonbooks.

Kogawa, Joy. 1981/1983. *Obasan*. Markham. Ont.: Penguin.

Kristeva, Julia. 1974a/1986. *About Chinese Women*. Trans. Anita Barrows. New York: Rizzoli.

————. 1974b/1986. "Stabat Mater." In *The Kristeva Reader*, ed. Toril Moi, 160–86. New York: Columbia Univ. Press.

Lauter, Paul. 1991. "The Literatures of America: A Comparative Discipline." In *Canons and Contexts*. 48–96. New York: Oxford Univ. Press.

Lew, Walter K. 1992. *Excerpts From: Dikte for Dictée*. Republic of Korea: Yeul Eum Publishing Co.

Li, David Leiwei. 1988. "The Naming of a Chinese American 'I': Cross-Cultural Sign/ification in *The Woman Warrior*." *Criticism* 30.4:497–515.

————. 1991. "The Formation of Frank Chin and Formations of Chinese American Literature." In *Asian Americans: Comparative and Global Perspectives*, ed. Shirley Hune, Hyung-chan Kim, Stephen S. Fugita, and Amy Ling, 211–23. Pullman: Washington State Univ. Press.

Lim, Shirley Geok-lin. 1990. "Japanese American Women's Life Stories: Maternality in Monica Sone's *Nisei Daughter* and Joy Kogawa's *Obasan*." *Feminist Studies* 16.2:289–312.

————. 1992. "The Tradition of Chinese-American Women's Life Stories: Thematics of Race and Gender in Jade Snow Wong's *Fifth Chinese Daughter* and Maxine Hong Kingston's *The Woman Warrior*." In *American Women's Autobiography: Fea(s)ts of Memory*, ed. Margo Culley, 252–67. Madison: Univ. of Wisconsin Press.

Loke, Margarett. 1989. "The Tao Is Up." *New York Times Magazine*, 30 April, Sec. D: 28, 50, 52, 55.

Lowe, Lisa. 1991. "Heterogeneity, Hybridity, Multiplicity: Marking Asian American Differences." *Diaspora* 1.1:24–44.

Lowe, Pardee. 1943. *Father and Glorious Descendant*. Boston: Little, Brown.

Magnusson, A. Lynne. 1988. "Language and Longing in Joy Kogawa's *Obasan*." *Canadian Literature* 116 (Spring): 58–66.

Miller, Margaret. 1983. "Threads of Identity in Maxine Hong Kingston's *Woman Warrior*." *Biography* 6.1:13–33.

Palumbo-Liu, David. 1990. "Discourse and Dislocation: Rhetorical Strategies of

Asian-American Exclusion and Confinement." *LIT: Literature Interpretation Theory* 2:1–7.

Pfaff, Timothy. 1980. "Talk with Mrs. Kingston." *New York Times Book Review*, 15 June 1980, 1, 24–6.

Quinby, Lee. 1992. "The Subject of Memoirs: *The Woman Warrior's* Technology of Ideographic Selfhood." In *De/Colonizing the Subject: The Politics of Gender in Women's Autobiography*, ed. Sidonie Smith and Julia Watson, 297–320. Minneapolis: Univ. of Minnesota Press.

Rabine, Leslie W. 1987. "No Lost Paradise: Social Gender and Symbolic Gender in the Writings of Maxine Hong Kingston." *Signs* 12:471–92.

Rose, Marilyn Russell. 1988. "Politics into Art: Kogawa's *Obasan* and the Rhetoric of Fiction." *Mosaic* 21 (Spring): 215–26.

Rose, Shirley K. 1987. "Metaphors and Myths of Cross-Cultural Literacy: Autobiographical Narratives by Maxine Hong Kingston, Richard Rodriguez, and Malcolm X." *MELUS* 14.1:3–15.

San Juan, E., Jr. 1991. "Beyond Identity Politics: The Predicament of the Asian American Writer in Late Capitalism." *American Literary History* 3.3:542–65.

Schenck, Celeste. 1988. "All of a Piece: Women's Poetry and Autobiography." In *Life/Lines: Theorizing Women's Autobiography*, ed. Bella Brodzki and Celeste Schenck, 281–305. Ithaca, NY: Cornell Univ. Press.

Smith, Sidonie. 1987. *A Poetics of Women's Autobiography: Marginality and the Fictions of Self-Representation*. Bloomington: Indiana Univ. Press.

Smith, Valerie. 1989. "Black Feminist Theory and the Representation of the 'Other.'" In *Changing Our Own Words: Essays on Criticism, Theory, and Writing by Black Women*, ed. Cheryl A. Wall, 38–57. New Brunswick, NJ: Rutgers Univ. Press.

Sollors, Werner. 1986a. *Beyond Ethnicity: Consent and Descent in American Culture.* New York: Oxford Univ. Press.

———. 1986b. "A Critique of Pure Pluralism." In *Reconstructing American Literary History*, ed. Sacvan Bercovitch, 250–79. Cambridge, MA: Harvard Univ. Press.

———. 1990. "Of Mules and Mares in a Land of Difference; or, Quadrupeds All?" *American Quarterly* 42.2:167–90.

Stephens, Michael. 1986. *The Dramaturgy of Style: Voice in Short Fiction.* Carbondale: Southern Illinois Univ. Press.

Sumida, Stephen. 1992. "Sense of Place, History, and the Concept of the 'Local' in Hawaii's Asian/Pacific American Literatures." In *Reading the Literatures of Asian America*, ed. Shirley Geok-lin Lim and Amy Ling, 215–37. Philadelphia: Temple Univ. Press.

Trinh T. Minh-ha. 1989. *Woman, Native, Other: Writing Postcoloniality and Feminism.* Bloomington: Indiana Univ. Press.

Wald, Alan. 1987. "Theorizing Cultural Difference: A Critique of the 'Ethnicity School.'" *MELUS* 14.2:21–33.

Wang, Veronica. 1985. "Reality and Fantasy: The Chinese-American Woman's Quest for Identity." *MELUS* 12.3:23–31.

Willis, Gary. 1987. "Speaking the Silence: Joy Kogawa's *Obasan*." *Studies in Canadian Literature* 12.2:239–49.

Wittig, Monique. 1969/1985. *Les Guérillères*. Trans. David Le Vay. Boston: Beacon Press.

———. 1973/1986. *The Lesbian Body*. Trans. David Le Vay. Boston: Beacon Press.

Wolf, Susan. 1986. "Theresa Cha: Recalling Telling ReTelling." *Afterimage* 14:11–13.

Wong, Jade Snow. 1950. *Fifth Chinese Daughter*. New York: Harper & Row.

Wong, Sau-ling Cynthia. 1988. "Necessity and Extravagance in Maxine Hong Kingston's *The Woman Warrior:* Art and the Ethnic Experience." *MELUS* 15.1:3–26.

———. 1991. "Kingston's Handling of Traditional Chinese Sources." In *Approaches to Teaching Kingston's "The Woman Warrior,"* ed. Shirley Geok-lin Lim, 26–36. New York: Modern Language Association.

———. 1992. "Autobiography as Guided Chinatown Tour? Maxine Hong Kingston's *The Woman Warrior* and the Chinese-American Autobiographical Controversy." In *Multicultural Autobiography: American Lives,* ed. James Robert Payne, 248–79. Knoxville: Univ. of Tennessee Press.

———. 1993. *Reading Asian American Literature: From Necessity to Extravagance.* Princeton, NJ: Princeton Univ. Press.

Yamada, Mitsuye. 1981/1983. "Asian Pacific American Women and Feminism." In *This Bridge Called My Back: Writings by Radical Women of Color,* ed. Cherríe Moraga and Gloria Anzaldúa, 71–5. 2d ed. New York: Kitchen Table/Women of Color Press.

SELECTED BIBLIOGRAPHY

EDITOR'S NOTE: In this bibliography I have included all the book-length primary works and most of the secondary works listed by the contributors in their separate bibliographies. I have also added entries on my own, especially of works published since the compilation of *Asian American Literature: An Annotated Bibliography* (Cheung and Yogi 1988). As this cumulative bibliography is not divided according to nationalities or themes, readers interested in a particular group or topic should consult the selected bibliography in the relevant chapter.

BOOKS BY ASIAN PACIFIC AMERICAN WRITERS

Accomando, Claire Hsu. 1993. *Love and Rutabaga: A Remembrance of the War Years.* New York: St. Martin's Press.

Agha, Shahid Ali. 1972. *Bone-Sculpture: Poems.* Calcutta: Writers Workshop.

———. 1979. *In Memory of Begum Akhtar.* Calcutta: Writers Workshop.

———. 1987a. *The Half-Inch Himalayas.* Middletown, CT: Wesleyan Univ. Press.

———. 1987b. *A Walk through the Yellow Pages.* Tucson, AZ: Sun/Gemini Press.

———. 1991. *A Nostalgist's Map of America.* New York: Norton.

———. 1992. *The Beloved Witness: Selected Poems.* New Delhi: Penguin India.

Ai. 1973. *Cruelty.* Boston: Houghton Mifflin.

———. 1979. *Killing Floor.* Boston: Houghton Mifflin.

———. 1981. *Conversations: For Robert Lowell.* Saint Paul, MN: Toothpaste Press for Bookslinger.

———. 1986. *Sin: Poems.* Boston: Houghton Mifflin.

———. 1987. *Cruelty/Killing Floor.* New York: Thunder's Mouth Press.

———. 1993. *Greed: Poems.* New York: Norton.

Albalos, Edward. 1953. *Bartered Corn.* New York: Exposition Press.

Alexander, Meena. 1976. *The Bird's Bright Ring: A Long Poem.* Calcutta: Writers Workshop.

———. 1977. *I Root My Name.* Calcutta: United Writers.

———. 1978. *Without Place.* Calcutta: Writers Workshop.

———. 1988. *House of a Thousand Doors: Poems and Prose Pieces.* Washington, D.C.: Three Continents Press.

———. 1989. *The Storm: A Poem in Five Parts*. New York: Red Dust.

———. 1991. *Nampally Road*. San Francisco: Mercury House.

———. 1992. *Night-Scene, The Garden*. New York: Red Dust.

———. 1993. *Fault Lines: A Memoir*. New York: Feminist Press.

———. 1995. *River and Bridge*. New Delhi: Rupa.

Amirthanayagam, Indran. 1993. *The Elephants of Reckoning*. New York: Hanging Loose Press.

Angeles, Carlos. 1963. *A Stun of Jewels*. Manila: Alberto Florentino.

Aying. 1960. *Fanmei huagong jinyue wenxue ji* [A collection of literature against the American exclusion of Chinese laborers]. Beijing: Zhonghua shuju.

Bacho, Peter. 1991. *Cebu*. Seattle: Univ. of Washington Press.

Bannerjee, Himani. 1982. *A Separate Sky*. Toronto: Domestic Bliss.

———. 1986. *Doing Time*. Toronto: Sister Vision Press.

———. 1991. *Coloured Pictures*. Toronto: Sister Vision Press.

Barry, Lynda. 1988. *The Good Times Are Killing Me*. Seattle: Real Comet.

Bedi, Susham. 1994. *The Fire Sacrifice*. London: Heinemann Educational.

Bergonio, Gemma. 1985. *"Mirror at Dawn" and Other Poems*. City of Industry, CA: L.A.C. Publishing.

Berssenbrugge, Mei-Mei. 1971. *Fish Souls*. New York: Greenwood.

———. 1983. *The Heat Bird*. Providence: Burning Deck Press.

———. 1989. *Empathy*. Barrytown, NY: Station Hill Press.

Bezine, Ching Yun. 1991. *Children of the Pearl*. New York: New American Library, Signet.

———. 1992a. *On Wings of Destiny*. New York: New American Library, Signet.

———. 1992b. *Temple of the Moon*. New York: New American Library, Signet.

Bissoondath, Neil. 1985. *Digging up the Mountains*. Toronto: Macmillan.

———. 1988. *A Casual Brutality*. Toronto: Macmillan.

———. 1990. *On the Eve of Uncertain Tomorrows*. Toronto: Lester & Orpen Dennys.

Brainard, Cecilia Manguerra. 1988. *Woman with Horns and Other Stories*. Quezon City, Philippines: New Day Publishers.

———. 1991. *Song of Yvonne*. Quezon City, Philippines: New Day Publishers.

———. 1994. *When the Rainbow Goddess Wept*. New York: Dutton.

———. 1995. *Acapulco at Sunset and Other Stories*. New York: Anchor/Doubleday.

Buaken, Manuel. 1948. *I Have Lived with the American People*. Caldwell, ID: Caxton Printers.

Bulosan, Carlos. 1942. *Letters from America*. Prairie City, IL: J. A. Decker.

———. 1943. *The Voice of Bataan*. New York: Coward, McCann.

———. 1946/1977. *America Is in the Heart: A Personal History*. Seattle: Univ. of Washington Press.

———. 1944. *The Laughter of My Father*. New York: Harcourt, Brace.

———. 1960. *Sound of Falling Light: Letters in Exile*. Quezon City: Univ. of the Philippines Press.

———. 1977. *The Power of the People*. Ontario: Tabloid Books.

———. 1978. *The Philippines Is in the Heart*. Quezon City, Philippines: New Day Publishers.

———. 1979. "Writings of Carlos Bulosan." *Amerasia Journal* (special issue) 6.1.

———. 1983a. *Bulosan: An Introduction with Selections*. Ed. Epifanio San Juan Jr.

Manila: National Book Store.

———. 1983b. *If You Want to Know What We Are: A Carlos Bulosan Reader*. Ed. Epifanio San Juan Jr. Minneapolis, MN: West End Press.

———. 1990. *"The Power of Money" and Other Stories*. Quezon City, Philippines: Kalikasan Press.

———. 1991. *"Now You Are Still" and Other Poems*. Manila: Kalikasan Press.

———. 1995a. *The Cry and the Dedication*. Ed. E. San Juan, Jr. Philadelphia: Temple Univ. Press.

———. 1995b. *On Becoming Filipino: Selected Writings of Carlos Bulosan*. Ed. E. San Juan, Jr. Philadelphia: Temple Univ. Press.

Caigoy, Faustino. 1974. *Bitter Sweet Chocolate Meat*. Los Angeles: Inner City Cultural Center.

Carunungan, Celso Al. 1960. *Like a Brave Man: A Novel*. New York: Farrar Straus.

———. 1963. *"Return to Gomora" and Other Stories*. Manila: Alberto Florentino.

Castro, Fernando. 1969. *Big White American*. New York: Vantage.

Cha, Theresa Hak Kyung. 1982/1994. *DICTEE*. Berkeley: Third Woman Press.

Chandra, G. S. Sharat. 1993. *Immigrants of Loss*. Somerset: Hippotamus Press.

Chandra, Vikram. 1995. *Red Earth and Pouring Rain*. New York: Faber.

Chang, Diana. 1956/1994. *The Frontiers of Love*. Seattle: Univ. of Washington Press.

———. 1982. *The Horizon Is Definitely Speaking*. New York: Backstreet Editions.

———. 1984. *What Matisse Is After*. New York: Contact II.

Cheong, Fiona. 1991. *The Scent of the Gods*. New York: Norton.

Chiang, Fay. 1979. *In the City of Contradictions*. Bronx, NY: Sunbury Press.

———. 1982. *Miwa's Song*. Bronx, NY: Sunbury Press.

Chiang, Yee. 1950. *The Silent Traveller in New York*. New York: John Day.

———. 1959. *The Silent Traveller in Boston*. New York: Norton.

———. 1964. *The Silent Traveller in San Francisco*. New York: Norton.

Chin, Frank. 1981. *The Chickencoop Chinaman and The Year of the Dragon*. Seattle: Univ. of Washington Press.

———. 1988. *The Chinaman Pacific & Frisco R. R. Co.* Minneapolis, MN: Coffee House Press.

———. 1991. *Donald Duk*. Minneapolis, MN: Coffee House Press.

———. 1994. *Gunga Din Highway*. Minneapolis, MN: Coffee House Press.

Chin, Marilyn. 1987. *Dwarf Bamboo*. Greenfield Center, NY: Greenfield Review Press.

———. 1994. *The Phoenix Gone, the Terrace Empty*. Minneapolis, MN: Milkweed.

Chin, Tsai. 1988. *Daughter of Shanghai*. New York: St. Martin's Press.

Chin, Woon Ping. 1993. *The Naturalization of Camellia Song*. Singapore: Time Books International.

Chock, Eric. 1978. *Ten Thousand Wishes*. Honolulu: Bamboo Ridge Press.

———. 1990. *Last Days Here*. Honolulu: Bamboo Ridge Press.

Choi, Sook Nyul. 1991. *Year of Impossible Goodbyes*. Boston: Houghton Mifflin.

———. 1993a. *Echoes of the White Giraffe*. Boston: Houghton Mifflin.

———. 1993b. *Halmoni and the Picnic*. Boston: Houghton Mifflin.

———. 1994. *Gathering of Pearls*. Boston: Houghton Mifflin.

Chong, Denise. 1995. *The Concubine's Children: Portrait of a Family Divided*. Toronto: Viking.

Chu, Louis. 1961/1979. *Eat a Bowl of Tea*. Seattle: Univ. of Washington Press.

Chuang Hua [pseud.]. 1968. *Crossings*. New York: Dial.

Chung, Frances. Forthcoming. *Crazy Melon*. New York: Kaya Productions.

Crusz, Rienzi. 1986. *A Time for Loving*. Toronto: TSAR Publications.

———. 1989. *Still Close to the Raven*. Toronto: TSAR Publications.

———. 1995. *Beatitudes of Ice*. Toronto: TSAR Publications.

Dabydeen, Cyril. 1982. *Elephants Make Good Stepladders: Poems*. London, Ont.: Third Eye.

———. 1986. *Islands Lovelier Than a Vision*. Yorkshire, Eng.: Peepal Tree Press.

———. 1988a. *Dark Swirl*. Yorkshire, Eng.: Peepal Tree Press.

———. 1988b. *To Monkey Jungle*. London, Ont.: Third Eye.

———. 1989. *Coastland: New and Selected Poems 1973–1989*. Oakville, Ont.: Mosaic Press.

Dalisay, Jose Y. 1992. *Killing Time in a Warm Place*. Manila: Anvil Publishing.

Davenport, Diana. 1994. *Shark Dialogues*. New York: Atheneum.

Desai, Boman. 1988. *The Memory of Elephants*. London: A. Deutsch.

Divakaruni, Chitra Banerjee. 1990. *The Reason for Nasturtiums*. Berkeley: Berkeley Poets Workshop and Press.

———. 1991. *Black Candle: Poems about Women from India, Pakistan, and Bangladesh*. Corvallis, OR: Calyx Books.

———. 1995. *Arranged Marriage*. New York: Anchor-Doubleday.

———. Forthcoming. *The Mistress of Spices*. New York: Anchor-Doubleday.

Fenkl, Heinz Insu. Forthcoming. *Mimosa Sector*. New York: Kaya Productions.

Feria, Benny. 1954. *Filipino Son*. Boston: Meador Press.

Feria, Dolores Stephens. 1991. *Red Pencil, Blue Pencil: Essays and Encounters*. Manila: Kalikasan Press.

Fong-Torres, Ben. 1994. *Rice Room: Growing Up Chinese-American: From Number Two Son to Rock 'n' Roll*. New York: Hyperion.

Foster, Sesshu. 1987. *Angry Days*. Los Angeles: West End Press.

———. Forthcoming. *City Terrace Field Manual*. New York: Kaya Productions.

Furuta, Soichi. 1980. *To Breathe*. Westbury, NY: Edition Heliodor.

Ghose, Zulfikar. 1964. *The Loss of India*. London: Routledge & Kegan Paul.

———. 1965. *Confessions of a Native-Alien*. London: Routledge & Kegan Paul.

———. 1967a. *Jets from Orange: Poems*. London: Macmillan.

———. 1967b. *The Murder of Aziz Khan*. London: Macmillan.

———. 1972. *The Incredible Brazilian*. New York: Holt, Rinehart & Winston.

———. 1984. *A Memory of Asia: New and Selected Poems*. Austin, TX: Curbstone Publishing.

———. 1991. *Selected Poems*. Karachi and New York: Oxford Univ. Press.

———. 1992. *The Triple Mirror of the Self*. London: Bloomsbury.

Ghosh, Amitav. 1993. *In an Antique Land: History in the Guise of a Traveler's Tale*. New York: Knopf.

Gonzalez, N. V. M. 1941. *The Winds of April*. Manila: Univ. of the Philippines Press.

———. 1947. *Seven Hills Away*. Denver: Alan Swallow/Manila: Halcyon House.

———. 1954/1977. *"Children of the Ash-Covered Loam" and Other Stories*. Manila: Bookmark.

———. 1956/1963/1975. *A Season of Grace*. Manila: Bookmark.

———. 1957/1964. *The Bamboo Dancers.* Denver: Alan Swallow.

———. 1963. *Look Stranger, On This Island Now.* Manila: Benipayo Press.

———. 1964. *Selected Stories.* Denver: Alan Swallow.

———. 1979. *Mindoro and Beyond: Twenty-One Stories.* Quezon City: Univ. of the Philippines Press.

———. 1990. *Kalutang: A Filipino in the World.* Manila: Kalikasan Press.

———. 1993. *"Bread of Salt" and Other Stories.* Seattle: Univ. of Washington Press.

Gool, Reshard. 1990. *Cape Town Coolie.* London, Ont.: Heinemann.

Gotanda, Philip Kan. 1983. *The Dream of Kitamura. West Coast Plays* 15–16: 191–223.

———. 1992. *The Wash.* Portsmouth, NH: Heinemann.

———. 1995. *Fish Head Soup and Other Plays.* Seattle: Univ. of Washington Press.

Gunesekera, Romesh. 1994. *Reef.* New York: New Press.

Hagedorn, Jessica. 1975. *Dangerous Music: The Poetry and Prose of Jessica Hagedorn.* San Francisco: Momo's Press.

———. 1981. *Pet Food and Tropical Apparitions.* San Francisco: Momo's Press.

———. 1990. *Dogeaters.* New York: Penguin.

———. 1993. *Danger and Beauty.* New York: Penguin.

———. 1996. *The Gangster of Love.* Boston: Houghton Mifflin.

Hahn, Kimiko. 1989. *Airpocket.* New York: Hanging Loose Press.

———. 1992. *Earshot.* New York: Hanging Loose Press.

———. Forthcoming. *The Unbearable Heart.* New York: Kaya Productions.

Hara, Marie. 1994. *Bananaheart and Other Stories.* Honolulu: Bamboo Ridge Press.

Harada, Margaret. 1960. *The Sun Shines on the Immigrant.* New York: Vantage.

Hartman, Yuki. 1970. *A One of Me.* Fenesis, NY: Grasp Press.

———. 1976. *Hot Footsteps.* New York: Telephone Books.

———. 1980. *Red Rice: Poems.* Putnam Valley, NY: Swollen Magpie.

———. 1984. *Ping.* New York: Kulchar Foundation.

Hartmann, [Carl] Sadakichi. 1908. *Schopenhauer in the Air: Twelve Stories.* Rochester, NY: Stylus Publishing.

———. 1913/1916. *My Rubáiyát.* St. Louis, MO: Mangan Printing/New York: G. Bruno.

———. 1915a. *Permanent Peace: Is It a Dream?* New York: G. Bruno.

———. 1915b. *Tanka and Haiku: 14 Japanese Rhythms.* New York: G. Bruno.

———. 1925. *Naked Ghosts: Four Poems.* South Pasadena, CA: Fantasia.

———. 1971a. *Buddha, Confucius, Christ: Three Prophetic Plays.* Ed. Harry Lawton and George Knox. New York: Herder.

———. 1971b. *White Chrysanthemums: Literary Fragments and Pronouncements.* Ed. George Knox and Harry Lawton. New York: Herder.

Hayslip, Le Ly, with Jay Wurts. 1989. *When Heaven and Earth Changed Places: A Vietnamese Woman's Journey from War to Peace.* New York: Doubleday.

Hayslip, Le Ly, with James Hayslip. 1993. *Child of War, Woman of Peace.* New York: Doubleday.

Hongo, Bob Noriyuki. 1958. *Hey, Pineapple!* Tokyo: Hokuseido Press.

Hongo, Garrett Kaoru. 1982. *Yellow Light.* Middletown, CT: Wesleyan Univ. Press.

———. 1988. *The River of Heaven.* New York: Knopf.

———. 1995. *Volcano: A Memoir of Hawai'i.* New York: Knopf.

Houston, Jeanne Wakatsuki. 1985. *Beyond Manzanar: Views of Asian American Womanhood*. Santa Barbara, CA: Capra Press.

Houston, Jeanne Wakatsuki, and James Houston. 1973. *Farewell to Manzanar*. Boston: Houghton Mifflin.

Huffman, Ivy, and Julia Kwong. 1991. *The Dream of Gold Mountain*. Winnipeg, Man.: Hyperion Press.

Huie, Kin. 1932. *Reminiscences*. Peiping: San Yu Press.

Huỳnh, Jade Ngọc Quang. 1994. *South Wind Changing*. Saint Paul, MN: Graywolf Press.

Hwang, David Henry. 1983. *Broken Promises: Four Plays*. [*FOB, The Dance and the Railroad, Family Devotions, The House of Sleeping Beauties*.] New York: Bard/Avon.

———. 1989. *M. Butterfly*. New York: Plume/Penguin.

Hyun, Peter. 1981. *Darkness at Dawn: A North Korean Diary*. Seoul: Hanjin Publishing.

———. 1986. *Mansei! The Making of a Korean American*. Honolulu: Univ. of Hawai'i Press.

Iida, Deborah. 1996. *Middle Son*. Chapel Hill, NC: Algonquin.

Ikeda, Patricia Y. 1978. *House of Wood, House of Salt*. Cleveland, OH: Cleveland State Univ. Press.

Imura, Ernest Sakayuki. 1976. *Sunrise–Sunset: A Continuous Cycle of Living*. New York: Vantage.

Inada, Lawson Fusao. 1971. *Before the War: Poems as They Happened*. New York: Morrow.

———. 1993. *Legends from Camp*. St. Paul, MN: Coffee House Press.

Ishimoto, Shidzue. 1935. *Facing Two Ways: The Story of My Life*. New York: Farrar Straus.

Itwaru, Arnold. 1987. *Entombed Survival*. Toronto: William Wallace Publishers.

———. 1990. *Shanti*. Toronto: Coach House Press.

———. 1991. *Body Rites*. Toronto: TSAR Publications.

Jelsma, Clara Mitsuko. 1981. *Teapot Tales*. Honolulu: Bamboo Ridge Press.

Jen, Gish. 1991. *Typical American*. Boston: Houghton Mifflin/Seymour Lawrence.

———. 1996. *Mona in the Promised Land*. New York: Knopf.

Kadohata, Cynthia. 1989. *The Floating World*. New York: Viking.

———. 1992. *In the Heart of the Valley of Love*. New York: Viking.

Kagawa, Bunichi. 1930. *Hidden Flame*. Stanford, CA: Half Moon Press.

Kakugawa, Frances. 1970. *Sand Grains*. San Antonio, TX: Naylor.

———. 1971. *Winter Ginger Blossom*. San Antonio, TX: Naylor.

———. 1976a. *Golden Spike*. San Antonio, TX: Naylor.

———. 1976b. *Path of Butterflies*. San Antonio, TX: Naylor.

Kamani, Ginu. 1995. *Jungle Girl*. San Francisco: Aunt Lute Books.

Kanazawa, Tooru. *Sushi and Sourdough*. Seattle: Univ. of Washington Press.

Kaneko, Lonny. 1986. *Coming Home from Camp*. Waldron Island, WA: Brooding Heron Press.

Kang, K. Connie. 1995. *Home Was the Land of Morning Calm: A Saga of a Korean-American Family*. Reading, MA: Addison-Wesley.

Kang, Younghill. 1931. *The Grass Roof*. New York: Charles Scribner's Sons.

———. 1937/forthcoming. *East Goes West: The Making of an Oriental Yankee*. New York: Charles Scribner's Sons. Rev. ed. New York: Kaya Productions.

Kikumura, Akemi. 1981. *Through Harsh Winters: The Life of a Japanese Immigrant Woman*. Novato, CA: Chandler and Sharp.

———. 1991. *Promises Kept: The Life of an Issei Man*. Novato, CA: Chandler and Sharp.

Kim, Chungmi. 1982. *Chungmi: Selected Poems*. Los Angeles: Korean Pioneer Press.

Kim, Myung Mi. 1991. *Under Flag*. Berkeley: Kelsey St. Press.

———. 1995. *The Bounty*. Minneapolis, MN: Chax.

———. Forthcoming. *Dura*. Los Angeles: Sun and Moon.

Kim, Richard. 1964. *The Martyred*. New York: George Braziller.

———. 1968. *The Innocent*. Boston: Houghton Mifflin.

———. 1970. *Lost Names: Scenes from a Korean Boyhood*. New York: Praeger.

———. 1989. *In Search of "Lost" Koreans in China and Russia*. Seoul: Eulyoo Publishing.

Kim, Ronyoung. 1987. *Clay Walls*. Sag Harbor, NY: The Permanent Press.

Kim, Willyce. 1972. *Eating Artichokes*. Oakland, CA: Women's Press Collective.

———. 1976. *Under the Rolling Sky*. n.p.: Maude Gonne Press.

———. 1985. *Dancer Dawkins and the California Kid*. Boston: Alyson Publications.

———. 1988. *Dead Heat*. Boston: Alyson Publications.

Kingston, Maxine Hong. 1976/1977. *The Woman Warrior: Memoirs of a Girlhood among Ghosts*. New York: Vintage.

———. 1980/1981. *China Men*. New York: Ballantine.

———. 1989. *Tripmaster Monkey: His Fake Book*. New York: Knopf.

Kiyooka, Roy. 1964. *Kyoto Airs*. Vancouver, B.C.: Periwinkle Press.

———. 1967. *Nevertheless These Eyes*. Toronto: Coach House Press.

———. 1975. *Transcanada Letters*. Vancouver, B.C.: Talonbooks.

———. 1977. *The Fountainebleu Dream Machine: 18 Frames from a Book of Rhetoric*. Toronto: Coach House Press.

———. 1982. *Wheels*. Toronto: Coach House Press.

———. 1987. *Pear Tree Pomes* (sic). Toronto: Coach House Press.

Ko, Song-won [Ko Won]. 1974. *The Turn of Zero*. Merrick, NY: Cross Cultural Communications.

———. 1984. *With Birds of Paradise*. Los Angeles: Azalea Press.

Ko, Taiwon. 1959. *The Bitter Fruit of Kom-Pawi*. Philadelphia: John C. Winston.

Kogawa, Joy. 1968. *The Splintered Moon*. Fredericton, N.B.: Fiddlehead Poetry Books.

———. 1974. *A Choice of Dreams*. Toronto: McClelland & Steward.

———. 1977. *Jerico Road*. Toronto: McClelland & Steward.

———. 1981. *Obasan*. Toronto: Lester & Orpen Dennys.

———. 1985. *Woman in the Woods*. Tucson, AZ: Mosaic Press.

———. 1992. *Itsuka*. Toronto: Viking.

———. 1995. *The Rain Ascends*. Toronto: Knopf Canada.

Kono, Juliet S. 1988. *Hilo Rains*. Honolulu: Bamboo Ridge Press.

Kudaka, Geraldine. 1979. *Numerous Avalanches at the Point of Intersection*. Greenfield Center, NY: Greenfield Review Press.

Kuo, Alexander. 1986. *Changing the River*. Berkeley: Reed & Cannon.

Kuo, Helena [Kuo Ching Ch'iu]. 1942. *I've Come a Long Way.* New York: Appleton.

Laiwan. 1984–5. *CAVE Caveat.* Vancouver, B.C.: Laiwan.

Larsen, Wanwadee. 1989. *Confessions of a Mail Order Bride: American Life Through Thai Eyes.* Far Hill, NJ: New Horizon.

Larsen, Wendy Wilder, and Tran Thi Nga. 1986. *Shallow Graves: Two Women and Vietnam.* New York: Perennial Library.

Lau, Alan Chong. 1980. *Songs for Jadina.* Greenfield Center, NY: Greenfield Review Press.

Lau, Carolyn. 1988. *Wode Shuofa: My Way of Speaking.* Santa Fe, NM: Tooth of Time Books.

Lau, Evelyn. 1989. *Runaway: Diary of a Street Kid.* Toronto: Harper Collins.

———. 1990. *You Are Not Who You Claim.* Victoria, B.C.: Porcepic Books.

———. 1992. *Oedipal Dreams.* Victoria, B.C.: Beach Holme.

———. 1994. *In the House of Slaves.* Toronto: Coach House Press.

———. 1995. *Fresh Girls and Other Stories.* Winnipeg, Man.: Hyperion Press.

Law-Yone, Wendy. 1987. *The Coffin Tree.* Boston: Beacon Press.

———. 1994. *Irrawaddy Tango.* New York: Knopf.

Lee, C. Y. 1957. *The Flower Drum Song.* New York: Farrar Straus.

Lee, Chang-rae. 1995. *Native Speaker.* New York: Riverhead Books.

Lee, Gus. 1991/1994. *China Boy.* New York: Penguin/Plume.

———. 1994. *Honor and Duty.* New York: Knopf.

———. 1996. *Tiger's Tail.* New York: Knopf.

Lee, Helie. 1996. *Still Life with Rice: A Young American Woman Discovers the Life and Legacy of Her Korean Grandmother.* New York: Simon & Schuster.

Lee, Li-Young. 1986. *Rose.* Brockport, NY: BOA Editions.

———. 1990. *The City in Which I Love You.* Brockport, NY: BOA Editions.

———. 1995. *The Winged Seed: A Remembrance.* New York: Simon & Schuster.

Lee, Marie G. 1992. *Finding My Voice.* Boston: Houghton Mifflin.

———. 1993. *If It Hadn't Been for Yoon Jun.* Boston: Houghton Mifflin.

———. 1994. *Saying Goodbye.* Boston: Houghton Mifflin.

Lee, Mary Paik. 1990. *Quiet Odyssey: A Pioneer Korean Woman in America.* Seattle: Univ. of Washington Press.

Lee, Robert. 1992. *Singing to Remember.* Produced and directed by Tony Heriza. New York: Asian American Arts Centre.

Lee, Sky. 1990/1991. *Disappearing Moon Cafe.* Vancouver, B.C.: Douglas & McIntyre/Seattle: Seal Press.

———. 1994. *Bellydancer: Stories.* East Haven, CT: Press Gang.

Lee, Yan Phou. 1887. *When I Was a Boy in China.* Boston: D. Lothrop.

Leong, Monfoon. 1975. *Number One Son.* San Francisco: East/West Publishing.

Leong, Russell. 1993. *The Country of Dreams and Dust.* Albuquerque, NM: West End Press.

Lim, Genny. 1989. *Winter Place.* San Francisco: Kearney Street Workshop Press.

———. 1991. *Paper Angels and Bitter Cane.* Honolulu: Kalamaku Press.

Lim, Paul Stephen. 1977a. *Conpersonas: A Recreation in Two Acts.* New York: Samuel French.

———. 1977b. *Points of Departure. Bridge* 5.2:27–9.

———. 1982. *Some Arrivals, But Mostly Departures.* Quezon City, Philippines: New Day Publishers.

———. 1985a. *Homerica: A Trilogy on Sexual Liberation.* Louisville, KY: Aran Press.

———. 1985b. *Woe Man: A Recreation in Two Acts.* Louisville, KY: Aran Press.

———. 1985c. *Flesh, Flash and Frank Harris: A Recreation in Two Acts.* Louisville, KY: Aran Press.

———. 1989. *Figures in Clay: A Threnody in Six Scenes and a Coda.* Louisville, KY: Aran Press.

———. 1992. *Mother Tongue: A Play.* Louisville, KY: Aran Press.

Lim, Paulino. 1988. *"Passion Summer" and Other Stories.* Quezon City, Philippines: New Day Publishers.

Lim, Shirley Geok-lin. 1989. *Modern Secrets.* London: Dangaroo.

———. 1994. *Monsoon History.* London: Skoob Books.

———. 1996. *Among the White Moon Faces.* New York: Feminist Press.

Lin, Alice Murong Pu. 1988. *Grandmother Had No Name.* San Francisco: China Books.

Lin, Tai-yi. 1958. *The Eavesdropper.* Cleveland, OH: World Publishing.

Lin, Yutang. 1948. *Chinatown Family.* New York: John Day.

Linmark, R. Zamora. 1995. *Rolling the R's.* New York: Kaya Productions.

Liu, Aimee, E. 1994. *Face.* New York: Warner.

Liu, Timothy. 1992. *Vox Angelica.* Cambridge, MA: alicejamesbooks.

Liu, William T. 1979. *Transition to Nowhere.* Nashville: Charter House.

Lo, Steven C. 1989. *The Incorporation of Eric Chung.* Chapel Hill, NC: Algonquin Books.

Lord, Bette Bao. 1990. *Legacies: A Chinese Mosaic.* New York: Fawcett Columbine.

———. 1996. *The Middle Heart.* New York: Knopf.

Louie, Andrea. 1995. *Moon Cakes.* New York: Ballantine.

Louie, David Wong. 1991. *Pangs of Love.* New York: Knopf.

———. Forthcoming. *The Barbarians Are Coming.* New York: Knopf.

Lowe, Pardee. 1943. *Father and Glorious Descendant.* Boston: Little, Brown.

Lum, Darrell H. Y. 1980. *Sun: Short Stories and Drama.* Honolulu: Bamboo Ridge Press.

———. 1990a. *Not Just the Funnies!: Stories by Darrell H. Y. Lum.* Honolulu: Bamboo Ridge Press.

———. 1990b. *Pass On, No Pass Back!* Honolulu: Bamboo Ridge Press.

Lum, Wing Tek. 1987. *Expounding the Doubtful Points.* Honolulu: Bamboo Ridge Press.

McCunn, Ruthanne Lum. 1981/1989. *Thousand Pieces of Gold.* Boston: Beacon.

———. 1985. *Sole Survivor.* San Francisco: Design Enterprises.

———. 1988. *Chinese American Portrait (Personal Histories: 1828–1988).* San Francisco: Chronicle Books.

———. 1995. *Wooden Fish Songs.* New York: Dutton.

Mara, Rachna. 1991. *Of Customs and Excise.* Toronto: Second Story Press.

Masumoto, David Mas. 1984. *Silent Strength.* Delray, CA: Inaka Countryside Publishers.

———. 1995. *Epitaph for a Peach: Four Seasons on My Family Farm.* San Francisco: Harper Francisco.

Matsueda, Pat. 1985. *The Fishcatcher.* Honolulu: Petronium Press.

Meer, Ameena. 1994. *Bombay Talkie.* New York: High Risk.

Mehta, Gita. 1993. *A River Sutra.* New York: N. A. Talese.

Mehta, Ved [Parkash]. 1972. *Daddyji*. New York: Farrar Straus.

———. 1986. *Three Stories of the Raj*. Berkeley: Scolar Press.

———. 1989. *The Stolen Light*. New York: Norton.

Miki, Roy. 1991. *Saving Face: Poems Selected, 1973–1989*. Winnipeg, Man.: Turnstone.

Min, Anchee. 1994. *Red Azalea*. New York: Pantheon.

———. 1995. *Katherine*. New York: Riverhead Books.

Minatoya, Lydia Yuri. 1992. *Talking to High Monks in the Snow: An Asian American Odyssey*. New York: HarperCollins.

Mirikitani, Janice. 1978. *Awake in the River*. San Francisco: Isthmus Press.

———. 1987. *Shedding Silence*. Berkeley: Celestial Arts.

Mistry, Rohinton. 1989. *Swimming Lessons and Other Stories from Firozsha Baag*. Boston: Houghton Mifflin.

———. 1991. *Such a Long Journey*. New York: Random House.

———. 1995. *A Fine Balance*. Toronto: McClelland & Stewart.

Mitsui, James [Masao]. 1974. *Journal of the Sun*. Port Townsend, WA: Copper Canyon Press.

———. 1975. *Crossing the Phantom River*. Port Townsend, WA: Graywolf Press.

———. 1985. *After the Long Train*. Minneapolis, MN: Bieler Press.

Miyakawa, Edward. 1979. *Tule Lake*. Waldport, OR: House by the Sea.

Miyamoto, Kazuo. 1957. *A Nisei Discovers Japan*. Tokyo: Japan Times Press.

———. 1964. *Hawaii: End of the Rainbow*. Rutland, VT: Bridgeway Press, Charles E. Tuttle.

Mootoo, Shani. 1933. *Out on Main Street*. East Haven, CT: Press Gang.

Morales, Rodney. 1988. *The Speed of Darkness*. Honolulu: Bamboo Ridge Press.

Morantte, P. C. 1982. *God Is in the Heart: Poetical and Symbolical Essays*. Quezon City, Philippines: New Day Publishers.

Mori, Kyoko. 1993. *Shizuko's Daughter*. New York: Henry Holt.

———. 1994. *Fallout*. Chicago: Tia Chucha Press.

———. 1995. *The Dream of Water: A Memoir*. New York: Henry Holt.

Mori, Toshio. 1949/1985. *Yokohama, California*. Seattle: Univ. of Washington Press.

———. 1979a. *"The Chauvinist" and Other Stories*. Los Angeles: Asian American Studies Center, Univ. of California.

———. 1979b. *Woman from Hiroshima*. San Francisco: Isthmus Press.

Mukerji, Dhan Gopal. 1923. *Caste and Outcast*. New York: Dutton.

Mukherjee, Bharati. 1972. *The Tiger's Daughter*. Boston: Houghton Mifflin.

———. 1985. *Darkness*. New York: Penguin.

———. 1988. *The Middleman and Other Stories*. New York: Grove.

———. 1989. *Jasmine*. New York: Grove.

———. 1993. *The Holder of the World*. New York: Knopf.

Mura, David. 1987. *A Male Grief: Notes on Pornography and Addiction*. Minneapolis, MN: Milkweed Editions.

———. 1989. *After We Lost Our Way*. New York: Dutton.

———. 1991. *Turning Japanese*. New York: Atlantic Monthly.

———. 1995. *The Colors of Desire*. New York: Anchor.

———. 1996. *Where the Body Meets Memory: An Odyssey Sexuality & Identity*. New

York: Anchor/Doubleday.

Murayama, Milton. 1959/1975. *All I Asking For Is My Body.* San Francisco: Supa Press.

———. 1994. *Five Years on a Rock.* Honolulu: Univ. of Hawai'i Press.

Murray, Sabina. 1990. *Slow Burn.* New York: Ballantine.

Nagata, Linda. 1994. *The Bohrmaker.* New York: Bantam.

Namjoshi, Suniti. 1981/1990. *Feminist Fables.* London: Sheba Feminist Publishers.

Naqvi, Tahira. *Attar of Roses and Other Stories.* Washington, D.C.: Three Continents Press.

Narayan, Kirin. 1994. *Love, Stars, and All That.* New York: Pocket Books.

Nazareth, Peter. 1972/1981. *In a Brown Mantle.* Nairobi: East African Literature Bureau.

———. 1984. *The General Is Up.* Calcutta: P. Lal.

New, Il-han. 1928. *When I Was a Boy in Korea.* Boston: Lothrop.

Ng, Fae Myenne. 1993. *Bone.* New York: Hyperion.

———. Forthcoming. *The S.S. Independent.* New York: Hyperion.

Ngor, Haing, with Roger Warmer. 1989. *Cambodian Odyssey.* New York: Warner.

Nguyen, Ngoc Ngan. 1982. *The Will of Heaven.* New York: Dutton.

Nguyễn Qúi Đú'c. 1994. *Where the Ashes Are: The Odyssey of a Vietnamese Family.* Reading, MA: Addison-Wesley.

Nguyễn Thị Thu-Lâm, with Edith Kreisler and Sandra Christenson. 1989. *Fallen Leaves: Memoirs of a Vietnamese Woman from 1940 to 1975.* New Haven: Council on Southeast Asia Studies, Yale Center for International and Area Studies.

Nguyen, Thi Tuyet Mai. 1994. *The Rubber Tree: Memoir of a Vietnamese Woman Who Was an Anti-French Guerilla, a Publisher, and a Peace Activist.* Jefferson, NC: McFarland.

Nguyễn, Văn Đài. 1990. *Ánh Sang và Bóng Tôi* [Light and darkness]. Westminster, CA: Văn Nghê.

Nieh, Hualing. 1981/1988. *Mulberry and Peach: Two Women of China.* Trans. Jane Parish Yang with Linda Lapping. Boston: Beacon.

Noda, Barbara. 1979. *Strawberries.* Berkeley: Shameless Hussy Press.

Noguchi, Yone. 1990. *Selected English Writings of Yone Noguchi: An East–West Literary Assimilation.* Ed. Yoshinobu Hakutani. Rutherford, NJ: Farleigh Dickinson Univ. Press.

Nunes, Susan. 1982. *"A Small Obligation" and Other Stories.* Honolulu: Bamboo Ridge Press.

Nunez, Sigrid. 1995. *A Feather on the Breath of God.* New York: HarperCollins.

Oishi, Gene. 1988. *In Search of Hiroshi.* Rutland, VT: Charles E. Tuttle.

Oka, Francis Naohiko. 1970. *Poems: Memorial Edition.* San Francisco: City Lights.

Okada, John. 1957/1979. *No-No Boy.* Rutland, VT: Charles E. Tuttle/Seattle: Univ. of Washington Press.

Okita, Dwight. 1992. *Crossing with the Light.* Chicago: Tia Chucha Press.

Okubo, Mine. 1946/1983. *Citizen 13660.* New York: Columbia Univ. Press/Seattle: Univ. of Washington Press.

Ondaatje, Michael. 1970. *The Collected Works of Billy the Kid: Left Handed Poems.* Toronto: Anansi.

———. 1976. *Coming Through Slaughter.* New York: Norton.

————. 1979. *There's a Trick with a Knife I'm Learning to Do: Poems 1963–1978.* New York: Norton.

————. 1982. *Running in the Family.* New York: Norton.

————. 1985. *Secular Love: Poems.* New York: Norton.

————. 1987. *In the Skin of a Lion.* New York: Knopf.

————. 1992. *The English Patient.* Toronto: McClelland & Stewart; New York: Vintage International.

Ota, Shelley Ayame Nishimura. 1951. *Upon Their Shoulders.* New York: Exposition Press.

Pahk, Induk. 1954. *September Monkey.* New York: Harper.

————. 1965. *The Hour of the Tiger.* New York: Harper.

————. 1977. *The Cock Still Crows.* New York: Vantage.

Pai Hsien-yung. 1990. *Crystal Boys.* Trans. Howard Goldblatt. San Francisco: Gay Sunshine.

Pai, Margaret K. 1989. *The Dreams of Two Yi-Min.* Honolulu: Univ. of Hawaiʻi Press.

Pak, Gary. 1992. *The Watcher of Waipuna and Other Stories.* Honolulu: Bamboo Ridge Press.

Pak, Ty. 1983. *Guilt Payment.* Honolulu: Bamboo Ridge Press and the Hawaii Resources Center, Talk Story, Inc.

Parameswaran, Uma. 1987. *Rootless But Green Are the Boulevard Trees.* Toronto: TSAR Publications.

————. 1988. *Trishanku.* Toronto: TSAR Publications.

————. 1990. *The Door I Shut Behind Me.* Calcutta: Writers Workshop.

Park, No-yong. 1934. *An Oriental View of American Civilization.* Boston: Hale, Cushman & Hunt.

————. 1937. *Retreat of the West.* Boston: Hale, Cushman & Hunt.

————. 1940. *Chinaman's Chance: An Autobiography.* Boston: Meador Publishing.

Peeradina, Saleem. 1992. *Group Portrait.* Madras/Oxford: Oxford Univ. Press.

Pei, Lowry. 1986. *Family Resemblances.* New York: Random House.

Pukui, Mary Kuwena, and Caroline Curtis. 1951. *The Water of Kane.* Honolulu: The Kamehameha Schools.

Ramanujan, A. K. 1966. *The Striders.* London: Oxford Univ. Press.

————. 1971. *Relations: Poems.* London and New York: Oxford Univ. Press.

————. 1976. *Selected Poems.* Delhi and New York: Oxford Univ. Press.

————. 1985. *Poems of Love and War: From the Eight Anthologies and the Ten Long Poems of Classic Tamil.* New York: Columbia Univ. Press.

————. 1986. *Second Sight.* Delhi and New York: Oxford Univ. Press.

————, trans. 1973. *Speaking of Siva.* Harmondsworth: Penguin.

Rau, Santha Rama. 1945. *Home to India.* New York: Harper & Brothers.

Reyes, Gracianus. 1986. *The Uncommitted.* Quezon City, Philippines: New Day Publishers.

Robles, Al. 1996. *Rappin' with Ten Thousand Carabaos in the Dark.* Los Angeles: Asian American Studies Center, Univ. of California.

Rosca, Ninotchka. 1970. *"Bitter Country" and Other Stories.* Quezon City, Philippines: Malaya Books.

————. 1983. *The Monsoon Coolection.* Santa Lucia and New York: Univ. of Queensland Press.

————. 1987. *Endgame: The Fall of Marcos.* New York: F. Watts.

————. 1988. *State of War.* New York: Norton.

————. 1992. *Twice Blessed.* New York: Norton.

Saiki, Patsy Sumie. 1977. *Sachie: A Daughter of Hawaii.* Honolulu: Kisaku.

————. 1982. *Ganbare!* Honolulu: Kisaku.

San Diego, Greg. 1956. *Soliloquies in a Philippine Garden.* San Francisco: Pisani Publishing.

Santos, Bienvenido N. 1955/1976. *You Lovely People.* Manila: Bookmark.

————. 1956. *The Wounded Stag.* Manila: Capitol Publishing.

————. 1960/1976. *Brother, My Brother.* Manila: Bookmark.

————. 1965/1986a. *Villa Magdalena.* Quezon City, Philippines: New Day Publishers.

————. 1965/1986b. *The Volcano.* Quezon City, Philippines: New Day Publishers.

————. 1967/1979. *The Day the Dancers Came: Selected Prose Works.* Manila: Bookmark.

————. 1979. *Scent of Apples: A Collection of Stories.* Seattle: Univ. of Washington Press.

————. 1982. *The Praying Man.* Quezon City, Philippines: New Day Publishers.

————. 1983a. *Distances in Time: Selected Poems.* Quezon City, Philippines: Ateneo de Manila Univ. Press.

————. 1983b. *The Man Who (Thought He) Looked Like Robert Taylor.* Quezon City, Philippines: New Day Publishers.

————. 1985. *Dwell in the Wilderness: Selected Short Stories (1931–1941).* Quezon City, Philippines: New Day Publishers.

————. 1987. *What the Hell For You Left Your Heart in San Francisco.* Quezon City, Philippines: New Day Publishers.

————. 1993. *Memory's Fictions.* Quezon City, Philippines: New Day Publishers.

Sasaki, Nanao. 1966. *Bellyfulls.* Eugene, OR: Toad Press.

————. 1983. *Real Play: Poetry and Drama.* San Juan Pueblo, NM: Tooth of Time Books.

Sasaki, R. A. 1991. *"The Loom" and Other Stories.* Saint Paul, MN: Graywolf Press.

Sasaki, Yasuo. 1968. *Ascencion.* Pasadena, CA: Balconet Press.

————. 1986. *Village Scene/Village Herd.* Cincinnati and Berkeley: Balconet Press.

See, Lisa. 1995. *On Gold Mountain.* New York: St. Martin's Press.

Seth, Vikram. 1986. *Golden Gate.* New York: Random House.

————. 1990. *All You Who Sleep Tonight.* Boston: Faber and Faber.

————. 1994. *A Suitable Boy.* New York: HarperCollins.

Shikatani, Gerry. 1973. *Barking of Dog.* Toronto: Missing Link Press.

————. 1975. *Haliburton.* Toronto: Missing Link Press.

————. 1978. *Ship Sands Island.* Toronto: Ganglia Press.

————. 1985. *A Sparrow's Food.* Toronto: Coach House Press.

Shikeguni, Julie. 1995. *A Bridge Between Us.* New York: Anchor/Doubleday.

Shiomi, R. A. 1982. *Yellow Fever.* West Coast Plays 13–14:1–44.

Shirota, Jon. 1965. *Lucky Come Hawaii.* New York: Bantam.

————. 1972. *Pineapple White.* Los Angeles: Ohara Publications.

Sidhwa, Bapsi. 1978/1992. *The Crow Eaters.* Minneapolis, MN: Milkweed Editions.

————. 1991. *Cracking India.* Minneapolis, MN: Milkweed Editions.

———. 1993. *An American Brat*. Minneapolis, MN: Milkweed Editions.

Skinner, Michelle Cruz. 1988. *Balikbayan: A Filipino Homecoming*. Honolulu: Bess Press.

Somtow, S. P. 1983. *Fire from the Wine Dark Sea*. Norfolk, VA: Starblaze Editions.

———. 1984. *Vampire Junction*. London: Gollancz Horror.

———. 1986. *Fiddling for Water Buffaloes*. Eugene: Pulphouse Publishing.

———. 1987. *Forgetting Places*. New York: Tom Doherty Associates.

———. 1989. *Moon Dance*. New York: Tom Doherty Associates.

———. 1994. *Jasmine Nights*. New York: St. Martin's Press.

Sone, Monica. 1953/1979. *Nisei Daughter*. Seattle: Univ. of Washington Press.

Song, Cathy. 1983. *Picture Bride*. New Haven: Yale Univ. Press.

———. 1988. *Frameless Windows, Squares of Light*. New York: Norton.

———. 1994. *School Figures*. Pittsburgh, PA: Univ. of Pittsburgh Press.

Sugimoto, Etsu Inagaki. 1925. *A Daughter of the Samurai*. Garden City, NY: Doubleday.

———. 1932/1968. *A Daughter of the Narikin*. Garden City, NY: Doubleday/ Rutland, VT: Charles E. Tuttle.

———. 1935. *A Daughter of the Nohfu*. Garden City, NY: Doubleday.

———. 1940. *Grandmother O Kyo*. New York: Doubleday.

Sui Sin Far [Edith Eaton]. 1912/1995. *Mrs. Spring Fragrance*. Ed. Amy Ling and Annette White-Parks. Urbana-Champaign: Univ. of Illinois Press.

Suleri, Sara. 1989. *Meatless Days*. Chicago: Univ. of Chicago Press.

Sze, Arthur. 1972/1981. *The Willow Wind*. Sante Fe, NM: Tooth of Time Press.

———. 1976/1984. *Two Ravens*. Santa Fe, NM: Tooth of Time Press.

———. 1982. *Dazzled*. Point Reyes Station, CA: Floating Island Publications.

———. 1987. *River, River*. Providence: Lost Road.

———. 1995. *Archipelago*. Port Townsend, WA: Copper Canyon Press.

Tagami, Jeff. 1987. *October Light*. San Francisco: Kearny Street Workshop Press.

Tamagawa, Kathleen Eldridge. 1932. *Holy Prayers in a Horse's Ear*. New York: Ray Long and Richard R. Smith.

Tan, Amy. 1989. *The Joy Luck Club*. New York: Putnam.

———. 1991. *The Kitchen God's Wife*. New York: Ballantine.

———. 1992. *The Moon Lady*. New York: Macmillan.

———. 1995. *The Hundred Secret Senses*. New York: Putnam.

Tanaka, Ronald. 1981. *The Shino Suite*. Greenfield Center, NY: Greenfield Review Press.

Tham, Hilary. 1992. *Tigerbone Wine*. Washington, D.C.: Three Continents Press.

Toer, Pramoedya Ananta. 1981. *This Earth of Mankind*. Trans. Max Lane. New York: Penguin.

———. 1990. *Footsteps*. Trans. Max Lane. New York: William Morrow.

———. 1991. *Child of All Nations*. Trans. Max Lane. New York: William Morrow.

Tran Van Dinh. 1983. *Blue Dragon, White Tiger: A Tet Story*. Philadelphia: TriAm Press.

Trask, Haunani-Kay. 1994. *Light in the Crevice Never Seen*. Corvallis, OR: Calyx Books.

Tsiang, H. T. 1937. *And China Has Hands*. New York: Robert Speller.

Tsuda, Margaret. 1972. *Cry Love Aloud*. New York: Poetica Press.

————. 1976. *Urban River*. Newark, NJ: Discovery Books.

Tsui, Kitty. 1983. *The Words of a Woman Who Breathes Fire*. San Francisco: Spinsters, Ink.

Tsukiyama, Gail. 1991. *Woman of the Silk*. New York: St. Martin's Press.

Ty-Casper, Linda. 1963. *"The Transparent Sun" and Other Stories*. Manila: Alberto Florentino.

————. 1964. *The Peninsulars*. Manila: Bookmark.

————. 1974. *"The Secret Runner" and Other Stories*. Manila: Alberto Florentino.

————. 1979. *The Three-Cornered Sun*. Quezon City, Philippines: New Day Publishers.

————. 1980. *Dread Empire*. Hong Kong: Heinemann.

————. 1981. *Hazards of Distance*. Quezon City, Philippines: New Day Publishers.

————. 1985a. *Awaiting Trespass (A Passion)*. New York and London: Readers International.

————. 1985b. *Fortress in the Plaza*. Quezon City, Philippines: New Day Publishers.

————. 1986. *Wings of Stone*. New York and London: Readers International.

————. 1987. *Ten Thousand Seeds*. Quezon City, Philippines: Ateneo de Manila Univ. Press.

Tyau, Kathleen. 1995. *A Little Too Much Is Enough*. New York: Farrar Straus.

Uchida, Yoshiko. 1982. *Desert Exile: The Uprooting of a Japanese American Family*. Seattle: Univ. of Washington Press.

————. 1987. *Picture Bride*. Flagstaff, AZ: Northland Press.

Uyematsu, Amy. 1992. *30 Miles from J-town*. New York: Story Line.

Uyemoto, Holly. 1989. *Rebel without a Clue*. New York: Crown.

————. 1995. *Go*. New York: Penguin.

Vassanji, M. G. 1989. *The Gunny Sack*. Portsmouth: Heinemann.

————. 1991. *No New Land*. Toronto: McClelland & Stewart.

————. 1992. *Uhuru Street*. Toronto: McClelland & Stewart.

Villa, José García. 1933. *Footnote to Youth: Tales of the Philippines and Others*. New York: Scribner's.

————. 1939. *Many Voices: Selected Poems by José García Villa*. Manila: Philippine Book Guild.

————. 1942. *Have Come, Am Here*. New York: Viking.

————. 1948. *Seven Poems*. Cambridge, MA: Wake.

————. 1949. *Volume Two*. New York: New Directions.

————. 1958. *Selected Poems and New*. New York: McDowell, Oblensky.

————. 1962a. *Poems 55: The Best of José García Villa as Chosen by Himself*. Manila: Alberto Florentino.

————. 1962b. *Selected Stories*. Manila: Alberto Florentino.

————. 1973. *Makata 3: Poems in Praise of Love*. Manila: Alberto Florentino.

————. 1979. *Appassionata: Poems in Praise of Love*. New York: King and Cowen.

Villanueva, Marianne. 1991. *Ginseng and Other Tales from Manila*. Corvallis, OR: Calyx Books.

Wadler, Joyce. 1993. *Liaison*. New York: Bantam.

Wah, Fred. 1991. *So Far*. Vancouver, B.C.: Talonbooks.

————. 1992. *Alley Alley Home Free*. Red Deer, Alta.: Red Deer College Press.

Wang Ping. 1994. *American Visa*. Minneapolis, MN: Coffee House Press.

Watanabe, Sylvia. 1992. *Talking to the Dead*. New York: Doubleday.

Watanna, Onoto [Winnifred Eaton]. 1910. *Tama*. New York: Harper and Brothers.

———. [anonymous]. 1915. *Me: A Book of Remembrance*. New York: Century.

Wei, Katherine, and Terry Quinn. 1984. *Second Daughter: Growing Up in China, 1930–1949*. Boston: Little, Brown.

Wichman, Frederick B. 1991. *Polihale and Other Kaua'i Legends*. Honolulu: Bamboo Ridge Press.

Wong, Angi Ma. 1995. *Night of the Red Moon*. San Francisco: Pacific Heritage.

Wong, Jade Snow. 1945/1989. *Fifth Chinese Daughter*. Seattle: Univ. of Washington Press.

Wong, Jan. 1996. *Red China Blues*. New York: Anchor/Doubleday.

Wong, Nellie. 1986. *The Death of Long Steam Lady*. Los Angeles: West End Press.

Wong, Norman. 1994. *Cultural Revolution*. New York: Persea Books.

Wong, Shawn. 1979. *Homebase*. New York: I. Reed Books.

———. 1995. *American Knees*. New York: Simon & Schuster.

Wong, Su-ling [pseud.], with E. H. Cressy. 1952. *Daughter of Confucius: A Personal History*. New York: Farrar Straus.

Wong-Chu, Jim. 1986. *Chinatown Ghosts*. Vancouver, B.C.: Pulp Press.

Woo, Merle. 1986. *Yellow Woman Speaks*. Seattle: Radical Women Publications.

Wu, Edna. 1994. *Clouds and Rain: A China-to-America Memoir*. Evanston, IL: Evanston Publishing.

Wu, Tingfang. 1914. *America Through the Spectacles of an Oriental Diplomat*. New York: Frederick S. Stokes.

Wu, William F. 1989. *Hong on the Range*. New York: Walker.

Yamada, Mitsuye. 1976. *"Camp Notes" and Other Stories*. Latham, NY: Kitchen Table/Women of Color Press.

———. 1988. *Desert Run: Poems and Stories*. Latham, NY: Kitchen Table/Women of Color Press.

Yamaguchi, Yoji. 1995. *Face of a Stranger*. New York: HarperCollins.

Yamamoto, Hisaye. 1988. *"Seventeen Syllables" and Other Stories*. Latham, NY: Kitchen Table/Women of Color Press.

———. 1994. *"Seventeen Syllables."* New Brunswick, NJ: Rutgers Univ. Press.

Yamanaka, Lois-Ann. 1993. *Saturday Night at the Pahala Theatre*. Honolulu: Bamboo Ridge Press.

———. 1996. *Wild Meat and the Bully Burgers*. New York: Farrar Straus.

Yamashita, Karen Tei. 1990. *Through the Arc of the Rainforest*. Minneapolis, MN: Coffee House Press.

———. 1992. *Brazil Maru*. Minneapolis, MN: Coffee House Press.

Yamauchi, Wakako. 1994. *Songs My Mother Taught Me: Stories, Plays, and Memoir*. New York: Feminist Press.

Yashima, Taro [Jun Atushi Iwamatsu]. 1943. *The New Sun*. New York: Holt.

———. 1947. *Horizon Is Calling*. New York: Holt.

Yasuda, Kenneth [under pseud. Shosun]. 1947. *A Pepper Pod: Classic Japanese Poems with Original Haiku*. New York: Knopf.

Yau, John. 1989. *Radiant Silhouette: New and Selected Work 1974–1988*. Santa Rosa, CA: Black Sparrow Press.

———. 1992. *Edificio Sayonara.* New York: Santa Rosa, CA: Black Sparrow Press.

———. 1994. *Hawaiian Cowboys.* Santa Rosa, CA: Black Sparrow Press.

Yep, Laurence. 1975. *Dragonwings.* New York: Harper.

———. 1990. *Pay the Chinaman.* In *Between Worlds: Contemporary Asian-American Plays,* ed. Misha Berson, 180–96. New York: Theatre Communications Group.

Yi, Sung-yol. 1988. *The Last Moon.* Los Angeles: Ace Publications.

Yip, Yuen Chung. 1990. *The Tears of Chinese Immigrants.* Trans. and intro. by Sheng-Tai Chang. Dunvegan, Ont.: Cormorant Books.

Yung, Wing. 1909/1978. *My Life in China and America.* New York: Arno.

ANTHOLOGIES OF PRIMARY WORKS

Abad, Gemino, et al., eds. 1991. *Flipside: Poems on America. Caracoa* (special issue) 24. Manila: Philippine Literary Arts Council.

Ancheta, Shirley, et al., eds. 1985. *Without Names.* San Francisco: Kearney Street Workshop Press.

Arkush, R. David, and Leo O. Lee, eds. 1989. *Land without Ghosts: Chinese Impressions of America from the Nineteenth Century to the Present.* Berkeley and Los Angeles: Univ. of California Press.

Aziz, Nurjehan, ed. 1994. *Her Mother's Ashes and Other Stories by South Asian Women in Canada and the United States.* Toronto: TSAR Publications.

Bay Area Filipino American Writers. 1985. *Without Names: A Collection of Poems.* San Francisco: Kearny Street Workshop Press.

Berson, Misha, ed. 1990. *Between Worlds: Contemporary Asian American Plays.* New York: Theatre Communications Group.

Brainard, Cecilia Manguerra, ed. 1993. *Fiction by Filipinos in America.* Quezon City, Philippines: New Day Publishers.

Bruchac, Joseph, ed. 1983. *Breaking Silence: An Anthology of Contemporary Asian American Poets.* Greenfield Center, NY: Greenfield Review Press.

Bulosan, Carlos, ed. 1942. *Chorus for America: Six Philippine Poets.* Los Angeles: Wagon and Star.

Camper, Carole, ed. 1994. *Miscegenation Blues: Voices of Mixed Race Women.* Toronto: Sister Vision Press.

Casper, Leonard, ed. 1966. *New Writing from the Philippines: A Critique and Anthology.* New York: Syracuse Univ. Press.

Chan, Jeffery Paul, et al., eds. 1991. *The Big Aiiieeeee!: An Anthology of Chinese American and Japanese American Literature.* New York: Meridian.

Chanoff, David, and Doan Van Toai, eds. 1986. *Portrait of the Enemy.* New York: Random House.

Chin, Frank, et al., eds. 1974/1991. *Aiiieeeee! An Anthology of Asian-American Writers.* New York: Mentor.

Chin, Marilyn, and David Wong Louie, eds. 1991. *Dissident Song: A Contemporary Asian American Anthology.* Santa Cruz: Univ. of California Press.

Chock, Eric, and Darrell H. Y. Lum, eds. 1986. *The Best of Bamboo Ridge*. Honolulu: Bamboo Ridge Press.

————. 1989. *Pake: Writings by Chinese in Hawai'i*. Honolulu: Bamboo Ridge Press.

Chung, C., Alison Kim, and A. K. Lemshewsky, eds. 1987. *Between the Lines: An Anthology by Pacific/Asian Lesbians*. Santa Cruz, CA: Dancing Bird Press.

Cooke, Miriam, and Roshni Rustomji-Kerns, eds. 1994. *Blood into Ink: South Asian and Middle Eastern Women Write War*. Boulder: Westview Press.

Cuyugan, Tina, ed. 1992. *Forbidden Fruit: Women Write the Erotic*. Manila: Anvil Publishing.

Dabydeen, Cyril, ed. 1987. *A Shapely Fire: Changing the Literary Landscape*. Oakville, Ont.: Mosaic Press.

————, ed. 1990. *Another Way to Dance*. Oakville, Ont.: Mosaic Press.

David-Maramba, Asunción, ed. 1965/1982. *Philippine Contemporary Literature in English and Pilipino*. Manila: Bookmark.

Francia, Luis H, ed. 1993. *Brown River, White Ocean: An Anthology of Twentieth-Century Philippine Literature in English*. New Brunswick, NJ: Rutgers Univ. Press.

Hagedorn, Jessica, ed. 1993. *Charlie Chan Is Dead: An Anthology of Contemporary Asian American Fiction*. New York: Penguin.

The Hawk's Well: A Collection of Japanese American Art and Literature. 1986. San Jose, CA: Asian American Arts Projects.

He Alo Ā He Alo/Face to Face. 1993. Honolulu: The Hawai'i Area Office of the American Friends Service Committee.

Hom, Marlon K., trans. 1987. *Songs of Gold Mountain: Cantonese Rhymes from San Francisco Chinatown*. Berkeley and Los Angeles: Univ. of California Press.

Hong, Grace, James Lee, David Maruyama, Jim Soong, and Gary Yee, eds. 1991. "Burning Cane." *Amerasia Journal* (special issue) 17.2.

Hong, Maria, ed. 1993. *Growing Up Asian American*. New York: William Morrow.

Hong, Maria, and David D. Kim, eds. 1992. "Voices Stirring: An Anthology of Korean American Writing." *Asian Pacific American Journal* (special issue) 1.2.

Hongo, Garrett, ed. 1993. *The Open Boat: Poems from Asian America*. New York: Anchor/Doubleday.

————. 1995. *Under Western Eyes: Personal Essays from Asian America*. New York: Anchor/Doubleday.

Houston, Velina Hasu, ed. 1993. *The Politics of Life: Four Plays by Asian American Women*. Philadelphia: Temple Univ. Press.

Howard, Katsuyo K., comp. 1990. *Passages: An Anthology of the Southeast Asian Refugee Experience*. Fresno: California State Univ., Southeast Asian Services.

Hsu, Kai-yu, and Helen Palubinskas, eds. 1972. *Asian American Authors*. Boston: Houghton Mifflin.

Hu, Zhaozhong, ed. 1970. *Maizhou Guangdong huagiao liuchuan geyao huiban* [A collection of folk rhymes popular among Cantonese in America]. Hong Kong: Zhendan tushu gongsi.

Hutcheon, Linda, and Marion Richmond, eds. 1990. *Other Solitudes: Canadian Multicultural Fictions*. Toronto: Oxford Univ. Press.

Huynh Sanh Thong, ed. 1988. *To Be Made Over: Tales of Socialist Reeducation in Vietnam*. New Haven: Council on Southeast Asia Studies, Yale Center for

International and Area Studies.

Kang, Hyun-Yi, ed. 1994. *Writing Away Here*. Oakland, CA: Korean American Arts Festival Committee.

Katrak, Ketu H., and R. Radhakrishnan, eds. 1988–9. "Desh-Videsh: South Asian Expatriate Writing and Art." *Massachusetts Review* (special issue) 29.4.

Kim, Elaine H., and Eui-Young Yu, eds. 1996. *East to America: Korean American Life Stories*. New York: New Press.

Kono, Juliet S., and Cathy Song, eds. 1992. *Sister Stew*. Honolulu: Bamboo Ridge Press.

Kudaka, Geraldine, ed. 1995. *On a Bed of Rice: An Asian American Erotic Feast*. New York: Anchor.

Lai, Him Mark, Genny Lim, and Judy Yung, eds. 1980. *Island: Poetry and History of Chinese Immigrants on Angel Island 1910–1940*. San Francisco: HOC DOI [History of Chinese Detained on Island] Project.

Laygo, Teresita, comp. 1978. *The Well of Time: Eighteen Short Stories from Philippine Contemporary Literature*. Los Angeles: Asian American Bilingual Center.

Lee, Bennett, and Jim Wong-Chu, eds. 1991. *Many-Mouthed Birds: Contemporary Writing by Chinese Canadians*. Seattle: Univ. of Washington Press.

Lee, Sky, et al., eds. 1990. *Telling It: Women and Language across Cultures, the Transformation of a Conference*. Vancouver, B.C.: Press Gang.

Lew, Walter K., ed. 1995. *Premonitions: The Kaya Anthology of New Asian North American Poetry*. New York: Kaya Productions.

Lim, Shirley Geok-lin, and Mayumi Tsutakawa, eds. 1989. *The Forbidden Stitch: An Asian American Women's Anthology*. Corvallis, OR: Calyx Books.

Lim-Hing, Sharon, ed. 1994. *The Very Inside: An Anthology of Writing by Asian and Pacific Islander Lesbian and Bisexual Women*. Toronto: Sister Vision Press.

Lumbera, Bienvenido, and Cynthia Nograles Lumbera, eds. 1982. *Philippine Literature: A History and Anthology*. Manila: National Book Store.

McGifford, Diane, ed. 1992. *The Geography of Voice: An Anthology of South Asian Canadian Literature*. Toronto: TSAR Publications.

McGifford, Diane, and Judith Kearns, eds. 1990. *Shakti's Words: An Anthology of South Asian Canadian Women's Poetry*. Toronto: TSAR Publications.

Makeda, Silvera, ed. 1993. *A Piece of My Heart: A Lesbian of Colour Anthology*. Toronto: Sister Vision Press.

Marin, Patricia, ed. 1953. *Love in Philippine Story and Verse*. Quezon City, Philippines: New Day Publishers.

Mirikitani, Janice, ed. 1980. *Ayumi: A Japanese American Anthology*. San Francisco: Japanese American Anthology Committee.

Morrison, Joan, and Charlotte Fox Zabusky, eds. 1980. *American Mosaic*. New York: E. P. Dutton.

Mukherjee, Bharati, and Ranu Vanikar, eds. 1986. "Writers of the Indian Commonwealth." *Literary Review* (special issue) 29.4.

Navarro, Jovina, comp. 1974. *Diwang Pilipino: Philippine Consciousness*. Davis: Asian American Studies, Univ. of California, Davis.

———. 1976. *Joaquin Legazpi: Poet, Artist, Community Worker*. El Verano, CA: Pilnachi Press.

Nguyen-Hong-Nhiem, Lucy, and Joel Martin Halpern, eds. 1989. *The Far East Comes Near: Autobiographical Accounts of Southeast Asian Students in America.* Amherst: Univ. of Massachusetts Press.

Nguyen Ngoc Bich, ed. 1989. *War and Exile: A Vietnamese Anthology.* Springfield, VA: Vietnamese PEN Abroad.

Oiwa, Keibo, ed. 1991. *Stone Voices: Wartime Writings of Japanese Canadian Issei.* Montreal: Vehicule Press.

Paper Doors: An Anthology of Japanese-Canadian Poetry. 1981. Toronto: Coach House Press.

Philips, Herbert, ed. 1987. *Modern Thai Literature: With an Ethnographic Interpretation.* Honolulu: Univ. of Hawai'i Press.

Phillips, J. J., Ishmael Reed, Gundars Strads, and Shawn Wong, eds. 1994. *The Before Columbus Foundation Fiction Anthology: Selections from the American Book Awards, 1980–1990.* New York: Norton.

Rafiq, Fauzia, ed. 1995. *Aurat Durbar (The Court of Women): Writings by Women of South Asian Origin.* Toronto: Second Story Press.

Ratti, Rakesh, ed. 1993. *A Lotus of Another Color: An Unfolding of the South Asian Gay and Lesbian Experience.* Boston: Alyson Publications.

Reed, Ishmael, Kathryn Trueblood, and Shawn Wong, eds. 1994. *The Before Columbus Poetry Anthology: Selections from the American Book Awards, 1980–1990.* New York: Norton.

Rustomji, Roshni, ed. 1986. "South Asian Women Writers; The Immigrant Experience." *Journal of South Asian Literature* (special issue) 21.1.

Rustomji-Kerns, Roshni, ed. 1995. *Living in America: Poetry and Fiction by South Asian American Writers.* New York: Westview Press.

Salanga, A. N., and Esther Pacheco, eds. 1986/1987. *Versus: Philippine Protest Poetry, 1983–1986.* Seattle: Univ. of Washington Press.

Santoli, Al, ed. 1985. *To Bear Any Burden.* New York: E. P. Dutton.

Silvera, Makeda, ed. 1991. *Piece of My Heart: A Lesbian of Colour Anthology.* Toronto: Sister Vision Press.

Srikanth, Rajini, and Sunaina Maira, eds. Forthcoming. *Contours of the Heart: South Asians Map North America.*

Stewart, Frank, ed. 1987. *Passage to the Dream Shore: Short Stories of Contemporary Hawaii.* Honolulu: Univ. of Hawai'i Press.

Uno, Roberta, ed. 1993. *Unbroken Thread: An Anthology of Plays by Asian American Women.* Amherst: Univ. of Massachusetts Press.

Vassanji, M. G., ed. 1985. *A Meeting of Streams: South Asian Canadian Literature.* Toronto: TSAR Publications.

Wand, David Hsin Fu, ed. 1974. *Asian American Heritage: An Anthology of Prose and Poetry.* New York: Washington Square Press.

Wang, L. Ling-Chi, and Henry Yiheng Zhao, eds. 1991. *Chinese American Poetry: An Anthology.* Seattle: Asian American Voices.

Watanabe, Sylvia, and Carol Bruchac, eds. 1990. *Home to Stay: Asian American Women's Fiction.* Greenfield Center, NY: Greenfield Review Press.

Wendt, Albert, ed. 1995. *Nuanua: Pacific Writing in English since 1980.* Honolulu: Univ. of Hawai'i Press.

Women of the South Asian Descent Collective (Sheela Bhatt, Preety Kalra, Aarti

Kohli, Latika Malkan, Dharini Rasiah), eds. 1993. *Our Feet Walk the Sky: Women of the South Asian Diaspora*. San Francisco: Aunt Lute Books.

The Women's Book Committee, Chinese Canadian National Council, ed. 1992. *Jin Guo: Voices of Chinese Canadian Women*. Toronto: Women's Press.

Wong, Shawn, ed. 1995. *Asian American Literature: A Brief Introduction and Anthology*. New York: HarperCollins.

Yabes, Leopoldo, ed. 1975. *Philippine Short Stories 1925–1940*. Quezon City: Univ. of the Philippines Press.

———. 1981. *Philippine Short Stories 1941–1955*. 2 vols. Quezon City: Univ. of the Philippines Press.

Yep, Lawrence, ed. 1993. *American Dragons: Twenty-Five Asian American Voices*. New York: HarperCollins.

Yoisho: An Anthology of the Japantown Arts and Media Workshop. 1983. San Francisco: Japantown Art and Media Workshop.

RESEARCH ON ASIAN PACIFIC AMERICAN LITERATURE AND CULTURE

Adair, Gilbert. 1989. *Hollywood's Vietnam*. London: Heinemann.

Adams, Timothy Dow. 1991. "Talking Stories/ Telling Lies in *The Woman Warrior*." In Lim, ed., 151–7.

Aguilar-San Juan, Karin. 1991. "Exploding Myths, Creating Consciousness: Some First Steps Toward Pan-Asian Unity." In *Pieces of My Heart: A Lesbian of Colour Anthology*, ed. Makeda Silvera. 185–92. Toronto: Sister Vision Press.

———, ed. 1994. *The State of Asian America: Activism and Resistance in the 1990s*. Boston: South End Press.

Aldama, Frederic Luis. 1994. "Spatial Reimaginations in Fae Myenne Ng's Chinatown." *Critical Mass* 1.2:85–102.

Alegre, Edilberto N., and Doreen G. Fernandez. 1984. *The Writer and His Milieu: An Oral History of First Generation Writers in English*. Manila: De La Salle Univ. Press.

Alexander, Meena. 1992. "Is There an Asian American Aesthetics?" *Samar* 1:26–7.

Alquizola, Marilyn. 1989. "The Fictive Narrator of *America Is in the Heart*." In Nomura et al., 211–17.

———. 1991. "Subversion or Affirmation: The Text and Subtext of *America Is in the Heart*." In Hune et al., 199–210.

Alquizola, Marilyn, et al., eds. Forthcoming. *Privileging Sites: Positions in Asian American Studies*. Pullman: Washington State Univ. Press.

Asian Women United of California, eds. 1989. *Making Waves: An Anthology of Writing by and about Asian American Women*. Boston: Beacon Press.

Aubrey, James R. 1991. "Women Warriors and Military Students." In Lim, ed., 80–6.

Aydelotte, William O. 1976. "The Detective Story as a Historical Source." In *Dimensions of Detective Fiction*, ed. Larry N. Landrum, Pat Browne, and Ray B. Browne, 68–82. Bowling Green, OH: Popular Press.

Azurin, Arnold Molina. 1993. *Reinventing the Filipino: Critical Analyses of the Orthodox Views in Anthropology, History, Folklore, and Letters*. Diliman, Quezon City: Univ. of the Philippines Press.

Balce-Cortes, Nerissa. 1995. "Imagining the Neocolony." *Critical Mass* 2.2:95–120.

Bannerji, Himani. 1992. *Unsettling Relations: The University as a Site of Feminist Struggles*. Boston: South End Press.

———. 1993. *The Writing on the Wall: Essays on Culture and Politics*. Toronto: TSAR Publications.

Bascara, Victor. 1993. "Hitting Critical Mass (or, Do your parents still say 'Oriental,' too?)." *Critical Mass* 1.1:3–38.

Birbalsingh, Frank. 1988. *Passion and Exile: Essays on Caribbean Literature*. London: Hansib.

———, ed. 1989. *Indenture and Exile: The Indo-Caribbean Experience*. Toronto: TSAR Publications.

Blinde, Patricia Lin. 1979. "The Icicle in the Desert: Perspective and Form in the Works of Two Chinese-American Women Writers." *MELUS* 6.3:51–71.

Boardman, Kathleen A. 1991. "Voice and Vision: *The Woman Warrior* in the Writing Class." In Lim, ed., 80–6.

Bow, Leslie. 1994. "Cultural Conflict/Feminist Resolution in Amy Tan's *The Joy Luck Club*." In Ng et al., eds., 235–47.

Briney, Robert E. 1970. "Sax Rohmer: An Informal Survey." In *The Mystery Writer's Art*, ed. Francis M. Nevins Jr., 42–77. Bowling Green, OH: Bowling Green State Univ. Popular Press.

Bruining, Anne Mi Ok. 1992. "Challenging the Lies of International Adoption by White Lesbians and Gays." *Color Life!* 28 June, 22–23.

Cachapero, Emily, et al., eds. 1975. *Liwanag: Literary and Graphic Representations by Filipinos in America*. San Francisco: Liwanag Publishing.

Campomanes, Oscar V. 1992. "Filipinos in the United States and Their Literature of Exile." In Lim and Ling, eds., 49–78.

———. 1995. "The New Empire's Forgetful and Forgotten Citizens: Unrepresentability and Unassimilability in Filipino-American Postcolonialities." *Critical Mass* 2.2:145–200.

———. Forthcoming. "Asian American Studies Beyond California and the Question of Imperialism." *Positions*.

Carter-Sanborn, Kristin. 1994. "'We Murder Who We Were': *Jasmine* and the Violence of Identity." *American Literature* 66:433–53.

Cha, Theresa Hak Kyung, ed. 1980. *Cinematographic Apparatus: Selected Writings*. New York: Tanam Press.

Chan, Jeffrey Paul, et al. 1981. "Resources for Chinese and Japanese American Literary Traditions." *Amerasia Journal* 8.1:19–31.

Chan, Jeffery Paul, and Marilyn C. Alquizola. 1987. "Asian-American Literary Traditions." In *A Literary History of the American West*, ed. J. Golden Taylor and Thomas J. Lyon, 1119–28. Fort Worth: Texas Christian Univ. Press.

Chang, Hsiao-hung. 1992–3. "Cultural/Sexual/Theatrical Ambivalence in *M. Butterfly*." *Tamkang Review* 23.1–4 (Part II): 735–55.

Chang, Juliana. 1993. "'Transform This Nothingness': Theresa Hak Kyung Cha's *Dictée*." *Critical Mass* 1.1:75–82.

Chen, Davina Te-min. 1994. "Naomi's Liberation." *Critical Mass* 2.1:99–128.

Chen, Tina. 1994. "Betrayed into Motion: The Seduction of Narrative Desire in *M. Butterfly*." *Critical Mass* 1.2:129–54.

Cheng, Ming L. 1994. "The Unrepentant Fire: Tragic Limitations in Hisaye Yamamoto's 'Seventeen Syllables.'" *MELUS* 19.4:91–108.

Cheung, Kai-chong. 1992–3. "Maxine Hong Kingston's Non-Chinese Man." *Tamkang Review* 23.1–4 (Part II):421–30.

Cheung, King-Kok. 1986. "Bienvenido N. Santos: Filipino Old-Timers in Literature." *Markham Review* 15 (1986):49–53.

———. 1988. "'Don't Tell': Imposed Silences in *The Color Purple* and *The Woman Warrior*." *PMLA* 103.2:162–74. Reprinted in Lim and Ling, eds., 163–89.

———. 1990a. "The Woman Warrior versus the Chinaman Pacific: Must a Chinese American Critic Choose between Feminism and Heroism?" In *Conflicts in Feminism*, ed. Marianne Hirsch and Evelyn Fox Keller, 234–51. New York: Routledge.

———. 1990b. "Self-Fulfilling Visions in *The Woman Warrior* and *Thousand Pieces of Gold*." *Biography: An Interdisciplinary Quarterly* 13.2:143–53.

———. 1990c. "Reflections on Teaching Literature by American Women of Color." *Pacific Coast Philology* 25:19–23.

———. 1991/1994. "Double-Telling: Intertextual Silence in Hisaye Yamamoto's Fiction." *American Literary History* 3.2:277–93. Reprinted in Cheung, ed., 161–80.

———. 1991–2. "Thrice Muted Tale: Interplay of Art and Politics in Hisaye Yamamoto's 'The Legend of Miss Sasagawara.'" *MELUS* 17.3:109–25.

———. 1993a. *Articulate Silences: Hisaye Yamamoto, Maxine Hong Kingston, Joy Kogawa*. Ithaca, NY: Cornell Univ. Press.

———. 1993b. "Talk-Story: Counter-Memory in Maxine Hong Kingston's *China Men*." *Tamkang Review* 24.1:21–37.

———. 1994. "Attentive Silence in Joy Kogawa's Obasan." In *Listening to Silences: New Essays in Feminist Criticism*, ed. Elaine Hedges and Shelley Fisher Fishkin, 113–29. New York: Oxford Univ. Press.

———. 1995. "The Dream in Flames: Hisaye Yamamoto, Multiculturalism, and the Los Angeles Uprising." In *Having Our Way: Women Rewriting Tradition in Twentieth-Century America*, ed. Harriet Pollack. Lewisburg: Bucknell Univ. Press; *Bucknell Review* (special issue) 39.1:118–30.

———. 1996. "Reading between the Syllables: Hisaye Yamamoto's 'Seventeen Syllables' and Other Stories." In Maitino and Peck, 313–25.

———. Forthcoming. "Of Men and Men: Reconstructing Chinese American Masculinity." In *Writing in the Borderlands*, ed. Sandra Kumamoto Stanley. Urbana-Champaign: Univ. of Illinois Press.

———, ed. 1994. *"Seventeen Syllables"* [by Hisaye Yamamoto]. New Brunswick, NJ: Rutgers Univ. Press.

Cheung, King-Kok, and Stan Yogi, eds. 1988. *Asian American Literature: An Annotated Bibliography*. New York: Modern Language Association of America.

Chin, Frank. 1976. "Backtalk." *Counterpoint: Perspectives on Asian America*, ed. Emma Gee et al., 556–7. Los Angeles: Asian American Studies Center, Univ. of California.

———. 1985. "This Is Not an Autobiography." *Genre* 18.2:105–30.

———. 1991. "Come All Ye Asian American Writers of the Real and the Fake." In Chan et al., 1–92.

Chin, Frank, and friends. 1992. "Uncle Frank's Fakebook of Fairy Tales for Asian American Moms and Dads." *Amerasia Journal* 18.2:69–87.

Chin, Frank, and Jeffery Paul Chan. 1972. "Racist Love." In *Seeing Through Shuck,* ed. Richard Kostelanetz, 65–72. New York: Ballantine.

Chin, Woon Ping. 1991. "Children of Chinese Diaspora: A Comparison of Lee Kok Liang's *Flowers in the Sky* and Maxine Hong Kingston's *China Men.*" In Hune et al., 265–76.

Chiu, Jeannie. 1993. "Uncanny Doubles: Nationalism and Repression in Frank Chin's 'Railroad Standard Time.'" *Critical Mass* 1.1:93–107.

Cho, Fiona. 1993. "Daddy, I don't know what you're talking." *Critical Mass* 1.1:57–62.

Ch'oe, T'ae-ung, et al. 1989. "Hankukmuntan 43 Nyunkwa Iminmunhak" [43 Years of Korean literature and immigrant literature]. *Yoksa Bip'an* [Modern praxis] 8 (Spring): 4–44.

Ch'oe, Yun-hong. 1989. "Mikuk Sok-e Hankukmunhak" [Korean literature in America]. *Yoksa Bip'an* [Modern praxis] 9 (Fall): 59–66.

Choi, Chungmoo. 1993. "The Discourse of Decolonization and Popular Memory: South Korea." *Positions* 1.1:77–102.

Chow, Rey, ed. 1993. *Writing Diaspora: Tactics of Intervention in Contemporary Critical Studies.* Bloomington: Indiana Univ. Press.

Christopher, Renny. 1992. "*Blue Dragon, White Tiger:* The Bicultural Stance of Vietnamese American Literature." In Lim and Ling, 259–70.

Chua, Cheng Lok. 1981. "Two Chinese Versions of the American Dream: The Golden Mountain in Lin Yutang and Maxine Hong Kingston." *MELUS* 8.4:61–70.

———. 1991. "Mythopoesis East and West in *The Woman Warrior.*" In Lim, ed. 146–50.

———. 1992. "Witnessing the Japanese Canadian Experience in World War II: Processual Structure, Symbolism, and Irony in Joy Kogawa's *Obasan.*" In Lim and Ling, 97–108.

Chuang, Jay. 1994. "Bone in Bone." *Critical Mass* 2.1:53–8.

Chung, Sue Fawn. 1976. "From Fu Manchu, Evil Genius, to James Lee Wong, Popular Hero: A Study of the Chinese-American in Popular Periodical Fiction from 1920 to 1940." *Journal of Popular Culture* 10.3:534–47.

Cobb, Nora Okja. 1994. "Artistic and Cultural Mothering in the Poetics of Cathy Song." In Ng et al. 1994, 223–34.

Cody, Gabrielle. 1989. "David Henry Hwang's *M. Butterfly:* Perpetuating the Misogynist Myth." *Theater* 20.2:24–7.

Crogan, Richard, ed. 1975. *The Development of Philippine Literature in English (since 1900).* Quezon City, Philippines: Alemar-Phoenix.

Crow, Charles. 1984. "Home and Transcendence in Los Angeles Fiction." In *Los Angeles in Fiction: A Collection of Original Essays,* ed. David Fine, 189–205. Albuquerque: Univ. of New Mexico Press.

———. 1986/1994. "The Issei Father in the Fiction of Hisaye Yamamoto." In

Opening Up Literary Criticism: Essays on American Prose and Poetry, ed. Leo Truchlar, 34–40. Salzburg: Verlag Wolfgang Neugebauer. Reprinted in Cheung, ed., 119–28.

Davé, Shilpa. 1993. "The Doors to Home and History: Post-Colonial Identities in Meena Alexander and Bharati Mukherjee." *Amerasia Journal* 19.3:103–16.

De Cristoforo, Violet Kazue Matsuda. 1993. "There Is Always Tomorrow: An Anthology of Wartime Haiku." *Amerasia Journal* 19.1:93–116.

Deeney, John J. 1993. "Of Monkeys and Butterflies: Transformation in M. H. Kingston's *Tripmaster Monkey* and D. H. Hwang's *M. Butterfly*." *MELUS* 18.4:21–40.

Demetrakopoulos, Stephanie A. 1980. "The Metaphysics of Matrilinearism in Women's Autobiography." In *Women's Autobiography: Essays in Criticism*, ed. Estelle C. Jelinek, 180–205. Bloomington: Univ. of Indiana Press.

Douglass, Lesley Chin. 1995. "Finding the Way: Chuang Hua's *Crossings* and Chinese Literary Tradition." *MELUS* 20.1:53–65.

Eakin, Paul John. *Fictions in Autobiography: Studies in the Art of Self-Invention*. Princeton, NJ: Princeton Univ. Press.

Eng, David L. 1994/1996. "In the Shadows of a Diva: The Commitment of Homosexuality in David Henry Hwang's *M. Butterfly*." *Amerasia Journal* 20.1:93–116. Reprinted in Leong 1996, 131–52.

———. 1994. "Primal Glances: Race and Psychoanalysis in Lonny Kaneko's 'The Shoyu Kid.'" *Critical Mass* 1.2:65–84.

Evangelista, Susan. 1993. "Jessica Hagedorn and Manila Magic." *MELUS* 18.4:41–52.

Feng, Peter. 1995. "In Search of Asian American Cinema." *Cineaste* 21.1–2:32–36.

Ferens, Dominika. 1993. "Contemporary Chinese American Writers versus the Perpetuators of Myths and Stereotypes." *Anglica Wratislaviensia* (Wroclaw, Poland) 25:49–59.

———. 1994. "Didacticism in Chinese American Literature: David Henry Hwang's *M. Butterfly*." *Anglica Wratislaviensia* 27:5–11.

Ferraro, Thomas J. 1993. *Ethnic Passages: Literary Immigrants in Twentieth-Century America*. Chicago: Univ. of Chicago Press.

Fischer, Michael M. J. 1986. "Ethnicity and the Post-Modern Arts of Memory." In *Writing Culture: The Poetics and Politics of Ethnography*, ed. James Clifford and George E. Marcus, 194–233. Berkeley and Los Angeles: Univ. of California Press.

Fisher, Dexter, ed. 1977. *Minority Language and Literature: Retrospective and Perspective*. New York: Modern Language Association of America.

Foster, Damon. 1995. "Yankee Dragons: A Laughable Look at American Martial Arts Movies." *Oriental Cinema* 7:4–31.

Freeman, James A. 1989. *Hearts of Sorrow: Vietnamese-American Lives*. Stanford, CA: Stanford Univ. Press.

Frye, Joanne S. 1988. "*The Woman Warrior*: Claiming Narrative Power, Recreating Female Selfhood." In *Faith of a (Woman) Writer*, ed. Alice Kessler-Harris and William McBrien, 293–301. New York: Greenwood Press.

Fujikane, Candace. 1994. "Between Nationalisms: Hawaii's Local Nation and Its

Troubled Racial Paradise." *Critical Mass* 1.2:23–58.

Fujita, Gayle Kimi. 1985. "'To Attend the Sound of Stone': The Sensibility of Silence in *Obasan.*" *MELUS* 12.3:33–42.

Fung, Richard. 1991. "Looking for My Penis: The Eroticized Asian in Gay Video Porn." In *How Do I Look? Queer Film and Video,* ed. Bad Object-Choices, 145–68. Seattle: Bay Press.

———. 1993. "Shortcomings: Questions about Pornography as Pedagogy." In *Queer Looks: Perspectives on Lesbian and Gay Film and Video,* ed. Martha Gever, Pratibha Parmar, and John Greyson, 355–67. New York: Routledge.

———. 1994. "Seeing Yellow: Asian Identities in Film and Video." In Aguilar-San Juan, ed., 161–71.

Garber, Marjorie. 1992. "The Occidental Tourist: *M. Butterfly* and the Scandal of Transvestitism." In *Nationalism and Sexualities,* ed. Andrew Parker et al., 121–46. New York: Routledge.

Gier, Jean Vengua. 1995. "'. . . to have come from someplace': *October Light, America Is in the Heart,* and 'Flip' Writing after the Third World Strikes." *Critical Mass* 2.2:1–34.

Gilead, Sarah. 1988. "Emigrant Selves: Narrative Strategies in Three Women's Autobiographies." *Criticism* 30.1:43–62.

Goellnicht, Donald C. 1989. "Minority History as Metafiction: Joy Kogawa's *Obasan.*" *Tulsa Studies in Women's Literature* 8.2:287–306.

———. 1991. "Father Land and/or Mother Tongue: The Divided Female Subject in Kogawa's *Obasan* and Hong Kingston's *The Woman Warrior.*" In *Redefining Autobiography in Twentieth Century Women's Fiction,* ed. Janice Morgan and Colette T. Hall, 119–34. New York: Garland.

———. 1992. "Tang Ao in America: Male Subject Positions in *China Men.*" In Lim and Ling, 191–212.

———. 1994. "Transplanted Discourse in Yamamoto's 'Seventeen Syllables.'" In Cheung, ed., 181–93.

Gong, Ted. 1980. "Approaching Cultural Change through Literature: From Chinese to Chinese American." *Amerasia Journal* 7.1:73–86.

Gonzalez, N. V. M. 1966. "The Filipino and the Novel." *Daedalus* 95:961–71.

———. 1976. "Drumming for the Captain." *World Literature Written in English* 15:415–21.

———. 1993. "Mindoro as Metaphor." *Asian America: Journal of Culture and the Arts* 1 (Winter):51–8.

Gonzalves, Theo. 1995. "'The Show Must Go On': Production Notes on the Pilipino Cultural Night." *Critical Mass* 2.2:129–44.

Gotera, Vicente F. 1991. "'I've Never Read Anything like It': Student Responses to *The Woman Warrior.*" In Lim, ed., 64–73.

Gottlieb, Erika. 1986. "The Riddle of Concentric Worlds in *Obasan.*" *Canadian Literature* 109:34–53.

Grewal, Gurleen. 1996. "Memory and the Matrix of History: The Poetics of Loss and Recovery in Joy Kogawa's *Obasan* and Toni Morrison's *Beloved.*" In Singh et al., 140–74.

Grewal, Inderpal. 1993. "Reading and Writing the South Asian Diaspora." In Women of the South Asian Descent Collective, 226–36.

———. 1994. "Autobiographical Subjects and Diasporic Locations: *Meatless Days* and *Borderlands.*" In *Scattered Hegemonies: Postmodernity and Transnational Feminist Practices*, ed. Inderpal Grewal and Caren Kaplan, 231–54. Minneapolis: Univ. of Minnesota Press.

Haines, David W. 1989. *Refugees as Immigrants: Cambodians, Laotians and Vietnamese in America*. Totowa, NJ: Rowman & Littlefield.

———. 1992. "The Contemporary Asian American Family on Television." *Amerasia Journal* 18.2:35–54.

Hamamoto, Darrell Y. 1994. *Monitored Peril: Asian Americans and the Politics of TV Representation*. Minneapolis: Univ. of Minnesota Press.

Har, Janie C. 1993. "Food, Sexuality, and the Pursuit of a Little Attention." *Critical Mass* 1.1:83–92.

Haslam, Gerald W. 1969. "The Subtle Thread: Asian-American Literature." *Arizona Quarterly* 25.3:197–207.

Hattori, Tomo. Forthcoming. "Psycho-linguistic Orientalism in the Criticism of *The Woman Warrior* and *Obasan.*" In *U.S. Women of Color and Literary Theory*, ed. Sandra Kumamoto Stanley. Urbana-Champaign: Univ. of Illinois Press.

Hidalgo, Cristina, and Priscelina Legasto, eds. 1993. *Philippine Post-Colonial Studies: Essays on Language and Literature*. Quezon City: Univ. of the Philippines Press.

Ho, Wen-ching. 1987. "In Search of a Female Self: Toni Morrison's *The Bluest Eye* and Maxine Hong Kingston's *The Woman Warrior.*" *American Studies* (Taipei) 17.3:1–44.

Ho, Wendy. 1991. "Mother/Daughter Writing and the Politics of Race and Sex in Maxine Hong Kingston's *The Woman Warrior.*" In Hune et al., 225–38.

———. 1996. "Swan-Feather Mothers and Coca-Cola Daughters: Teaching Amy Tan's *The Joy Luck Club.*" In Maitino and Peck, 327–45.

Holstein, Michael E. 1982. "Creative Writing as Comparative Criticism: Maxine Hong Kingston and the Vision of the Bicultural Writer." *American Studies* (Taipei) 12.3:73–88.

Hom, Marlon K. 1983. "Some Cantonese Folksongs on the American Experience." *Western Folklore* 42.2:126–39.

———. 1984. "A Case of Mutual Exclusion: Portrayals by Immigrants and American-born Chinese of Each Other in Literature." *Amerasia Journal* 11:29–45.

———. 1987. *Songs of Gold Mountain: Cantonese Rhymes from San Francisco Chinatown*. Berkeley and Los Angeles: Univ. of California Press.

Homsher, Deborah. 1979. "*The Woman Warrior*, by Maxine Hong Kingston: A Bridging of Autobiographical Fiction." *Iowa Review* 10.4:93–8.

Honma, Todd. 1995. "Ting-A-Ling-A-Ling: A Sexual Wake-Up Call." *Critical Mass* 2.2:121–8.

Hongo, Garrett. 1994. "Asian American Literature: Questions of Identity." *Amerasia Journal* 20.3:1–8.

Hosillos, Lucila V. 1969. *Philippine-American Literary Relations 1989–1941*. Quezon City: Univ. of the Philippines Press.

Houn, Fred [Fred Ho]. 1987. "The Revolutionary Writings of H. T. Tsiang." *East Wind* 6.1:39–40.

Hune, Shirley, Hyung-Chan Kim, Stephen S. Fugita, and Amy Ling, eds. 1991. *Asian Americans: Comparative and Global Perspectives*. Pullman: Washington State Univ. Press.

Hunt, Linda. 1985. "'I Could Not Figure Out What Was My Village': Gender vs. Ethnicity in Maxine Hong Kingston's *The Woman Warrior*." *MELUS* 12.3:5–12.

Ileto, Reynaldo Clemena. 1979. *Pasyon and Revolution: Popular Movements in the Philippines, 1840–1910*. Quezon City, Philippines: Ateneo de Manila Univ. Press.

———. 1982. "Rizal and the Underside of Philippine History." In *Moral Order and the Question of Change: Essays on Southeast Asia*, ed. David Wyatt and Alexander Woodside, 274–337. New Haven: Yale Univ. Southeast Asia Studies.

Inada, Lawson Fusao. 1976. "The Vision of America in John Okada's *No-No Boy*." In *Ethnic Literatures since 1776: The Many Voices of America*, ed. Wolodymyr T. Zyla and Wendell M. Aycock, 275–87. Lubbock, TX: Interdepartmental Committee on Comparative Literature, Texas Tech Univ.

———. 1982. "Of Place and Displacement: The Range of Japanese American Literature." In *Three American Literatures: Essays in Chicano, Native American, and Asian American Literature for Teachers of American Literature*, ed. Houston A. Baker Jr., 254–65. New York: Modern Language Association of America.

Islas, Arturo. 1983. "Maxine Hong Kingston." In *Women Writers of the West Coast: Speaking of Their Lives and Careers*, ed. Marilyn Yalom, 11–19. Santa Barbara, CA: Capra.

Itwaru, Arnold. 1989. *Mass Communication and Mass Deception*. Toronto: Terebi.

———. 1990. *The Invention of Canada: Literary Text and the Immigrant Imaginary*. Toronto: TSAR Publications.

Joaquin, Nick. 1988. *Culture and History: Occasional Notes on the Process of Philippine Becoming*. Manila: Solar Publishing.

Jones, Manina. 1990. "The Avenues of Speech and Silence: Telling Difference in Joy Kogawa's *Obasan*." In *Theory between the Disciplines: Authority/Vision/Politics*, ed. Martin Kreiswirth and Mark A. Cheetham, 213–29. Ann Arbor: Univ. of Michigan Press.

Juhasz, Suzanne. 1979. "Towards a Theory of Form in Feminist Autobiography: Kate Millet's *Flying* and *Sita*; Maxine Hong Kingston's *The Woman Warrior*." *International Journal of Women's Studies* 2.2:62–75.

———. 1985. "Maxine Hong Kingston: Narrative Technique and Female Identity." In *Contemporary American Women Writers: Narrative Strategies*, ed. Catherine Rainwater and William J. Scheick, 173–89. Lexington: Univ. of Kentucky Press.

Kalogeras, Yiorgos. 1996. "Producing History and Telling Stories: Maxine Hong Kingston's *China Men* and Zeese Papanikolas's *Buried Unsung*." In Singh et al., 227–44.

Kang, L. Hyun Yi. 1994. "The 'Liberatory Voice' of Theresa Hak Kyung Cha's *Dictée*." In Kim and Alarcón, 73–99.

Kaplan, Caren, and Inderpal Grewal, eds. 1994. *Scattered Hegemonies: Postmodernity and Transnational Feminist Practices*. Minneapolis: Univ. of Minnesota Press.

Kennedy, Colleen, and Deborah Morse. 1991. "A Dialogue with(in) Tradition: Two Perspectives on *The Woman Warrior.*" In Lim, ed., 121–30.

Kim, Elaine H. 1982. *Asian American Literature: An Introduction to the Writings and Their Social Context.* Philadelphia: Temple Univ. Press.

———. 1987. "Defining Asian American Realities through Literature." *Cultural Critique* 6:87–111.

———. 1990a. " 'Such Opposite Creatures': Men and Women in Asian American Literature." *Michigan Quarterly Review* 29.1:68–93.

———. 1990b. "Defining Asian American Realities through Literature." In *The Nature and Context of Minority Discourse,* ed. Abdul R. JanMohamed and David Lloyd, 146–70. New York: Oxford Univ. Press.

———. 1994a. "Poised on the In-between: A Korean American's Reflections on Theresa Hak Kyung Cha's *Dictée.*" In Kim and Alarcón, 3–30.

———. 1994b. "Asian American Literature." In Ng et al. 1994, 207–9.

———. 1994c. "Room for a View from a Marginal Site: Texts, Contexts, and Asian American Studies." *Critical Mass* 1.2:3–22.

Kim, Elaine H., and Norma Alarcón, eds. 1994. *Writing Self, Writing Nation: A Collection of Essays on DICTEE by Theresa Hak Kyung Cha.* Berkeley: Third Woman Press.

Kim, Illsoo. 1981. *The New Urban Immigrants: The Korean Community in New York.* Princeton, NJ: Princeton Univ. Press.

Kingston, Maxine Hong. 1982. "Cultural Mis-Readings by American Reviewers." In *Asian and Western Writers in Dialogue: New Cultural Identities,* ed. Guy Amirthanayagam, 55–65. London: Macmillan.

———. 1991. "Personal Statement." In Lim, ed., 23–5.

Kondo, Dorinne K. 1990. "*M. Butterfly*: Orientalism, Gender, and a Critique of Essentialist Identity." *Cultural Critique* 16 (Fall): 5–29.

———. 1995. "Poststructuralist Theory as Political Necessity." *Amerasia Journal* 21.1 and 2:95–100.

———. Forthcoming. *About Face: Race, Orientalism, and Performance.* New York: Routledge.

Kosasa-Terry, Geraldine E. 1994. "Localizing Discourse." In Ng et al. 1994, 249–51.

Koshy, Susan. 1994. "The Geography of Female Subjectivity: Ethnicity, Gender, and Diaspora." *Diaspora* 3.1:69–84.

———. 1996. "Mother-Country and Fatherland: Re-Membering the Nation in Sara Suleri's *Meatless Days.*" In *Interventions: Feminist Dialogues on Third World Women's Literature and Film,* ed. Brinda Bose and Bishnupriya Ghosht, 47–63. New York: Garland.

Lai, Him Mark, Genny Lim, and Judy Yung. 1980. *Island: Poetry and History of Chinese Immigrants on Angel Island 1910–1940.* San Francisco: HOC DOI [History of Chinese Detained on Island] Project.

Lall, E. N. 1983. *The Poetry of Encounter: Three Indo-Anglican Poets.* New Delhi: Sterling.

Lam, Maivan Clech. 1992. "Resisting Inside/Outside Classism." *Forward Motion* 11.3:59–63.

Lau, Joseph S. M. 1981. "The Albatross Exorcised: The Rime of Frank Chin."

Tamkang Review 12.1:93–105.

Lee, Quentin. 1994. "Cyborg Identity/Metamorphosis/Skin." *Critical Mass* 1.2:103–22.

Lee, Rachel C. 1995. "Claiming Land, Claiming Voice, Claiming Canon: Institutionalized Challenges in Kingston's *China Men* and *The Woman Warrior*." In Ng et al. 1995, 147–59.

———. 1996. "The Erasure of Places and the Re-Siting of Empire in Wendy Law-Yone's *Coffin Tree*." *Cultural Critique* 35.

Lee, Robert G. 1991. "*The Woman Warrior* as an Intervention in Asian American Historiography." In Lim, ed., 52–63.

———. 1992. "In Search of the Historical Guan Gong." *Asian America: Journal of Culture and the Arts* 1:28–47.

Leong, Russell, ed. 1991. *Moving the Image: Independent Asian Pacific American Media Arts*. Los Angeles: UCLA Asian American Studies Center and Visual Communications.

———. 1994. "Dimensions of Desire." *Amerasia Journal* (special issue) 20.1.

———. 1996. *Asian American Sexualities: Dimensions of the Gay and Lesbian Experience*. New York and London: Routledge.

Lew, Walter. 1992. *Excerpts from DIKTE for DICTEE*. Seoul: Yeul Eum Sa.

Li, David Leiwei. 1988. "The Naming of a Chinese American 'I': Cross-Cultural Sign/ification in *The Woman Warrior*." *Criticism* 30.4:497–515.

———. 1990. "*China Men*: Maxine Hong Kingston and the American Canon." *American Literary History* 2.3: 482–502.

———. 1991. "The Formation of Frank Chin and Formations of Chinese American Literature." In Hune et al., 211–23.

———. 1992. "The Production of Chinese American Tradition: Displacing American Orientalist Discourse." In Lim and Ling, 319–31.

———. 1992. "Filiative and Affiliative Textualization in Chinese American Literature." In *Understanding Others: Cultural and Cross-Cultural Studies and the Teaching of Literature*, ed. Joseph Trimmer and Tilly Warnock, 177–200. Urbana, IL: National Council of Teachers of English.

Li Shu-yan. 1993. "Otherness and Transformation in *Eat a Bowl of Tea* and *Crossings*." *MELUS* 18.4:99–110.

Lidoff, Joan. 1991. "Autobiography in a Different Voice: *The Woman Warrior* and the Question of Genre." In Lim, ed., 116–20.

Lightfoot, Marjorie. 1986. "Hunting the Dragon in Maxine Hong Kingston's *The Woman Warrior*." *MELUS* 13.3–4 (Fall–Winter): 55–66.

Lim, Shirley Geok-lin. 1990a. "Japanese American Women's Life Stories: Maternality in Monica Sone's *Nisei Daughter* and Joy Kogawa's *Obasan*." *Feminist Studies* 16.2:289–311.

———. 1990b. "Twelve Asian American Writers: In Search of Self-Definition." In Ruoff and Ward, 237–50.

———. 1991. "Asian American Daughters Rewriting Asian Maternal Texts." In Hune et al., 239–47.

———. 1992a. "The Ambivalent American: Asian American Literature on the Cusp." In Lim and Ling, 13–32.

———. 1992b. "The Tradition of Chinese-American Women's Life Stories:

Thematics of Race and Gender in Jade Snow Wong's *Fifth Chinese Daughter* and Maxine Hong Kingston's *The Woman Warrior.*" In *American Women's Autobiography: Fea(s)ts of Memory,* ed. Margo Culley, 252–67. Madison: Univ. of Wisconsin Press.

———. 1993a. "Assaying the Gold: Or, Contesting the Ground of Asian American Literature." *New Literary History* 24.1:147–69.

———. 1993b. "Feminist and Ethnic Literary Theories in Asian American Literature." *Feminist Studies* 19.3: 571–96.

———. 1993c. "Hegemony and 'Anglo-American Feminism': Living in the Funny House." *Tulsa Studies in Women's Literature* 12.2:279–87.

———. 1994. "Asian American Literature: Race, Class, Gender, and Sexuality." *Multicultural Review* 3.2 (June): 46–53.

———. 1996. "'Growing with Stories': Chinese American Identities, Textual Identities." In Maitino and Peck, 273–91.

———, ed. 1991. *Approaches to Teaching Kingston's "The Woman Warrior."* New York: Modern Language Association of America.

Lim, Shirley Geok-lin, and Amy Ling, eds. 1992. *Reading the Literatures of Asian America.* Philadelphia: Temple Univ. Press.

Lin, Patricia. 1991. "Use of Media and Other Resources to Situate *The Woman Warrior.*" In Lim, ed., 37–43.

Ling, Amy. 1982. "A Rumble in the Silence: *Crossing* by Chuang Hua." *MELUS* 9.3:29–37.

———. 1983–4. "Thematic Threads in Maxine Hong Kingston's *The Woman Warrior.*" *Tamkang Review* 14.1 (Part I): 155–64.

———. 1986. "Writers with a Cause: Sui Sin Far and Han Suyin." *Women's Studies International Forum* (London) 9.4:411–19.

———. 1987. "I'm Here: An Asian American Woman's Response." *New Literary History* 19.1:151–60.

———. 1989. "Chinamerican Women Writers: Four Forerunners of Maxine Hong Kingston." In *Gender, Body, and Knowledge: Feminist Reconstructions of Being and Knowledge,* ed. Alison Jaggar and Susan Bordo, 309–23. New Brunswick, NJ: Rutgers Univ. Press.

———. 1990a. *Between Worlds: Women Writers of Chinese Ancestry.* New York: Pergamon Press.

———. 1990b. "Chinese American Women Writers: The Tradition behind Maxine Hong Kingston." In Ruoff and Ward, 219–36.

———. 1991. "'Emerging Canons' of Asian American Literature and Art." In Hune et al., 191–7.

———. 1992. "Creating One's Self: The Eaton Sisters." In Lim and Ling, 305–18.

———. 1995a. "The State of Asian American Studies in Wisconsin." In Ng et al. 1995, 195–206.

———. 1995b. "Maxine Hong Kingston and the Dialogic Dilemma of Asian American Writers." In *Having Our Way: Women Rewriting Tradition in Twentieth-Century America,* ed. Harriet Pollack. Lewisburg: Bucknell Univ. Press. *Bucknell Review* (special issue) 39.1:151–66.

Ling, Jinqi. 1995a. "Race, Power, and Cultural Politics in John Okada's *No-No*

Boy." *American Literature* 67.2:359–81.

———. 1995b. "Reading for Historical Specificities: Gender Negotiations in Louis Chu's *Eat a Bowl of Tea*." *MELUS* 20.1: 35–51.

———. Forthcoming. *Negotiating Transformations: Ideology and Form in Post–World War II Asian American Literary Discourse*. New York: Oxford Univ. Press.

Linton, Patricia. 1994. "'What Stories the Wind Would Tell': Representation and Appropriation in Maxine Hong Kingston's *China Men*." *MELUS* 19.4:37–48.

Liu, Lydia H. 1993. "Translingual Practice: The Discourse of Individualism between China and the West." *Positions* 1.1:160–93.

Loo, Chalsa. 1989. "M. Butterfly: A Feminist Perspective." *Asia Week* 14 July.

Lowe, Lisa. 1991a. *Critical Terrains: French and British Orientalisms*. Ithaca, NY: Cornell Univ. Press.

———. 1991b. "Heterogeneity, Hybridity, Multiplicity: Marking Asian American Differences." *Diaspora* 1.1:24–44.

———. 1993. "*Des Chinoises*: Orientalism, Psychoanalysis, and Feminine Writing." In *Ethics, Politics, and Difference in Julia Kristeva's Writing*, ed. Kelly Oliver, 150–63. New York: Routledge.

———. 1994. "Unfaithful to the Original: The Subject of *Dictée*." In Kim and Alarcón, 35–69.

———. 1995. "Canon, Institutionalization, Identity: Contradictions for Asian American Studies." In Palumbo-Liu, ed., 48–68.

———. 1995. "On Contemporary Asian American Projects." *Amerasia Journal* 21.1 and 2:41–52.

———. Forthcoming. "Decolonization, Displacement, Disidentification: Asian 'American' Novels and the Question of History." In *Cultural Institutions of the Novel*, ed. Deidre Lynch and William Warner. Durham, NC: Duke Univ. Press.

———. Forthcoming. "Imagining Los Angeles in the Production of Multiculturalism." In *Multiculturalism?* ed. Avery Gordon and Christopher Newfield. Minneapolis: Univ. of Minnesota Press.

———. Forthcoming. *Heterogeneity: On Asian American Cultural Production*. Durham, NC: Duke Univ. Press.

Lumbera, Bienvenido. 1984. *Revaluation: Essays on Philippine Literature, Cinema, and Popular Culture*. Baguio City, Philippines: Index Press.

Luu, Khoi T. 1994. "A Heart of Sorrow? Exposing the Lighter Side of the Vietnamese American Experience." *Viet Nam Forum* 14:321–32.

Lye, Colleen. 1995. "*M. Butterfly* and the Rhetoric of Antiessentialism: Minority Discourse in an International Frame." In Palumbo-Liu, ed., 260–89.

Ma, Sheng-mei. 1991. "David Henry Hwang's *M. Butterfly*: From Puccini to East/Western Androgyny." *Tamkang Review* 21.3:287–96.

McAlister, Melanie. 1992. "(Mis)Reading *The Joy Luck Club*." *Asian America: Journal of Culture and the Arts* 1:102–18.

McBride, Paul W. 1991. *The Woman Warrior* in the History Classroom." In Lim, ed., 93–100.

McDonald, Dorothy Ritsuko. 1979. "After Imprisonment: Ichiro's Search for Redemption in *No-No Boy*." *MELUS* 6.3:19–26.

McDonald, Dorothy Ritsuko, and Katharine Newman. 1980/1994. "Relocation and Dislocation: The Writings of Hisaye Yamamoto and Wakako Yamauchi." *MELUS* 7.3:21–38. Reprinted in Cheung, ed., 129–42.

Magnusson, A. Lynne. 1988. "Language and Longing in Joy Kogawa's *Obasan*." *Canadian Literature* 116 (Spring): 58–66.

Maitino, John R., and David R. Peck, eds. 1996. *Teaching American Ethnic Literatures*. Albuquerque: Univ. of New Mexico Press.

Manalansan, Martin IV. 1993. "(Re)locating the Gay Filipino: Resistance, Postcolonialism, and Identity." *Journal of Homosexuality* 26:53–72.

Manuud, Antonio, ed. 1967. *Brown Heritage: Essays on Philippine Cultural Tradition and Literature*. Quezon City, Philippines: Ateneo de Manila Univ. Press.

Mathur, Saloni. 1992. "Broadcasting Difference." *Samar* 1 (Winter): 2–5.

Matsumoto, Valerie. 1987. "Desperately Seeing 'Deirdre': Gender Roles, Multicultural Relations, and Nisei Women Writers of the 1930s." *Frontiers* 12.1:19–32.

Mayer, David R. 1990. "Akegarasu and Emerson: Kindred Spirits of Toshio Mori's 'The Seventh Street Philosopher.'" *Amerasia Journal* 16.2:1–10.

Meissenburg, Karin. 1987. *The Writing on the Wall*. Frankfurt: Verlag für Interkulturelle Kommunikation.

Melton, Judith M. 1991. "*The Woman Warrior* in the Women's Studies Classroom." In Lim, ed., 74–9.

Miller, Lucien, and Hui-chuan Chang. 1984–5. "Fiction and Autobiography: Spatial Form in *The Golden Cangue* and *The Woman Warrior*." *Tamkang Review* 25.1–4 (Part II): 75–96.

Miller, Margaret. 1983. "Threads of Identity in Maxine Hong Kingston's *Woman Warrior*." *Biography* 6.1:13–33.

Min, Yong Soon. 1988. "Whirl War." *New Observations* 62.

———. 1990. "Territorial Waters: Mapping Asian American Cultural Identity." *New Asia: The Portable Lower East Side* 7.2.

———. 1991. "Comparing the Contemporary Experiences of Asian American, South Korean, and Cuban Artists." In Hune et al., 277–87.

Mistri, Zenobia Baxter. 1990/1994. "'Seventeen Syllables': A Symbolic Haiku." *Studies in Short Fiction* 27.2 (1990): 197–202. Reprinted in Cheung, ed., 195–202.

Mitchell, Carol. 1981. "'Talking-Story' in *the Woman Warrior*: An Analysis of the Use of Folklore." *Kentucky Folklore Record* 27.2–3 (January–June): 5–12.

Morantte, P. C. 1984. *Remembering Carlos Bulosan (His Heart Affair with America)*. Quezon City, Philippines: New Day Publishers.

Mostern, Kenneth. 1995. "Why Is America in the Heart?" *Critical Mass* 2.2:35–66.

Mukherjee, Arun. 1988. *Towards an Aesthetic of Opposition: Essays on Literature Criticism and Cultural Imperialism*. Toronto: Williams-Wallace.

Moy, James S. 1993. *Marginal Sights: Staging the Chinese in America*. Iowa City: Univ. of Iowa Press.

Mura, David. 1991. "Mirrors of the Self: Autobiography and the Japanese American Writer." In Hune et al., 249–63.

Mura, David. 1992. "What Is an Asian American?" *Artpaper* 12.2.

———. 1994. "A Shift in Power, A Sea of Change in the Arts: Asian American

Constructions." In Aguilar-San Juan, ed., 183–204.

———. 1995. "The Margins at the Center, the Center at the Margins: Acknowledging the Diversity of Asian American Poetry." In Ng et al. 1995, 171–84.

Myers, Victoria. 1991. "Speech–Act Theory and the Search for Identity in *The Woman Warrior*." In Lim, ed., 131–7.

Needham, Lawrence. 1992. "'The Sorrows of a Broken Time': Agha Shahid Ali and the Poetry of Loss and Recovery." In Nelson 1992, 63–76. New York, Westport, and London: Greenwood Press.

Nelson, Emmanuel S., ed. 1992. *Reworlding: The Literature of the Indian Diaspora.* New York, Westport, and London: Greenwood Press.

———. 1993. *Writers of the Indian Diaspora: A Bio-Bibliographical Critical Sourcebook.* Westport, Greenwood Press.

———. 1994. *Bharati Mukherjee: Critical Perspectives.* Hamden, CT: Garland.

Ng, Franklin, Judy Yung, Stephen S. Fugita, and Elaine H. Kim, eds. 1994. *New Visions in Asian American Studies: Diversity, Community, Power.* Pullman: Washington State Univ. Press.

Ng, Wendy L., Soo-Young Chin, James S. Moy, and Gary Y. Okihiro, eds. 1995. *Reviewing Asian America: Locating Diversity.* Pullman: Washington State Univ. Press.

Nguyen, Viet Thanh. 1995. "The Postcolonial State of Desire: Homosexuality and Transvestitism in Ninotchka Rosca's *State of War*." *Critical Mass* 2.2:67–94.

Nishime, Leilani. 1995. "Engendering Genre: Gender and Nationalism in *China Men* and *The Woman Warrior*." *MELUS* 20.1:67–82.

Nomura, Gail M., Russell Endo, Stephen H. Sumida, and Russell C. Leong, eds. 1989. *Frontiers of Asian American Studies, Writing, Research, and Commentary.* Pullman: Washington State Univ. Press.

Okamura, Jonathan Y. 1980. "Aloha Kanaka Me Ke Aloha 'Aina: Local Culture and Society in Hawai'i." *Amerasia Journal* 7.2:119–37.

Okihiro, Gary Y., Shirley Hune, Arthur A. Hansen, and John M. Liu, eds. 1988. *Reflections on Shattered Windows: Promises and Prospects for Asian American Studies.* Pullman: Washington State Univ. Press.

Omura, James. 1989. "Japanese American Journalism during World War II." In Nomura et al., 71–80.

Oyama, Richard. 1987. "'Ayumi: 'To Sing Our Connections.'" *A Gift of Tongues: Critical Challenges in Contemporary American Poetry*, ed. Marie Harris and Kathleen Aguero, 249–56. Athens: Univ. of Georgia Press.

———. 1994. "The Oriental Art of Torture." *Critical Mass* 1.2:59–64.

Palumbo-Liu, David. 1990. "Discourse and Dislocation: Rhetorical Strategies of Asian-American Exclusion and Confinement." *LIT: Literature Interpretation Theory* 2:1–7.

———. 1991. "Toshio Mori and the Attachments of Spirit." *Amerasia Journal* 17.3:41–8.

———. 1994a. "Los Angeles, Asians, and Perverse Ventriloquisms: On the Functions of Asian America in the Recent American Imaginary." *Public Culture* 6 (Winter): 365–81.

———. 1994b. "Representing the Other as Self: Problematics of Self-Representation in Asian American Literature." *Cultural Critique* 28 (Fall): 75–102.

Reprinted in *Making Barbarians for Civilization: An Interdisciplinary Anthology*, ed. Mary Layoun and Jane Tylus. Madison: Wisconsin Univ. Press.

———. 1995a. "Theory and the Subject of Asian American Studies." *Amerasia Journal* 21.1 and 2:55–65.

———. 1995b. "Universalism and Minority Culture." *Differences* 7.1:188–208.

———. 1995c. "The Ethnic as 'Post-': Reading *Reading the Literatures of Asian America*." *American Literary History* 7.1:161–8.

———. 1996. "The Politics of Memory: Remembering History in Alice Walker and Joy Kogawa." In Singh et al., 211–26.

———. Forthcoming. *Narrating Asian America: Cultural Politics and Subjectivities*. Stanford, CA: Stanford Univ. Press.

———. Forthcoming. "Model Minority Discourse and the Course of Healing." In *Minority Discourse: Ideological Containment and Utopian/Heterotopian Potentials*, ed. Abdul JanMohamed. New York: Oxford Univ. Press.

———, ed. 1995. *The Ethnic Canon: Histories, Institutions, and Interventions*. Minneapolis: Univ. of Minnesota Press.

Pao, Angela. 1992. "The Critic and the Butterfly: Sociocultural Contexts and the Reception of David Henry Hwang's *M. Butterfly*." *Amerasia Journal* 18.3:1–16.

Park, Clara Claiborne. 1980. "Ghosts on a Gold Mountain." *Hudson Review* 33 (Winter): 589–95.

Payne, Robert M. 1993/1994. "Adapting (to) the Margins: *Hot Summer Winds* and the Stories of Hisaye Yamamoto." *East–West Film Journal* 7.2 (1993): 39–53. Reprinted in Cheung, ed., 203–18.

Perez, Benjamin. "Sisters." *Critical Mass* 2.1 (1994):71–8.

Peterson, Marlyn, and Deirdre Lashgari. 1991. "Teaching *The Woman Warrior* to High School and Community College Students." In Lim, ed., 101–7.

Portales, Marco A. 1984. "Literary History, A 'Useable Past,' and Space." *MELUS* 11.1:97–102.

Price, Darby Li Po. 1994. "'All American Girl' and the American Dream." *Critical Mass* 2.1:129–46.

Quinby, Lee. 1992. "The Subject of Memoirs: *The Woman Warrior*'s Technology of Ideographic Selfhood." In *De/Colonizing the Subject: The Politics of Gender in Women's Autobiography*, ed. Sidonie Smith and Julian Watson, 297–320. Minneapolis: Univ. of Minnesota Press.

Rabine, Leslie E. 1987. "No Lost Paradise: Social Gender and Symbolic Gender in the Writings of Maxine Hong Kingston." *Signs* 12:471–92.

Radhakrishnan, R. 1994. "Is the Ethnic 'Authentic' in the Diaspora?" In Aguilar-San Juan, ed., 219–33.

Rafael, Vicente. 1984. "Language, Identity, and Gender in Rizal's *Noli*." *Review of Indonesian and Malaysian Affairs* 18:110–40.

———, ed. 1995. *Discrepant Histories: Translocal Essays on Filipino Culture*. Philadelphia: Temple Univ. Press.

Rathbun, David. "Ways of Knowing a Curriculum: Literature by Asian Americans." *Teaching the Humanities* 1.1 (1995): 37–48.

Revilla, Linda A., Gail M. Nomura, Shawn Wong, and Shirley Hune, eds. 1993. *Bearing Dreams, Shaping Visions: Asian Pacific American Perspectives*. Pullman:

Washington State Univ. Press.

Reyes, Soledad, ed. 1991. *Reading Popular Culture*. Quezon City, Philippines: Ateneo de Manila Office of Research and Publications.

Rolf, Robert T. 1982/1994. "The Short Stories of Hisaye Yamamoto, Japanese American Writer." *Bulletin of Fukuoka University of Education* 31.1:71–86. Reprinted in Cheung, ed., 89–108.

Rose, Marilyn Russell. 1988. "Politics into Art: Kogawa's *Obasan* and the Rhetoric of Fiction." *Mosaic* 21 (Spring): 215–26.

Rose, Shirley K. 1987. "Metaphors and Myths of Cross-Cultural Literacy: Autobiographical Narratives by Maxine Hong Kingston, Richard Rodriguez, and Malcolm X." *MELUS* 14.1:3–15.

Ruoff, A. LaVonne Brown, and Jerry W. Ward, eds. *Redefining American Literary History*. New York: Modern Language Association.

Rustomjee, Roshni. 1985. "Expatriates, Immigrants and Literature: Three South Asian Women Writers." *Toronto South Asian Review* 4.2. Reprinted in *Massachusetts Review* 29.4 (1988–9): 655–65.

Sadana, Rashmi. 1993. "Making a Space for Women in the Third World: Displacement and Identity in Suleri's *Meatless Days*." In Women of the South Asian Descent Collective, 320–4.

Saeki, Karen. 1994. "Untitled: *Obasan*." *Critical Mass* 1.2:123–8.

Said, Edward S. 1978/1979. *Orientalism*. New York: Vintage.

Sakurai, Patricia A. 1993. "The Politics of Possession: Negotiating Identities in *American in Disguise, Homebase*, and *Farewell to Manzanar*." *Critical Mass* 1.1:39–56.

San Juan, E., Jr. 1971. *The Radical Tradition in Philippine Literature*. Quezon City, Philippines: Manlapaz Publishing.

———. 1972. *Carlos Bulosan and the Imagination of the Class Struggle*. New York: Oriole Editions.

———. 1983. *Bulosan: An Introduction with Selections*. Manila: National Bookstore.

———. 1984. *Toward a People's Literature*. Quezon City: Univ. of the Philippines Press.

———. 1986. *Crisis in the Philippines*. South Hadley, MA: Bergin & Garvey.

———. 1991a. "Beyond Identity Politics: The Predicament of the Asian American Writer in Late Capitalism." *American Literary History* 3.3:542–65.

———. 1991b. "Mapping the Boundaries: The Filipino Writer in the U.S.A." *Journal of Ethnic Studies* 19.1:117–31.

———. 1991c. *Writing and National Liberation: Essays on Critical Practice*. Quezon City: Univ. of the Philippines Press.

———. 1992a. *Racial Formations–Critical Transformations: Articulations of Power in Ethnic and Racial Studies in the United States*. Atlantic Highlands, NJ: Humanities Press International.

———. 1992b. *Reading the West/Writing the East*. New York: Peter Lang.

———. 1993. "Symbolizing the Asian Diaspora in the United States: A Return to the Primal Scene of Deracination." *Border/Lines* 24/25:23–9.

———. 1994. "The Predicament of Filipinos in the United States: 'Where Are You From? When Are You Going Back?'" In Aguilar-San Juan, ed., 205–18.

———. 1995a. "In Search of Filipino Writing: Reclaiming Whose 'America?'" In Palumbo-Liu, ed., 213–40.

———. 1995b. *Hegemony and Strategies of Transgression: Essays in Cultural Studies and Comparative Literature.* New York: State Univ. of New York Press.

———. 1996. "Searching for the Heart of 'America.'" In Maitino and Peck, 259–72.

Santillian-Castrence, P. 1967. "The Period of Apprenticeship." In *Brown Heritage: Essays on Philippine Cultural Tradition and Literature,* ed. Antonio G. Manuud, 546–74. Quezon City, Philippines: Ateneo de Manila Univ. Press.

Santos, Bienvenido N. 1977. "The Filipino as Exile." *Greenfield Review* 6:47–55.

———. 1982. "Pilipino Old Timers: Fact and Fiction." *Amerasia Journal* 9:89–98.

Sarkar, Sheila. 1994. "Cynthia Kadohata and David Wong Louie: The Pangs of a Floating World." *Critical Mass* 2.1:79–98.

Sato, Gayle K. Fujita. 1990. "The Island Influence on Chinese American Writers: Wing Tek Lum, Darrell H. Y. Lum, and Eric Chock." *Amerasia Journal* 16.2:17–33.

———. 1991a. "Ghosts as Chinese American Construct in Maxine Hong Kingston's *The Woman Warrior.*" *Haunting the House of Fiction: Feminist Perspectives on Ghost Stories by American Women,* ed. Lynette Carpenter and Wendy K. Kolmar, 193–214. Knoxville: Univ. of Tennessee Press.

———. 1991b. "*The Woman Warrior* as a Search for Ghosts." In Lim, ed., 138–45.

———. 1992. "Momotaro's Exile: John Okada's *No-No Boy.*" In Lim and Ling, 239–58.

Schenck, Celeste. 1988. "All of a Piece: Women's Poetry and Autobiography." In *Life/Lines: Theorizing Women's Autobiography,* ed. Bella Brodzki and Celeste Schenck, 281–305. Ithaca, NY: Cornell Univ. Press.

Schmidt, Jan Zslotnok. 1980. "The Other: A Study of the Persona in Several Contemporary Women's Autobiographies." *CEA Critic* 43.1:24–31.

Schueller, Malini. 1989. "Questioning Race and Gender Definitions: Dialogic Subversions in *The Woman Warrior.*" *Criticism* 31.4:421–37.

Schweik, Susan. 1989. "The Pre-Poetics of Internment: The Case of Toyo Suyemoto." *American Literary History* 1.1:89–109.

———. 1991. *A Gulf So Deeply Cut: American Women Poets and the Second World War.* Madison: Univ. of Wisconsin Press.

Sharpe, Jenny. 1995. "Is the United States Postcolonial? Transnationalism, Immigration, and Race." *Diaspora* 4.2:181–99.

Shen, Shiao-ying. 1989. "Ancestors and Descendants of Charlie Chan." *Tamkang Review* 20.2:217–34.

Shih, Shu-mei. 1992. "Exile and Intertextuality in Maxine Hong Kingston's *China Men.*" In *The Literature of Emigration and Exile,* ed. James Whitlark and Wendell Aycock, 65–77. Lubbock: Texas Tech Univ. Press.

———. Forthcoming. "Nationalism and Korean American Women's Writing: Theresa Hak-Kyung Cha's *DICTEE.*" In *Speaking the Other Self: American Women Writers,* ed. Jeanne Campbell Reesman. Athens: Univ. of Georgia Press.

Shimakawa, Karen. 1993. "'Who's to Say?' Or, Making Space for Gender and Ethnicity in *M. Butterfly.*" *Theatre Journal* 45.3:349–62.

Singh, Amritjit, Joseph Skerrett, and Robert Hogan, eds. 1996. *Memory and Cultural Politics: New Approaches to American Ethnic Literatures*. Boston: Northeastern Univ. Press.

Skloot, Robert. 1990. "Breaking the Butterfly: The Politics of David Henry Hwang." *Modern Drama* 33.1:59–66.

Sledge, Linda Ching. 1980. "Maxine Hong Kingston's *China Men*: The Family Historian as Epic Poet." *MELUS* 7.4:3–22.

———. 1990. "Oral Tradition in Kingston's *China Men*." In Ruoff and Ward, 142–54.

Slowik, Mary. 1994. "When the Ghosts Speak: Oral and Written Narrative Forms in Maxine Hong Kingston's *China Men*." *MELUS* 19.1:73–88.

Smith, Julian. 1975. *Looking Away: Hollywood and Vietnam*. New York: Charles Scribner's Sons.

Smith, Sidonie. 1987. *A Poetics of Women's Autobiography: Marginality and the Fictions of Self-Representation*. Bloomington: Indiana Univ. Press.

Solberg, S. E. 1981. "Sui Sin Far/Edith Eaton: First Chinese-American Fictionalist." *MELUS* 8.1:27–40.

Spivak, Gayatri. 1987. *In Other Worlds*. London: Routledge.

Spelman, Elisabeth V. 1982. "Woman as Body: Ancient and Contemporary Views." *Feminist Studies* 8.1:109–31.

Srikanth, Rajini. 1994. "Gender and Images of Home in the Asian American Diaspora: A Socio-Literary Reading of Some Asian American Works." *Critical Mass* 2.1:147–82.

Stephens, Michael. 1986. *The Dramaturgy of Style: Voice in Short Fiction*. Carbondale: Southern Illinois Univ. Press.

Su, Karen. 1994. "Jade Snow Wong's Badge of Distinction in the 1990s." *Critical Mass* 2.1:3–52.

Suleri, Sara. 1992. *The Rhetoric of English India*. Chicago and London: Univ. of Chicago Press.

Sumida, Stephen H. 1986. "Waiting for the Big Fish: Recent Research in the Asian American Literature of Hawaii." In *The Best of Bamboo Ridge: The Hawaii Writers' Quarterly*, ed. Eric Chock and Darrell H. Y. Lum, 302–21. Honolulu: Bamboo Ridge Press.

———. 1988. "Hawaii, the Northwest, and Asia: Localism and Local Literary Developments in the Creation of an Asian Immigrants' Sensibility." *Seattle Review* 11:9–18.

———. 1989a. "Asian American Literature in the 1980s: A Sampling of Studies and Works." In Nomura et al., 151–8.

———. 1989b. "Japanese American Moral Dilemmas in John Okada's *No-No Boy* and Milton Murayama's *All I Asking For Is My Body*." In Nomura et al., 222–33.

———. 1991. *And the View from the Shore: Literary Traditions of Hawai'i*. Seattle: Univ. of Washington Press.

———. 1992a. "Sense of Place, History, and the Concept of the 'Local' in Hawaii's Asian/Pacific American Literatures." In Lim and Ling, 215–37.

———. 1992b. "Protest and Accommodation, Self-Satire and Self-Effacement, and Monica Sone's *Nisei Daughter*." In *Multicultural Autobiography: American*

Lives, ed. James Robert Payne, 207–43. Knoxville: Univ. of Tennessee Press.

———. 1994. "Centers without Margins: Responses to Centrism in Asian American Literature." *American Literature* 66.4:803–15.

Suzuki-Martinez, Sharon. 1995. "Trickster Strategies: Challenging American Identity, Community, and Art in Kingston's *Tripmaster Monkey.* In Ng et al. 1995, 161–70.

Sze, Julie. 1994. "Have You Heard?: Gossip, Silence, and Community in *Bone.*" *Critical Mass* 2.1:59–70.

Tajima, Renee E. 1989. "Lotus Blossoms Don't Bleed: Images of Asian Women." In *Asian Women United of California,* 308–17.

Taliaferro, Frances. 1980. "Spirited Relatives." *Harper's* 261: 76–7.

Tapping, Craig. 1992. "South Asian Writes North America: Prose Fictions and Autobiographies from the Indian Diaspora." In Lim and Ling, 285–301.

Tenhula, John. 1991. *Voices from Southeast Asia.* New York: Holmes & Meier.

Tran, Qui Phiet. 1992. "From Isolation to Integration: Vietnamese Americans in Tran Dieu Hang's Fiction." In Lim and Ling, 271–84.

———. 1993. "Exile and Home in Contemporary Vietnamese American Feminine Writing." *Amerasia Journal* 19.3:71–83.

Trask, Haunani-Kay. 1993. *From a Native Daughter: Colonialism and Sovereignty in Hawai'i.* Monroe, ME: Common Courage Press.

Trinh, T. Minh-ha. 1989. *Woman, Native, Other: Writing Postcoloniality and Feminism.* Bloomington: Indiana Univ. Press.

———. 1991. *When the Moon Waxes Red: Representation, Gender, and Cultural Politics.* New York: Routledge.

———. 1992. *Framer Framed.* New York: Routledge.

Trường, Monique Thuy-Dung. 1993. "The Emergence of Voices: Vietnamese American Literature 1975–1990." *Amerasia Journal* 19.3:27–50.

Tsang, Daniel C. 1994. "Notes on Queer N' Asian Virtual Sex." *Amerasia Journal* 20.1:117–29.

Tu Wei-ming, ed. 1995. *The Living Tree: The Changing Meaning of Being Chinese Today.* Stanford, CA: Stanford Univ. Press.

TuSmith, Bonnie. 1993. "The 'Inscrutable Albino' in Contemporary Ethnic Literature." *Amerasia Journal* 19.3:85–102.

———. 1994. *All My Relatives: Community in Contemporary Ethnic American Literatures.* Ann Arbor: Univ. of Michigan Press.

Uba, George. 1992. "Versions of Identity in Post-Activist Asian American Poetry." In Lim and Ling, 33–48.

———. 1993. "Friend and Foe: De-Collaborating Wendy Wilder Larsen and Tran Thi Nga's *Shallow Graves.*" *Journal of American Culture* 16.3:63–70.

———. 1995. "The Representation of Asian American Poetry in *The Heath Anthology of American Literature.*" In Ng et al. 1995, 185–94.

Ueki, Teruyo. 1993. "*Obasan*: Revelations in a Paradoxical Scheme." *MELUS* 18.4:5–20.

VanSpanckeren, Kathryn. 1991. "The Asian Literary Background of *The Woman Warrior.*" In Lim, ed., 44–51.

Wang, Alfred S. 1988. "Maxine Hong Kingston's Reclaiming of America: The Birthright of the Chinese American Male." *South Dakota Review* 26.1

(Spring): 18–29.

Wang, Jennie. 1995. *Tripmaster Monkey*: Kingston's Postmodern Representation of a New 'China Man.'" *MELUS* 20.1:101–14.

Wang, L. Ling-Chi. 1976. "The Yee Version of Poems from the Chinese Immigration Station." *Asian American Review* 117–26.

Wang, Veronica. 1985. "Reality and Fantasy: The Chinese-American Woman's Quest for Identity." *MELUS* 12.3:23–31.

Wenquan. 1982. "Chinatown Literature during the Last Ten Years." Trans. with an introduction by Marlon K. Hom. *Amerasia Journal* 9.2:75–100.

Westfall, Suzanne R. 1992. "Ping Chong's Terra In/Cognita: Monsters on Stage." In Lim and Ling, 359–73.

White-Parks, Annette. 1989. "Women's Force: Between Image and Reality of Chinese Immigrant Women in Literature." In Nomura et al., 201–9.

———. 1995a. *Sui Sin Far/Edith Eaton: A Literary Biography.* Urbana-Champaign: Univ. of Illinois Press.

———. 1995b. "A Reversal of American Concepts of 'Other-ness' in the Fiction of Sui Sin Far." *MELUS* 20.1:17–34.

Williams, A. Noelle. 1995. "Parody and Pacifist Transformations in Maxine Hong Kingston's *Tripmaster Monkey: His Fake Book*." *MELUS* 20.1:83–100.

Willis, Gary. 1987. "Speaking the Silence: Joy Kogawa's *Obasan*." *Studies in Canadian Literature* 12.2:239–49.

Wilson, Rob. 1981. "The Languages of Confinement and Liberation in Milton Murayama's *All I Asking For Is My Body*." In *Writers of Hawaii: A Focus on Our Literary Heritage*, ed. Eric Chock and Jody Manabe, 62–5. Honolulu: Hawaii Commission for the Humanities and the Hawaii Foundation for the Arts.

Winks, Robin W., and James R. Rush, eds. 1990. *Asia in Western Fiction.* Honolulu: Univ. of Hawai'i Press.

Wolf, Susan. 1986. "Theresa Cha: Recalling Telling ReTelling." *Afterimage* (Summer): 11–13.

Women of the South Asian Descent Collective (Sheela Bhatt, Preety Kalra, Aarti Kohli, Latika Malkan, Dharini Rasiah), eds. 1993. *Our Feet Walk the Sky: Women of the South Asian Diaspora.* San Francisco: Aunt Lute Books.

Wong, Eugene Franklin. 1978. *On Visual Media Racism: Asians in American Motion Pictures.* New York: Ayer.

Wong, K. Scott. 1995. "Chinatown: Conflicting Images, Contested Terrain." *MELUS* 20.1:3–15.

Wong, Sau-ling Cynthia. 1988a. "Necessity and Extravagance in Maxine Hong Kingston's *The Woman Warrior*: Art and the Ethnic Experience." *MELUS* 15.1:3–26.

———. 1988b. "Tales of Postwar Chinatown: Short Stories of *The Bud*." *Amerasia Journal* 14.2:61–79.

———. 1988c. "Teaching Chinese Immigrant Literature: Some Principles of Syllabus Design." In Okihiro et al., 126–34.

———. 1989. "What's in a Name?: Defining Chinese American Literature of the Immigrant Generation." In Nomura et al., 159–67.

———. 1991. "Kingston's Handling of Traditional Chinese Sources." In Lim, ed., 26–36.

———. 1992a. "Ethnic Dimensions of Postmodern Indeterminancy: Maxine Hong Kingston's *The Woman Warrior* as Avant-garde Autobiography." In *Autobiographie und Avant-garde*, ed. Alfred Hornung and Ernstpeter Ruhe, 273–84. Tübingen: Gunter Narr Verlag.

———. 1992b. "Autobiography as Guided Chinatown Tour? Maxine Hong Kingston's *The Woman Warrior* and the Chinese-American Autobiographical Controversy." In *Multicultural Autobiography: American Lives*, ed. James Robert Payne, 248–79. Knoxville: Univ. of Tennessee Press.

———. 1992c. "Ethnicizing Gender: An Exploration of Sexuality as Sign in Chinese American Immigrant Literature." In Lim and Ling, 111–29.

———. 1993a. *Reading Asian American Literature: From Necessity to Extravagance.* Princeton, NJ: Princeton Univ. Press.

———. 1993b. "Diverted Mothering: Representation of Caregivers of Color in the Age of Multiculturalism." In *Mothering: Ideology, Experience, and Agency*, ed. Evelyn Nakano Glenn, Grace Chang, and Linda Rennie Forsie, 67–91. New York: Routledge.

———. 1993c. "Subverting Desire: Reading the Body in the 1991 Asian Pacific Islander Men's Calendar." *Critical Mass* 1.1:63–74.

———. 1995a. "'Sugar Sisterhood': Situating the Amy Tan Phenomenon." In Palumbo-Liu, ed., 174–210.

———. 1995b. "Denationalization Reconsidered: Asian American Cultural Criticism at a Theoretical Crossroads." *Amerasia Journal* 21.1 and 2:1–27.

———. Forthcoming. "Chinese/Asian American Men in the 1990s: Displacement, Impersonation, Paternity, and Extinction in David Wong Louie's *Pangs of Love*." In Alquizola et al.

Wong, Shelley Sunn. 1994. "Unnaming the Same: Theresa Hak Kyung Cha's *Dictée*." In Kim and Alarcón, 103–40.

Wu, William F. 1982. *The Yellow Peril: Chinese Americans in American Fiction.* Hamden, CT: Archon Books.

Xu, Ben. 1994. "Memory and the Ethnic Self: Reading Amy Tan's *The Joy Luck Club*." *MELUS* 19.1:3–18.

Yabes, Leopoldo Y. 1977. "Pioneering in the Filipino Short Story in English (1925–1940)." In *Philippine Writings*, ed. A. G. Hufana, 370–89. Manila: Regal Publishing Co.

Yalom, Marilyn. 1991. "*The Woman Warrior* as Postmodern Autobiography." In Lim, ed., 108–15.

Yamada, Mitsuye. 1981/1983. "Asian Pacific American Women and Feminism." In *This Bridge Called My Back: Writings by Radical Women of Color*, ed. Cherríe Moraga and Gloria Anzaldúa, 71–5. 2d ed. New York: Kitchen Table/ Women of Color Press.

———. 1996. "Experiential Approaches to Teaching Joy Kogawa's *Obasan*." In Maitino and Peck, 293–311.

Yamamoto, Traise. 1995. "Different Silence(s): The Poetics and Politics of Location." In Ng et al. 1995, 137–46.

Yau, John. Forthcoming. *The Life and Times of Anna May Wong*. New York: Kaya Productions.

Yeh, William. 1993. "The Liminality of John Okada's *No-No Boy*." *Amerasia Journal* 19.1: 121–34.

Yin, Xiao-Huang. 1991. "Between the East and West: Sui Sin Far – the First Chinese-American Woman Writer." *Arizona Quarterly* 47 (Winter): 49–84.

Yogi, Stan. 1989/1994. "Legacies Revealed: Uncovering Buried Plots in the Stories of Hisaye Yamamoto." *Studies in American Fiction* 17.2:169–81. Reprinted in Cheung, ed., 143–60.

———. 1992a. "The Collapse of Difference: Dysfunctional and Inverted Celebrations in John Okada's *No-No Boy*." *Revue Française D'Etudes Americaines* [French Review of American Studies] 53:233–44.

———. 1992b. "Rebels and Heroines: Subversive Narratives in the Stories of Wakako Yamauchi and Hisaye Yamamoto." In Lim and Ling, 131–50.

———. 1996. "Yearning for the Past: The Dynamics of Memory in Sansei Internment Poetry." In Singh et al., 245–65.

———. 1996. "'You had to be one or the other': Oppositions and Reconciliation in John Okada's *No-No Boy*." *MELUS* 21.2.

Yoshikawa, Yoko. "The Heat Is on *Miss Saigon* Coalition: Organizing Across Race and Sexuality." In Aguilar-San Juan, ed., 275–94.

Yun, Chung-Hei. 1992. "Beyond 'Clay Walls': Korean American Literature." In Lim and Ling, 79–96.

INDEX